DEMOCRATIC GOVERNMENT AND POLITICS

CANADIAN GOVERNMENT SERIES

General Editors

R. MacG. Dawson (1946–58), J. A. Corry (1958–61)
C. B. Macpherson (1961–   )

Democratic Government and Politics

BY

J. A. CORRY
Principal, Queen's University, Kingston

AND

J. E. HODGETTS
Professor, Department of Political Economy,
University of Toronto

THIRD EDITION, REVISED

TORONTO

UNIVERSITY OF TORONTO PRESS

PREFACE

The last forty years has produced a large and constantly growing literature on democratic government and politics. The ever widening activities of government, the changes made in structure and operation of democratic governments to carry the expanding functions, and the spread of a variety of anti-democratic forms of government in the world have compelled a thorough reconsideration of democratic creed and practice. There has been a great continuing debate on democratic government and politics.

The discussion which forms the content of this debate is scattered through many books and journals, and much of it is wrapped in a technical idiom. In 1946, when the first edition of this book was published, no introduction to this discussion which was suitable for Canadian students beginning the study of government had been made available.

The first edition attempted to provide such an introduction. In it, a comparison of the structure and working of government in Britain, the United States, and Canada was combined with an elementary analysis of the problem of democratic government under present-day conditions. It thus had a concern for analysis and political theory, on which descriptive works on government often lay little or no stress, and it also had a concreteness of reference that is often lacking in introductory books on political science.

The second edition was prepared in 1951 when it had become clearer than ever that we live in an era of profound social and political change where almost nothing can be taken for granted. A still closer examination of democratic theory and the relationship of democratic institutions and practice to that theory seemed to be called for. Accordingly, while the second edition retained the main content of the first, it offered four new chapters devoted mainly to fundamental issues. Also, a special effort was made throughout to relate the structure and operation of the governments of Canada, Britain, and the United States to these fundamental issues in a way that would be understandable to beginning students.

Events since 1951 all seem to confirm the judgment which determined the content of the second edition. The interest shown in that edition has been taken to justify another revision along the same essential lines. The book has been carefully brought up-to-date and attempts have been made to clarify obscurities and to sharpen analysis on particular points.

What was said in the prefaces to the earlier editions should be repeated here. The book does not purport to be an original contribution to the subject and is very largely based on the work of others. To have acknowledged these obligations extensively would have overburdened the text with footnotes. Most of the data can be found in standard works on the governments in question. The footnotes are mainly limited to references to a number of more specialized studies on which heavy reliance was placed. Still other, but by no means all, debts to specialized studies will be found in the Selected References at the end of the volume.

In the second edition gratitude was expressed to Professor J. E. Hodgetts for "corrections, telling criticisms, and illuminating suggestions." Professor Hodgetts has made a still greater contribution to this third edition, carrying the main burden of its preparation. He joins in signing this preface as co-author.

J. A. CORRY

J. E. HODGETTS

CONTENTS

DEMOCRATIC GOVERNMENT AND POLITICS

CHAPTER I

THE STUDY OF GOVERNMENT

IF each of us were solitary and self-sufficient, each could rule himself, and would have no need to control the actions of others, or to be controlled for the sake of others. There would be no need of government which in its simplest and most superficial appearance is the ruling of some aspects of our conduct by others for the sake of others. Nor would we have to concern ourselves with politics which is a term for a particular set of processes by which we try to bring the actions of others under the control of government, or try to divert or modify the application of government to ourselves.

SOCIETY AND GOVERNMENT

However, we are neither solitary nor self-sufficient. Man is a social creature. To flourish, or even to survive, in isolation from his fellows, he would have to be an utterly different creature from what he is. All history testifies to his need for society. We cannot alter this verdict, nor would we want to do so. The child could not survive to become the man without the family. The man could not flourish without easing the burden of securing food, clothing, and shelter through co-operation with others. If each of us had to produce unaided with our hands all our material needs, we would lead a barren and precarious existence. In economic co-operation with others, we produce wealth and not merely subsistence.

The Need for Society

Without society, there would never be the rich heritage of art and literature and practical knowledge needed to improve man's estate. Even if there were, it is only by living in society that it can be transmitted from one generation to another. If each had to learn for himself the hard way about everything we should never know or enjoy very much. Then, beyond all the selfish calculations about what a good bargain society is for the individual, there is the need for fellowship. Where one seeks his own company in solitude, thousands want to be with their fellows for purposes that run all the way from religious communion to idle gossip.

Society, as the term is used here, is not a name for an agglomeration of people like a public meeting or the residents of a particular nation. Nor is it a name for particular groups of persons organized for some purpose such as the Red Cross Society or the Society for Prevention of Cruelty to Animals. Such groups are called associations, or simply groups. Society is a term for designating the entire network of social relationships between individuals, whether within or without groups, between groups, or between individuals and groups. Thus the total of social relationships in Canada constitutes Canadian society. The word "community" will be used here from time to time in a similar sense to mean the totality of any group whether it be the people of Canada, or of a particular province, district, or city. The context will always have to be kept in mind to make clear whether it is the national community or some lesser community that is being discussed.

We enter into varied and innumerable relationships with our fellows expecting advantages and satisfactions of various kinds. If these expectations are not always to be frustrated, there must be some order and regularity in the behaviour of those participating. It is true that much of the attraction of a game is suspense about the result, an unpredictable element depending on chance or skill. But the game loses all point if there are no rules, or if everybody plays according to different rules. Even a game of chance is spoiled if somebody cheats. The social relationships that constitute society depend on some measure of order and regularity.

Economic co-operation in the factory will not satisfy expectations unless the workers come and go at fixed hours, work co-operatively and accept such direction as is needed for the common tasks. The same is true of the family, the church, the club, the school. The relationships must be based on some kind of order, must exhibit a pattern that can be relied on. While no one wants social relationships to have the faultless regularity of a machine, each must know, within limits, what to expect of the others, and these expectations must not be too often disappointed. Men must live in society in order to live at all. To maintain society, to prevent a breakdown of social relationships through wholesale failure of the expectations on which they rest, we must be disciplined in orderly social co-operation in predictable ways.

The Need for Government

This conclusion is indisputable, but it does not of itself alone prove the need for government and politics. A multitude of social relationships follow an orderly pattern which has been established and maintained without any obvious control being exercised by anybody over anybody, or at least without any control being exercised by governments. Many of our social relationships are established by custom and maintained by habit. The elementary courtesies of waiting our turn, exemplified at a high level of perfection by the English queue, rest on custom and habit. So do most of the relationships of family life. Other social relationships are based on conscious and deliberate agreement. Clubs and associations are formed and the terms of association are agreed on by the members. Of course, there is control and direction exercised by the parents in the one instance and by the officers of the club in the other. But the control is voluntarily accepted for the most part; the co-operation is spontaneous. Much of our life in society is ordered in these ways. It is even conceivable that all social relationships might be ordered on the bases of custom, habit, and agreement, that we might learn to do voluntarily all that is needed to ensure the satisfactions of social life, and thus make government and politics unnecessary.

While this is conceivable, it seems most unlikely. The history of human societies is a history of conflict as well as of voluntary co-operation. Unruly elements seem deeply rooted in human nature. Children quarrel over the terms of their play and fight for the possession of toys. These dispositions, however moderated and disciplined by social life, continue in grown-ups. The established social relationships are always frustrating to many people, and frustration leads to aggressive and unpredictable behaviour. Modern psychology pictures us all as potential aggressors, because life can never give any of us all we are capable of demanding.

Even if most of us are pacific and co-operative, the violent and unpredictable behaviour of a few is capable of disappointing most of the expectations of social life. Voluntary co-operation rests on confidence, and fear dissolves confidence. A few thugs and burglars operating without restraint can disrupt social relationships and paralyze the social life of a community. So there must be an organization to maintain order and suppress violence through the possession, and use where necessary, of coercive restraining power. This organization, in its concrete tangible form, is government. The primary and indispensable function of government is to ensure a firm framework of public order within which men can order their social life on the bases of habit, custom, and agreement. Ordinarily, it does this by making laws forbidding acts that imperil public order, and restraining those who break the law, by force if necessary.

It is not enough for the effective maintenance of public order merely to support custom and habit and the established ways of society. A community that sets itself against all change is static, asserting that the old ways cannot be improved on. The communities with whose governments this book is primarily concerned are dynamic, bent on progress and improvement. That means acceptance of the principle of change in social relationships but not necessarily any agreement on what, when, or how. The process of social change is infinitely complex but its main features are a matter of everyday observation. We have already noted that many people feel frustrated in their established social relationships. There are always individuals and groups bent on particular changes while other individuals and groups resist. This leads to friction and conflict which if not moderated by some external authority may disrupt public order just as seriously as the activities of thugs and burglars.

Much of the adjustment of this kind of conflict can be—and is—carried through by voluntary agreement of the individuals and groups affected. However, where society consists of the relationships of millions, or tens of millions, of people spread over a great territory, it is too complex for adequate adjustment always to be made by voluntary agreement. An example may be taken from the economic field. If the coal miners want a change which will give them higher wages and shorter hours of work, such a change does not merely affect them and their employers. It affects all householders and all industries that use their coal, and ultimately it affects all the consumers of goods produced by those industries.

It affects everyone in the country, and people in other countries as well. If the attempt to get higher wages and shorter hours involves a prolonged strike in the coal-mining industry, again everyone is affected. It is not possible, even with the best will in the world, for all the groups and individuals affected to adjust such a conflict by general voluntary agreement. At every turn, one will find that changes in the relationships of particular persons and groups have repercussions on many other persons and groups as well. These latter need some agency that speaks for them and protects their interest in the outcome of the conflict.

Here is another great function of government: presiding over the struggle for social change of whatever kind. Its main purpose here is to ensure that the struggle does not imperil public order. A higher price for coal is embarrassing and annoying to many but it is not likely to endanger public order, unless the rise in price is astronomical. On the other hand, prolonged strikes in the coal industry will paralyse industry and transportation and threaten public order, and government will be required to intervene to protect it. It is through the government that society, threatened by failure of a supply of coal or by any other conflict between individuals and groups, can bring pressure for a solution of the conflict, and dictate and enforce its terms if necessary. The very fact that the reserve power of government always overhangs the scene disposes the parties to the conflict to find a solution.

If we are to live in society with some assurance that it will not be disrupted by individual and group aggressions, government is necessary. Its essential function determines its character. It is an organization for controlling human action, mainly through the enforcing of rules, by sheer physical force if necessary. Present-day governments carry on many activities which seem to have little or no connection with making and enforcing of rules of conduct, just as a drugstore handles many lines besides drugs. But to understand the essential character of government and the prevailing attitude of individuals and groups towards it, it is necessary to keep its essential function always in mind. Politics is a term for describing the varied methods by which individuals and groups try to move the government to stop conduct that is disturbing public order, to compel the settlement of some conflict that is threatening public order, to enforce some social change they want, or to refrain from enforcing some social change they dislike.

Besides the danger of disruption from within, a society is exposed to attack from without, and this will continue until war has been eliminated from human affairs. Society has to take steps to protect itself from external enemies. The example of the countries that have been overrun by war in the last forty years vividly illustrates this need. Government is a necessary agent for meeting this need through the maintenance of military and naval establishments. It is the organization to which the control and application of naked force is given whether in relation to internal or external matters.

STATE AND GOVERNMENT

When the rules enforced by the government restrain us from doing things we want to do, we tend to regard it as an alien force imposed on us from the outside. We actually see some few men who form the government for the time being apply its power to control the conduct of other men. However, government is not alien and external to society. It is an essential instrument of men in society for ensuring an adequate measure of stability in society. There must be order, dictated by government decree if need be. In time past, men have supported absolute governments over which they themselves had no control because these governments ensured order. They have even regarded absolute monarchs as gifts from God for this indispensable service.

But government does not undertake to define all social relationships by law; it does not try to dictate the terms of all social co-operation by government decree. That would scarcely be possible. In any event, it is not necessary because men always want to be together in society and they exert themselves to find ways to make it possible, such as custom, habit, and voluntary agreement. Because these alone do not suffice, they support government as well to act at critical points and at critical times. All have an interest in seeing that government does its essential job. When it is doing its essential job, it acts for us all in furtherance of common interests and common purposes.

In effect, what we do, at least in democratic countries like Canada and the United States and Britain, is to become members of a compulsory mutual insurance association to ensure one another against external enemies who would ravage us by war, against private aggression within society, and against disruption of social relationships by individual and group conflict. The taxes we pay are the premiums for protection by this kind of insurance. This association is called the state.

It is an association for limited specific purposes, working by methods appropriate to those purposes. If we want to associate together for some other purposes, such as religious worship, business, or recreation, we join quite different kinds of associations working by quite different methods. Every association consisting of large numbers of persons must have a constitution prescribing how it is to act and who is to act for it in protecting the common interests and carrying out the common purposes of its members. The association that is the state has a constitution prescribing the organs of the state and the methods for selecting the persons through whom these organs find expression. These organs and persons constitute the government about which we have been talking.

The state is the expression of one aspect of society. The government as a whole is the organ of the state, and thus an instrument of society. The government at any moment has concrete and tangible form; we can hear its voice and we can see the members of Parliament, the judges, and government officials. The state is always an abstraction, a sign, or a shorthand term, for bringing into the focus of attention the discussion of the preceding pages. It denotes the "order" aspect of society. It points to unseen but important realities behind the concrete manifestations of government, helping to clarify our understanding of the place of government in society.

The State Defined as an Association

Many definitions of the state, varying in their emphasis, have been attempted. The one which best provides the emphasis wanted here may be quoted and given some comment:

The state is an association, which, acting through law as promulgated by a government endowed to this end with coercive power

external conditions of social order.[1]
maintains within a community territorially demarcated the universal

The state is concerned with order in a given territory. Its rule is universal in that territory. Everyone there must obey the law of the state, and only the government or its delegates are entitled to apply physical coercion. The monopoly of coercive power wielded by the state is called sovereignty. Membership of the state depends on the constitution and is at least as extensive as the right to vote. One cannot escape from the laws of the state and the control of the government merely by resigning one's membership. Indeed, the only effective way to resign is to take up membership in another state. Even then, unless one removes physically from the territory of the state in question, one remains subject to its control. The state does not create all social order by its coercive apparatus. Much of the order found in society is spontaneous. The primary concern of the state is with the outward conditions needed to nourish the inward impulses for orderly social relationships.

All persons have a common interest in social order. In this matter, the state can act for all its members with their approval. In fact, wherever its members discover a common interest or a common purpose, the state can appropriately act to protect that common interest and promote that common purpose. So the state can be defined rather more widely than in the foregoing definition as an association for promoting the common interests and common purposes of its members, always remembering that it is the guardianship of social order that gives the state its special and unique characteristics, and that most common interests are related, in one way or another, to the maintenance of social order.

The world is divided territorially among a number of states. The definition of the state quoted here is not valid in all its terms for all the states of the present day, nor for many of the states that have existed in the past. We shall see later why this is so. It is, however, correct for those states which have democratic governments, and the primary concern of this book is with democratic states and governments.

Strictly speaking, then, the definition is a description of a par-

[1]R. M. MacIver, *The Modern State* (Oxford University Press, Oxford, 1926), p. 22.

ticular kind of state as it now exists. It does not purport to explain the essential character of all states that have ever existed. Nor does it purport to explain the historical origin of the state. Historically, the state always arises in response to a need for order. But its first manifestations rarely take the form of an association. It has generally begun as an organization of naked power controlled by a small, imperious clique imposing order on its people as *subjects*, exploiting them harshly at the same time, and refusing them any participation in the state as *citizens*. The definition is valid only for states that have been tamed and made directly responsible to the people on whose behalf order is being provided.

Society, State, and Government

To sum up this preliminary discussion, society is the total of social relationships within the given area of the earth's surface on which attention is focused. The state is one particular constellation of social relationships, men associating together to provide the indispensable conditions of public order. The state is therefore less than society, an instrument of society for its purposes. The government is the concrete embodiment of the state consisting of the organs and persons who carry out the purposes of the state. For democratic countries at any rate, the government at any particular moment is less than the state. It is the agent of the association that directs and controls it.

It is necessary here, however, to anticipate a possible confusion about the use of the term "government." The word is widely used, and will be used here, in two different senses. First, it is used in a narrow sense as when we speak of the government of the day. It is common to speak of Mr. Diefenbaker's Government. In this sense, one could speak of President Eisenhower's Government, meaning President Eisenhower's Administration. The narrow meaning designates the executive branch of government which will be described in chapter VI. Second, the word is used in a general inclusive sense to denote the whole set of institutions through which some command and others obey. It is in this wide sense that the word is used in the title of this book, or when we speak of the study of government, ideals of government, forms of government, and so on. In a particular sentence in this book, it may not be immediately obvious in which sense the word is used. The context as a whole, however, will make it clear and the reader must attend to the context to avoid confusion.

WHY STUDY GOVERNMENT?

Government affects almost every aspect of our lives. We have already seen that it ensures for us the advantages and satisfactions of life in society. Properly designed and used, it can nourish the highest level of civilization. Clumsily and ignorantly managed, it can—and often has—led men to think it is intolerable because of the burdens it puts upon them. It always takes from us in taxes money for which we have infinite uses of our own. It can block our most cherished designs and suppress us ruthlessly if we pursue them in the face of its interdict. It can require us to sacrifice our lives in war. Normally, we can only escape it by submitting to another government somewhere else in the world which may deal with us still more harshly and summarily. If we want to know anything about our world, if we want to know what we can plan for or expect in the future, we must try to understand government.

In democratic countries, we enjoy the privileges of citizenship. Through voting in elections and other methods to be discussed later, the citizens who are members of the state collectively decide in broad outline what government will do and how it will behave. The actions of the citizens are decisive, as much by their ignorance and inattention as by their understanding and sustained interest. The man who neglects to vote is also helping to decide. It is broadly true in a democracy that we get the government we deserve. If it is bad, the first step for each of us is to deserve better by earnest effort to understand and to influence what government does.

Citizenship is more than an opportunity: it is also a responsibility. There have always been critics of democracy, government under the control of the many, who were sure it could not endure permanently because the mass of citizens would not live up to the high responsibilities it entails. It is not necessary, or even possible, for every citizen to understand the nature and problems of government. But democracy will certainly be a failure unless there comes forward voluntarily in each generation a large number of citizens prepared to give the time and thought necessary to the understanding of government and then to participate actively in political life. By the attitude we take towards this responsibility, we decide the fate of democracy.

Hitherto, there has not been enough well-informed participation by the citizens of democratic countries. Too many have assumed that they could have the advantages of "government of the people, for the people, and by the people" without their taking up the responsibilities it involves. The men who struggled from the eighteenth century onward to secure the right of participation for all would have found this most difficult to understand. They and their forebears had had a long experience as subjects of states whose governments they could not control, or even persuade to listen to them. The frustrations and humiliations of this condition led them to think that full citizenship, the right of participation in the state, was the greatest gift that could be made to man, and that men who had it would cherish it and exercise it to the full.

They, who knew the unpleasantness of the alternatives, would have deemed it incredible that the privileges and responsibilities of citizenship should be taken lightly. We, who have enjoyed for a long time the right of participation in the state, have let the unpleasantness of the alternatives fade from our minds and have taken the responsibilities of citizenship lightly. In large measure, we have done this because of the enormous success of democracy in the latter part of the nineteenth century and in the early years of the twentieth century. For a time, democracy seemed almost certain to sweep the world and to become the prevailing, if not the universal, form of government. In these circumstances, it was easy to take it for granted and forget the unpleasantness of the alternatives.

However, the late grisly episodes of dictatorship in Nazi Germany and Fascist Italy and the established Communist dictatorships in Russia, Eastern Europe, and most recently in China have warned us again that the alternatives are very real and very unpleasant. We cannot take democracy for granted. If democratic government is to maintain itself as a genuine alternative to dictatorship, it must be able to draw deeply on the informed understanding and vigorous participation of a large number of its citizens. This gives a special urgency to the study of democratic government.

Democratic government has not fulfilled all the high hopes of those who first established it in the modern world. It is even probable that some of these hopes were naïve and not capable of realization in full. Some of the indifference of citizens towards their privileges and responsibilities may be due to disillusionment. The purpose of this book is to reveal the essential characteristics of democratic government as experience seems to show them to be by describing and comparing in broad outline the governments of Canada, the United States, and Britain. Note will be taken of the defects and limitations democratic government has so far exhibited in these three countries that have practised it most successfully. An effort will be made to show what it does achieve despite its defects and limitations, and to suggest what we can fairly expect it to accomplish.

WAYS OF STUDYING GOVERNMENT

It will help to make clear the scope and limitations of this book if we look briefly at the different ways in which state and government, or particular aspects of them, can be studied. Enough has been said already to show that state and government are very complex, as complex as the total sum of social relationships with which they are in one way or another concerned. Even if one wants to understand state and government completely, one cannot study all aspects of them at once. It is necessary to isolate particular aspects or branches of the study, and focus intensively on each one separately, hoping later to combine these separate pieces of learning in a fuller understanding. Also, particular persons may be interested in one aspect of government and not in another. There have come to be a number of different branches, or foci of interest, in the study of government.

The first and most fundamental thing to note is the distinction between a study of what government actually is and does in any one or several countries, and a study of what government ought to be and ought to do. The difference is one between fact and theory. The focus of interest of each is different, and the method of study appropriate to each is different.

Government as It Is

One can study the government of Canada as it actually is, read its constitution and its laws, learn how the legislature is composed and how it makes laws, fix in one's mind how the executive, the courts, and the civil service are organized. This is a study of existing structure and machinery, and is not very revealing in itself. The next necessary step to understanding the government of Canada is to observe how men act in relation to their government whether as private citizens or as part of the government. Here one studies the behaviour of men in political parties, in elections, in pressure groups, in their dealings with various branches of the government, trying to get the government to do this, or not to do that. This is the study of political behaviour, the dynamics of government.

The examination of structure and dynamics together constitutes the study of the government of Canada, or Canadian Government. But interest is not exhausted and understanding is incomplete with the mere collection of facts. As particular facts are turned up and recorded, the student will ask how this came to be. The constitution of Canada makes no mention of or provision for political parties. Yet political parties are facts of undeniably first-rate importance in the government of Canada. Why did political parties develop? Why are there three national parties, and not four or more? For that matter, why did Parliament pass one particular law and not another? The questions that can be asked are almost endless. Asking them assumes that the facts in question have causes that can be identified. If these causes can be identified, understanding is deepened.

So the study of a particular government to be meaningful must go beyond the collection of facts to inquire into the meaning or significance of facts. This involves analysis, an attempt to discover the relation, if any, between one fact, or set of facts, and another fact. However, both description of the facts and their analysis are concerned with seeing and understanding what government actually is in a particular country.

This focus of interest and this method can be applied to one government after another, or to two or more in combination. There is a special advantage in comparing side by side two or more governments which have at the same time both marked similarities and striking differences. For example, both Britain and the United States have had two-party systems that are similar in a general way, and yet show very striking differences in their detailed structure and working. What accounts for the similarities and for the differences? Some comment will be offered on this question later. The point to be noted now is that such comparison can be hoped to deepen the analysis of cause and effect, and thus improve the understanding of the essentials of both governments. Study conducted on these lines is known as Comparative Government. This book falls largely, though by no means entirely, in that category.

Government as It Ought to Be

Then there is the study of government as it ought to be, the search for standards for judging the rightness or wrongness of particular governments as they actually exist and work. Presumably life has a purpose or purposes, and government, if it makes any sense at all, must be an instrument of these purposes. What are the ideals or goals at which we should aim? Is government necessary to help towards these goals? If so, in what way can government help or hinder; what should it do? When should it bring its monopoly of coercive power to bear on individuals, and when should it refrain? Who should be allowed to participate in governing and how best can government be organized to achieve the purposes we have decided it should pursue?

These and similar questions have been asked again and again since the first beginnings of government. Academic philosophers have asked them as academic questions and tried to find answers for them. Both philosophers and ordinary men have asked them as agonizingly practical questions when they were trying to decide whether it was their duty to obey their government, or to resist it when they themselves thought what it was doing was wrong. There is an immense literature recording what men in the western world have thought on these questions in the last 2,500 or more years. The study of this record, and of original thought on these questions, with a view to finding answers to problems of our own times is called Political Philosophy, or Political Theory. One's conclusions on it may lead one to deny the rightness of one's own government and to demand that it be changed.

In every stable society, there is a widely-held set of beliefs, or ideals, of what government should be, and they exercise a pervasive and powerful influence on the structure and working of government in that society. There is a democratic political theory which seeks to justify democratic government and also to determine the uses to which a democratic government will be put. A study of the governments of Britain, Canada, and the United States which ignored the ideals that have largely determined the present structure, and press constantly on the daily working, of these governments would be incomplete. Accordingly, the following chapter attempts to outline democratic political ideals, and to contrast them in a summary way with the beliefs that have motivated some modern dictatorships. Succeeding chapters will try to show in what ways the structure and the working of the governments of these three democratic countries are responses to the democratic ideals.

Government as Cause and Effect Will Make It

There is a third approach to the study of government and politics, which is concerned not only with understanding what is, but also with predicting what will be. It does not focus on the issue of what men should do in government and politics, but on what their fundamental human nature will lead them to do in specific sets of circumstances. We are all given to predictions of this kind in every field of human activity. We say that certain things cannot be done because they are against human nature, or that particular kinds of behaviour are inevitable, given human nature. Such forecasts are based on the assumption that human nature, or at least certain elements in it, are constant, and do not change from person to person and from time to time. The public opinion polls take a sample composed of the opinions of a few thousand people and on this basis predict how several millions will vote. The predictions are not always right but they are always based on an assumption of constancy in human nature and human behaviour.

The interest in prediction is always present in the study of government, as distinct from the study of political philosophy. Whenever we say that political facts A and B in combination cause political event C, we are asserting cause and effect relationships which are the basis of all prediction. It will be suggested later that the fact of political parties, and some at least of the behaviour of men in parties, is the inevitable outcome of human nature in a certain kind of political and social environment. To say, as is sometimes said, that the president of the United States should have the power to dissolve Congress and call a new congressional election at any time instead of having fixed election dates as at present assumes that political behaviour reacting to these changed circumstances would bring predictable beneficial results.

Our power of prediction in politics is markedly defective, partly because of the complexity of both human nature and of the circumstances and conditions to which human nature reacts. Also, we have not been able to determine how far men are conditioned by their nature and by circumstances, and how far each is free to direct his actions by conscious and deliberate aim. Presumably men are in some measure conditioned or there would be no sense in talking about cause and effect, or in trying to make any predictions, in human affairs. Presumably men are in some measure free to choose or there would be no point at all in the thousands of years of talk about what government ought to do, or ought not to do. To talk in this way assumes that men are free, to some degree at least, to decide how their government shall be organized and what it shall do. But we do not know where the line between determinism and free will really lies.

The science of psychology is trying to discover how far human behaviour can be predicted. Psychologists amass great bodies of data from which they draw generalizations about how men can be expected to act in certain defined sets of circumstances. This method can be, and is being, applied to the study of political behaviour in elections, in the relations between political leaders and followers, and so on. There may some day be a reliable science of political behaviour but at present it is still in its early, although distinctly promising, stages.[1]

Materials for attempting predictions in the field of government and politics can be drawn from history as well as from psychology. History reveals to us a long record of the vicissitudes of states and governments. In the course of history, there have been a great number of states and governments, and we know a good deal about

[1]For a recent stimulating study of this kind, see Sebastian De Grazia, *The Political Community* (University of Chicago Press, Chicago, 1948).

how they arose, how they developed and flourished, how they were torn by civil war or revolution, how they fell, or how they have endured for varying lengths of time. By a study of this record, we may be able to discern constantly recurring patterns in history according to which states rise, thrive, and fall.[1] To take specific examples, it has been urged, on the basis of historical record, that men have always been ruled by an élite, a small governing class, who always make their will prevail whatever the forms of government, and further, that they always will be so ruled.[2] A fascinating study of a number of political revolutions in the past shows them all going through several remarkably similar stages,[3] tempting one to predict that future revolutions will also go through these same stages. Communism claims the warrant of history for its predictions about the outcome of our times, although not resting its case by any means on history alone.[4]

A study that finds laws by which to predict what will happen in politics in carefully defined sets of circumstances differs markedly from both the study of Government and the study of Political Theory, and is appropriately called Political Science. "Science" is here used in the sense of a body of knowledge that enables us to make accurate predictions on the analogy of the natural sciences, notably physics and chemistry. The identifying mark of these two sciences is the power of prediction.

To talk of political science in this sense is somewhat pretentious because in the present state of knowledge our ability to predict the course of political events is very limited indeed. One has only to ask how much reliable forecast there is in one decade of the major political events of the next decade. We think that careful analysis has given us some insight into causal relationships in government and politics, and the patient intensive study of political behaviour will no doubt give us further and deeper insights. At present, however, political science in this strict sense has not advanced very far. It represents an aspiration to a deeper knowledge of political forces rather than any substantial body of reliable generalizations.

[1]Arnold Joseph Toynbee, *A Study of History*, Abridgement of Vols. I-VI by D. C. Somervell (Oxford University Press, London, 1946).

[2]James Burnham, *The Machiavellians* (The John Day Co., New York, 1943).

[3]Crane Brinton, *The Anatomy of Revolution* (Allen and Unwin, London, 1939).

[4]See pp. 51-63, *post*.

Political Science as Systematic Study of Government

The term, political science, is more often used in a wider and looser sense to cover the entire study of government and politics in whatever aspect and by any of the methods outlined above. Very often a university course in Political Science will cover a general description of the forms of government, of constitutions and the different organs of government, an analysis of the state as an aspect of society, and a consideration of theoretical views on what governments ought to be and ought to do. In this wider sense, the identifying mark of "science" is in the methods of study used: painstaking accuracy in observation and in collection of facts, and systematic analysis by close logical reasoning. Defined in this way, any comprehensive systematic body of knowledge about a specified area of inquiry may be called a science.

In this sense, there is a political science, and this book at least attempts to be scientific. When, as often happens, universities put the label, Political Science, on one or more of their courses in government and politics, they are generally using "science" in this sense. Much of the argument and difference of opinion on whether the study of government is, or can be, a science turns on sharply different definitions of what is a science. It is only when the narrow definition is accepted that a serious issue arises. There is nothing to be gained by pursuing that particular issue further here.

For anyone to satisfy his own mind whether the study of government is, or can be, a science, he needs first of all to master the existing body of knowledge about government and politics. This book is at most an introduction to a part of that body of knowledge. Then he would need to learn what history and psychology and several other branches of systematic knowledge tell us about human behaviour in the past and in the present. With that knowledge, he will be fully aware of the difficulties of deciding. Without it, he cannot make any useful judgment on the issue. As in everything else, one must begin at the beginning.

The purpose here is to make a beginning with one particular kind of government, democratic government, trying to make clear in an elementary way what its essential features are, how it works, and how it is related to the ideals it is supposed to be furthering.

CHAPTER II

IDEALS OF GOVERNMENT

IN a developed society, we are conscious of having some freedom of choice in our actions. At a given moment, we can decide to do this rather than that. In order to make the choice, we must believe that one course of action is right and another wrong, or at the very least, that one is more worthwhile than another. Without such beliefs, we could not order our activities into any coherent pattern. These beliefs express a set of values for which we live, define a system of ends, or ideals, towards which we direct our efforts. These ends or values give meaning to life; without them, we develop disordered personalities.

THE NEED FOR COMMON IDEALS

It is not enough for each individual to have a private set of values as an exclusive possession. Each would then be cut off from his fellows, tortured by the loneliness that often afflicts the stranger in a great city. One cannot feel at home in the world without friends, and friendship is essentially a sharing of interests and values secured only by living in society. More than that, even the private aims and satisfactions through which we express whatever individuality we have are made possible almost entirely by social co-operation in an ordered society. At the peak of self-expression, the artist is largely dependent on others for the leisure and the materials his art requires. To free the poet for his art, others must work at more prosaic tasks. To get any spontaneity in co-operation, the participants must be somewhat in agreement on the ends to be served by their integrated effort. They must share common objectives, or at least have similar aims which induce them to work in concert.

A complex society such as ours involves an immense amount of social co-operation on an extended plane. For men to establish common schools to educate their children, they must have some common conception of what education is for. Participation in the division of labour as we now know it brings us into far-flung co-operation with millions we never know and never see. What kind of a system of organized mass coercion would be required to bring to the assembly line of the great automotive plant the varied materials it needs, or to ensure the delivery of all the items in the T. Eaton Co. catalogue? There must be some widely accepted version of the larger purposes to be served by economic co-operation on this scale. There must be some steadying vision seen together, some music to which men respond in unison.

Although their lives are largely guided by them, relatively few individuals can give a coherent account of the common values of their society. Because these values are generally accepted, they go unnoticed by most people. Much of our conduct is brought into harmony with them by habit, habit which is inculcated by the family, school, and church in our formative years. They often lie below the level of consciousness. In so far as they are consciously held, it rarely occurs to us that we might hold different ones. We think of these values almost as part of the order of nature, meriting comment no more than the landscape we see every day, and no more subject to modifying criticism than the weather.

These common values are part of the social inheritance passed on from generation to generation. Their roots lie very deep in the past. In the main, they are not indigenous to Britain and North America. They were slowly developed and refined by Western European civilization. It is increasingly common now to refer to them comprehensively as the Western political tradition. It is also true that we have become increasingly more articulate about them in recent years. The Fascist regime in Italy, the Nazi scourge in Germany, and the Communist system in Russia all rejected the main elements of the Western tradition and challenged its validity. If we must defend our way of life with our lives, it is important to know whether it is worth that price and why. We want to know what is the essence of the common ideal.

First, however, it should be emphasized that the common ideals set standards for government too. The state has been defined as an association for achieving common purposes. Therefore co-operation in government, as in other forms of social co-operation, depends on shared ideals. Men may indeed submit to providing sport for the gods, but the governors will first have to implant the idea that they are gods. There must be some congruence between what government is doing and what seems good to the governed.

This does not mean that every action of government must be calculated to win unanimous applause. We know that all governments have the power to apply coercion, use the threat of coercion to get obedience, and where that fails, actually bring physical force to bear on substantial numbers of people. Even at the best, there are always some who will not observe the minimum conditions of social life or do not agree with the common view of what these minimum conditions are. Thus government from time to time has to take drastic action which dismays and/or angers very substantial numbers of the governed. Coercion has its difficulties, and even the threat of coercion has nasty aspects. For this reason, it is necessary for governments to have a line of credit on which to draw. All credit depends on confidence. The credit of government depends on satisfaction with its general aim and on a conviction that its general aim is not seriously falsified by its record of performance.

A government which lacks credit with its people soon finds that it has to maintain itself by force at every turn. While sheer force may serve in the short run, it is self-defeating in the long run. This truth is expressed in the common saying that you can do anything with bayonets except sit on them. All governments which endure depend in some measure on consent. Even governments which keep a significant portion of their people in slave labour camps must have some popular support however secured. It may be secured by propaganda and fraud. But government cannot get on without unifying ideas any more than society will endure in their absence.

THE DEMOCRATIC ULTIMATE: RESPECT FOR INDIVIDUAL PERSONALITY

Our concern here is with the deeply embedded beliefs that support and justify present-day democratic government, and with the rejection of these beliefs that has brought modern dictatorship to the fore. There are, it is true, significant differences in emphasis in the ideals actually honoured in different democratic countries, and the modern dictators vary in the raucousness of their repudiation of Western thought. Yet there is a common core of values that supports all functioning Western democracies, and a basic similarity in the negations of the dictatorships.

This common core has been shaped through a long period of history. The beginnings of the Western tradition from which Britain, Canada, and the United States derive their ideals of government can be traced to Greek political thought five centuries before the Christian era. Significant features of it come from Hebrew thought introduced into the West by Christianity. The Western tradition began to take distinctive shape with the mingling of Graeco-Roman and Hebraic-Christian elements in the later days of the Roman Empire. The fusing of these elements went on in Western Europe for a thousand years before the beginning of the modern age, and produced a remarkable synthesis in the political thought of the Middle Ages.

The modern age ushered in by the Renaissance and Reformation rejected the medieval synthesis and went back again to the classical age of Greece and Rome and to earlier Christianity for inspiration. Another four hundred years of thought and reflection went into the formulation of the democratic ideal as we know it in Britain and America. While the formulation is different and distinctive, it was not made out of whole cloth. In large measure, it is another synthesis achieved by reworking ideas long current in Western thought. Because of the great emphasis it puts on individual liberty, it is most accurately described as the liberal democratic ideal.

A brief sketch cannot do justice to a synthesis that rests on two thousand years of thought and reflection. It can only attempt to state the essentials, ignoring many of the qualifications and refinements of statement needed for precision. Unfortunately, a bald statement of essentials lumps together a number of beliefs that seem on superficial appearance and in everyday unreflective experience to be mutually contradictory. Democrats believe in individual freedom and in social order, in individual freedom and social equality. Yet it often appears that the demands of one can only be met at the expense of the other.

It is not possible here to phrase a reconciliation of these beliefs. Actually, that reconciliation is one of the perennial and never-ending tasks of democratic politics. But it is necessary to see how a reconciliation is possible. The possibility exists because not all the various ends, purposes, values, and objectives cherished by democratic society are regarded as having equal rank or worth. Some are held because they are thought to contribute to the achieving of still other higher ends. Thus we believe in freedom and social equality, not for themselves alone but rather because they are both needed in varying proportion to create the best environment for the development of individual personality.

A wide range of individual freedom enables some to get rich while others remain poor, thus producing sharp social inequalities. Intervening in this situation for the purpose of enforcing some measure of equality will limit individual freedom. The clash between the claims of individual freedom and social equality can be resolved by asking what combination of freedom and equality is needed to promote the purpose that is higher than either of them, the full and rich development of individual personality.

If all other values are subordinate to the claims of individual personality, then it is the superior value, the highest of the democratic ideals. But why should it be the ultimate? Should not our highest aim be to do the will of God, or to serve Truth and Goodness? The ideals of democratic government, that is, government controlled by the people for their purposes, must be widely accepted and believed by the people or they cannot, by definition, be democratic ideals. Respect for individual personality is the maximum on which it has been possible to get widespread agreement. If we say our highest ideal is to do the will of God, that raises the question of what God's will is. If we say our highest ideal is to serve Truth and make it prevail, that raises the question of what Truth is. Answers to these questions will turn on religious or philosophical views about the nature of the universe and man's place in it. And when we ask what is the final scheme of things and man's place in it, we meet divergent answers and hot dispute. We are in the midst of the controversies of the ages, and beyond the area in which general agreement is possible in our present state of knowledge.

Disagreement on Cosmic Ultimates

We cannot frame or hold a common ideal that depends on the prior settlement of questions we cannot presently settle. It is not an accident that all the functioning democracies are committed to religious toleration. Also, it is of the highest significance that modern democracy did not begin to develop and flourish until the commitment on religious toleration was made. For it is in the sphere of religious belief that views on first and last things find passionate and diverse expression. In taking religion out of politics, three assumptions vital to modern democracy were made.

First, by virtue of their common humanity, men have enough common interests, and can find a sufficient basis of common beliefs, to found a system of order without having to be committed to dogmatic answers to all the ultimates. Second, the profoundest need of all men is for self-expression (in selfless as well as self-regarding forms) and all the various interests they struggle to defend and promote are means to that end. Third, they can agree to concede to others the claim to personality that they make for themselves on the ground that, given mutual trust and confidence, this is the best way to protect their own most cherished claims and promote their own deepest needs, including their need for fellowship with others of their fellow-men.

From the point of view of democracy, the highest value, *the ultimate for politics*, is the liberation of and respect for individual personality. In the cosmic sense, there are other values to which men may make personal commitments. For example, the communist thinks himself to be in possession of a cosmic truth, a final purpose toward which all creation moves, and which he wants to see vindicated through political action at whatever cost to individual men and women here and now. But from the point of view of democracy, government is a mundane affair, primarily concerned with a framework of order which will serve the concrete needs and interests of an earth-bound humanity. If men will make the adjustments necessary to secure firmly for one another these needs and interests, they are freed in their persons for the pursuit of the various forms of excellence that seem good to them. If one's vision is solitary, he can hitch his wagon to the star of his choice. If he finds others of like mind, they can go forward in voluntary and satisfying fellowship. If the vision fades for some, they need go no further. But when government is harnessed to a cosmic purpose, all are required to go in the same wagon to the same star, willy-nilly.

Freeing Persons to Pursue Higher Values

Making individual personality the ultimate value for politics does not deny the existence of other higher values for individual or group activity.[1] On the contrary, it frees men to pursue them. If the highest value is to glorify God, God is best glorified by willing servants who submit freely to His demands as they see them. If the highest value is Truth, it must be discovered by individual minds free of constraint, building on the insights of other free minds. Truth, it is said, will set us free, but we must be free to search for it in the first place. And if Truth is to prevail throughout the world, it must suffuse individual personalities with a sense of its imperative. Belief cannot be coerced; it must be freely given.

What we apprehend of these values, whether it be Goodness, Truth, or Beauty, is crystallized for us by the religious, intellectual, and artistic expression of individual personalities. It is true that individuals give diverse, and often conflicting, interpretations of these values. If it is recognized that each has a right to his own view as long as he respects the equal right of others to their views, competitive expression in these matters enriches our lives. To put it another way, art, literature, and science are debased, and the artist and scientist are defiled, when instead they conform slavishly to the dictates of a government which claims to be the final authority on first and last things. So the fundamental goal of democratic politics is the securing of the conditions needed for the realization of individual potentialities. Perhaps this goal can never be fully achieved because it makes stupendous demands on human nature. Yet it is the pursuit of this goal that gives meaning to political life in the democracies.

[1]Nor does it deny that, in the final analysis, belief in the value of individual personality must rest on some view of cosmic ultimates, framed in religious or philosophical terms. It merely reiterates that we are far from any agreement on ultimate truth. For example, Christians affirm that belief in the importance of individual personality and in the related values of individual freedom, responsibility, and equality depends on acceptance of the Christian view of man and the universe; positivists deny it; and sceptics beg leave to doubt. All that is affirmed here is that democracy has been made a going concern in Britain, Canada, and the United States with individual personality as the ultimate for politics and has managed, over a long period, to get a common loyalty both from those who profess ignorance or doubt about cosmic ultimates and from those who claim to know the final answer but differ as to what it is.

Stoic and Christian Emphasis on Personality

In committing itself to the value of individual personality, democracy is carrying forward one of the most persistent themes of the Western tradition. Before the Christian era, the Stoic philosophers in Greece asserted the brotherhood of men, the claims of a common humanity which makes us all members one of another. They urged the duty of the individual to realize Truth and Goodness in his own life, to enlighten the understanding of his fellows by precept and example, and to attest his faith in human dignity by succouring the unfortunate.

The central features of the Christian message are the infinite worth of the individual soul, the denial of all distinctions of rank or place, and the redemption of mankind through pity and love. Christianity asserted too the awful responsibility of the individual to God, and the necessity of rendering an account of his stewardship at the Last Judgment. In the final balance of the soul, duty to an earthly king would not be an excuse for failing in the service of God. While Christianity admits that Caesar is entitled to his due, it is not Caesar who sits at the Last Judgment. Religious duty has a higher claim than any earthly authority.

Translated into secular terms, the Christian emphasis on the unique value of the individual soul expresses itself as a profound concern for human personality. The imperative of love for one's neighbour and the denial of social distinctions, issue in a demand for the creation of the conditions of self-realization for all, for rough equality of opportunity. The overriding duty to supernatural authority expresses itself in a demand for the limitation of the power of governments so as to ensure to the individual a sphere of private judgment in which his conscience is his guide. Conscience speaks peremptorily but with a different voice to different people. This accounts for much of the bewildering differences of opinion in democratic politics.

Thus the ideal of democracy, although stated in secular terms, has a powerful religious sanction for its main tenets. There is much of the passion which religious feeling evokes in the support ardent democrats give to the claims of personality. There is much of Christian compassion in the demand for a large measure of social equality. Christian belief in the responsibility of the individual to God gives strong support to the claim for individual freedom.

The Ideal of Individual Freedom

At later points in this book we shall be concerned with the political significance of the claim to individual freedom and private judgment, and the consequent proliferation of diverse opinions. At present we are concerned with the ideals on which there is a large measure of agreement, verging on a religious dogma. In so far as there is a persistent enduring ideal, it is respect for personality. Liberty and equality are also democratic ideals but they are honoured when they subserve the claims of personality, and limited and qualified insofar as they do not contribute to this purpose. The claims of personality provide the criterion for testing the validity of all other ideals in the political sphere.

Individual freedom or liberty is the necessary condition for the realization of the potentialities of personality. The sheltered, protected person, like the slave whose choices are made for him by others, is likely to be a colourless, starved, and even weak, personality. It is the making of moral choices in which we assess the alternatives and then abiding by the consequences of the decision that develop character and make life rich and meaningful. The long struggle for individual freedom arose from the claims of ever larger numbers of men seeking to secure for themselves this means to the enrichment of their lives.

It must be added at once that the ideal of respect for personality does not support and justify every claim for freedom. It justifies only that freedom which is exercised responsibly, which respects the equal claims of other personalities to the conditions of self-realization. The criminal law expresses a thousand limitations on the freedoms of those who are disposed to disregard the claims of others. Some basic order and physical security from violence is at once seen to be necessary if we are to live in society and enjoy the enrichment of our lives that society makes possible. More controversially, if the freedom of the business man to do as he likes with his own property can be shown, in present-day conditions, to blight and frustrate the lives of many people, there is a case for its limitation. The ideal of freedom is therefore not an absolute, not an end in itself, but rather a means to the liberation of personality and justified only to the degree that it serves that purpose. This is the key to the reconciliation of the rival claims of freedom and order.

Where there are millions of individuals each bent on securing and defending his claims to self-realization, there is bound to be continual competitive striving and collision. The peaceful harmonizing of freedom and order may seem an impossible task. It is impossible if each thinks only of himself without regard to the claims of others and blindly refuses to consider the mutual benefits of participation in a society inspired by mutual respect. But the democratic ideal postulates a decent respect for others, an admission that each must exercise his freedom responsibly, and therefore a willingness at least to discuss the validity of his claims and to refer them to some tribunal for settlement. It permits each to argue his case tenaciously, yet counsels him to concede something to the reasonable claims of others reasonably put forward. If this attitude were not widely held, the widespread discussion that goes on in newspapers and legislatures and on election platforms would never take place. Men who are not prepared at some point to contemplate concessions will not be willing to debate. The very fact of debate implies a willingness to "listen to reason," and a recognition by the participants that they will have to moderate their demands if these are shown in discussion to be inconsistent with some generally accepted principle.

THE BELIEF IN RATIONALITY

In other words, the democratic ideal assumes that man is a rational being, capable of finding principles of action and subordinating private desires to those principles. This assumption is of basic importance. If men will not "listen to reason," democracy cannot be an enduring form of government. The conflicting aims and interests of numerous individuals cannot be arbitrated and harmonized by discussion and debate unless there are generally accepted rules to decide who wins the debate. The simplest and most obvious of these rules is that the majority carries the day. But the bare principle of majority rule is just as irrational as the proposition that might is right. We choose ballots—and the process of discussion involved therein—rather than bullets because the former makes room for rational procedures. For example, in discussion of rival claims, it is common to ask each claimant what he would expect to get if he were in the other's shoes. This is an appeal to a principle, the principle of equality of treatment for all who stand in the same position.

In a society where there is mutual respect for individual personality, men have some confidence that when the majority is making up its mind, the appeal to principles will not go entirely unheeded. To be more specific, there is some confidence that when a case is shown to rest on erroneous statements of fact, it will be discredited, that when it is shown to conflict with some widely accepted principle, it will be held to be a bad case. On the other hand, there is some confidence that when a case rests on proved facts and accepted principle, it will be given favourable consideration.

Of course, none of us shows full respect for facts and logic all the time. Some men are always immune to reason, and there are times when emotional appeals seem almost to drive reason from the field. Men are also creatures of feeling and not mere logical machines. But the peaceful interplay of free personalities requires a substantial measure of rationality. The democratic ideal therefore has to assume that, through effort, men can move from the plane of feeling to the plane of reason, there to talk out their differences and settle them on some basis of principle.

THE IDEAL OF EQUALITY

Another vital democratic ideal is equality. Just as in the case of individual freedom, there is the widest possible divergence of interpretation as to what this ideal requires. Some democrats interpret it narrowly, saying it requires only equality before the law, and equal political rights in voting. At the other extreme, it is held by some to require social and economic equality, putting everyone on the same level of income and obliterating all social distinctions. Much of the struggle in contemporary democratic politics is concerned with this issue.

Every attempt to define the ideal of equality with precision raises the problem of harmonizing it with the ideal of liberty. It is obvious that men are not equal in natural endowment, whether it be health or stature or intelligence. So, if they are left free to make of themselves what their inborn capacities make possible, they will turn out to be unequal in artistic perception, intellectual accomplishment, economic status and what not. Accordingly, an attempt to enforce a dead level of economic and social status will involve the sharpest of restrictions on individual freedom. Even if the emphasis is on pulling the weaker up, a uniform level can only be reached by holding the stronger down. On the other hand, the lifting of all restrictions on individual liberty would mean, in practical effect, the abandoning of the ideal of equality. How are liberty and equality to be reconciled?

Reconciling Liberty and Equality

They are to be reconciled by remembering that both liberty and equality are subordinate means to the end of releasing the potentialities of individual personality on the widest possible scale. The development of a rich variety of personalities requires a large measure of liberty and forbids all attempts to impose a dead level of social and economic equality. On the other hand, if men are to live together with mutual respect and harmonize their differences by peaceful discussion, they must be able to meet on some plane of equality. For the purposes of discussion, they must treat one another as if they were equal. Even in the midst of differences in natural endowment and in social and economic position, the assumption of equality for the purpose of discussion need not be a fiction. The Christian and Stoic doctrines of the brotherhood of man, if strongly held, dwarf all differences between men, and make their membership one of another a vivid aspect of existence. Differences of natural endowment and of social position can become almost irrelevant if there is a sufficiently keen appreciation of what they have in common.

However, we know that, for most of us, the consciousness of brotherhood needs to be buttressed by the sharing of common experience. The antagonism that exists between classes even in democratic countries clearly illustrates this point. So also does the fact that there is more give and take within nations than between nations. Where there are wide distinctions of economic status and social position, the feelings of superiority and inferiority that emerge make discussion between the two extremes almost impossible. It is impossible for the depressed poor to debate on anything like equal terms with the very rich. Even with good will, the experience of life of the two groups is so different that they can scarcely understand each other. They belong to different worlds and cannot find enough common ground for discussion.

The convention of equality vitally necessary for the purposes of discussion can scarcely be maintained where social and economic inequalities are so great as to be a standing refutation of it. Discussion moves most easily in a society where these inequalities are kept within bounds. Under the impulsion of the ideal of equality, democratic societies have been moving steadily for over fifty years to reduce existing social and economic inequalities. In this movement, the aim has not been to reach a flat level of economic equality but rather to create a rough equality of opportunity so that each individual, no matter how circumscribed his origins, may by his efforts bring his innate capacities to fruition. Phrased in this way, the ideals of liberty and equality can be reconciled in the service of personality. The actual reconciliation at a particular time and place has to be worked out through discussion in the political process.

To sum up, the ideal of equality has insisted that men are politically equal, that all citizens are equally entitled to take part in political life, to exercise the franchise, to run for and hold office. It has insisted that individuals shall be equal before the law, that when the general law confers rights or imposes duties, these rights and duties shall extend to all; or conversely, that the law shall not confer special privileges on particular individuals or groups such as exempting football stars from the law of assault and battery. For the rest, the emphasis has not been on an enforced flat level of actual equality but on a liberating equality of opportunity.

THE IDEAL OF JUSTICE

No account of the ideals of government would be even superficially adequate without some discussion of the ideal of justice. Those who struggled to establish democratic government in the world and those who have struggled to improve it have been inspired by a quest for justice. Indeed, Western political thought for more than 2000 years can be represented as a ceaseless effort to define justice so that governments and other social arrangements could be directed towards achieving it. Every form of government we have known has been defended on the ground that its rule was just, and has also been attacked because it maintained intolerable injustice. There is a universal human yearning for justice.

Yet despite the protracted debate about justice, no general and lasting agreement on a definition of justice has been reached. To take only the question of the distribution of economic rewards, some have tried to show that justice requires payment according to merit, others have insisted that the standard must be payment according to need, leaving, be it noted, both merit and need still to be defined. Still others have urged standards as diverse as equality of incomes, on the one hand, and what the market will bear, on the other. Equally divergent and clashing views are held on what justice requires in social relationships outside the economic field. One can almost say that each has his own private dream of a just society, and that that dream defines justice for him. Just as men disagree about Truth, Beauty, and Goodness, so they disagree about Justice. And a common ideal requires agreement rather than disagreement.

Yet it is not possible to dismiss the discussion of justice in this way. From the time of Aristotle there has been a persistent tendency to define justice as some kind of a proportion between merits on the one hand, and rewards and recognition on the other. For example Justinian in his codification of Roman Law in A.D. 525 defined justice for the legal system as the giving to every man his due. Even this, of course, remains vague for it presupposes a standard for weighing merit and assessing rewards.

Men are not satisfied to get merely what some authority external to themselves thinks they deserve. So the establishing of merit in a way that will be accepted as just requires men to be free to try to prove their own valuation of themselves as correct. Equally, since one man's meat is another man's poison, they must be free to say what they regard as fitting reward or recognition. If what wage-workers really want is a share in the control of their working conditions, the demand cannot be met by merely raising their wages. In other words, justice as a democratic ideal is in part subsumed under the ideal of freedom.

Justice and Equality

The notion of justice as a proportion also implies equality in the sense that persons of equal merit should get equal reward and recognition. Phrased in this general and comprehensive way, the ideal of justice almost comes to a nice refining of the ideal of equality. If governments were asked to enforce justice in this comprehensive sense, some authority would have to be set up that would decide exactly what each was worth and what each should get. But where the dominating political ideal is the liberation of personality, men will not agree to this, and the ideal of justice so phrased would be a profoundly disrupting force rather than a unifying ideal.

As was suggested earlier, the political ideal of democracy is not the vindication of cosmic truth. Neither is it the vindication of some conception of exquisite and exact justice, to be enforced though the heavens fall. Its primary concern is rather the establishment of order and security adequate for the free development of personality. It expresses a faith that once men are secure in their persons, they will learn to treat one another with respect and even become friends. Friends do not need to demand justice of one another because that—and more—is freely given without the asking.

But none of this can come to pass without a solid framework of order and security. Moreover, in this vital sphere, all should be treated equally. We all need the protection that order affords, and therefore we must all be made to observe its requirements. Its requirements can only be met by measuring every action against standards laid down in advance by law. The law should be general, playing no favourites and laying down reciprocal rights and duties for all. If it exempts some from the duties it imposes on others, it creates privilege. If the judge, in applying a general law, excuses some but not others from the obligations it imposes, he creates favouritism.

When Justinian said justice aimed to give every man his due, he was declaring against legal privilege and against favouritism in applying the law. It is highly significant that when we think today about an impartial law being impartially applied, we talk about the administration of justice. The most specific meaning given to justice in the Western tradition is justice according to law, which in the main means equality before the law. Here the elusive notion of justice as a proportion between merits and deserts is brought down to earth. All merit equal treatment in the vital sphere of order and security protected by law. Also, as we have seen, it is widely believed that all merit some rough equality of opportunity.

THE IDEAL OF RULE BY LAW

The ideal of an impartial law impartially administered is, of course, conceived as a buttress to individual personality. No one can have any security for his claims as a person, no one can plan his life or take the risk of the responsibility for his own actions, unless he knows what he has a right to try to do, and what demands others can effectively make on him. But if he is forearmed with this knowledge he has a chart for his voyage. He can anchor his personality firmly with the cords of the law. Of course, no one can expect to have charts and anchorage supplied solely for his convenience. Each must submit to rule for the benefit of others embarked on the adventure of life. Realizing the potentialities of personality requires freedom but always freedom under law.

To have to submit to capricious and forcible interference is an indignity as well as a frustration. In submitting to the law, however, one submits to a principle which makes equal demands on all. In this, there is no indignity and only such frustration of individual desires as is equally suffered by others for the sake of an ordered society.

The individual needs to know the limits of his rights and duties in relation to his fellow-citizens. He also needs to know the limits of his rights and duties in relation to his government. There is little point in being free from the caprice of private persons if one remains subject to unlimited and unpredictable demands by the government. There is no essential difference between being bullied by a bully and being bullied by a policeman, a customs official, or an income tax inspector. Capricious action by a government can be far more oppressive than capricious action by private persons because governments have far more power, a longer reach, and much greater resources for persecution.

On this view of things, the good life is not to be secured by finding a wise ruler and then blindly obeying whatever orders he thinks good for his subjects. Rather, it is to be secured through obedience to a law which defines clearly what the government as well as private persons can and cannot do. Five centuries before the Christian era, Aristotle explained why it was better for the citizens to be ruled by a fixed law than by the imponderable wisdom of even a wise ruler. Ever since then, Western political thought has been developing and strengthening this conviction. The ideal of rule by law, of "a government of laws and not of men," has been one of the strongest beliefs in the democratic creed.

RULE BY LAW AND CONSTITUTIONALISM

Closely related to the ideal of rule by law is the ideal of constitutionalism. Starting from the conviction that government action should be in accordance with law carefully laid down beforehand, it holds that the best way to accomplish this is to establish a fundamental law which defines the organs of government, prescribes how they shall function, and outlines the basic relationships between government and the private citizen. Government is then denied the power to change this fundamental law, and required to observe its terms. Actually, of course, constitutionalism is a means for achieving the ideal of rule by law. But in the democratic world, the constitution has become a symbol around which men who are in disagreement on other points can be rallied. A special sanctity attaches to the constitution, and a special revulsion to unconstitutional actions or proposals.

It is worth while to note how deep the roots of constitutionalism are in Western culture. Greek political thought was profoundly concerned with the notion of a constitution which would regularize the actions of government but it did not put special emphasis on the rights of individuals against governments. Strong emphasis on this point was supplied by Stoic and Christian thought. The Stoic philosophers worked out a conception of a law of nature unconditionally binding on all men at all times in all places because it expressed the permanent demands of their innermost nature. That is to say, it was thought of as a fundamental law binding on rulers and ruled alike. Christian thought asserted that God rules the world and that the commandments He gives His creatures form the Divine law. Rulers should obey this fundamental law as part of their duty to God. Moreover, individuals cannot render to God that which is God's if Caesar is allowed to use his power to prevent them doing so. Government, therefore, must be limited by a law higher than any commands it makes. Secular and religious elements in the Western tradition combine to support rule by law and constitutionalism. To trace the Bill of Rights, and related provisions about civil liberties in the constitutions of Britain, Canada, and the United States, to their sources in human thought would take us back to Stoic philosophy and basic Christian doctrine.

DISAGREEMENT DESPITE COMMON IDEALS

It has been said that these are the motivating political ideals of democracy. It cannot be said, however, that they are graven on the heart of every citizen of a democracy. There are always substantial numbers who are little moved by ideals of any kind. Even those who acknowledge these ideals do not always give automatic and undivided loyalty to them just as sincere professing Christians do not always live up to the high professions of their faith. Moreover, since the ideals all celebrate the importance of individual personality, they invite individual self-expression. Individuals earnestly bent on developing and expressing their inherent capacities will often find it difficult to draw the fine line between legitimate expression of themselves and unwarrantable interference with the claims of others for opportunities to realize *their* capacities. Indeed, it is so difficult that some serious thinkers in every age have deemed it impossible and have urged the necessity of authoritarian government to keep everyone in his place.

Most important of all, these ideals are vague and do not lay down specific rules for harmonizing the infinity of conflicting claims that may easily arise. What should the government do in specific terms to encourage the widest possible realization of individual capacities? At what point does individual freedom become disruptive of order and thus require limitation? How far can the government go in trying to redress grave social inequalities without shackling initiative and destroying incentive? Rules of thumb cannot be laid down for these or for a thousand other issues because almost everything depends on the social and economic circumstances of the time when and the place where the question arises.

The ideals provide us only with a goal. They tell us little about the means of reaching or approaching it.

To be still more specific, does the industrial factory and wage system where the many spend their working day under the direction of a few frustrate the personalities of the many? And if it does, what alternative organization of the complex division of labour will be at once less frustrating and also compatible with the maintenance of the conditions of freedom? If a partial answer to this question is the compulsory recognition of trade unions and compulsory collective bargaining, at what point if at all, does the power of the trade union to withhold labour in a strategic industry imperil social order and deny the reasonable expectations of consumers and workers in other sectors of industry? A comprehensive system of social security helps to redress social and economic inequalities, promotes equality of opportunity and ensures basic necessities to exposed groups in the community. At what point, if at all, does the security thus provided reduce incentives in the recipients? At what point does the high taxation necessary to finance such measures seriously reduce initiative and enterprise in the taxpayer? (Insofar as either result occurs, productivity falls and the economic means available to the community are reduced.)

These and many others are questions on which honest men, all equally agreed on the political ideals of democracy and all equally anxious to direct the actions of government to these ideals, differ. Such questions cannot be answered with the convincing assurance that supports the solution of a problem in mathematics. The answers will turn partly on questions of fact on which it is always very hard to get adequate evidence, and partly on estimates of how human beings will behave in given circumstances. In many matters that vex our present politics, it is impossible to say with certainty what to do, and impossible to get general agreement on what to do.

Here then are the reasons why, despite broad general agreement on goals, there is so much diversity of opinion, confusion of counsel, and cross-purposes in action in democratic life. The ideals postulate freedom and therefore diversity: they welcome self-expression. Yet we must co-operate to satisfy our need for society, and to preserve and improve the conditions for a further approach to the ideals. Co-operation in politics, in deciding what shall be undertaken and enforced in the name of all, runs into a considerable measure of indifference, a good deal of individual selfishness, honest ignorance of the effects of our actions on the legitimate claims of others, and honest disagreement about what can or should be done.

This last presents peculiar difficulties. Men of high purpose who hold strongly to ideals generally also have strong opinions on how to achieve them. Conscience is thus brought into play and sharpens the clash when disagreement is discovered. For example, Christians who feel a profound responsibility for making the will of God manifest in history find a special urgency in many political issues. It leads some to press passionately for the extension of governmental action and others to press passionately against encroachment by government on the sphere of private judgment.

Agreed Procedures for Dealing with Disagreements

What prevents this diversity of immediate aims and confusion of counsel from disrupting society and degenerating into violence? The widespread acceptance of common ideals helps to dispose men to study together the reasons why they differ on means. It is here that the agreement on certain procedures for handling differences is of vital importance. First, there is the agreement that when the state acts, it must act through law laid down beforehand in accordance with procedures established in the constitution. Individuals and groups who object to a proposed law always have a chance to protest and state their objections before coercive state action is taken. Second, there is the agreement, resting on mutual respect, that differences must be submitted to discussion and debate. Indeed, the process of law-making always involves debate in the legislature, and often involves long preliminary discussion in innumerable groups, in the press and on the radio, within political party organizations, and between parties on election platforms. Third, there is the assumption that one's fellows are, within limits, rational beings and will submit their differences to the tests of fact, logic, and principle.

There are always two sides to a story. Discussion undertaken in a reasonable and accommodating spirit is likely to be fruitful, revealing some common middle ground on which, it is true, no one gets his own way entirely but each gets some concession in reward for cogent facts and argument, and for his reasonable attitude. Fourth, there is the agreement to conclude the debate at some stage by taking a vote, and then to abide the decision of the majority. Minorities agree to accept majority decision because they have reason to hope that majority decision reached after a fair hearing in a reasonable spirit will incorporate some concessions to their points of view, and because they know their right to reopen the debate is not affected by the decision.

Fundamentally, the democratic political process is one of discussion, accommodation, and compromise. Many persons of imperious, inflexible temperament dislike it and resist it. But as long as the great majority insist on submission to the procedures just outlined, the democratic political process is reasonably secure against disintegration from within.

The Place of the State in Democratic Ideals

Given these ideals of government, it can be seen why the state is defined as an association for securing the common interests and promoting the common purposes of the individuals who are its members. Since the principal point of general agreement and common purpose among the members is liberation of individual personality through individual freedom, the genuinely shared interests and purposes cover only a small part of the interests and purposes entertained and pursued by the members. The greater, and the more cherished, part of human activity must go on outside the state in the area of freedom it is designed to secure. Moreover, the only way to find out what is genuinely shared is through discussion and vote of the members. Even then, the inherent diversity of views noted above compels continuous compromise in deciding on the scope of action for the state. Two conclusions follow.

First, the state is an instrument of its members to be controlled to that end and criticized when it falls short in performance. The government, meaning the men who direct the activities of the state at a given time, cannot assert that it has exalted purposes beyond the criticism and understanding of its members. The state cannot be set up as an end in itself. Even when it calls on individuals to sacrifice their lives in a war, the sacrifice is justified only on the ground that it is necessary to protect the society without which individuals cannot realize any of their purposes. That is to say, the supreme demand that the state can make is for the securing of a common interest in maintenance of the society, and rests on the tragic fact noted by Mr. Justice Holmes that societies are founded on the death of men.

Second, because of its restriction to common purposes, it cannot be an instrument through which particular individuals and groups realize all their purposes. Each has to share the state with others. Because the state has to do something for everybody, it cannot be all things to anybody. No one can expect to bend it to the comprehensive service of his particular purposes.

At the same time, men will only give their best to purposes which they, for whatever reason, find good. This is the essential significance of free personality. It follows that men cannot hope to realize their loftiest aims through the state. While the state is necessary for social life and therefore to make the realization of our fondest dreams possible, we have to find the principal meaning of our lives outside it.

The state therefore is not an exalted communion in which men lose themselves gladly and spend themselves prodigally. That calls for spontaneity and there is little spontaneous enthusiasm left after the processes of discussion and compromise necessary for defining the sphere of state action have been carried through. Discussion consumes time and delays decision. The compromises reached seem to many to be tainted with mediocrity. Decisions reached by compromises are rarely executed with single-minded devotion.

The state therefore does not inspire reverence and unthinking obedience. It may evoke respect, and even affection, but it is the affection a man has for a tool that serves his purpose. When a tool begins to turn in his hand or does injury rather than service to the user, he does not submit to its imperfections but turns critically to remedy its defects and dangers. So will we consider the state as long as we are moved by the ideals of government sketched above.

The state is also too remote from the lives of most men for them to find in it the principal meaning of existence. The modern states number their citizens in tens of millions dispersed over a great area. The only active and direct participation of most citizens is in periodic elections. Even with the present wide range of state activities, most citizens have little active contact with the state. Most of them never see Congress or Parliament in action, never see even the outsides of the buildings in Washington, London, or Ottawa where the great decisions are taken and administration is carried on.

There is, of course, wider and more sustained participation in state, provincial, and municipal government, but even there only a very few of the citizens expend a significant portion of their effort in the work of government. If all had to find the deepest significance of life in the association that is the state, they would lead an intolerably barren existence.

Contrast with the Ancient City-State

If the state is small in numbers and area, fellowship in the state may have a larger meaning for the citizen. In the city-state of ancient Athens, where the citizens were few, lived cheek by jowl in relative freedom from economic pressure through the use of slave labour, and participated directly and frequently in political life, citizenship came closer to being a full-time job. In those conditions, more things were shared in common and the state was the active supervisor of the common life. The city had an official religion. To put it in our terms, church and state were one. The combined political and religious regulations and ceremonies pervaded almost every aspect of the citizen's life. In this respect, the city-state of Athens resembled the early New England town meeting which undertook not only the political functions of order and general security but also the supervision of morals and religious observances. Thus the reflective minds of Athens were led to say, in effect, that the purpose of the state was to teach men how to live the good life.

Just as a school which opens the windows of the world for the growing mind can absorb almost the whole life of the adolescent, so the Athenian might be expected to find his life and work as a citizen almost completely absorbing. There was an intimacy in the Greek city-state which made it more like a close-knit family than like the Canadian nation or the United States of America. Just as a family bound together by loyalty and affection and sharing a common household can often provide the solidest satisfaction for its members, so it could be claimed that fellowship in the city-state was the transfiguring experience for individuals.

Of course, whatever the values of this close fellowship it had its costs as well. The citizen was so busy participating in politics, submitting to the routine of custom and the regimen of religious observance, that he had little time to be himself. A powerful, almost fierce, communal spirit demanded a high degree of conformity from individuals. Even Socrates, the symbol of liberated intelligence, paid his respects to the gods of the city.

Whether or not this fellowship was worth the price, the choice is not open to the citizen of the modern state. The modern state is too remote from him. While it is well adapted to caring for interests that are common to all, it is not able to meet the particular diverse needs to which the family, for example, can minister. The state can build vast armies for the common defence and equip the soldier adequately for that purpose. But it has the greatest difficulty in catering to the diverse needs of soldiers as individual human beings.

The Importance of Voluntary Association

Yet men need fellowship almost as much as they need their individuality. They cannot realize their individuality except through society. If membership in the state cannot supply fellowship, it must be found in other ways. Where the ideals supporting democratic government have been accepted, it has been found through voluntary association. The interests of personality cannot be served at all without allowing like-minded individuals to club together for common purposes. As we shall see in detail later, freedom of association is one of the principal freedoms derived from the democratic ideals of government and supported by constitutional guarantees.

Historically, the critical step was taken when religious toleration was accepted. Its acceptance meant that each man was entitled to his own views on religious questions, and to join with others of similar views to establish a communion of their own. In other words, the church became a voluntary association providing both freedom and fellowship. Once freedom of association was conceded in the field of religion, there was no reason for withholding it in any other field of legitimate human activity. An ever-growing number of voluntary groups came into existence, each to further purposes shared in common by its members.

Because each association is devoted to some end that seems good to its members, it helps to give meaning to the lives of the members and in return gets some of their loyalty and allegiance. Particular groups can spend themselves on objectives that seem trivial or even reprehensible to outsiders as long as their activities do not imperil the common interest in public order and general security. They can move faster to their objectives because there is relatively little diversity of views among the members to be discussed and compromised. The dissenters can always resign from the voluntary association whereas they cannot resign from association in the state except by leaving the country. Freedom and fellowship are reconciled through the voluntary association.

THE WAR OF IDEAS BETWEEN DEMOCRACY AND DICTATORSHIP

It was said earlier in this chapter that Fascist Italy, Nazi Germany, and the Soviet Union had rejected the main elements of the Western political tradition. Something will be said later about the forms of government in these three states which have earned the label of dictatorship. The immediate concern here is with the ideas and ideals activating these governments. Preliminary to that purpose, it is enough to recall that for over a generation the world has been racked by the antagonism between democracy and dictatorship. The first phase culminated in World War II where Fascist Italy and Nazi Germany went down before a coalition of democratic powers with the Soviet Union. In the second phase now in progress, Communist Russia is ranged against the Western democracies in the cold war. The antagonism between democracies and dictatorships is deep-rooted.

The antagonism has always rested partly on a conflict of material interests, but it is also a conflict of ideas. The cold war at present involves a good deal of manoeuvring for strategic advantage but it is essentially a war of ideas, a battle for men's minds. The Soviet Union tries to win converts in the democracies. The democracies have almost despaired of making contact with minds behind the iron curtain but they are deeply aware of the need to try.

There was also, of course, a bitter antagonism between Fascist Italy and Nazi Germany on the one hand, and Communist Russia on the other. The Fascists and Nazis were fiercely anti-Communist. Even today, the most abusive epithet in the great arsenal of Communist invective is "fascist." But all three have been remarkably alike in the means they employ, and substantially at one in their negations of Western political ideals.

Nazi and Fascist Negations

The Fascist and Nazi philosophies consisted almost entirely of negations. Widespread resentment, frustration, and despair in Italy and Germany, arising largely out of World War I, led to disillusionment with democracy and rejection of the Western tradition without bringing any alternative constructive system of ideas. Moreover, the Fascist and Nazi dictatorships have run their course, and such positive ideas as they embodied are most unlikely to be resurrected in the same form again. Attention here will be concentrated on the negations with a view to sharpening the essential significance of the democratic ideals.

The fundamental negation of the Fascists and Nazis is the denial of individual personality as the ultimate for politics. Indeed, these creeds went to the point of denying that the individual, as such, has any significance at all except as means to ends beyond and above him. In part, this view rests on a low estimate of human nature. The great mass of individuals are engrossed in their private lives and are utterly lacking in any conception of the public interest. They live on an emotional level in continual conflict over squalid, selfish aims. If one waits for people of this quality to conceive and carry through great projects, no grand, heroic achievement is possible. The Fascist and Nazi movements had their substantial share of impatient visionaries with vague designs for human betterment who could not wait for a slow, fumbling humanity to realize the vision. It is not difficult but fatally easy to despise and even hate people who cannot live up to the plans you have made for them.

Mussolini, the Fascist dictator of Italy, scoffed at public opinion and one of his favourite epithets for the people was "mud." In *Mein Kampf*, the Nazi bible, Hitler stated bluntly his estimate of human beings. Individually, they were ignoramuses and incompetents, collectively a rabble, marked by indolence, stupidity, and cowardice. Individuals are therefore to be regarded as means and not as ends in themselves.

This comes out most clearly in the attitude of Hitler and Mussolini toward persuasion in the political process. The democratic ideal assumes the rationality of man. On this assumption, the individual has a claim to be persuaded by reasonable arguments before he gives his consent and support. However many democratic politicians fall short of this in practice by appealing to the passions of their listeners, they all pay lip-service to logic and truth. Hitler and Mussolini paid no such tribute. On the contrary, they paid tribute to falsehood, holding that the more audacious the lie, the more likely it is to be believed. The crudity of their propaganda was an insult to the intelligence of their listeners.

Their appeals to their people were not fireside chats: they were mass spectacles in which music, colour, ritual, symbols, the atmosphere of church and theatre, combined with hypnotic suggestion to overwhelm the minds of the listeners. The heckler who pricks pretentious bubbles with a question or ribald comment was brutally silenced. Questioning provoked violence rather than discussion. Indeed, it was unsafe not to applaud.

This shows better than anything else the Fascist and Nazi contempt for individual personality. It shows too their unqualified denial of the rationality of man. The success of their methods suggests that there is much truth in their estimate of the susceptibility of man to emotional appeal. (There is, in fact, independent evidence from the science of psychology to show that the democratic ideal has underestimated the irrational factors in human nature.) This may be acknowledged while pointing to a still further lesson to be learned from the Fascist and Nazi episodes.

The dignity of the individual cannot survive this unqualified denial of his rationality. If he cannot be appealed to on the basis of facts and reasoning, he has to be appealed to on the vague grounds of sentiment and feeling where obscurantists and liars have an overwhelming advantage. If these will not suffice, he has to be bludgeoned by force. The democratic ideal is compelled to hold to the faith that he can be persuaded—and further educated— to take thought about the alternative courses of action before him.

Society and State over the Individual

If the Fascists and the Nazis denied the value of individual personality, what goal did they ask men to strive for? They asserted the unqualified pre-eminence of society over the individual. The Italian Fascists put it bluntly: "Society is the end, individuals the means, and its whole life consists in using individuals as instruments for its social ends." Equally categorical statements abound in Nazi literature. The individual was to realize himself by submerging himself in loyal unquestioning service and boundless sacrifice for society.

Society, for them, was identical with the nation. Their one unvarying appeal was to a strident jingoistic nationalism. Mussolini was always promising to revive the glories of the Roman Empire. Hitler's supreme aim was to rouse the German nation to a sense of its racial superiority, and of its world mission consequent on that superiority. Literally, the dictators demanded that every Italian and German submit himself to severe military discipline for the achievements of these ends. Their watchwords were authority and obedience. No more than any other military commander did they propose to let the private soldiers discuss and decide the plan of campaign.

Three highly important consequences follow from what has been said so far. First, grandiose schemes of this kind require concerted effort on a grand scale. The state was the only agency that could undertake the comprehensive co-ordination needed. Hence the state became supreme, in the name of society. Mussolini gave the formula: "Everything in the state, nothing against the state, nothing outside the state." Hitler was generally careful to insist that the state was only an instrument in the service of the Germanic

Folk. But in practice, the Nazi state was far more imperious than the Fascist.

This brings us to the second consequence. Vague goals like the welfare of society or a world mission do not define any specific programme of action. It is still necessary for someone to decide step by step in great detail what to do. If individuals here and now do not matter, the welfare of society has nothing to do with them. If they are lazy, stupid, and self-centred, they are incapable of entertaining a heroic design, let alone thinking clearly and systematically about the means of promoting it. So the Fascists and the Nazis rejected majority rule by elected representatives in a legislature.

The effect of this was to relieve the state from all responsibility to the people. It followed inevitably that the decisions leading to action had to be taken by the state without reference to what the body of citizens might think were common interests or common purposes. The state decided in its utter discretion what were the desirable social ends, what was the world mission, and how to set about them.

But who or what, it may be asked, is the state? Obviously, it is no longer what adherence to democratic ideals makes it, an association of the people in a given territory for furthering the interests they share in common. It has become identical with the small group of persons who control its power and operate its machinery. State and government become one and the same thing. This is the third consequence. Political power is concentrated in the hands of a small élite, the dictator and those he gathers round him. And this, as all Fascist and Nazi literature insists, is as it should be. "World history is made by minorities." They alone have the vision, the courage, and the relentless will to struggle against the inertia of the masses, to inspire them with their vision and example, and to drive them when they will not be led. The élite alone have the right to rule.

Only one comment on these arrogant claims is needed here. Having elevated themselves so far above their fellows, beyond the reach of responsibility, the leaders can pursue their visions. But having no obligation to listen to anyone or to win consent through rational discussion, they have no way of knowing whether their visions are anything but bad dreams. They have nothing but their own powers of self-criticism (a scarce commodity among visionaries, prophets, and crusaders) to keep them from confusing their private prejudices, hatreds, and ambitions with the great social ends, always vague and undefined, by which they justify their irresponsible power. The sordid realities of the Fascist and Nazi regimes are not at all surprising. They merely confirm the ancient wisdom that no man is good enough to be trusted with absolute power.

Denial of Freedom and Equality

The remaining negations of democratic ideals by the Fascists and Nazis can now be stated quickly. Having denied the worth of individual personality, they could find no value in individual freedom. Mussolini sneered at the "putrescent corpse of the Goddess of Liberty." Hitler talked much about freedom but it was freedom for the German nation to be gained by denying freedom to individual Germans now. Individual freedom could not be claimed against the state. It existed only insofar as the state allowed it to exist. We shall see later how the systematic destruction of individual freedom was carried out.

Their contempt for individuals in general and their glorification of the élite were, in substance, a denial of human equality. The dictators saw clearly the facts of inequality but lacked the deeper sense of the brotherhood of man which is needed to reduce the significance of the more obvious natural and social inequalities. Denying the need for discussion and debate, they had no reason to treat men as if they were equal for any purpose. On the contrary, they glorified inequality. "Fascism," said Mussolini, "asserts the irremediable and fertile and beneficial inequality of men." The Nazi creed of inherent Nordic racial superiority denied the rights of full-blooded Jews to be citizens. Cross-breeding between Germans and Jews produced "bastards," an inferior group that must be eliminated. Furthermore, the aristocratic principle which identifies superior and inferior races also distinguishes between superior and inferior persons within the master race, "putting the heads above the masses and subjecting the masses to the heads." In Nazi and Fascist practice, the consequences of these views were fully worked out in the abolition of equality in political and civil rights.

In conclusion, the Fascist and Nazi negation of democratic ideals was categorical and complete. As a result, the individual becomes defenceless before the state. In the place of a state with limited functions which he as a citizen helps to define, he is faced with a state that undertakes to organize every aspect of his existence when and how it likes. He no longer has a realm of freedom in which he realizes his potentialities outside the state. He has to find the meaning of life in abject surrender and unquestioning obedience. The state is all, the totality, and hence the Fascist and Nazi states were called totalitarian. In place of the ideals of Liberty, Equality, and Fraternity which inspired the French Revolution and the succeeding democratic age, they put Responsibility, Discipline, and Hierarchy.

COMMUNIST IDEALS OF GOVERNMENT

The ideals professed by the Soviet Union must be discussed more fully. They are now competing with the democratic ideals for men's allegiance all over the world. They thus have a topical urgency which the Fascist and Nazi negations lack, even though we can all recognize in our midst, if not in ourselves, the impatience and intolerance that lead to them. The Communist ideals were not hastily thrown together to justify power-hungry men in doing what they had already done or determined to do anyway. The Communist Bible is the writings of Karl Marx. Marx died in 1883 and his theories were anxiously worked over for almost fifty years after his death by a large body of disciples before attempts to put them into practice began in Russia in 1917. Furthermore, for Karl Marx and innumerable of his followers, Communist theory was not a negation of the basic ideals of the Western tradition but rather, in their view, the necessary means to their full realization. Any examination of Communist ideas must begin with Marx.

Marx Compares Democratic Ideal and Economic Reality

Marx was a German philosopher deeply influenced by the Western political tradition. In his youth, he shared with most of the young intellectuals of his time an enthusiasm for the ideals of the French Revolution. But he quite early became acutely conscious of the immense gap between these ideals and the political and social realities of the time. In the Europe of his day, the masses of peasants and urban workers were sunk in degrading poverty, entirely dependent, so it seemed, on the whims of large landowners, and of the capitalists, the owners of commercial and industrial establishments. Formal slavery did not exist but the practical condition of the masses was little improvement on serfdom.

The struggle for a bare existence was so exhausting that the great bulk of the lower ranks of the people had no opportunity to realize whatever possibilities they may have had as individuals. Even in Britain, where individual liberty had been formally acknowledged for over a century, countless thousands of lives were being blighted by the horrors of the early factory system. Theories about the essential dignity of the human person seemed a travesty in the light of these facts. Fired by a genuine passion for human dignity and freedom, Marx set out to discover why things were as they were and how they could be changed.

He concluded that the cause of the plight of the masses was economic. One cannot be a person, one cannot have the freedom to do anything, or be anything, living on the verge of destitution. But the means of production on which the masses had to rely for any improvement in their condition were private property in the hands of landowners and capitalists who did not give them enough in the form of wages or other return to make meaningful freedom possible. More than that, the owning classes took advantage of their superior position in the social structure to exploit their workers.

Evidence to support these conclusions was easily found in Europe in the middle of the nineteenth century as it can still be found in Europe and elsewhere. But it would take a considerable knowledge of early nineteenth-century German philosophy to explain the larger and more general conclusions Marx reached after he saw the importance of economic factors in social life. He concluded, in effect, that this economic exploitation had always been inevitable but also that it was fated to pass entirely away. Mankind having lived thus far in the "realm of necessity," plagued by the economic struggle, would move in the near future into the "realm of freedom" where the exploitation of man by man would cease.

Starting from certain highly abstract formulations in German philosophy, he developed an all-embracing philosophy of history to show how all creation moves in a predestined direction. He worked out a theory of social development comparable in certain ways to Darwin's theory of biological development. But while Darwin limited himself to explaining the course of evolution in the past, Marx undertook to show the course of evolution of human society in the future. It was as if Darwin, after showing how the apes came down out of the trees and became men, had gone on to demonstrate that men would now, at the next stage, sprout wings and become angels. The vitally important part about Marx was his prediction of the future.

The Theory of Economic Determinism

Attempts to sketch briefly a philosophy of history generally end in misrepresentation. Having noted that danger, Marx's destiny of mankind may be looked at under three headings. First, there is the theory of economic determinism. The known ways and means of meeting material needs such as food, clothing, and shelter at any given time determine all significant aspects of social and political organization. If these "forces of production," as they are called, are to be fully employed, certain relationships between the different members of society must be established. Those with the know-how must direct the productive effort, and all others must be subordinated to them.

The drive to satisfy material needs is so strong that it forces the division of men into economic classes. The significant classes are the directing class whose rule has generally been enforced by its members taking over the means of production and distribution as their private property, and the servile classes who are dependent on the directing class. The dominant class always comes, sooner or later, to systematic exploitation of the subordinate classes. The most important fact about any society is the economic class structure.

With the discovery of new resources and new techniques of production, there always comes sooner or later a radical change in the mode of production which forces a change in economic organization and a new alignment of economic classes. The feudal aristocracy formed the dominant exploiting class in the days of self-sufficient agriculture in the Middle Ages. With improvements in the means of transportation and the arts of navigation, and with the discovery of the New World and its new resources, the feudal lords had to give way to the merchants, traders, and adventurers who alone could organize an economy based primarily on specialization of labour and widespread exchange of goods.

At first, the merchants and traders and adventurers formed a new class, the middle class, midway between lords and serfs. With the coming of the Industrial Revolution and the developing factory system, the middle class was enlarged and consolidated in the capitalist class. With the drawing of the peasantry from the countryside into the factories in rapidly growing urban centres, an entirely new dependent and exploited class, the urban industrial wage worker, came into existence. Marx identified the capitalists and the urban proletariat, the industrial working class, as the two significant classes for our time.

But economic organization determines all other aspects of social and political organization. To ensure the dominant and directing class in its control of the forces of production and to prevent revolts by the exploited classes, a policing organization is necessary. This is the state, and this is its indispensable function. The state, according to Marx, is not an association for furthering the common interests of the citizens as a whole: "it is an executive committee for managing the affairs of the governing class as a whole." The laws enforced by the state and all significant aspects of political life are direct consequences of the form of economic organization.

This is only a small part of the story. The ideals of government that hold sway at a particular time arise also from economic sources. The dominant theory about what government should and should not do is always the one that protects the interests of the exploiting class. On this analysis, Marx would say that the decisive feature of the democratic values discussed earlier in this chapter was the emphasis on freedom. He would say that the significant thing about this ideal of freedom was that it upheld the freedom of the capitalist to do as he liked with his property, i.e., to continue the exploitation of the working class. And he would go on to say that this chapter completely misrepresents the relationship of ideals to action when it treats the ideals or values as determining what the state shall and shall not do.

The state always does whatever is necessary to protect the position of the dominant economic class. In their main aspects, the democratic ideals are a sort of reflex of the economic system, a set of elaborate afterthoughts justifying the rule of the capitalist class. The stress on human equality and on the essential worth and dignity of individual personality is largely hocus-pocus for hoodwinking the exploited masses and persuading them to accept their subordinate role. When it is pointed out that many democratic values are rooted in religious beliefs, Marx makes his famous retort that "religion is the opiate of the people." It too is cunningly adapted to keeping the people quiet. The dominant religion at any time is also a reflex of the economic structure.

To put it shortly, Marx banished God from the scheme of things and put "the forces of production" in His place as the final cause. The Calvinist interpretation of Christianity pictured an all-wise and all-powerful God who governed the universe in every detail. He left men no freedom of action but determined even before their birth whether they were to be saved or damned. This was the doctrine of predestination. Marx also believed in predestination where everything is preordained by the forces of production. Men are the pawns of these forces which determine not only what they shall do but also what they shall believe. This is the theory of economic determinism.

The Theory of Class Conflict

Second, there is the theory of class conflict. The forces of production divide society into dominant and subordinate classes, into exploiters and exploited, between which there is unceasing and irreconcilable antagonism. There are no common interests uniting all men in society. There are only conflicting class interests. The significant classes for our era are the capitalist owners of the means of production and distribution, and the urban industrial proletariat who must sell their labour and work for a wage in order to live. Their antagonism is illustrated by the need of the capitalist to buy labour as cheaply as possible, and the need of the proletariat to sell labour as dearly as possible.

Each class develops a set of beliefs and values which justify its place in the economic structure—or its aspirations to a better place. Marx thought he was discovering the theory appropriate to the aspirations of the proletariat. The capitalist class justifies itself by reference to democratic ideals which, of course, were formulated and won widespread adherence in the period of its dominance. These are the ideas which the forces of production predestined the capitalist class to believe.

Generally speaking, the members of this class and its adherents sincerely believe in democratic values, and also believe that private property in the means of production and distribution is the best way to a further realization of these values. For these and other reasons, the capitalist class refuses to give up its privileged position, and it will fight the aspirations of the proletariat to the bitter end. If the proletariat is to realize its aspirations, it must be prepared to overthrow the capitalist class by violence. This is the theory of class conflict which denies that there are, or can be, any common interests or common values, any common ground on which men can meet to compose their differences, as long as they are divided into economic classes.

The Theory of Dialectical Materialism

If the rule of the capitalists has been predestined by the forces of production, what hope of ousting them can be entertained? This brings us to the third heading for discussion, the theory of dialectical materialism. Dialectical materialism is the core of Marx's philosophy of history. The materialism involved in substituting "the forces of production" for God is obvious enough. The dialectic can be described for present purposes as an inner mechanism of the material world which ensures the full working out of economic and social change. Through the ceaseless contention of rival economic classes, it brings new economic and social arrangements into existence in somewhat the same way as logical argument, or dialectical dispute, between opposing sides in a debate often opens up new truth. In a cunning way, it even makes the capitalist class create the conditions which will ultimately destroy it.

Freedom of individual economic enterprise brought the Industrial Revolution. To reap the full benefits of the Industrial Revolution, the capitalist class had to create the factory system, and ultimately the mass production system. For this purpose, they drew the peasants to the towns and created the urban proletariat. Production on the assembly line in the great factory is an intensely co-operative kind of work and the capitalist system trained the workers to co-operative action. Incidentally, the workers learned also to co-operate in resisting the efforts of the capitalists to exploit them.

The only effective motive the capitalist class can bring to the processes of production is the desire for private profit and gain. This drives the capitalists to suppress competition among themselves and to combine in monopolies. But the effect of monopoly in their hands is restrictive; it thwarts the potentialities of the great productive equipment they themselves have brought into existence. To realize these potentialities, it is necessary to abolish private property and the profit motive, and to give unrestricted scope to co-operative impulses and techniques. The only class which has been trained to exploit co-operative production to the full is the industrial proletariat. God, that is to say, "the forces of production," will not be mocked. The very forces which once gave mastery to the capitalist class must now confer it on the proletariat. The industrial working class is destined to become the vanguard of progress. This is the outcome thought to be guaranteed by the theory of dialectical materialism.

Freedom and Equality in the Classless Society

As his own theories show, Marx did not expect the capitalist class to recognize that it was headed for the dustbin. He anticipated rather that the capitalists would use every means including the repressive power of the state to maintain their position. There was no reason to expect they could be ousted by measures short of revolution. The proletariat could not count on being able to take up its historic role without the use of violence. To protect itself against counter-revolution by the capitalists, it would be necessary to set up and maintain during a transitional period a dictatorship of the proletariat. In reality, this would be a new kind of state for protecting the interests of the proletariat and for liquidating capitalist remnants. One might have expected, again on Marx's own theories, that it would continue indefinitely as the "executive committee" of the new governing class.

But Marx expected the capitalist system in its last days to drive almost everyone except a few great capitalists and their hangers-on into the exploited proletariat. Thus he envisaged something new in history once the threat of capitalist counter-revolution had been removed, a society in which there is only one significant economic class. He predicted the emergence at long last of a classless society. Since there would no longer be a submerged class or classes to exploit, there could not be an exploiting class. With the disappearance of economic classes, there would no longer be anything to divide men in bitterness and conflict. In place of irreconcilable class interests, there would be at last a genuine and all-absorbing common interest in raising co-operative production to the highest possible level for the benefit of all. Like many other creators of Utopias, he looked to see men live together like one happy family.

If the sole cause of contention among men is economic and that cause is removed, the problem of maintaining public order and security is solved. The state and government no longer have any reason for existence. As Engels, Marx's collaborator said, the state withers away and "the government of persons is replaced by the administration of things and the direction of the process of production." Also, the study of government and politics fades from the university curriculum. It becomes as dead as a dead language.

The long sad record of the exploitation of man by man will then be closed, and the violation of human dignity through poverty, oppression, and violence will cease. That is to say, freedom will at last become meaningful because there is no longer a dominant class whose freedom rests by necessity on the exploitation of subordinate classes, and no longer subordinate classes whose freedom is thwarted by the necessities of the economic system. Mankind moves from the "realm of necessity" into the "realm of freedom." Marx's ideal of freedom and equality is realized in the age of Communism where everyone contributes to society according to his capacities and receives according to his needs.

Communism in Practice

This is the merest outline of Marx's philosophy, properly known now as Communism. The main emphasis here has been put on the economic and political implications. It should be noted, however, that Marx thought he had found the key for explaining every significant aspect of human society. Not only economics and politics but art, literature, science, philosophy, religion, all are to be explained and understood in terms of economic classes. A body of doctrine which uses one key to unlock all mysteries is a religion. Communism has become a religion to Marx's followers. This goes far to explain their untiring zeal, their sacrificial devotion, their dogmatism and intolerance.

As already noted, Marx's doctrines were systematically developed by his followers into what is known as Marxism, or Communism. Just as interpreters of the Bible claim always to be faithful to the sacred text, so Marx's followers have claimed never to add or diminish a word of what Marx has said. Just as in the interpretation of the Scriptures, there has been endless dispute as to what Marx really meant. In particular, his followers have disagreed on whether Marx believed that revolution would be necessary to oust the capitalists and bring the proletariat into its own. There are passages in Marx's writings which suggest that he had not ruled out the possibility of a peaceful transition. However, the main trend of his arguments and most of his explicit statements support the interpretation that revolution will be necessary. Also, the successful practitioners of Marxism, the masters of the Soviet Union, the Communist party in the Soviet Union and in the other countries that now have Communist governments, all support this interpretation. It is they who make Communist ideas a power in the world, and they who determine what Communism means today.

The revolutionary wing of the Russian followers of Marx seized power in Russia in 1917 and proclaimed the dictatorship of the proletariat. The social and economic system they set up cannot be discussed here. For the moment, it is sufficient to say that although the capitalists in Russia were always few and were fully liquidated thirty years ago, the state has not withered away and the "government of persons" is still an active enterprise. For example, some millions of persons are being governed in forced labour camps. Something will be said later about the continuing dictatorship in the Soviet Union as a form of government. Here the focus of interest is in the ideas behind government.

Consequences and Tendencies in the Communist Creed

It was said earlier that Communist thought in practice rejects the Western political tradition in the same way as Fascist and Nazi doctrine. These negations are nowhere bluntly stated in Communist doctrine; indeed, it affirms the same fundamental values as the Western tradition and promises the full realization of them in the future. The negations arise from certain consequences and tendencies in the Communist creed which must now be stated.

First, in so far as Communists are loyal to their doctrine, they cannot give any allegiance to democratic values as these are understood in the Western world until the exploiting capitalist class is overthrown and the proletariat has come to power. Before the revolution, before the emergence of the classless society, freedom, equality, and justice are meaningless terms. To labour for the realization of these values within the framework of a society made up of conflicting economic classes is to pursue a phantom. Bernard Shaw, who understood Communist theory sympathetically, once said that democracy was a big balloon put aloft to attract the gaping attention of the populace while the exploiting class picked their pockets.

That is to say, working for these ideals is merely playing the capitalist game of keeping the masses quiet and submissive. It distracts attention from the vital task of undermining the old system and making way for the new. For this purpose, class antagonisms must be heightened, not lessened. Improving the lot of the masses within the capitalist society tends to lessen them. For the sake of the future, it is necessary to forget about the values of human personality here and now.

If Communists are loyal to their creed, the important unit is not the individual, but the economic class which is the instrument of destiny. The worth of individuals and the treatment to be accorded them is determined by their class affiliation. Those with capitalist mentality are obstacles stubbornly blocking the new world that awaits its birth. They are in the way, and they must be removed like any other rubbish that gets in the way. The proletariat are the vanguard of the new society, the expendable soldiers important now as means and not as ends in themselves. In fact, of course, many members of the proletariat are deaf and inert to the call of destiny. How long must the "realm of freedom" wait for them to respond? After all, at this stage of history, they are merely means, the class structure prevents them from realizing themselves as persons. In the outcome, the temptation to drive the masses when they will not be led is almost as strong for Communists as it was for Nazis and Fascists.

Secondly, if the real interests are always class interests in a class-divided society and if these interests are irreconcilable, it follows that all discussion aimed at composing these diverse interests is useless. Any agreement that might be reached is certain to violate the interests of one or other of both classes and will have to be broken if economic classes are to perform their inevitable role in history. Actually, on Communist theory, genuine agreement is impossible. It is impossible to convince the capitalist that his part on the stage of history is finished, because his economic interest, his membership of his class, determines his beliefs. Blinded by class interest, he cannot see the truth.

Equally, no Communist can agree with propositions put forward by persons of capitalist mentality because he knows in advance that, however plausible they appear on the surface, they must be fallacious and perverse. Discussion and debate will never reveal a common interest which men can agree to pursue together because no such common interest exists. In a class-divided society, there are only capitalist interests and capitalist truth, proletarian interests and proletarian truth, and never the twain shall meet!

Whatever the view about the rationality of man in the classless society of the future, Communist theory denies the possibility of rational discussion in a society divided into economic classes. Men do not think freely and make up their minds on the basis of logic and evidence. Their thinking is just a reflex induced in them by their role in the economic system. This too leads to the denial of the worth of human personality. Individuals cannot treat one another with mutual respect unless there is some common ground of experience and values on which to meet, discuss, and compose differences.

Third, the Communist thinks he has grasped the inner meaning of the world, the final truth about man and society. Communism is a kind of religion. Its adherents are so utterly certain of their truth and so intoxicated with the beatific vision of the kingdom of heaven that they become an easy prey to religious intolerance. Their first loyalty is to the truth that will ultimately bring all men to salvation and freedom. Their first duty is to make that truth prevail. The sacred word of Marx, according to the prevailing interpretation, says that the inevitable way is through intolerance, conflict, and violence. Their impatience with the willful obstructors, the lazy who do not care, and the blind who cannot or will not see, becomes almost unendurable. Consequently, there is a strong tendency to ruthlessness, a disposition to regard the great end as justifying any means. This will not surprise anyone who recalls how the rack and the stake were used in the name of Christian love and charity until we learned the lesson of religious toleration. The democratic ideals are inextricably bound up with religious toleration. Religious intolerance of whatever kind is an utter negation of them.

Bad Means Frustrate Good Ends

The result of these consequences and tendencies in Communist theory is to subordinate individuals to the claims of society, the classless society of the future, just as Fascist and Nazi theory subordinated individuals to the existing Italian and German society. Because all three theories lack respect for individual dignity here and now, the rejection of democratic ideals goes point for point the same. In Communist theory, individual freedom is not for the present but for the future. Thus far, wherever Communists have come to power, inequalities that rest on distinctions of economic class have been abolished and a multitude of regulations made to enforce social equality without regard for the claims of individual freedom. The essential feature of this equality is an equal subjection to an all-powerful government. The one kind of equality that is fundamental in the democratic ideals, equality before the law, is rejected. A small Communist élite, those who have the vision and the hard determination, seize control of the machinery of government and exercise unlimited power over individuals.

This involves the rejection of majority rule in any meaningful sense, the rejection of constitutionalism, of rule by law, of all the procedures that ensure discussion and peaceful accommodation of conflicting interests in the democracies. These ideals and procedures are all denied for the sake of getting into power and establishing the dictatorship of the proletariat. Once in power, the élite resists all attempts to limit its power, and the dictatorship of the proletariat becomes dictatorship over the proletariat.

At any rate, this seems to be the conclusion to be drawn from the course of events in the Soviet Union. Forty years after the Revolution, the Soviet Union has not yet realized the realm of freedom. As we shall see in detail later, the state has not withered away but has grown to monstrous proportions. The state in the Soviet Union under Communism is as totalitarian as the Fascist or Nazi states, perhaps more so. Marx and countless of his disciples have been moved by a generous passion for humanity. But they adopted a theory and a set of procedures which inevitably frustrate the high ideal.

This underlines an important lesson which could be illustrated in many ways. Ideals may come to nothing unless the means appropriate to their realization are chosen and carefully observed. Procedures are almost as important as the ideals themselves. The means used to reach an end cannot be divorced from the end desired. Much of the discussion in this book will be focused on the procedures by which the Western democracies have been trying, however inadequately, to realize the democratic ideals. Consideration of procedures may be usefully prefaced with the analysis of various forms of government which will be taken up in the next chapter.

CHAPTER III

FORMS OF GOVERNMENT

EVEN in the most primitive societies, government exists in some rudimentary form. There are always leaders who exercise authority, patriarchs or priests if not kings or politicians or dictators. Government in each society has distinctive characteristics, and as a society develops and changes, government usually passes through several transformations. History is a rich storehouse of forms and types of government, which political thinkers ever since the time of the Greeks have been trying to classify.

There are many different classifications of government, none of which has been generally accepted as satisfactory. In these circumstances, it would merely be confusing to the beginning student to enumerate and discuss them. It will be worth while, however, to discuss briefly one famous classification, an adaptation of that made by Aristotle in his study of the Greek city-states. It is still perhaps more widely accepted than any other, and it illustrates sufficiently the difficulty of classifying different kinds of governments.

The criterion used by this classification for distinguishing types of governments is the number of persons who rule, or share the ruling power. Where one governs, the government is a monarchy. Where rule is shared by a relatively small section of the population, the government is an aristocracy. Where control of government is vested in the citizens generally, the government is a democracy. Accordingly, every government is either a monarchy, an aristocracy, or a democracy.

It should be pointed out that this is both an adaptation and simplification of Aristotle's classification. It is an adaptation, because some of the terms used had not the same meaning for him as for later classifiers. Democracy, for example, meant to him something approaching mob-rule, and was a perversion of a good form of government, which he called polity. His term polity meant something pretty close to what we would call democracy. It is a simplification because Aristotle's classification identified at

least six forms of government, some of which were true forms, or
models, while others were recurring perversions of these models. He
also noted the occurrence of a variety of mixed forms. There have
been, of course, many variations on Aristotle's classification but
most of them treat monarchy, aristocracy, and democracy as the
basic forms.

The difficulty about this threefold classification lies in its
application. In one sense, British government is a monarchy.
In strict constitutional law, the king is the ruler. The ministers
who exercise the powers of government derive their formal
authority from the king and cannot act without it. Relying on
this aspect of the British constitution, some have concluded that
the British government is a monarchy—a limited monarchy, it is
true, but still a monarchy.

However, as we shall see, a large part of the British constitution
is made up of customary rules which settle the way in which the
formal legal powers of the king are to be exercised. The customary
rules have been closely adhered to for over a hundred years and
they give the king only a negligible influence over the appointment
of his ministers and the powers they exercise. Briefly, they provide
that the king must choose ministers who have—and can hold—the
confidence of Parliament, and that he must accept their advice.
The House of Commons, the effective part of Parliament, is made
up of the elected representatives of the electorate, which, in turn,
comprises the whole body of adult citizens. On these grounds,
many classify British government as a democracy.

If substance rather than shadowy forms is to be the criterion, the
British form of government is a democracy, and a highly effective
one as matters go in an imperfect world. But if we brush aside
forms to follow substance, there are serious difficulties in applying
the classification. When, as has often happened, the king shares
his rule with his mistresses, is the government still a monarchy?
More important, no monarchy has ever been able to maintain its
rule without the support of at least a small group or class in the
community. These do not give their support without sharing in,
or imposing limitations on, the powers of the monarch. There are
republics where the forms clearly point to democracy but the
practice points equivocally to rule by one or a few, and not to rule

by the many. The communist case against the democracies of the present day is that they are masked oligarchies, in which the relatively small owning capitalist class are the effective rulers. An attempt to classify according to the inward practice rather than the outward forms often raises difficult questions and interminable debate on what the realities are.

The governments of all but the most primitive societies are complex institutions and they cannot be sorted neatly into simple categories. Almost all of them reveal some combination of two or more of the three forms. Some governments combine monarchy and aristocratic elements; others combine aristocratic and democratic, and so on. Attempts at classification are important for the scientific study of government in general, but discussion of these attempts cannot usefully precede careful detailed study of particular governments.

Those who tried to classify governments as either monarchies, aristocracies, or democracies then proceeded to discuss the merits and demerits of each. By the end of the nineteenth century, this discussion had become largely academic. Democracy defined as rule by the many and marked by wide extensions of the franchise had triumphed in the Western World. Whether it was the best form of government or not, there was no prospect of a return to aristocratic or kingly rule.

If this conclusion requires any confirmation, it has been provided by the course of events since the first world war. After World War I, a new form of government—or a very old form of government in a new dress—appeared in Europe. As the result of revolutions in Russia in 1917, in Italy in 1922, and in Germany in 1933, the great modern dictatorships were established. Somewhat similar forms of rule were set up in Turkey, Poland, Spain, and other countries. Then, after World War II, Communist dictatorships modelled on the pattern of the government of the Soviet Union were set up in China and in the countries of East Central Europe. Most of these regimes have reviled the existing democracies but have paid them the compliment of regarding them as presenting a serious rival form of government. Monarchy and aristocracy, as the world has hitherto understood the terms, they dismissed with a shrug of contempt.

Although the great modern dictatorships are worlds apart in many respects, they have certain striking similarities, particularly in methods of gaining and maintaining power. These methods have proved so successful that aspiring revolutionaries are bound to copy them in the future. Where democracy proves to be an inadequate form of government, it seems almost certain to be succeeded by the modern type of dictatorship.

World War II is not seriously misrepresented as a titanic struggle between two forms of government, democracy and fascist dictatorship. Although the democracies and the Communist dictatorship in the Soviet Union were allies in the war, they fell into distrust and bitter rivalry as soon as their common enemy had been overcome. As we have already seen, their fundamental beliefs about government and politics are sharply opposed. They now confront each other "in a posture of war" in every part of the world. The only classification of forms of government which seems at all closely related to current realities is that which distinguishes between democracy and dictatorship.

Dictatorship has been spreading through the world in the past generation, replacing some democratic governments and threatening others. Superficially, it appears as a new form of government in the western world, threatening the older established democratic forms. But in the perspective of history, democracy, as we know it today, is a newer and rarer form than monarchy, aristocracy, or dictatorship. The human race has had a much wider and longer experience of government imposed by one or a few than it has had of democratic self-government.

EARLY FORMS OF GOVERNMENT

Before the Christian era, the prevailing form of government over an extensive territory was the despotic empire. For several thousand years, the Middle East, or large parts of it, were ruled successively by the Assyrian, Egyptian, Babylonian, and Persian Empires, headed by kings who were gods or demigods as well as kings. They maintained a precarious kind of order throughout their dominions, and levied crushing taxes and tribute in return. Apart from the dubious public order they provided, they did little for their people, who lived in fear of the tax-gatherer. Their polyglot subjects had no participation in or control over the government. The short-lived empire of Alexander the Great was of this kind.

In the millennium before Christ, many small city-states grew up in the Mediterranean basin, the most famous of which were Athens and Rome. Initially at any rate, their territory was always small, limited to a few square miles. In the course of their history, they ran the gamut of the forms of government, from monarchy to aristocracy to democracy to dictatorship. The democratic phases were very short in contrast to the duration of the other phases. During their brief appearance, however, the Greek and Roman democracies gave to the world the idea of free and equal citizenship.

At the dawn of the Christian era, the Roman Republic was transformed into the Roman Empire, the greatest and longest-lived empire the world has known. It extended citizenship to all the subject people of the Empire, and it ruled the known world for 400 years. However, there were no effective institutional devices by which the citizens could participate in government and control the Empire. The power of the emperor became absolute, and the very office of Emperor became the plaything of the praetorian guard in Rome, who set up and tore down the emperors at their will. There was nothing democratic about the forms of government under the Roman Empire.

The Empire disintegrated in Western Europe in the fifth century of the Christian era. Civilization collapsed and government itself almost disappeared for about 500 years in the Dark Ages that followed. What government there was certainly was not democratic. In the Middle Ages (roughly A.D. 900 to A.D. 1500) Western Europe revived under the feudal system. In its political aspects, feudalism was an extremely decentralized form of government. Europe was broken up into thousands of little principalities, many of which would not make a large farm by modern standards. The feudal lord both owned the principality, or farm, and provided the government for his tenants and serfs. There were some elements of popular participation in feudal government, but it was everywhere predominantly monarchical or aristocratic in essential form.

Throughout the Middle Ages, individual feudal lords and their descendants steadily expanded their holdings by a variety of methods, and the more successful of them finally set themselves up as kings. In this way, a number of large territories were each brought under the sway of a single central government. The process of consolidation first brought the kingdoms of England, France, Spain, Austria, and so on, into existence, and then continued until all the modern states of Europe as we have known them were established. The final consolidation of Germany and Italy was not completed until after the middle of the nineteenth century.

However, by the end of the fifteenth century, feudalism had lost its vigour, and rule by a king or monarch was becoming the typical form of government in Europe. The Middle Ages came to an end and the modern era began. From the sixteenth to the nineteenth centuries, most of Europe was ruled by absolute monarchs who treated their people as subjects rather than as citizens. Indeed, the Czar of Russia, the German Kaiser, and the Austrian Emperor continued to claim almost absolute power until they were all overwhelmed in World War I.

THE RISE OF DEMOCRACY

Absolute monarchy never really established itself in Britain. The attempts of the Stuart kings so to assert themselves were defeated in the seventeenth century. From then until the Great Reform Act of 1832, which extended the franchise to the propertied middle classes, Britain was ruled by a landed aristocracy. Full manhood franchise was not reached in Britain till 1884. The American Revolution in the late eighteenth century was a popular revolution, but manhood franchise was not fully realized in the United States until about 1840. Similarly, the aspirations for democracy expressed in the French Revolution at the end of the eighteenth century were not fully realized until after the middle of the nineteenth century.

Democracy in the city-states of the ancient world was a brief interlude in the long record of government by one or a few. Modern democracy, as we shall see, is sharply different from ancient democracy, particularly in its ambitious application to an enormous territory and to tens of millions of population. This kind of democracy is entirely new in the world. Its effective establishment dates from about the middle of the nineteenth century. We have had at most a century of experience with it, while other forms of government, in various manifestations, have lasted thousands of years.

Once established, however, modern democracy spread very quickly. Monarchic and aristocratic governments were everywhere giving way before it in the years preceding World War I. President Wilson represented World War I as a struggle "to make the world safe for democracy" against monarchical and aristocratic reaction. Victory in this struggle was interpreted as the final victory of democracy over the older forms of government. All new governments established in Europe after that war (excepting always the Soviet Union) were set up under thoroughly democratic constitutions. No sooner did its victory seem assured and complete than a pronounced reaction set in against democracy. This reaction has given us the modern dictatorships.

Reaction against Democracy

So far, the actual supersession of democratic government by dictatorship in our day has been in countries where democracy was entirely new, as in Germany, or insecurely established, as in Italy, or undermined by agents of the Soviet Union, as in Czechoslovakia. Democracy has never been voluntarily abandoned by countries in which it had been efficiently established. The desperate eagerness of the leaders of the Soviet Union and of the East European countries now under Communist dictatorship to prove that their governments are genuinely democratic shows that the popular aspiration for democracy is still very strong.

In actual fact, however, democracy has failed to work in many of the countries in which it has been tried. Even in the countries where it has been longest established and works best, the events of the last thirty years have made many wonder if it will be as transitory in the modern world as it was in the ancient world. Why have its prospects declined so rapidly? Why does it work in some countries and not in others? Under what conditions can it be expected to work, and under what conditions is it likely to fail? The first step in trying to find answers for these questions is to examine the structure and working of democratic government in countries where it has worked best.

THREE MODERN DEMOCRACIES

Whatever the difficulties of identifying a government as a democracy, Britain and the United States are acknowledged to be the leading democracies. A comparison of the governments of the two ought to bring out some of the essential characteristics of democracy as a form of government. The governments of the two countries operate under markedly different constitutions, in sharply different geographical and cultural environments. Britain is a small island with a homogeneous population, a population habituated for centuries to a common way of life. The United States spans a continent of widely varying conditions. Its people are of diverse origins and are still struggling to adjust themselves to a common way of life. When differences in the working of the two governments are observed, it is not always clear whether they are due to differences in constitution or environment.

Canada, like the United States, grew out of British colonial status into a democracy in a geographical and cultural environment resembling that of the United States. On the other hand, Canada adopted a constitution modelled as far as could be on the British constitution. At the points where the British model does not fit Canadian needs, Canada has relied heavily on American experience and practice. Canadian government cannot be justly appreciated without an understanding of British and American government. Moreover, the working of Canadian government reveals the adaptation of the British model to continental North American conditions and affords some index to the relative influence of constitutional forms and environment.

The succeeding chapters are mainly devoted to an introductory comparison of these three governments, showing how they work, similarly or dissimilarly as the case may be, and throwing, it is hoped, some light on the possibilities and limitations of democracy as a form of government. At certain points, principally in this and the final chapters, the characteristic features of modern dictatorship are considered and some of the striking contrasts between democracy and dictatorship are pointed out.

Even if an exact definition of democracy as a form of government is difficult to frame, certain common features of the three democracies in question are readily seen. They have little in common with the democracies Aristotle studied. He was concerned with the Greek city-states, societies with the area of a county and the population of a smallish city, of whom only a minority were citizens entitled to take part in government. The modern democracies have an enormous territory and millions of population. Substantially all who live in the territory are citizens and almost all adult citizens enjoy full political rights.

The ancient democracies were direct democracies. Each citizen participated directly in making laws, and could expect to come to public office from time to time by lot or rotation. The democracies to be discussed here are called representative democracies, because the common form of participation of the citizen in the control of government is in voting for representatives who govern on his behalf. Other significant ways of influencing the government are open to the citizens generally and are exercised by some, but the periodic election of representatives is the principal decisive method the many have for enforcing their rule.

There are a host of other differences between the characters of the ancient and modern democracies. The environment, economic, social, and cultural, is entirely different. However much the liberal democratic ideals owe to the political theory of the Greek city-state, they are a modern formulation profoundly influenced by Stoic and Christian thought which did not make their impact on the world until after the decline of the Greek city-state. Thus little would be gained in trying to compare governments which are not at all comparable. It is true that the closer we approach the fundamental problems of modern democracy the more relevant become the reflections on democracy of the ancient political thinkers. Some patterns of political behaviour appear to be repeated throughout the ages. However, we cannot approach these fundamental problems until some appreciation of the concrete institutions and actual working of modern democracy has been gained.

THE MODERN DICTATORSHIPS

Dictatorship is not a new term in the language of government and politics. At times of crisis in the ancient Roman Republic, immense, although not quite absolute, power was often put in the hands of a single man, a dictator. But his rule was limited to a very short period of time and was subject to some other limits and restraints as well. The powers of the dictator came automatically to an end and the normal agencies of republican rule were restored. /The modern dictatorships, on the other hand, are forms of absolute rule and are not subject to any predetermined limits of time or subject matter./

While the modern dictatorships are quite unlike the old Roman institution from which the name is derived, they are not entirely new phenomena. One of the ancient forms of government was known as tyranny. At many times and places in the world of the Greek city-states, the government fell into the hands of tyrants. Originally, the word tyrant meant merely ruler, and there were good and bad tyrants just as there have been good and bad kings. However, the word gradually came to be a term of abuse, as has bureaucracy in our own day, used to describe a despotic ruler who seized power by fraud or force, often with the support of the submerged masses of the population. Thus Plato described tyranny as the worst form of government and as the most probable outcome of democracy, which he was disposed to regard as an unworkable form of government. Aristotle regarded tyranny as a perversion of monarchy, the tyrant as a ruler who ruled by demagogic tricks rather than by the kingly virtues of wisdom and forbearance.

It is this form of government which modern dictatorship most resembles. The modern dictators are usually persons of obscure origin, whose first political successes were in the leadership of crowds. They seize power by unconstitutional means, exercise it in despotic fashion, and, at the same time, go to extraordinary lengths to persuade the masses to support them. To read Aristotle's account of how tyrants maintain their power, one would think he had been ng at first hand the actual methods of Mussolini and Hitler.[1] way in which these two men and their associates exploited the aknesses of the faltering democracies of Italy and Germany gives sombre significance to Plato's account of how democracy can degenerate into tyranny.[2]

It has already been noted that the three great modern dictatorships are markedly different in many ways. The description just given above is not a wholly accurate statement of the origins of the communist dictatorship in Russia. It overthrew a degenerate monarchy rather than a degenerate democracy, and the most striking native quality of Lenin and Stalin was not the leadership of crowds. But the methods of exercising and maintaining power are substantially the same for all three. As we saw in the preceding chapter they are, for practical purposes, at one in rejecting democratic ideals.

It is impossible at the outset to state with any approach to precision the principal distinctions between the democracies in question and the modern dictatorships. That must wait at least until democratic government has been examined in some detail in the succeeding chapters and the essential institutions of the dictatorships have been sketched in the last chapter. The most that can be done here is to make some impressionistic contrasts which will be sharpened later, and to suggest some salient features for the emergence of which the reader should be on the watch.

One very important distinction, if not the basic one, has been best phrased by a wit with no pretence to learned scholarship. In the democracies, he said, what is not forbidden is permitted, while in the dictatorships, what is not forbidden is compulsory. That is to say, the democracies have been regimes of freedom. In the main, government in the democracies has been concerned to forbid and punish various forms of serious anti-social conduct and not to command a precise pattern of behaviour on all matters. Murder and wife-beating are forbidden. On the other hand, no one is ordered by the government to love his neighbour as himself or to produce ten children for the glory of the state. Even where the government commands people to do precise and specific things,

[1]Aristotle, *Politics,* Bk. v, ch. vIII.
[2]Plato, *The Republic,* Bk. viii.

such as sending their children to school or submitting to compulsory vaccination, the professed object is to enlarge the freedom of the individual.

Government in the dictatorships not only has forbidden a wide range of actions, but has also limited severely individual free choice by ordering many of the details of life from the cradle to the grave. While these minute regulations are explained to the individual as being for his own good, they enforce on him the dictator's conception of that good, and prevent him very largely from following his own. In effect, the regimentation is for the glory of the small ruling group, or, at any rate, for something other than the enlargement of the life of individual citizens.

The Constitutional Tradition of Modern Democracy

If the ensuing discussion of democratic government and the comparisons made with the dictatorial regimes in the concluding chapter are to be understood clearly, this distinction must be kept continually in mind. The structure of democratic government is still largely determined by certain beliefs of ancient lineage but now identified mainly with the Renaissance of the sixteenth century. These beliefs exalt the individual and depreciate—sometimes excessively—the collective restraints which society puts upon him through custom, law, and government. They are deeply influenced by the Christian insistence on a higher law than the law of the state, whether it be the dictates of an organized church or the promptings of private conscience. The claims of a church can sometimes be so imperious as to threaten public order, and private conscience sometimes leads us to an outrageous disregard of others. So, these beliefs do not reject all restraints. They recognize the necessity of some minimum of government. We all have impulses which must be restrained and we are never sure when our own inhibitions, our limited understanding of the claims of others to an equal freedom, and our desire to be thought well of by our fellows will need to be supplemented by the threat, or by the actual use, of the organized force of the community. So there must be government and it must have the ultimate power to apply direct coercion to individuals.

This power to apply force must be a monopoly, because to allow two or more independent centres of coercive power in a community is to create the conditions for civil war. But according to these beliefs, such a monopoly has grave dangers. The obverse of a belief in the importance of the individual is a fear of government which unless controlled can crush him—and more often than not has done so. Government, though necessary, is potentially one of the greatest evils. Like fire, it is a good servant and a bad master. And it is always potentially master because of its monopoly of naked force. What prevents the government of the day from using the army and the police to enforce on us its conception of our own good is the knowledge that its power is contingent and may be taken away at the next election, and the further knowledge that if it pursues its own whims in these matters it will soon find itself violating the law which binds the government as well as the citizens. In other words, government is held in check by the procedures briefly outlined in the preceding chapter.

It will be quickly and properly objected that the Trumans and the Eisenhowers, the Attlees and the Macmillans are not the clay from which dictators can be swiftly moulded. This is equally true of the Roosevelts and the Churchills although, of course, the leaders which the democracies call up in a crisis are likely to have some of the qualities of resolute leadership which undoubtedly mark the crisis-born dictators. Here it is necessary to remember that a system of government attracts and chooses as its leaders the type of men who are temperamentally suited to work within its limitations. It is extremely unlikely that any of these men would ever have come to power in a dictatorship. On the other hand, the Nazis in Germany were drawn to politics and encouraged to pursue power by violent means because of the prizes congenial to their taste which control of the government offered. Four years before Hitler came to power, the devices for assuring that government should remain servant and not master had ceased to work and the country was governed by executive decree. That is to say, the riches of the earth lay open to those who could somehow get control of the government. Whenever this happens, the power-hungry, the ruthless, the doctrinaire zealots who want to impose their conception of the good life on everybody are all attracted to politics as the bees to the flowers. But where the people are determined that government shall be servant and not master and the machinery of government is constructed to that end, the imperious are little attracted to politics and do not get far even when they try.

So in approaching the study of democratic governments, the centuries-long tradition of government as servant must be kept to the fore, and the machinery of government understood as a means to that end. This draws attention at once to the constitution, which sets the structure of government conformably to the purpose of keeping it under control. The democratic constitution is a body of fundamental rules which the government of the day cannot change of its own free will, and which is, at the same time, a censor of governmental actions. The constitution gives sanctity to the law which cannot be changed without the consent of the legislature, and it also provides that the government and its agents must obey the law or expose themselves to punishment through the courts.

It follows that the democratic constitution is not merely a set of rules by which the people are governed; it is also a device by which the people govern their rulers, by which they ensure that the state remains an instrument for furthering genuine common interests. It is true, of course, that many details of the constitution are neutral on this point. Whether or not women have the vote, whether the life of the legislature is five years or two, whether judges hold office for life or must retire at the age of seventy are questions that matter little from this point of view. But the main features of the democratic constitution are designed to ensure that those who exercise the powers of government shall act with a sense of responsibility. The phenomenon of governments conforming to the dictates of a settled constitution is known as constitutionalism. The democracies to be considered here are called constitutional democracies. Their governments are constitutional governments.

The dictatorships have no constitutions, in the sense of a body of rules that limit and control what the government can do. What passes for a constitution is no more than a set of rules for the division of the work of the government. Every large organization must have rules for internal management, even if there are no rules for imposing external control upon it. Otherwise, civil servants would not know what to do in their day's work and would be falling over one another all the time. But these rules for internal house-keeping are in no way a restraint upon the rulers. They can change them all by decree just as a business corporation can change the rules by which it manages its own affairs or as the owner of a slave plantation could reshuffle the tasks of his slaves. As far as governmental forms are concerned, power is utterly concentrated. The one abiding rule is authority from the top downward, obedience from the bottom upward. Constitutionalism does not exist in the dictatorships. The governments of the dictatorships are not constitutional governments. This is true of the Soviet Union as well as the others. An elaborate constitution was adopted in the Soviet Union in 1936. Despite claims that it guarantees to its citizens a greater range of rights than any other constitution, it has never been an effective restriction on the power of the small group that run the Russian state.

Democratic countries also must divide the work of government for the sake of efficiency. There is a geographical distribution which delegates certain powers to municipalities while the residue of powers is in the hands of the central government. Sometimes this distribution is made more complex by introducing a third and intermediate level of government, as in the federal systems where state governments have exclusive control of a wide range of matters. At each level of government, there is always a functional division, generally identified as legislative, executive, and judicial, with still more elaborate division or departmentalization within the executive branch. Such divisions of work, whether geographic or functional, invite disagreement and cross-purposes, and therefore every constitution must define the relations between the different levels and functions so as to limit friction and provide an assured means of breaking deadlocks.

However, these divisions, though necessary for efficiency, are not solely directed to that purpose. In the democracies, they are designed for, and contribute in considerable measure to, preventing the concentration of power in the hands of a few. The legislature is a check on the executive; the judges are independent and commonly are sharp critics of the executive. They cannot even be said to be always sympathetic to the legislature. In a federal system, the state governments are a check on the federal government, and the existence of municipal governments sets limits to the ambitions of state governments.

In the dictatorships, such division of authority as exists does not serve this purpose at all. In Germany, for example, the Nazis destroyed the federal system, eliminating the separate states. They destroyed the autonomy of the municipalities, giving them over to the charge of Nazi party bosses. The legislature was a complete farce without power and the judges were the tools of the leaders. The divisions of authority in the Soviet Union come to the same thing. As was said before, the concentration of power at the apex is utter and complete. In the light of this contrast, the squabbling which goes on within and between governments in a democratic country ceases to look entirely deplorable.

LIBERALISM AND DEMOCRACY

It might be concluded from the emphasis of this contrast that the democratic peoples are so much in fear of government as such that they would deny it any significant range of power, holding that the best government is the one that governs least. The men who framed the American constitution and those who laid down the main lines of the modern British constitution after the expulsion of the Stuart kings in 1688 were much of this mind. However, they were not democrats. They believed in constitutional government and a wide range of individual liberty but not in the control of government by the many. They feared that extension of the franchise to the ignorant masses would result in the destruction of all liberty. They believed rather that the franchise should be restricted to the upper and middle ranks of the population.

British government in the eighteenth century was an aristocracy, and the relatively few who controlled it sometimes confused their own narrow interests with the public interest. But they did banish arbitrary government from Britain, and a by-product of their success was a large measure of civil liberty for individuals. Continental European admirers of Britain in the eighteenth century constantly spoke of it as a land where men were secure in their persons and property from arbitrary governmental action and could think and express themselves freely. It is true that men could still be impressed into the service of the navy against their will and that Roman Catholics and dissenters from the doctrines of the Church of England were subject to disabilities on the ground of religion. These and other restrictions were deviations from the liberal ideal. Yet, in comparison with earlier times and other countries, the British constitution of the eighteenth century provided a striking vindication of individual liberty. British government which operated within the strict confines of the constitution could be fairly described as liberal government.

One of the grounds of complaint that lay behind the American Revolution was that British subjects in America were denied liberties which British subjects were accorded at home. Accordingly, steps were taken in the American Constitution, and in the first group of amendments thereto in 1791, to secure the content of these and other liberties for American citizens. Without attempting a complete catalogue, it is to be noted that the American Constitution contains guarantees against arbitrary interference with person or property and specifically assures freedom of religion, freedom of speech, freedom of the press, and freedom of peaceable assembly. The framers put themselves on record as unqualified believers in liberal government. Yet few of them believed in democracy, defined as adult male suffrage.

Adult male suffrage, subject to certain minor qualifications which need not concern us here, came in Britain, United States, and Canada in the course of the nineteenth century. It was won by convinced democrats, relying on the freedom to discuss and agitate afforded by liberal constitutional government. These convinced democrats were also convinced liberals and individualists who asked little of government except that it should protect individuals in the widest possible freedom of action. They wanted manhood suffrage because they thought this was the only way to ensure permanently that government would not restrict freedom in the interests of a narrow class. Thus democracy in Britain and North America inherited beliefs in individual liberty and constitutional government and made them a central part of its own creed. In the beginning, it feared government as such, and thought of manhood suffrage as an additional device for keeping it under control. The principle

of laissez faire, the belief that government should be confined to a
very narrow sphere of action, was a dogma of first importance
through the greater part of the nineteenth century.

Therefore, the governments of Britain, the United States, and
Canada are appropriately described as liberal democratic governments. Those who have lived under them and have had no
experience of other regimes think, if common speech is any index
to belief, that they are sufficiently described as democratic governments, assuming that liberty and democracy inevitably go arm in
arm. However, we have just seen that it is possible to conceive of,
and to maintain for a time at least, governments which are liberal
without being fully democratic. In the strict meaning of words,
democracy means merely rule by the many. And it is always
possible to have a democracy in which there is little respect for
individual liberty. Some of the ancient democracies degenerated
into mob-rule. Mobs are composed of large numbers who do not
behave liberally or constitutionally.

There is always danger of intolerant majorities denying liberty
to individuals and minority groups that have aroused their hostility.
The record of democracy in the United States, Canada, and
Britain is by no means free of blemishes of this kind. It can be said
with assurance that the principal check on intolerant majorities is
the widespread mutual respect engendered in men, despite their
differences, by the liberal democratic ideal. The modern dictatorships have not been lacking in certain democratic elements,
because the dictators have gone to great pains to secure, by one
means or another, mass support for their rule. These masses often
behaved like mobs, and Mussolini and Hitler encouraged them so
to behave. Yet there is no denying the large elements of popular
support, however secured.

Whatever the democratic element in the dictatorships, they have
not been liberal any more than they have been constitutional. On
every hand, the individual is subordinated to some overriding purpose, relentlessly pushed, if not entirely conceived, by the leaders.
We have already seen what Mussolini and Hitler thought about
freedom for individuals. The Communist dictatorship in the Soviet
Union scorns bourgeois liberty as found in the liberal democracies
on the ground that it is merely the liberty of the few to exploit the

many. It holds forth the promise of a larger liberty which liberals must acknowledge as a noble ideal, but thus far it has not delivered any significant instalments on account.

DEMOCRACY AND THE POPULAR WILL

Whether liberal or not, a democracy is not a democracy unless it responds to the will of the people. With the broadening of the franchise, government in Britain, the United States, and Canada did so respond, making laws in accordance with the aspirations of the newly enfranchised groups. After manhood franchise had been achieved and people got some confidence that government was an instrument they could use for their purposes, some of the earlier fear of government as a necessary but regrettable evil began to disappear. At the same time, a variety of circumstances which will be considered later suggested a good many purposes which governments could be used to further./The belief in laissez faire began rapidly to decline and democratic electorates loaded the government —their servant—with new tasks, new powers, and new obligations/ until ancient despots might well envy democratic governments their range of authority.

The steadily accelerating tendency to call on government for solutions to any and every social problem is perhaps the most remarkable social phenomenon of our time. The rapid growth of government action was well under way by 1900. It was accelerated by World War I, it slackened in the 'twenties, gathered speed again in the long depression of the 'thirties, and came, during World War II, almost to match the scope of governmental functions in the dictatorships. While government activities have fallen away sharply from this peak in Canada and the United States, and to a lesser extent in Britain, it is unlikely that there will be a return to the 1939 level given the present international tensions and the massive defence requirements. The people no longer show any great fear of government, although there is growing uneasiness about /the power of the electorate to control and direct its operations. /

This raises another important distinction between democracy and dictatorship. In a dictatorship, the leader and a small clique around him decide what government shall do. They are able to act with great rapidity and often with a high degree of consistency, because there are only a few minds to be made up. /In a democracy, the ultimate decision about what the government is to do rests with the millions of which the widely scattered electorate is composed./ Cumbersome machinery that consumes a great deal of time and effort is necessary to consult the wishes of the sovereign electorate. More important still, it is exceedingly difficult for millions of people to come to a common mind or a majority decision about anything. When one considers how long a small committee can debate before coming to any agreement about the simplest matters, it is astonishing that the electorate ever manages to agree on instructions to its government. When it is realized how many things democratic governments do nowadays, it is understandable why the will of the people is not always manifest in what is done. What needs explaining is how the electorate is able to transmit coherent instructions to the government at all.

Democracy inherited its devices for restraining governments from the presumptuous abuse of power. It did not inherit its mechanisms for eliciting and transmitting to the government the positive measures it wants to see carried out. It had to create them, feeling its way by trial and error. The chief of these mechanisms is the organized system of political parties. Its workings are far from giving general satisfaction. A great deal of the dissatisfaction with political parties and with democracy arises from a failure to understand the difficulty of what is being attempted.

The discussion that follows has two principal themes. First, the need for restraints on government as such, and the instruments by which democratic peoples have maintained these restraints. Second, the problem of deciding, in a democracy, what the government is to do in the name of all, and the instruments through which the authentic voice of the electorate is to be heard and translated into action. The two themes cannot always be discussed separately, because the same instrument is often used for both purposes. For example, the legislature is both a check and a spur to government. And, as we shall see, decisions emerging from the electorate that government should be spurred on to a more positive programme of action often require that the reins by which government is checked should be slackened.

In fact, democratic constitutions have been considerably modified in the last fifty years to allow government to carry out the widening activities it is expected to perform. The adaptation has gone so far that some will challenge the accuracy of the description of democratic constitutions given here. They will say that democratic constitutions are no longer to be understood as devices for restraining governments but rather as instruments for carrying out the will of the people, for ensuring that government does what electoral majorities want it to do. Furthermore, they will contend that any portion of the constitution which does not promote this latter purpose is outmoded and should be changed forthwith. For the past thirty or so years, a great debate has been raging in democratic countries over this question. Some of the considerations bearing on it will be brought out later.

CHAPTER IV

CONSTITUTIONS AND THE SEPARATION OF POWERS

THE governments of Britain, the United States, and Canada are constitutional governments and it is necessary first to look at the constitutions within which they work. But we should emphasize that it would be quite unrealistic to suppose that a description of the constitution is about all that an intelligent person needs to know about a government. We must realize that a constitution is no more than the skeleton or essential frame of orderly government. The constitution defines and provides for the establishment of the chief organs of government. It outlines the relation between these organs and the citizen, between the state and the individual, and between the organs themselves. Being concerned mainly with the pedigree of governmental organs and the relationship between them, it does not create the government or make it work. By itself, it is inert and lifeless, and only when clothed with flesh and blood (human passions and active agents) does it begin to win friends and enemies and influence people. We learn very little about a government merely by examining its skeletal structure. We have to study the complex functional system installed in it, and also the hopes, fears, aims, and prejudices, the fundamental drives and conflicts of the individuals and groups whose actions influence the government of the day and provoke governmental action. We must go beyond anatomy to physiology and psychology—vastly more difficult subjects.

The figure may be varied. The constitution is the frame or chassis in which the working engine of government is set. Within a certain tolerance, the type and structure of the engine can be modified without changing the frame. A constitution generally will accommodate a considerable adaptation of the working mechanisms of government. The engine itself will not run without fuel. Human needs and dreams are the fuel on which governments run, and what governments do depends to a large degree on the tangled motives of politicians and on the foibles and cross-purposes as well as the agreements of the individuals and groups making up society.

While much always depends on the intelligence and skill of the operators, the structure of the engine nevertheless determines what can be used as fuel. Liberal democratic government will not run on the aspirations of a multitude of would-be dictators. It requires, among other things, a tolerant mentality of its people.

On the other hand, the frame within which the working engine of government is set determines the ways in which the power generated can be transmitted, and the kind of operations to which it can be effectively harnessed. A liberal democratic constitution is not a very good frame for transmitting power for twentieth-century wars. So much improvising for the purpose of war organization has to be done that one can almost say the constitution is temporarily set aside. Most motor vehicles do not lend themselves to amphibious operations, and a constitution of the liberal-democratic type is not designed for travelling at high speed to the new Utopia.

In the study of a particular government, therefore, we have to examine the frame or constitution, to see the essential design. We have also to study the working mechanism of government within the constitution. We have to take account of the character of the people and the beliefs and the wants on which the government feeds, which calls for an understanding of human nature in general and also of the unique qualities of the particular society in question. The government of a people, like the history of that people, is the study of a lifetime. Whatever introductory simplifications may be resorted to, the inherent complexity of the subject must be emphasized.

This suggests why all sorts of contradictory statements can be made about government, with a show of truth. For example, many close observers of liberal democratic governments have described them and their operations as enforcing the will of the people. On the other hand, many critics have described them as tools of an economic oligarchy—instruments for maintaining the rule of the capitalist class. Honest, intelligent exponents of both these views can be found, and they can both produce impressive evidence to support them. The truth is that so great a variety of forces and motives enter into government in the twentieth century and the response of government to these is so complex that a plausible case for a great many propositions can be made out. No one key will unlock the mysteries of government and we must always beware of thinking we know more than we really do.

If, in his initial approach to government, the student tries to comprehend it in all its complexity he will be completely baffled. A play-by-play description of what goes on at the national capital on a single day would convince him that he should stick to a tidy subject like mathematics. Difficult subjects can only be handled by isolating and studying one at a time the elements involved. One can begin with the anatomy of government—the framework to be found in the constitution. That will occupy the attention of the present chapter and parts of the succeeding chapters. At the next level of difficulty, one can isolate the organs and agencies of government and see how they function within the framework. Finally, one can consider how far this functioning is a response to the environment in which government operates, to what extent government action reflects the interplay of the social forces of the community. In the later chapters, some consideration, inevitably incomplete, will be given to the physiology of government and to the reaction of the organs to the environment.[1]

WHERE TO LOOK FOR THE CONSTITUTION

The British constitution is always said to be unwritten. This is not to say that it has nowhere found expression in the printed word, but rather that the principles and detailed rules of the constitution have never been collected together in a formal document solemnly adopted at a specific date. The British people have never made a sharp revolutionary break with their past. Freedom—and everything else political in nature—has slowly broadened down from precedent to precedent. The present-day constitution has been worked out over centuries by trial and error. What endures is what has been found workable. Magna Carta, A.D. 1215, although overrated in popular oratory, is the earliest, and still a significant, document of the constitution. The Petition of Right, 1628, the Bill of Rights, 1689, the Act of Settlement, 1701, the great Reform Act, 1832, are others of prime importance. In terms of bulk, the

[1]The use of the biological analogy must not be taken to suggest that biological laws are in any way applicable to the state. As the analogy becomes more forced in later pages, this will probably become sufficiently obvious.

greater part of it is to be found in the form of statutes enacted by Parliament. Almost all the momentous changes of the past century have been thus brought about, such as the extension of the franchise, the method of elections, and the defining of the rights and duties of public officials.

Many basic principles, however, rest on the Common Law, that vast body of English law based on custom and reshaped to new needs by succeeding generations of judges. The principles that rest on the Common Law have to be spelled laboriously out of the decisions of the courts in particular disputes. Finally, a considerable and important portion of the constitution has no other basis than comparatively recent custom. The conventions of the constitution, as these are called, concern mainly the relation of the cabinet to Parliament ensuring that the government is always carried on conformably to the will of the majority in Parliament. Thus a first-hand exploration of the British constitution would take one through ancient charters, scores of statutes, hundreds of judicial decisions, and finally into the biographies and correspondence of statesmen, which often provide the only written evidence for the conventions of the constitution. Its elusiveness is excused by saying it is unwritten. The logically minded who want everything in precise black-and-white throw up their hands and say, "The British constitution! There's no such thing!"

The American Revolution was a fairly clean break with the past and the Americans got from it a written Constitution. But they did not write on an entirely clean slate. Both in what they accepted and what they rejected they were decisively influenced by their past. This remarkably short constitution—a document of only five thousand words—is not, however, by any means the whole of the American constitution of today. To make the paper Constitution work in practice and adapt it to the changing American scene, much improvising had to be done. Twenty-two formal amendments to the Constitution have been adopted. With the passage of time, many usages for which there is no warrant in the written text and which it takes a substantial volume to describe, have acquired an importance and sanctity scarcely less than that of the Constitution itself. Also, the very terseness of the written Constitution left a number of gaps, which have been filled by Acts of Congress. For example, Acts of Congress established the ten executive departments and fixed the basic structure of the federal courts. Legislation on matters as fundamental as these is a part of the working constitution.

The Supreme Court of the United States, which has the last word on the meaning of the Constitution, has added a wealth of meaning to many of the terse phrases of the written document. It has held, for example, that some matters not expressly mentioned therein are necessarily implied. As a result, no conceivable feat of imagination would suffice to gather from the written text what 150 years of interpretation have made it mean. It takes hundreds of pages to describe even summarily the contribution of the Supreme Court and thus there is some warrant for the frequent jibe that the Constitution is what the Supreme Court says it is.

It is commonly said that the Canadian constitution is contained in certain statutes of the British Parliament, the British North America Acts of 1867-1952. But here again the great bulk of the constitution and many of its most important provisions are to be found elsewhere. An examination of the British North America Act of 1867 will show that it is mostly concerned with outlining the constitution of the new Dominion thereby created and with fixing the relationships between, and the respective powers of, the new Dominion and the provinces. The only substantial qualification on this arises from the fact that Confederation involved the breaking up of the old province of Canada into two entirely new provinces, Ontario and Quebec, and the constitutions of these two new provinces had to be provided for in the Act. The other provinces either retained the constitutions they had already received as British colonies or, as in the case of the Prairie Provinces, later received their basic constitutions from Acts of the federal Parliament.

Yet this is by no means all. British colonies have always been deemed to hold, as a right, such portions of the British constitution, particularly those resting on Common Law and custom, as are not incompatible with their situation. The provinces (but not the Dominion) are empowered by the British North America Act to add to or modify their constitutions and they have often exercised the power. So the provincial constitutions, except those of Ontario and Quebec, are either Imperial Orders in Council (providing for the government of the colony before Confederation) or Dominion statutes (bringing post-confederation provinces into existence), worked into an amalgam with provincial statutes, English Common Law, and the conventions of the British constitution.

If we leave the provincial constitutions entirely aside, only a part of the constitution of Canada is to be found in the British North America Acts. The Act of 1867 refers to the Governor General but does not create his office. The executive government and Privy Council are provided for but there is no mention of the cabinet. Provision for the cabinet has to be spelled out of the preamble of the British North America Act which recites the desire of the colonies for a constitution "similar in principle to that of the United Kingdom," certain statutes of the federal Parliament, and the conventions of the British constitution relating to cabinet government. Equally, most of the Common Law principles of the British constitution are applicable. Numerous other matters, such as the privileges of Parliament, the franchise, election laws, and the constitution and powers of the Supreme Court of Canada, depend on statutes enacted by the federal Parliament under powers specially given in the British North America Act of 1867.

This sketch indicates the sources and some of the range and variety of constitutional provisions. It also suggests that if a search for the essential elements of a constitution is not to lose itself in a welter of confusing materials, some categories of classification and analysis will have to be adopted. Just as the amateur botanist, lacking a principle of classification, wanders among the flowers and gets only the impression that nature is wonderful, so the student of government without categories for sorting out his material may decide that the subject is incomprehensible.

THE SEPARATION OF POWERS

The distinctive feature of government is the exercise of power by some men over other men, and a classification of the kinds of power thus exercised, though artificial to a degree, aids understanding. At the simplest level of discussion, a familiar classification, as old as Aristotle, is available for use. There are, it is said, three distinct kinds of governmental power, legislative, executive, and judicial. Legislative power consists in making laws, general rules of conduct supplementing or replacing some of the older rules based on custom or unwritten law. Executive power consists in the executing or carrying out of the laws and the carrying on of the manifold public activities and services, the daily drudgery that exhausts the civil servant. Judicial power consists in interpreting the laws or, more concretely, deciding in the event of dispute what specific acts are permitted or required or forbidden in execution of the law.

While it is impossible thus to classify all the varied powers exercised by modern governments, these categories will serve for immediate purposes. Montesquieu, a French writer of the mid-eighteenth century, adopted this classification and made himself famous by arguing that the secret of civil liberty lay in the separation of these powers, in the reserving of each type of power to different persons or bodies of persons. One man or group of men should exercise substantially all legislative power and at the same time have no extensive share in or control over executive or judicial power. Men will always push what power they have to the limit, and if those who make the laws also enforce them, they can tyrannize over their fellows. The result will be the same if either executive and judicial, or legislative and judicial, powers are joined in the hands of the same persons. No one body of men, according to this argument, can be trusted with the monopoly of force possessed by government.

According to Montesquieu, assurance that government shall be servant and not master depends on the separation of powers. This, he argued, is the essence of an effective constitution. He thought he discerned a proof of his argument in the British constitution of the eighteenth century. Britain enjoyed individual liberty, while on the Continent, where absolute monarchs had gathered all power into their hands, no one had any sure tenure of freedom. He saw the independent status of the judges in Britain, ensured by the Act of Settlement in 1701. He saw in Parliament a legislative authority independent of the executive and he thought he saw in the king, his advisers, and servants an independent executive authority. He was in substantial error on this last point, but the British constitution did conform to the classification and there was then some measure of separation of powers.

The Americans could not find the civil and political liberty they wanted under the British constitution in the days of George III. Yet they were deeply impressed with Montesquieu's analysis, if not with the particular proof he offered. They were the more impressed because Locke, the philosopher of constitutionalism, had pointed to a similar conclusion. Moreover, the conservative-minded fathers of the Constitution feared the excesses of popularly elected legislatures as much as they feared a powerful executive. Accordingly, they set out to fashion a new government composed of three powers, each of which would be separate and, at the same time, a check on the others. So whatever of enduring wisdom there is in the separation of powers, it is a principle closely associated with the rise and spread of modern constitutional government. The constitutions of the modern world which have tried to hold governments strictly to account have relied heavily on the British and American models. This is reason enough for using Montesquieu's doctrine for preliminary analysis. Its value can be more justly assessed at a later stage.

Very early in British constitutional history, the powers of government exercised by the Norman and Angevin kings began to be differentiated along lines resembling the threefold classification, and distinct organs for their exercise emerged. The Great Council, composed of the great feudal lords and meeting three times a year, "advised" the king largely by trying to set limits to royal action, as in Magna Carta. With the addition of representatives from the counties and boroughs, the Great Council developed into Parliament. The redress of grievances and the imposition of limitations on the king took the form of laws enacted with the consent of the king.

Apart from the Great Council, the king was advised by an inner council composed of his trusted lieutenants, the heads of an embryonic civil service only slowly differentiated from the king's personal household. This inner council, generally called the Curia Regis, carried on all the executive work of government, doing the will of the king everywhere except where blocked by the Great Council. As government business increased, several groups of these officials specialized in settling disputes and interpreting the law applicable to them. At first, they were merely committees of the Curia Regis but after developing an organization and procedure of their own, they became distinct and separate courts of law, although until 1701 the judges still held office at the king's pleasure. Within the Curia Regis itself, increasing size brought the need for a small executive committee—hence the Privy Council, close to the king. The Privy Council became the real executive council, and even today the formal authority of the cabinet derives from their being sworn "of the Privy Council."

Leading Principles of the British Constitution

Thus distinct legislative, executive, and judicial organs took shape. It would, however, be misleading to suggest that the judges never made laws and that the legislature and executive always refrained from judging, and wrong to think that each organ had a well-marked sphere of authority in which it was separate and independent. In part at any rate, the struggle between Parliament and the Stuarts arose out of the indefiniteness of the relationship between these organs which was only cleared up by the constitutional settlement after the Revolution of 1688. The judges once appointed were made independent of the executive. It was settled that only Parliament could change the law or make a new law such as the levying of a tax—which, in effect, made Parliament supreme. The power of governing the country subject to the limitations thus imposed by law, the administration of the colonies, and the conduct of foreign relations remained with the king and his advisers appointed by him. It took most of the eighteenth century to establish beyond question the rule that the king must choose ministers who enjoy the confidence of Parliament. Montesquieu can be excused for thinking in 1748 that the executive was separate and independent.

But there has been no excuse in the last hundred years for anyone's thinking that the British constitution exhibits a sharp separation of powers. The basic principle of the British constitution is the supremacy of Parliament. Any and every law passed by Parliament is constitutional. It has been said that Parliament can do anything except make a man a woman. This is an understatement. If Parliament were to declare that henceforth women were to be treated in all respects as if they were men, the executive and the courts would be obliged so to treat them, even in the face of nature. Women would then have to be called up under the military service law hitherto applicable only to men. Obviously, this means that Parliament can turn absurdities into laws and can work its will on the other two organs of government. It could pass a law dismissing all servants of the Crown and taking into its own hands the entire executive power. It could abolish the judiciary. So it can enlarge or diminish at pleasure the sphere of the executive and judiciary. It can—as it has increasingly done in the last seventy-five years—delegate law-making powers from itself to the executive. There is no ban on law-making by the executive if only Parliament will authorize it. It can—and does with great frequency —take the power of interpreting particular laws away from the judiciary and give it to the executive.

Of course, as long as the House of Commons, which is the effective part of Parliament, represents the electorate and depends on it for re-election, there are many things it will not dream of doing. There is, in practice, a considerable separation of powers although there are no formal constitutional provisions ensuring its close observance. If we look at the strict legal forms of the constitution alone, Parliament can change any law by majority vote, and it can change the constitution in the same way. But the British constitution is largely made up of custom and convention which often seem to nullify the legal forms. Constitutionalism and the constitutional practices on which it rests are preserved in Britain by custom and the deeply conservative habit of the British people. They resist rapid and drastic change. They believe in limits on governmental power and those who represent them in Parliament have not been allowed to forget it. As we shall see later, drastic constitutional change is not ordinarily undertaken by Parliament until the proposed change has been made a direct issue in a general election.

The electorate, however, has not insisted on a sharp separation of legislature and executive. It has rather approved an intimate connection and interdependence between them. The executive is directly responsible to Parliament. The ministry, composed of more than one hundred ministers, heads the various departments of government and directs all the energies and activities of the civil service. A varying number of the more important ministers, generally about twenty, composes the cabinet. Since the cabinet—and the other ministers also—must have seats in Parliament, it is, in reality, a committee of Parliament for the executive management of the nation's affairs. When this committee loses the confidence of the House of Commons, it must either abandon the direction of affairs of state and resign, or seek a dissolution of Parliament in the hope that a newly elected House of Commons will give it renewed confidence. In formal constitutional theory, at any rate, the executive is dependent on Parliament. The cabinet is, in Bagehot's words, a buckle, a hyphen, a combining committee, for ensuring harmony between the detailed execution of the laws by the civil service and the will of the majority in Parliament. The executive and legislative powers are not separated but almost completely fused.

The judges are appointed by the king on the advice of his ministers, but the appointment is for life and during good behaviour. They can be removed only by an address of both Houses of Parliament. Because of a high standard of judicial rectitude and impartiality, this power has almost never been used and the judicial power has enjoyed a high degree of independence. It must be remembered, however, that Parliament has the power to declare that any and every interpretation of law made by the judges is wrong and, by an amendment, to substitute its own authoritative interpretation.

Although there is no formal separation of powers, it would be incorrect to think that these organs do not act as some check on one another. The heads of the civil service sometimes find obstacles to doing what Parliament wants to do. The courts not infrequently interpret the laws to mean something different from what Parliament intended and the executive hoped. Even the majority in Parliament that supports the cabinet is sometimes reluctant to support particular ministers. The essential point is that if Parliament really makes up its mind, nothing can stand in its way.

There is another fundamental principle of the British constitution called the Rule of Law. It is the concrete British embodiment of the liberal democratic ideal of rule by law. Although its exact significance is a matter of much debate, it is clearly of critical importance. The Rule of Law means, at least, that all actions of government must conform to the law and an individual cannot be prejudiced in person or property by the government or anyone else except in accordance with existing law. It has commonly been thought that, in addition, officials had to justify their actions by the law generally applicable to all citizens before the established judiciary, which is free of all suggestion of executive influence.

A hundred years ago there was much more warrant for this last proposition than there is today. For a long time now, Parliament has been granting to officials special powers to take action not justified under the ordinary law, and it has been limiting the right of the citizen to have the actions of officials scrutinized by the judicial power. Yet there has been no general removal of officials from judicial surveillance, and it remains true in most cases that anyone who asserts that he has been wronged by the action of a government official can bring that official before the courts of law to answer for his conduct. The official may justify himself by pointing to an act of Parliament that gives him a special privilege to do what he has done. But he cannot turn aside the complaint merely by asserting an exalted official status and an inscrutable executive expediency in what he has done. The state can throw away the conscript's life but it cannot conscript him in the first instance on the plea of high policy or public expedience except as supported by a law sanctioned by Parliament. The Rule of Law, although qualified today by the grant of special powers to officials, remains an indispensable instrument for ensuring that government remains servant.

Parliament, being supreme, could abolish the Rule of Law to-morrow. As long as Parliament is concerned to keep the executive under control, it is unlikely to do so. Yet the fact that the Rule of Law does not now mean what it meant a hundred years ago indicates that the really fundamental principle of the British constitution is the supremacy of Parliament.

THE CONSTITUTION OF THE UNITED STATES

Although only a part of the constitution of the United States is now to be found in the written document and in the twenty-two formal amendments, it is still the most basic part and attention will, for the present, be directed primarily to the written document.

In looking at it, one must always remember that it is an instrument establishing a new national government and it takes the constitutions of the separate states of the Union almost completely for granted. For the most part too, it takes for granted the main principles of the Common Law that the colonists imported from Britain and adapted to their use. Some significant features of the American constitutional system are derived from the Common Law. With the Revolution, the thirteen states modified or repudiated their charters as British colonies. Before 1789, most of them had adopted republican written constitutions. These constitutions as since revised and added to by the admission of thirty-seven new states form an important part of the American constitutional system. But their bulk forbids discussion here, and, in any event, on the more fundamental questions they are faithfully paralleled by the Constitution of 1789.

The more important principles of the constitution may now be sketched. The first is its federal character arising from the preservation of the integrity and substantial independence of the separate states. The thirteen states that had made the Revolution had need of unity if they were to protect their nascent republicanism in a world of powerful monarchies. Yet they were not prepared at all to submerge themselves in a new state giving all authority to a single central government. The result was a compromise federal system in which a new national government was to have certain specific powers in aid of the broad general objectives stated in the preamble, viz., "to establish justice, insure domestic tranquility, provide for the common defense, promote the general welfare and secure the blessings of liberty." The separate states, on the other hand, as Amendment x adopted in 1791 makes clear, were to continue to exercise such authority as was not specifically granted to the national government, expressly prohibited to the states, or withdrawn from the reach of all governments. Most of the written Constitution is taken up with defining the new national authority and distributing powers between it and the states. The special features of federalism will be considered later.

Constitutional Limitations on Government

The second principle is that of limited government. Whereas the supreme legislative power under the British constitution can regulate every aspect of social life, the American constitution tried to put certain claims of individuals that were thought to be sacred human rights beyond the reach of Congress. It limited the area of human affairs over which the federal government, and in some cases the states, could exercise power. This sprang, in part, from the eighteenth-century doctrines about the natural rights of man, so prominent in the French Revolution and the revolutionary constitutions in France. In part, it sprang from the more earthy concern of the conservative framers of the Constitution who feared the radical ferment stirred up by the American Revolution.

These general limitations on government are to be found principally in the original Constitution of 1789 and in the first ten amendments adopted in 1791. Some of them take the form of abstract "natural" rights. For example, Congress is forbidden to interfere with freedom of religion, of speech, of the press, and of peaceable assembly.[1] Other provisions struck at particular abuses, the usual weapons of arbitrary governments, such as general search warrants, bills of attainder and *ex post facto* (retroactive) laws,[2] while still others sought to preserve against encroaching governments particular institutional procedures that had been useful in the English and American struggles for liberty, such as habeas corpus and trial by jury.[3]

Most of these and numerous other limitations are applicable only to the federal government and do not bind the state governments. Of those mentioned above, only the prohibitions against bills of attainder and *ex post facto* laws apply to both levels of government.[4] However, since most of the state constitutions, in the group of clauses known as the Bill of Rights, go as far as or farther than the federal Constitution in imposing limitations, it is substantially correct to think of all these restrictions as being generally applicable. By judicial interpretation of the due process and equal protection of the law clauses in the Fourteenth Amendment, which apply to the states, substantially all the limitations in the Bill of Rights, except the guarantees of indictment by grand jury and trial by jury, are also effective against the states.

[1]Constitution of the United States, Amendment I.
[2]*Ibid.*, Art. I, s. 9 and Amendment IV.
[3]*Ibid.*, Art. I, s. 9 and Amendments V, VI, and VII.
[4]*Ibid.*, Art. I, s. 10.

The most famous of all these restrictive provisions is one imposed by the federal Constitution on state and federal governments alike. The Fifth Amendment forbids the federal government, and the Fourteenth Amendment forbids the states, to "deprive any person of life, liberty or property, without due process of law." The phrase "due process of law" can be traced back into the early history of English law and is reminiscent of the tone of Magna Carta, which stipulated that free men should not be proceeded against except in accordance with the law of the land. The Petition of Right in which the English Parliament in 1628 petitioned Charles I to respect the rights of his subjects uses the two phrases, "the law of the land," and "due process of law," interchangeably. The Declaration of Independence pronounced "life, liberty, and the pursuit of happiness" to be inalienable rights. The exact phrase used in the Constitution, however, comes from John Locke, the philosopher of constitutionalism, who declared "life, liberty and property" to be fundamental natural rights of man. But the past fame of these phrases pales before the notoriety they have gained in the American Constitution. The Supreme Court of the United States has been deeply divided over their meaning and this in turn has aroused sharp political debate throughout the country. These simple phrases have been storm centres of controversy over the last fifty years.

Some restrictions were laid upon the state governments only. In the turbulent period during and after the Revolutionary War, the legislatures of many of the states had been enacting laws that impaired the rights of creditors under existing contracts and/or made the almost worthless paper currency legal tender for payment of debts. It is said that harassed creditors often took to the woods to evade their vindictive and relentless debtors who sought to pay them off in inflated currency. Accordingly, the framers of the Constitution, among whom the creditor interest was well represented, inserted clauses providing that no state should pass any "law impairing the obligation of contracts," and forbidding states to coin money, emit bills of credit, or make anything but gold or silver legal tender.[1]

---

[1]*Ibid.*, Art. I, s. 10.

These are some of the more important of the clauses illustrating the principle of limited government. In Britain, by contrast, Parliament could lawfully enact each and all of these measures forbidden in the United States. It has not done so. Britain has been no less free of legislative tyranny than the United States. The effective guarantee is not found in a written constitution but in the settled constitutional habit of the British people, of which Parliament is itself an expression. Thus far it has been reasonably adequate. There has not been any significant agitation for written constitutional guarantees against the power of Parliament.

Separation of Powers

The third fundamental principle is the separation of powers. The Constitution of 1789 takes Montesquieu's classification for granted. Without defining the nature of the three powers in any way, the first three articles of the document assign legislative, executive, and judicial power to three separate organs. Article I provides that all legislative powers granted therein shall be vested in Congress; Article II that the executive power shall be vested in the President; Article III that the judicial power shall be vested in one Supreme Court and in such inferior courts as Congress may establish. It is also stipulated that no member of Congress shall, during his term in Congress, be appointed to any civil office, and that no person holding any such office shall be a member of Congress. Thus no one can share in the exercise of more than one of the three powers at the same time. Neither the President, nor his cabinet, nor any executive officer, can be a member of Congress. The executive power of the United States is exercised, not by a committee of the legislature responsible to the legislature, but by an independently elected President aided by such advisers outside Congress as he sees fit to consult. The President is required to keep Congress informed of the state of the union, to advise it about the administration of national affairs, and to recommend such legislation as he thinks necessary. He has power, in certain circumstances, to convene Congress and to fix a date for its adjournment, but beyond this he is not expected to shape or participate in its deliberations.

The judiciary is appointed by the President with the advice and consent of the Senate. But once appointed, judges hold office during good behaviour. Congress cannot intimidate them by reducing their salaries during their continuance in office. They can be removed by Congress, but only through impeachment for and conviction of a serious offence. It would appear that the powers of government are parcelled out among the three organs and kept separate by the unscalable walls of the constitution. In the United States, Montesquieu's principle received its fullest expression.

Each organ was to have a will of its own and as little ability as possible to influence the choice of the personnel who exercise the other two powers. Even so, the framers feared the popularly elected legislatures that had run riot in the revolutionary period, and they still feared a strong executive who might get it in his head to be a king. It was thought that dividing the Congress into two Houses, each to be elected by a different method and for different periods, would tend to divide and moderate the legislative will. By providing for indirect election of the President, that office would be shielded from demagogues who notoriously abuse even the widest mandate.

It was thought advisable to have still further checks on power, and this abundance of caution led the framers to introduce some qualifications on the clear-cut separation of powers. Bills passed by a majority of the two Houses of Congress require the approval of the President in order to become law and can only be made law over his veto by a two-thirds vote of both branches. The President was given some share in legislative power. The President, Vice-President, and other executive officers can be removed from office by impeachment in the House of Representatives and conviction in the Senate, thus giving the latter some judicial power. The declaration of war, an executive act, can only be made by Congress. The Senate shares with the President the powers of treaty-making and of the appointment of high officials, also executive acts. While the President and Senate appoint the federal judges, the Senate can remove them by conviction on impeachment. The constitution of all courts inferior to the Supreme Court is confided to Congress. These checks and balances, as they are called, were not set up to knit the three powers together for concerted action but rather to ensure that the "several constituent parts [of the government] may by their mutual relations, be the means of keeping each other in their proper place."[1]

To those who do not know the history of the disorder of the revolutionary period, the predominantly conservative temper of the framers, and the emphasis put by the prevailing political philosophy of the time on the natural rights of individuals and on the natural propensity of government to tyranny, much of this will seem not merely abundance but excess of caution. Indeed, there is no doubt that the separation of powers and checks and balances have had unfortunate effects on American government, and there is doubt whether this complex scheme would have worked at all but for the rise of mediating institutions not contemplated by the authors of the Constitution. But the various effects of the scheme on the operation of government and the important modifications that custom has brought about in the last hundred and fifty years, largely through the rise of political parties to all-pervasive influence, must be left for succeeding chapters.

The Principle of Judicial Review

The last of the important features of the American constitution to be sketched here is judicial review, the power of the judiciary to declare acts of Congress or of the state legislatures to be unconstitutional and therefore of no more legal effect than if they had never been passed. The courts cannot range across the statute book on their own motion slaying legislation at will. But when, in a dispute between parties properly brought before them, the decision is found to turn on the terms of some act of a legislature, the judges (state and inferior federal as well as Supreme Court) will inquire whether the legislation is contrary to state, or federal, constitutions, and if so, the party relying on its terms will fail through the ensuing declaration of unconstitutionality. An act of a state legislature may be struck down on the ground that it could only be enacted by Congress, or vice versa, and is thus a violation of the federal principle. A statute may be attacked before the courts on the ground that it violates one or the other of the two

[1] *The Federalist*, no. 51.

"due process of law" clauses, or some other fundamental guarantee and thus infringes the principle of limited government. An act of Congress may be challenged on the ground that it violates the principle of the separation of powers. Indeed, any legislative act deemed by them to be prohibited by the constitution may be held invalid by the courts.

This is in the sharpest contrast with the treatment of legislation in the British courts. The latter may misinterpret an act of Parliament but they can never question the power of Parliament to do anything that Parliament has manifestly done. The Rule of Law in Britain means no more than the enforcement as law of what Parliament has said. The Rule of Law in the United States means also the enforcement of the "higher law" of the constitution against both the legislature and the executive.

Strangely enough, this power of the courts is not explicitly stated in the Constitution but is one of the powers that the Supreme Court has long held to be necessarily implied from the provisions *(a)* that the constitution and the laws of Congress made in pursuance thereof shall be the supreme law of the land and *(b)* that the judges of the United States and of the several states are required to swear to support the constitution.[1] The necessity of the implication has often been challenged but, in any event, custom has made judicial review as much a part of the constitution as if it were explicit in the document. Hundreds of state and federal laws, chiefly the former, have been held unconstitutional. In this censorship of legislation, of course, the Supreme Court, being the highest court of appeal, has the last word.

Congress acting alone has no power to amend the Constitution. The framers did not want their handiwork to be easily marred and they made formal amendment extremely difficult. Noting the difficulty and rarity of amendments, many have said that it is the constitution that is supreme in the United States. Others, noting the relative ease with which the Supreme Court has from time to time found unsuspected meanings in the clauses of the Constitution, have said that it is the "nine old men" who make up the Supreme Court who are supreme. Still others, seeing the numerous cases in which the ruling interpretation given by the Supreme Court

[1] Constitution of the United States, Art. vi.

rests on the narrow majority of five judges for and four against, make still more disturbing comments. Such remarks are significant, but no simple statement will uncover the locus of supreme power in the United States. As a matter of form, supreme power rests with the bodies that Article v of the Constitution authorizes to make amendments. But thus far relatively little of the amending and developing of the Constitution has been carried out in this way.

CONTRASTS IN THE CANADIAN CONSTITUTION

The Canadian constitution was modelled as closely as could be on that of Britain. Before the union of 1867, the principal colonies had been granted self-government in internal affairs and they were learning how to govern through a cabinet that was responsible to the legislature. The great bulk of the people in the colonies were doggedly loyal to the British connection and they copied wherever they could. However, the Canadian constitution created a federal union for which no native British model was available. In these circumstances, the colonial statesmen who framed the broad outlines of the British North America Act preparatory to its sanction by the British Parliament were influenced by the example and experience of the United States. Keeping in mind that the Canadian constitution is an attempt to adapt British forms of government to the conditions of a federal state, a few basic considerations may be outlined.[1]

First, because of the federal character of the constitution the Parliament of Canada is far from enjoying the unqualified legal supremacy of the British Parliament. There is a very large sphere in which the provincial legislatures only can enact laws. Secondly, once the distribution of legislative authority imposed by federalism is clearly ascertained, the national Parliament and provincial legislatures each enjoy, within their own area of competence, substantially the same supremacy as the British Parliament. There are no bills of rights in the written constitution of Canada such as are found in the United States. The British North America Act contains, it is true, certain special guarantees of minority rights in

[1]See Robert MacGregor Dawson, *The Government of Canada*, ch. IV, for an account of the salient features of the Canadian constitution.

education and language. Frequent collisions between the French-speaking Roman Catholic and English-speaking Protestant groups had occurred before the union, and special guarantees covering the main points of friction were necessary assurances written into the terms of union.[1] Subject to these restrictions, the appropriate legislature can do anything by majority vote.

Thirdly, the separation of powers is flouted to almost the same degree as in Britain. Cabinet government modelled on that of Britain knits together the legislative and executive powers. The judges are appointed by the Governor-General on the advice of the Dominion cabinet and they are removeable by an address of both Houses of Parliament. It should be added, however, that in Canada the mode of appointment and removal of judges is fixed by the British North America Act, and the tenure of judges of the Superior Courts cannot be altered by the legislature.[2]

Fourthly, the principle of the Rule of Law, subject to the qualifications already noted in the case of Britain, is a part of the Canadian constitution. Indeed, this principle has a wider recognition in Canada because a substantial, though limited, judicial review of legislation takes place. Whenever federal or provincial legislation is in issue before the courts, the judges will consider its constitutionality, whether or not it violates the federal division of legislative power set out in the British North America Act. Judicial review is not nearly so extensive as in the United States because so few rights are guaranteed by the constitution and no strict separation of powers operate as limitations on legislative power. The only question the courts can ask of legislation other than its meaning is whether it violates the terms of the British North America Act, which, like the Constitution of the United States, is binding on all legislatures. Also, as in the United States, judicial review rests on judicial practice, and on judicial assertion as a necessarily implied term of the Constitution. The power of judicial review is nowhere expressly stated in the British North America Act.

By considering this point further we can review in summary important contrasts between the three constitutions. When the Quebec legislature enacted the Padlock Law authorizing the

---

[1]British North America Act, ss. 93 and 133.
[2]*Ibid.*, ss. 96 and 99.

government to lock up buildings used in the distribution of Communist literature, when the Alberta legislature tried to regulate the newspaper business, and when the Ontario legislature declared certain contracts between the Ontario Hydro Electric Power Commission and some Quebec power companies to be no longer binding on the Commission, the Canadian courts had to consider one constitutional question only: whether the provincial legislatures had invaded a field of legislation reserved to the federal Parliament or to another provincial legislature. In all three situations, as recently as 1958 in the first one, the legislation was found to be such an invasion and therefore null and void. In Britain, the courts could not have reviewed such legislation as this on any ground; they could only have considered its meaning. In the United States, on the other hand, in addition to the federal question, the courts would also have had to consider very seriously whether the legislation in question did not invade freedom of speech and peaceable assembly, infringe freedom of the press, and impair the obligation of contracts respectively, and in all the cases, whether a deprivation of liberty or property without due process of law, or a denial of equal protection of the laws, was involved. If so, the legislation would have been null and void, even though it did not violate the federal distribution of powers.

Formal Amendment of Constitutions

So far we have considered constitutions as if they were frozen and static, imposing a rigid frame within which the powers of government are exercised. Obviously, a high degree of stability in a constitution is necessary because order and security depend, in part, on being able to anticipate what governments can do or can be required to do. On the other hand, only a static, caste-ridden society could tolerate an unchanging constitution. As long as social change, or progress, continues, it is vital that the constitution should respond to decisive social transformations. A too rigid constitution may stifle, or distort the direction of, change. At the other extreme, the forces dammed back by it may gather enough force to break it by revolutionary means. As an alternative to violence, there is stealth. The constitution may be evaded by pretending it does not apply to a particular situation or even by pretending it is not there. If the pretence is accepted for a considerable time without effective protest, it amounts to an unacknowledged change in the constitution. It is important, therefore, to see what formal methods of amendment, if any, constitutions specifically provide for. Then certain types of informal amendments, changes by stealth, will be considered.

As the British Parliament is utterly supreme, it follows that it can change the constitution as it sees fit. An ordinary law passed by a simple majority suffices to make the profoundest constitutional change. However, the recently developed doctrine of the mandate, to be considered later, is an important modification imposed by custom on this sweeping power of Parliament.

Article v of the Constitution of the United States provides for four methods of amendment, all of great difficulty. More correctly, perhaps, there are two ways of proposing amendments, each of which offers an alternative method of ratification. A two-thirds majority in Congress may propose an amendment that may be ratified either by three-fourths of the state legislatures or by approving conventions called for the purpose in three-fourths of the states. The legislatures of two-thirds of the states may require Congress to call a convention for proposing amendments, and any amendment it proposes may be ratified in either of the ways mentioned above. Thus far, all twenty-two amendments have been proposed by Congress. The first twenty, and the twenty-second, were ratified by the state legislatures. The twenty-first, repealing the eighteenth, or prohibition, amendment, was ratified by conventions in three-quarters of the states.

The difficulty of formal amendment is thus fairly obvious. If one can judge from experience since the Civil War, it generally takes about a quarter-century of agitation to get an amendment launched with any hope of success and the issue must be one that can be dramatized so as to arouse widespread popular interest and feeling. Forbiddingly technical matters, whatever their importance, will scarcely ever muster the necessary support. There were some who thought it would be impossible to repeal the eighteenth amendment even though every man, woman, and child carried his own flask. However, the issue turned out to be one of broad popular appeal and the repeal went through quickly. The Constitution is generally regarded as much too rigid and most changes have been worked by informal methods. One-quarter of the fifty states representing about five per cent of the population can block an amendment. Although thousands of resolutions for amendments have been introduced in Congress, only twenty-seven have obtained the necessary two-thirds majority, and of these, five failed to get adequate support in three-quarters of the states.

The mixture of rigidity and flexibility in the Canadian constitution has already been noted. Broadly speaking, the appropriate legislature, national or provincial, can amend any portion of it except the clauses of the British North America Act establishing and defining the federal division of power. The provincial constitutions, excepting the provisions relating to the office of Lieutenant-Governor, the formal executive head of the provincial Governments, can be amended by the provincial legislatures.[1] The Canadian Parliament, by an ordinary majority, can alter any portion of the Constitution that is not put beyond its power by the British North America Act. In 1949, however, the Parliament of Canada without consulting the provinces requested and secured from the British Parliament an amendment to the British North America Act. As a result, those parts of the Act itself which concern federal matters only and do not express powers, rights, or privileges of the provinces can also be amended by a simple majority in the national Parliament. The rigid parts of the constitution today are the clauses of the British North America Act which fix the status of the provinces in the Canadian federation. These clauses still can be amended only by the British Parliament which passed the Act in the first place.

Intervention by the British Parliament is a formal requirement only. In 1931, in the Statute of Westminster, the Magna Carta of the British Commonwealth of Nations, the Dominions were given full power to repeal or amend any act of the British Parliament

[1]*Ibid.*, s. 92.2.

applicable to them. This would have located in Canada power to amend the British North America Act. Because Canadians could not agree on the mode of exercise of such power if they had it, the Federal Parliament had to ask that this badge of independence be not pressed upon the country and the provision of the Statute of Westminster referred to above was not made fully applicable to Canada.[1] Nevertheless, the British Parliament would not dream of amending the Act without a request from Canada and it seems probable that it would accept no less and require no more than a request from the Federal Parliament. These requests have always been made by the Canadian cabinet and since 1886 they have always been preceded by a resolution of both Houses of the Federal Parliament. In recent years, some provinces, at least, have feared that the enlarging activities of the federal government would result in encroachment on the provincial sphere. Clearly, if the Federal cabinet alone has the power to request amendments that are never refused, it could use its substantial control of the amending power to cut away provincial autonomy. So there is much insistence that the provinces be consulted and even that the unanimous consent of provincial governments is necessary before an amendment is sought.

A practice of consulting the provinces on at least those amendments that affect the provinces directly is fairly well established and, as a matter of practical politics, it is almost inconceivable that amendments reducing provincial powers should be sought without first getting the consent of most of the provinces, and, in some instances, where racial, linguistic, and religious matters are involved, without getting their unanimous agreement. Yet the practice has not hardened into a custom of the constitution and the practical political necessities cannot be defined with any precision. Details belong to a later discussion of federalism. Meanwhile, when it is said that Canada lacks power to amend the vital parts of her constitution, the jibe means only that Canadians have yet to settle on a method of originating and ratifying amendments to those parts of the Act expressly excluded from the operation of the amending procedure established in 1949.[2]

[1]See Statute of Westminster, 1931, 22 George V, ch. 4, s. 7.
[2]Important excluded sections are ss. 20, 50, 92, 93, 95, and 133.

INFORMAL AMENDMENT OF CONSTITUTIONS

A constitution that provides for one particular method of amendment, by implication forbids all other methods. Informal amendment is, therefore, a paradox. It is a development of the constitution by unconstitutional means. This raises the large question of the nature of political processes that often rely on devious pretence rather than straightforward rational attack. Yet wherever there is life, this informal development of the constitution goes on ceaselessly. In the working of a constitution, new problems are always being met. The instinct for a quiet life predisposes the men who are working it to modify its application to the circumstances, or to read into it particular answers to questions on which it has no answer at all, rather than to cry out that the constitution is unworkable unless amended. But the process of patching, stretching, and twisting goes on until it finally becomes clear to everyone that a change has come about and has been generally accepted. The individual men who begin and carry along the piece-meal adjustments often do not appreciate their creative role or perceive the general direction of their labours. Like the polyps on the coral reef, they work silently below the surface building atolls and islands and archipelagos of which they never dreamed.

Informal amendment comes about either through custom or judicial decision. Custom is much more widespread in its operation because it works more silently over longer periods. A notable example are the conventions, or customs, of the British constitution that enforce the responsibility of the cabinet to the House of Commons. For centuries, the king chose whom he would as his advisers and ministers. But it has been clear for over a hundred years that ministers who lose the confidence of the House of Commons must either resign or secure a dissolution of Parliament hoping to find renewed support in a newly elected House of Commons. In effect, the king must now choose as his ministers persons who can carry the House of Commons. The various conventions that ensure the workability of cabinet government were worked out slowly over many years.

It has already been stated that the power of Parliament to amend the constitution has been qualified by the convention that requires Parliament to have a mandate from the electorate for making any fundamental constitutional change. This convention is a very recent one resting almost entirely on the practice of the last fifty years. But it gets its real authority from an inner logic. If Parliament were to use its undoubted power to make any law whatsoever to force through unpopular and drastic changes in the constitution, it would be soundly punished by the electorate at the first opportunity. Thus it is the part of wisdom for Parliament to refer all proposals for drastic change to the electorate at a general election. Like all constitutional changes resting on custom, its limits are hard to define. How does one identify changes so fundamental as to require a mandate? In 1936, the Public Order Act in Britain put some very substantial restrictions on freedom of assembly. One might have thought this was a fundamental constitutional question, yet no mandate from the electorate was sought.

It is also difficult to know when a decisive change has been effected by custom. Up until 1940, no President of the United States save Theodore Roosevelt had ever been even nominated for a third term of office and it was generally said that custom had made a third term unconstitutional. Yet, President Franklin Roosevelt sought and obtained a third term in 1940 and a fourth in 1944. Did this mean there was no rule against a third term or was it merely an application of the maxim, *inter arma leges silent?* The question is academic now, because in 1951 the Twenty-second Amendment to the Constitution restricted election to the Presidency to two terms of office.

The method of election of the President of the United States is a striking instance of a decisive change brought about by crystallization of usage. The written Constitution provides for indirect election of the President through a body of electors who were clearly intended to exercise their own judgment. Through the operation of the political party system, these electors are now chosen by popular means and are pledged to cast their votes for the presidential candidates put forward by their respective parties. Indeed, the activities are now in some instances regulated by formal legal rules, are extra-constitutional growths depending on custom.

political parties themselves in the three countries, although their

The other method of informal change is judicial decision. In

Britain, United States, and Canada, the judges are required to interpret the constitution when it is in issue in disputes coming before them. He who interprets authoritatively sets the measure of the law, be it constitutional or otherwise. In each of the three countries, part of the constitution is found in the Common Law, which is derived entirely from judicial decision and which is subtly modified thereby. The judges also interpret statutes, many of which may be said to be part of the constitution; but they do not interpret those conventions of the constitution that depend on modern custom. Until 1949, the British North America Act was finally interpreted by the Judicial Committee of the Privy Council in Britain and there have been endless complaints that it has imposed on Canada by its interpretation a constitution vastly different from what the framers of the Act intended. Whether or not this charge can be substantiated in full, there is no doubt that the Privy Council made significant modifications.

In the United States, for over a hundred years the Supreme Court has had to be continuously deciding what the brief and often vague phrases of the written document mean in relation to the development of a continental domain by a restless and almost inexhaustibly resourceful people. A little reflection on the movement and variety of American life and the transformations of the last century will show that the judges could not possibly find all the answers in the short written document. It now takes volumes to do justice to the meanings that the Supreme Court has read into it.

Two illustrations in brief and inadequate form must suffice here. Article I, section 8, of the Constitution gives Congress power "to regulate commerce with foreign nations and among the several states. . ." All commerce that is not interstate must be regulated, if at all, by the state legislatures. The river-boat, pack-horse, and wagon-freight days of 1789 have given way to the age of steamships, railways, motorized road transports, and airliners; local industries serving a local market have been replaced by prodigious enterprises making products shipped to every state in the Union. How much of this activity is interstate commerce? Who would know from an examination of the words alone that an insurance company that ensures clients who live in other states is not engaging in interstate commerce[1] whereas the transportation of lottery tickets across state lines is interstate commerce,[2] and therefore subject to regulation by Congress?

The Constitution does not say expressly that Congress has power to regulate trusts and combines as affecting interstate commerce, but the Supreme Court has held that Congress may do so. On the other hand, in 1918, the Supreme Court decided that Congress could not forbid or regulate child labour as used in making goods that go into interstate commerce.[3] In 1941 it reversed this decision[4] and Congress can now regulate child labour in such circumstances. This is why it can be said with some show of reason that the Constitution means what the Supreme Court says it means. It now takes a book to explain fully what the interstate commerce clause means.

The Fourteenth Amendment, adopted in 1868, forbade the states to "deprive any person of life, liberty or property without due process of law." The primary purpose of the amendment, it appears, was to protect the newly enfranchised Negroes in the Southern states in the exercise of their newly acquired political and civil rights. The amendment was not vigorously used for this purpose, but for forty years the Supreme Court interpreted it as forbidding a variety of efforts by state legislatures to regulate various aspects of economic life on the ground that legislation interfering with economic freedom except as obviously police or health measures, was a deprivation of liberty or property, or both, without due process of law.[5] The "due process" clause was bent to the service of laissez faire, the doctrine that government should leave business alone. In recent years, however, with a considerable change in the personnel of the Supreme Court, there has been a

---

[1]The Supreme Court so decided in 1869 in *Paul v. Virginia*, 8 Wall. 168. But in 1944, in *United States* v. *South-Eastern Underwriters Association*, 322 U.S. 533, it held that such an insurance company is engaging in interstate commerce. The 1944 decision stands today as a clear illustration of how the Supreme Court modifies the Constitution.

[2]*Champion* v. *Ames*, 188 U.S. 321 (1903).

[3]*Hammer* v. *Dagenhart*, 247 U.S. 251 (1918).

[4]*United States* v. *Darby*, 312 U.S. 100 (1941).

[5]E.g. in 1905, in *Lochner* v. *New York*, 198 U.S. 45, the Supreme Court held a New York statute fixing maximum hours of work in bakeries to be unconstitutional on this ground. For a similar decision on the constitutionality of minimum-wage legislation, see *Adkins* v. *Children's Hospital*, 261 U.S. 525 (1923).

marked retreat from this position[1] and a restoration of emphasis on the protection of minorities from attacks on their political and civil rights. The forty years that the Supreme Court spent in protecting the freedom of economic enterprise from the more controversial forms of state interference may turn out to have been no more than an episode in constitutional development. In any event, it is a striking illustration of amendment by judicial interpretation.

This discussion does not pretend to be an outline of the constitutions under review, or even a comparison of all their salient points. It gives no clue at all as to how governments actually operate within these constitutions. It merely marks a number of points of departure and tries to cut a few exploratory paths through the jungle that modern government presents to the student. All classifications and categories are tentative, to be tested with increasing knowledge as that comes from further elaboration of detail. It is hoped that it reveals the inadequacy of engineering and biological analogies. The constitution is a framework constructed for a conscious purpose, but it is one that is constantly being revised and modified by a process that bears an analogy to growth. It is the bony structure or anatomy of government, but it is modified at times by deliberate purposeful intelligence, and here the tempting analogy is mechanics and not biology. The application of other possible analogies would show that a constitution is *sui generis*.

---

[1]E.g. the Supreme Court reversed its earlier decisions on minimum-wage laws in *West Coast Hotel Co.* v. *Parrish*, 300 U.S. 379 (1937).

CHAPTER V

THE EXPANSION OF GOVERNMENT ACTIVITIES

THE main lines of the British and American constitutions were laid down in the eighteenth century. Prominent among the factors determining those lines was the view then taken as to what it was either possible or desirable for government to do. The role government can play in human affairs is physically limited by the means of transport and communication and by the productiveness of the economic system. Obviously, governments cannot let the numbers of their employees outrun the food supply. The role government ought to play within the limits of the physically possible is determined by the views of the politically powerful of the time and place.

In the eighteenth century, modern developments in transport and communication had hardly begun, and the modern industrial economy that has so increased productivity was still in embryo. There were many serious physical limits to governmental action from which we have now been freed. Also, the dominant political thought of the eighteenth century favoured individual liberty of action with corresponding restrictions on governmental action. Thus these constitutions did not envisage government's taking on a wide range of functions.

In the first half of the nineteenth century, the means of transport and communication were greatly improved and extended, and there was an enormous increase in economic productivity. The inescapable limitations on the range of governmental action were greatly diminished, and governments did take on some new functions. But the political theory of laissez faire, the theory that government ought to be restricted to a very narrow sphere of operation, steadily gained strength and reached its zenith about 1860. The amazing material progress of the time was generally attributed to the abandonment of government regulation in economic and social matters. It was in this atmosphere that Confederation was achieved in Canada. So the Canadian constitution, although adopted just as the belief in laissez faire began to decline, is a product of much the same outlook that fashioned the constitutions of Britain and the United States.

LAISSEZ FAIRE AND ITS DECLINE

Generally speaking, the laissez-faire philosophy held that government should restrict itself to protection of the community from external enemies, maintenance of internal order, and a few great essential public works. Maintenance of order may involve much or little. Laissez faire interpreted it narrowly, calling it the police function and invoking only the technique of the criminal law. By general laws, it was intended that the legislature should forbid conduct disruptive of order, leaving us to rely on the policeman and the courts to punish law-breakers. Faced with the certainty of detection and punishment, all but a few would be deterred from anti-social behaviour. There would be enough jails (essential public works) to look after the incorrigibles. Within the limits thus imposed, individuals were to be free to direct their energies as they saw fit. Of course, engagements freely entered upon must be kept. The judiciary was to award damages for breach of contracts, and also for a variety of minor transgressions known as torts, not serious enough from a public point of view to merit the proscriptions of the criminal law.

Therefore, public works and military establishment apart, government was to be mainly occupied in making general laws applicable to everybody and enforcing the judgments of the courts on transgressions as they appeared. The state, as thus envisaged, has been aptly described as the negative state, imposing restraints at the margins of socially permissible conduct. The believers in laissez faire never were able to restrict the operations of government to the narrow sphere prescribed by their beliefs. But they had a profound influence on the scope of government action throughout the greater part of the nineteenth century. The negative state was not merely an academic theory; it was largely realized in the scope and character of nineteenth-century governments.

After the middle of the nineteenth century, however, a combination of forces steadily undermined the laissez-faire tradition. Except in Britain, where free trade ruled until 1931, important sections of the business community wanted—and got—government interven-

Ways in which government intervened

complexity of government can

tion in the form of tariffs to aid industrial development. In continental Europe, agriculture as well got tariffs to protect it against the competition of cheap wheat from America. The shift of population from rural isolation to rapidly growing industrial cities brought many new social problems. Elementary education became a necessity; public health measures had to be improved. Later it was seen, for example, that a system of employment exchanges was necessary to give the necessary mobility to labour. These are only examples of the services, necessary to an industrial society, that the government has been asked to provide or to supervise.

With increasing economic specialization and further minute division of labour, the social structure became more complex and individuals became less able to control the factors affecting their destiny and more dependent on the actions of others that they could not control. The self-sufficient farmer of earlier times who produced his own food and most of the other necessities of life was mainly dependent on the weather, and it did not occur to him that the government could do much about it. The highly specialized farmer of today is dependent on distant markets for his income, and on other specialized producers for many of the necessaries of life. The industrial wage earner is dependent on markets too, and also on a multitude of decisions taken by his employer and others.

The farmers and workers as individuals cannot control these factors any more than they can control the weather, but it is at least plausible for them to think that the government, which has the longest reach of any agency in the community, can do something to control them. Accordingly, they, and many other groups as well, are disposed to appeal to the government. Economic and social interdependence gives an impetus to government intervention.

Moreover, it was gradually realized that unrestricted individual enterprise did not bring about the degree of social justice that had been expected of it. While wealth and productivity increased at an astonishing pace, a large section of the population was still condemned to grinding poverty and/or acute insecurity. At the same time, competition proved an inadequate regulator in various branches of industry. Large-scale organization produced monopolistic features in industry where entrenched interests levied toll on the public.

These facts gave at least an appearance of deliberate exploita-

Measures adopted by government.

tion, and two types of measures were adopted to combat it. First, regulations of various kinds, ranging from factory legislation requiring safety devices in factories to the fixing of rates and standards of service for railway companies, were imposed by governments on industry. The government was to regulate industry so as to ensure operation in the public interest. Secondly, an attempt was made to reduce the glaring inequalities of income and improve the security of the less fortunate members of society through social services or social security measures such as health insurance, unemployment insurance, and old-age pensions. These measures are administered and financially supported by governments. Through taxation, income is taken from the taxpayer and transferred to the recipients of these services. The movement towards social security and regulation of business was greatly accelerated by the extension of the franchise to the adult male population. The mass of the people had no firm conviction that laissez faire was an advantage to them, and they did see the advantages to be had from social services. Politicians learned the connection between votes and the services desired by large groups in the population.

Once significant breaches were made in the principle of laissez faire, its inhibiting power was greatly diminished and finally almost disappeared as an influence on public policy. Government had proved amenable to popular control through a democratically elected legislature. Government provided valuable services and there seemed to be no reason why it should not be used to correct all kinds of maladjustments. Britain and America had been the great strongholds of laissez faire, but by 1939, even in these countries, almost every significant social group in the community was enjoying some service or privilege provided by government.

In 1840, it had been agreed that the job of government was through general laws to maintain equal rights for all before the law and special privileges for none. Before 1940, the cynics had coined a new slogan, "special privileges for all and equal rights for none." For many years, socialists have urged that governments must go still further and plan and manage the economic system as a whole rather than merely intervene at particular points as they were doing prior to the outbreak of war in 1939. During World War II, we saw this done, although not with the measure of public ownership socialists desire. The scope of government functions has narrowed somewhat since the war but is unlikely to return to the 1939 level. For present purposes, it will be sufficiently revealing to give some indication of how matters stood at that date and to take general note of post-war developments.

The war period also revealed, in a striking way, how the sheer physical limitations on government action have declined. Transport and communications are now so highly developed that central governments can overcome the handicaps of time and space sufficiently to direct the energies of half a continent. And productivity is now so great that government can absorb for its purposes, including war, well over half the national income and still leave the civilian population a tolerable standard of living.

The negative state is now only a memory and we are faced with what is called, by contrast, the positive state. The government is not merely imposing restraints; it is acting positively to accomplish a wide range of purposes. In peacetime, it is charged with attaining a minimum standard of education, with ensuring public health, with guaranteeing individuals security against a wide range of misfortunes, and with regulating economic life in the public interest. In war, it must direct all the activities of the population; it must keep the common goal in sight and improvise methods of reaching it. It must do for the nation what the plantation owner did for his estate. This task requires vast resources of energy, foresight, and initiative, which, in the negative state, were largely supplied by individuals operating on their own account. But even before World War II, the government was carrying on a great many activities of vital importance to the community calling for qualities of a similar character, though to a lesser degree.

It has been difficult to adapt the constitutions framed on the assumptions of the negative state to the demands of the positive state. In fact, the fighting of the two World Wars substantially required the temporary suspension of these constitutions. The purpose of the separation of powers, for example, was to secure effective restraints on government even at the expense of efficiency. When efficiency and national self-preservation become the prime considerations, the separation of powers is an embarrassment. The tripartite division of powers, while it may have been an adequate instrument of analysis a hundred years ago, is defective for an understanding of the complex operations of government today. It is widely contended that these laissez-faire constitutions are outmoded and will have to be very substantially revised. And it is also urged in many quarters that simple analyses such as those outlined in the last chapter do not get us at all close to the realities of present-day government. This argument will be assessed in later chapters. Here we must sketch in outline the tasks that governments are now called on to perform.

THE NEWER FUNCTIONS OF GOVERNMENT

The broad patterns of government functions in Britain, United States, and Canada are strikingly similar. Britain, with a more mature industrial system, has moved faster and further in the provision of social security, but the United States and Canada have been catching up rapidly in recent years. On the other hand, government in North America has been called on to assist in opening up the resources of a new continent—an activity for which there has been no scope in Britain. It has not merely been a matter of building canals, roads, and railways. Governments have assisted and encouraged land settlement, agriculture, mining, lumbering, and fishing in a great variety of ways. The trend now, of course, is toward conservation and more efficient use of natural resources, and there is more similarity in the three patterns in this respect than formerly. In Britain, there is a distribution of tasks between central and municipal governments. In North America, federalism requires a three-way distribution between federal, provincial or state, and municipal. Attention here is focused on the activities of central governments, including provincial and state but not municipal. No attempt will be made at this stage to distinguish state and federal functions.

In view of the similarity of pattern it will be adequate to sketch the newer activities of central governments in a general way without attempting a separate catalogue for each of the three countries.[1] While some of the specific functions pointed to may not be carried

[1]For an outline of these newer functions in Canada, see J. A. Corry, *Growth of Government Activities Since Confederation*; for Britain, see F. M. G. Wilson, *The Organization of British Central Government, 1914–1956* (ed. D. N. Chester); for the United States, see William H. Young, Ogg and Ray's *Introduction to American Government* (11th ed.; 1956), chs. 19–25.

on in all three countries, other functions comparable to them are almost certain to exist and the general impression will be reasonably accurate for each of them.

Regulation of Business. Regulation of business is either of a broad pervasive character affecting business generally or of a more specific kind affecting directly only particular kinds of trade or business. General regulation of business is accomplished by tariffs and by control of currency and credit. Tariffs are now much more than the fixing of import duties and the policing of the borders to ensure their collection. The government is charged with delicate and frequent adjustment of tariff schedules to the end that native industries shall not be driven out of business by the dumping of cheap foreign goods on the domestic market. Government must be continually collecting and revising statistics on the cost of production of domestic industries, because this knowledge is necessary for intelligent adjustment of the tariff to the end desired. In this way, the government substantially protects investment in established industry and gives the employed worker in these industries at least the illusion that his livelihood is also being protected. The tariff has a powerful influence in determining what industries, and what enterprises within an industry, shall be established or maintained.

Expansion or contraction of business is determined by a great variety of factors. One of the most powerful is the interest rate, the cost of borrowing money to carry on business. This is primarily fixed by the banks as the main lending institutions. The banks are subject to close supervision and inspection by government. Also, the central banks—the Federal Reserve System in the United States, the Bank of England in Britain, and the Bank of Canada in Canada—have been established to control the banking and credit business. The central bank has powers that enable it to exert a most powerful influence on the lending policy of the banks. And whether or not the central bank is directly a department of government, the government can exert, in turn, a powerful influence on its policy. In fact, in the long run, the central bank must accommodate itself to the main lines of government policy. Moreover, the government, either directly or through the central bank, determines the rate at which the domestic currency shall be exchanged for foreign currency. In this way, apart altogether from tariffs, the trend of imports—and exports—can be modified. This in turn has profound effects on the economy as a whole. The central bank, and departments of government associated with its work, must be gathering statistics incessantly on domestic and international trade and conducting research continually into their significance in order to know how to use their powers intelligently.

A third general kind of regulation of business is aimed at trade combinations, trusts, and monopolies in the production and distribution of goods and services. It seeks to dissolve those combinations whose activities are clearly detrimental to the public interest and to prevent particular unfair trade practices by trade associations that otherwise are thought to serve legitimate purposes. In order to keep track of the trade agreements and monopolistic practices in various industries and estimate their effect as well as to secure the evidence necessary for prosecuting offending combinations, government must maintain a staff of economists and accountants continuously engaged in investigation and research.

Various trades and types of business have been singled out for more specific regulation. The most important group are the public utilities, those industries producing an essential service for the public but which, for one reason or another, have a tendency to monopoly with its attendant evils. All transport and communication enterprises are in this class: railways, tramways, motor and air transport, shipping, telegraph, telephone, radio, and television. The gas, water, and electric power industries also fall in this class. A great variety of regulations that cannot be detailed here are imposed on them by government.

Generally speaking, no one can enter into any one of these businesses without getting a licence or a certificate that additional facilities in the industry are needed for the public convenience. The rates to be charged and the extent and quality of the service to be rendered are subject to minute governmental control. These rates cannot be fixed without taking into account the rates of return that particular enterprises are to be allowed to earn for their owners. In the transportation businesses, a great many regulations are concerned with safety: licensing of pilots and airfields, the load line on ships and the licensing of masters and pilots, inspection of brakes, speed limits, level crossings, and the like. It will not do for a government to make haphazard decisions on these matters. It obviously must have at its command a great array of economic, accounting, and engineering talent in order to decide on rates of return, rates to be charged to the public, standards of service, and safety measures. And the job cannot be done once and for all. As costs fluctuate, adjustments must be made in the rates to be charged. Technical advances will call for repeated revision of the standards of service and safety.

The financial enterprises of insurance, trust, and loan companies are subject to close government supervision designed to ensure fair dealing and to safeguard their financial position. They must secure an annual licence and often are required to make deposits with the government covering a portion of their obligations to their clients. They must make annual returns describing their operations and undergo annual inspection by government officials. If their financial practices have been reckless or their financial status is seriously impaired, their licences may be modified or cancelled.

Before a corporation can be formed to conduct any enterprise, the promoters must secure a charter, or grant of incorporation, from government. All corporations which, on incorporation or during reorganization, wish to sell an issue of securities to the public, are required to make a fair disclosure of the facts relevant to the enterprise. Through refusal to authorize particular issues of securities, and through regulation of brokers and stock exchanges, governments try to prevent reckless and fraudulent misrepresentation in the issue and sale of corporate securities.

Scores of other kinds of businesses are subjected to licence and inspection generally for police, health, or safety purposes. The regulations involved need not be described as they do not profoundly affect the economic life of the community and do not require the accumulation of records, the marshalling and interpretation of statistics, or the intricate economic and engineering knowledge needed for the working of the more far-reaching controls already described.

Regulation of Employer–Employee Relations. The bringing of workers into factories or shops to work for an employer or manager has raised many acute social and economic problems with which governments have tried to deal. Government officials frame—and enforce through periodic inspection—factory, shop, and mine regulations designed to ensure safe and sanitary working conditions, and to regulate hours of work and working conditions for women and children. Government administers an insurance scheme whereby employers are compelled to provide compensation and rehabilitation for their injured workers whatever the cause of the injury may have been. The burden of industrial accident and industrial diseases, which used to fall mainly on the worker and his family, has been turned through government action into a cost of production that falls on the purchasers of the products of industry.

Minimum wages and maximum hours are fixed by the government in great detail for most industries in Britain and Canada. In the United States, such regulations have been limited, in the main, to the employment of women and children, because until quite recently minimum wage laws for adult males were held to be unconstitutional deprivations of liberty without due process of law.[1] In all three countries, government enforces an immigration policy that limits the entrance of foreign workers into the country to compete for jobs with the native-born. Governmental measures in support of the unionization of labour and collective bargaining have been introduced. Government also provides a conciliation service for mediating in industrial disputes and, in some vital industries, it insists on a public investigation and strenuous effort at settlement before a strike or lockout can be called.

Government is thus involved in continuous study of wages, costs of living, standards of living, the trade cycle, industrial diseases, and safety devices. If it is to perform adequately the functions it has undertaken, it must be steadily revising its regulations in the light of accumulating knowledge and changing conditions, and it must put drive and energy into its inspection to detect, punish, and prevent evasions.

Government Economic Enterprises. In some industries, government tries to get a simple solution of the complex problems of business and labour regulation by direct government ownership and operation. Where not so long ago there was only the post office, there are now many varied enterprises managed by the government. Apart altogether from the ownership of waterworks, gasworks, tramways, and electric power plants by municipalities, central governments in one or more of the three countries in question own

[1]See p. 113, n. 5, and p. 114, n. 1, *ante.*

and operate railways, canals, air lines, telegraph, telephone, radio and television transmission systems, electric power, and liquor distribution systems. While governments have undertaken a wider range of economic enterprises in Britain and Canada than in the United States, the Tennessee Valley Authority is the most diversified government economic enterprise to be found in any of the three countries.

In such undertakings, government sets out to make itself a model employer as well as a model producer and distributor of goods and services. To do this, it has to wrestle with the same problems that plague private enterprise and that call for sympathy and imagination. It has to find the energy and resourcefulness, which alone make any enterprise efficient, and it has to find them without the incentives of profit and the spur of competition that have done much to maintain healthy vigour in private enterprise. When government goes into business, business methods have to be carried over into government. These methods are not the methods of the policeman and the judge. Here perhaps more than anywhere else, the requirements of the positive state are made clear.

Agriculture. In North America particularly, government now takes the lead in promoting the application of science to agriculture. Most of the measures take the form of free services to farmers. Relatively few of them are police regulations, although falling into this category are those long-standing regulations for control of animal diseases and plant pests, which give the government powers of quarantine and wholesale destruction of plants and animals to check the spread of such threats to agriculture. The effort spreads out as far as the control of the commercial poisons offered to combat pests and to the supervision of nurseries that distribute stock. There can be no traffic in queen bees unless they have a certificate of health from the department of agriculture. Alongside these powers goes continuous research into the origins and causes of, and the means of controlling, plant pests and animal diseases. For example, decades of research have been put into the development of strains of wheat that will resist rust and the sawfly.

This, however, is only a small fraction of governmental research into agricultural matters. Attempts are made to improve every breed of agricultural product, whether plant or animal. The search for champion hens and champion cows, longer bacon pigs, longer ears of corn, and smaller *petits pois*, never ends. Experimental farms carry this work into the field and explore the methods of culture best suited to particular districts. Soil surveys discover deficiencies of soil and aid in other extensive governmental efforts to deal with drought and erosion.

Improved methods are of little value unless widely adopted, and education of the farmer is pushed in various ways by illustration stations, extension services, agricultural fairs, county agents, distribution of pure-bred stock, and a barrage of bulletins. Increased production needs wider and better markets. Government tries to find new markets at home and abroad and provides a marketing and intelligence service that analyses market trends and possibilities. Reliable grades and honest packaging are important aids to marketing. Government now requires that most agricultural products going outside a local market should be sold according to specified grades and in standard packages, and it devises the specifications and employs an inspectorate to see that the regulations are obeyed. Continuous research must go into the establishment and improvement of grades if they are to have their maximum usefulness. Some of these grading regulations are pure-food regulations and thus are matters of public health to be considered later.

The middleman who markets farm produce has always drawn the wrath of the farmer. Government now intervenes at many points in the marketing process on behalf of the farmer. It imposes regulations on stockyards, and on commodity exchanges such as the grain exchange. It puts its influence and authority behind schemes for co-operative marketing, and for stabilization of prices and production, of a number of agricultural products. For example, in the United States, the Agricultural Adjustment Act of 1938, as amended, attempted, by an intricate set of measures covering the six principal agricultural products, to limit acreage, to fix marketing quotas, and to facilitate the storage of surpluses. The purpose was both to maintain prices and to ensure growers something like an annual average return in good years and bad. It supports, if it does not enforce, efforts to limit acreage and thus to maintain prices. The Canadian Wheat Board indicates how far such measures may go. The Board is solely entrusted with marketing, at politically deter-

[margin note: education of farmers for their particular job.]

mined prices, the wheat, oats, and barley produced in Western Canada. Similarly, in all three countries, the laws of supply and demand are challenged by the laws of the government in fixing the price and regulating the distribution of fluid milk in urban areas.

The range and variety of government activity in relation to agriculture defy summary description. Enough has been said to afford further illustration of the main points that government provides many valuable services and privileges to different groups in the community, and that effective provision of these services makes demands on governmental organization and personnel that were never dreamed of in the days of the negative state.

It may be added here that the other producers of primary products in the forest and fishing industries also get similar assistance from government. However, these types of aid have been launched only recently and, in the nature of things, cannot develop as luxuriantly as the agricultural services. It is enough to recall that other groups get similar assistance from government.

Public Health. Public health has long been a charge of government, but measures to promote it remained rudimentary until the scientific discoveries of the last century revealed the causes of a great variety of diseases and the means necessary to control them, and they remained relatively unimportant until urban concentration and rapid means of transport changed entirely the problem of public health. Since that time, health services of a range and variety comparable to the activities noted in the last section have been developed. The bulk of these are still carried out by the municipal governments, but central governments exercise close control and supervision over the municipal health agencies. Sanitation measures must meet government standards and every municipality must maintain a public health organization that meets certain minimum specifications. These standards are enforced by frequent inspection. Furthermore, governments enforce many precautions against the spread of infectious diseases, and the outbreak of an epidemic brings extraordinary powers of the central government into action.

Government makes available a great many health services for local governments and for individuals. Diagnostic clinics aid in the discovery and identification of diseases. Laboratory analysis of a great variety of noxious specimens is offered and vaccines and serums are manufactured and distributed. Research is carried on in the fields of sanitary engineering and preventive medicine. Statistics are collected and studied and a programme of public education in health matters is advanced by demonstrations, exhibits, bulletins, and motion pictures.

Besides making grants to aid in the maintenance of general hospitals, government provides special clinics and hospitals for those suffering from particular diseases such as tuberculosis. It maintains institutions for the mentally ill and the mentally defective. Special health services are given to school children and special attention to maternal and child welfare.

Pure-food laws establish standards of quality designed to prevent dangerous adulteration of food. Samples of food offered for sale are collected and analysed and frequent inspections of food-processing plants are made. Government inspectors are permanently installed in the canning and meat-packing plants. The sale of patent medicines and narcotic drugs is subject to regulation. Numerous other interventions in the field of public health could be cited.

Social Security and Other Social Services. Governmental research into the incidence and causes of disease proved the close connection between poverty and ill-health and was thus one of the prime causes of the demand that government should supplement charitable relief of poverty. Except in Britain, the chronically poor remain, as they have been for centuries, the responsibility of municipal governments and philanthropy. Central governments have, however, undertaken to ensure individuals against misfortune arising from certain specified causes. Sometimes the technique is that of compulsory insurance, requiring persons to contribute to a fund that the government supplements, as in the case of insurance against unemployment. Sometimes it takes the form of outright grants from the public treasury, as in the case of allowances to deserted or widowed mothers, assistance for needy and neglected children, and relief to unemployed workers not covered by unemployment insurance. But whether through compulsory insurance or through outright assistance, government comes to the aid of the aged, the blind, the permanently disabled, and other classes of needy persons, as well as the ones mentioned above.

Other social services of a somewhat different character may be mentioned here. Government maintains an employment service that assists workers in search of a job. Substantial grants are made to municipal governments in aid of elementary, secondary, and *government and education* vocational education. Central governments fix the curriculum and try to maintain standards of instruction by inspection and examination. Governments make grants to colleges and universities and sometimes operate them as state institutions.

Although elementary and secondary education is primarily a function of local governments, its vital importance in a democracy has led central governments in all three countries to pay increasing attention to it. Grants in aid of education by the central government in Britain, and by the state and provincial governments in United States and Canada, have increased steadily. Along with the increase in grants, these governments have extended greatly their control over the local education authorities. To exercise their control intelligently, they must give sustained attention to the varied problems of the educational system, which, viewed as a whole, is a huge undertaking. In the United States—but in Canada only with respect to university grants—the federal government has shown a serious interest in education. The federal Office of Education not only provides certain grants, largely for vocational education, but also makes surveys of existing educational facilities, conducts research in certain educational problems, and offers advice to the local and state authorities concerned with education.

Conservation of Natural Resources. Public health and social security measures are aimed at conservation of human resources. In recent years in North America there has been a steadily growing substantial effort by governments to conserve dwindling natural resources. Restrictions on the taking of fish and game have been tightened and steps toward enforcing a more careful timber-cutting policy have been taken. Fish and game are also ravaged by disease, while fire and insects are the heaviest users of the forest. Forest protection services have been established by government and, at the same time, reforestation projects are being launched, pollution of rivers and streams is being curbed. Fish hatcheries and wild-life sanctuaries are government enterprises. Strenuous government action is being taken to restore the lands ravaged by drought and erosion and to regulate those who delve beneath this land for minerals, oil, or natural gas.

Such measures are not likely to bring significant results unless action is guided by scientific knowledge. So intensification of research goes hand in hand with preventive and restorative action. Even then, the co-operation of the public must be enlisted and government takes up the role of educator and propagandist for conservation. Conservation is no longer a matter of sprinkling the country with a few fish and game wardens. It requires a dozen different kinds of scientists and research laboratories, a large field service staffed by men with highly specialized training for their jobs, a diverse apparatus for fighting fires and insects and assisting nature to multiply. In another direction, it develops into a large project of public education. Enforcement of conservation measures by policemen and judges is now a minor, though necessary, part of the conservation programme.

Other Functions and the General Trend. This is a comprehensive but by no means an exhaustive enumeration. The list of public works that governments maintain or subsidize goes far beyond those contemplated by the laissez-faire tradition. For example, a great network of highways and not merely a few trunk roads for military purposes is now maintained by central governments. Also, the taxes now levied by governments are not limited to the amounts required by the government to finance its direct expenditures. Federal governments levy taxes and make grants to the provinces and states to assist the latter in carrying out their extensive functions. State and provincial governments, in turn, levy taxes in order to make equalizing grants to municipalities of disparate financial capacity so that all municipalities can maintain a certain minimum level of services. In this way, as well as by direct social security measures, governments are engaged in an extensive compulsory redistribution of the national income.

Each of the functions of government enumerated here is a matter of common knowledge, although few perhaps realize the grand sweep of the operations as a whole. In the main, these are the activities that governments in the United States, Canada, and Britain carried on at the outbreak of World War II, and almost none of them were carried on in 1850. For the purpose of prosecuting the war, all three governments went very much further with a great range of activities designed to meet the emergency. Since the end of the war in 1945, a common pattern in new government functions is hard to find. The United States liquidated most of its wartime emergency activities very quickly in an effort to return to the pre-war situation. Canada tried to do the same at a somewhat slower pace. Britain, much more badly shaken by the war, maintained many of the wartime functions of government. Moreover, a Labour government came to power in 1945 with a socialist programme most of which could only be carried out by large extensions of government action.

By 1950, indeed, the Korean crisis and the dark shadow of cold war compelled all three countries to re-introduce a number of wartime controls. In addition, since World War II in all three countries, there has been an extension of activity in the provision of public housing, social security, and in regulation of agricultural prices, with Britain going much further than the United States and Canada in housing and social security. All three countries have undertaken public ownership and development of atomic energy. All three governments are committed, as far as solemn statements of high policy can commit them, to the maintenance of a high level of employment and purchasing power.

This last is the most important development common to all three countries. Governmental planning for war purposes after 1939 quickly ended the depression conditions of the 'thirties and brought an unprecedented level of employment and production. Public opinion came easily, perhaps too easily, to the conclusion that if governments could make and carry out effective economic planning for war, they could do it for peace as well. This conception, if it is to be carried out with vigour and effect, requires a new strategy to be adopted by governments in relation to all their activities. The piecemeal and sporadic intervention of the last sixty years designed to deal with particular maladjustments in a limited way will no longer be enough. Government will have to undertake a large measure of continuous, co-ordinated over-all planning of all its activities with a view to maintaining the economic life of the nation at a high level.

The socialist government of Britain took this particular responsibility seriously. It was not alarmed by the prospects of comprehensive economic planning by governments, a policy which socialists have been advocating for at least a generation. It regarded economic planning as an essential part of the programme of socialization it pressed between 1945 and 1951. During that period, the nationalization of the electric power industry which had been in progress for many years was completed. The iron and steel industry, gas enterprises, rail, motor, and air transport were all taken into public ownership. The coal mines and the central bank, the Bank of England, were nationalized in the same way.

Under a Conservative Government the socialist trend in Britain has been only mildly reversed through the de-nationalizing of the steel industry. In the United States and Canada the dislocations caused by World War II and the confusion caused by the seemingly permanent tension between the Western World and the Soviet Union give little reason to suppose that the continuing expansion of government activities will abate.

It was said at the outset, and specific illustrations have emphasized the point, that in the United States and Canada some of these activities are carried on by the federal governments and some by the state or provincial governments. To have specified throughout which are federal and which are state activities would have required a digression to examine the federal distribution of powers in the two constitutions. A later chapter will discuss this subject and describe the impact on the federal systems of the great growth in the functions of both federal, and state or provincial, governments.

No judgment is expressed here on the wisdom or unwisdom of any of these governmental activities, and little has been said about the causes that underlie their introduction. Obviously, however, almost all of them are responses to problems that needed to be met somehow. Whether they should have been met in these particular ways, or indeed by governmental action at all, is deliberately left an open question. Some conclusions may suggest themselves later, but for the moment these activities are facts that shape the structure and profoundly influence the operations of government and therefore must be accepted and kept in mind at every turn.

THE INDIVIDUALIST—SOCIALIST DEBATE

There has been no lack of judgments about the wisdom or unwisdom of the growth of government activities. All the while, there have been wide discussion and controversy about the appropriate range of government action, in the course of which almost every conceivable judgment one way or the other has been made.

The focus of the controversy is on the relationship of government and business, or economic life, although wider issues are always involved. On the question of the relations of government and business there are four distinct bodies of opinion. The division is not entirely clear-cut because within each group there are divergent views. First, there are the extreme individualists who are almost anarchists in believing that government is inherently evil. They hold to laissez faire. Economic enterprise should be almost entirely free of governmental control. But laissez faire is dead, if we can judge from the record of the preceding pages, and its supporters are voices crying in the wilderness.

Second, there are the moderate individualists most of whom approve, reluctantly or otherwise, of almost all the activities of government undertaken in Britain, Canada, and the United States up until World War II. They are the group whose policy has been reflected in the action of these three governments in the first fifty years of the century. They are least moved by doctrinaire theories and counsel a tentative, experimental attitude toward the question of the appropriate functions of the state.

Third, there are the evolutionary socialists who advocate a gradual transition from capitalism to socialism through the piecemeal transfer of the major industries from private ownership to public ownership, where they would be, directly or indirectly, under the control of the government. They are somewhat doctrinaire in thinking that political democracy, government of the people by the people, must somehow bring in its train economic democracy, the operation of the economic system not only for the benefit of the people but by the people, or at any rate by their chosen agents rather than by private owners, or capitalists. But they do point to the stubborn tendency of private industry to combine in ever larger units in fewer and fewer hands. They argue that these concentrations of power in private hands are just as destructive of democracy in the long run as is the monopoly of governmental power in the hands of kings and aristocrats. Because of their undoubted loyalty to democracy they are also called democratic socialists.

The democratic socialists accept Marx's prediction of the trend to monopoly and agree with him in expecting it to have dire consequences. But they do not follow him in the further contention that the grip of monopoly capitalism will almost certainly have to be broken by violence. On the contrary, they believe that the capitalists can be compelled to submit to the will of the people through the peaceful processes of democratic politics. Consequently, they see no need to wipe out every vestige of private ownership in the means of production. They are prepared to leave substantial sectors of relatively small industry in private hands.

The vital need, as they see it, is to transfer the great public utilities in the transport and communication and energy fields, the massive financial and commercial institutions, and the heavy industries like coal and iron and steel, from private hands to public ownership. It is in this sector that private monopoly is so pervasive and menacing because of the enormous power it puts in a few hands. In fact, this body of opinion has tended in recent years to trim its demands for socialization because they see, first, that many of the vexing problems of the economic system are not solved by nationalization and second, that there are grave dangers in the state running everything. Nevertheless, this body of opinion wants government action to go far beyond the scope outlined above. It is not satisfied with government regulation of the economic system. It wants a larger measure of public ownership and operation.

The Labour party in Britain which formed the British Government between 1945 and 1951 was largely composed of people of this mind. As we have just seen, it carried through a piecemeal socialization of key industries in Britain. Thus far, the democratic socialists seem to have been right in rejecting Marx's programme of violent overthrow of the capitalist system. There is little evidence in Britain that the big capitalists feel able, or seriously disposed to try, to resist socialization by violent non-democratic means. The really critical problems at the moment seem to be how to run these industries efficiently after they have been socialized, how to replace the incentives for production that moved both owners and workers under private ownership.

Fourth, there are the Communists, the revolutionary socialists in the Marxist tradition. As was seen in chapter II, they believe that all capitalists must be destroyed root and branch and the means of production fully socialized. They think this is necessary in order to free society from the festering bitterness and conflict of class struggle, and to release the full potentialities of the productive system. Their literature has always suggested in vague terms that the management of industry in the classless society would be carried on by the voluntary co-operation of all workers whether by hand or brain.

Their practice thus far in the Soviet Union is quite the contrary. The state, which is in the hands of a relatively few, plans and directs the entire productive system. No private person can hire the labour of others in production. Even agriculture has been socialized. The state has become the sole employer and substantially all economic life is directed by the government. As far as realities as distinct from forms go, it would not be misleading to describe the system as state capitalism. Whether or not the productive system is run for the benefit of the people, it is certainly not run by the people in voluntary co-operation. This is not "the realm of freedom," whatever else it may be.

Moderate Individualists v. Moderate Socialists

Setting communist theory and practice aside, it is important to see that the disagreements among the other three groups are about means rather than ends. The individualists, whether moderate or extreme, and the democratic socialists are mostly agreed in wanting to prepare the social ground in which human personality can grow to its fullest flowering. They are even agreed that a wide range of individual freedom is necessary for that purpose. They differ on the questions how much freedom is necessary, how far economic freedom is necessary to the maintenance of other freedoms such as freedom of expression and occupation, how far we can go in enlarging the power of the state without making it our master.

The democratic socialists think that economic freedom as it now exists, say in Canada and the United States, sours the social soil and dwarfs the lives of countless people. On the one hand, the economic freedom which is largely concentrated in the hands of the owners of the means of production is much greater than is needed for the purposes of individual self-realization. It is, in fact, the power to control a large part of the lives of those who work for them for wages. It is more power than they are able to use wisely with proper respect for the claims of others for self-realization. On the other hand, the economic freedom formally conceded to everybody to dispose of his time and labour as he sees fit is illusory and unreal for large sections of the population. The freedom of the working man to choose his occupation has little meaning if over an extended period he cannot get a job at all. Even when he has a job, he is a hired tool, generally employed in routine operations which he had no share in planning and has no power to modify. He lacks a sense of creative and free participation. He is, they insist, almost a slave of the complex process in which he is enmeshed.

In place of these two unsatisfactory kinds of economic freedom, the democratic socialists want gradually to introduce a large measure of ordered planning in economic matters. The planning of economic life will end many of the frustrations of unemployment, strikes, and lockouts. It will greatly increase productivity and provide more goods, amenities, and leisure with which to draw out a rich variety of personal achievement in cultural and other fields. By diminishing economic freedom, more freedom of better quality can be assured in other aspects of social life. Moreover, the worker in a publicly owned industry is a part of the public, and therefore a part owner. He will have a sense of sharing in the work and purpose of the industry that is now denied him. He will participate much more than he does now in controlling the conditions under which he works.

Democratic socialists think that social and economic inequality is a major cause of frustration of human possibilities. They are prepared to limit individual freedom in various fields for the sake of greater equality. Thus the socialization of industry is aimed at the elimination of profits and the raising of wages. Furthermore, they demand heavy taxation to maintain comprehensive social security measures, thus levelling incomes.

The democratic socialists doubt the capacity of democratic government to regulate private monopolies successfully in the public interest but are confident that it can devise successful means of running public monopolies. As ardent democrats, they believe that the will of the people can control and direct the state, even in the massive task of running the key industries of the country. Thus, they see no reason to fear the state. They do not believe that economic freedom, the dispersion of ownership in many hands— and it is many hands despite the features of monopoly—has any significant relation to the other freedoms that they think are more important.

The individualists, on the other hand, think freedom is the main buttress of human personality. The extreme individualists think that those who cannot thrive on freedom are dead losses anyway, and that there is no sense in sending good money after bad. They recognize, of course, that all freedom depends on a framework of order and security and they approve the criminal law which restricts the "freedom" of the criminally minded and by that very fact enlarges the freedom of everybody else. But it is hard to convince them that the need for order and security goes much beyond the protection afforded by the criminal law.

The moderate individualists are less sure that freedom always serves the interests of personality. For example, whatever the effect of unemployment insurance, maximum hours laws and factory legislation may be on individual freedom, they see these measures as justifiable, or even necessary, protection to the human claims of industrial workers. But when it comes to widespread public ownership of economic enterprise, they pause. They suspect strongly that there is some close connection between economic freedom and individual freedom in other fields. They remember that absolute monarchy in Europe between the sixteenth and nineteenth centuries went hand in hand with detailed intervention in economic life by the state. They remember that the triumph of liberal democracy in the nineteenth century was achieved in a period when there was very wide freedom of economic enterprise, and that its triumph was greatest in those countries where the state had least to do with economic life. They cannot forget that the Fascist, Nazi, and Communist dictatorships which denied all forms of individual freedom in our own day also took over decisive direction of economic matters.

Independently of this kind of evidence, the moderate individualists still fear the state because they think all great concentrations of power tend to override the claims of individuals to live their own lives. For that matter, they fear the concentration of economic power in private hands. They approve the increase of governmental power mainly as a counterpoise to big business, for the purpose of regulating and limiting monopolistic tendencies. They hope to achieve a balance in some kind of mixed economy composed of some private ownership, some public ownership, some governmental economic planning, and considerable governmental regulation of private enterprise. They think extensive socialization of private industry would tip the scales far too much.

The moderate individualists have difficulty in seeing how the electorate can control the operation of great publicly owned industries through the ballot box. They are not sure that the people could ever reach a united will on matters as complex as the operation of an industry. They are not convinced that the average industrial worker will find much more creative satisfactions in working for a mammoth public enterprise than for General Motors. It would appear, for example, that public ownership of the railways and the coal mines in Britain has not worked any great transformation in labour-management relations in these industries.

The moderate individualists agree with the democratic socialists on the dangers of gross social and economic inequality. They support substantial social security measures as a means of narrowing inequalities and providing rough equality of opportunity. But their recipe for enriching human personality has more freedom and less equality than the democratic socialist.

The controversy between the individualists and the democratic socialists is largely one of means. At one in fundamental purposes, they differ in their judgments on human psychology, the lessons of history, the possibilities of directing the economic system through the political process, and a hundred other complex questions that cannot be adverted to here. These questions are debated, and will continue to be debated, on the assumption that the discovery of more facts, a better knowledge of psychology and of political processes will bring some measure of agreement. The continuing experiment with socialism in Britain is bound to produce persuasive evidence one way or the other on many points. The important point to note here is that adherence to liberal democratic ideals and democratic procedures compels this kind of discussion about the appropriate range of state action.

The actual merits of the many issues debated between individualists and socialists cannot be discussed here. Many of the considerations involved are too complex for satisfactory discussion in the early stages of the study of government. The present purpose is to describe and analyse the machinery and processes of liberal democratic government. Whatever action government undertakes, it has to be carried out by this machinery and these processes. Is the machine suitably designed, or can it be adapted, for the purpose of running a socialist economy under democratic control?

One further significant comment should be made. While the extension of government activities of the last fifty or so years has been somewhat influenced by the highly technical and theoretical arguments of individualists and socialists on the subject, it does not appear to have been primarily determined by them. It has followed rather a tentative experimental course. Social and economic maladjustments occur and persist. After a time, government is moved to take action about them. The action taken does not proceed so much from theoretical convictions as from the pressure of various elements in the electorate that, for one reason or another, want something done about the maladjustment. The action taken is always tentative. It is later modified and adjusted, or even abandoned, in the light of the results it seems to have obtained.

The New Functions and the Will of the People

One argument sometimes made in support of these activities should be given attention. All these projects were launched by governments that were supported by a legislative majority, and almost all of them have survived changes of government and reversals of party fortunes. So, it is often argued, they have the support of a majority of the people and from them there is no appeal in a democracy. If plebiscites were taken on particular measures separately one by one, however, it is doubtful how many of them would find majority support. Generally speaking, the truth is that many of these activities directly benefit particular individuals and groups and, in an immediate material sense at any rate, place a burden on other individuals and groups.

Social security measures benefit the recipients and are a burden to the taxpayers. A new customs duty benefits some industries and some groups of workers at the expense of the rest of the community. When price supports are provided for agriculture, they must be paid for by the taxpayer. A workmen's compensation scheme benefits industrial workers and the cost of it is passed on to the purchasers of the goods and services they produce. It may be that, in each case, there are general benefits to the community as a whole that are shared even by those on whom the burden immediately falls. But these benefits are indirect and difficult to trace and establish. Outside those who think they will be directly prejudiced or advantaged by a particular measure, very few members of the public pay attention to it and, of those, only a fraction attempts the intricate calculations necessary to trace out the effects of the measure.

Thus, in relation to almost any proposed new activity of government, there is an active interested minority pushing for it, supported less strongly by a larger group who think social justice or economic efficiency will be served by it. There is an active interested minority opposed to it, passively supported by a larger group that vaguely objects. In most cases, unless the measure is very widespread in its obvious effects or has been effectively dramatized by supporters or opponents, the great mass of the electorate are sufficiently neutral not to take a stand either way. Minorities are often able to get measures in their favour, not because of active support of a majority of the electorate but because the majority in the legislature think it is a good thing and that, on balance, it will mean more gain than loss in electoral support.

This analysis does not apply to every new function of govern-

/ ment, and even where it is applicable it does not begin to do justice to the complexity of the forces behind legislative action. More will be said about it later. At present, we are concerned only with its general significance, namely, that modern legislation is greatly influenced, and often determined, by the push and pull of interest groups. Economic specialization has created almost innumerable groups, each with a special economic interest. Ease of transport and communication has enabled the like-minded across the country to seek one another out and form associations on the basis of their special interest. A thousand religious, philanthropic, cultural, economic, and recreational associations flourish, and they all have purposes that can be promoted by one kind of government action and impeded by another.

The twentieth-century phenomenon of governments undertaking activities for the benefit of special groups is partly due to the ubiquity of special interests and partly the cause of further strengthening of these group interests. They thrive on the benefits they can get from the government for their members and on the defence they can put up against legislation prejudicial to their interests.

Normally, most individuals identify themselves more closely with their own special interests—they may belong to any number of different interest groups—than with the general common interest of the community. The immediate loyalties are continuous and intense, the wider loyalties and interests are tenuous and only spasmodically cross the threshold of attention. The industrial worker, the manufacturer, the farmer see much more clearly the advantages of a rise in their money income as producers than they do their corresponding disadvantages as consumers (a general common interest) that result from the successful effort of each group to raise its own income.

There should be no need to illustrate this point. During the war, when the most obvious and vital of general community interests were at stake, we saw producer groups of every kind demanding legislation that would maintain or raise their money income despite the patent fact that, to win the war, the general standard of living had to be lowered. This is not due to a callous indifference to the general interest but to the greater immediacy and clarity of our special interest and to the difficulty of comprehending that our narrow advantage may be at variance with the general interest. So, much of the extension of government activity in the twentieth century comes, not from a widespread general conviction that the public interest will be served thereby but from the demands that interest groups, in combination or competition, press upon the government and the legislature.

AGGRANDIZEMENT OF THE EXECUTIVE

One other general result of great significance involved in the burgeoning of government activities must be attended to here. The positive state and the nature of the tasks it undertakes have aggrandized the executive branch of government. For example, fifty years ago the law, as given content by judicial application of common law principles or as enacted by the legislature, defined in general terms the circumstances under which an employee could recover damages from his employer for injury suffered in the course of his employment. If he suffered injury and the employer denied responsibility, the employee had to bring an action in the courts where a judge decided the issue and awarded the damages, if any. Whatever damages he got, he then spent either in paying his doctor or having a day at the races as he saw fit. The executive had no part in the process at all unless the employer refused to pay the damages the court had awarded.

The result is entirely different with the present-day workmen's compensation laws already briefly described. The legislature has outlined in a general way a scheme of compulsory insurance against industrial accident and disease, requiring a fund to be built up by contributions from employers. The carrying out and enforcing of this law is given to an executive agency, a Workmen's Compensation Board or Industrial Accidents Commission. Injured employees make claims to the Board, which has substantial discretion as to liability and amount. The courts have no longer any extensive functions in this field. The Board is instructed to devote the amount awarded to the rehabilitation of the worker. It is expended on maintenance of his family, medical expenses, and retraining for a new job as the Board sees fit.

The Board also has important preventive powers. It can order the use of safety devices in a factory and it can increase the premium payable by employers with a bad record of accidents. This involves not only a field force of inspectors going from place to place but also the compilation of statistics, an engineering branch, and a staff for research into the causes and incidence of industrial accident and disease. The Board soon knows more about industrial accidents than anyone else and therefore can contribute more ideas for the amendment and improvement of the workmen's compensation laws than the legislature.

Moreover, its statistics and its researches show that the health conditions of the worker outside the factory, his education and training, even his biological inheritance, are important factors in the incidence of industrial accident and disease. That is to say, a Board that wants to do a really effective job will be pressing constantly for an extension of its powers, and if it were not checked by the legislature it might soon bring public health, education, and eugenics within its purview. As it is, the administration of the workmen's compensation fund brings a significant enlargement of the executive including an inspectorate, a claims division, an engineering division, medical advisers, a social-welfare service, and a research bureau as well as many routine and clerical workers. This agency speaks with great authority on its operations, and its voice is likely to be heard in favour of rather than against an enlargement of its powers.

This matter is so important that, even at the risk of boredom, another illustration must be given. Not so long ago, the regulation of public utilities, those essential industries enjoying for one reason or another monopoly advantages, was left to the legislature and the judiciary. The law provided merely that railway, telegraph, telephone, and electric-power companies must provide reasonable services to the public and must not charge unreasonable rates. Anyone who was aggrieved by the rates or service had to bring an action in the courts asking for a decision that the rate charged him was too high or the service given him inadequate. Now the legislature makes provision for an executive agency, a transport commission, or a public utilities commission.

Aggrieved persons apply to this agency and not to the courts. It determines rates in great detail. To do this, it has to decide what is a reasonable return on the investment of the public utility company. It is thus necessary to decide what the investment shall be taken to be, the nominal capital, the actual value of the assets committed to the adventure (i.e. ruling out watered stock), replacement value of the assets, or the amount prudent men would have invested in this particular enterprise. Allowances for depreciation and obsolescence have to be calculated. The commission lays down precise regulations about standards of service. A railway may be required to run more trains, or more cars per train, or forbidden to discontinue particular trains. An electric utility may be required to step up its voltage or extend its lines. This involves finding a very nice balance between public needs in the way of service and the ability of the company to furnish them. New capital seeking entrance to the industry must satisfy the commission that it is in the public interest that the industry should expand, a judgment that calls for a great range of knowledge. This executive agency must go deeply into the economics of the industry, the financial history of particular companies, and relate these to what it is thought the public needs, i.e. the public interest. Expert staffs of economists and accountants are needed.

Moreover, safety is an element in reasonable service, particularly in the transport utilities. The commission must develop minute regulations regarding the safety measures to be taken. The devising and improving of these regulations and the enforcement of them require an inspectorate and an engineering staff always at work surveying existing facilities in the industry, investigating accidents, and testing new safety devices.

Here again, a large staff is built up; its activities give it unique knowledge about the public utility industry and reveal new ways in which it can improve its regulation by extending the scope of its control. Its experience is always suggesting changes in the laws for the regulation of public utilities and thus it has great, and often decisive, influence when the legislature comes to amend the law.

In almost all the functions of government outlined in this chapter, similar enlargements of the executive have taken place. The New Deal alone in the United States swelled the civil service by some 350,000 persons. The large staffs that carry out the intricate detail of these tasks of government are generally referred to as the administrative, and some have described it as a fourth power alongside the legislature, executive, and judiciary. In fact, it is a part of the executive although it has swollen that power out of all recognition and radically changed its character. Where the executive formerly was something of an automaton carrying out the dictates of legislatures and courts, it now does a great deal of detailed legislating on its own in the course of administration, it is a powerful influence in the determining of legislative policy, and it has everywhere encroached on the judiciary. Its size and the scope of its operations have created a new problem of internal management. How is the President of the United States to co-ordinate and direct the energies of well over two million civil servants in the employ of the federal government? No matter what problem of present-day government is under consideration, it will be found to have been intensified, if not entirely created, by the remarkable developments we have been considering.

This great service and regulatory apparatus called the administrative is also known, in terms of alarm or contempt, as the bureaucracy. It is not always understood that it is the necessary concomitant of the positive state. Most people approve of some or other of these new functions of government and almost all castigate bureaucracy, associating it with those activities of government of which they disapprove. But the general effect of the great extension of state action on government, and particularly on democratic government, has never been adequately explored. Later chapters will indicate trends and suggest probabilities.

CHAPTER VI

THE EXECUTIVE—THE MAINSPRING OF GOVERNMENT

WE HAVE distinguished one of the organs of government as the executive and described its function as executing or carrying out the law. It is now necessary to carry the distinction further and define the function more precisely. In the broadest sense, the executive includes all those engaged in or associated with the active manipulation of men and things in the name of the government. The discussion of the scope of modern government action has indicated the extraordinary range of activity involved.

The executive in this wide sense includes the chief of state, be he king or president. It includes the small group who, through their positions as heads of the great government departments, are in direct command of the manifold activities of government. This is the ministry or cabinet, known in Britain as the government, in the sense of Mr. Macmillan's Government, and in the United States as the administration, in the sense of Mr. Eisenhower's Administration. For convenience of nomenclature, we may call them the temporary, or political, executive. The executive also includes the tens, and even hundreds, of thousands of civil servants who may be described as the permanent executive because, in the main, they do not now change with a change of government. It also includes the armed forces and police who, while they cannot be said to carry out the law, do act as agents of the government in whatever they do.

Indeed, it is a gross understatement of the function of the executive to say that it carries out the law. It is often said that the executive carries out the will of the state. If we leave aside the metaphysical question whether the state has an identifiable will, the statement is helpful because it directs attention, not to specific laws that are enforced but to a complex total of actions of a bewildering variety, many of which are not the execution of laws but discretionary actions that the law permits without commanding. For example, the executive runs the vast household of the modern state, buying rope for the navy and pens, ink, and paper for the civil service, hiring servants, constructing or renting office space, and a thousand other jobs of domestic management. The government provides a great many services that cannot always be described as the carrying out of mandatory laws. There is ordinarily no law requiring the government to conduct research in astronomy, diagnostic laboratories, or experimental farms. They are lawful because the appropriate legislature, national or provincial, has granted money for the purpose.

The Executive as the Mainspring of Government

In sheer numbers, the executive far outstrips the other two powers. Where judges are numbered by dozens and legislators by hundreds, the executive counts in tens of thousands. Its importance is not merely numerical. In the typical nation-state of today with a central government exercising a wide authority over an extensive territory and millions of people, the executive is the mainspring of government. Nazi Germany and Fascist Italy proved, for example, that nation-states can continue in some fashion without a functioning legislature and without a judiciary of significant independence. But when the executive breaks down, the central government collapses.

The reasons for this are quite simple. We know that large business enterprises will not run without the guidance of great executives. Government today, in terms of the scope of its operations, is the largest of all enterprises. It therefore must have leadership. That leadership must be continuous, always devising and revising. It must be informed leadership. It must know the objectives of all the activities carried on. It must also know, or have readily available, detailed information on the problems government is supposed to be solving. Government cannot undertake to improve public health or public education unless it knows in detail what is wrong. It cannot regulate and promote agriculture unless it knows a great deal about agriculture. Even then, the problem is often so complex that trial and error is the only way to approach solutions. So, in order to decide intelligently what to try next, the knowledge gained in the course of administration is indispensable.

There is a steady accumulation of this kind of information in every government department that is effectively organized, and there is often much more of it concentrated there than anywhere else. It is not that the executive knows best what should be done; generally it does not. But it has a body of information that is indispensable in deciding what can and what cannot be done. The legislature usually does not have it, and this explains why so much legislation today is framed by the executive and why the role of the legislature is increasingly that of criticizing, rejecting, or approving executive proposals. Much more will have to be said about this later. For the moment, the point is that if the vast apparatus of present-day government is to perform satisfactorily the tasks laid upon it, there must be continuous initiative by a body that knows the detail of the work and imparts drive and direction. This initiative must come from the executive itself. The legislature is too far away from the complexities of administration; it is not continuously and exclusively absorbed in the study of these matters and it is always too numerous and often too distracted by partisan battles to give unified and vigorous direction to the daily work of government.

The fact is that the emphasis in the literature of the last hundred years on the vital role of the legislature in maintaining democratic control of government has led many to the unwarranted belief that the legislature is the government. Reference to history as well as to current realities should correct this mistaken impression. Historically, the first origin of central government almost everywhere is in a war leader or a conqueror who seizes control of a territory and uses the reserve of force at his command to control the population for ends that need not be inquired into here.

At this stage, the analogy is the slave plantation and the executive is everything. The limitations on it are the limitations of nature and the passive or other resistance of the population. There are no internal restraints. To take only one but not an isolated example, the government of William the Conqueror in England was not distinguished from his own personal household. Legislative and judicial institutions emerged later and only slowly became effective brakes on executive action. The essence of government is an executive. The legislature and judiciary are merely the instruments for keeping it responsible.

No matter how fully representative a legislature may be, it cannot govern the country. The great weakness of the Third, as of the Fourth, Republic in France, whatever the deeper causes of their collapse, was that the legislature would not abide a strong executive. Lacking effective leadership the country was unable to prepare to meet the Nazi menace or the postwar problems of rehabilitation.

One of the most serious defects of the Articles of Confederation, the first attempt at a national government for the United States, was the failure to provide for distinct organization of the executive power, all powers granted being placed in the hands of the Congress. Similarly, the state constitutions as maintained throughout the nineteenth century, did not provide for effective organization of the executive power. While they established the office of Governor, they denied him any substantial authority, dispersing executive power into many hands. The result was a weak executive and a very low level of efficiency in state government. The efficiency of state government did not begin to rise until the movement to reorganize the state executive power was launched in 1917.

To insist on the executive as the essence of government is not a depreciation of the legislature and judiciary. Rather it reveals the tremendously important and only effective role of the legislature as a check or brake on an energetic executive. This is vital for the maintenance of constitutionalism; an importance underlined by Lincoln's doubt whether a government (i.e. an executive) that was strong enough for surmounting emergencies would not be too strong to be kept under effective control by its people. With the aggrandizement of the executive through the great extension of governmental action, and its need for vigour if it is to do efficiently all the tasks assigned to it, the need for checks on the executive is greater than ever before in the history of liberal democratic government.

Accepting the necessity for strong executive leadership, it should be clear that that leadership is not provided by the executive in the broad sense including tens of thousands of civil servants. Leadership is always the function of one or a few. Too many cooks spoil the broth, and what holds for soup holds for government as well. Every numerous body that wants to accomplish anything has to set up an executive committee, and there is ample testimony that if such a committee is to give really vigorous direction to affairs it should not exceed ten and had better be five. There is indeed an argument that a plural executive suffers too much from cross-purposes and indecision, and that the executive should be headed by a single person. Neither the shareholders nor the board of directors of a great business enterprise try to run the daily affairs of the enterprise. They appoint a general manager who is popularly known— and revered and despised by turns—as a "big executive."

In the preceding paragraph a quite different but commonly used sense of the word "executive" emerges. Executive means commanding men and directing affairs rather than the direct and immediate carrying out of particular objectives in all their detail. This latter aspect of the work of big organizations, be they business or government, is called, by contrast, administration. The executive generally means the small group, the cabinet, who head the great departments of government and thus direct the multifarious efforts of the civil service and who, because they are in command, must supply the initiative and leadership that is necessary. On the one hand, they furnish drive and direction for governmental administration. On the other hand, the civil service funnels to them the continuous stream of information and experience gained in the course of administration from day to day. Using this information to develop their own conception of public needs and keeping in mind what the legislature wants or will stand for, the executive matures legislative proposals for the consideration of the legislature.

In these functions, they are greatly aided by a small group of higher civil servants, their immediate subordinates in the departments, and it is almost impossible to disentangle the separate contributions of the two groups. There are some who say that these few higher civil servants make by far the greater contribution and are the real governors of the modern state. However, because the executive has the responsible command and is always contributing fresh ideas not gleaned from the civil service, they may justly be described as the mainspring. Therefore, the discussion in this chapter will be directed to the executive in the narrow sense.

THE CHIEF OF STATE IN BRITAIN

Discussion of the British executive must first take up the position of the King or Queen, as the case may be.[1] In wraith-like legal formalism devoid of substance, the King is the executive. The members of the cabinet are His Majesty's ministers tendering him advice. While they take full responsibility for actions of the government, legally their acts are the acts of the King. The judges are His Majesty's judges, though no king since the Stuarts has interfered with the course of justice. The King must assent to bills before they become law, but the last refusal was in 1707. The King is the head of the state, but it is an office devoid of power. The legal rule that the King can do no wrong, combined with the conventional rule that the King must act on the advice of his ministers, shifts both responsibility and power to the ministers. The legal forms are merely echoes of a time when the King had the reality of power.

Out of the wreck of his former pre-eminence the King has saved what Bagehot called, "the right to be consulted, the right to encourage and the right to warn." Because his consent is required for statutes and many other official acts, he could not well be deprived of all contact with affairs of state. His ministers keep him advised on major issues and they receive in return such counsel and caution as he cares to give them. Governments change and ministers come and go. A king who has had many years on the throne has the opportunity for a wide grasp of public affairs. If to ability he joins study and effort, his position obviously enables him to wield great influence. His hand is strengthened by the social popularity with the masses of the people that the Monarchy has enjoyed in the present century. Queen Victoria exercised these three rights to the full and not without effect. Both she and Edward VII had very substantial influence in foreign policy. George V took a great interest in domestic matters and had an influence which only now his biographers are beginning to assess.

In addition, the King has certain ill-defined personal prerogatives, chiefly relics of the past, which are still competent to his office. He appoints the Prime Minister and is under no obligation to

[1]The reader should substitute Queen for King wherever subsequent references in the text make this appropriate.

accept advice as to the choice. As long as one party has a clear majority in Parliament and that party has an acknowledged leader, he has, in reality, no choice, but must accept that acknowledged leader as Prime Minister. However, in the case (typified by the resignation of Sir Anthony Eden in 1957) where the Prime Minister resigns and the majority party has no acknowledged leader, the Queen then has the personal responsibility of picking a successor— power as well as influence. This function may assume critical importance if three or more political parties become a permanent feature. For example, George V is credited with a leading role in the formation of the National Government coalition under Ramsay MacDonald in 1931.

The King has the formal legal power to dismiss his ministers, and it is sometimes argued that he may constitutionally dismiss them on his own motion if he believes that the cabinet, while holding the support of the majority in Parliament, has decisively lost the support of the electorate. More accurately, it is suggested that the King, if he so believes, may threaten dismissal as a means of securing the consent of the Prime Minister to a dissolution of Parliament, thus bringing on an election to test the matter; and that if the Prime Minister refuses, he may dismiss the cabinet.

Some authorities also maintain that in certain circumstances the King may refuse the request of the Prime Minister for a dissolution if he has grounds for thinking that an alternative government can get the parliamentary support the Prime Minister has lost—a situation likely to arise where there are three or more relatively equal parties in Parliament. It is contended that in such circumstances the King is the guardian of the constitution and that if a government is flouting the will of the people, he may intervene.

All matters touching the relationship of King, cabinet, and Parliament are supposed to be settled by the conventions of the constitution, resting on past precedents and practice. But, with respect to the power of dismissal and the right to refuse advice, there is disagreement among the experts as to the conditions in which the exercise of the personal prerogatives are justified. Without going into this issue, it can be said that royal intervention has far greater dangers for the constitution than those it is intended to meet. If the King turns out to be wrong in his judgment and the country supports the government he threatened to dismiss, or if his alternative government cannot get sustained parliamentary support and the ensuing election returns to the House of Commons a clear majority supporting the party leader to whom he refused a dissolution, relations between the King and that leader's party are bound to be seriously strained. The King will be blamed for taking sides, and if the political party that stood to benefit from this intervention does not repudiate his action, they will be turned into a party of the king's friends—a return to the days of George III![1]

In trying to guard the constitution, the King may wreck it. If he is to retain his throne in a system of parliamentary government he must, at all costs, retain his neutrality. He must bide his time and wait for the electorate to say whether the cabinet has lost its sympathy. Even at the expense and confusion of an unnecessary election, he must let the electorate punish an over-crafty cabinet. Of course, if the actions of the cabinet amount to an attempt to subvert the constitution, the King would obviously be justified in bringing his personal prerogatives to bear.

Yet if the traditional two-party system were to splinter into three or more parties of comparable strength an alarming burden would be placed on the Chief of State. He has to find a Prime Minister who must be someone who can either throw together a coalition or form an acceptable minority government. At times it will be tempting, and even on occasion legitimate, to try other combinations without resorting to a dissolution and a new election every time a government is defeated in the House. The genuinely important present-day function of the King is to stand as a symbol of unity, and there is a natural disposition to hope that he may express that unity at times when the factiousness of numerous parties threatens to make orderly government impossible. No doubt he can appeal to whatever unity underlies party faction and, in so far as it exists, exert a moderating influence and perhaps tide the country over particular crises. The continuity and security of his office should enable him to take an objective view not always reached by the leaders of political parties. However, if and when the two-party system splinters, that is symptomatic of a deeper disunity, and then

[1]See Harold J. Laski, *Parliamentary Government in England*, ch. VIII, for the full weight of the argument on these issues.

the King may get little more for his pains than charges of partisanship.

The effectiveness of the King as a symbol of unity, as long as the exigencies of his office do not require him to take sides, is not open to question. Steady allegiance to Country, Nation, Community, is difficult to obtain because most people are not greatly moved by abstractions. The living figure brings the argument for subordinating our desires to the good of the whole down to the level of common experience. The King can call men to arms more effectively than can the Country or the Nation. The good that governments do can be ascribed, through the King, to the people; the evil they do can be pinned on the ephemeral government of the day. The opposition which obstructs that government maintains its prestige more easily because it is His Majesty's Loyal Opposition. It is loyal to the permanent common interests and fundamental aspirations of the people while opposed to the audacity of a temporary parliamentary majority.

In fact, the symbol has triumphed over the person. As the abdication of Edward VIII revealed, a king who does not outwardly conform to the proprieties that move the bulk of the nation must go. Some are disposed to think the symbolism too powerful. The King is inevitably a symbol of conservatism, of what has been revered in the nation's past. By nurturing that reverence and projecting it strongly into the present, the King may retard necessary social change. He cannot lead in a new attitude toward divorce; he must be a symbol of old attitudes. Yet there is no doubt that in Britain he is identified with the fundamental aspirations of the British people. Even the Labour party, which wants to change much in Britain, does not want to abolish the Monarchy.

The King is a symbol of unity not only for Great Britain but for the Commonwealth of Nations as well. The British Government and Parliament no longer have any control over its members. The Dominions are autonomous and independent.[1] They are bound to Britain and to one another only by the invisible ties of a common tradition as former British colonies. The King is the only living figure common to most if not all and thus the only visible link

[1]For a summary of the position of the Dominions in the British Commonwealth of Nations, see Robert MacGregor Dawson, *The Government of Canada*, ch. III; for the special constitutional position of newer members in the Commonwealth, see Nicholas Mansergh in *Commonwealth Perspectives*, ch. I.

between them. The strength of this symbolic link is hard to estimate, but no doubt it is considerable.

THE CHIEF OF STATE IN CANADA

The Chief of State in Canada is the Governor-General. He no longer represents the British Government but is the personal representative of the King. He is appointed by the King solely on the advice of his ministers in the Dominion of Canada. According to the Imperial Conference of 1926, at which the Prime Ministers of Great Britain and the several Dominions met and recorded many of the constitutional practices of the British Commonwealth of Nations, he holds "in all essential respects, the same position in relation to the administration of public affairs in the Dominion as is held by His Majesty the King in Great Britain. . ." In so far as he represents the King, he is the Canadian concretion of the symbol of unity and of the continuity of government.

But in his own person, he cannot hope to have the influence that it is open to the King to exercise in Britain. His term of office is short, and if he is not a Canadian his knowledge of Canadian affairs will be limited. Most important, he is chosen by the King on the advice of the Canadian cabinet and may be removed by the King on its advice before his term of office expires. While the cabinet keeps him advised of its policy, it is not likely to be greatly impressed by his counsel. He can scarcely take a stand against it. And if he makes gestures in its support, his action will be regarded as a prostitution of his office for the benefit of the government of the day. Now that a Governor-General may frequently be a Canadian it will be more hazardous for him to intervene because he will rarely be able to isolate himself entirely from domestic partisan disputes.

Indeed, there is more likelihood that Canadian politics will be bedevilled by three or more parties than are British politics and the Governors-General may well have critical roles thrust upon them. Because they are temporary partisan appointments and not hereditary kings they are even less likely to perform such functions satisfactorily. They cannot claim to speak for the Canadian people in the way the King may on occasion claim to speak for the British people.

The only functions that can be safely ascribed to the Governor-General are purely formal. He must concur in the summoning, proroguing, and dissolving of Parliament. The Prime Minister and the cabinet receive their authority at his hands and the formal acts of government are done in his name. He issues proclamations and orders-in-council, appoints the judges and pardons criminals, but always on the advice of his ministers.

The Chief of State and Chief Executive in the United States

It has been said that while the king of Great Britain reigns but does not govern, the President of the United States governs but does not reign. Being an elected person involved in partisan considerations, he arouses antagonism as readily as devotion. The Constitution comes much closer to being the symbol of unity in the United States than does the President. Since the President lacks the divinity that hedges a king, the Americans have had to find their symbol in an abstraction. The Civil War was fought to preserve the Union, not the kingdom of Abraham Lincoln.

Yet the President is the formal Chief of State who performs many of the legal and ceremonial functions of the King. He opens public buildings, charity drives, and the baseball season. He receives ambassadors from, and is the official medium of intercourse with, foreign countries. He is the commander-in-chief of the armed forces. He gives formal assent to legislation although his veto may be overridden by a two-thirds vote of Congress. If he neither assents nor vetoes, the measure automatically becomes law after a lapse of ten days provided Congress is still in session; if it has adjourned in the meantime, the bill is killed by such inaction. The regular sessions of Congress are fixed by law and he cannot change them, just as he cannot prorogue or dissolve Congress. The principle of the separation of powers limits his interference with Congress to the calling of special sessions in emergent circumstances. He may pardon criminals, and formal acts of government are performed in his name.

Also, the President holds the executive power of the United

States and thus he governs within the ambit of power given by the Constitution. It is impossible, in fact, to make any clear distinction between his functions as Chief of State and as chief executive. Thus he not merely signs the pardon that frees a convicted criminal; he also decides with the assistance of the Attorney-General whether a pardon shall be granted. This latter is a function that, in Britain and Canada, rests, not with the King or Governor-General but with the Home Secretary and Minister of Justice respectively. The President not only promulgates ordinances, he decides upon and takes responsibility for their content. It will be convenient, therefore, to go on at once to the official functions of the executive of the United States, remembering always that he cannot begin to give personal attention to the compass of his office and that, in most matters, the advice of subordinates has to be accepted.

The President is elected for a four-year term by an electoral college to which each of the states contributes a number of electors equal to the total number of senators and representatives to which the state is entitled in Congress. These electors, chosen as the laws of the separate states prescribe, meet and ballot for the candidates for the Presidency. The ballots are then sent to the capital and opened and counted by the president of the Senate in the presence of Congress. The person getting a majority of the electoral votes is declared to be President.

Thus far goes the written Constitution, which intended the electors to exercise their personal judgment in casting their ballots. But the development of two strong political parties has resulted in a complete change in the substance behind these forms. At national conventions called for the purpose, the two parties each choose a party candidate for President. In each state, state laws enable each party to nominate a complete slate of candidates (usually prominent party workers) for election to the electoral college. On the day fixed for the presidential election, the electorate in each state chooses by plurality (usually majority) vote either the Democratic or Republican slate of candidates for the electoral college in that state. When the electors so chosen meet, they always plump for either the Democratic or Republican candidate for the Presidency. But since they are pledged from the beginning to vote for the candidate of the party that nominated them, the result is a foregone conclusion as soon as it is known which complexion of electoral slate has been chosen in each state. The later formalities —the electors' meeting to cast their votes, the dispatch of these ballots to Washington, and the grave proceedings there—are now empty forms whose only justification is the necessity of complying with the precise requirements of the written Constitution. The spirit changes but the letter remains.

In effect, the President is elected by popular vote. This is not quite accurate because it is still the number of electoral votes that counts and it is possible for a candidate to win a majority of the votes of the electors without having a majority of the popular vote. Woodrow Wilson in 1912 and Truman in 1948 came to office without a popular majority. But even when the President gets a majority of the popular vote it cannot always be said that he is the popular choice because the process of nominating presidential candidates often produces candidates whose decisive merit is that they are inoffensive to the important diverse elements in the party.

The framers of the Constitution did not want to create a replica of George III, but they were fully aware that an executive must be able to act with energy and undivided purpose. To that end, they vested the executive power in one man. But one man could not run even the United States Government of 1789. Executive assistants had to be provided. From time to time, Congress has created departments of the executive, now ten in number, each of which is headed by a secretary. These heads of departments early became known as the President's cabinet. He has to rely heavily on them for directing the executive work of government for which he is responsible. His appointments to the cabinet must be approved by the Senate, but the Senate almost never refuses to ratify his choice. It has taken the view that the President as the responsible executive should not be restricted in his choice of those on whom he must rely.

As far as the Constitution goes, the President's choice is limited only by the separation of powers, which prevents a member of Congress from holding an office under the United States. In practice, a number of political factors influence his appointments. He almost always picks men who are members of his own political party but usually he does not pick more than one or two of them from among the principal political leaders of the party. In contrast to the situation in Britain, a political career in the United States is not significantly advanced by elevation to the cabinet. Whether as cause or consequence of this, Presidents tend to consider other qualifications such as executive capacity and experience as being more important than political leadership.

Cabinet posts generally go to men who have been active in party politics without becoming distinguished party leaders. They must be distributed with an eye on the different wings or factions of the party. The great geographical sections of the country and the great economic interests of labour, agriculture, and capital also claim representation and cannot be entirely denied. The Departments of Agriculture, Commerce and Labor must generally be headed by men who have the respect, if not the confidence, of agriculture, capital, and labour respectively.

In addition, there are always some more personal considerations. One cannot be elected President without accumulating obligations to staunch lieutenants and supporters. It would be ungracious as well as impolitic to forget these obligations entirely in forming a cabinet. And there is almost always an intimate personal friend whom the President takes into his cabinet. A great many factors have to be considered and balanced in selecting the cabinet.

THE HEAVY BURDENS OF THE PRESIDENT

The members of the cabinet direct the work of the departments and advise the President on matters coming within his charge. Each has his own department to administer within the limits laid down by congressional legislation and by the President's decisions on broad questions of policy. The weekly meetings of the cabinet with the President serve two main purposes. First, they provide a forum for discussion and settlement of questions that affect two or more departments. The scope of present-day government activities ensures that there will always be some interdepartmental questions to be discussed. Secondly, they enable the cabinet to discuss together and advise the President on matters of policy on which he wants advice.

Discussions in cabinet are informal and confidential. Until Eisenhower created a Secretary to the cabinet, in 1954, no record of discussions was kept. It still rests with the President what public announcements, if any, are to be made as a result of discussions. Views that the members agree in expressing are not executive decisions marking out lines of policy but merely recommendations to the President. He may treat the members of the cabinet as colleagues whose combined judgment he is willing to follow. But there is nothing in the Constitution making them colleagues who share the power and responsibility for decision. Rather, they are his subordinates and subject to his command.

Accordingly, he may ignore their advice. He may make decisions affecting their departments without consulting them. Often, his most confidential advisers are not in the cabinet at all. Even when the entire cabinet votes against his proposal, he may say, as Lincoln did, "Noes, seven, Ayes, one: the Ayes have it!" The cabinet is not collectively responsible with the President for the decisions taken. He is the executive and he alone carries the responsibility.

Consequently, the President can do little to shift the burdens of his office. No interest of power and consequence is willing to accept a denial of its demands from the head of a department. It insists on having a decision from the President. Because the cabinet cannot compel him to take account of their views, they often do not give him the blunt, candid criticism he needs. Not being responsible along with him, they can be at times irresponsible and unco-operative. He can dismiss them, but it is often politically inexpedient to reveal a rift in the cabinet. There is constant danger that they—and his unofficial advisers—will become sycophants flattering him with too ready confirmation of his views. Like all men who reach a high pinnacle of authority, the President is likely to be isolated and lonely.

The steadily growing burdens of the office and the weakness of the cabinet as an advising and deliberating body led to the establishment in 1939 of a White House office. This office provides a personal staff or secretarial service for the President and is composed of six administrative assistants, a press secretary, an economic adviser, various military aides, and a large clerical staff. Their function is to collect information relevant to the countless decisions the President has to make and to furnish liaison with Congress, the numerous executive agencies, and the public.

A brief summary cannot give a just impression of the scope of the presidential office. The Constitution charges the President to see that the laws are faithfully executed. Today, this means that he must supervise the vast range of regulation and services of the positive state in so far as they are federal and not matters for the separate states. Congress annually piles new duties on the executive, many of which are really of a legislative nature.[1] Whether through delegation by Congress or through the inherent ordinance power of the executive, the President must now make ordinances and regulations which, in sheer bulk, dwarf the output of Congress into insignificance. He must see to the appointment and direction of the officers necessary for the tasks in hand. The Senate shares in appointments to the "higher" offices, which including the judiciary still number twenty-two thousand. The "lower" offices are mostly filled by heads of departments under civil service regulations. Yet the President must often attend, perfunctorily or otherwise, to a vast number of appointments in the course of a year. Subject to civil service regulations, he has power to discipline and remove the executive officers of the United States.

He has charge of the conduct of foreign policy, subject to Senate approval of treaties and to congressional support by way of necessary appropriations and legislation. While Congress declares war, it is his task to see that the war is fought with energy and intelligence to a successful conclusion. Much discretionary power and heavy responsibility lie with him to deal with all emergencies affecting the nation, whether war or civil disturbance. In addition under present conditions, he must give much of his time to the developing of legislative policy, despite the separation of powers. More will be said on this point later. Finally, the administrative organization of the government of the United States is now so huge that it is a tremendous task to combat its inertia, subdue its internal

[1]The natural query whether this does not violate the separation of powers will be considered later.

rivalries, and erase its cross-purposes. Testimony is almost unanimous that the President's burden is too great for any man to carry.

It has already been said that the positive state has everywhere aggrandized the executive. The American Presidency is a striking illustration of this truth. The executive must actually perform the tasks of modern government, tasks of such importance to the economy and community life that inefficiency or failure is serious. The President is responsible, and his powers tend to become commensurate with the responsibility. In any crisis that requires something to be done, almost everyone looks to the President. The country, it is said, needs leadership and knows it. Congress, for reasons that will appear, is peculiarly unfitted to give this leadership, and so it must come from the President.

The clearest and most dramatic proof of this comes in the field of foreign affairs. Congress can legislate the country into isolationism, and the Senate can reject all entangling alliances. Yet the President actually conducts foreign policy and he may take irrevocable steps which in effect commit the country to intervention. While he cannot make treaties, he can make executive agreements with foreign states, which often are as effective as treaties. His power to recognize, or refuse to recognize, newly established governments can be used with decisive effect. In short, his conduct of foreign affairs, as one interpretation of Franklin Roosevelt's policy from 1939-41 would have it, may make war inevitable. And when it comes, the President who has been preparing for it while Congress has not, is likely to have the major share in deciding how it is to be fought.

President Roosevelt and his advisers, and not Congress, framed the New Deal. It is true this was an emergency like war, but Theodore Roosevelt and Woodrow Wilson exercised similar, if not as great, influence on legislation. The legislation of today is often enacted in general terms. Its detailed application depends more and more on rules and regulations and particular discretionary decisions taken by the executive. The President, or his subordinates over whom he has power of control, exercise these discretionary powers, and the great interests of the country find they must deal with the President as well as with Congress.

At every turn, eyes are focused on the President. His constitutional powers are not at all equal to what he is expected to do.

Despite this, he often has decisive influence. He can reach everybody through radio, television, and press conferences. Everybody listens when he speaks. The White House has been called the biggest pulpit in the country. The man who can sway this congregation has something better than formal power. The more serious issue is whether one man can do what is now expected of the President.

A brief account of the executive of the United States must concentrate on the President, with whom all executive power and responsibility lie. But the great executive organization at the apex of which he stands must not be forgotten. The White House office already mentioned is only a part of a much larger establishment, the Executive Office of the President, which also contains the Bureau of the Budget, the Council of Economic Advisers, the National Security Council, the Office of Emergency Management, and the Office of Defence Mobilization.

Each of the ten departments is in itself a massive organization. In addition, there are now more than sixty administrative agencies of the federal government outside the ten departments. These boards, commissions, administrations, and authorities have been established, for the most part in the last fifty years, to administer and supervise some of the newer activities of government. Many such bodies have been designed to cope with emergencies like depression and war and have not been permanent. Yet when some are abolished, other new agencies take their place and the total number of the extra-departmental agencies has not fallen below sixty for many years. Some aspects of this great executive organization will be taken up in later chapters.

The Cabinet as the British Executive

In Britain, the executive, in the narrow sense under consideration here, is the cabinet. It consists of the Prime Minister and about twenty colleagues who are appointed heads of the more important departments of the government. It has now almost twice as many members as it had a hundred years ago. As the activities of government expanded, important new departments (labour and national service, power, education, transport, and so on) were organized, and room had to be found in the cabinet for their heads. It is now admittedly too large for effective discussion and decision, but the only feasible way to reduce its size is to reduce the number of important departments by amalgamation.

The King calls on the leader of the majority party in the newly elected House of Commons to be Prime Minister. The Prime Minister is then free to choose his cabinet. The only constitutional limitation is that the persons he chooses must either have a seat in Parliament or get one without delay. The linking of the cabinet with Parliament is vital to the British system.

The British Parliament is composed of two chambers, the House of Commons and the House of Lords. While members of the cabinet may be chosen from either House, the great majority are always from the House of Commons. As we shall see later, the House of Lords is not representative of the electorate and has lost most of the powers it once had. The House of Commons represents the electorate and only by retaining its confidence can the cabinet retain office. Accordingly, most, although not all, members of the cabinet are chosen from the House of Commons. It is said that the cabinet is responsible to Parliament, but it would be more accurate to say it is responsible to the House of Commons.

As a matter of practical politics, the Prime Minister in picking his cabinet has to give weight to the same kind of considerations as affect the President's choice of a cabinet. The Scots and the Welsh and the various sections of England must not be forgotten. Important social and economic interests cannot be passed over. Certain alliances within the party support the Prime Minister's leadership of his party. These must be held together and the bargains on which they are based must be kept. In addition, the Prime Minister's choice is further limited by factors that the President can ignore. Not only must the British cabinet be chosen from Parliament but certain members of Parliament, particularly of the House of Commons, have special claims to consideration. Members of former cabinets, members who are able parliamentarians and effective critics when the party is in opposition, are difficult to exclude. It may even be necessary for the Prime Minister to include in the cabinet an unsuccessful rival for the leadership of the party. There may be some claimant for cabinet rank whose only recommendation is that it will be safer to have him inside than outside. Many exceedingly delicate decisions must be made, for the Prime Minister, unlike the President, must pick a team of colleagues who will work together and always defend one another in public, who can command the respect of the House of Commons and retain the confidence of the majority therein, who can defend their departments effectively in Parliament as well as direct them efficiently.

The members of the cabinet are all ministers of the Crown, a body of equals because each is equally commissioned to advise His Majesty. They need to be united by mutual respect, if not by affection. It is, of course, impossible for twenty men genuinely to agree on all major issues. At the same time, it will not do for foreign policy to commit itself to preparation for war while financial policy insists on a sharp cut in all government expenditures. Major policy is a unity; the ship of state cannot sail in different directions at one and the same time. Hence the conventions of the constitution, which seek to get from the team the concerted action that a king or a president can supply.

While each minister is responsible individually to Parliament for the operation of his department, all members of the cabinet are responsible collectively for each department and for general policy. This does not mean that all decisions are taken collectively; that would be physically impossible today. It does mean that when a minister has taken an important decision on his own initiative, the others must either stand by and defend him in the face of parliamentary criticism or throw him to the wolves. As a result, each hesitates to take important decisions without prior consultation with the Prime Minister at least, and each takes a personal interest in what the others are doing. Every decision taken in cabinet must be supported by all. A minister who is doubtful of the wisdom of a decision must either conceal his misgivings or part company with his colleagues. Lord Melbourne is reported to have told his cabinet on one occasion that he did not much care what decision was taken as long as they all told the same story. Mistakes in policy are not likely to be as immediately disastrous to confidence in Parliament and in the country, as are evidences of internal disagreement.

It is therefore vitally important for the Prime Minister to pick a good team and hold them together. The greatest single advantage he can have in his selection is to be able to pick them from a single political party. This ensures, to begin with, a certain similarity of view and temperament. All have strong loyalties to the party and hesitate to jeopardize its fortunes by open dissension. Equally important, the political fortunes of each are bound up with those of the party. Each knows that the party will punish revolts, and this disciplines toward agreement. These favourable conditions do not exist when a cabinet is chosen from a coalition of parties. In 1932, the cabinet of the National Coalition could not agree on tariff policy, and they publicly announced an agreement to differ on this question. Such a formula will work only within very narrow limits, and it weakens a government dangerously.

As long as it works within the confines of a two-party system, the British cabinet is a remarkably successful device for combining vigorous and unified direction, joint counsel, and mutual criticism, and for the maturing of decisions through discussion. When working satisfactorily, the cabinet system provides for each of its members the frank discussion and blunt criticism that the President of the United States needs so badly. But it will not work satisfactorily when the cabinet has to be pieced together from two or more parties.

Every team needs a captain, and this leadership is accorded to the Prime Minister. It is commonly said that the only significance of the "prime" is to make him first among equals. This phrase, however, means nothing unless it means he is something more than an equal. With the coming of the popular franchise and strongly disciplined political parties, it was inevitable that the acknowledged leader of the majority party would have significant pre-eminence in the cabinet. He is a key figure in the central organization of the party, he leads the party in Parliament and in election campaigns, and so has an immense influence on the policy and platform of the party. There is much drama in leadership and little in complex policies no matter how important they may be for the country. That section of the electorate which is not rigidly frozen in its party allegiance, does not—as indeed you cannot—separate men from measures. Thus general elections have tended to become personal contests between the leaders of the rival parties, and the verdict at the polls to become the choice of a Prime Minister by the people. He has a mandate to lead which his colleagues lack.

The Prime Minister's pre-eminence is evident at every turn. He is the channel of communication between the cabinet and the King. In sudden emergencies that do not give him time to consult the cabinet, he will act on his own initiative. Particular ministers after consulting him will often take decisions they would not risk on their own judgment. The House of Commons and the country expect him to make all important statements on policy. On advice from him, the King will dismiss a minister. Most important, it is now settled as a result of the practice of recent years that the decision to advise a dissolution of Parliament rests solely with him. This is a heavy weapon to keep hanging over the heads of a cabinet that cannot make up its mind.

Yet he remains the captain of a team and has not become a chief executive for two main reasons. First, the other ministers of the cabinet are equally responsible to Parliament and thus have an equal personal stake in policy. He has to carry them with him. Secondly, his leadership of the government depends on maintaining control over the House of Commons. He cannot risk frequent resignations and dismissals, nor weak and unconvincing support of policy by his colleagues on the floor of the House, for that will undermine the solidarity of the party majority. The knowledge that they must all hang together or hang separately not only disposes them to earnest effort at agreement, but also limits what the Prime Minister can do with his unquestioned pre-eminence. It ensures the fullness of discussion and candour in criticism that the President of the United States often fails to get in his cabinet.

THE FUNCTIONS OF THE BRITISH CABINET

The broad functions of the cabinet can now be stated very briefly. As heads of departments, they furnish direction and drive to the activities of the civil service. They defend the actions of their departments in Parliament, discharging their responsibility to Parliament by answering without demur the most trivial questions in minute detail. No civil servant is ever asked or allowed to defend himself in Parliament. The minister is responsible for every action, and he does not shirk it unless, of course, he can plead actual insubordination by a civil servant. Collectively, they must co-ordinate the work of their separate departments, ironing out inter-departmental disputes and thus integrating the diverse activities of hundreds of thousands of civil servants.

As an executive committee of Parliament, they must organize the work that the House of Commons particularly is expected to do in a session. They allot the time to be spent on particular matters, prepare the budget and the legislative programme that the House is to consider. They pilot government bills through the House, explaining their purpose and meaning and defending them against criticism. Through their pervasive control, they channel the energies of the House, which otherwise would be largely dissipated in discussion, into concrete accomplishments in the form of legislation.

It is through the cabinet that Parliament effects its criticism and surveillance of daily administration. On the other hand, the cabinet brings to Parliament the accumulated knowledge and experience which the civil service collects in the course of administration and which is a vital ingredient in the making of policy for the future. It brings these data forward not in a heterogeneous mass, but transmuted into either proposed amendments to existing laws or matured plans for new legislation. It almost invariably persuades Parliament to accept its programme without substantial modification because it can rely on a party majority in the House of Commons, fortified in its loyalty by the threat of a dissolution of Parliament. This gives rise to the charge that the cabinet dictates to a subservient House of Commons—an indictment that will be considered later. At present, it is sufficient to see why Bagehot described the cabinet as a buckle linking Parliament and the executive (meaning the executive in the broad inclusive sense), and why it can also be described as the mainspring of government.

Directing the work of a department in a government which engages in such a wide range of activities is in itself a heavy burden on a minister even when he can rely on a number of able senior civil servants. When the tasks of co-ordinating the work of all departments, defending his department and general government policy in Parliament, maturing policy and guiding legislation through Parliament are added, it can be seen why the cabinet is said to be overworked and the job of the Prime Minister to be an exhausting one. The Prime Minister does not normally take on the work of a heavy department, but he has a host of other concerns from which his colleagues are free. There are several other posts that are sinecures, such as Lord Privy Seal and Lord President of the Council. The Prime Minister generally gives these to men whose advice and assistance on general policy are needed but who do not wish to carry exacting administrative burdens. Despite this, a number of devices to ease and simplify the work of the cabinet have had to be introduced.

Easing the Burdens of the Cabinet

For many years, it has been the practice to appoint one or more parliamentary secretaries in each of the important departments of the government. The parliamentary secretaries are members of the ministry but not of the cabinet. Such posts are generally given to promising younger men in the party to keep them satisfied for the moment and train them for higher things. They assist the ministers in administration, and in answering questions and defending their departments in the House.

As the volume of decisions to be taken by the cabinet grew and as these decisions came to involve more and more considerations, cabinet meetings became more frequent and discussions more prolonged, interfering with the time available for other pressing duties. Some relief has been found in the use of small committees of cabinet. Many problems concern two or more departments very closely and others in minor degree or scarcely at all. Small committees of cabinet are set up to try for agreement on such issues, thus saving the time of the larger body for more general questions. If the committee can agree, the cabinet as a whole seldom needs to spend time on the matter. Committees are now an established feature of cabinet procedure, even flowering out into subcommittees where the issues are complex. This procedure helps to meet the mounting pressures of the positive state, but its use is limited by the fact that the ministers whose departmental duties are heaviest will generally be those having to carry the major burden of committee work.

As already noted, the cabinet is now at least twice as large as it should be for effective discussion and speedy decision—another reason for seeking relief through small committees. The delay involved in reaching decisions becomes quite intolerable in time of war. Lloyd George summed it up by saying you cannot wage war with a Sanhedrin. When he became Prime Minister in the First World War, he set up a small War Cabinet of five members (later enlarged). These had no departmental duties and devoted themselves to planning the conduct of the war. As almost every aspect of domestic policy was necessarily subordinated to the dominant aim of winning the war, the War Cabinet was, in effect, the cabinet. It made wide use of committees and subcommittees for investigating and reporting on the multitudinous matters it had to decide. The use of this small inner cabinet made for more rapid dispatch of business, but the divorce of deliberation on policy from the direction of administration in the several departments proved to be most unsatisfactory.

A War Cabinet was again set up in World War II. It did not follow the earlier precedent in this respect, but was largely composed of ministers who headed the departments most vitally concerned with prosecuting the war. The best decision on what to do next cannot be made without knowing in detail what is now being done and bringing that experience to bear on the decision. The solution of the problem of the overlarge and overworked cabinet is not to be found in separating the thinking from the doing.

At the end of the war, a Labour Government came to power. It had a large programme which involved much greater government activity and much greater congestion of cabinet business than existed at the outbreak of war. Six entirely new, presumably permanent, departments of government concerned with the public interest in food, fuel and power, civil aviation, supply, national insurance, and town and country planning came into existence between 1939 and 1948. The total number of departments increased sharply. On the other hand, Mr. Attlee reduced his Cabinet to seventeen members. The ministers of the new departments, and some others as well, were excluded from the cabinet.

This makes necessary still further use of committees. Many weighty questions on which the cabinet must decide will involve departments whose heads are not in the cabinet. These latter are drawn into discussion and decision of matters affecting their departments through membership in appropriate cabinet committees.

No device has yet been found to reduce the cabinet to the most effective size of perhaps ten or twelve. One way would be to amalgamate two or more closely related departments into a single department. For example, the three departments concerned with army, navy, and air force could be made into a single department of defence. This would, of course, greatly increase the work and responsibility of the cabinet ministers at the head of the mammoth departments and compel still further delegation to parliamentary secretaries and senior civil servants. At present, this kind of amalgamation is not being seriously considered.

Instead, the British are experimenting with another somewhat similar device. In World War II, Prime Minister Churchill created, and occupied with great distinction, the office of Minister of Defence. This office was not an amalgamation of the departments concerned with army, navy and air force. They remained intact, but Mr. Churchill as Minister of Defence took over the strategical conduct of the war with such overall supervision and co-ordination of the fighting services departments as was required for the purpose.

The Ministry of Defence Act, 1946, aims to adapt this arrangement for permanent use. It provides for a Minister of Defence who is charged with formulating and applying a unified policy for all the armed services of the country. Since his appointment under this Act, the Minister of Defence has been a member of the cabinet, and the First Lord of the Admiralty, the Secretary of State for War, and the Secretary of State for Air have ceased to be members of the cabinet. The Minister of Defence has been given supervisory powers over them and their departments.

Here perhaps is the first instance of a new kind of organization, a super-ministry charged with co-ordination of a number of departments whose heads are not in the cabinet and who will almost certainly be subordinated to the super-minister. The cabinet may come some day to be composed largely of such super-ministers. A further tendency in this direction can be detected in the conferring on the Chancellor of the Exchequer of a co-ordinating role in matters of economic policy. Furthermore, although the War Cabinet has disappeared, there is still a small inner group in the Cabinet on whom the Prime Minister places special reliance. This may well be a super-ministry in embryo. At any rate, the effective working of the cabinet system under present circumstances seems to require a still further concentration of responsibility and power on fewer men.

The congestion of cabinet business is not merely a wartime problem. The peacetime scope of government action piles up work of comparable magnitude for the cabinet. The greatly expanded scope and complexity of cabinet duties is underlined by the establishment of a cabinet office under a secretary to the cabinet. Originally the cabinet was a cabal whose very existence was not free from doubt. The doubt has vanished, but the deliberations have remained secret in the highest degree. Throughout the nineteenth century, however, the proceedings of the cabinet were most informal. A minister who wished to raise a matter notified the Prime Minister beforehand and then spoke to the point at the meeting. The agenda was in the Prime Minister's head and the only record of decision was the minute made by the Prime Minister for the purpose of informing the King. This gives some indication of the easy tempo of British government in the nineteenth century.

This lack of system became unworkable in World War I. A secretary to the cabinet was appointed in 1917, and has continued since that time. He prepares the agenda for, and keeps the minutes of, cabinet meetings. Except in cases of urgency, a minister who wants to bring a matter to cabinet must first consult the other departments concerned and then prepare a memorandum setting out the matter in detail. The cabinet office then circulates the memorandum several days before the meeting at which it will be raised. Thus all members of the cabinet are apprised in advance of the nature of the question and those particularly concerned have had time to develop their views on it. A dozen or more higher civil servants will have posted their particular ministers on how the matter affects their departments. Business can be dispatched more rapidly and with a fuller knowledge of what is involved in the decision. Extraordinary precautions are taken to ensure the secrecy of these memoranda and of the minutes of cabinet meetings.

THE CANADIAN CABINET

Canadian government, apart from its federal aspect, is modelled on British government. The Canadian cabinet performs the same functions and stands in the same formal relationship to Parliament as the British cabinet. The acknowledged leader of the majority party in a newly elected House of Commons becomes Prime Minister. He picks his colleagues from the supporters of his party in Parliament. The cabinet so selected is individually and collectively responsible to Parliament for the conduct of administration. Yet in the construction of a cabinet and in its methods of working, there are significant differences from the British practice.

Most of the differences spring from two sources. First, Canada is a federation of ten distinct provinces, a fact that must always be remembered when a new federal cabinet is being formed. Secondly, the national government in Canada, apart from the emergencies of war, has never thus far engaged in a range of activities comparable to those carried on by the British governments. A substantial proportion of the governmental functions carried on in Canada are in the hands of the ten provincial governments. So, while the federal cabinet has always had to keep in mind the bearing of its actions on provincial governments and politics—considerations from which the British cabinet is free—it was not compelled, until World War II, to adjust its procedure to a congestion of business comparable to that which piles up before the British cabinet. Attention will be limited here to the principal points of difference.

When a party leader is called on by the Governor-General to form a cabinet, he has to attend to the same kind of considerations which guide the British Prime Minister in his selection. Yet these can scarcely be said to be his primary concern. Well-established custom which has almost hardened into a convention of the constitution requires him to distribute cabinet posts so as to give representation to the provinces, and even to minorities and sections within provinces. Representation in the federal cabinet is accorded to provinces as regions, to the portion of the electorate that resides in a particular area, and not to provincial governments as such. For example, when a Liberal government is in power in Ottawa, the cabinet minister from Alberta is not in any sense a representative of the Social Credit government in Alberta.

Broadly speaking, there is a minimum representation from each province: four each from Quebec and Ontario, and one from each of the other provinces. In actual practice in recent years, Prince Edward Island has often been without a representative in the cabinet while Ontario and Quebec each have managed to get six places. It is generally recognized that three of the minimum four from Quebec must be French-speaking Catholics and the fourth a representative of the English-speaking minority in Quebec. When the actual Quebec representation rises to six, the practice allows a second English-speaking representative. The considerable French-speaking population outside Quebec is usually represented, and the English-speaking Catholics of the country usually find a spokesman, often in one of the ministers chosen from Ontario. In addition, certain sections of the country have established claims to particular departments. For example, ministers of agriculture have been drawn from the Prairie Provinces for many years, and the Maritime Provinces generally provide the ministers of fisheries.

The exact distribution of cabinet posts along these lines varies from time to time, but the sectional, ethnic, and religious diversity of the country is always recognized in the composition of the Canadian cabinet. If one can judge from the practice of the past, this scheme of composition is the first imperative in cabinet-making and any radical departure from it is likely to weaken the prospects of the offending political party with the sections or groups whose expectations have been slighted.

The necessity of giving the cabinet a federal character limits the Prime Minister's choice of colleagues in two ways. On the one hand, it is often hard to find cabinet timber among the members of his party returned to the House of Commons from particular provinces or by particular minorities. Since he scarcely dares to pass them over, the quality of the cabinet is sometimes lowered. On the other hand, by the same token, he may be compelled to pass over able parliamentarians who could almost insist on inclusion in Britain. One result is that the Canadian national parties do not always manage to maintain a corps of recognized party leaders with long experience in Parliament and in office. Cabinet posts often have to go to men whose previous political career has been undistinguished or limited to one province. Men who are relatively or entirely unknown in national politics commonly turn up in the cabinet, particularly after an election that brings a change of government.

It will be explained later that the national political parties in Canada are not close-knit, well-disciplined organizations as they are in Britain. It will suffice here to note that the federal cabinet is not so much composed of a body of recognized leaders of a national party as it is of representatives of provinces and of ethnic and religious groups. Consequently, the attitude of the cabinet on the national questions it has to decide is often strongly influenced by sectional and other particularistic considerations.

A minister always has to state the view of the province or other group he represents. For example, when tariff policy is being considered in the cabinet, the minister of agriculture representing one or other of the Prairie Provinces must remind his colleagues of the special prairie attitude on tariffs. In all matters of federal administration affecting a particular province, that province has a friend at court in the person of the minister from that province. Appointments to federal jobs in a province are generally made on the recommendation of the minister from that province.[1] As we shall see later, the men who framed the Canadian federal union intended the Senate, the upper chamber of the legislature, to represent the interests of the several provinces in the councils of the Dominion, in much the same way as the United States Senate was intended to give special representation to the several states. As things have turned out, the Senate has no great influence and it does not in any marked way represent provincial points of view. But the champions of provincial interests have established themselves in the seats of power in the cabinet.

The relatively modest peacetime functions of the federal cabinet have also affected its structure. Except under the stress of war, the number of departments in the Government of Canada has rarely

---

[1]Only, of course, in the case of jobs that are not controlled by the Civil Service Commission.

risen as high as twenty while in Britain the number of departments, major and minor, is never less than twenty-five. Moreover, until the aftermath of World War II, the peacetime load of departmental work in the Dominion government was never so great as to establish the practice of appointing junior assistant ministers, while in Britain there have long been roughly as many of these as there are ministerial heads of departments. So the British ministry is always sixty or more, of whom about twenty of the important ministers form the cabinet.

In Canada, with negligible exceptions, all ministers have been members of the cabinet and also heads of departments. In World War I, three parliamentary secretaries (the equivalent of junior ministers) were temporarily appointed, but no further use of this device for easing the burdens of ministers was made until the appointment of a number of parliamentary assistants, as they are now called, in World War II. Nowadays the demand for ministers who are to contribute wisdom without sharing administrative burdens is so slight that the number of ministers without portfolios, i.e., without departments, is normally not more than two. One minister without portfolio is regularly appointed from the Senate because of the need to have a spokesman for the cabinet in the Senate. Thus in times of peace, the numbers in the Canadian cabinet have fluctuated between fifteen and twenty.

World War II seems to mark an important turning point in the structure of the Canadian cabinet and in the organization of its work. Prior to that time (always excepting the period of World War I) the relatively light burden of departmental duties had led to certain characteristics in the cabinet. First, it made it possible—although by no means wise or useful—for the cabinet to give much closer attention to the details of administration than was possible in Britain. Minutiae which in Britain were left to the discretion of a minister had to be dealt with by order-in-council in Canada, i.e., a decision of the cabinet was necessary. There was a strong tendency for ministers to be immersed in minor detail at the expense of the quality of thought given to the larger issues of policy. Everyone who contrasted the Canadian and British cabinets was struck by this difference.

Second, the Canadian cabinet did not find it necessary to rely to any significant extent on committees. Almost all issues went to the full cabinet for discussion and decision. Third, there was no compelling need to establish a cabinet secretariat. Fourth, although parliamentary secretaries as assistants to busy ministers were often promised, the ministers were never so busy as to force the taking of this step. The Canadian cabinet managed to maintain up till World War II the informality and easy pace that the British cabinet had had to abandon a generation earlier.

World War II called for a level of national government activity never before contemplated and the Canadian cabinet very quickly took up the expedients adopted earlier in Britain. A War Committee of the cabinet was set up in 1939 and it was followed by the establishment of a number of other cabinet committees for urgent purposes. In 1940, a special committee was set up to deal with the routine detail which under many statutes and prevailing practice still had to be dealt with by order-in-council. In the same year, a secretary to the cabinet was appointed. With the development of a staff to assist the secretary, his office rapidly became a cabinet secretariat. And in 1943, parliamentary assistants to seven of the ministers with the heaviest parliamentary duties were appointed. In 1959, an act of Parliament adopted the title "parliamentary secretary" for the office but made it clear that the occupant would have neither cabinet rank nor ministerial status.

Since the end of World War II, the activity of the Canadian government has diminished greatly but nevertheless has remained at a much higher level than ever before in peace time. The expedients adopted for the purposes of war have been continued and appear now to be part of the permanent organization. As the wartime committees were disbanded, others concerned with peacetime problems were set up. Minor detail requiring formal cabinet action goes to a small committee for final disposition except where some significant question of policy is involved. The cabinet secretariat has been continued as an indispensable auxiliary to the cabinet. The number of parliamentary assistants has increased rather than decreased since the war. In these ways, the Canadian executive has adapted itself to the requirements of the positive state.

CHAPTER VII

THE LEGISLATURE: ITS FUNCTIONS AND PROCEDURE

IN THE tripartite division of powers, the legislature makes the laws. This function includes the imposing of taxes and the appropriating of money to particular items of expenditure. The legislature is in theory the most august authority within the constitution. In Britain, as we have seen, Parliament has the formal power to amend the constitution, although, of course, the exercise of the power is restricted by the conventional requirement of a mandate from the electorate. By making laws and appropriating public money the legislature sets the tasks of the executive, determines what public services are to be rendered, and within what limits the government is to operate. In democratic theory, the legislature represents the people, or the community, and is supposed to exercise general surveillance over the executive to see that, in its actual administration, government is for the people and not against them. In the United States, despite an independently elected executive, the legislature is expected to give close scrutiny to the actions of the executive. This surveillance works through the cabinet system in Great Britain and Canada; in the United States it works through the detailed legislative control of finance and administration and increasingly through investigation carried out by legislative committees.

The powerful weapon of impeachment is also available in the United States, the Constitution authorizing the Senate to remove executive officers from the President down by this method. However, it has been used so rarely that it cannot be said to be a working method of the legislature for controlling the executive. There have been only twelve cases of impeachment proceedings launched under the federal constitution. Only four of these resulted in convictions, and the convicted parties in every case were federal judges and not members of the executive. It may well become as obsolete as it has in Britain, where the last case of impeachment of a minister before the House of Lords was in 1805. Although the House of Lords no longer exercises this power, it has other judicial functions that have persisted. Until 1948 it tried all peers accused of serious offences and it is still the final court of appeal for Great Britain and Northern Ireland. These have been or are historical survivals and need no extended comment. The making of laws and keeping watch over the executive are the significant functions so far as the legislature is concerned.

The high significance of the law-making function should be underlined by recalling the discussion of liberal democratic ideals of government in chapter II. The ideal of individual freedom involves the right of private judgment. The democratic ideals, taken as a whole, are phrased in such general terms that when men exercise private judgment there is a wide diversity of opinion on what government should and should not do. The ideal of the rule of law as expressed in constitutional provisions requires governments to act in accordance with law. Individual freedom must not be abridged except through law. Respect for individual personality requires discussion and debate as a means for composing differences of opinion on what to do to further the ideals. Finally, it is assumed that men are sufficiently rational to undertake discussion and to submit to persuasion on the basis of logic and evidence.

The liberal democratic legislature is an institution constructed under the compulsion of these ideals and designed to promote their realization. The millions of persons in a society cannot all meet for discussion. Through the electoral system, they elect to the legislature persons who are supposed to represent their views. This representation is admittedly imperfect but it does bring together some kind of cross-section of the principal diverse views in the community. If some significant body of opinion is deeply dissatisfied with the existing state of affairs and fails to get the adjustment it wants through discussion and voluntary action at a lower level, it will sooner or later find a way of proposing a law to the legislature. The legislature has no magic formula for dealing with such proposals. It is itself representative of diverse views and interests and therefore has no agreed view on the matter, in the initial stages at any rate. It can only proceed in patient pedestrian fashion by hearing what is to be said on both sides and collecting as much data as it can on the issue in question. Ultimately, of course, it will have to come to a decision because it is the final authority for composing the clashing demands of private judgment, conscience, and interest. The only appeal beyond its decision is to force and violence which dishonour and frustrate human personality. So it has to find a solution that will at least be tolerable to almost all concerned. Only rarely will any one course seem both acceptable and obviously right to the legislators who have to decide. Law-making is normally a compromise based on debate and majority decision.

The liberal democratic legislature is organized with a view to performing this supreme function. It has a structure of committees for collecting facts and for giving detailed examination to issues. It has rules of debate designed to allow the frankest expression of views, and, at the same time, to prevent that unfettered licence of expression which destroys mutual respect among the members. In addition to trying to provide the proper atmosphere for rational discussion, the rules of debate aim to guide discussion along orderly lines. The liberal democratic legislature also has rules for compelling at some point an end to discussion, and then a decision by majority vote. Finally, it has a system of political parties which runs the organized machinery of the legislature and in the end submerges the private reservations of members in majority decisions.

THE COMPOSITION OF UPPER CHAMBERS

The British Parliament and the federal legislatures of the United States and Canada are all bicameral, composed of upper and lower chambers. The lower or popular chamber is in each case made up of representatives of territorial units, or constituencies, chosen by substantially adult suffrage. Attempts are made—with indifferent success—so to draw the lines of the constituencies that each member represents roughly an equal number of individuals. The lower chamber is popular in the sense that it mirrors the nation, the nation being regarded as a number of collections of individuals resident in particular territorial areas. In the United States, the lower chamber, the House of Representatives, is chosen for a fixed period of two years, being regularly renewed at the

end of that time by a fresh election. In Britain and Canada, the
maximum life of the House of Commons is five years, but it may
be cut short at any time by a dissolution of Parliament leading to a
general election.]

The House of Lords, the upper chamber in Britain, antedates
the period of deliberate devising of political institutions and is a
relic of the insistence of the feudal barons that they should advise—
and control—the king, whose centralizing ambitions always threatened to cut down their local perquisites. By the rule of primo-
geniture, the eldest son of the feudal lord succeeded to his father's
estates and to his place on the Great Council advising the king.
Today the hereditary peerage makes up by far the greatest part of
the membership of the House of Lords. Of course, it must be
remembered that most of the great feudal houses are long since
extinct; the Bohuns, Mortimers, Mowbrays, and DeVeres are "in
the urns and sepulchres of mortality." The peers are mostly
parvenus, their peerages having been created by royal letters patent
since the seventeenth century.

Indeed, the character of the peerage has almost completely
changed since the Reform Act of 1832. Most of the existing
peerages have been created since that time, almost half of them
since 1900. The new peers of the nineteenth century were mostly
men who had succeeded in industry and commerce rather than
great landlords. And increasingly now, peerages are granted for
"political and public services." Conspicuous service to the state in
the civil service, in the armed services, in diplomacy, or in the
professions may be rewarded by elevation. Political services meriting a peerage are of various kinds. Politicians may crown their
careers by going to the House of Lords. Men of eminence whose
counsel is wanted in the cabinet but who will not fight elections or
undertake departmental responsibilities may be made peers to give
them the necessary qualification for inclusion in the cabinet. And,
of course, it is widely asserted that many have been ennobled in
return for handsome contributions to party campaign funds.

Ennoblement is not a personal prerogative of the King. The
Prime Minister, taking such suggestion and advice as he deems fit,
recommends names to His Majesty. The King may object to the
inclusion of particular persons or urge a candidate of his own

and may on occasion win his point. But, generally speaking, peerages are in the gift of the political party in power.

In addition to the hereditary peers, the House of Lords includes the princes of royal blood, princes of the church (twenty-six bishops and archbishops of the Church of England), representative Irish and Scottish peers, and nine Lords of Appeal, the latter being eminent lawyers and judges who are given life peerages to carry on the judicial work of the House of Lords. In 1958 a new category of "life peers" was added and the male monopoly on the upper house was broken when, amongst the first appointments, three baronesses were chosen.

The Senate of the United States has one hundred members, two from each state in the Union. The constitution originally provided for their election by the state legislatures. But in 1913, pressure for more direct democratic choice combined with indignation at the manipulation of the state legislatures by would-be Senators forced the Seventeenth Amendment to the Constitution providing for popular election of the Senators in each state. They are elected for a term of six years, but one-third retire every two years and are replaced by new elections, thus combining a degree of continuity with frequent elections.

The Senate of Canada consists of 102 members chosen to represent the four great geographical sections of the country. The Maritimes, Ontario, Quebec, and the Western Provinces are each assigned twenty-four senators. This representation is broken down still further. Each of the four Western Provinces is assigned six senators, New Brunswick and Nova Scotia each have ten, and Prince Edward Island has four. When Newfoundland came into the Dominion in 1949, it was allotted six senators, raising the total number from ninety-six to the present 102. Senators are appointed for life by the Governor-General on the advice of the Prime Minister. Membership in the Senate is in the gift of the party in the majority in the House of Commons, and the power to appoint is used for party purposes. Considerations similar to those prevailing in Britain determine the choice, though, of course, it is limited by the number of vacancies and the requirement that those chosen must be residents of the areas for which vacancies have occurred. Under these limitations, the exigencies of party leave little room for recognizing distinguished public service which is not of a specifically political nature.

A minister who has outlived his usefulness in the cabinet can be promoted to the Senate. The pain of being dropped from high office is assuaged if one falls into a soft seat in the Senate. Just before an election—and also just after an election in which effective service to the cause of party has been demonstrated—it is common for a number of politicians of the party in power to abandon active practice and go to the Senate. Others who have been active in the service of party although not in the front line as members of Parliament are also remembered. It would be difficult to say how much party management is eased by having a few senatorships to dangle as prizes or consolations, but no doubt they help significantly. The use of such appointments for such purposes is not necessarily to be condemned. Politics generally demands heavy material sacrifices from those who make it a life-work, and a seat in the Senate is not a generous compensation in many cases. If criticism is to be made, it should be at the frequency of appointment of rich men of powerful business connection for services of an unspecified character. Present indications, however, are that wealth and powerful business connections are of declining importance as qualifications for appointment to the Senate.

The upper chambers of the United States and Canada were deliberate constructions with aim and purpose. Sheer imitation of the British system and colonial precedents were factors in both cases, but two other considerations were decisive. First, in each case, a number of states or provinces of greatly unequal size and population were being federated under a national government. Representation in the lower federal chamber was to be on the basis of population, and it was thought that giving the states or provinces equal, or something approaching equal, representation in the upper chamber would safeguard the interests of the less populous in the general councils of the nation.

These anticipations have been largely disappointed. In each case, the Senate has become at least as much representative of economic and social interests of a nation-wide extent as of particular geographic sections. While the smaller states in the United States still cherish the defences offered by the Senate, in Canada, as the last chapter indicates, other more effective means have been found for representing provincial and sectional interests in the federal government. This does not mean that sectional interests are ignored in the Canadian Senate nor that the provinces themselves do not cherish the notion of equality of regional representation. There are always vigorous champions of sectional interests in the Senate, and from time to time they succeed in moving the Senate in defence of these interests.

Secondly, the American and Canadian constitutions were formed, one at the outset, and the other in the early stages, of extension of the franchise towards adult suffrage. It was widely feared that the people and the representatives they chose for the lower chamber would be easily swayed by gusts of emotion and even moved by the baser passions of envy and cupidity. It was thought to be important for stability, for the security of minorities, propertied and otherwise, that an upper chamber representing more conservative elements and not chosen by popular vote should check the vagaries and the envious appetite of the lower chamber. It was for this reason that indirect election and appointment for life respectively were chosen as the methods of recruitment.

In this too, anticipations have been wrong. Lower chambers have not been nearly so passion-ridden as was feared. It is true that for many years before the change to popular election in the United States, the Senate was a bulwark of the great business interests against regulation by government and was popularly derided as "a millionaires' club." But this was due, perhaps, as much to the general domination of all American political life by big business in that period as to the indirect election of Senators. Since direct popular election was introduced in 1913, the Senate has come increasingly to be moved by the impulses at work within the electorate as a whole.

In Canada, the membership of the Senate has been of a predominantly conservative cast (in a social rather than a political sense) according an exaggerated representation to business interests, but the political influence of the Senate has steadily declined almost to the vanishing point. Lacking entirely a popular basis in the electorate, it rarely has enough confidence in its convictions to stand firmly against what it regards as radical innovation. More important, the cabinet is responsible to the House of Commons and must bend all its energies to placating and holding the confidence of the lower chamber where the banns are read and all the solemn vows are taken.

The Senate of the United States, on the other hand, has by no means declined into political impotence. The President does not find it necessary every day to cater to the lower house while he is continually compelled to woo the Senate. For the Senate shares with him in the appointing and treaty-making power, thus gaining prestige and influence. Senatorial courtesy, a well-settled usage of the constitution by which the Senate normally refuses to confirm certain presidential appointments unless the President has first consulted the Senators of his party from the state concerned, in effect assures to Senators of the President's party, control over a considerable number of appointments to government jobs in their respective states. This forges for them a powerful connection with the political party machines in the states, enabling them to influence, and even at times to control, party nominations of candidates for the lower chamber.

A six-year term frees them from frequent distraction over re-election from which, by contrast, a member of the House of Representatives with a two-year term is scarcely ever free. The continuity of membership afforded by staggered senatorial elections every two years is a great advantage. The fact that the Senate has less than a quarter of the number of members of the lower chamber contributes greatly to the quality and effectiveness of debate. All these factors, in turn, make the Senate attractive to able men. Members of the House of Representatives aspire to, and frequently achieve, the Senate, thus giving it greater resources of mature political experience.

As a result, the Senate is much more than a check on the lower chamber. Although the constitution gives both chambers equal powers in legislation except for reserving to the lower chamber the initiation of all revenue bills, the Senate is the dominant partner in legislation. It amends at will legislation coming up from the lower chamber, smothers many such bills in committees, and originates a large share of those finally enacted. When the two chambers disagree on a bill and a compromise has to be arranged through a conference committee, the Senate generally makes the fewest concessions. Thus the widespread doubts about the effectiveness of upper chambers do not apply to the Senate of the United States. In prestige and power, it rivals the British House of Commons.

THE FUNCTIONS OF UPPER CHAMBERS

Generally, however, there are grave doubts about the utility of upper chambers in Canada and Britain. Acceptance of the democratic principle that the will of the majority should prevail made it inevitable that any forthright challenge of that will by an upper chamber should be regarded as insolent presumption. So when a trial of strength came in Britain over Lloyd George's budget in 1909, the result was the Parliament Act of 1911, an ignominious defeat for the House of Lords. By the Act, its power over money bills, which had already been modified by convention, was completely removed. A bill certified by the Speaker of the House of Commons to be a money bill no longer needed the Lords' consent before becoming law. They retained a veto on non-money bills, but this could be over-ridden by the House of Commons passing the measure three times in three successive sessions in a period of not less than two years. The House of Lords thus came to have only a suspending power.

Another trial of strength occurred in 1947. The Labour party came to power in 1945 pledged to introduce a large measure of socialism. Fearing that the conservative-minded House of Lords would veto important socialist measures and hold them up for two years, the Labour party majority in the House of Commons passed a bill reducing the period of the suspensive veto of the House of Lords from two years to one. The House of Lords rejected this bill. The House of Commons passed it again in 1948 and in 1949, thus making it law within the terms of the Parliament Act of 1911. A bill now becomes law over the veto of the House of Lords by being passed twice by the House of Commons in two successive sessions.

The Canadian Senate, which has equal legislative powers with the House of Commons (except perhaps for money bills, a question on which there is some debate among the constitutional authorities), has escaped a like clipping of its wings by refraining from flying too often in outright defiance of the House of Commons.

The upper chambers in Britain and Canada are now restricted to very narrow functions. It is sometimes suggested that they can be revivified and made highly useful by making them elective as in the case of the United States Senate. But if they are elected at the same time and on the same franchise as the lower house, they are likely to reflect much the same electoral opinion as the lower house and therefore to be superfluous. If they are elected at different times, or on different franchise, they may represent different popular moods or different general convictions respectively. The result would either be deadlock or, as the experience of the United States suggests, the practical primacy of one house over the other.

The alternative reform, which can be accommodated to an almost infinite variety of ways of appointing the upper chambers, is the one adopted in Britain of deliberately reducing the powers of the upper chamber to a mere suspending power. The majority in the lower chamber, either in the first flush of victory or in the hectic dying hours of a busy session may well pass measures that, on maturer consideration, they would regret. So an upper chamber can usefully check such legislative impulses without doing violence to the democratic dogma.

Also, the lower chamber in countries with parliamentary government is badly congested because of the enormous grist of legislation, and because it is a forum for criticism of the executive and for party manoeuvers, which take up a great deal of time. The upper chamber does not suffer much from these latter distractions. By sheer oversight, bills coming from the lower chamber sometimes lack provisions necessary to their effective administration or contain clauses involving unnecessary difficulties or hardships for particular groups. Sometimes some of their phrasing is obscure, leaving doubts what the new law really is. The upper chamber has time to spend in trimming and polishing the measures which come rough-hewn from the lower chamber.

These suspending and revising functions are the main functions now performed by the House of Lords and the Canadian Senate. Yet even these are subject to criticism. No major legislative proposal, except in wartime, goes through the lower chamber without being preceded by extensive discussion there and in the country. There is, it is often urged, no justification for permitting the House of Lords to postpone the enactment of such a proposal for another year.

However, it may be doubted whether any reform is of such great urgency that an additional year spent in broadening consent to it through the slow erosion of opposition is not well spent. For democracy is as much a matter of gaining the consent of minorities as it is of giving effect to the will of the majority. There is much to be said for the suspending function. The revising function also is important and is reasonably well performed considering the conditions under which it has to be done. Most bills must originate in the lower chamber, and few reach the upper chamber till late in the session, when they come in with a rush. The upper chamber is idle and overwhelmed by turns, so that many bills must either be rejected outright or enacted substantially unchanged. Also, many of the amendments made in the upper chamber are sponsored, or at any rate accepted, by the government. On this ground it is sometimes urged that the revising function could be as well or better performed by a special revision committee of the House of Commons.

Nevertheless, the handicap of an uneven flow of bills into the upper chamber could be largely overcome. And there is much to be said for a second chamber which has time for searching inquiry into the confused and complex facts that give rise to proposals for legislation. As we shall see later, one of the chief defects of legislatures today is that they rarely know enough about the facts to frame the laws most effectively. Neither the House of Lords nor the Senate in Canada has made full use of its time and talents for this purpose. But it is true that the Canadian Senate has made an important contribution to the legislative process through the investigations made by its committees into economic and social issues.

A very important function of the upper chamber in Britain and Canada is not legislative at all but consists in helping to lubricate the party system. As already noted, it often helps party leaders in forming or reforming a government and in executing other essential party manoeuvers to be able to kick someone upstairs. We do not know how the mechanics of the party system would work without this patronage, but some equivalent for it would clearly have to be found. This is not an argument for retaining an upper chamber so much as a warning that few political institutions are purely vestigial, to be removed without any adverse organic effects. The resource of democratic politicians is infinite; they can even find uses for second chambers!

Political parties that are bent on rapid and radical innovation are naturally deeply hostile to upper chambers. The great majority of the members of the House of Lords and the Senate of Canada have found the *status quo* good and will resist its wholesale dissolution. Most of the British peers never attend the sessions of the House of Lords except on occasions of ceremony or to vote against some measure that threatens drastic change. If and when the electorate gives a socialist party a clear mandate for a constitutional revolution, the upper chambers of Britain and Canada will find it hard to survive. The cry will be for extinction rather than reform, but a compromise on the basis of popular election for a short term might be worked out. Until that moment comes, the issue is likely to lie uneasily quiet, for raising it would raise a storm. It will not be discussed here because other matters of greater immediate and long-run importance must be considered.

THE ROLE OF POLITICAL PARTIES IN THE LEGISLATURE

The eighteenth century threefold division of governmental powers takes no account of political parties as organs of government because parties of the contemporary type did not then exist. The constitutions of the three countries in question here do not mention them at all, and only in the United States is there any law regulating their activities. Actually, political parties as they now operate are far-reaching modifications of these constitutions through usage and convention. Close attention will have to be given to their organization and functions in later pages. The immediate concern here is with legislatures, and parties are brought into the discussion only because they affect very deeply the working of the House of Commons in Britain and Canada, and of the United States Congress.

The influence of the parties on the legislature is markedly different in the three countries, owing to constitutional and other differences. To put it briefly, political parties in Britain are highly disciplined associations with strong central organs that shape decisively the working of the House of Commons. In the United States, political parties are strong in the localities and in the several states, but the national party associations are relatively weak and they do not dominate Congress as in Britain. In the Canadian House of Commons, political parties appear as fairly successful understudies of the British parties. Outside the House of Commons, their strong links with local and provincial interests make them resemble the American parties. So it is impossible to give a general description of the effect of political parties on the legislature that would be true for all three countries. The British and American situations must be outlined separately, and some attention given to the midway position in Canada.

Parties and the Legislature in Britain

In Britain, candidates are normally chosen by the local party associations but, as localism is not strong in national politics and the candidate need not be resident in the constituency he hopes to represent, the central party organization strongly influences the choice and often actually provides the candidate.

In choosing a candidate, each party in Britain is careful to pick, among other things, a sound party man, one who is loyal to the leadership and principles of the party. In recommending its candidate to the constituency, each party always justifies him by reference to the statesmanlike leadership and sound platform of the party. The candidate himself modestly subordinates to this praise of his party his own claim to merit and preferment. He dwells on his party's past record, its present promises, the integrity of its leaders and the wisdom of their policies. He might well repeat the self-depreciation of the hymn, "Nothing in my hand I bring." It is assumed throughout that the voting is not merely, or even mainly, to choose a person to represent the constituency, but to get the verdict of the voters on the party, its leaders, and its platform.

There have been normally only two significant political parties

and one or other of them gets its members elected to a majority
of the seats in the House of Commons. The executive, the cabinet,
is chosen from the leaders of the majority party. The rank and
file of this majority party responds to its leaders and presents a
united front on almost all issues. The making of laws and other
important decisions in the House of Commons are decisions of
the majority party under persuasion and pressure by the cabinet.
Often, particular members of Parliament belonging to the majority
party are personally opposed, more or less strongly, to the line
their party proposes to take. Yet they almost invariably vote for
the party line.

All this is common knowledge, but its far-reaching significance
is not always grasped. Members of Parliament are often chided
for meekly following their party when public opinion in their constituencies is strongly opposed to the line the majority party is following. It is forgotten that the member never held himself out to be
individually responsible as a mouthpiece for his constituents but
rather professed always to be the loyal member of a party. The
party takes the responsibility for the man and for the platform, and
the constituency is invited to make its reckoning with the party
which, of course, it can effectively do by rejecting the candidate of
this particular party at the next election. The political parties have
planted themselves between the electorate and the legislature.
Moreover, the bulk of the electorate show their approval of this by
voting for a party, for a party leader, and for a party platform
rather than for an individual candidate.

It would be both foolish and futile for a political party to
invite responsibility in this way unless there was a prospect of
power to make good its promises. Actually, if a well-disciplined
party wins a majority of the seats in a legislature where decisions
are taken by majority vote, it has the power to carry out its
promises. To make that power good, it must keep its members
in line.

In Britain, each party in the House of Commons has a number
of party whips, members of the party whose function it is to
maintain close liaison between the leaders of the party and its
rank and file. The party whips move constantly among the party
members in the House of Commons, sounding opinion among

them, informing them of the matters which must be decided, and mobilizing them for a vote when a decision is about to be taken in the House. The job of the whips is to ensure the united front of the party and to bring to the attention of the party leadership not only breaches of party loyalty but also any serious murmurs of the rank and file against the policies of the leaders.

The whips try to placate and persuade disgruntled members. If, despite this, members vote against their party on serious issues, they will almost certainly not be nominated as candidates for their party at the next election. These methods of ensuring support generally suffice. Almost all bills introduced in the House of Commons are part of a unified programme of the majority party and get disciplined support from the members of that party. Moreover, the majority party compels the House of Commons to work to an exacting time-table and to accept an order of priority of business that the party deems essential to the fulfilment of the responsibility it has accepted. It thus controls all significant action in the House of Commons.

Of course, the member of Parliament, of whatever party, keeps in close touch with his constituents and always furthers their interests where he can consistently with the party line. The vital communication has not been between the member and his constituents as individuals. It is between him, the local association of his party, and the central organization of his party, and takes the form of a steady flow of information, advice, explanation, and expostulation. If the intelligence thus coming in from all parts of the country indicates that the current party line should be modified, it is not revised through open desertion of it by members of the party in debate in the House of Commons. The revision is made unobtrusively in secret conclave of the parliamentary leaders of the party, where the sensitive antennae of the party organization that reach into all parts of the country register the shifts of opinion that must be heeded.

In fact, both of the major parties in Britain have established an elaborate apparatus of committees made up of parliamentary "backbenchers" and organized them on the basis of special subjects or areas of continuing legislative concern. These committees discuss with the leaders any adjustment of party policy. In this way,

with the party whips acting as intermediaries, the views of the rank
and file are brought to the attention of their parliamentary leaders
and the leaders, in turn, are able to work out a party line agreeable
to the whole parliamentary group. Through such private and other
informal consultations the substance of party policy is hammered
out in Britain. Quietly behind the scenes and not in open debate
in the legislature, members of Parliament show what independence
and courage they have. In party meeting or committee, and in
discussion with party whips, facts ably argued and convictions
powerfully expressed may change opinion and alter the party line.
Any such alteration is to ensure that all members will support their
party in the voting in the House of Commons. In this way, party
discipline is made effective, the majority party controls the House
of Commons, and carries out the bulk of the promises it has made
to the electorate.

Parties and Congress

By contrast, party discipline in the United States Congress is
weak. Well-established custom has made it an inflexible requirement that candidates for election to Congress must reside in the
election district they seek to represent. The candidates are almost
all chosen in direct party primaries, preliminary elections within
each political party to decide who shall be the party candidate.
This device was adopted in most of the states between 1900 and
1910 to reduce the influence of party organization, as distinct from
that of the rank and file of the party, in the choice of candidates.
Whatever the influence of local and state party organizations in the
primaries may be, the central organizations of the national parties
have never controlled nominations to Congress and have rarely had
any significant influence on the choice of candidates. Localism
has always been extremely strong in this matter.

As a result, the personalities of those seeking nomination, and
their personal attitudes on questions of keen local and sectional
concern, rather than their firm stand on the generalities of the
platform of their national party, are always highly important and
generally decisive. The member of Congress, once elected, is as
much a representative of a locality as he is of a national political
party. As we shall see in detail later, it follows that the national

parties in the United States do not take the heavy responsibilities for candidates and for the enforcement of party platforms that British parties accept.

The central organizations of the national parties in the United States do not maintain direct and continuous contact with the election districts. Liaison between the parties in the legislature and the districts is primarily furnished by the individual members of Congress, each of whom tries to gauge the drift of opinion in his district. Each party has its own organization within Congress for getting within its own ranks what agreement and discipline it can.

The members of each party in Congress meet in caucus, or party conference, from time to time. In recent years, the caucus has not been much used for deciding the party line on issues of proposed legislation. Its principal importance now is in dealing with matters of the internal organization of Congress and issues of party tactics in the political manoeuvering within Congress. The nominee of the majority party caucus is invariably elected Speaker of the House of Representatives. The caucus also appoints a steering committee for each chamber, headed by a floor leader who commands the party forces on the floors of the chambers. Subject to the rules of legislative procedure which will be discussed later, the steering committee takes the responsibility for pushing through legislation, determining the priority of measures, and limiting debate. It has, however, much less control over the actual terms of the laws it pushes through than has the leadership of the majority party in Britain.

The minority party also appoints a strategy committee and a floor leader for its party in each chamber. Each party has party whips whose functions are similar to those in Britain. But they are less effective than whips in Britain in shepherding their flocks through the division lobbies because on many matters there are no generally agreed party lines. Indeed, on many bills in Congress, discussion and voting do not follow party lines at all. On other bills, one or both parties seeks a united front for or against, but it often cannot be secured or maintained.

Breaches of party discipline cannot be punished by preventing the selection of the culprit as candidate of the party at the next election because the national parties have no control over selection of candidates. So many excuses have been recognized as justifying a member in flouting the majority decisions of his party caucus that the caucus has almost ceased to be a means of securing party regularity on controversial issues. Of course, the leaders of the parties in Congress have a number of means of persuasion they can employ, and according as these are effective, the strength of party discipline in Congress varies from party to party and from time to time. But even at its highest, it falls far short of that enforced in the British House of Commons.

Nevertheless, in matters relating to the organization of the work of Congress, the party system is the dominating factor. The majority and minority floor leaders in consultation together arrange the allotment of time and of speakers in debate. The party caucuses select the all important standing committees. In the House of Representatives, the majority party selects the Speaker who in turn exercises a pervasive control over the proceedings of the House. In both chambers, the chairmen of committees are always of the majority party.

Parties and the Legislature in Canada

Candidates for the Canadian House of Commons are generally chosen by party nominating conventions in each constituency, the convention usually being composed of prominent local supporters of the party elected as delegates for the purpose. As in Britain, there is no requirement that candidates must be resident in the constituency they hope to represent. But local feeling is very strong in Canada and most candidates for election are "home-town boys." While the candidate wants to associate himself firmly with his party and its programme, he also wants to appear as a champion for local interests. So does his opponent, and in many Canadian constituencies elections are fought, not on the record and platforms of the rival parties, but on some local issue. Because of the strength of localism, the central national organizations and leaders of the parties have less influence on the choice of candidates than in Britain. It would be wrong, however, to think that they are as powerless in this respect as the national party organizations in the United States. National party leadership can make its pressure felt in the choice of party candidates in Canada, but it has to be more cautious and judicious in applying that pressure than in Britain.

The result is that almost all those who become members of

Parliament in Canada have some minimum of acceptability to the leaders of the party to which they belong. Consequently, they are considerably more amenable to party discipline than are members of the United States Congress who are primarily the spokesmen of local and sectional interests. Voting almost invariably follows party lines in the Canadian House of Commons. While members of Parliament may on occasion vote against their party on a minor issue, it is now unknown for party lines to break seriously on major issues. On the surface, at least, the machinery of party control, caucuses and whips, seem to work as effectively as in Britain. The difference is that in order for the parties to get steady support in this way in Canada, the party programme must show considerably more tenderness to local and sectional feeling than is necessary in Britain. The platforms of Canadian parties have more generalities and fewer firm commitments than their British counterparts.

However, once the party lines are marked out, there are strong sanctions available for enforcing party discipline. Failure to support the party line on major issues will be punished by withdrawing the assistance of the central party organization in the next election. Indeed, the party leaders are likely to go further and apply pressure to prevent the renomination of the dissenter at the next election. While they have not the acknowledged right of veto of candidatures under the party label, they nevertheless can persuade strongly.

Apart altogether from the effectiveness of party discipline on the voting habits of members of Parliament, the party system dominates the organization and procedure of the Canadian House of Commons in much the same way as we have already noted for the British House of Commons and the United States Congress. None of these legislatures can be understood without keeping constantly in mind the role played by political parties.

The Legislature when Party Lines are Drawn

The role played by political parties is the cause of much of the public impatience with legislatures. If and when party lines are really drawn, as they almost always are in Britain and Canada, the legislature is not the active centre of decision where great speeches sway opinion and make history. When the party leaders speak, they speak to the country as a whole, or at any rate to groups outside

THE LEGISLATURE 197

the legislature. Many members do not speak at all; most of them speak but little and then mostly to their constituencies. Their vital function when party lines are drawn is to vote in accordance with party considerations. This is a very large part of the explanation of the empty seats (except when the party whips descry an approaching division or roll-call), the seeming triviality of debate, the scant attention, the almost discourteous lack of attention, to what is being said.

Parties are arrayed against each other in competition for power, for the sweets of office, as well as for the power to carry out the programme wanted by the interests in the electorate that support them. The psychological atmosphere thus generated is one of struggle, and when the parties are fully deployed in the legislature they tend to contest every inch of ground, whether or not truth and the public interest are at stake. In these clashes, personal feuds and rivalries tend at times to overshadow issues of principle as the inspiration for debate. As long as parties continue to play their present role, legislative proceedings will be deeply affected by them. Yet many people expect legislatures to behave as if political parties did not exist.

The overshadowing significance of parties, where it exists, must not be taken to mean that the legislature is no more than a Punch and Judy show where the puppets move through the unseen manipulations of parties. We should be in bad case indeed if laws were made and announced by a secret junta like a party caucus without possibility of appeal. Many men will acquiesce in private in decisions they would not defend in debate. When they know that they must justify their proposals in what is, despite all detraction, the greatest forum in the country, before an opposition that will pounce on the slightest offence to the public sense of decency, a restraining influence of immense weight comes into play. One great service of the opposition lies not in its spoken criticisms, but in the mere fact of being there.

As well, there are always two or more sides to a story, and the majority party has not heard all of the other side until the opposition has had its say. Concession to the arguments of the opposition follows oftener than is generally believed. The public, despite its disillusionment, gets from the dramatic clash of parliamentary debate a grasp of the great issues of public policy which it cannot get in any other way until much larger resources are thrown into political education. Finally, the new laws made each year are only a tiny fraction of the old ones which are being administered day by day. Oppressive, wasteful, or neglectful administration will be a black mark against the party that presently controls the executive power if its behaviour can be given wide publicity. Questions in the House of Commons in Britain and Canada and investigations by the United States Congress expose such matters to the public gaze and the executive proceeds warily. Here again, it is not the actual gleanings of legislative surveillance which are of supreme importance but the ever-present threat of investigation.

The discussion of many matters relevant to a well-rounded account of the place of the legislature in modern government must be postponed to later chapters. Here we are primarily concerned with the legislature as a distinct organ of government, and the main emphasis will be on internal organization and procedure and on the role of parties in it. The emphasis will be highly selective and partial. The internal workings of each of the legislative bodies under review is a study in itself, and only the briefest sketch designed to bring certain important features into relief can be offered.

Legislative Committees

The growing torrent of legislation that must be enacted to meet the demands of the positive state puts increasing pressure on legislatures. Even though party organization formulates almost all of the new legislation (except in the United States) and guides it to the statute book, these measures must be explained to the legislature and enacted by it, and time must also be found for debating general policy and examining the trend of administration of the manifold activities of government. It is not only a question of time but also of the sheer size of the legislature. Aside from the United States Senate, the Canadian House of Commons is the smallest active assembly with 265 members. The British House of Commons has over six hundred members. Each of them is too large for effective deliberation. Consequently there is increasing reliance on committees to divide the labour and thus to provide for more effective discussion.

Committees in Congress

In each of the chambers of the United States Congress, a well-developed system of committees antedates the rush of legislation, which has been rising for seventy-five years. This elaborate organization into committees was rendered necessary by the absence there of a general executive committee like the cabinet in Britain and Canada. Many standing committees were formed, each to carry some part of this function of examining proposals for legislation and deciding which of them should be recommended to the chambers. As the mass of legislative work mounted, these committees came to dominate Congress in somewhat the same fashion as that in which the British cabinet dominates the House of Commons. The standing committees are appointed after each congressional election for a period of two years. In each chamber, there is a standing committee for each of the important recurring subjects of legislation. The number of standing committees has varied from time to time. The Legislative Reorganization Act of 1946 provided for a sharp reduction in the number of standing committees, from forty-eight to nineteen in the House of Representatives and from thirty-three to fifteen in the Senate.

Each party is entitled to membership on each committee proportionate to its strength in the chambers. When the time comes to appoint committees, the members of each party in each chamber meet in party caucus and select a committee on committees. Each committee on committees then nominates members of its party to fill the quota to which the party is entitled on the standing committees of the chamber. These nominations are ratified almost as a matter of course, first by the appropriate party caucuses and then by the appropriate chamber as a whole.

As we shall see later, the standing committees of Congress substantially make the laws. Thus those who effectively choose the standing committees have a great influence on what laws are made. The committees on committees are composed in each case of a small group of party leaders or their nominees. This gives some indication of the extent to which the party system, if not the majority party, can control Congress. In fact, the majority party can control the decisions of the standing committees when it chooses. In addition, chairmanship of each standing committee goes almost automatically to the member of the majority party in the chamber who has had the longest continuous service on the committee. A skilful chairman who has had a long experience on a committee and has accumulated a wide knowledge of the range of matters with which the committee deals can exercise a powerful influence on its deliberations.

All bills and proposals for legislation go automatically to the standing committees before being considered by the House as a whole. To aid them in reaching the recommendations they will make to the House, the committees hold hearings, public or private, where civil servants, disinterested experts, and lobbyists representing the interests concerned are heard pro and con on the subject. Enormous numbers of proposals for legislation are quietly smothered in committee. Only about ten per cent of those referred to committee ever emerge therefrom. Those not killed in committee are often subjected to major operations re-making them in such a way that their sponsors would hardly know them. Of course, the majority party can control the committee and compel it to report to Congress bills which the party is backing, or that the President, provided he is of the same party, urgently wants to go forward. Use of this so-called "discharge rule" is, however, extremely rare.

The vital work of the United States Congress is done in the standing committees. Once the public hearings are over and representatives of protesting groups have been heard, each committee usually meets in "executive session" where, discussions being private, speeches are to the point and not to the constituencies. The form in which the bill is finally reported out is generally satisfactory to the majority party, and Congress rarely makes significant changes in any bill that is positively recommended by the standing committees. In other words, the committees are performing some of the functions of the British cabinet, although there is much less often a party line to which to hew.

In this way, the labour of the legislature is divided and a bigger harvest of legislation is produced. However, it must be said that in so far as the effective decisions are taken by small committees ranging in number from nine to fifty members, the representative character of deliberation on law making is greatly impaired. Attempts are made to distribute membership of committees geographically, but that does little to repair the damage to the representative principle. Also, the system suffers from the nemesis that pursues all divisions of labour—the difficulty of combining the separate specialized efforts into a harmonious whole. The practice of dividing the standing committees into many sub-committees —they now number over 150—only accentuates this difficulty. Very effective work is done on specific pieces of legislation but not always with sufficient recognition of their relation to general policy. The cabinet system, by concentrating responsibility for the formulation of all aspects of policy on a single body, keeps the necessity for integrating the legislative programme in the foreground, and the House of Commons in Britain and Canada therefore is marked, as Congress is not, for debates of high quality on the general policy of the government.

The Legislative Reorganization Act of 1946, as previously noted, substantially reduced the number of standing committees in both Houses. The legislative work of Congress has been divided among these committees in such a way that each committee in each chamber has a well-defined area of jurisdiction corresponding closely to the field of operations of particular departments and agencies of the executive. The Act also authorized the appointment of staffs of experts to assist these committees in their work. These, and other provisions of the Act to be referred to later, are improving the effectiveness of the detailed work of the standing committees in particular fields of public policy. They are not likely to improve greatly the quality of the attention Congress gives to general policy.

In addition to standing committees, select committees are appointed to inquire into special issues of concern as they are thought to require it. Also, the fact that the two chambers are equal in power often brings them to deadlock on some piece of legislation. Since both must accept a proposal before it can become law, some compromise acceptable to both has to be found. The usual device is a conference committee consisting of members of both chambers who search—sometimes long—for a solution.

Finally, no account of committees in the United States Congress would be complete without reference to the rules committees, particularly the Rules Committee of the House of Representatives. This small committee of twelve persons controlled by, though not wholly representative of, the majority party, determines, in effect, when the formal rules of the House are to be departed from for the time being, what priorities are to be observed in the agenda and the time limits on debate. It is a most important agency of majority party control and its chairman wields authority second only to that of the Speaker.

Committees in the British House of Commons

The British House of Commons, always averse to standing committees on the ground that in practical effect they make inroads on the supremacy of a representative Parliament, managed to avoid any substantial development in this direction until the beginning of the twentieth century. It was able to do so for two reasons. First, the cabinet is largely a committee of the House for framing and guiding legislation. Second, the practice of resolving the whole House into committee for various purposes gave some of the advantages of committee procedure.

Committee of the whole, as it is called, is formed by the Speaker's leaving the chair and giving over his duties to a less exalted chairman of committees. Party reins are slackened and the rules of debate are relaxed. For example, members may speak more than once to the point under discussion and the majority cannot summarily saw off debate by moving that the previous question now be put. All financial proposals, and other bills of unusual importance, still go to committee of the whole.

The pressure of work, however, has necessitated supplementation of the committee of the whole. After some exploratory use of standing committees, they came into general use in 1907. Varying in number from two to six, ordinarily now there are four. Aside from one that specializes in Scottish affairs, these are general-purpose committees, taking whatever assignments are given them by the Speaker on the advice of the committee of selection. To provide for expert assistance and specialist interest, the committee of selection may add members temporarily for the purpose of considering a particular bill.

The committee of selection is nominated by the party leaders and confirmed by the House at the beginning of each session. The committee, in turn, nominates the standing committees, taking counsel with the party whips. The chairmen are not necessarily of the majority party, and while the party whips are not brandished in committee, party persuasion is still within call.

Normally, all public bills (including private members' bills but not private bills, of which more will be said later) that are not financial bills are referred to the standing committees after second reading in the House of Commons. However, the second reading approves the general principle of the bill, narrowing the scope of discussion in committee to details, many of which are of a technical character. Often the decision on these matters of detail will turn on questions of fact or scientific judgment.

The discussion in committee must be restricted to these details. For example, if the bill in question is one to establish a code of safety and sanitary measures in industrial establishments, the committee cannot debate the issue whether the law should interfere with the way in which industrial employers run their factories, for that question has already been answered in the affirmative on the second reading. The committee must settle down to deciding what particular sanitary and safety measures are necessary to preserve health and prevent accidents.

So there is not so much room for division on party lines, and there is not much temptation to make speeches to the country at large in a committee whose proceedings get very little publicity. Members even of the majority party supporting the government may press for modifications, and within limits the government will concede them if the argument in committee is cogent or if the debate on second reading has indicated a strong case for some adjustment. But the leaders of the majority party are far from giving the committee its head, and they can apply closure to speed it towards its report. Unlike the practice in the United States, the committees do not provide hearings for the private interests concerned. However, while the bill is in committee, the private interests may press their views strongly on the cabinet.

The British committees lack the power and prestige of their American counterparts. They cannot smother bills and they cannot make major amendments that cut into the principle of the bill, e.g. they cannot eliminate from the factory bill all requirements for sanitary precautions. On the whole, membership in them is not sought but evaded. Being general-purpose committees, they make no appeal to members with specialized knowledge or interest, and members who go on a committee for the narrow purpose of a single piece of legislation will often ask to be relieved once it has been reported to the House.

The House of Commons is jealous of the committees. Yet it could not do its work without delegating this discussion of detail, and its only alternative is to extend still further the growing practice of limiting legislation to a statement of general principle and delegating the power to fill in the details to government departments. The significance of this practice will be taken up later and it will suffice here to say that it too is irksome to the House. So the trend towards greater reliance on committees continues.

It is often urged that specialized standing committees should be set up to attract the sustained effort of members according to their interest. To each such committee would be assigned the scrutiny of one of the great government departments. It would consider the legislative proposals and the annual estimates of that department and make a close study of its administrative operations. In this way, Parliament would move towards a better understanding and a more effective control of the complexities of government.

The experience of some of the democratic governments of continental Europe (which cannot be considered here) and the dominant position of committees in Congress in the United States clearly indicate that such committees would compete with the cabinet for primacy, and it is likely that the party leaders, in order to preserve intact their instrument of unified action, would have to make the practical scope of such committees much narrower than is suggested. There is also the question already noticed, whether concentration on specialized competence in these committees would not detract from the quality of discussion the House of Commons now provides on general policy. These considerations have apparently been less relevant so far as financial control is concerned for, as a later chapter will show, special committees on public accounts and estimates have long been used by parliament.

A word must be said about the treatment of private bills. A private bill is a proposal to make a special law or dispensation for a particular person or group or for a particular locality. Thus, when divorces were granted by Parliament instead of by the courts, the procedure was by private bill relieving particular husbands and wives from the requirement of the general law that matrimony is a fight to the finish.

In Britain, most private bills originate in the application by municipalities or public utility companies for additional powers to clear a slum, to construct new tramways, to borrow money for some unusual capital expenditure, or to extend their facilities. Private bills after two readings in the House go to a private bills committee of the House. These committees do give hearings at which all the parties interested in the subject matter are heard with the assistance of very expensive parliamentary counsel. They are small and disinterested committees, rarely being influenced by party considerations. But this procedure is cumbrous and expensive and it is being replaced by another technique for reaching the same result—one that aggrandizes the executive at the expense of Parliament by authorizing the Minister of Health, for example, to decide whether particular municipalities shall have power to clear slums and on what terms.

Frequent use is also made in Britain of select committees of the House to inquire into particular subjects of great importance, or to give special consideration to particular bills that propose drastic change. Their function is inquiry into complex issues rather than the discussion of legislative detail. Accordingly, they are always small committees of fifteen members or less, chosen for their knowledge of or interest in the particular subject matter. They hold hearings at which interested parties appear and give evidence. When expressly authorized by the House they may compel the attendance of witnesses and require the production of documents. Detailed records of their proceedings are kept and printed along with their formal reports. In short, their function is similar to that of a royal commission of inquiry although performed in a less pretentious manner.

Committees in the Canadian House of Commons

The committee system in the Canadian House of Commons has responded to both British and American influences but has developed distinctive features of its own. As in Britain, money bills go to committee of the whole, being introduced there in the form of financial resolutions. Select committees are used more extensively than in Britain. Seventeen standing committees (three of which are joint committees with the Senate) are set up in each session, each to deal with one of the recurring topics of discussion or legislation. A special committee of the House composed of the leaders of the political parties prepares a list of the members to be assigned to each of the committees and their choice is confirmed by the House. The standing committees, composed of from twelve to sixty members, reflect the relative standing of the different parties in the House and, as in the United States, the chairmen—with the notable exception in 1958 of the Public Accounts Committee— always of the majority party. A minister may be selected as chairman, although the practice is now less common than it used to be.

When bills are referred to them, the standing committees may call witnesses and hear representations from interested parties—a copying of American practice. Their membership is usually thirty or more and their proceedings are discursive. Despite the fact that the chairman and a majority of the committee belong to the party supporting the cabinet, discussion and voting have often been markedly non-partisan. Although they have no power to smother bills, committees have at times failed to report to the House before the end of a session, thus postponing action. Ministers who wish to hasten the progress of bills through committee cannot always arrange for a summary closing of discussion, and they sometimes find a committee proposing amendments they are reluctant to accept. Standing committees have exhibited greater independence of partisan control and cabinet suggestion in Canada than in Britain. Whether for these or other reasons, many standing committees of the Canadian House of Commons are inactive or little used. As will be explained later, this difference arises from a difference in the nature of the political parties in the two countries. However, it must be added that there is evidence in recent years of stronger party control being exercised over the proceedings of committees.

After second reading in the House, most bills are referred to select committees set up to study them, or to committee of the whole. Reference of bills to committee of the whole does not relieve the House of its burdens in any way. However, the Canadian House of Commons has not in the past been nearly as hard pressed as the

British House of Commons. Moreover, frequent use of committee of the whole is a recognition of the sectional diversities of the country. It enables the representatives of every part of the country to press their points of view at committee stage of the bill.

RULES OF PROCEDURE IN THE LEGISLATURE

A glance at the rules of procedure in legislative assemblies should now enable us to sketch the process of law making in the legislature. Every deliberative body needs rules of procedure to expedite business and also to protect the right of speech and protest from abridgement or abuse. Rules against the abuse of the right of speech are particularly required to maintain the equable temper of discussion without which deliberation cannot be carried on at all.

In the long course of its development, the British House of Commons built up an impressive body of customary rules of procedure. These remain the basis of its procedure at the present day, but they have been extensively supplemented by deliberately adopted written rules, known as standing orders, covering the order of business, the time to be allotted to various kinds of business, the stages of debate on measures, and other matters. By majority vote, the House may suspend or repeal any rule of procedure as it sees fit. Thus the majority party controls the procedure of the House. Standing orders give government business about nine-tenths of the time of the House, and a session rarely goes by without the cabinet's having to encroach still further on the limited time left for private members' business.

By the adoption in standing orders of the various forms of closure early in this century, the cabinet can use its supporting majority to close discussion at once or at a definite future hour, and to select which of a number of proposed amendments to a bill shall be discussed and which rejected without discussion. Closure is a drastic power but, as a result of the demand for more and more legislation and government action, the hard choice is between more talk and less completed business, or more business disposed of and less talk. One may sympathize generally with the latter alternative, but it must not be forgotten that the real function of Parliament is to talk reluctant people into consent to measures they dislike.

Closure is a necessary instrument under present circumstances, but if it is not used sparingly and with wisdom it will strangle a deliberative assembly.

The colonial legislative assemblies of North America followed the British rules of procedure of the time, and Congress has been deeply influenced by them. Thomas Jefferson, when Vice-President, drew up for the Senate a famous *Manual of Parliamentary Practice* based on the British model. The House of Representatives adopted this manual in 1837. It is still the core of congressional procedure although now surrounded by many modifications and additions. Both the House of Representatives and the Senate can change their rules by majority vote. The two committees on rules, dominated by the majority party, propose changes which the chambers accept. The House of Representatives has rules corresponding to the British closure provisions, and they are used not only to limit but at times to strangle debate.

For long, the Senate made no provision in its rules for restricting freedom of debate and recognized the right of minorities to continue talking indefinitely in protest against majority measures. On occasion, senators have turned in prodigious performances, speaking many hours at a stretch, supplementing ideas and arguments with the poets and, working in relays, keeping the house in continuous session around the clock. These filibusters, as they are called, sometimes accomplish their purpose of wearing out the majority and defeat the legislation, but they have not been so common in recent years. The reasons, in part, are that in 1917 the Senate adopted a rule for enforcing a mild form of closure, and that in 1933 the short session of Congress with a fixed date for its termination was abolished. As none of the sessions now end on a fixed date, it is harder for senators to talk until the sands run out. Closure has been used in the Senate only four times and, since the latest revision in 1949 which requires the affirmative vote of sixty-four senators, it has never been used. Whatever the influence of the threat of closure may be, actual enforcement of it has had no significant influence on debate in the Senate, and filibusters still take place. Of course, the relatively small membership of the Senate reduces somewhat the necessity for restrictive measures and debate is often held within limits by unanimous agreement that a vote shall be taken at a definite future time.

In Britain, the cabinet containing the leaders of the majority party takes the leadership in expediting business within the framework of the rules. It has a programme prepared at the opening of every session. It takes up most of the time of the House and sees to it that the important items on its programme are dealt with and brought to some conclusion. In the United States, the executive does not lead in Congress, and its place is taken by the floor leaders and steering committees of the majority party.

In fact, in each chamber, each party has a small steering committee. Naturally, the steering committee of the majority party is the significant one, as the pushing of party measures, the allotting of time, and changes in the order of business generally originate there. The chairman of the committee is usually floor leader for his party, and is aided by the whips who herd the members of their party into the chamber for roll-calls. If some members of the party are wavering on an issue that seems to call for party solidarity, the caucus meets and tries to work to a position that all will be willing to support.

Procedure in the Canadian House of Commons is modelled on the procedure of the British House of Commons. There are, however, significant variations in the rules, and also in the way in which the same rule is applied. Broadly speaking, the majority party does not keep as tight a rein on the House as in Britain. Debate is more prolix and loquacious. A form of closure was introduced in 1913, but it has since been used only six times. The cabinet, until 1955, did not insist on the House working to a timetable. As a result, the Canadian House of Commons in World War II found itself unable to give anything like adequate attention to the conduct of the war. Even in times of peace, the end of a session almost always finds the House rushing through important business without giving it the careful consideration it deserves.

It is widely held that the cabinet in consultation with the leaders of the parties in the House of Commons should take the responsibility of rationing debate. In 1955, the House approved a modest version of the British rules for curtailing discussion. Six Mondays were allotted to private members, twelve days for debating supply motions, ten for the debate on the Address in reply to the Speech from the Throne, and eight for the Budget debate. These changes reveal that the Canadian cabinet is now confronting pressures on its timetable similar to those with which the British had to contend earlier. However, as we shall see, party discipline will not bear as much strain in Canada as in Britain, and there will probably have to be a much more extreme congestion of business in the House before the Canadian cabinet could enforce as rigid a timetable as has been possible in Britain.

It is evident then that the majority party everywhere has procedure within its control and can enforce its will by drastic methods. However, drastic action is not often openly resorted to, although the threat of it is always there. Both parties know that they are participants in a system of deliberation that will not work without give and take. The minority expects soon to be a majority, when it will want the decks cleared for action on its programme. The majority will generally make some concession to a determined opposition pressing arguments that seem likely to appeal to a wide section of the public as sensible and just. So changes in the order of business and limitations on the time of debate are often by arrangement between the leaders of the parties. It is only when some contentious issue provides a reason for releasing deep conflicting passions—as in the Canadian pipeline controversy—or when an impatient new party appears in the legislature that obstruction and disorder, and the consequent bludgeoning by the majority, make their appearance.

Formal Steps in Law Making

The process of law making will now be outlined. In Britain, government bills, almost the entire grist of public bills, are drafted by the executive. The department whose special concern a bill is consults with the other departments affected, civil servants contribute their experience and work out specifications of the technical means required to reach the desired end. When a completed draft of what is wanted has been approved by the cabinet, it goes to the parliamentary counsel to the Treasury, a drafting expert who fits the bill with legal clothing or, more precisely, drafts a bill that will accomplish legally the desired results.

First reading in the House of Commons follows. It is generally reading by title only and never more than notice of motion to bring the bill forward for discussion at a later date. On second reading, the principle of the bill, the general question whether such legislation as this is necessary or desirable, is discussed. While it is not unknown for the government to withdraw a bill after an onslaught on it at second reading, it is extremely rare. After all, the government claims a mandate from the people to pursue its policy, and its bills are the central part of that policy. The bill is passed on second reading and is referred to a standing committee.

As already explained, the committee considers the bill in detail clause by clause, making amendments at its own, but mainly at the government's behest. When this overhauling is completed, the bill is reported back to the House. At report stage, as it is called, the House considers the bill in detail. But if the time saved in committee is not to be wasted at the report stage, this consideration must be limited and fewer amendments are moved at report stage than in committee. As soon as report stage is finished, the third reading may be moved. At this final stage, only verbal amendments may be introduced, so that the debate on the third reading tends to rehearse the debate on the second reading. Despite the reservations of the House about standing committees, the really thorough consideration of the bill in detail is given in committee. After passage by the House of Commons, the bill goes to the House of Lords. It may be added that private members draft their own bills, but this is of little import as such bills have almost no chance of becoming law.

The formal steps in law making are much the same in the Canadian as in the British House of Commons. Significant differences to be noted are that a high proportion of bills go to committee of the whole rather than to a standing committee, and that even when a bill goes to a standing committee it is next referred to committee of the whole before coming to the report stage.

In the United States, bills considered desirable by the President may be drafted in the government departments and introduced into one or other chamber of the legislature by a member of Congress who is of the President's political party. A high proportion of the important measures put before Congress are now initiated in this manner. Congress, however, considers many measures that are not inspired or even favoured by the executive. Any member may introduce a bill, and the committees often have proposals before them that they wish to put in the form of a bill looking toward legislation. For long, Congress had to find its resources of draftsmanship where it could, but some years ago provision was made for the appointment of legislative counsel as officers of Congress to draft bills for its committees and members. In addition, the Legislative Reference Service of the Library of Congress provides congressmen with research assistance. Special interests wanting legislation on their behalf often draft their own bills and have them presented to Congress. This extensive private enterprise by individual members of Congress and outside groups in introducing bills explains why such heavy slaughter of bills occurs in committees.

All bills introduced are given first reading by title only and are immediately referred to the appropriate committee. In the Senate, first and second readings, both quite perfunctory, are commonly given at the same time before the bill goes to committee. The real deliberative effort, it will be recalled, takes place in committee. The House of Representatives, when a bill is reported to it favourably by committee, generally contents itself with acceptance, rejection, or minor amendment on second reading with little debate. If serious debate and amendment are desired and are acceptable to the steering committee of the majority, the House resolves itself into committee of the whole for the purpose. Third reading immediately precedes final passage and occurs without debate.

In the more individualistic Senate with fewer members and less restrictive rules of procedure, bills favourably reported by committee are likely to get closer examination and more discussion. Amendments are freely offered and debated; whether they have a chance of acceptance depends on whether the measure is one respecting which party lines are drawn. Third reading immediately precedes the final vote on the bill.

In a constitutional regime, all taxation must be approved by legislation, and no expenditure of public money can be made without authorization of the legislature. Taxing and appropriation measures are legislation of vital importance, subject to some special rules. As the course of financial legislation brings out most clearly the working relationship of the executive and the legislature, discussion of it will be postponed to a chapter devoted to those relationships. For the same reason, discussion of legislative surveillance of administration might be postponed, as some attention will have to be given to it there in any case. On the other hand, a description here of the mechanisms used and the time available for inquiring into administration will help to round out discussion of the legislature and to clear the ground for undivided attention to the essence of legislative-executive relationships.

CONTROL OF ADMINISTRATION BY THE LEGISLATURE

In Britain and Canada, the executive is in the legislature and responsible to it. A vote of censure of its administrative performance may cause the downfall of the cabinet just as well as rejection of a government bill. In practice, a motion of censure is rarely successful, because the government can generally rely on its majority to preserve it from such disasters and its demands on the time of the House do not leave much time for the debating of administration. Despite the enormous range of the present-day activities of government, the time available for discussing administration in the normal, annual session of Parliament is estimated at less than thirty days in Britain and not much longer in Canada.

A more effective means of criticizing the administration is the right to ask questions of the executive. In Britain, a period is set aside each day for questions addressed by a member to a minister. The rules of the Canadian House of Commons do not provide for a daily question period, but a substantial amount of time is made available for questions. In Canada, the questions almost invariably seek information, often in such great detail that it can be adequately given only in writing. Apparently the view is that if enough data are elicited they will reveal something about the distribution of jobs or awarding of contracts that will be embarrassing to the government.

In Britain, the questioner may be seeking sheer information, but more often he picks on some incident of administration, perhaps the grievance of one of his constituents against a minor government official, or on some unwary remark of a member of the government in the House or elsewhere, in the hope of forcing the minister into a damaging statement about the policy of the department he is administering. He wants an oral reply and he needs the right to ask supplementary questions of a minister who makes an evasive reply. The question hour is a battle of wits, the minister trying to score off the hecklers and they trying to skewer the minister with a question that cannot be answered without putting him and his department in a bad light. It is an important technique of opposition. Ministers always fear that if there is a chink in their armour, questions on successive days will probe for it until it is found. Civil servants (whom the minister protects loyally in the House but whom he excoriates afterwards for their mistakes) are extremely wary in what they do. Where thousands of civil servants are dealing daily with hundreds of thousands of citizens, it is important to have a forum where grievances against their conduct can be aired and misdeeds corrected.

The House of Commons would be swamped with questions if each member were not strictly limited in the number to which he can demand oral answers. Only a fraction of the opportunities for grilling the executive for its administrative actions can be followed up. And, of course, many of the best opportunities are missed even in Britain because most members of Parliament are not at all conversant with the details of administration. For that matter, the minister himself does not know too much about them, but he is coached by civil servants who know vastly more about these details than anyone else. The actual contest is on unequal terms. The real control is the knowledge that gross maladministration will sooner or later be exposed on the floor of the House and thus broadcast to the public.

Members of Congress in the United States cannot question the executive on the floor of the legislative chambers, but they do debate administrative action and vote critical resolutions making specific recommendations. They go further at times and enact detailed laws directing the minutiae of administration. In recent years, the congressional committees, particularly the appropriations committees, have developed a practice of attaching to their reports to Congress a variety of instructions and limitations meant to control very closely the expenditure of some portions of the money appropriated. Most important, Congress appoints from time to time committees of investigation to explore the conduct of some branch of the executive. These committees ask, and often get, from the executive access to books, papers, and documents, although they cannot compel the President to give it to them.

They require government officials as well as private citizens to appear and testify before them.

Newspapers and television give almost hysterical publicity to these investigations, thus unfortunately turning them into witch-hunts or sensational trials of particular individuals rather than sober investigations into public administration. They are sporadic rather than continuous, and often they are not launched until after the horse has been stolen. Nevertheless, Senate investigations particularly are educators of public opinion, and the executive has a well-founded fear of the probings of the Senate. They are perhaps as effective as the separation of powers permits them to be. At any rate, they confirm the anticipation of the framers of the Constitution in that they fan the latent hostility between the legislature and the executive.

The Legislative Reorganization Act of 1946, which, as already noted, provided for expert staffs to assist the standing committees, also authorized the standing committees to maintain continuous oversight of administration in the field of public policy assigned to each committee. Thus the committees of the two chambers, which originally studied and reported a particular legislative proposal, are now charged with sustained scrutiny of administration of that legislation. With the aid of expert staffs, the committees are in a position to give closer and steadier attention to the conduct of administration, if they do not indeed try to exercise detailed supervision of it. This will make for closer contact between the legislative and executive, but not perhaps for more harmonious relationships.

WHAT IS WRONG WITH THE LEGISLATURE

Present-day democratic legislatures are ridiculously over-worked. Despite the increasing length of sessions, the legislatures cannot give careful consideration to many of the laws they enact, and they can find only a limited time in each session to examine the vast administrative machine of the government. Moreover, they could not accomplish what they do if they were not guided and controlled by a relatively small group of men, the leaders of the political parties. Important decisions have to be delegated to committees which are not really representative, and debate has to be curtailed.

It is scarcely true nowadays to say, in more than a formal sense, that legislatures make the law.

Yet legislatures are vitally necessary as censors of the parties and of administration. There is great need to improve the quality of their work. No doubt their procedure, which is still redolent of more leisurely bygone days, could, and must, be improved. But if the demands of the positive state are to continue to mount, it cannot be emphasized too strongly that the greatest need is to improve the legislators' knowledge of the complexities with which they are asked to deal. The average member does not stand very far above the general standard of the good citizen, often called the man in the street. This is the kind of censor of government that a democracy wants, not a talking encyclopaedia so devoted to the accumulation of information that he loses the common touch. Unfortunately, it would require a superman without any other distractions to understand what is involved in the present-day range of legislation and administration. And if the legislature does not understand what the government is doing, constitutionalism can only have a precarious existence.

If the legislature is once more to have a reasonably clear understanding of what the government is doing, its members will have to be provided with expert assistance. The appointment of expert staffs to aid the standing committees of Congress in the United States is a recognition of this need. In Britain and Canada, it would probably be a mistake to build up permanent expert staffs to serve committees of the House of Commons because of the danger already noted, that these committees would then be led to challenge the primacy of the cabinet. The political parties themselves have undoubtedly chosen the better alternative of developing expert staffs for the service of their own members in the House of Commons, thus enabling them to get a better grasp of the nature of the tasks facing the legislature. The parties in Britain have made much greater advances, in this respect, than Canadian parties.

It is often complained that the quality of legislators has declined, that today none can compare with the gigantic figures of the statesmen of the past. Close observers who have tried to measure the eminence of the legislators of earlier days are almost unanimous in denying the decline. If the quality of deliberation and legislative action has dropped, the clue is to be found, not in the quality of the legislators but in the extraordinary expectations of what it should be possible to accomplish by legislation. When the accomplishments fall short of the expectations, as they often do, the tendency is to blame the legislators. Rarely is sufficient allowance made for the inherent difficulty of what they are expected to do.

CHAPTER VIII

POLITICAL PARTIES

THE way in which political parties have inserted themselves between the electorate and the legislature has been pointed out. Some indication of their influence over legislative proceedings and decisions has been given. Even if there were no other evidence of their central importance, we already have enough to show that a study of liberal democratic government that ignores them would be quite unreal. There is, however, other evidence. The growing democratization of government in the nineteenth century was everywhere accompanied by the rapid development and intensive organization of nation-wide political parties. Wherever democratic government has flourished, two or more political parties have been active participants in government. Invariably, the first step of dictators in destroying democratic government has been to forbid all political parties but one. There is ample reason for suspecting that political parties are somehow essential to the working of democratic government.

It is, however, far too important a matter to be left in the realm of reasonable conjecture, particularly because many people of genuinely democratic instinct are deeply hostile to the party system and are convinced that most of the troubles of democratic countries are caused by the spirit of faction which competing parties foster and promote. An attempt must be made to lay bare the connection between liberal democratic government and political parties. This requires some fairly abstract analysis based on certain assumptions about the prevailing condition of the electorate. It does not require at this stage any further description of the organization and general behaviour of political parties. Such description will be much more meaningful once the essential functions of parties are made clear.

The analysis will assume the existence of two parties only, partly for the sake of simplicity and partly because the most effective democratic governments have, until very recently, had two-party systems. The multiplicity of parties has a weakening effect on the democracies of continental Europe and it is not at all clear that democratic government will work permanently where there are numerous parties of roughly equal strength. The reasons for this doubt will emerge later.

THE FUNCTIONS OF PARTIES IN A DEMOCRACY

The basic fact for this analysis is adult suffrage. There are, it is true, minor restrictions on the suffrage, varying from country to country. In the United States, where the minimum qualifications for voting are fixed by state laws, the restrictions vary from state to state. In some states, a significant number of adults are effectively excluded from voting. Yet in the three countries generally, almost every adult citizen has a vote to add to the total from which the will of the people for some common action has to emerge. Unfortunately, the people are far from finding spontaneous agreement, or even spontaneous majorities, on what ought to be done. The important basic assumption made here about the prevailing condition of the electorate is that, given the freedom of thought, expression, and association which has marked the liberal democracies, individuals and groups produce a great variety of opinions on political as well as other matters.

It has already been argued in chapter II that even where there is widespread agreement on fundamental ideals, there seems inevitably to be a wide range of disagreement on the means of furthering the ideals. Extensions and improvements of education may well diminish this disagreement but are not likely to abolish it.

If ten men are asked what should be done to save the country, there will be several opinions: soften the banks, abolish trade unions, forbid the sale of goods on credit, teach religion in the schools. Even when patterns of partial agreement are found, such as the socializing of the means of production and distribution, a little further inquiry reveals a multitude of counsel about the pace of advance towards, and the means for reaching, the desired end. Socialists, practising utter self-abnegation, have yet quarreled bitterly for two generations and broken into a dozen camps over the question of means. The electorate, even after years of education by political parties, is still a mass of various opinions looking for salvation in different directions. The essential function of two competing parties is to draw the electorate together into majorities so that men can be governed by their own consent. The great merit of government by consent is not that it always makes justice prevail but that it makes naked and arbitrary force unnecessary. As long as men can govern themselves by consent, they can keep government under control and ensure for themselves a large area of individual liberty within which they can struggle for justice and truth as they see it.

Left to themselves, how would the voters in a constituency pick a representative to the legislature and instruct him on what should be done there to further the common interest? At worst each voter would vote for himself and his own panacea. At best there would be numerous candidates, and one of them supported by a small faction that had agreed momentarily to back him would get more votes than any other candidate. Only in the rarest circumstances would any candidate get a majority of all votes or any majority opinion emerge on what should be done to further the public interest. The members of the legislature thus chosen by haphazard and temporary combinations in each constituency across the country would themselves be of various opinions, and their accomplishments in the legislature less constructive and more disillusioning than at present.

The two-party system does to this incoherent electorate what the magnet does to the iron filings—it organizes the voters around two poles, orients them in relation to specific alternative programmes of political action. It selects programmes more or less clearly outlined, it chooses candidates, and given a majority in the legislature one or other party proceeds with its programme. Without the parties, there would be no stable majority in a legislature, and without the support of an enduring majority it would be impossible to maintain steady drive behind a programme for even a month, let alone three or four years. When government performs so many important functions and builds up permanent public expectations, such a situation would be serious indeed.

How do the parties do it? Each sets itself primarily to the task of constructing a majority. Party politicians are not, and cannot be, crusaders, men of single-minded passionate purpose, who drive straight to the realization of their ideals. They are not even generally the inventors of the ideas they expound. In the aptest phrase yet applied to them, they are brokers of ideas.[1] They are middlemen who select from all the ideas pressing for recognition as public policy those they think can be shaped to have the widest appeal and, through their party organization, they try to sell a carefully sifted and edited selection of these ideas (their programme) to enough members of the electorate to produce a majority in the legislature.

It puts the activities of the politician at their lowest to say that he seeks to gain power and a livelihood through traffic in the beliefs and ideas of others. It is well to see things at their starkest. In fact, most politicians have their own conception of the public good which they would like to see carried out. That is impossible without power, and power has been dispersed among a numerous electorate.

It can only be concentrated in a democratic way by massing votes behind leaders and a programme. The party politician, unlike some others, has learned about the facts of life; he knows, as another happy phrase has put it, that votes are not delivered by the stork. Voters have to be attracted and organized. Only when this has been done by nation-wide effort and co-operation of many politicians can any one of them hope to make some of his ideals come true. And then he can never hope to realize more than a fraction of them politically. For to get the co-operation of other politicians whose ideals differ from his, each has to give hostages. Each has to give up some portion of the good he sees, to make room for some of the good that others see.

When the politicians united in a party come to appeal for the votes of a vast electorate, the programme has to set aside much that the politicians personally think desirable in order to accommodate something of the diverse goods held dear by the members of the electorate, and by the organized interest groups within the electorate. In so far as the initial assumption of a radical diversity of

[1]A. Lawrence Lowell, *Public Opinion and Popular Government* (Longmans, Green and Co., New York, 1914), rev. ed., ch. v.

opinion in the electorate stands, it is clear that the wider the appeal, the lower will be the highest common factor on which united action can take place.

Perhaps the simplest illustration of the necessity for such accommodation is to be found in Canadian politics. The people of the Province of Quebec, overwhelmingly French-speaking and Roman Catholic, make up about one-quarter of the population of Canada. Therefore, it is only rarely that a political party can win power without getting substantial support in Quebec. But Quebec opinion on what the national Parliament should be instructed to do for the common good shows marked divergences from the lines of policy for which majorities can be found in the rest of Canada. Accordingly, political parties must modify their programmes to find a compromise that will produce a nation-wide majority. This compromise will be something that neither Quebec nor the rest of the country would plump for if each were going its own way.

It is not the fact of Quebec alone that makes this process necessary, although the French-English diversity provides its most striking illustration. The process is at work in every constituency and in every province across the country. The use of this technique of accommodation is, in varying degree, a skill required of democratic politicians everywhere. Britain, with greater social homogeneity than Canada or the United States, gets on with less watering down of programmes of political action, but is far from avoiding it entirely.

In the United States, the Republican and Democratic parties have both drawn traditional support from different regions and diverse interest groups, and framed their electoral appeals to attract votes from almost all sections and interest groups. The Democratic party has first to compromise within itself to hold together the conservative-minded agricultural and business interests of its Southern wing and the more radically inclined elements of its traditional support in the urban industrial North. Then, to win a majority, it has to woo the predominantly agricultural West whose interests differ markedly from those of both Southern and Northern Democrats. The Republican party has won its greatest successes as an alliance of Northern business interests, industrial workers, and Western farmers.

The political combinations involved are much more complex than this statement indicates, and their patterns have changed from time to time. The main point, however, is that both parties appeal to almost all sections and classes. A notable exception was the Republican party which, when it first took shape in the eighteen-fifties, was entirely a combination of Northern interests. Its first victory in 1860 did not take account of Southern interests and demands. At the same time, the Democratic party failed to maintain its former nation-wide basis of compromise, thereby leading to the Civil War.

Party politicians, therefore, are brokers in another sense. They are always arranging deals between different sections of opinion, finding compromises that "split the difference," and thus concentrating votes behind the programme of their political party. As long as the sovereign electorate is of numerous diverse opinions, this is the only way majorities can be constructed and power gained to push through any political programme in a democracy.

It may be objected that the argument proves too much. If opinion were naturally so diverse, the parties could never herd the bulk of the electorate into one or other of two camps. In fact, this is precisely what the democratic politicians of continental Europe have always been unable to do, and parties always tend to become more instead of less numerous. In Britain and the United States a two-party system was established while the electorate was still small in numbers and politics was, much more than now, a game between the ins and the outs (where there are naturally only two sides). Large sections of the electorate became habituated to allegiance to one or other of the two parties and deeply attached to its leaders and traditions.

Once the two-party system was firmly established, a number of factors discouraged the setting up of additional parties. Everyone has had cause to remark the plausibility of the politicians. Their programmes are devised with generally recognized problems in mind. Their arguments seem convincing to an electorate that knows little about the nature of those problems and has given little attention to the ways of meeting them. Most people find that after earning their daily bread and keeping track of the adventures of their favourite television idols, they have little time for the serious study of politics. Their interest and conviction are not strong enough to make them launch new parties unless there is a pronounced failure of the established parties to meet obvious and urgent problems.

The voter who has not time to study politics has not time to start an organization to promote his views. If his vote is to count at all, he must attach himself to one of the vote-gathering organizations already in the field with some prospect of winning. He is the more disposed to do this, because everyone likes to put his money on the winning team. Third parties are launched from time to time, but unless they rapidly come within striking distance of a majority, their support is likely to fall away. The older parties are deeply entrenched in the community. Their organizations are alert to thwart or undermine the competition of any new political party that emerges. Additional factors that have supported the two-party system in the past will be considered in other contexts.

The first essential function of the party system then is to organize voters into majorities behind platforms and leaders. The voters get alternatives from which to choose, and the electorate can reward the party that appears to be deserving and be sure that both parties will strive to merit reward. This is the only way in which a numerous electorate can exercise effectively the power which democratic theory assigns to it. Also, as earlier discussion shows, the parties by their activity in the legislature contribute to the political education of the electorate. They turn talk into legislation, and legislation into concrete regulation and services through administration.

By concentrating votes for themselves, the political parties concentrate responsibility on themselves. It would be difficult to exaggerate the importance of this. The majority party has power to implement its promises, to meet problems as they arise, and to administer laws wisely and fairly. In so far as it is judged in the sequel to have failed, there is no doubt who is responsible and who is to be punished. The people can bring home responsibility to a determinate group of men.

If there were no parties and a crisis arose that was not appropriately met, everybody would be equally responsible, i.e. nobody would be responsible. If there were only one party, the responsibility would be clear but it could not be brought home because there would be no alternative government. And the chief defect of the multiple-party system is that in the shifting coalitions it involves, responsibility is blurred and the electorate can scarcely determine where it lies. The two-party system does not enable the sovereign electorate to govern the country. It does enable it to participate in the process of government, to choose and rule its masters and to make government responsible. Those who know the history of government among men will not be disposed to belittle this achievement.

The Indictment against Parties

Yet the everyday spectacle of party politics rouses widespread disgust and distaste. To many, politicians are the lowest form of life, and all appreciate Artemus Ward's recommendation of himself, saying, "I am not a politician and all my other habits are good." In part, this disgust results from a failure to understand why the democratic politician does not summarily enforce the opinions of the critic and have done with it. In great measure, however, it is a reaction to certain unsavoury aspects of political life. The indictment against parties must be heard and a verdict considered and given.

The unsavoury features arise mainly from the fact of widespread suffrage, although it must not be inferred from this that politics had a better smell when the franchise was limited to the well-born. It had a different odour, but by no means a better one. In politics, men are always trying to get their hands on the instruments of legalized coercion and on the sweets of office. It is therefore the most ill-clad struggle for power short of open war and is likely to be unmannerly and sometimes unscrupulous. Politics is also the arena where passionately held views of right and wrong clash and men are tempted to make the end justify the means. It is rash to think that the political process can ever be turned wholly to sweetness and light.

When the franchise was narrow and gentlemen were born to politics, there was little evidence of the existence of parties outside the legislature. In Parliament itself, the members of the parties made their deals in secret caucus and the only outward evidence of these were the principles the members expounded. It was in these circumstances that Edmund Burke framed his famous definition of a political party as "a body of men united for promoting the national interest on some particular principle on which they are all agreed." Of course, the parties tried to extend their membership and influence to the constituencies in the hope of altering or maintaining the complexion of Parliament at the next election. But the candidate often knew all the voters personally, and in any event could canvass them all himself. Elaborate party organization was unnecessary under these circumstances.

All this has been changed by universal suffrage. Where the voters in a constituency numbered dozens or hundreds, they now number thousands and tens of thousands. The candidates cannot personally canvass more than a few of them. Yet their votes are necessary for victory. The party must come to the aid of its candidate with money and scores of tireless workers. For there is much to be done as an election approaches. The voters must be harangued and canvassed. Wavering voters must have the issues at stake specially explained to them. Campaign literature must be prepared and widely distributed. Space in the newspapers and time on the radio and television must be arranged and paid for. Transport must be provided to carry the eager voters to the polls.

An organization that does all this efficiently cannot be thrown together on the eve of an election. It becomes necessary to maintain permanent party committees in each constituency. Nor is this enough. The parties carry on nation-wide campaigns on a national platform and the greatest possible number of seats must be won. A central organization for over-all direction is necessary for maximum results. Local party organizations are sometimes slack and need coaching and encouragement. Doubtful constituencies are the sectors where the front breaks, and the central organization must mobilize strategic reserves. Research is undertaken in problems of public policy and party speakers across the country are supplied with facts, arguments, and statistics.

The most important work of the central organization, however, is not in fighting this election but in planning the next one. Therefore, it should be a permanent organization with a substantial permanent staff. The platform of the party must have the widest possible appeal and it must not be settled on until the contours of opinion in the constituencies have been plotted. The central organization collects much of the data that the leaders must take into account in drafting the programme. It gives attention to alternative plans of campaign and to the strategy and tactics appropriate to each. It keeps in touch with constituency organizations, bolstering their morale, explaining the government's policy if the party happens to be in power, the government's lack of policy if the party is in opposition. Analogies are always misleading, but it comes close to being the directing brain of the party.

In different countries, the vigour of the central party organizations varies. They are strongest in Britain, attending to all the matters described and others as well. In the United States and Canada, the national central party organizations are but pale reflections of the picture drawn here. That is because the strongest and most effective party organizations are state or provincial in scope. In many of the provinces and states, central party organizations attempt most of the functions described above.

In any case, permanent central and constituency organizations are necessities if the parties are to make the most of the possibilities. The maintaining of these organizations and the fighting of periodic elections are a heavy expense to the parties. Thousands of party workers are needed to garner in the vote at elections. In so far as funds are lacking to pay them, the party has to persuade volunteers to help for the sake of the party. At the very best, large sums are needed to pay party workers and a multitude of other expenses. Money is the root of much evil in political parties as elsewhere. The parties find it too cramping, if not impossible, to rely on the small contributions of a large number of party supporters and much easier to get large contributions from a relatively few people. This philanthropy is not always pure, and there are lively hopes of favours to come when the party gets into power. Also, it is found that volunteer workers are more numerous and zealous if the party can give concrete recognition of their services. The loyal workers who do the party drudgery are often aspirants for favours that will be in the gift of the party when it is victorious. The party cannot be successful without a vigorous organization, and organization depends on benefactors and loyal workers.

Party organization has other disillusioning features. All organization has a tendency to fall under the control of a few. The organization tends to become autonomous, to exist for its own sake and for the satisfactions it provides for its active personnel even at the expense of its principles and original purpose. Most of the supporters of the party have little interest in humdrum matters of organization, and their attention to party affairs subsides between elections. Party organization in the constituency falls into the hands of an interested few who try to control it. The national party leaders naturally have a commanding influence in the national organization.

These local and central leaders, along with the permanently employed officials of the party, come to regard the organization as important for its own sake. Since the organization flourishes on victory and languishes in defeat, principles tend to become subordinated to success at the polls. The benefactors and the party workers often make a similar judgment. The former often show how much they care about the principles of the party by making equal contributions to both parties. The party workers and those benefactors who bet their horse on the nose cannot be rewarded without victory. Furthermore, the sheer delight of battle stirs everyone connected with the parties to put victory first. There have been times, in North America at any rate, when these influences made the party system primarily a struggle between the ins and the outs. The only safeguard against this degeneration at any time is some minimum of intelligence and interest in the electorate.

There is clear support of this estimate in the search of the parties for issues that will capture the vote. Since neither party can escape the necessity of encouraging one section of opinion to expect some things that, if stressed too much, will repel other sections of opinion, each party looks for red herrings to draw across the trail, specious issues that divert the public and force the other party to a more favourable battleground. Such manoeuvres can only be prevented by a public that knows too much to let itself be deceived.

Two of the counts in the indictment against the party system used to be fraud in the buying of votes and the stuffing of ballot boxes. Election laws have been tightened up and party managers have lost a good deal of their interest in such piecemeal methods. Improvements in the art and media of propaganda make it easier to attempt wholesale stampedes of voters, and bribery now tends to take the form of promising large sections of the population benefits from the public treasury.

After the election has been won by such methods, those who have deserved well of the party are rewarded. The benefactors who have earned a reward are given profitable government contracts, tariff increases, and other advantages. Some of the party workers get government jobs, often through the dismissal of employees of the government who were just learning how to do their work reasonably well. The patronage or spoils system has many unfortunate effects, which are too well known to need discussion. It must be acknowledged, however, that the worst excesses of the spoils system have latterly been curbed by reasonably effective reforms.

Thus it is claimed that the parties are run by small cliques of politicians who take pains to exclude men of better will than themselves from influence in party councils or in framing the party platform. They deceive the public and frustrate the will of the people for better government. They saddle the public with incompetent servants and use their control of the government to enrich themselves, their friends, and supporters.

THE VERDICT ON PARTIES

If a verdict has to be given on the charges summed up in the last paragraph, it will be neither "guilty" nor "not guilty," but "greatly exaggerated." Occasional politicians enrich themselves at the public expense, but most of them live and die poor. Corrupt bargains with benefactors are fewer than is generally supposed. Many men give large sums to their party without expectation of a concrete return, although it would not be correct to say that party policy has been unmindful of the source of contributions to party funds. Loyal workers are rewarded with jobs wherever possible, but the critics of this practice have rarely taken adequate account of the difficulty of finding alternative sources of energy for running the party organizations.

The hard fact is that the parties need funds and workers for their indispensable function of organizing the electorate. Job-seekers are the bane of the politicians' existence and there is nothing more welcome than utterly voluntary service to the party. It is equally certain that they would prefer to get party funds that entailed no obligation. These have not come forward in sufficient volume from the rank and file of the supporters of the parties, and they have received but little supplement from those who rebuke the politicians for making what shift they can.

It cannot be emphasized too much that the party organizations in a democracy are flexible and necessarily responsive to currents of opinion. Those who are sure that party practices outrage common decency can dedicate themselves to reform of those practices. The obstacles they face are nothing compared to those which vital social movements have overcome in the past.

It is true that a small group of leaders tries to control the party, but that is a general feature of all human organization, not limited to political parties. Men of good will are not excluded from party councils, but they often exclude themselves because they are too inflexible to make the compromises essential to the gathering of votes. The parties do not frustrate the will of the people, because it is only rarely that even a transient majority of the people is genuinely of one mind about a specific political problem. The parties deceive the public, but so do propagandists of every kind. The deception does not often arise from cynicism but rather from zest for the game itself, a general human trait. It may be said generally in conclusion that the evils in the party system are not peculiar to it but are the outcome of general human frailties. Indeed, it is hard to see how the parties that must woo the electorate with success can do other than reflect its virtues and its vices. Perhaps it is people as much as institutions that need to be reformed.

These charges and the verdict on them have been general and they make no allowance for differences in the party system in different countries. Nor do they take account of differences between the parties in the same country. In the last eighty years, at any rate, the spoils system and unsavoury bargains with party benefactors have been much more common in North America than in Britain. Moreover, many of the charges levelled at the party system are much less applicable to the new third and fourth parties —the parties of protest.

These latter parties are maintained by a generous idealism which finances the party and supplies the workers for the sake of the cause. This is a tremendous gain and the supporters of these parties, socialist and otherwise, assure us that it is because they appeal to the best rather than to the worst in people. This is not the whole reason. As long as these third parties are a long way from power, it is easy for them to be pure. No one tempts them with donations in return for favours and concessions at public expense. The party workers work hard because until they approach the threshold of power it is possible for each to believe that the party will bring his ideals to fruition. It is only when you have to try to please everyone in order to catch and retain votes that the sickening compromises begin and the disillusionment that saps enthusiasm among the supporters of the older parties sets in.

PARTIES AND PEACEFUL CHANGE OF GOVERNMENT

As long as we adhere to the rule that ultimate power rests with a diffused electorate, political parties are necessary to frame issues and bring public opinion to a focus. However, political parties, two or more in number, perform other even more fundamental functions for democracy. They make peaceful change of government possible and thus eliminate the necessity for the armed *coup d'état* as a means of changing government, and the counter-necessity of ruling by force and terror to prevent such a *coup d'état*. A glance at two striking episodes in the Nazi and Soviet dictatorships will help to make this point clear. It has already been noted that the Soviet Union permits only one party, the Communist party. Likewise, in Germany under the Nazis, the Nazi party was the only party allowed to exist and participate in the processes of government.

In 1934, the Nazi party in Germany purged itself of scores of prominent members of the party by shooting them down under the pretence that they were resisting arrest. Between 1936 and 1938, there were repeated purges in the Communist party in Russia. Several dozens of the old distinguished members of the party who suffered imprisonment and exile for the sake of the revolution under the Czarist regime were tried for treason and either executed or imprisoned. In each case, these actions were the result of a serious split in the party.

The Nazi party had in it many genuine socialists who wanted to make the party the instrument of out-and-out socialism. In order to win power, however, Hitler had made infamous bargains with anti-socialist elements which he found it expedient to honour for a considerable time after gaining power. The socialist wing, including a minority of important leaders, regarded this as a betrayal of their hopes and of promises that had been made them. Although the exact circumstances and sequence of events are not clear, it seems that this group was threatening to contest Hitler's leadership of the party when Hitler struck first.

There is also confusion as to what happened in Russia. The accused were charged with and convicted of conspiring with Germany and Japan to overthrow the Soviet government. If they did so conspire, it is clear that the conspiracy was the consequence of a conviction that Stalin had betrayed the revolution. For years there had been a widening rift in the party between those who held with Stalin that a strong socialist state must first be established in Russia before trying to convert the rest of the world, and those who sympathized with Trotsky's view that Stalin's policy was bound to fail and that it was necessary to get on with world-wide revolution without a day's delay. In other words, they disagreed profoundly over the means by which the desired end, world-wide socialism, could be reached.

There are strong reasons for thinking that such purges are a periodic necessity in the one-party system. Whether or not they will require bloodshed depends on how deeply and passionately the leaders are divided and how determined both factions are to make their will prevail. But purges of some sort are necessary where free elections are not used to settle disputes over government policy. For, to set up a one-party system is to say that there is only one right way to govern the country and that the way is clear and unmistakable. If there were any reasonable doubt, the sensible thing to do would be to allow two or more parties and let them experiment in turn with their solutions to the country's problems. The one party monopolizes all political activity and it can entertain only one policy. Any man with political ambitions or with strong views on what the government ought to be doing must get into the party and try to work his way to influence and authority.

Nazis and Communists, like other people, are of diverse opinions. There is disagreement over policy within the party. When neither group can convince the other and neither will give in, the single party has, in fact, split into two parties. The peaceful way out is to allow the dissenting minority to secede openly and set up party organs of its own, and then to agree to let the people arbitrate this and any subsequent conflict between them, awarding control of the government to the group that wins the confidence of the electorate for the time being. The alternating governments of the democracies are made possible only by the unflinching and unhesitating acceptance of the convention that the party in power always accepts the verdict of the polls.

The frank adoption of this solution is barred in the one-party state because the zealots who set it up are agreed on one thing at least; they know what government policy should be and there is nothing for the public to arbitrate. How could it be otherwise with men who think they have perceived the only valid goals of human life and society? It is a betrayal of their vision to allow the perverse and the stupid to organize against them. Nothing will be gained and everything may be lost by reasoning and discussing with the obstructors who, if they had any reason or good will in them, would have seen the light long ago. For such as these, the zealots have only a burning impatience and contempt. So they destroy without a qualm all organizations and persons which might talk or act against their views.

Men who are willing to obliterate all other parties but their own generally will not shrink from obliterating opposition elements within the party. It becomes a question which faction will shoot first. There is no ground for thinking that Hitler enjoyed shooting old friends who had shared his struggle or that Stalin found much satisfaction in the judicial liquidation of comrades with whom he had fought and suffered for an ideal. The logic of the one-party system compels it from time to time.

So when it is asked whether the country can afford to have half its able leaders always obstructing in opposition, the real issue is whether they are more useful there than in the cemetery. The shooting of old friends would not necessarily be bad for the body politic if there were any assurance that those who are quick on the draw somehow have also the better political opinions. There is no evidence that this is an index to statesmanship.

The prime advantage of the two-or-more-party system is that it applies the only rational test of statesmanship, the testing of policies through their practical application. The public will support one party for a while and then another. Each party experiments with its ideas while in power, and if the results are satisfactory the opposition party acknowledges this by continuing the measure after it comes to power. In the past, at any rate, relatively little legislation has been repealed on a change of government. This fact is of great importance. It suggests strongly that the liberal democratic processes of discussion are effective means of enlarging the area of agreement among men and confirming their sense of unity if they have the patience to thresh out their differences on terms of mutual respect.

Those who come to politics with white-hot convictions will always be impatient with government by trial and error. Before they reject it, they may well examine the alternative and ask whether they wish to put their faith to the test of violence. For violence not only degrades the personalities of those on whom it is practised. It also destroys the basis of mutual trust and respect on which the pursuit of liberal democratic ideals depends. Those who admit that there may be reasonable differences of opinion on how best to further these ideals will find merit in the open flexible system. Those who lay store by constitutionalism will cling to the party system because alternating governments are the effective device for keeping power contingent. The people can govern their rulers and hold them responsible only as long as they can dismiss them and find at once a workable alternative government.

THE PARTY BATTLE AS A SHAM BATTLE

It is often complained that the party battle is a sham battle and that the parties are not divided on real issues. In part, but by no means entirely, the party battle in a working democracy *is* a sham battle. This is just another way of saying that the parties and the bulk of the people are sufficiently agreed on a few fundamental issues that they do not have to regard their political opponents as deadly enemies to be fought to the bitter end. The party battle will become really satisfying to the pugnacious only when the issues dividing the parties cleave down through the fundamentals.

When the parties are committed to sharply opposed views about the basic principles of a just society, they are compelled to regard one another as dangerous enemies of the state, to be separated from the control of the army and police at any cost. The convention of unhesitating acceptance of the verdict of the electorate breaks down. When all the elements of sham have disappeared, all parties but one will be proscribed. That one party will proclaim that all true men are united behind it to protect the fundamental aims of society. This is precisely what has happened in the modern dictatorships because of a dogmatic assertion by a ruthless group that they alone know the fundamental aims of society. In fact, of course, the establishment of a one-party system is a living proof that men are less united than before. Mutual trust and respect between individuals and groups of differing views have broken down.

If the party system of a liberal democracy comes to take the form of a socialist party committed to extensive and rapid socialization as soon as it comes to power and an opposing party that mobilizes all the anti-socialist sentiment, the convention on which alternating governments depend will face a very severe test. It might be thought that this test confronted Britain in 1945 when the Labour party, professedly socialist, faced a Conservative party which was strongly anti-socialist. In the event, however, the British genius for compromise prevailed, and neither party pressed its dogmas to the point of endangering the unity of the community.

In fact, it would appear that several of the important socializing measures enacted by the Labour majority were not resisted by the Conservative Opposition on grounds of principle but rather on grounds of methods and timing. Many British conservatives are moderate rather than extreme individualists, and most British socialists are evolutionary socialists. As we saw in chapter v, the differences between these two groups are often differences over means and do not involve cleavage over fundamentals. Moreover, the Labour party has become less doctrinaire in recent years. Many of the voters who helped to put it in power in 1945 were not socialists and would not have supported out-and-out socialism. The Labour party always knows it will need these votes in the future. The overthrow of the Labour Government by the Conservatives in 1951 has provided no additional evidence for assuming that the easy-going tolerance found in all ranks of the British people has been unable to survive the test of recent acute party strife.

It is time for someone to remark that this discussion has reached the point of complete contradiction. The argument began by finding the justification for two or more parties in the inability of the electorate to reach general agreement on what the government should do. It has now reached the conclusion that two or more parties will not work except where the people are agreed on certain fundamental matters. This paradox will bear a great deal of reflection, for whoever resolves it will have laid bare the secret of democratic politics. It is still a secret, for there is no generally accepted analysis. Some hold that the necessary agreement on fundamentals is very slight, requiring no more than an agreement to disagree peaceably,[1] and to observe certain procedures in negotiating about disagreements when these can no longer be ignored but must be resolved. But people will scarcely respect one another sufficiently to agree to disagree unless they are conscious of sharing some ultimate objectives in common. Here the few general and widely held ideals of liberal democracy are of decisive importance.

[1] C. J. Friedrich, "Democracy and Dissent" *Political Quarterly*, 10 (1939), 571-82.

All that can be said here is that government by consent is not possible unless there is some minimum of agreement on the ends and purposes of social life. This is a very considerable achievement. However, the agreement on ends, which is generally the unconscious result of tradition and education, seldom encompasses means, which are always consciously devised and differently conceived. Since people hold diverse and often uninformed views on what to do and how to do it in detail, political parties are necessary to organize the electorate.

The much-debated question that asks when a coalition government is necessary or justified may throw some light on the matter. When the nation is fighting a war for its very existence, all other aims and interests must be subordinated to the one overriding purpose of winning the war. The means necessary to win it are largely a matter of technical calculation, and despite the ubiquity of armchair strategists most people are constrained to allow those who understand the problems to make the decisions. There appears to be sufficient general agreement on aims and purposes to enable the parties to coalesce and unite their energies and abilities.

In actual practice, it turns out not to be so simple. We know from our own experience that the various interests do not all accept subordination, because they are unable to appreciate the connection between the sacrifice demanded of them and the winning of the war. There is still disagreement on the necessary means for reaching the agreed end. Winston Churchill, before he knew that he would lead a national coalition in World War II, made an adverse judgment on the British coalition government of World War I. The bringing together of men of diverse temperaments and views in the cabinet slowed, and sometimes watered down the vigour of, cabinet decisions. The differences of opinion that are normally fought out in the elections and on the floor of the House of Commons had to be fought out inside the cabinet.

There is no doubt a point at which the position of the nation is so obviously desperate that these differences of temperament and view cease to be a decisive factor. Britain reached that position in 1940 but never consciously faced it in 1914-18. In all emergencies short of this, coalition is a detriment rather than an aid to efficient government because of the incorrigible variety of opinion on what ought to be done.

This abstract discussion can be summed up by saying that until human nature is greatly changed and education and knowledge are greatly improved and extended, the party system performs two indispensable functions for a democracy. First, it enables the sovereign electorate to participate in the operation of government. Secondly, it makes constitutionalism and ultimate control of government by the electorate possible by enabling the people to change their masters when they see fit to do so. The matter can be left at this point for the present and attention turned to political parties as they are found in Britain, the United States, and Canada.

PARTY ORGANIZATION IN BRITAIN

A comprehensive description of political parties in any country requires a review of the political history of that country for the past hundred years, at least. Political parties cannot be clearly understood unless seen in relation to their development in their environment. Their policies and platforms cannot be appreciated except in relation to the social and economic structure that reveals their sources of support. The present purpose being limited to a preliminary study of the mechanisms and functions of government, a wide survey of political parties cannot be undertaken. The main emphasis will be on party organization.

It seems probable that the Liberal party in Britain is doomed and that its supporters will be distributed between the other two parties, the Conservative party and the Labour party. But in any case, Liberal and Conservative organizations are so similar in pattern that a description of one will serve for the other. Also, the organization of the Labour party steadily grows more like that of the others. It will be sufficient to note a few salient divergences. The basic unit in all three parties is the local constituency organization composed of all those who formally join the party and maintain their membership. The active and effective part of the local association is the small executive committee, which, in turn, is very powerfully influenced by its secretary and a paid party agent, whose job it is to win the constituency in the election.

The local associations are in each case united in a national union, which maintains a central party office and holds an annual conference made up of delegates from the constituency organizations. The conference elects a national executive committee, which directs the work of the central office. The central office, it will be recalled, is an over-all directing and co-ordinating agency devoted to the planning and winning of elections. In theory, the conference is a representative party legislature for establishing the policy of the party. But like Parliament itself, it has come under the powerful influence of its executive committee and civil service (the permanent staff of the central office). The central office works in the closest relation with the party leaders in Parliament. The party programme is drafted by the leader of the party in Parliament, the chairman of the executive committee, and the chief official of the central office. Headquarters rarely fails to have this draft approved by the annual conference of the party.

Nor does the conference choose the leader of the party. He is chosen by those members of the party who are in Parliament. Since he is their leader in the critical party struggles in Parliament, it is most desirable that he should be their choice. Equally, those who lead the party in Parliament and who have, or will have, the responsibility of making and enforcing government policy are sternly set against having the annual conference saddle them with a policy that is impracticable or impossible of application. This helps to explain the centralized party machine. The natural tendency towards oligarchy in human organization and the inherent logic of responsible cabinet government both contribute to it.

The main divergences of the Labour party from this pattern of organization arise from the connection of the party with the trade unions. Trade unions and local trades councils as well as individuals are members of the party entitled to distinct representation in local and national organization. The local party agent is often a trade-union official. Because the trade unions are powerful principalities within the party, the central organization cannot dominate the party so fully. The annual Labour party conference discusses party policy more fruitfully. Yet the conference cannot force a policy on the parliamentary group of the party. After all the debate is over, they must approve the policy before it becomes official. The parliamentary group also choose the person who is to lead them in Parliament. His position is somewhat less secure than that of the leaders of the older parties because he must be re-elected each session and he has no acknowledged claim to be Prime Minister when the party comes to power.

As part of their duties in planning and executing election campaigns, the central organizations insist that every candidate who represents the party be approved by them, making judgments on his orthodoxy in cases where doubt arises. Central party officials often want seats in Parliament, and these—and others—are recommended to the local associations. It is very rarely, however, that the central office will try to force a candidate on a local committee that is determined to pick its own, although the central office may refuse its imprimatur to a particular choice. Ancillary to its principal duties, the central office carries on research in the problems of government, grinds out party literature, manages the party funds, and nurses the party press. It is active continuously and not merely at election time.

Much less is known in detail about the sources of campaign funds in Britain than in America. The two older parties rely mainly on substantial contributions from men of substance. Explicit bargains for a *quid pro quo* are not common, partly because of a high standard of political morality, partly because until very recently Britain has not maintained a protective tariff and British governments have not engaged in active promotion of economic development. Unlike governments in North America, British governments have not had vast natural resources to give away and have not been subsidizing desirable private economic enterprises such as railways. However, titles of honour have been a significant substitute for railway concessions, timber limits, and tariff increases. The parties exploit social snobbery instead of the natural resources of the country. The Labour party, for obvious reasons, has had little part in such traffic. It has drawn its funds in small amounts from a vast body of supporters, particularly through the trade unions.

The merit system of appointment to the civil service covers most government jobs and it is loyally and honestly applied. There is therefore very little room for operation of the spoils system. The patronage appointments do not begin to provide rewards for doing the drudgery of the party. In so far as voluntary workers do not come forward in sufficient numbers, they must be paid a wage. Here the Labour party has an advantage because it has the largest reserve of crusading enthusiasm. On the other hand, it is at a disadvantage on election day because few of its supporters can supply motor cars to take the voters to the polls.

The count in the indictment against political parties that sticks best to British parties is, therefore, the charge of domination by a few. Step by step with the extension of the suffrage has come progressive concentration of control in the central organs of the party. The movement is also closely connected with the increasing range and complexity of the functions of government. The amateur student of politics, let alone the average party supporter, cannot distinguish what seems desirable from what is possible, either in the technical sense of the administratively feasible or in the political sense of attracting a majority of the votes. Thus the professional party worker who makes it his business to study such matters advances rapidly in power and prestige.

The rank and file cannot directly write the programme and choose the leaders of their party. The chief guarantee that the central organization will be sensitive to the wishes of the rank and file is, of course, the existence of the opposition party. As long as the opposition is there, eager to capitalize on dissatisfaction in the ranks of its opponents, the central office and the parliamentary leaders will give anxious and courteous attention to representations from the local associations and will try to anticipate the temper of the annual conference.

PARTY ORGANIZATION IN THE UNITED STATES

It is impossible to give a simple description of party organization in the United States. Parties perform their functions in each of the fifty states as well as in national politics, and the necessity for linking state and federal party activity fosters complexity. Although the Republican and Democratic parties are national parties, the state is, for each of them, the vital unit of organization, and the structure of each party varies from state to state.

Furthermore, there are more elections in the United States than in any other country. In the national field, there is a presidential election every four years and congressional elections every two years at fixed dates. At state elections, generally held at the same time as the national elections, the voters must choose a governor and a state legislature. In addition, many state and municipal executive and administrative posts which in Britain and Canada are filled by appointment are elective offices in the United States. Also, in many states the law now requires each party to hold direct primaries (preliminary elections within the party) for the purpose of choosing party committees, party candidates, and even delegates to conventions that will choose candidates. There is almost always an election in the offing for which preparation must be made.

The numerous elections and the state-national division account in large part for the hyper-organized condition of political parties and for the large numbers of professional politicians in the United States. Here, more than in any other democratic country, there is justification for calling party organization a machine, because of its intricate articulation and smooth efficiency. The professional politician handles the machine with a sure and delicate touch, and the necessity for making the machine work well and almost continuously encourages apprenticeship in the profession of politics.

Yet this organization stops short of full perfection. Despite the fact that the principal popular excitement is over national issues and national elections, party organization at the national level is temporary, haphazard, and almost entirely lacking in the discipline revealed at the state level. Party organization and activity are much regulated by law, but these laws are almost all state laws. For example, state laws determine how party candidates to Congress and party delegates to national as well as state nominating conventions shall be chosen.

This emphasizes the fact that it is the state and local organizations of the parties which are significant. Although we are mainly concerned with national and not with local, provincial, or state government, it is necessary to give close attention to the party organization within each state. Fortunately, there is a general pattern to which both parties conform in most states. The pattern only will be sketched and what is said about it must be prefaced with the warning that the description will not be fully accurate for all, nor perhaps for any one state or party.

Party Organization in the States

The lowest general unit of organization of the party is the local committee of the city, town, or township, formally chosen by the interested supporters of the party in a party caucus or primary. The members of these committees are all active party workers, many of whom hold municipal office or jobs in the state government when their party is in power. In the larger cities, organization goes farther down into the wards and the polling subdivisions (called precincts). The ward and precinct committees are often dominated by ward bosses and precinct captains, and the more important of these figures find their way into the city organization of the party.

In the larger cities, city organization is generally linked directly with state organization of the party. In the smaller centres of population, the local committee is subordinate to the county committee, which is formally chosen by a county convention or primary. Still higher stands the state central committee, chosen through a primary election or by a convention to which delegates from the constituencies go. One can count on finding the more important of the local committeemen on the state committee.

It would be hazardous to say how far this formal organization, much regulated by law, represents the reality. The situation varies from state to state and often differs as between the two parties in the same state. In some of the larger cities, the party that is in the ascendant is controlled by a city boss who may hold no office in the party at all. For reasons that cannot be discussed here, the city bosses are steadily losing their power, but they are still a significant factor in American politics. In the past, they found the best soil for their growth in those cities with a large non-English speaking, foreign-born population. These masses were generally poor and always in need of the elementary necessities of life. They were ignorant of American institutions and ways of life and thus frequent violators of laws and regulations. They were utterly bewildered by the complexities of the political system in which they were asked to participate.

In these circumstances, the city bosses were those who proved to be the best friends of the harassed immigrant and his family, who reasoned that those who spice concrete assistance in time of need with human sympathy and consideration are to be trusted to give sound advice in political matters. Unfortunately, such assistance has to be financed somehow. A man who can swing numerous votes has political power and can use it to tap the public treasury through various kinds of graft and corruption. The more votes he controls, the greater his leverage on the treasury; and the greater his financial resources, the more voters who appreciate his qualities and his advice on politics. There are many sordid aspects of the power of bosses. These are well enough known without enumeration while the mitigating, if not redeeming, facts are not so widely appreciated. In any event, the present concern is with the key to the power of the bosses.

The boss who collects a large following in this way becomes a king-maker, if not a king. Without holding any party position, he can often determine the make-up of local party committees through his control of the deciding votes in party caucuses and primaries, and he is a power to be reckoned with in the state party machine.

Control by bosses is not limited to cities with large populations of foreign origin. Indeed, the foreign-born are not as numerous as they were in the days before large-scale immigration was terminated at the close of World War I. But every community has its poor and also the many who are perplexed by the intricacies of American politics. Organization is always affected by a tendency to oligarchy, and the special features of American politics already noted feed the tendency. Another contributing factor is the extensive patronage still available largely but not entirely in state and local government. United States Senators who control the federal patronage for their state have now and then used this and other levers to become the state bosses of their party. While state bosses have been rare, county bosses have not been uncommon.

Even where power in the party is not gathered into a single hand, the most prominent and skilful of the local party leaders generally have a large enough following to get themselves chosen for the state central committee, and that following often enables them to decide who shall be elected to the local and county committees. Thus, power does not always go with the titles to authority and, even where it does, it is often secured by manipulation rather than by the chaste methods prescribed by the democratic ideal. It must suffice to say that the realities are often very different from what the forms would indicate.

The state central committee, or the person or persons who control it, exercises functions and imposes discipline much as the central office and the parliamentary leaders of the party do in Britain. The party platform for the state is made by a party convention composed of delegates from the localities. The central committee influences the choice of delegates and guides them in their deliberations. Candidates are chosen by conventions or in party primaries over which the central committees have a varying influence. The central committee plans the campaign, raises the necessary funds, and supervises the work of the local committees in striving for victory.

It is also active in national, as distinct from state, politics. It must see to it that party delegates to the presidential nominating convention are chosen by convention or direct primary as the law requires. It must conduct direct primaries for choosing the party candidates for Congress. And in the presidential and congressional elections, much of the work of carrying on the campaign, although not so much of its planning, falls to the state central committees. Generally speaking, party organization in the several states is highly centralized, strongly disciplined, and extremely efficient in converting a heterogeneous electorate into party majorities.

National Party Organization

After the complexities of the state organization of the parties, their national organization is simple. It can almost be said that there is no permanent national organization but only a succession of temporary committees for fighting presidential elections every four years. It is true that, for the biennial congressional elections, the party caucuses in the House of Representatives and the Senate pick campaign committees, but these committees do not run the congressional elections. Their activities mainly consist in co-operating with the state party committees.

Thus the chief national organization is the national committee, nominally picked by the national convention that every four years chooses a party candidate for the presidency. This national committee consists of one man and one woman from each state and territory and—in the case of the Republicans—additional members as a "bonus" to staunchly Republican states. The national convention always ratifies the nominations made by the state party organizations. It plans the presidential election, collects a campaign fund, and co-ordinates the nation-wide party effort to elect a President. Once the debris of the presidential election is cleared away, the national committee lapses into quietude and rallies only once when it issues a call for another presidential nominating convention some three years later. In recent years, however, both parties have maintained permanent headquarters and staffs in Washington. Although these staffs are greatly reduced in size after an election, they do carry on some research to aid members of the parties in Congress and help in various ways with the continuing problem of party organization.

The chairman of the national committee is the personal choice of the presidential candidate of the party, because he is chiefly responsible for managing the candidate's campaign. The national committee under his direction plans the larger strategy, deciding which are the doubtful states into which money, speakers, and propaganda must be poured. However, the national chairman is scarcely a commander-in-chief who passes orders to the field commanders, the state party leaders. These latter are remarkably independent, like the leaders of well-organized guerilla bands, and the authority the chairman can exercise over them depends much more on his personality and his infectious energy and enthusiasm than on his position. If the party wins the presidency, the national chairman is likely to remain active as the national party instrument for distributing patronage and implementing pre-election arrangements.

The effective authority of the national committee is limited to the presidential campaign. The committee pays little attention to the concurrent congressional elections beyond making available a portion of its campaign funds for use in them. It does not frame the national platform of the party nor share in the choice of the party candidate for president. These functions are performed by the presidential nominating convention composed of delegates chosen by the state party organizations, either in primaries or conventions. The national organizations of the American parties do not carry on planning and research between elections on the same scale as do the central organizations of the British parties.

It is common to represent any elaborate organization as a pyramid rising from its base on the local organization to the apex of national authority. Such a figure for the American party system would show the chairman of the national committee at the apex and the ward and precinct committees at the base. However, if the pyramid is to represent the realities of authority, the apex must be cut off at the state level. Below this level, party discipline is generally sharp and effective. But there is little discipline imposed on the state organizations from above. The party that wins the presidency finds that it cannot escape some responsibility for the policy of the national government and thus must accord leadership to the President. The President, armed with this authority and the control of patronage, is a power to be reckoned with in his party, but whenever he has tried to use his power to purge the party of rebellious elements he has almost always failed.

At most, the primacy of the President is a temporary situation in the party. On his retirement or defeat, the state leaders will be again without superiors. Indeed, it may be that the prejudice against a third term (which persisted for a long time before it resulted in a constitutional amendment forbidding a third term) was based, not on the precedent of Washington's refusing a third term but on the studied purpose of state party leaders to prevent the building up of a national leadership that might dominate the party.[1] Generally then, authority flows from the state leaders upward as well as downward. The presidential candidate and the national platform of the party are the results of bargains between them.

The national party conventions in the United States are, it is universally agreed, like nothing else on earth. They always end with impressive demonstrations of party unity and solidarity. However, the way to that happy conclusion is marked by sharp struggles over the platform, subtle manoeuvres by state delegations over the nomination, and much secret horse-trading. If these features are studied, it will be seen that the national convention also resembles an international conference in which separate nations haggle over a treaty of friendship or alliance.

The fact is that the federal system that leaves the states a large measure of autonomy has provided even more autonomy for state party organization. The great sections of the country have varying

[1] E. E. Schattschneider, *Party Government* (Farrar & Rinehart, New York, 1942), p. 156.

interests that it is the business of each political party to try to reconcile. Thus the national party platforms and the presidential candidates of both parties are compromises dictated by this necessity. The national party is a loose confederation of the state parties.[1] This is one reason why national party organization is a temporary coalition of the state parties for winning the presidency and the spoils of office that go with it.

Another reason is the separation of powers enforced by the Constitution. This division of authority works against the emergence of well-disciplined, permanently organized, national parties. As we have seen, the President is the national leader of his party for the time being. If he is a strong personality and an astute mediator between factions in his party, he exerts a unifying influence on it. But the separation of powers limits his effectiveness. If the executive were closely linked to the legislature as in Britain and the President had the power to dissolve the legislature, the members of his party in Congress would be much more disposed to work with him in trying to ensure discipline in their party, and the opposition party would have to meet this attempt at concentration of power with a comparable attempt.

As matters stand, however, Congress is elected by constituencies strongly aware of their sectional interest and, lacking any strong counteracting pressure, members of Congress are the unruly levies of sectionalism rather than the disciplined troops of national parties standing for national policies. So the members of the parties in Congress resist party discipline at the national level for most purposes except the distribution of patronage.

Another reason for the lack of consistency in the policies of the national parties in the United States is the fact that the framing of the party platform and the implementing of it rests in each party with different groups of men. The party platform is determined by the delegates to the presidential nominating convention. The implementing of the platform depends on the action of the men who are elected to Congress on the party ticket. How many of the leaders of the majority party in Congress will also have been members of the platform committee of the nominating convention of their party is almost entirely a matter of accident. In these

[1]See Pendleton Herring, *The Politics of Democracy* (Norton, New York, 1940), ch. xv, which has influenced strongly the interpretation of political parties offered here.

circumstances, consistency in the framing and executing of party policy is extremely difficult to achieve and maintain.

It is true that sectionalism is nurtured by the state party leaders who can often make and unmake members of Congress. The power wielded by these leaders would largely disappear if party leadership were centralized at the national level as in Britain. On these grounds, it is sometimes argued that the elimination of local and state party bosses would open the way to disciplined national parties. However, sectionalism is something more than a racket organized and maintained by party bosses at the state level. As the parallel in Canadian party organization suggests, it is inherent in the variety of life in a country of continental sweep. Even if state party leadership were always secured in a fully democratic way, it would still give expression to sectional interests, although probably not as strongly as at present.

A great deal could be said about campaign funds and patronage in the American party system, but the abuses are sufficiently notorious to need little description. The most important thing that can be said is that the abuses are by no means the universal practice. The patronage appointment of public officials is more widespread than in any other Western democratic country. However, it is being steadily diminished by extension of the merit system, and there have always been volunteer workers who did not ask or expect reward.

The campaign funds of the parties are not raised by contributions from the rank and file of their supporters. Exception must be made, however, for the practice of assessing the party supporters who have got government jobs through the good offices of the party. The main reliance is on substantial contributions from business interests, legitimate or otherwise, and from men of means who often, but by no means always, expect something in return. The facts that there has always been a customs tariff to be manipulated and that governments in the United States have always been promoting the economic development of a great country have ensured extremely close relations between business and government. It has not been unknown for campaign managers frankly to solicit contributions from business men on the ground that these were policies of insurance on their businesses, and many business men take out insurance with both parties.

The state legislatures, and to some extent Congress, have tried to regulate campaign funds by law. The most frequent provisions are aimed at securing publicity concerning the source and use of party revenues, forbidding contributions by corporations and compulsory assessment of office-holders, forbidding certain kinds of expenditures, and limiting the amounts to be spent by candidates. Most of the provisions are easily and consistently evaded, and there is no adequate inspection or other machinery for enforcement. The chief value of these laws, which must not be underestimated, is to interest the public in the questions where the money comes from and where it goes.

The control of party organization at the state and city level by bosses or small cliques is a common occurrence in the American party system. The deplorable consequences cannot be denied, but they should not be exaggerated. The power of the cliques and bosses is always contingent, and they will be supplanted if they do not keep their ears to the ground and attend to clearly expressed and general demands of the supporters of the party. This will be true as long as there is another party searching everywhere for available support. For example, it is pretty clear that the leaders of the Republican party did not want Wendell Wilkie as their presidential candidate in 1940. But they did not think it prudent to pull the wires necessary to defeat him, because he had caught the popular imagination. The party machines have been in a similar quandary before over Woodrow Wilson and both the Roosevelts.

If the rank and file of the supporters of a political party could, of their own resources, precipitate a majority opinion on men and measures, the party bosses and wire-pullers would get short shrift. Unfortunately, it is only rarely that they can. Yet a candidate must be chosen and a platform adopted. This is what gives the wire-pullers their opportunity. It also reveals their function. They act as catalysts, always ready to precipitate by seeming legerdemain a majority opinion on particular issues facing the party.

PARTY ORGANIZATION IN CANADA

It is more difficult to speak about the pattern of organization of political parties in Canada because they have not had the close detailed study given to parties in Britain and United States. It is easy enough to say that one or other of the parties has a particular organization in a particular province or constituency, but that is not to say that this is the general pattern. In so far as a pattern can be discerned, it shows resemblances to both the British and the American, but it is not a copy of either.

On the one hand, cabinet government in Canada has tended towards a centralized discipline in the hands of the party leaders in Parliament and in the provincial legislative assemblies. On the other hand, the general environment in which Canadian parties have carried on their functions resembles much more that in the United States than that in Britain. The North American influences are not only a federal political system in a continental country but also a heterogeneous population, a firmly rooted patronage system, and very intimate relations between government and business because of a long history of tariff protection for industry and vigorous government assistance of private enterprise in economic development. Without any conscious copying, these factors have made for resemblances to American party organization.

The resemblances, however, are limited. Municipal elections have rarely been fought on party lines in Canada, so that normally the parties have only two elections to fight in a four-year period. The parties themselves have never adopted the direct primary system. Thus the Canadian parties, unlike the American, do not need to be in continual tension preparing for the next election. Local party organization is much more casual, and there are few professional politicians because they cannot find steady employment in the field of politics unless elected to the legislature. Canadian political parties have been like those of the United States in their reliance on patronage, their close association with business interests, and in the fact that the national parties are federations of the provincial parties of the same label. The provincial parties are unlike the state parties in being less highly organized and less responsive to the touch of professional politicians.

From the formation of the Dominion of Canada in 1867 until the last few years, the Canadian political scene has been dominated by two parties, the Liberal party and the Conservative party. Between 1931 and 1957 the Conservative party suffered many reverses, being in power only once during that time. In 1943, incidental to a serious attempt to revise its policies and improve its fortunes, it changed its name to the Progressive Conservative party. Under that banner it successfully contested for power in June, 1957, and nine months later in another general election captured a massive majority in the House of Commons.

At the close of World War I, dissatisfaction with the two older parties led to the organization of third parties in several of the provinces. Since that time, third-party movements of various kinds have continued to emerge in provincial politics and have had a varying success in elections in some of the provinces. Only one of them, the Co-operative Commonwealth Federation party organized in 1933, appears to have established itself as a significant national party.

The Co-operative Commonwealth Federation party is a moderate socialist party with a programme similar to that of the Labour party in Britain. In organizing for this purpose, however, it has had to adjust itself to the political realities of the Canadian federal system. Therefore, despite many differences in detail, the broad outlines of the formal structure of its organization are similar to those of the two older parties. The principal features of the organization of the two older parties will be sketched first and some significant deviations of the Co-operative Commonwealth Federation party noted briefly later.

The Two Older Parties

The lowest unit of party organization in the two older parties is the polling subdivision, and party fortunes in elections depend to a great extent on the wit and zeal displayed within these small cells of the party. For the purpose of a brief outline of party structure, the basic unit of organization may be taken to be the constituency, or riding, association to which the interested supporters of the party belong. A small executive committee of the local association directs local party affairs in most matters. The rank and file of party supporters in the constituency participate in the nomination of candidates, but generally the decisions as to how the election is to be fought and how party affairs are to be managed between elections rest with the executive committee.

Party candidates for national or provincial elections are chosen by conventions made up of party supporters in each constituency.

(This statement is not entirely correct for Quebec where the local or district party organization often settles the nomination without calling a convention.) In the rural constituencies where party organization is very loose, there is likely to be a genuine contest for the nomination, which is decided on the floor of the convention. In the urban constituencies, the executive of the local association of the party along with a few other actively interested party members generally manage to get their choice of candidate approved by the convention.

The active members get their way because the rank and file of party supporters are rarely sufficiently interested and sufficiently united to concentrate their votes on an alternative candidate. Moreover, if and when popular opinion does appear to be swinging to a particular person, the local party leaders are likely to respond to it. The local party leaders have not the strong grip on party organization that their counterparts often have in the United States. With rare exceptions, Canadian cities have been free of party bosses of the kind so common in the United States.

The candidate of the party and the executive of the local association have charge of the party effort in the election. They get advice and assistance, but rarely instructions, from the provincial headquarters of the party. It must be recognized, of course, that the assistance may not be forthcoming unless the advice is followed. In some provinces, there are regional or district party organizations standing between the provincial and local organizations, which help to co-ordinate election campaigns in their area of the province. Because of patronage problems and other connections between the government and the constituency, the executives of the local associations of the party in power at Ottawa or at the provincial capitals are likely to remain active, in greater or less degree, between elections. But the local associations of the defeated party often become somnolent and are only revived by the immediate prospect of another election. Local party organization is not in a continuous state of tension as it is in the United States.

Above the riding associations stands the provincial association of the party, composed of the active supporters of the party. Meetings of the provincial association are mainly made up of delegates from each of the provincial constituencies, members of the party who have seats in the national Parliament or the provincial legislature or who were unsuccessful candidates for such seats in the last elections, and representatives of the youths' and women's organizations of the party.

The provincial association meets annually, or even less frequently, to discuss the affairs and fortunes of the party. It elects an executive and provides for a provincial party council, or management committee, which is supposed to give close attention to party affairs. The provincial council not only contains the acknowledged leaders of the party but also representatives from the constituencies and the auxiliary organizations of the party. Its membership is so numerous and scattered that it is hard to convoke it for frequent meetings and it is too unwieldy for effective discussion. As a result, it does not usually exercise much more control over party affairs than does the provincial association.

In these circumstances, the members of the party who have seats in the provincial legislature, and particularly the leaders of the party there, are the most active persons in party decisions. But the party leaders do not always have the commanding influence that their counterparts have in Britain. Their influence depends greatly on whether the party is in power, controlling the legislature and the cabinet. If the party is in power, the party leaders in the legislature have a very strong position in the provincial council and the provincial association. If the party is out of power, there is obviously something wrong that needs correction, and party policy and leadership are much more open to the criticisms of the members of the council and of the association.

The party leaders do not make the official party policy or choose the official provincial leader of the party. These functions are performed by a meeting of the provincial association of the party or by a province-wide party convention called for the purpose. The use of a representative convention to choose the party leader is in sharp contrast to the British practice of choice by the parliamentary group of the party. It is no doubt partly a copying of American practice and partly a response to the demands of democratic theory. Here again, however, it can be said that the degree of influence that the parliamentary group can exert on the choice of a new leader or on the revision of the party platform depends greatly on whether the party is in or out of power at the time.

The executive of the provincial association appoints a secretary who is a salaried official and who is normally the official provincial organizer for the party. The secretary has charge of the central party office and staff, which is usually very small except at election times. The secretary and the central party office are at all times under the direction and close control of the provincial leader of the party. Their chief function is to prepare for elections and to co-ordinate the campaign throughout the province. Between elections, they pay more attention to patronage and related matters, and much less to research and education in party principles, than do the central offices of the parties in Britain.

The provincial party headquarters have yet to publish books and organize party schools and conferences to explain what the parties are about. Until very recently, the issues with which provincial governments and politics have had to deal have been few and simple compared with those arising in Britain. Consequently, party policies and platforms have not been taken so seriously. Provincial politics often look like a game between the "ins" and the "outs," with a marked tendency in several provinces for one party to dominate over a long period.

The party leadership maintains discipline over the members of the party in the legislature and exerts great influence in the general councils of the party. This is particularly true of the party in power. For most of the rank and file, the requirements of the game are satisfied as long as the party is in power and they do not make concerted challenges to the leadership. The leader of the party as Premier has the power to dissolve the legislature, and that helps to keep the members of the party in the legislature in line. There is considerable patronage to be distributed, and control of this patronage is one of the strongest holds the member has on his constituency. Those who revolt against the leadership of their party are usually deprived of their control over patronage, and they cannot count on assistance from the central organization of the party in the next election. For these reasons, the leadership and central headquarters of the provincial parties are often described as "machines."

With uncommon exceptions, this is invective rather than accurate description. Party discipline is not as strong and pervasive as in Britain. Party organization does not fall into the grip of political bosses such as are commonly found in United States. It should be noted particularly that the party leadership and central office have not the acknowledged power to veto the candidature of particular persons in the constituencies. Of course, the party leadership may, in the case of particular rebels, persuade the local constituency organizations not to renominate them. But the task of persuasion would be too great if there were anything approaching a general revolt in the party against the party leadership.

The contingent nature of party leadership becomes apparent when the party is defeated in the election after having had control of the government for a time. Then there is commonly a reckoning that brings new ideas and new personalities to the fore in the party and generally involves significant changes in the party programme and party leadership. Genuine machine politics with firmly seated political bosses in control are most likely to be found only in those provinces where one party has managed to stay in power continuously for a long period.

Our concern here is with the national organization of Canadian political parties. However, it has been necessary to describe the provincial organization because it is in the provinces that effective durable organization is found. The parties rely on it for fighting federal as well as provincial elections. The national organizations of the parties are built on their provincial organizations. The former have been changed so frequently that it is difficult to say that there is any settled permanent form.

The National Liberal Federation, set up in its present form in 1932, is, as the name indicates, a linking together of provincial Liberal parties. Elected representatives from provincial Liberal associations and Liberal members of Parliament are the principal elements in its composition. The National Conservative Association, formed in 1924, consisted of all those who paid membership fees, but it was unsatisfactory because it did not secure, in practice, sufficient representation from the provincial Conservative parties in the outlying provinces. In its reorganized form as the Progressive Conservative Association, it is largely made up of elected representatives from the provincial Progressive Conservative associations and Progressive Conservative members of Parliament.

These national associations of the parties meet annually to

discuss party affairs. They adopt resolutions on party policy and other matters which, while not rigidly binding on the leadership, have strong moral authority because they come from the most widely representative organization of the party. They do not, however, choose the leader of the party. In the last thirty years, a practice has grown up of calling a special national party convention to choose a new leader when a choice becomes necessary.

The convention comprises delegates from all the federal constituencies. In addition to selecting a leader, the convention also overhauls the party platform. The parliamentary leaders of the party are not able, as their counterparts generally are in England, to control the resolutions of the nominating convention or annual party assembly on party policy. They are therefore unfriendly to the practice because their sense of the possible tells them that the formulae that emerge from such gatherings often cannot be implemented in important particulars.

Fortunately for them, pronouncements on party policy have not been taken in the past as seriously in Canada as in Britain. In the first place, the interest of the electorate in national policy has not been as keen or intelligent. Secondly, the national platform of a party in a country with Canada's sectional diversities must be such as will attract votes in all sections and repel as few as possible. Accordingly, the party platform is always the result of bargaining between the provincial parties associated together as a national party and thus has tended to be made up of vague general resolutions.

It resembles the national party platforms of the United States much more than those of Britain. But party resolutions on policy that cannot be implemented cause more embarrassment to party leaders in the Canadian Parliament than to party leaders in Congress because, as already explained, the cabinet system concentrates the responsibility for government policy on the party in power. Leaders may therefore be taunted for failure to carry out the announced policy of the party.

Each party maintains a party organizer and a central party office or headquarters in Ottawa. The party organizer is the personal choice of the party leader and both he and the headquarters staff work under the direction of the party leader. The organizer and the central office are very active during preparations for a federal election, planning the campaign in conjunction with the parliamentary leaders of the party. But the national parties in Canada are federations of provincial parties and they rely very heavily on provincial organization in conducting the campaign. Generally, there is a federal organizer appointed for each province, but of necessity he has to work with and through the provincial organizations. On occasion, the national party may have to contemplate a separate federal organization in a particular province, but it could scarcely do so for all provinces. The central party office uses the campaign funds it collects to provide campaign literature and to bolster doubtful provinces and constituencies with money, speakers, and propaganda. A federal election campaign is, in each party, a number of provincial efforts with some central assistance and co-ordination. The role of the national party office and organizer thus has a rather closer resemblance to that played by the national committee and national chairman in the United States than to that carried on by the central party office in Britain.

Between elections, the national party headquarters maintain only skeleton staffs performing routine services for the party, keeping records of membership, sending out party literature on request, issuing press releases, and so on. Their main function is to fight elections and not to co-ordinate their respective national parties. They do not undertake extensive research into issues of public policy and they do not contribute greatly to the political education of the electorate.

The connection between the national central party office and the parliamentary leaders of the party is very close. There are, however, limits to the discipline that this combination can impose on the party members in Parliament. The leaders of the party in power are obviously in a better position to control their followers than are the leaders of the opposition. The Prime Minister has the power of dissolution. The members of the party who refuse to follow the party line may lose their control over patronage, and they may be denied the assistance of the national party organization in the next election. But these threats are used sparingly and are rarely enforced except where the insurgents flout or repudiate the leadership of the party.

In neither national party has the central party office the

acknowledged power to veto the candidature at the next election of
those who stray from the party line. However, the party leadership
can often apply effective informal pressure to prevent the constituency organization from re-nominating them. The decision as
to when this pressure can be applied effectively without serious
adverse consequences is a delicate one. If the views for which the
dissenter stands have a strong backing in his province and his
constituency, his defections are more likely to be overlooked. Even
if the maverick is thus deprived of the federal nomination, his
political career in the party is not necessarily ended, as it is in
Britain. He may still have a strong position and a career in the
provincial party. Something also depends on how strongly the
leader is entrenched in the leadership of his party. A leader with
the prestige of years of successful leadership can apply pressure,
and perhaps even a personal veto, in a way that is not open to a
leader who lacks such prestige.

At any rate, it must be said that party loyalty, supplemented by
the prospect of the sanctions just discussed, generally suffices to
maintain an impressive party discipline on the floor of the House
of Commons. In these matters, the main difference between Britain
and Canada is that the policies of the national parties in Canada
are always being adjusted to the demands of provincial and sectional interests. To take the case of the majority party, the cabinet
itself, being representative of provinces and sections, must always
compromise within itself on policy. The private members of the
party from particular provinces often meet in provincial caucus on
important matters. In this way, provincial points of view can be
impressed on members of the cabinet from particular provinces
while the cabinet is deliberating on the line for which it hopes to
get support. The party leadership takes considerable pains to
ensure that its line does not raise seriously divisive issues among
its followers. Through compromises and concessions, the yoke of
party discipline is made tolerable for almost all members of the
party.

In summary, it is readily seen why the older national parties in
Canada are described as federations of provincial parties. National
party organization is, in the main, a linking together of provincial
party organizations. The latter carry the main burden of federal

as well as of provincial elections. Even the cabinet is in some measure an alliance of representatives of provincial interests. This provincialism is general, but is, of course, most marked in the case of Quebec, because, of all the provinces, it has the most distinctive outlook on national political issues.

Some of the consequences of the federal character of the national party organizations will be considered later. It should be said here, however, that in the period between the two world wars at any rate, the signal importance of provincial political organization corresponded to significant political realities. In that period, the provincial governments were much closer to the people than the national government, and thus the party organizations that alternately controlled the provincial governments were much closer too than any national party organization.

Provincial governments shared with the municipal governments the administration of social security measures. When the merit system of appointment in the federal civil service was widely extended at the end of World War I, the provincial governments became the main source of patronage appointments. After the railway building and colonization era came to an end, the active role of the central government shrank, and its affairs became of less importance to business interests. On the other hand, the provincial governments took up the building of highway systems, a source of lucrative contracts, and they have, of course, had control of the public domain of the country. Parties that have, or may have, control of highway contracts, water-power sites, mining resources, and timber limits always attract financial support whether they seek it or not. These are some additional reasons why provincial party organizations have been so important.

The course of events since 1939 may well be working a significant change in the relative importance of federal and provincial party organizations. During World War II, as we have already noted, the Government of Canada took over the organizing of the country for war and determined the direction of economic life. Since the war it has relaxed but never really relinquished this direction. Apart altogether from temporary measures for post-war reconstruction, the national government has pursued vigorously a number of complementary fiscal, monetary, and trade policies designed to maintain a high level of employment and income for Canadians. It has exercised a pervasive influence on almost all aspects of economic life, and the exigencies of national defence suggest that it will continue, and even extend, this influence for an indefinite period in the future. Finally, it has become the dispenser of important social security benefits.

Whereas many significant interests in the country used to be mostly concerned with the activities of provincial governments and with provincial politics, almost all interests now find—and have been finding for the last twenty years—that they are vitally concerned with the activities of the central government, and therefore with national politics. It is too early to say what the effects of these striking changes will be but they are clearly enhancing the importance of national party organizations at the expense of the provincial organizations. For example, there was a period in the 'twenties and 'thirties when national party organizations were heavily dependent on provincial organizations for the raising of campaign funds. There is ground now for thinking that this dependence has been greatly diminished.

No attempt will be made to lay bare the sources of campaign funds or to describe the part played by traffic in government jobs in getting voluntary service to the parties. North American influences already referred to have made Canadian practice in these matters closer to that of the United States than of Britain. The abuses have been less sensational if for no other reason than that Canada is a much poorer country than the United States. The provincial civil services still provide a large field for patronage although thorough house-cleanings on the occasion of a change of government are rare. The older parties rely much more on substantial contributions for their campaign funds than on the small donations of a multitude of supporters and many of the benefactors expect a return even if they do not expressly bargain for it.

The C.C.F. Party in Canada

Of the several newer third parties in Canada, only the Co-operative Commonwealth Federation can be described at present as a national party. Although there are many differences in detail, the broad outlines of the formal structure of C.C.F. party organization are similar to those of the older parties. The greatest differences are in the way in which the organization works. Some of the major differences in structure and operation may be pointed out.

The C.C.F. regards itself as a movement as well as a party. As a movement, it has a sense of mission which the older parties lack. The mission is the achievement of democratic socialism. Holding, as it does, that democracy in the older parties is a sham, there is great emphasis on making party organization democratic. Being unable to rely on habitual support from the voters, unceasing efforts are made to educate the electorate away from their unthinking allegiance to the older parties. Since socialism obviously cannot be achieved merely by voting for it, there is great emphasis on research into political, economic, and social problems. C.C.F. organization is at present directed more towards these aims than to winning elections.

The basic unit of organization is the local C.C.F. club with social and educational as well as political purposes. The one or more clubs in a given constituency form the constituency association. Candidates are nominated by a convention composed of the members of the association. The provincial and national organizations built on the constituency associations have careful constitutional provisions for ensuring that the rank and file of party members will be represented and heard. The party leadership, whether provincial or national, is formally subject to control and detailed direction by their respective party associations. Because the rank and file are deeply interested and highly articulate, this control is at present rather more effective than in the older parties. Annual provincial and biennial national party conventions, which are widely representative, insist on the leaders giving a full account of their stewardship, even to the point of opening the office of leader to a new election at each convention. Many matters which in the older parties would be settled in caucus by the party members of Parliament and of the legislative assemblies are dealt with in the C.C.F. party by the representative associations and conventions.

The central offices of the party, both provincial and national, are, on the whole, more continuously active than those of the older parties. In addition to preparing for and conducting elections, they are extensively engaged in research, the production of party literature, and the distribution of it to the local clubs for dissemination among their members and the public. They organize lecture tours and summer schools for education in party principles.

Alongside the insistence on democracy and education, there are provisions looking to the maintenance of strong party discipline. The central party organizations have authority to veto candidatures and to oust individuals and constituency organizations from the party. Every candidate must pledge himself to abide by the party platform and the general aims of the party. These devices are necessary, not only because the party will need strong discipline to establish a socialist society but also because, at present, there is constant danger that opportunists and hostile elements will work their way into the party and try to wreck it.

The federal nature of the Canadian constitution and Canadian politics have compelled the C.C.F. to organize on a provincial basis for provincial elections. Actually, the C.C.F. is unfriendly to provincialism. Few members of the C.C.F. have a vested interest in the *status quo* for which provincialism furnishes a strong defence. Thus the outlook of the C.C.F. is more specifically national than that of the older parties. Moreover, the central planning which a socialist system requires must be planning by the national government. Thus they must create a well-disciplined national party if they are to accomplish their aims. While provision is made for discussion and criticism at the formative stage of policy, there is sharp insistence that the party line be adhered to once it is formally drawn.

The national organization is not built directly on the provincial organizations, and it is not, therefore, in formal terms a federation of the provincial parties. However, the persistent diversity of Canadian political life presents the national C.C.F. party with much the same problem of reconciling the divergent outlooks of the provincial wings of the party as faces the two older national parties. A significant provincialism still persists—even among those who are not conscious of specifically provincial loyalties—and is further enhanced by the fact that the only political victories of the C.C.F. have been at the provincial level.

In its attempt to ensure that the party organization shall work democratically, the C.C.F. has thus far been free from the embar-

rassment which comes from accepting large donations from benefactors. Party funds are raised mainly by collecting annual fees
from the mass membership of the party. Like the Labour party
in Britain, it invites affiliation with trade unions and gets some
revenues from that source. Some donations are always received
but these come from well-wishers and enthusiasts. The C.C.F. has
had no traffic with business interests. Its war chest is much smaller
than that which the older parties can generally raise but most of
its work is done voluntarily and enthusiastically for the sake of the
cause.

There are other contrasts with the older parties which could
be drawn but most of them are merely consequences of the general
influences which have been illustrated. It is impossible to say now
whether the austere democracy at which C.C.F. organization aims
will endure. Like other human institutions, political parties are
corrupted by power and the C.C.F. has not yet been exposed
seriously, on a national scale at least, to this baneful influence. It
is clear, however, that in its emphasis on research, education, and
continuous intensive effort it has grasped what present-day conditions require of democratic parties. The C.C.F. may not be what
the country needs but it does bring into sharp relief some of the
defects of the older parties.

CONCLUSION

In conclusion, the scope of the foregoing treatment of political
parties should be re-stated. Attention has been concentrated
almost entirely on the functions of political parties in a democracy,
and on the organization that parties have worked out for fulfilling
these functions. It has been urged that the only practicable method
so far discovered for eliciting the will of the people as a whole is
to have political parties compete for the support of the electorate.
This is the essential function of political parties. They cannot
perform the function without extensive and intricate organization.

It is difficult to energize a football team by pointing out the
broad social functions of sport and recreation. The team needs a
more immediate concrete objective, the winning of the next game.
Party organization also needs an immediate objective, the winning

of the next election. Many of those who are active in party organization regard it as primarily, if not solely, an instrument for gaining power. The immediate objective necessarily looms large in party calculations, a fact that can best be appreciated by looking at the scale and character of party organization.

Much of the criticism of political parties, and of democratic government, arises from the belief that both parties and government are the playthings of small cliques of rival politicians. In any assessment of democratic government and politics, it is necessary to attend to criticisms of this kind. A complete investigation of such charges would take us far afield, but the first step is to describe party organization with a view to seeing who exercises power in it, who makes the effective decisions, and under what limitations and controls. These questions are not easy to answer, but at least it has been seen that whatever power small groups may exercise in political parties from time to time, their power is always contingent, can be undermined, and therefore must be used with both eyes on the electorate.

As already pointed out, concentration on the functions and organization of political parties leaves aside much that is necessary to an understanding of the political parties in any one of the three countries. From the point of view of the politics of a particular country, the policies for which the parties stand are of primary significance. But these policies cannot be understood without reviewing political history and the vicissitudes of party fortunes, explaining the social and economic structure, and outlining the current politics of the country in question. Such an extensive treatment cannot be undertaken here.

CHAPTER IX

REPRESENTATION

THIS chapter is an excursion through a number of plans for improving democratic government that time has laid to rest. Political democracy has never fulfilled the hopes of its more sanguine believers. For a long time, they laid these disappointments to defective machinery and put great ingenuity into devices for making the will of the people manifest and effective. The staple of theoretical political discussion, in the Anglo-Saxon world at any rate, for the fifty years preceding 1930 was how to make democracy more democratic. A number of plans for accomplishing this were advocated and tried in various parts of the world. As a result of their failure, faith in them has almost entirely disappeared and thus they need not be discussed in detail. However, the criticisms of legislatures and political parties which these devices embodied and the defects from which they themselves were shown to suffer throw very significant light on democratic politics. Also the dissatisfaction that gave rise to the proposals still remains.

The central issue is the problem of representation, and some general remarks on it must first be made. Subject to a few unimportant exceptions, the members of the lower houses of the legislatures in Britain, United States, and Canada are chosen by the voters in single-member constituencies. The candidate with a plurality, i.e. the largest number of votes though not necessarily a majority of the votes cast, is elected. He is said to represent the constituency even though, in a three-or-more-cornered fight, he may get much less than an absolute majority. Whether he has an absolute majority or not, those who voted against him are disposed to think of themselves as unrepresented, while many of those who voted for him regard him only as the lesser of two or more evils. When we remember how various opinions are, it is clear that no member of Parliament can begin to represent them all and that a good deal of dissatisfaction is inevitable.

What Does the Representative Represent?

To understand what this so-called representation is or can be, it is necessary to recall some history and venture some analysis. The democracies of the ancient world practised direct democracy. The citizens of the city-state participated directly in the making of laws and the governing of the city. Lacking the device of representation, the Roman Republic was unable to provide for effective popular participation in government when it expanded too far beyond the confines of the city. Representation is a medieval invention apparently originating in the practice of the early Christian Church in calling together representative councils to deal with matters affecting the government of Christendom. With the emergence of kings in the feudal societies of Europe, the custom of calling representatives from the communities under their sway developed. Simon de Montfort called representatives of the shires and boroughs to Westminster in 1265, with momentous results, but he did not invent representation. It was widely used in the medieval world.

In the thirteenth century, and in most instances up to the nineteenth century, the shire or borough was a close-knit community with a high degree of economic self-sufficiency in which individuals were bound together by customary relationships. What division of labour and economic specialization there was, was local, not national and international. Without the modern means of communication, there was little movement of individuals from one community to another, and little intercourse between communities. People lived and died and found the entire meaning of their lives in a single area. The dialects, which often differ from shire to shire, testify to the distinctiveness of these communities that were represented.

They were social unities in much the same sense in which today, rightly or wrongly, we attribute unity to the nation. We have little difficulty in thinking that the government or an ambassador can represent the common interests of the nation in international negotiations. It used to be just as easy, and perhaps easier, to think that a representative could represent the shire or borough in the councils of the king. He could air the grievances of his community and combine with other representatives in petitioning the king to redress them.

A constituency today is not such a community with a distinctive unity of its own which one man can represent. Constituencies are now strips of territory in which so many voters live, and their boundaries are always being readjusted so as to give representation by population. This practice of readjusting the boundaries of constituencies gives the clue to the modern theory of representation. It is individuals and not communities which are represented.[1] This is partly due to the modern emphasis on individualism. But the older theory could not be maintained today because there are no longer local communities with a distinctive unity to be represented. Economic specialization transcends the local community and also the nation. The vital interests of individuals are linked to persons, circumstances, and events far beyond the locality.

Modern transport and communications have given extraordinary mobility to the population, making them a nation of transients without deep consciousness of locality. As has already been pointed out, the great ease of communication has facilitated the organization of many communities of interest, economic, social, and cultural, which are at least nation-wide and not connected with any locality. The local undertaker is now likely to be at least as much interested in the shop-talk of the annual embalmers' convention as in the death of his neighbours. The result is that the older social unity based on territory has been broken into a multitude of diverse specialized interests. And governments today are engaged in all sorts of activities that can help or harm these specialized interests, thus inviting people to mix calculations concerning their narrow interests with their opinions about public policy.

The older localism and the theory of representation appropriate to it have been outmoded. It may help to emphasize the change to point to a remaining vestige of the older theory. The constitutions of the United States and Canada give equal, or something approaching equal, representation to the states and provinces in the upper chambers of the federal legislatures. The states and provinces are still regarded as communities that can be represented, and are entitled to be represented as such, and not merely as heterogeneous collections of individuals. But even here, the forces

[1]Practice does not entirely accord with theory. The member of the legislature does represent certain common interests of his constituency, as when he manages to secure a new highway or a new post office.

just discussed have been at work, and the unity of particular states and provinces in the federations is somewhat artificial.

The situation today is profoundly different in another respect. As long as the king was in reality the government he expressed the general interests of the nation, however defective that expression may have been. Even if he was no more than a leader in war he made and executed the policy of national defence. The representatives to his councils acknowledged this, although grudgingly. Their function was to act as a check on him, limiting the demands made by the whole on the parts. The king and his civil service withstood these pressures, asserting their interpretation of what was needed to maintain the unity and integrity of the country.

When the king was reduced to a figurehead or dethroned, the legislature composed of representatives of local interests became supreme. If the members of the legislature represented only their constituencies, who now spoke for the nation? It was a recognition of the inescapable necessity of some body with a unified conception of the national interest which led the framers of the first republican Constitution of France to declare that the deputy (i.e. the member of Parliament) belongs to the nation. He must represent the nation, and speak for it and not for the narrow purposes of his constituency.

The same provision appeared in the Constitution of the German Republic of 1919. However, despite some distinguished advocacy of it, this view never caught hold in Britain and North America, where it is the general assumption that the member of Parliament represents the electors of his constituency. Despite this seeming defect in Anglo-American theory, Britain, the United States, and Canada have not suffered as much from lack of national unity as have continental European countries. The explanation is that theory is of little account unless it is workable in practice, and to say that the deputy belongs to the nation accomplishes nothing unless the deputy and a majority of his fellows can agree on what should be done on behalf of the nation. Continental democracies, generally speaking, have never reached this agreement, always being plagued by a multiple-party system, while the two-party system in Anglo-American countries has almost always produced a majority view of the national interest.

Without going into the many factors of history and geography that are responsible for this difference, the short explanation is that most of the democracies on the continent of Europe have always been split by so many deep cleavages that they could never get to the point of agreeing that there were only two important sides to the story. There were always many important sides to the story requiring to be narrated at length by many political parties. Britain, the United States, and Canada have had a deeper political unity, a wider acceptance of the liberal democratic political ideals outlined in chapter II. Partly because of this, they have always been the foremost experts in working out practical procedures for mediating differences. With the possible exception of Switzerland and the Scandinavian countries, the processes of discussion have always worked more temperately and more fruitfully in the Anglo-American world than anywhere else.

At any rate, the important point for present purposes is that when the king lost his power and gave up his function of integrating the parts of the country as a whole, political parties took his place. We have said that the executive and civil service govern the country; but their ability to do it depends on the support of a political party that has won a majority of the electorate. As has already been argued, political parties in a two-party system are not divisive but unifying influences. In their never-ceasing search for votes they build bridges across local and personal prejudices, sectional and occupational antagonisms. In a democracy, which cannot fall back on some authoritative statement of the national interest but must always manufacture the national interest out of the consent of the people, the unifying function is indispensable. In societies where the ultimate political ideal is the releasing of individual personality in conditions of freedom, the political parties are a procedural device for integrating the inevitable diversity of views into the unity of action that is vital for the running of any government. European experience indicates that where political parties fail to perform this task, dictators arise who do. But, as we have already seen, they do it by destroying spontaneity and stifling diversity, i.e. by negating the liberal democratic ideals.

The dilemma should now be clear. The dominant theory and the social structure of our time combine to insist that the member of Parliament must represent the individuals in his constituency. Because these individuals have differing views and conflicting interests, the member of Parliament cannot represent them all. The fundamental impossibility of representing heterogeneous individual opinions and group interests through representatives chosen by a plurality of votes in single-member constituencies has caused profound dissatisfaction and numerous panaceas.

The aim of most of these schemes is to make the legislature reflect more accurately the diversity of opinions and interests in the electorate. This diversity is increased and made much more complex by the luxuriant development of organized groups in which the like-minded gather together to further a common occupational or cultural interest. These groupings cut across the territorial constituency and seek to express themselves politically in other ways than through their votes. They always promote narrow purposes and often clash with one another, thus adding to the babel of individual opinions and the collision of group interests.

The integrating function is difficult to perform under the best of circumstances. Any scheme of representation that does not enable it to be performed makes representative government impossible. The reformers generally have not understood this, and almost all their schemes are discredited because they make integration more difficult, if not impossible. With these points in mind, we may look at some of these reforms, their tendencies and results.

As long as there are only two parties and two candidates in a constituency, one will always receive an absolute majority of votes cast. However, when there are three or more parties the victor will often be elected by less than an absolute majority, and the more parties there are, the smaller the fraction of the vote that will suffice to elect. A candidate who could never have wheedled an absolute majority of the voters into voting for him may be elected.

The devices for meeting this specific defect are the second ballot and the alternative vote. The second ballot involves an immediate second, or "run-off," election between the two candidates who got the greatest number of votes in the first election. It has been used in some countries of continental Europe. It is also used in the direct primaries in about a dozen southern states of the United States. The law in these states requires that the candidates chosen in the primary shall be nominated by a majority of those who vote, since nomination in a one-party state is tantamount to election. Accordingly, where the first ballot fails to produce a candidate with a majority, a second "run-off" election takes place between the two at the top of the poll. It ensures that an absolute majority of those who voted in the primary regard the candidate as at least a tolerable choice.

The alternative vote, which is also known as preferential voting, requires the voters to mark 1 opposite their first choice on the ballot, and if they wish to express second and third alternative choices, to mark 2 and 3 opposite the names of these choices. Then, if the counting of first preferences of all voters does not give any candidate an absolute majority, the candidate at the bottom of the poll is eliminated from the contest and the second choice of the voters who voted for him as first choice are distributed according to their preferences. A second counting of ballots then follows to see if the totals of the first and second choices give any candidate an absolute majority. If not, the process of dropping candidates from the foot of the poll continues until an absolute majority for some one candidate emerges. The ultimate result achieved is the same as that reached by the second ballot.

The alternative vote was used in provincial elections in the Canadian provinces of Alberta, Manitoba, and, for a short period, in British Columbia. Some eleven states in the United States at one time or another also experimented with it for primary elections but ultimately discarded it. They found that a very large percentage of the voters "plumped" for one candidate and did not indicate second and third choices. The alternative vote is, however, apparently found to be satisfactory in Australia where members of the House of Representatives are elected in this way.

Preferential voting, if the voters really indicate an order of preference, prevents the election of candidates by a mere plurality. It has therefore some advantages where three or more parties become a persistent feature of political life. It has, however, some undesirable tendencies in enabling any two parties to combine at the polls to knock out a feared third party. If the two older parties act in concert against a third radical party, they may stifle the party without removing the dissatisfaction that caused its rise. Third and fourth parties are, of course, undesirable, but the effective way to deal with them is for the older parties to make accommodation for minority protest rather than by trying to evade the issue by election dodges.

Neither of these devices has had much appeal to the vigorous reformers because it still leaves in every constituency a substantial or large minority whose candidate or candidates were defeated and who think they are denied representation. It is even possible in a two-party fight for one party that wins its seats by small majorities and gathers a very light vote in the seats it loses, to win a majority of all seats with less than a majority of the total vote. This will rarely happen, but it is not uncommon for a party to win a much smaller proportion of the seats than its proportion of the total vote would warrant if it is individuals who are being represented.

The situation is aggravated by the emergence of third and fourth parties, because a minority of votes will elect a candidate and two or more substantial minorities will claim to be unrepresented. The C.C.F. party in Canada has suffered heavily in this way. In 1949, it took over thirteen per cent of the popular vote and won less than five per cent of the seats. Moreover, this inequitable apportionment is also apparent in the excessive number of seats captured by the victorious majority party. In 1949, the Liberals with fifty per cent of the popular vote held seventy-three per cent of the seats in the House of Commons. Such disparities have been a regular feature of national elections in Canada as three or more parties continue to bid for office. They have been less usual in Britain and the United States where the two-party tradition, at the national level, has been more secure in recent years.

PROPORTIONAL REPRESENTATION

Starting from the assumption that representation in the legislature ought to be a true image of the nation regarded as a collection of individuals, the reformers of the late nineteenth century sought to devise a scheme that would give representation to every significant body of opinion in proportion to its numbers. They sought equity in representation and not merely endorsement of candidates by an absolute majority. Some three hundred different schemes of proportional representation have been devised, but they are of two main types. One is known as the single transferable vote, also known as the Hare system after its original inventor, and the other is the list system. Each requires for its working multiple-member constituencies with enough members so that any substantial minority can expect to elect at least one of its candidates. The constituencies are necessarily very large in area and population if the number of members of the legislature is to be kept within reasonable limits.

The single transferable vote requires a constituency with at least five members if it is to achieve its purpose of enabling each substantial minority to elect a member. Voters mark their choices in order of preference, 1, 2, 3, 4, and so on. The quota of votes necessary for election is determined,[1] and as soon as that number of first preferences is counted for particular candidates, they are declared elected and the remaining ballots for those candidates as first choice are transferred to the second choice and so on. When all surplus ballots have thus been transferred, the candidate with the smallest total is eliminated, and all his ballots transferred to the candidate who is the next choice on each. This process of transferring surpluses and eliminating the weaker candidates proceeds until the quota has been reached by as many candidates as there are seats to be filled.

Thus any party whose disciplined supporters vote the party ticket throughout will waste no votes and will elect one of its candidates every time it fills a quota. Every minority that can fill a quota will elect a member. Variants of the single transferable vote, of which there are many, are used in a few municipal elections in the United States. The single transferable vote was used in provincial elections in Alberta (until 1957) and Manitoba (until 1958) in the multiple-member constituencies of Calgary, Edmonton, and Winnipeg. Eire is today probably the most consistent adherent of this system.

There are also many variants of the list system currently being used by a number of European countries. The most thoroughgoing of these was used in Germany under the Weimar Republic. Germany was divided into thirty-five mammoth constituencies ranging from one to two million voters each. These constituencies were grouped together, generally in pairs, into eighteen larger areas called unions, and the unions in turn were lumped into one national constituency

---

[1] The quota is determined by dividing the number of votes cast by the number of seats to be filled plus one, and then adding one to the result.

called the Reich. Each of the thirty-five constituencies was to send eleven members to the Reichstag; each union, and also the Reich, to send an indefinite number, depending on the voting. Each party prepared lists of candidates for the constituencies, the unions, and the Reich. Elections were held in the thirty-five constituencies only. The voter was required to select his party and vote for the whole list or not at all. A quota of 60,000 votes elected a candidate for the party.

If the X party got 230,000 votes for its list in Y constituency, the first three candidates on its list were elected with 50,000 votes to spare. In the Z constituency, grouped with Y constituency in a union, the party might elect two members and have 45,000 votes left over. The two surpluses were then transferred in a book-keeping transaction to the union and added together, giving the party an elected member on its union list with 35,000 votes unused. The union surpluses of each party were added together in the same way and transferred to the Reich, where they would elect another party candidate for every 60,000 votes transferred. Ignoring minor qualifications such as the untransferability of small surpluses, and visualizing the process at work in each constituency and for each party, it is clear that no single party could waste more than 59,999 votes in the entire country. Party representation in the Reichstag mirrored almost exactly its voting strength. In spite of this or, as some say, because of it, came Hitler! Nevertheless, the West German Republic of today still elects half its legislature by proportional representation.

Proportional representation obviously accomplishes its prime purpose of giving representation to minorities. This may be admitted to be a gain in so far as well-established parties in a two-party system ignore the interests of small bodies of opinion. In addition, the mathematics of the scheme prevent wasted votes and correct the tendency of the single member district system to award seats out of all proportion to the total votes cast. Enlarged electoral districts may also give a wider range of choice to voters and provide a larger arena from which competent candidates can be selected.[1]

However, the perils to which proportional representation exposes

---

[1]For a detailed examination of the merits of proportional representation, as well as a full account of its application in many countries, see Enid Lakeman and James D. Lambert, *Voting in Democracies* (London, 1955).

democratic government outweigh any possible advantages. Its main undesirable tendencies are two: first, the splintering of political parties and secondly, the increase in centralized control of the electorate by political parties. The list system is more dangerous in these respects than the single transferable vote system. The extent to which the latter promotes these undesirable tendencies depends on the size of the multiple-member constituencies and the number of members each of them is to elect. If a multiple-member constituency elects no more than three members, the damage may not be serious. It has been pointed out, however, that it must elect about twice this number if it is to effect its main purpose of giving fair representation to minorities. The following comments are applicable to both systems except as noted.

Undesirable Tendencies of Proportional Representation

To establish the tendency of proportional representation towards a multiplication of parties, one could rely on the actual results in the countries of continental Europe that used proportional representation. For example, in Germany before the adoption of the list system in 1919, there were only half a dozen significant political parties. When Hitler abolished all parties in 1933, there were twice that number of significant parties as well as a number of sects endeavouring to assert themselves as political parties. Such results could be, and to a large extent no doubt were, due to other causes. So it is important to see why the tendency must be in that direction.

Where only two parties are in the field, each knows it must work for a majority in the constituency and in the country. Each knows it must put out bait for the wavering voters, generally the moderates who look at both sides of a question. Each must court significant minorities, and these necessities make for a middle-of-the-road platform and for candidates who have a general appeal. That is to say, minorities are not ignored and they are not entirely unrepresented, because one or other of the party platforms takes their less extreme demands into account.

This is the party system working at its best. It compels everyone to concentrate on what he shares in common with others, to search for the unifying ideas and policies. It compels everyone either to forget differences or to minimize and compromise them, instead of

exaggerating them. And since both parties are competitively engaged in the same task, looking for a basis of unity on which to
construct a majority, it draws them closer together rather than
forcing them further apart.

On the other hand, minority groups of opinion know that their
chances of electing members of their own are slim except where
they happen to be heavily concentrated in particular constituencies. They tend to swing to one or the other of the two parties,
hoping for some consideration in return for support and often
bargaining for it. While the middle-of-the-road programme may
not attract them, it does not positively repel. With reluctance, yet
with some minimum of consent, they come into the fold. Extreme
views do not construct a party for their propagation unless conditions are such as to encourage them over a long period of time.

When proportional representation makes it possible for minorities
to count confidently on getting at least a few seats, they reject
middle-of-the-road programmes and set out in full cry to realize
their interpretation of the good life. Once a small bloc gets into
Parliament, a minority has a forum from which to expound its
gospel, and it hopes, as sects always do, to win the world to the
obvious truth of its views. Once the core of a party is formed, it
tends like all organizations to become important for its own sake as
well as for its purposes and thus to perpetuate itself.

When the minorities begin to withdraw their support from the
two old parties, these, in turn, change their character. The premium
paid for moderation diminishes, and they tend to take more dogmatic positions, hoping to hold a following with strong convictions.
If the French-speaking people of Canada were to consolidate in a
minority party of their own, the two old parties would naturally
become more truculent in their expression of English-speaking
Protestant views. Such action repels still other groups, e.g. the
Irish Catholics, which then seek self-expression. As the number of
significant parties grows, it becomes unlikely that any one party
will get an absolute majority of the seats in the legislature. Not
expecting to have the sole responsibility of governing, parties are
no longer under the necessity of working out a practicable platform.
Since responsibility can no longer be concentrated on them, they
cease to feel a sense of responsibility. They devise their programmes
to attract a fervent following whose particular interests they push,

rather than to provide an acceptable policy for the country as a whole.

In periods of unrest, the spectacle of extreme views making headway in the country rouses opposing schools of extremism. When the extreme left steadily increases its representation in the legislature, panic rises on the extreme right, and a party, or parties, appears to combat the danger of revolution, real or imagined. The violent demeanour of this reactionary element pushes the moderate left toward the extreme left. Some such pattern of development was seen in both Italy and Germany during the rise of Fascism. This degeneration of politics into open warfare was not solely caused, but it was actively fostered, by proportional representation.

The parties are therefore not only splintered, but they also become dogmatic sects and rabid factions promoting their own narrow creeds. French experience with the workings of proportional representation after World War II revealed, for example, how easy it was for the Communist party to take advantage of the system to form a rabid, vocal bloc in the Assembly. As a result, recent electoral reforms have substantially modified the system, with a consequent reduction in the seats captured by the Communists. All parties become radical, in one sense or another, and less disposed to the inevitable compromises of a democratic system. While few of the economic groups—farmers, workers, manufacturers, and a thousand lesser occupations—set up their own parties, they exact concessions from the parties much more easily than under a two-party system. A strong economic interest may win one of the small parties to its views on economic matters because the small party, unlike the great parties of the two-party system, does not have to consider the reaction of opposing interest groups. It will never have the unquestioned power to implement the bargain. In this way, the economic and other group interests pick their champions and expect them to stand firm on the floor of the legislature. This increases the intransigence of parties.

The inevitable result of a multiple-party system is weak government. All governments are coalitions chosen, not by the country in the election, but through huckstering in the legislature. The several parties in the coalition, backed by opposing interests of various kinds, often find that the only thing they can agree to do is to do nothing. Their policies are more colourless than those of governments in a two-party system. At best, governments are short-lived compromise arrangements, and at worst they are paralytics. If resolute government action must be taken, it can only be taken by relieving the government from responsibility to the legislature, i.e. by executive decree. Such was the actual course of events in Germany and Italy. Workable democratic government had become impossible before the Nazis and Fascists came to power. They did not so much destroy democracy as fill a gap left by its demise.

Government by short-lived coalitions of several parties makes it impossible for the electorate to enforce responsibility. If the government fails to do what it should obviously have done, each party retorts that it never had the power to do it and blames the other parties in the coalition for the failure. It is rarely clear who should be punished at the next election. The gap between the electorate and the government—too wide under the best of circumstances—is still further widened. In the two-party system, the party that wins the election drives forward something resembling its announced policy, and the opposed ranks of voters across the country feel triumph and chagrin if the policy works well, and disappointment and prophetic insight if it works ill. After all, this is what they voted for or against. But the policy of a compromise coalition is always one on which they never were asked to express an opinion. Apathy and disgust deepen with the sense of remoteness from the whole process of governing.

These evils of group coalition government are all likely to be realized in any thoroughgoing system of proportional representation. Under the list system, it is harder for groups to get the initial organization necessary for preparing party lists in a number of constituencies across the country. But if this hurdle can be jumped, it promotes thorough fragmentation of the political parties. The Hare system, on the other hand, is not likely to result in so numerous splinter parties. However, it makes it much easier to take the initial steps. A candidate for a new party can be put up at any time in one constituency and, even if he fails to win, the votes for him are not wholly lost but transferred to second or third choices. If he does win, the group is encouraged to take further easy steps in other constituencies.

The problem of coalition government is peculiar to parliamentary systems of the British type where the executive sits in the legislature and is responsible to it. Factional division in the legislature, which makes majorities there unstable or impossible, is directly reflected in the executive. Without a resolute majority in the legislature, there cannot be a resolute executive. Thus any disintegrating tendency that proportional representation may have will manifest itself most sharply and most quickly in a parliamentary system. Germany and Italy were both trying to work parliamentary systems of the British type.

Under the United States Constitution, the executive, i.e. the President, is, in effect, directly elected. To win the Presidency, it is necessary to concentrate a clear majority of the votes of the electoral college in favour of one candidate. This, in turn, compels each party to aim at winning a majority of the popular vote. This necessity has contributed to, if indeed it is not one of the main factors responsible for, maintaining the two-party system in national elections.

Proportional representation obviously could not be introduced in presidential elections. If it were introduced for congressional elections, the desire to win the Presidency, and the fact that it can only be won in an election by getting a clear majority of the votes of the electoral college, would work against the disintegrating tendency of proportional representation. It is impossible to say whether the tendency would be combated effectively.

It can be said, however, that one of the serious present-day defects in the national government of the United States is the weakness of legislative-executive co-ordination. When the President and the majority in Congress are of the same party, as is usually the case, the weakness arises largely out of lack of discipline in the majority party. Any electoral reform that would tend to increase and strengthen blocs and factions within Congress would be undesirable.

Proportional representation undermines the intimate connection of the member with his constituency. In the single-member constituency, he is likely to be a prominent person widely known, and he can visit every section of it. He can make contact with all groups and learn the configuration of opinion. In the large multiple-member constituency, which may have hundreds of thousands of voters, relatively few voters know the candidates and the candidates cannot cover the whole constituency. Each cultivates his own sect, which confirms his prejudices rather than enlarging his outlook. More rigid doctrinaires, and fewer flexible persons of broad sympathy and general electoral appeal, go to the legislature. Lacking broad support in their constituency, they have no foundation for an independent stand in the councils of their party. The supporters of the Hare system have always claimed that it would send more independent-minded men to Parliament. This can mean, in reality, no more than that they would be independent of the discipline of the parties in the two-party system. They are likely to fall under a narrower and sharper discipline in the splinter parties that support them. These sects are likely to tolerate independence even less than the old parties, which were invariably seeking an over-all majority rather than some special brand of salvation.

This brings us to the second undesirable tendency of proportional representation, the tendency towards more strongly disciplined control of the party by the central party machine. The list system cannot help but work in this direction. In Germany, under proportional representation, the central party organizations strengthened their influence over their respective parties. It is much more practicable to centralize control of local party organization when constituencies number in tens instead of hundreds. The officers of the party and their favourites then get their names at the head of the party list, and since voters must vote for the list and not for particular candidates they, at least, are always sure of election.[1] Young men are thus greatly handicapped in advancing to leadership, while everything favours the perpetuation of the old guard and the extension of its influence over the party. Independent-minded candidates must not be put on the list, because their presence there may make voters reject the whole list.

The parties become much less responsive to opinion in the constituencies. Members are not in close touch with their constituencies and, as has been remarked, they are not sufficiently sure of solid personal backing in the constituency to press insistently for revision in party policy. By-elections, which are such useful barometers of opinion, are not possible under proportional representation.

[1] Belgium, Holland, and Norway use a variant of the straight list system that permits the voter to indicate on his party's list the order of his choices, thus partially overcoming this criticism.

The old guard who head the party lists are always sure of election and need not cultivate the constituencies carefully at all. Because they do not have to wage a stern fight for election, they remain active and influential much longer than would otherwise be possible. Men who represent new currents of opinion in the party and thus threaten the established leadership cannot get on the party list at all, or if they do, are likely to be removed when their rivalry becomes serious. Party leadership becomes unresponsive, rigid, and bureaucratic. The Hare system when it works through large constituencies has similar tendencies although, in the absence of the rigid list, they are not likely to be nearly so marked.

The fact that democracy fared ill in certain European countries that used proportional representation does not prove that the electoral device was the effective cause of what happened. The evidence that proportional representation contributed greatly to the downfall of democracy in Germany and Italy is very strong.[1] But, as already stated, there were other deeper forces working in the same direction that, by themselves might well have been decisive. Neither country had an effective liberal democratic tradition. Both were racked by the economic and social dislocations of war and both suffered severely from internal disunity.

Both Italy and Germany had numerous political parties before proportional representation was introduced. The experience of these countries does not demonstrate that the introduction of it elsewhere would necessarily cause a splintering of the party system. In the Scandinavian countries, for example, proportional representation has presumably worked successfully, largely because united communities have checked excessive splintering of parties and supported relatively stable coalitions. The limited use of the single transferable vote in the United States and Canada does not afford any positive evidence one way or the other as to the possible splintering effects of the scheme. The use of it, until quite recently, in the Canadian provinces was limited to three urban multiple-member constituencies and therefore it never did invite attempts to form new parties. It has been used for a considerable period in municipal elections in a few cities in the United States. The results, judged by estimates

[1]See F. A. Hermens, *Democracy or Anarchy? A Study of Proportional Representation,* Review of Politics, Notre Dame, 1941, on which the above discussion of proportional representation relies heavily. See also the same author's *The Representative Republic* (Notre Dame, 1958).

made of them, have been mixed.[1] The device has helped non-partisan citizens' organizations to break control of city government by party machines. While it has encouraged racial groups to vote together to elect members to municipal councils in some instances, it has not shown any tendency to splinter the party system.

However, as long as the frame of the national and state organization of the existing parties remains undisturbed, splintering tendencies introduced at the local level are not likely to have any effect. The disintegrating tendencies argued to be implicit in proportional representation require a larger field than a single city in which to operate. Like-minded minorities are scattered across the country. Proportional representation would have to be adopted on a state, or perhaps even on a national, scale to give them an effective opportunity to organize.

Also, a multiplicity of divisive political issues is needed to provide impulses for division. It has already been pointed out that the great increase in central government activities creates this multiplicity of issues and that conscious group interests tend to form and express themselves as these issues give them common ground. The rapid growth in the number of organized pressure groups and their incessant search for ways and means of influencing the political process, which will be discussed in the next chapter, at least suggest that such groups would welcome the undoubted opportunities afforded by proportional representation. Anything that tends to give freer rein to these divisive influences rather than checking them is undesirable, and the working of liberal democracy is more likely to be prejudiced than improved by this electoral device.

THE REAL DILEMMAS IN REPRESENTATION

It will be asked, then, whether there is no cure for the defective representation of opinion in democratic representative government. The discussion has already suggested that minority views are not completely unrepresented in the two-party system. The electorate is, as the electoral reformers argue, made up of a great many opinions and groups of opinion. Each party must try to conciliate

[1]Compare Hermens, op. cit. pp. 359–419 and Joseph P. Harris, "The Practical Workings of Proportional Representation in the United States and Canada," *National Municipal Review*, XIX, 335-83.

enough of these views to win a majority of the seats in the legislature, and that means taking these views into account in its platform. That is why party programmes seem to the holders of strong views to be lacking in vigour. Of course, no party that expects to have the sole responsibility for governing can embrace many of the extremes of minority opinion, if for no other reason than that they are often contradictory and inconsistent. No party can put an anti-vaccinationist plank in its platform and at the same time meet the demands of more enlightened opinion for effective protection of public health. A little reflection will bring many similar possible clashes to mind. Proportional representation can find representation for diverse views of all kinds because it ignores the necessity of finding a single coherent and consistent public policy for the country as a whole.

We come again to some hard realities that were mentioned earlier. Government action is collective action taken on behalf of the whole and, if it is not to be self-defeating, it cannot give expression to *all* the crosspurposes entertained by particular members and parts of the whole. Presumably, something is to be accomplished by common action and, if it is to be done with consent, it cannot pander to extremes. Also, the immediate effect of much of government policy is to shift burdens from one set of shoulders to another. As long as this is so, there will be disgruntled minorities even though they get direct representation in the legislature. Even if the majority in the legislature agree to do nothing, minorities that had hoped to shift their burdens will be disgruntled.

There is therefore no cure. The best that can be offered is a palliative to be found through government's being limited in its actions in so far as is humanly possible to matters on which something approaching a community of view can be found. Democratic government may not survive unless action is so limited, and unless a sensitive mechanism is available for discovering which policies of action can hope to find a broad base of consent. The two-party system is the best instrument so far found for this delicate task. There may be others, but they have not yet appeared.

It will be retorted that election by a mere plurality in contests between three or more parties is intolerable. That may be our conclusion if such contests are to become a general and permanent feature of political life. It is not at all clear, however, that degeneration into a multiple-party system is inevitable. All our social institutions must face periodic crises. The sick do not always die and institutions often surmount their crises. An electorate that has had experience of the ease of fixing responsibility under the two-party system and cabinet government is likely to abandon a party that shows, by running third in several successive elections, that it has little chance of gaining a majority. Less rational considerations such as the desire to be on the winning side work in the same direction. It is probable that this fate has overtaken the Liberal party in Britain, its proportion of the popular vote having declined from twenty per cent in the 'twenties to less than three per cent in the 'fifties. The excision of such a party is painful, as all surgical operations are, but those who genuinely cherish democratic government will not shrink from it if it ensures the continued life of the two-party system. In Canada, the third and fourth parties of protest do not seem as great a threat to the two-party system as they were ten years ago.

The United States lacks the cabinet system as a device for clearly fixing responsibility, but it has a most effective substitute for the maintenance of the two-party system in its national politics. As has been pointed out, the Presidency cannot be won by a plurality but only by a majority of the votes of the electoral college. Parties that cannot come within striking distance of this great prize have always been brushed aside and are likely to continue to get scant support.

A return to a two-party system will not be of any great advantage to democracy if, for example, a socialist party determined on wholesale socialization faces as its sole competitor a Conservative or Liberal party determined to preserve the *status quo*. In such circumstances, solid community of view is extremely problematical, even among the socialists themselves. What a democratic government does in the name of all must be limited to things that a substantial majority either actively approve or regard as tolerable. Here we come upon a factor that should have been mentioned much earlier. It would not do to blame proportional representation entirely for the splintering of parties in those countries in which it has been used. An underlying influence of great strength has been the continually extending range of the activities of government.

In the heyday of laissez faire, it was relatively easy to come to some community of view on government policy because the possible courses of government action under the restraining influence of that philosophy were sharply limited. Once it was generally admitted that it might be desirable for government to intervene in any or all sectors of social life, the possible courses of government action reached infinity and tended to produce a sharper diversity of view in the electorate. Groups that could formerly agree on foreign policy and on the aims and means of maintaining internal order began to divide on issues affecting economic and social welfare. Is the government to aid industry or agriculture, or both, with concrete privileges? Is it to discourage trusts and combines and to encourage small businesses with loans at low interest? Is it to fix wages but not profits or agricultural prices? Is it to provide social security for the industrial wage earner but not for the independent worker on his own account? The alternative possibilities are almost endless.

Some reflection on the contents of chapter v will show that measures which benefit one group are an immediate burden to another group and that, in so far as the people judge government action by immediate consequences and considerations of narrow advantage, the increase of government activities tends to multiply greatly the divisions of opinion in the electorate. In fact, if people judged solely by these criteria, democratic government would have expired long ago. No one will suggest that the electorate is uninfluenced by such criteria, and hearkening to them makes it difficult to prevent either the breaking up of the two-party system into an agglomeration of interest groups or its degeneration from a sham battle into a real battle between left and right.

The fact that government now does so much that affects intimately the life of everyone is at the root of much of the dissatisfaction over the existing system of representation. In a constituency of diverse economic occupations and interests, many of which are directly regulated or assisted and all of which are in some peculiar way affected by government, how can one man know enough about these interests to share in making the laws governing them or have wide enough sympathies to represent their points of view in criticizing administration? Where farmers, industrial workers, industrial employers, independent tradesmen, and so forth, feel the impact of government action in diverse ways, how can the member of the legislature who may be doctor, lawyer, worker, or employer represent all their interests fairly? It is not a problem of the representation of precious sects but of representing legitimate interests engaged in the necessary work of making a livelihood for themselves and producing the material needs of the community. In the nature of things, the member of the legislature has only his partial and limited experience to go on. Yet he and others like him make the laws affecting these interests and supervise their administration.

Often it is not so much the question of principle but the detailed application of admitted principle that is involved. It is generally agreed that monopolies should be regulated but not, in most cases, that they should be dissolved. Just what should be done to protect the public interest without unnecessarily interfering with the productive functions that the monopoly is, in effect, licensed to perform is a matter of great intricacy. Employers may accede to the general view that minimum wage laws are necessary, but the application of such laws in all their ramified detail may only harass industry without effectively protecting the workers unless a high order of intelligence and a wide range of knowledge are brought to bear. There is no dissent at all from the proposition that safety devices in factories should be enforced, but the safety regulations must be worked out to meet the conditions in every kind of factory and for every kind of machinery.

In each of these cases and in many others, the interests directly concerned, whether workers, employers, or whatever, have some unique knowledge and experience relevant to the choice of effective means. Yet generally the laws in question are made and administered by legislators and civil servants who cannot fully grasp the import of this knowledge and experience. The point is sufficiently clinched by the story of the steamship company that found itself compelled to carry two sets of lifeboats, one set to satisfy rigid governmental specifications and the other to save the lives of its passengers in the narrow choppy seas in which the company operated. If representation through the electoral system is inadequate where the problem is only one of means, it is still less satisfactory in fields where sharp conflicts over principle make representation of the views of the interests at stake still more urgent.

OCCUPATIONAL VERSUS TERRITORIAL REPRESENTATION

This is a much more searching criticism than that put forward by the advocates of proportional representation. It was ably developed and widely discussed in many quarters in the first thirty years of the twentieth century. It denies that individuals as such can be fully represented by anyone. It is not only that the industrial worker cannot be represented in the legislature by the lawyer who is retained by his employer; he cannot be represented even by a fellow worker because they rarely share more than a few interests in common. Outside his working hours, he is devoted to Christian Science, horticulture, and the promotion of temperance legislation. The man who works next to him is a rank materialist who invests his modest savings in shares of a distillery company and whose enthusiasms are prize fighting and compulsory state medicine. A third fellow worker who is a candidate for the legislature plays host to another set of leisure interests. He cannot fully represent the other two if only because their interests outside the factory are either inconsistent or unsympathetic to one another. At most, he can merely represent the common interests of their working hours.

According to this analysis, the much deplored apathy of the electorate cannot be overcome as long as sole reliance is placed on the attempt to represent individuals in territorial constituencies. In an election campaign, voters are expected to give attention to and reach sensible conclusions on a great many issues of different kinds. Interest cannot be aroused for the obvious reason that no one can come to an intelligent answer on matters of which he has little or no knowledge and on which his experience of life affords no guide. Thus, for one issue that touches off thought and informed reflection in a voter, there are dozens that do not rouse a flicker of attention.

This lack of attention is the common-sense retort of the sensible man who recognizes his limitations and thinks it better to mind his own affairs as best he can, trusting that there are others who can judge the merits of such complicated issues. The ideal of the citizen who makes the public interest the over-riding concern of his life is impossible, at least in a complex civilization where central governments are involved in a multitude of activities, because it would leave him no time for his own unique functions in society. To which one might add that the wholly public man has no private life and is therefore likely to be an unhappy, if not an unbalanced, person.

The analysis accordingly concludes that in addition to the blundering of the amateur legislator in highly technical legislation and his inability to represent the many sides of many-sided individuals, there is the inability of the voter to register an intelligent vote. In a highly specialized society, government is bound to be a highly specialized matter too. The attempt to bring all issues to an amateur level of discussion and decision denudes them of content. The questions on which the public should arbitrate between the parties are so many and so recondite that only a few of them—and these in garbled and unreal versions—are ever put to the public. Consequently, if the vital functions in the hands of distant central governments continue to increase and are subject only to the shadowy popular control now possible, government will become steadily more bureaucratic and unresponsive until, in the end, it becomes irresponsible as well as unrepresentative.

This criticism, of which only a brief and therefore inaccurate outline has been given, was developed in great detail in the first two decades of this century. It received its fullest and most telling expression from the guild socialists in Britain. This group was certain that economic life must be fully collectivized in order to secure social justice. They were equally concerned that socialism should be thoroughly democratic. In those days before socialists became wholly captivated by the idea of central planning, the guild socialists were convinced that the nationalizing of industry under control of the central government would not bring the workers significantly closer to the democratic control of industry. They would only be exchanging one imperious employer, the big corporation, for a bigger and more imperious employer, the state, because the workers could not hope to control the publicly owned industry through the existing machinery of representative government. That is to say, the problem, as the guild socialists saw it, was substantially similar to the one to which their arguments have been applied here.

The guild socialists thought of each industry, whether agriculture, mining, lumbering, fishing, or one of the manufacturing or distributive trades, as performing an economic function for society. They proposed that each such function should be governed by a guild or association of those who worked by hand or brain in the particular industry. Legislation for and administration of the industry would be in the hands of a representative council elected by the members of the guild. Not only producers but also consumers and cultural interests of various kinds should have similar institutions of government. Each person would then have a voice in a producer, a consumer, and such cultural, associations as attracted his interest.

Most of the highly specialized activities now performed by the general national government should be transferred to the more competent specialized representative councils, which would be more amenable to democratic control. The legislature of the central, or national, government should be made up of representatives from the governing councils of the various guilds and associations. Because all the industries and important functions in the society would be governing themselves much as municipalities now govern themselves, the central government would have very few functions beyond those of defence, police, and the settling of disputes between the various self-governing guilds and associations.

The electorate for each of these representative councils, including the national legislature, would be automatically determined by function. These electorates, because they would be asked to rule on matters relating to their intimate daily life and only on those matters, would bring knowledge, experience, and a lively interest to their decisions. The representatives they chose for the governing councils would not only have this knowledge, experience, and interest, but would also fully represent their constituency because of the complete identity of its interest with theirs. The result would be a revitalizing of democracy.

The plans of the guild socialists and of others who took up their underlying idea proposed that functional or occupational representation should supersede the outmoded territorial representation. Every important specialized interest or function would form a separate electorate and choose representatives to a council that would govern its affairs. The national legislature with which we are concerned here would be composed largely of representatives of the organized functions and not of the people living in particular territorial areas.

This is the alarming final logic thought to be involved in a highly specialized society. Neither territorial communities nor individuals but only functions can be represented. Function becomes so important that it obscures the individual. Also, too much preoccupation with the clear articulation and vindication of function weakens the sense of community, of pelonging to something that contains but transcends the function. The deputies do not belong to the nation or even to the individual voters in the constituencies but only to their separate functions.

The guild socialist proposals, of which there were several varying in detail,[1] were never adopted in Britain, and the movement has disappeared. Ironically enough, the only concrete applications of their ideas have been by dictators and not by democrats. Soviet organization in Russia has several kinds of councils representative of functional groups. Nor are their ideas necessarily tied to socialism. Nazi Germany organized numerous councils representative of economic interests, professedly to provide for self-government of industry and trade. Fascist Italy set up the most complete structure of this kind and in 1939 the National Council of Corporations, chosen by occupational representation, superseded the Chamber of Deputies, which had always been chosen by territorial representation. As Mussolini explained, this was the corporate state. Corporatism was a marked feature of the Dollfuss dictatorship in Austria. Its current exponent is the Salazar regime in Portugal.

The Vices of Occupational Representation

The details of these functional institutions are not vitally important for present purposes. All the guild socialist proposals had inherent defects that ensured their discredit. They suffered from the vice of too much complicated machinery, none of which gave any reasonable assurance of safeguarding and enforcing the general interests of the whole against the parts for whose self-expression such anxious care was taken. To put it in the terms of the discussion at the beginning of this chapter, there was no adequate provision for ensuring a strong over-all authority with a unified conception of the national interest. It is, by the way, a realization of this that has

[1]G. D. H. Cole, *Guild Socialism Re-stated* (Allen and Unwin, London, 1920). This volume outlines one proposal for guild socialist organization.

won the socialists over to central planning by a strong central government.

Firmly seated dictators enforce on every group and function a view of the national interest, whether or not one agrees with their interpretation. Thus they have no need to fear such self-expression of functional organizations as they allow. The dictators are in the position of the kings already adverted to, who found it politic, and even necessary, to have representation of the communities under their rule. There is no doubt that present-day communities have functional as well as territorial habitations, and dictators need the co-operation of group interests. However, democracies do not want to employ a dictator to decide for them what should be done in the national interest, particularly because the democratic political ideals encourage individual self-expression and the cultivation of the wide range of diverse interests that enrich personality. Accordingly, the basic difficulty about adopting full-fledged functional representation is that it would eliminate the party system, the democratic instrument for producing and enforcing unified views of the national interest. It cannot be repeated too often that the capital problem of politics in a democracy is integration, drawing people into an effective unity on the collective action that government is to undertake in their name, while at the same time cherishing and protecting diversity in their private lives.

It should not be necessary to offer extended proof for this assertion. It is always easier to see the narrow interests which divide us than the common ones which unite us. As the case for functional representation so clearly shows, it would arouse a vivid interest where political parties now fail to do so. A system of representation that invites this diverse self-expression would be disruptive of party loyalties which now bridge many of the chasms between group and sectional interests. The representatives chosen by the groups would be chosen because they were ardent champions of the interests and not because they were benevolent, yielding, and conciliatory. They would be held sternly to their task by a united constituency agreed on what it wanted. There would be as many parties as there are interests.

To put it in its broadest terms, the representatives of the great interests, labour, management, and agriculture, would stand by the

demands of their constituencies, and the most likely result would
be, as in the case of proportional representation, paralysis. If a
would-be dictator were planning to make his strong-arm methods
indispensable, he could scarcely do better than promote functional
representation.

The conclusion on functional representation is the same as that
on proportional representation. In a democracy, the collective
action undertaken by government must put its main emphasis on
what unites rather than on what divides. There is no need, then,
for every interest to be specially represented in political decisions.
It is only when the government runs everything and everybody
that the demand of every interest for representation becomes
legitimate. Within a framework of order firmly maintained by
consent because it is in the main limited to those things on which
consent, however grudging, can be gained, all sorts of diversities
may be permitted self-assertion. Individuals may live rich lives
engrossed in a great variety of interests, even though these interests
lack direct political representation. The present scheme of representation through single-member territorial constituencies seems
better calculated to meet the imperative requirements demanded
of a representative system in a democracy than any of the schemes
so far proposed for supplanting it.

Yet it is sufficiently clear that the common interest almost
always requires the circumscription or regulation of particular
interests or mediation by the government between conflicting
interests. In an interdependent society with an advanced technology like ours, this regulation and mediation are always complex
questions and, as the argument for occupational representation
shows, the interests involved need to be represented in some way.
Fortunately, there are other ways of representing them, and also
the minority groups of opinion on whose behalf proportional representation is asked, than by giving them seats in the legislature.
Interests may—and do—organize lobbies to influence the government and the legislature. They can be—and often are—represented
on advisory committees attached to the government departments
that administer the laws affecting group interests. They even get
representation in the administration itself, as when the board
enforcing minimum wage laws includes representatives of employers

and employees. These forms of participation in government by organized interests and pressure groups will be discussed in later chapters.

THE INITIATIVE AND THE REFERENDUM

Dissatisfaction with representative institutions led to still another proposal for making democracy more democratic: initiative and referendum. The diagnosis behind this proposal made the political parties the villains of the piece, attributing the ills of democracy to the fact that the parties got between the electorate and the legislature. The legislators forgot their pledges, enacted bad, or failed to enact good, legislation because the parties that dominate the legislature serve interests other than those of the people. Underlying this analysis was the assumption that the electorate could be counted on for wisdom and a unified conception of the public good if only it were enabled to express itself. The opportunity could be created by authorizing the voters to by-pass the parties and the legislature and participate directly in law making.

The referendum is applied by requiring that, on petition of a small percentage of voters, particular laws enacted by the legislature shall be suspended until the whole electorate has voted on them. The initiative similarly enables some fraction of the voters to petition for a particular law to be drafted and submitted to the electorate for their decision. These two devices, which generally go together, were in use in several of the democracies of continental Europe, although Switzerland is now the only country in which they are still frequently used. In the first three decades of this century, some twenty states of the United States adopted them.[1] The movement spilled over into Western Canada, but the sole remnant of it in Canada today is the Direct Legislation Act of Alberta providing for the initiative and referendum. Many Canadian provinces, however, have made use of the plebiscite for getting an expression of popular opinion on particular issues, particularly the liquor question.

---

[1] A third instrument of direct democracy—the recall—has also been adopted by a dozen states in the United States. The recall of an elected official is usually initiated on petition of twenty-five per cent of the voters. In the province of Alberta a recall act was repealed in 1937, and the Dominion Elections Act makes it illegal for any candidate to bind himself to recall provisions imposed by his party—a practice that is still legal in Saskatchewan.

In Britain, significantly, demands for direct legislation have never got any substantial support. It was realized that direct legislation is incompatible with the practice of responsible parliamentary government. The cabinet is responsible to the legislature for its administration of the law, and the cabinet will decline to take responsibility unless the legislature enacts the laws it thinks necessary. Direct legislation by the people on vitally important matters or in any substantial volume would make this kind of government impossible. It would either deny to the cabinet the legislation that the cabinet thinks necessary, or it would impose on the cabinet responsibility for the administration of laws the cabinet dislikes. Under these conditions, a sensible cabinet would either resign or seek a dissolution of the legislature.

Worse still, since the laws to be made by the people are to correct the errant will of the legislature, the cabinet would find the legislature pushing it one way and the people pulling it another. The cabinet must enforce the law made by the people, but it can also be voted down by the majority in the legislature. Thus, the effective introduction of direct legislation into the parliamentary system would require the abolition of the rule that the cabinet must retain the confidence of the legislature, i.e. the abolition of responsible parliamentary government.

It is clear that Canadian experimenting with direct legislation results from the influence of American thought and example. Where there are fixed election dates, where the legislature and executive are separated and may be deadlocked, there is perhaps some room for direct participation of the people. At any rate, direct legislation is not so obviously incompatible with the American form of government. The experience of many American states with political corruption and boss-controlled legislatures provided a great temptation for popular intervention. Direct legislation by the electorate has put some useful legislation in force in some states, and as a standing threat against parties and legislatures that have eluded popular control it may be of some use. However, there are other ways of restoring a measure of popular control, and the defects of direct legislation outweigh its advantages.

In the first place, law making in a complex society is not a simple process. To many, the moral issue in proposals for prohibition may be quite clear. The effectiveness of such legislation if enacted depends on its detailed provisions such as the definition of "intoxicating," what is a "medicinal use," the apparatus for controlling import and manufacture, and the question whether it is purchase and sale only, or use as well, which are to be prohibited. These are complex questions. And if use is prohibited, enforcement depends on how far the police are to be authorized to search premises and persons on suspicion. Who will say that such interference with the right of privacy is not another and more complex question?

Legislation of this kind and in this detail cannot be got on the ballot paper in readily understandable terms, let alone terms enabling the public to discern the deeper issues involved. Complex legislation should only be enacted after extended debate and discussion have eliminated crudities and obscurities, foreseen difficulties and provided for them, and tempered the wind as much as possible to the particular private interests that are to be shorn by the law. Direct legislation requires the voter to take it or leave it in the raw form in which the zealots framed it, without any modification by minority protests.

Proposals of this kind assume that the laws that should be made for the common good are simple questions on which a unified popular will infallibly singles out the correct answer. In fact, the electorate entertains many views shaded in various ways, and a majority opinion has to be created by organization and propaganda. The parties are professional organizers of opinion and they do not ignore such opportunities. The multiplying of the occasions of voting is not likely to diminish greatly the power of party machines. The special interests that will be directly advanced or prejudiced by the proposed law spend money and pour out propaganda. For example, experience shows that both the temperance and the liquor interests can be counted on for zeal and overstatement, and they bombard the electorate with biased information and arguments in plebiscites on the liquor question. The influence of parties and special interests is by no means eliminated.

Direct legislation is supposed to educate the citizen and revive his interest in public affairs. But experience in the United States does not support this argument. Many voters who go to the polls and vote for candidates for office do not vote at all on the laws submitted for their decision on the same ballot. Measures have often been passed or rejected with little more than a quarter of the electorate voting. This suggests that many voters feel themselves more competent to choose men than to make laws. The instinct is sound. If the candidates put forward by the parties are not to their liking, those who feel keenly the need to improve the quality of political life can take more effective steps than resort to direct legislation. Through active participation in party affairs, they can influence the choice of candidates with a much smaller expenditure of time and energy than it takes to learn enough to vote wisely on particular measures.

Reverting to the discussion of the last chapter, it is clear that direct legislation flies in the face of the principle that the political parties take the responsibility for public policy and for administering and enforcing the laws, and that the voters do all they can as voters when they examine the stewardship of the parties at election times. The people cannot directly make the laws and govern the country. Perhaps a prohibition law cannot be enforced at all. Certainly it cannot be enforced except when the executive, the government of the day, puts great vigour and determination behind it. If the people want the laws enforced, the only way open to them is to concentrate responsibility for the detailed provisions of the laws and their administration on the political party that currently enjoys the support of a majority, and then punish it for its failures at election time. Between elections they can warn their parties of their desires and intentions by influence on the local party associations. The members of the parties in the legislature are, or can be made, extremely sensitive to clearly expressed opinion in the country.

Belief in the efficacy of direct legislation appears to be declining in the United States. Most of the states that adopted it did so before 1914 under the impulse of the Progressive movement and, although the scheme is likely to be retained, there has been no new adoption of it by any state in recent years. In part, this may be because its purposes have been largely accomplished. The features of American politics against which it was a protest are much less prominent than they were a generation or more ago. Also, no doubt, its defects have been an important factor. Another influence in its decline is more speculative. As already remarked, belief in the efficacy of direct legislation depends on a belief in a united popular will. It is probably significant that in America, at any rate, direct legislation was mainly adopted in states where one interest, that of agriculture, was predominant. In these states, it was possible, although not wholly correct, to think that a united popular will would emerge.

At the very same time, in the highly specialized industrial society of Britain, the guild socialists were expounding the inherent diversity of interest in the nation. The emphasis of discussion in the last three decades on the clash of interests in the nation and on the inevitability of class war has brought to the fore a new generation of reformers who assume that the people are irreconcilably divided into classes, and that therefore no united will for the common good can emerge without the surgery of revolution. The pendulum swings between extremes, and this view may turn out to be as unwarranted as the more naïve democratic beliefs of the nineteenth and early twentieth centuries about the united will of the people. Some considerations bearing on the question will be introduced in the next chapter.

The conclusions on the reforms discussed in this chapter may be summarized. As far as machinery goes, the two-party system offers the best, if not the only, means for maintaining liberal democratic government. Single-member territorial constituencies, where every voter has one vote regardless of his interests, provide the best mode of representation for encouraging the continuance of the two-party system. This kind of representation is admittedly defective at several points, and many of the criticisms rehearsed here are partially valid. However, if democracies are to meet the substance of these criticisms, the attempt should be made with means other than the radical reforms of the electoral system which have been discussed in this chapter.

CHAPTER X

PRESSURE GROUPS

A NUMBER of considerations touched on in earlier chapters must now be drawn together. In particular, it is necessary to recall what was said in chapter II about some of the consequences of accepting the liberal democratic ideals of government. Men need fellowship with one another almost as much as they need their individuality. In the great modern nations, they cannot find this fellowship in the state because it is too remote and impersonal. At any rate, they cannot find it in the liberal democratic state because it is mainly limited to the purposes that all share in common. They must seek it in voluntary associations which cater to the diverse interests of free personality. Those who share a particular skill, experience, or outlook on life will always respond to one another if they are given the chance.

Modern democracy has provided very wide freedom of association, and the ease of transport and communication makes it possible for persons with common or similar interests, experience, and outlook to organize on a national and even international scale. The result has been a spontaneous group life without parallel in history. The great hotels in the centre of networks of transportation are rarely free from the raucous fraternity of conventions. These groups are of a great variety and are not limited, as discussion sometimes seems to suggest, to those that share a common interest based on the intense economic specialization of the modern world.

Although economic interest groups are of special, and perhaps even fateful, significance when government reaches out to regulate many aspects of economic life, they are not necessarily the most active and powerful groups. Activity depends more on intensity of conviction, and this is often strongest in crusading fraternities with no economic axe to grind. The power of any group, in democratic politics at any rate, depends on the degree of vigour and single-mindedness it exhibits, and on numbers. Other things being equal, the bodies with the largest membership are likely to be the most effective because they can muster the most votes. Thus war veterans' organizations, in so far as they can agree on what they want, are extremely powerful although not organized around a common economic interest or function. Of the economic interest groups, one might hazard that agricultural associations and trade unions will exert the strongest push and pull on public policy in the future. An organization of consumers that naturally includes everyone would overtop all other economic interest groups. But for reasons already suggested, the consumer interest is extremely difficult to harness in an effective organization. The most successful form of consumers' organization has been the consumers' co-operatives. The importance of this movement in giving concrete expression to common interests shared, but not adequately realized, by producer groups of diverse and often conflicting special interests is often overlooked.

The Pros and Cons of Lobbying

Moreover, the widening range of governmental action affects most of the organized interests in ways that they think favourable or adverse. Every time the government intervenes in economic or social matters, it sets going a chain of consequences which affects the welfare of a number of groups. Organized interests think that their aims and purposes can be advanced or retarded by legislation. Thus, at every session of the legislature, legislation is proposed which some groups want to support and others want to defeat or modify. Groups that have not yet obtained advantages from governmental action are encouraged to organize for the purpose of securing it.

It must also be remembered that most laws do not become settled issues merely because a majority in the legislature approves them. Most modern legislation requires continuous administration to accomplish its purposes. Unlike the law of gravity, it is not self-enforcing. To fit the law to the almost infinite variety of situations, the government is given substantial discretionary power by the legislature. The complexity of the conditions that government undertakes to regulate are such as to make it impossible for the government to know fully what it is about unless it can draw on the knowledge and experience of the interests affected. In many fields, it is quite possible for government to cause serious damage as well as unnecessary nuisance to the interests being regulated, without accomplishing the purpose intended by the regulation. Therefore day-to-day administration is of even more vital concern to the interest groups than the enactment of the legislation itself.

These are the circumstances underlying the demand for representation of interests in some way that will connect the affected interests directly with the processes of government and not limit their communication to what can be expressed in voting for a candidate in a territorial constituency once in two or three or four years. In countries where the agitation for functional representation in the legislature made no headway, the interest groups have sought other means of access to government. Unable to take a hand directly in the making of laws and in the daily administration of them, they have resorted to influence and pressure. What is familiarly known as lobbying is the most notorious but not the only method by which group interests of various kinds communicate with the government. These methods will be discussed here and in a later chapter dealing with the administrative process. First, however, some cognizance must be taken of the widespread view that lobbying and kindred practices are improper topics for genteel discussion.

Lobbying of the government and the legislature by special interests rouses much indignation and alarm. Some of it is clearly justified because the lobbying interests have sometimes stooped to bribery and corruption. Also, the clandestine character of much of the lobbying arouses natural suspicion. Backstairs influence always smells of intrigue, and is objectionable in method if not in content. The average citizen who has no one to lobby for him is angered by the ease with which organized interests maintain close and intimate connection with government, and he comes to the common-sense conclusion that they would not continue the practice unless it paid dividends. Undoubtedly, organized interests get results from their contact with government, often at the expense of unorganized interests. For example, the price controls established by the United States government during World War II were quickly liquidated at the end of the war because of heavy pressure from manufacturing and other business interests, although there is strong ground for thinking that a majority of the American people favoured continuance of price control for a further period. However this may be, the consumer interests, largely unorganized, always pay for the services that government provides for producer groups.

These and other points form the case against lobbying. But the real question is whether the practice should be suppressed or encouraged to become more respectable. In so far as it is thought to be essentially evil, consultation between government and the interests will rely greatly on backstairs methods. If consultation is recognized as legitimate and even necessary, and required to be carried on openly, it will become as respectable as general community opinion demands. Moreover, the answer to the pressure of selfish interests may be counter-pressure of other interests with diverse aims. One of the pillars of the democratic way of life is freedom of association, and the answer to organization of special interests is counter-organization. The only thing preventing any significant social interest, economic or otherwise, from enjoying consultation with the government is lack of energy and initiative to organize for that purpose. Everyone who has leverage on a bloc of votes can get himself heard by democratic governments.

Lobbying and the Popular Will

The objection to lobbying, however, goes beyond these immediate considerations. The truth is that the practice is a denial of certain widely held beliefs about democracy. These beliefs are that the people, free of oppression by arbitrary governments and privileged classes, all want the same things of government. They want government to act for the good of all and not for any narrow, selfish purpose. That is to say, the sovereign people are essentially devoted to the public good, and the will of the people, if not corrupted or deflected, unerringly concentrates in a general will, a unified will for the good of all. Somehow—it was never very clear how—the people in electing representatives to the legislature informed them of the content of the general will and suffused them with a sense of its imperative. It was believed that a legislature so

chosen and insulated from all outside influence except the mandate
of the voters at the polls would produce in its legislation the highest
possible expression of the common good. Therefore, it was wrong
for any individual or group to rush to the capital and try to explain
the bearing of things to the legislature and the government. Either
they had the presumption to think they had some private revelation
of the common good or they were trying to nourish a special interest
at the expense of the public interest. Such beliefs are not always
clearly articulated, but unqualified objections by democrats to
consultation between government and the interests of which society
is made up must rest on the assumption that the will of the people
makes it sufficiently clear what should be done for the common
good.

Earlier discussion has indicated that this picture of a people
wholly absorbed in the public as distinct from the private good,
and of a general will, an agreed conception of the common good
arising from that absorption, is untrue to the facts. If it were true,
there would be no more room for political parties than for lobbying. People are not absorbed in public questions, and it is difficult
to see how the mass of citizens in a modern democracy could ever
give more than a minor fraction of their time to them. The citizens
of the Greek city-state had leisure, based on slavery, for this absorption. It was pointed out in chapter II that the diverse interests of
free personality cannot find their principal expression in and through
the sprawling modern territorial state. So the citizen must largely be
absorbed in concerns outside the specific sphere of government.

The true public interest does not spring, fully formed, from the
hearts of the people. It may be that a supreme being standing
above the struggles of life, or that men who are able to eliminate
all passion from their deliberations, could perceive *the* public
interest purged of all contamination from narrow special interests.
But the men who can achieve such detachment are rare, and divine
revelations of the common good vouchsafed to men appear to be
various and are far from bringing them to a consensus. It is true
that most of the members of the community, or nation, will whatever is necessary to preserve the community and to realize the
shared ideals, but that will often lacks specific content. While it
enables us to agree to resist a foreign aggressor, it does not tell us

how to do it or at whose expense. No more does it tell us what laws to make on a given day in peace time.

Therefore, as a practical matter of deciding what government is to do in the common or public interest, the choice is between meek submission to some dictated formula, and a formulation, always partial and incomplete, that emerges from the competition, clash, and compromise of a great variety of individual and group interests. A democracy must choose the latter because it has its origin and main justification in this diversity. The question that then faces us is: How can a legislature insulated from all contact with the varied interests of men, except what the members of the legislature bring to it, relate the common good to the particular "goods" that men pursue? Does the common good consist of a partly informed guess of the legislature at the general will of the people, or in arbitration between interests in the light of all the data that can be discovered from whatever source? If the latter is even partly correct, government must make contact with all interests that are strong enough to make their voices heard.

DIVERSE GROUP INTERESTS AND DEMOCRACY

The above analysis is far from doing justice to all the factors involved. It needs to be qualified by recalling what was said in chapter II about the unifying influence of the liberal democratic ideals. There is a large measure of agreement about the higher goals of political action. Much of the competitive striving between groups is concerned with exploring the means of giving fuller expression to the claims of personality. Also, this analysis leaves aside for later discussion the important role of political leadership in finding amid the clash of interests the compromises that reconcile unity and diversity and thus attract the support of majorities. It perhaps suggests by its emphasis that all organized interests are narrowly selfish interests, which of course is not true.

Many organized groups find their binding common interest in being their weaker brothers' keepers. All three countries have active associations for penal reform, birth control, child welfare, world peace, and prevention of cruelty to animals. Britain has its Council for Preservation of Rural England, its League for Endowment of Motherhood, and so on. Comparable examples in the United States are the Women's Christian Temperance Union, the American Eugenics Society, and the Society to Maintain Public Decency. Canada has the Women's Christian Temperance Union, the John Howard Society, the Imperial Order Daughters of the Empire, the Lord's Day Alliance, and so on.

The analysis certainly suggests that interest groups are more single-minded than they really are. Few people find full expression of themselves in one interest, and thus most of those who share a particular interest are reluctant to push it to the limit because that would jeopardize other interests they cherish. The organized farmers (except those mainly or solely engaged in dairying and stock-raising) are interested in a high price for grain. If this were their only interest, they would push for unlimited manufacture and sale of liquor so as to assure a greater demand for their grain. In fact, however, most of them feel they have a stake in a temperate, or even an abstemious society, and this moderates the agricultural lobby. A study of the membership of any interest group would show that almost every member has other interests that moderate his support of this particular interest. The multiplying of interests not only enriches life but also provides an automatic check on extremism. A peaceful society becomes possible—although not guaranteed—through a delicate equilibrium of interests without demanding the agreement of everybody on everything.

It should be clear from these considerations that we have only scratched the surface of the question of the place of interest groups in a democracy. It might be argued, at least for the sake of argument, that what has been called democracy in the last hundred years could never have flourished if there had been on every issue the manifest general will which many yearn for. A society in agreement in detail as to what was right would have muzzled the cranks, throttled discussion, and trampled on minorities, exhibiting all the earmarks of a totalitarian regime and impoverishing life for the sake of a few hard and fast conceptions of what was good.

A Balance of Power

Government by discussion and peaceful adjustment of differences finds its significance in the fact of numerous diverse interests.

Each interest is convinced of its own worth and therefore determined to survive and thrive. Being unable—and also unwilling—to ensure its position through a domination of all other interests, it is compelled to seek accommodations with some of these interests and, through a series of shifting combinations, to try to prevent any one interest from dominating all the others.[1] To put it in the terms of international politics, it is the technique of balance of power, so deplored by those who believe in a general will of all good nations for an international common good. One important reason why the balance of power between nations is so much more precarious than the equipoise of interests in a democracy is that the members of the nation have put all their eggs in one basket—"my country, right or wrong!" The egoism of nations is not moderated by the factor that moderates the thrust of interest groups—the divided allegiance of their members. Another important reason has already been pointed out. Most of the members of the diverse interest groups want to preserve the community. They thus recognize the necessity of eventual accommodation between diverse groups.

This digression is a luxury of which we can afford only a taste. It does tend to confirm the suggestion that the existence and lively activity of interest groups are closely connected with democracy. At any rate, democratic government has always been involved in maintaining an equilibrium between groups. This has never been an easy task and it requires the continuous services of a number of highly skilled politicians searching for the accommodations that will attract majority support. Thus democracy is not something that can be won today and guaranteed for posterity. It is always on trial. The trial becomes increasingly severe as government activities expand and affect more and more deeply the welfare of an ever larger number of interest groups.

As the two previous chapters indicate, the job of appeasing interests by giving them privileges that are immediately, if not ultimately, at the expense of others has a divisive rather than a unifying tendency, and it becomes harder to mobilize majorities that will

[1]James Madison, in *The Federalist*, no. 10, foresaw the effectiveness of such automatic checks on extremism. For further discussion, see Henry M. Magid, "Freedom and Political Unity" *Journal of Ethics*, 51 (1941), pp. 144-57.

accept all these activities as contributions to the common good or the public interest. Yet whether government activity declines or continues to expand, democratic governments must mediate between interests. The mediating will be most successful if it is done in the light of all the available information, including that tendered by the interests themselves.

FACTORS AFFECTING LOBBYING

Much more is generally known about the activities of pressure groups in the United States than in Britain or Canada. There are a number of reasons for the great quantity of data available on the United States. It is a country of "joiners," where the fullest advantage has been taken of freedom of association. No other government has to take account of so wide a range of diversity of interests, most of them organized. In no other country do pressure groups so openly approach the government. The process of law making is a free-for-all. The majority party does not monopolize the defining of public policy and the executive does not monopolize the drafting of an authoritative legislative programme. The laws are made by Congress and its numerous committees. The committees are always open to suggestion and afford hearings to interested parties. Accordingly, an organized interest can hope to influence legislation by lobbying individual congressmen and by putting its case before the appropriate congressional committees. Because the activities of pressure groups are so open and obvious, they get a great deal of publicity and much careful study by students of government.

In Britain and Canada, where the cabinet formulates policy and party discipline ensures its adoption in substantially the form proposed, pressure groups cannot hope to get far by lobbying individual members of Parliament or urging their case on parliamentary committees. These avenues of influence are not entirely neglected, but the most important representations must be made directly or indirectly to the cabinet. Little is publicly known of what goes on when the cabinet receives delegations or written representations, and still less can be said certainly of their influence on the cabinet's final decision. Equally little is known of what takes place in secret party caucus where the cabinet has to clear serious modifications and adjustments of policy with its supporters. Thus pressure groups work more unobtrusively and with less publicity than in the United States. Where the party and the cabinet insist on making policy and have to take full responsibility for it, there is less candour in acknowledging the influence of pressure groups. Also, frequent congressional investigations of lobbying in the United States have brought a good deal of information to light and encouraged further private investigation and research.

For these reasons, much less is known in detail in Britain and Canada than in the United States about the collaboration of interests with government. It is known that they are at work and that they do influence legislation, but the influence is hard to measure. In the United States it is often possible to describe the provisions of a particular law in terms of a compromise between the numerous groups that lobbied openly on both sides. In Britain and Canada, on the surface at any rate, the law represents the agreed policy of the majority party and the cabinet. The account of the activities of pressure groups given here deals largely with the American experience.

Pressure Groups in the United States

It is impossible to say how many organized group interests are in active contact with the national government at Washington, but it runs into thousands. Hundreds of different groups maintain offices in Washington. However, by no means all of these organizations are really effective, recognized by congressmen as being genuinely representative of the interests concerned and possessed of sufficient voting strength and propaganda power to compel anxious consideration. While all the groups with offices in Washington maintain a representative to look after their interests, only the larger and stronger groups are equipped with all the modern means of research and propaganda. They also employ professional lobbyists, or legislative agents as they prefer to be called, and pay them highly for their services. Some 4,500 such lobbyists filed reports, as required by law, with the Clerk of the House in 1957 alone. These agents must be well versed in the intricacies of legislative procedure, at home in the labyrinths of administration, and reeking with plausibility. They are generally journalists, lawyers, former civil servants and ex-congressmen—the latter being deemed especially desirable because they have access to the floor of Congress.

The Range of Organized Interests

The groups that exert pressure in Washington are organized to promote a bewildering variety of purposes. It would be difficult to classify them in a limited number of categories. Without attempting a classification it may be said that the more powerful groups are trade associations (representing industrial and commercial interests), organized labour, agrarian interests, professional associations, the bureaucracy, foreign policy associations, national women's organizations, various reform leagues, and a number of veterans, patriotic, ethnic, and religious organizations.[1] Perhaps the most broadly inclusive and effective of the commercial and industrial organizations are the United States Chamber of Commerce and the National Association of Manufacturers, which in 1906 formed the National Industrial Council to supply expert lobbying against labour legislation and later participated in setting up the Department of Commerce and other agencies in the federal government. Agricultural interests have found expression in many groups, notably the American Farm Bureau Federation, which has held the "farm bloc" together in Congress; the National Grange; and the National Farmers' Union, the most militant in recent years in its fight for legislative action in aid of agriculture.

The three principal large groups representing organized labour are: the recently created fifteen million member A.F.L.–C.I.O., a merger of the American Federation of Labour (which played an active and influential role in the formulation of legislation concerning employers' liability and workmen's compensation) and the Congress of Industrial Organizations; the four Railroad Brotherhoods which, among other things, secured the passage of the Adamson eight-hour law in 1916; and the United Mine Workers, under the colourful leadership of John L. Lewis.

The professional organizations are not as powerful as the economic interests because they lack the financial resources of the business groups and the numbers of the labour and agricultural

[1]Hugh A. Bone, *American Politics and the Party System* (2nd. ed.; McGraw-Hill, New York, 1955), chs. IV–VIII, for a discussion of pressure groups in the United States under these headings.

associations, but they do possess an asset that is of prime importance in public affairs, namely, technical knowledge. This knowledge enables them to exert considerable influence upon legislators and administrators. For example, the American Medical Association with a membership approaching the 150,000 mark was particularly active in securing the adoption of the pure-food laws. It has exerted pressure for the establishment of a federal department of health, the reorganization of the health activities of the national government, and against social insurance laws, particularly those providing for health insurance. In 1949, it collected $2 million from its members to fight against President Truman's proposal for compulsory health insurance. Another professional organization, the National Education Association, has pushed plans for a federal department of education and has favoured such reforms as a law prohibiting profits on the manufacture and sale of munitions, a law providing for unemployment insurance, a federal child-labour law, and laws for the protection of freedom of speech for teachers in the classroom.

The women's organizations, particularly the General Federation of Women's Clubs and the League of Women Voters, have brought a large and influential opinion to bear in favour of measures for the censorship of books and moving pictures, and have campaigned for better homes, conservation, civil service reform, prohibition enforcement, education, social legislation, Americanization, and international co-operation for peace. In many of these agitations, they have co-operated with other reformist groups found in the United States. Of these, perhaps the most outstanding in the whole history of pressure groups was the Anti-Saloon League of the organized churches, which was largely responsible for the enactment of temperance legislation from 1893 on, and often drafted such legislation.

The associations for promoting the interests of different ethnic groups in the United States are not usually as well organized as the economic and philanthropic groups, but they do exert considerable political pressure from time to time. There are at present approximately 175 ethnic organizations. On domestic issues, they press for simplification of electoral procedures and for increased immigration from the countries of their origin. In the field of foreign policy, they strive for good relations between the United States and their countries of origin. After World War I, the pressure of American Poles, Czechs, and Yugoslavs on President Wilson's administration influenced the creation of new states in Central Europe. The German-American Bund and a number of Irish organizations tried to prevent the entry of the United States into World War II.

The interests of the Negroes are championed primarily by the National Association for the Advancement of Colored People and the Urban League. They press for fair treatment of Negroes in the courts, for integration in public education, for appointment of Negroes to public offices, and oppose discrimination against Negroes in voting, private employment, and housing.

Some of the principal religious organizations of national scope are the National Council of Churches in Christ (U.S.A.), which speaks for several influential Protestant groups, the national Catholic Welfare Conference and the Legion of Decency (Roman Catholic), the General Zionists and the American Jewish Congress (Jewish). They are actively interested, often on different sides, in public policy relating to education, marriage and divorce laws, birth control, literary censorship, prohibition, diplomatic representation at the Vatican, establishment of a Jewish state in Palestine, and so on.

Looking at the extraordinary range of interests represented by organizations in Washington and noting their frank, persistent, and widespread legislative activity, observers have described them as a third House of Congress, operating outside the Constitution, it is true, but not lacking effectiveness on that account. They do not limit their activities to national government and politics. They work in a similar way in state government and politics. The present study is concerned only with the national scene, but it is important to remember that pressure groups do not neglect any government that has power to affect their interests.

These pressure groups conduct their campaigns on four fronts. They try to influence congressional nominations and elections. They maintain direct contact with, and apply pressure on, members of Congress, and also on officials—sometimes even on the judiciary. They pour out propaganda in the hope of influencing public opinion.

The Techniques of Pressure

Pressure groups often act on the theory that simpler and more effective control over legislation is to be had by securing the nomination and election of friendly legislators than by attempting to influence them after they are elected. It does not matter whether candidates or prospective candidates are Democrats or Republicans; they are supported or opposed according to their stand on the questions in which the particular lobby is interested. Those who aspire to Congress are questioned on their views and, if willing to give pre-election promises, they are given support in the campaign in various ways, including money contributions to the candidates' campaign funds. Both the "wets" and the "drys" in the struggles over prohibition supported candidates financially. Big business, which is often long on money and short in numerical voting strength, commonly contributes to the campaign funds of particular candidates.

It should be noted that this traffic is encouraged by the lack of clear, precise party programmes and the weakness of party discipline. If the parties had clear, firm policies, the promise of a candidate to support the special claims of a pressure group would not be worth buying. If the central party organization had, as in Britain, a virtual veto on the candidature of particular aspirants, the tools of special interests would have great difficulty in getting a nomination. The weakness of the national parties is the opportunity of diverse interests of every kind.

If an interest group has a large membership, its delivery of effective support in an election campaign is simpler. If it is well organized and able to persuade its members how to vote, it can bring heavy pressure to bear in any constituency where it has significant voting strength. The A.F.L.–C.I.O. and its predecessors, because of the size and compactness of their membership, have been successful in ensuring the election of particular candidates friendly to labour and in defeating hostile candidates. Labour's Committee on Political Education, which grew out of the C.I.O.'s Political Action Committee, endeavours to obtain labour votes for candidates who will endorse labour's objectives. The Farm Bureau Federation has also had signal success in influencing elections. The Bureau keeps a close check on the legislative record of congressmen from agricultural constituencies and brings that record to the attention of voters at the next election. This is a procedure also followed by organized labour.

Alone or in combination with other groups, interests can ensure the election of a number of favourably disposed congressmen who form a bloc in Congress, supporting what the interests want with little regard for party lines or party platforms. If these legislators do not live up to their promises, they are marked for defeat at the next election. However, this is not enough. Countless pressures from all directions play on all congressmen and it is necessary to supply sympathizers with data and to counteract other pressures. The lobbies maintain offices in Washington because they want to be close to Congress to express their views directly on all measures that interest them and to maintain contact with such members of Congress as they hope to impress.

The oldest form of direct pressure on legislators is the social lobby, which still persists although its results are generally thought to be meagre. Members of Congress are often wined and dined by legislative agents just for the sake of getting acquainted. New members particularly are singled out and the lobbies do much to make them feel at home in Washington. But members of Congress cannot be bought for the price of a meal and there is no attempt to do so. The purpose is to establish friendly relations as a prelude to feeding the legislator with information and persuasive arguments.

It has already been pointed out that legislators today are inadequately informed on most of the subjects with which they have to deal. Devices for supplying them with accurate data are lacking or inadequate and busy lawmakers cannot do more than a fraction of their own research. But lobbyists on both sides of almost every question are well supplied with information and eager to impart it. They are the chief source of information pro and con on many issues that come before Congress. The members of Congress whose minds are already made up can draw supporting data and arguments from this source. Those who are in doubt and conscious of their ignorance can be fairly sure that they will get much of the relevant data and arguments by listening to all sides of the story from the interest groups concerned. Naturally, the information is biased, but some of the truth always emerges from the clash of opposites.

The real work of legislation, as we have seen, is done in the congressional committees, and therefore lobbyists take special pains to educate members of the committees whose field of work affects them. The committees hold hearings at which they invite evidence from all the interests concerned in a particular bill. These hearings often have a good deal of resemblance to the proceedings of a court, with lobbyists appearing as counsel and witnesses on both sides and the members of the committee acting as judge and jury. Of course, the committees are expected to gather information from all possible sources, and officials from the government departments appear to put governmental data and points of view at the disposal of the committee. The evidence of officials may not be wholly impartial either, but it will correct many of the exaggerations and partial truths of the pressure groups.

The well-organized groups go to great pains to convince congressmen that their constituents are solidly behind the group demands. They persuade their own members and all the prominent citizens who are sympathetic to their point of view to shower congressmen with letters, telegrams, memorials, and resolutions urging the legislators to vote for or against particular measures. Even though the opinions expressed in the "form letters" often used are clearly inspired by interest groups, the congressmen cannot afford to ignore them completely, because the senders may have espoused the opinion expressed in them. Such organizations as the Chamber of Commerce, the Farm Bureau Federation, and the A.F.L.–C.I.O. with huge memberships can pour an avalanche of letters and resolutions on legislative bodies. The professional associations can also make an impressive showing. When the American Medical Association (supported by 145,000 doctors all organized locally into about 2,000 county units) asks its members to write, and to persuade their friends and patients to write, to their representative at Washington, a heavy mail can be anticipated.

The reform organizations also use the same technique. One Anti-Saloon League official claimed that he alone had arranged for the sending of 900 telegrams in a single day. On one occasion in the nineteen-twenties, when the Naval Affairs Committee of the

House of Representatives was considering the proposals of the administration for a naval building programme, the National Council for the Prevention of War bombarded the committee with letters and telegrams until the committee decided to cut the programme by two-thirds. The night before the Senate voted on the question of American adherence to the World Court in 1935, Father Coughlin, the radio priest, persuaded thousands of his listeners to telegraph their senators, urging rejection. The Senate did reject it and the telegrams are believed to have been an important factor in that decision. A related technique is the sending of delegations to impress the legislature. In 1927, delegates from ten national women's organizations who were joined together in the Conference on the Cause and Cure of War marched to the Capitol, and presented to the Senate 10,000 resolutions of women's organizations across the country supporting the ratification of the Kellogg Pact to outlaw war.

Pressure groups not only inspire and support legislation they favour; they often draft it and present it to congressional committees. They also maintain direct contact with the administration which, through its discretionary powers, can do much to help or harm the interests of the various groups. How to work your way through the bureaucratic maze at Washington to the official who can and will deal with your problem instead of referring you to someone else is a distinct branch of learning, and all the important pressure groups employ experts who have made this province of knowledge their own. They negotiate with officials, investigate administrative practices, and inform officials of the point of view of their groups on such practices. This is an extremely important part of the work of pressure groups and it will be considered in more detail when the administrative process is discussed in a later chapter.

Finally, pressure groups try to mould public opinion. The surest guarantee of success is to convince a large section of the electorate of the justice of their group's claims. Almost every channel of communication is used to proclaim the gospel of the group to the public. Speeches are prepared for sympathetic members of Congress. Advertising and public relations agencies are brought into play to help "engineer consent." (The American

Petroleum Institute—to mention one outstanding example—has recently been spending fifty million dollars a year on public relations). Special articles and news releases are supplied to the press. Radio and television are used, and the motion pictures are not neglected. Speakers are supplied to churches, schools, luncheon clubs, and public forums. When the public utility industry was trying to discredit public ownership of public utilities, it not only used all these common methods of trying to influence public opinion but also tried to mould the educational system to its purposes. It made extensive efforts to eliminate public school textbooks that spoke favourably of public ownership and supplied the schools with hundreds of thousands of specially prepared booklets. It endowed public utility research bureaux in universities, which were expected to find facts supporting its views. The grand scope of its activities is indicated by the fact that in one year it sponsored more than ten thousand addresses, which were heard by an estimated million and a half people.

Most pressure groups, of course, work on a much smaller educational programme and few of them think it worth while to try to work through the schools and universities, because they want quick results on current issues. But they are all anxious within the limits of their resources to influence public opinion.

It has been argued at length here that as long as government is expected to carry on its present wide range of functions affecting the welfare of interest groups, close contact between the interests and the government is legitimate and even necessary. That does not mean that all the methods used by pressure groups should be approved or even tolerated. Bribery and corruption have long been offences against the criminal law. The problem of dealing with such methods is one of detection and punishment. Sinister influences in elections are already outlawed in most states but, as has already been noted, these laws are very difficult to enforce.

Respecting the non-criminal methods of persuasion and propaganda brought to bear on Congress, public officials, and public opinion by pressure groups, believers in democracy (which is, at bottom, government by persuasion) will find it difficult to distinguish between forms of persuasion that are legitimate and those that are not. The important issue at stake arises out of other distinctions, the distinction between interests that are effectively organized for pressure and those that are not, and perhaps the distinction between those interests with lavish funds and those without. This last is doubtful because small financial resources can often be compensated for by organization and numerical voting strength. The problem is how to protect the unorganized interests, and specifically in the economic field, how to organize the general consumer interest to counterbalance the whole range of producer interests. Aside from the difficulty of defining what is evil in the genuinely persuasive practices of pressure groups, the really forbidding difficulty is that of enforcing any law that might be made.

These considerations help to explain why, despite many years of agitation for the regulation of lobbying by law and the frequent introduction of bills and resolutions in Congress for that purpose, no law on the subject was enacted by Congress until 1946. As part of the 1946 legislation for the reorganization of Congress, provision was made for the registration of lobbyists and the disclosure of the source of their employment and the amount of their compensation. The terms of the law are restricted to professional lobbyists who try "directly" to influence Congress or its committees. Therefore the law does not cover persons who limit their pressure to the executive branch of the federal government or any organized association whose officers do its lobbying incidentally to carrying on the general purposes of the association. While almost five thousand persons have registered, this registration is not, because of the restricted coverage of the law, a reliable index to the number of persons who, at one time or other, bring the pressure of organized groups to bear on the government of the United States.

The purpose of the law is to identify the source of pressures and to make it a matter of public knowledge who is paid for doing what, and how much. The reliance is on publicity, a weapon not to be underestimated in a democracy. Significantly, there is no attempt to distinguish between the methods used by lobbyists, forbidding some and regulating others. It is a matter of the greatest difficulty to get sufficient agreement on what should be forbidden and what should be permitted.

During the last quarter-century or so, lobbying has become much more respectable. Less is heard nowadays about outright corruption and backstairs intrigue. The relation between lobbying and the complex functions of government is better understood, and the operations of most of the more effective pressure groups are increasingly conducted in the open. Yet, even if some of the moral stigma has been removed, genuine alarm about the total effect of the activities of pressure groups on the national government has perhaps increased rather than diminished.

Largely as a result of the increased governmental activities of the New Deal and World War II, the number of pressure groups operating in Washington has increased at a very rapid rate. Their pressure on government has become more pervasive and continuous. There is much fear that their push and pull will rob Congress of any sense of national purpose and make it mainly an instrument for registering the resultant of all the dispersive influences brought to bear on it.

The fear is by no means groundless. As we shall see in the next chapter, Congress has generally found it difficult to reach and maintain a coherent, consistent view of national policy. The persistent lobbying of many powerful groups with divergent demands increases the difficulty. However, it was suggested in chapter vIII that the cause of the difficulty is the failure of the national parties to develop clear-cut specific programmes and firm party discipline. The majority party is potentially in a position to control Congress and to resist the demands of interest groups, but it generally lacks a firm comprehensive programme which it can agree to enforce in the national interest. If this is correct, the enactment of repressive laws against lobbying is not likely to accomplish much. What is needed are party lines that do not falter or break before the thrusts of interest groups. Such party lines do exist in Britain, and although the phenomenon of organized interest groups is comparable to that found in the United States, the activities of these groups do not cause nearly so much alarm.

PRESSURE GROUPS IN BRITAIN

In Britain, there are hundreds of organized interests taking the form of business, labour, professional, agricultural, reform, philanthropic, and other associations.[1] In the range of interests thus served, as indeed in total numbers of organizations, the British pheno-

[1]See the compilation of S. E. Finer, "Interest Groups and the Political Process in Great Britain" in *Interest Groups on Four Continents* (ed. Henry W. Ehrmann; University of Pittsburgh Press, Pittsburgh, 1958), pp. 117–24.

menon is comparable to that of the United States. On the economic side alone, there are hundreds of associations representing commercial, manufacturing, transport, shipping, agricultural, mining, and financial interests. Most of these are in turn linked together in a few great national federations like the Federation of British Industries, the Association of British Chambers of Commerce, and the National Farmers' Union. The numerous labour unions have a common organ in the General Council of the Trades Union Congress.

No one of these large federations speaks with a single voice except on a few matters of broad general concern. On many if not most specific issues, the associations in a particular federation will speak discordantly. Professional and philanthropic interests are highly organized often with national headquarters established close to the governing departments in Whitehall and to Parliament at Westminster. Their purpose in every case is to advance the interests of their members and this generally involves the securing of legislative favours. As we shall see in chapter xviii, the numerous associations of municipal governments and municipal government officials are among the most effective pressure groups in Britain.

The Techniques of Pressure

For reasons already discussed, the working of party government with the cabinet in the driver's seat defeats attempts by interest groups to influence policy through winning over individual members of Parliament. The interests do on occasion try to influence the choice of candidates in particular constituencies and to exact pledges from candidates by promising support or threatening opposition. Generally speaking, they cannot influence the choice of candidates because the local party associations know they must choose good party men. And the candidate, once in the field, must resist all pressure groups which would bind him to action contrary to the party line. So he refuses to give pledges. In Parliament, members almost always vote with their party. The interests cannot break its grip nor are they allowed to appear before the standing parliamentary committees as in the United States.

The interests therefore must work within and through the parties instead of outside and against them. While many groups remain outwardly non-partisan, some associate themselves directly with one or other party. The trade unions led the van in forming the Labour party and still form its main strength. The bulk of the election expenses of Labour candidates are provided by the trade unions associated in the Trades Union Congress. A Labour Government is therefore particularly sensitive to the claims of organized labour. The national Farmers' Union gives a measure of support to the Conservative party. The President of the Union not only was himself chosen and elected as a Conservative candidate in 1935, but was also a member of a standing committee which later examined and reported favourably on a bill to assist the livestock industry. Without committing themselves fully, the commercial and industrial groups are generally sympathetic to the Conservative or waning Liberal rather than to the Labour party, and they often endorse candidates. Among the professional associations the National Union of Teachers and the British Medical Association, for example, pledge support of one or more candidates sympathetic to them, but they are strictly non-partisan.

The mere fact that an interest group manages to smuggle a number of its sympathizers into Parliament under the cloak of one or other of the parties does not ensure it any great influence. Private members, standing alone, are quite insignificant, as the time afforded and the treatment given to private members' bills clearly shows. Most of the legislation sought by interests involves the expenditure of money, and private members cannot introduce money bills at all. If a private member's bill is unopposed in the House, as bills sponsored by the Royal Society for Prevention of Cruelty to Animals generally are, it may go through easily. But most private members' bills meet opposition, which means they must be debated. The time allotted for such debates is so short that only a few private members' bills ever reach the discussion stage. Finally, the cabinet has to be persuaded; the civil servants on whom the cabinet relies have to be convinced. Consequently, it is something of an occasion when a private member's bill actually becomes law.

The interests seek to introduce bills through private members mainly for the purpose of getting publicity and building up an agitation that will persuade the government to act. They know they must persuade the cabinet. They also know that the cabinet is extremely susceptible to the temper of public opinion and of opinion in the House. So they supply members of the House with their literature and encourage their sympathizers in the House to proselytize and to initiate questions and debates bearing on the claims of the group.

This indirect pressure on the cabinet is not the most important activity of interest groups. All the great organized interests are also in close and almost continuous contact with particular ministers and with the cabinet, presenting their facts and urging their point of view. They often appoint a committee to make direct representations to the cabinet or to a particular department of the government. They watch all legislative proposals, and before a bill adverse to their interests goes to Parliament they make strong representations against it to the cabinet.

Consultation of Interests

The cabinet, to ensure itself as much as possible against opposition in the House, generally consults all the organized interests concerned while the bill is being drafted. For example, when the bills for nationalizing the coal mines, the air lines, and the railways were being drafted, the Labour Government consulted both the management and the trade unions in these industries. Representations are heard on both sides, the criticisms made are subjected to examination by experts, and adjustments and concessions are made by the cabinet as far as it finds it possible to do so. When bills are before the standing committee, parliamentary spokesmen for various interests raise innumerable amendments concerning details and the government may make further modifications in the bill. After the legislation is enacted, the interests are generally represented on an advisory committee which is associated with the government department administering the legislation. The committee makes suggestions and criticisms which often lead to substantial amendment of the legislation at a later date. The picture of the cabinet as a dictator thus requires even more qualification than earlier discussion indicated. It is continually mediating between a great range of interests, each of which claims to be representative of the public interest. It tries to find accommodations that are acceptable or tolerable to the interests concerned and that still enable it to carry out the pledges of the party.

When extremely contentious issues arise on which the government wants fuller knowledge of facts before committing itself, a royal commission of inquiry, to which a number of persons who know and can speak for the major affected interests are appointed, is often set up. These bodies perform a function somewhat similar to that of congressional committees in the United States when they afford public hearings for the various interests on some legislative proposal. If the commission can produce a unanimous report, the government has some ground for hoping that the interest groups will accept its proposals.

In any case, the interests are again consulted by the government before the government frames its bill on the recommendations of the commission. For example, the Minister of Transport submitted the Report of the Royal Commission on Transport of 1931 for comment and criticism to five local government associations, fifteen transport associations, four motoring associations, four trade unions, the Association of British Chambers of Commerce, the Federation of British Industries, the Mansion House Association on Transport, and the National Federation of Iron and Steel Manufacturers. These interests could not agree. The railway companies and the road transport associations were far apart, as might be expected. The Minister was not yet prepared to state a policy of his own for action by the cabinet and Parliament. He called a conference of representatives of the interests in conflict, which did agree on a proposal, although the road transport associations still refused to accept it. In the end, the Road and Rail Traffic Bill produced by the government diverged somewhat from the recommendations of the Commission and also from the proposal of the conference. This illustrates the kind of negotiation that generally precedes the introduction of complex and controversial legislation into the House of Commons.

Important though organized interests are in the initiation of legislative proposals, their importance as critics of such proposals is even greater. As soon as a bill is published, the cabinet and the appropriate government departments get representations from all the interests that conceive themselves to be affected. It is often impossible to consult all interests before a bill is drafted. Those that were not consulted, and those that were but are still dissatisfied, urge their views as strongly as they can. If representations to the government are not effective, the interests then circularize the members of Parliament and get sympathetic members to urge their friends to protest. If the issue is one on which a general public opinion might be raised, that too is tried. A combination of these tactics is sometimes effective. To take only a few instances, the Incitement to Disaffection Bill, 1934, and the Population Bill, 1937, were very substantially altered by the government, and the operation of the Teachers' Superannuation Bill of 1956 and the Rent Bill of 1957 were postponed, because of widespread dissatisfaction with them in the House of Commons. Organized interests had a considerable part in fostering this dissatisfaction. The objective of interest groups in Britain is always to convince the cabinet or the department concerned that proposed legislation should be passed, amended, or rejected.[1] They have a large share in shaping legislation, although it is not as important a share as in the United States and is achieved by different means.

PRESSURE GROUPS IN CANADA

In Canada, the organized interests follow the pattern of the United States and Britain but are much fewer in number. Of the economic interest groups, the Canadian Federation of Agriculture is the most highly organized and most cohesive. It speaks generally for the farmer and represents most branches of agriculture. The Canadian Manufacturers' Association (representative of the manufacturing interest only) and the Canadian Chamber of Commerce (representative of trade and industry generally) are both highly organized, but they are both federations of such a variety of associations that they do not often agree on concrete measures. Organized labour is split into several groups, some of them purely Canadian, but most of them affiliated with American unions. The Canadian Labour Congress, a merger of the Trades and Labour Congress and the Canadian Congress of Labour approved in 1955, has over one million affiliated members. All the well-established trades and industries have their own associations. Professional, reform, veteran, and philanthropic organizations also flourish.

As in Britain, the aim of pressure groups is to persuade the government, but their tactics are not always identical. In Canada

[1]Sir Ivor Jennings, *Parliament* (2nd. ed.; Cambridge University Press, Cambridge, 1957), ch. VII. The above sketch of pressure groups in Britain is largely drawn from this volume. For more detailed illustrations of the "consultation" procedure between ministries and interests, see J. D. Stewart, *British Pressure Groups* (Oxford University Press, Oxford, 1958).

more effort is put into trying to influence elections. Even more than in Britain, many of the larger groups can always count on having a considerable number of supporters in the House of Commons. Canada has so many constituencies, and even large regions, where one industry is so overwhelmingly predominant that the elected member, whoever he is or whatever party he adheres to, has no choice but to represent a particular interest. Almost every member from the Prairie Provinces, for example, is necessarily a spokesman for agriculture. Then, too, party discipline is not so strict as in Britain. As a result of these two facts, the important interests can generally find a group of members sympathetic to their point of view on issues that come up. The interests try to create opinion in the House and in the country by publicity, but lavishly financed propaganda is not common.

The principal reliance of the interest groups is on direct contact with the government. Some of the highly organized groups have their headquarters in Ottawa, but many have not, and rely instead on the sending of occasional deputations or on securing the services of a parliamentary agent. There are few permanent lobbies in Ottawa of the kind found at every turn in Washington. The pressure of interest groups on the federal government tends to be sporadic rather than continuous, making itself felt as particular issues arise. Of course, the groups keep in touch with sympathetic members of Parliament and with ministers and permanent senior officials, supplying them with information on request. The Canadian Federation of Agriculture, for example, keeps members of Parliament informed of its views and has a strong influence on those representing agricultural constituencies, but it does not threaten them with defeat at the next election or attempt to organize a farm bloc in the House of Commons. It carries great weight with the Department of Agriculture, for it occupies a prominent position on the influential National Advisory Committee on Agriculture. Active pressure is applied by it and other groups when particular questions of policy come up, as when the customs tariff is to be revised.

The relatively lighter and more intermittent pressure of Canadian interest groups on the Dominion government, at least in the period between the two world wars, was not due to the self-restraint of these groups. It was due primarily to the fact that the national government, apart from the emergency of war, has not engaged in such a wide range of activities as the British, or the United States federal, government. Despite rapid growth in recent years the range of government functions is still not as great in Canada as in Britain and the United States, and, of those functions undertaken in Canada, a very high proportion are carried out by the provincial governments on their own responsibility. In the United States, the states also perform many functions, but there has been more centralization at Washington than at Ottawa. Consequently, the Government of Canada acts in a narrower field; the laws it makes and administers touch fewer interests and their impact is less pervasive and continuous. The pressure of interest groups on the government varies directly with the scope and intensity of governmental activities. Many of the organized interests have only occasional business with the national government and therefore do not find it necessary to maintain permanent offices in Ottawa. It should be noted, however, that the activities of the central government since World War II have been on a greater scale than ever before, and the organized interests are already moving into much closer relationships with the government.

Also, because the Canadian bureaucracy is relatively small and not excessively complicated, it is easy for outsiders to find their way around. Government officials and even ministers are more accessible than in London or Washington. Interest groups can send a representative or a deputation and reach the persons they want to see without the aid of professional guides and intermediaries. Thus there are only a few professional parliamentary agents in Ottawa, and although they have a considerable clientele they are not highly successful in negotiating favours. In addition to these methods, representations may be made to the government and pressure applied to members of Parliament by inspiring numerous letters and telegrams complaining about one course of action or urging another.

When contentious measures are under consideration, the government consults with the organized interests affected, and this consultation takes much the same form as in Britain. In one respect, it goes further, enabling interest groups to appear before and give evidence to parliamentary committees. The federal civil service is not as well supplied with experts in all fields as is the British civil service, and yet, even in Britain, much reliance has to be put on the information gathered from the organized interest groups. Such reliance is all the more necessary in Canada. On highly controversial and technical issues, a royal commission of inquiry is often appointed to inquire into the facts and make recommendations.

In Canada, as in Britain and the United States, the interests seek to be heard, not only on what laws should be made, but also on how the laws should be administered and enforced. In fact, as will be shown in detail later, they are as closely connected with the process of administration as with law making. The various interests that make up modern society have found means of access to government which ensure that their knowledge, experience, and point of view will not be overlooked. The arguments for proportional and occupational representation have largely been met in these countries by arrangements that, although by no means free of abuses, are less dangerous to democratic institutions. It should also be clear that the present-day phenomenon of assertive pressure groups arises from the wide range of governmental functions and that it is only in this context that the significance of lobbying and kindred practices can be appreciated.

Pressure groups, of course, have a significant influence on the actions of both executive and legislature. They supplement the activities of political parties in moulding the exercise of both legislative power and executive power. Neither legislature nor executive operates in a vacuum. To borrow a mechanical analogy, each can be thought of as a cylinder connected by several series of many pipes to political parties and pressure groups. The thrust developed in the cylinders, which pushes out laws, decrees, and orders, always bears a relation to the pressures pushing in.

Nor is this all. Legislature and executive are each connected with the other by another series of pipes. These pipes, however, are fitted with gauges (the relevant provisions of the constitution) which limit and ration the pressure each can exert on the other. To speak, as we did at the beginning, of the legislature making the laws which the executive in turn merely carries out is an oversimplification. The two branches work always in close relationship to one another, and to this relationship we must now turn.

CHAPTER XI

THE RELATIONSHIP BETWEEN THE EXECUTIVE
AND THE LEGISLATURE

THE legislative and executive organs have been described and their distinct functions have been outlined. The legislature makes the laws, levies taxation, appropriates public revenues for the executive to spend and keeps some check on the activities of the executive. The executive cannot pursue any course of action affecting the rights of citizens except as authorized by law to do so. The legislature sets the tasks of the executive and is thus superior to it even where the rigid separation of powers makes them co-ordinate organs. The executive runs the household economy of the government, carries out the laws, and supplies the services authorized by legislation.

As we have already seen, however, this is an over-simplification Many of the objects and purposes pursued by governments today are not accomplished merely by making laws. A law and an appropriation of public revenue to the purpose is essential, but the vigour of administration by the executive sets the measure of success. Much legislation in the positive state is to no purpose unless the legislature can transmit to the executive the impulse that put the law on the statute-book. The executive, in turn, often finds the laws cannot be made to work with the best economy of effort, or at all, unless they are amended, and the executive must be able to transmit its experience in administration to the legislature. Indeed, the question whether a particular law is workable, or even desirable, may turn on the data and experience accumulated by the executive in trying to enforce it.

As we shall see later, there is even ground for saying that the making of laws and the administration or enforcement of them are not two distinct processes. Most laws enacted nowadays are attempts to correct some social abuse or to ease the tension caused by some conflict of interests. The legislature never knows all the factors involved. It is clear that something should be done, but it is not clear what or how. Accordingly, it often legislates in vague general terms, instructing the executive to exercise a discretion and experiment with possible solutions. The executive makes detailed rules and regulations which are law tentatively, to be modified and recast in the light of the results. Wartime legislation affords the clearest example. The laws for controlling prices in the United States and Canada in World War II were not made full-fledged at the time when the fixing of prices was first introduced. Something had to be done. It was not clear what should or could be done, and the general policy was launched with much fear and trembling. The law of price control was developed and refined in great detail by the executive in a continuous stream of rules, amendments, and interpretative orders as experience suggested or compelled. As someone has put it concisely, the law was being made while it was being administered and enforced, and it was being administered while it was being made. The same is true of much of the legislation of the past sixty years.

Of course, it was never possible to separate completely the legislature and executive, and it was never attempted. Today, the scale and importance of governmental action make it imperative to have a very considerable degree of co-ordination between the two organs. It is not enough that they should check one another; everyone expects them to work together as a team to promote the good life. Therefore, the working relationships between them are an important subject of inquiry. The relationships in Britain and the United States are in marked contrast. An examination of the contrast should illuminate the much-debated question of merits and demerits of presidential and parliamentary systems of government and give some insight into the workings of democratic government. In broad essentials, the Canadian follows the British system, and it will be sufficient to indicate significant variations from time to time.

LEGISLATURE AND EXECUTIVE IN BRITAIN

The British legislature and executive are not separated but almost entirely fused. The cabinet as a committee of the legislature links the administration to the legislature. The impulses that move the legislature move the executive also, and the information and experience gained in administration are readily available to the legislature in its deliberations on policy. This fusion might not be particularly significant if it were not for the fact that both legislature and executive are in the grip of the same political party. Without party control, the executive committee of the House of Commons might be of one view while the majority of the members took another view; or more likely, there would be several factions differing in opinion with the cabinet and among themselves. In reality, it is the party which links the executive and legislature. The Prime Minister and his colleagues in the cabinet are the leaders of the majority party in the House of Commons. As we have seen, these leaders have already gained, through the party councils, party adherence to a platform that they themselves had a very large share in making. They come to the House of Commons with a programme, a disciplined majority to support it, and a mandate from the electorate to use the majority to push the programme.

At bottom, however, parties in a democracy are unstable combinations and the concurrence of a majority with the cabinet would often be uncertain were it not for the power of dissolution. The Prime Minister has the right to ask the King for a dissolution of Parliament at any time and it is only under extraordinary circumstances, if at all, that the King would be constitutionally justified in refusing it. Members of Parliament do not want to face the election that follows a dissolution because it is expensive, makes heavy demands on energy, and is uncertain in result. These liabilities apply as well to the government, and dissolution is rarely invoked for this purpose—knowledge of its potential threat generally being sufficient to hold the waverers in line. As long as the political situation gives one party a clear majority in the House of Commons, Parliament lives out the greater part of its allotted span of five years, and during that period the party programme is steadily pushed forward under the leadership of the cabinet.

The cabinet monopolizes the drafting of legislation, bringing to the task all the information, experience, and expertness of the civil service. Subject to minor qualifications, the cabinet gets what legislation it wants from Parliament and prevents the enactment of laws it does not want. Thus the cabinet is prepared to enforce vigorously all the laws enacted. The fact that a single body, the cabinet, moulds the legislative programme ensures at least a minimum of coherence and unity in that programme so that the administrators are not called on to enforce measures that are contradictory or inconsistent with each other. In so far as modern legislation and administration are inseparable, the British system of government is admirably adjusted to meet the situation.

Party Government versus Parliamentary Government

However, British government is no longer parliamentary government in the classic sense. A hundred years ago, the cabinet was continuously dependent on the will of the legislature, which might be asserted against it at any time. The power of the legislature to deny support to the cabinet and the power of the cabinet to dissolve the legislature maintained a balance in which direct responsibility of the executive to the legislature was assured and frivolous obstruction and irresponsible self-assertion by the legislature was prevented. Both legislature and executive were compelled to estimate closely the temper of the electorate. If the executive found itself hampered by attitudes in the House of Commons that it thought would not get support from the electorate, it would demand a dissolution. If the executive took a line that the House thought the electorate would reject, it would challenge the executive. Government in close correspondence with electoral opinion was assured. Also, predominance in government went to the body best able to estimate electoral opinion. In the absence of strong central party organization to keep it informed, a dozen or so men in the cabinet could not hope to guess as accurately at electoral opinion as could the House of Commons. Government therefore was parliamentary government.

With the extensions of the franchise, electoral opinion became harder to estimate and easier to mould. Central party organization was developed to perform these tasks. With its emergence, the leaders of the majority party, who either are in the cabinet or work closely with it, ceased to be inferior to the House of Commons in their guesses at public opinion. At the same time, the central party organizations reached out to influence the choice of candidates and the content of the party programme and to associate candidates and programme with the party leadership, until elections came to be primarily contests between the party leaders. There is no great exaggeration in saying that the Prime Minister is elected by the people and given a popular mandate to carry out the announced policy of the party. At least, the members of the cabinet now have direct relations with the electorate and are not merely a committee of the House of Commons.

In these circumstances, the House of Commons inevitably lost its pre-eminence, and British government became party government. In this view of the matter, it has been suggested that the Parliament Act of 1911, which stripped the House of Lords of its powers, was not so much a victory of the House of Commons over the House of Lords as it was the final triumph of party government over parliamentary government.[1] The last obstacle to control of Parliament by the parties was removed. In the last fifty years, only two governments have fallen through a vote of lack of confidence, and neither of these had the support of a single party with an over-all majority in the House of Commons.

Those who focus attention solely on events in the House of Commons see a disciplined party majority invariably supporting the proposals of the cabinet and conclude that Britain has been governed for half a century or more by a series of four-year cabinet dictatorships. The average member has lost his independence and his influence on legislation, and he is grimly compelled to vote the party line on most occasions. Some even argue that the House of Commons is fast becoming, as the King and the House of Lords have already become, a dignified rather than an effective part of the British constitution.

Cabinet Dictatorship

If we keep in mind some salient points of the preceding chapters, we can make some estimate of this charge of cabinet dictatorship. The executive is the one indispensable element of any government. The more things a government is expected to do, the more important executive leadership becomes, and the widespread activities of present-day governments have everywhere aggrandized the executive. If a government is to be democratic,

---

[1]See Don K. Price, "The Parliamentary and Presidential Systems" *Public Administration Review*, 3 (1943), pp. 317-34. This article prompted a critical reply by Harold J. Laski in *Public Administration Review*, 4 (1944), pp. 347-59. See also Don K. Price, "A Response to Mr. Laski," *ibid*, pp. 360-63. This interchange provides and illuminating discussion of the two systems.

political parties must organize majorities and find the policies that majorities will support. The party with the majority must rule, and the legislature must register its decisions as long as it holds a majority. Any organization as large in number and as complex in function as a political party becomes a prey to oligarchical tendencies, and the leaders of the party are the active deciding elements in many issues. When the party wins power in an election, the party leadership makes or becomes the cabinet. The executive is undoubtedly the mainspring of the British system of government.

To estimate whether the cabinet exercises a dictatorship during its period of office, one must look beyond the House of Commons to see who rules the ruling party. The discussion in an earlier chapter indicates that this is not an easy question to answer. The central organization and the parliamentary leadership of the party have enormous leverage on the party. On many matters, they have their way either because the rank and file of the party supporters do not know what is involved or because they cannot agree on instructions to the leadership. This is far from saying that the leaders can do what they like with impunity. There are always rival would-be leaders in the party who will swim into prominence and power on any strong current of opinion in the party if the present leaders do not canalize the current by making accommodations for it. Even if they are adept at heading off revolts among the rival would-be party leaders, they always face the danger that disgruntled elements of their popular support, unable to get concessions to their point of view, will transfer their allegiance to the opposition, thus imperilling their party's chances in the next election.

That is to say, the power of the party leaders, although it is impressive at a given moment when the party line has been settled and always effective against individual malcontents, is always contingent on their holding the leadership of the party and securing a majority for the party at the next election. They are therefore responsive to all pronounced trends of opinion in the party or in the electorate; anxious, indeed, to anticipate them. The ease or difficulty with which they hold majority support in the House of Commons is the measure of their success. The fact that the party majority always supports the cabinet may not mean much more than that the cabinet has correctly interpreted the will of that majority.

The necessity of running the gauntlet of debate and criticism in the House of Commons always disposes the cabinet to caution and moderation. Not infrequently, bills introduced by the cabinet are modified, or even withdrawn, because of criticism by the opposition and pressure from members of the majority party. Even during World War II, when Britain's desperately critical position might have been expected to bring full acquiescence in cabinet leadership, there were many instances of this kind. Moreover, it is not repeated trials of strength between the horse and the fence that keeps the horse in the pasture but the fact that the fence is there and the horse knows it. The opposition as well as the party majority in the House has an influence over the cabinet that cannot be measured by counting the number of collisions between the cabinet and the House. No simple cliché suffices to describe the relations between the cabinet and the House of Commons.

Party government in Britain has ensured the co-ordination of legislature and executive necessary to meet the demands of present-day governmental activities. It enables the legislature to enact, and the executive to administer effectively, complicated and far-reaching measures of social and economic adjustment. It is the only method thus far discovered for combining strong vigorous government with democratic control. Of course, it has inevitable costs and these may become so high as to bankrupt democracy. The consistency and coherence of its public policy for which the system is praised involves uniformity of treatment that often cannot take sufficient account of special needs and special circumstances. For example, the British government did not respond effectively to the needs of the depressed industrial areas of the country in the nineteen-twenties. The individual members of Parliament for the depressed areas could not escape from the discipline imposed by their parties to combine in a bloc for special concessions to their constituencies. It may be inevitable, but it is not an unmixed good to have the policy of the country framed in party councils rather than in Parliament. Among other things, it unfortunately reduces the prestige of Parliament in the eyes of the country. Other disadvantages will be considered later.

The most serious danger does not arise from the fusion of

executive and legislature but from the fact that it becomes increasingly difficult for the electorate, the rank and file of the party, and even for members of Parliament to understand what is involved in the policies that the party leadership works out in conjunction with the numerous experts in the civil service. This difficulty, however, arises out of the demands for governmental action rather than out of the form of political organization.

Legislature and Executive in the United States

In the United States, the executive and legislature are sharply separated. Neither the President nor any member of his cabinet can sit in the legislature. The legislature is cut off from any direct access to the information and experience that the executive accumulates, and the executive cannot participate directly in the framing and pushing of legislation. The terms of office of each are fixed by the Constitution and cannot be cut short by any ordinary exigency of politics. The legislature therefore cannot bring the executive to terms by the threat of a vote of lack of confidence. It has to work indirectly through its control of appropriations and its committees of investigation, through senatorial refusal to confirm presidential appointments, or through enactment of laws in such detail that they confine the executive to exactly prescribed tasks. The executive cannot persuade the legislature to come round to its view, or halfway to that point, by threatening dissolution. It has, of course, a veto power to prevent any legislation that cannot summon a two-thirds majority in Congress, and hints dropped to congressional leaders that it might be used are sometimes effective. The President can always get some leverage on Congress by delaying patronage appointments and by appealing directly to the people over the head of Congress. None of these threats, however, can be of more than occasional use in special circumstances.

The formal constitutional relationships work against rather than for the co-ordination that has been premised as necessary. The President who gets some kind of an over-all view from the information flowing to his desk from the administration and from the country cannot help trying to give a lead in legislation and, as usual, the efforts of one or a few to tell the many what to do cause almost continual tension between him and Congress. As a rule, it takes an emergency, such as war or depression, to secure for the executive the legislative leadership that the British cabinet normally enjoys. The leadership exercised by Abraham Lincoln, Theodore Roosevelt, Woodrow Wilson, and Franklin Roosevelt is explained, in large measure, by certain critical conditions in the period of their rule, and there are other instances of less dramatic interest.

In fact, the federal government has oscillated between presidential leadership and congressional leadership with such regularity as to prompt the suggestion that this oscillation rather than rule by alternating political parties is the striking feature of American politics.[1] When Congress leads, it does not lead vigorously in any particular direction but gives itself over to the play of sectional, local, and group interests. The country tires of the bickering and of the combinations of selfish interest that get their way in Congress. When a crisis looms, attributable sometimes in part to the lack of political leadership, a President comes to power with a popular mandate for action. With this popular support, an astute President can for a time master the diverse forces in Congress and push a legislative programme like the New Deal, unified in purpose if not in all its concrete detail.

But in the past, at any rate, these periods of effective legislative-executive co-ordination have been short. Many sectional and group interests are inevitably alienated or disappointed, the mood for united action and concentrated leadership passes, and the President's pre-eminence vanishes. At the next election, the country chooses, almost deliberately it would appear, a chief executive who is unfitted by ability and temperament for vigorous leadership. One trend, however, is discernible in these oscillations. The executive grows steadily in functions and importance and the authority of the President, when it declines, never falls back to the previous low point.

Most of the time, Congress leads and its leadership is divided among the congressional committees. Chairmanships of these committees go by seniority to those of the majority party with the longest continuous service on the respective committees. The men who are continually returned to Congress generally come from safe

[1]E. Pendleton Herring, *Presidential Leadership* (Farrar & Rinehart, New York, 1940), ch. i.

constituencies where opinion changes slowly, where common sectional or local interests return the same champion again and again. Thus the most powerful men in Congress are often representative of "backwater" areas of the community little stirred by changing currents of opinion in the nation as a whole. In these circumstances, there is no unified national leadership, and party discipline, while it keeps business moving through Congress, has comparatively little effect on the content of that business.

Lobbies and sectional interests launch bills in committees and work up combinations, which generally do not follow party lines, to support them. In the securing of appropriations to be spent for local amenities in the constituencies, members of Congress cooperate in supporting each other just as the pioneer settlers assisted one another in rolling up logs for buildings, or to be burned. Logrolling, also known as pork-barrel politics, is always a prominent feature of congressional leadership in financial and other legislation.

The President, elected by the country as a whole and representing the nation, tries to rally his party in Congress against this kind of legislation and may check the more cynical bargains by his veto. He cannot always prevent the enactment of legislation he dislikes and often cannot get support for legislation he thinks desirable. He may even be required to administer legislation that cannot be made effective because administrative experience and data were ignored in the framing of it, or because adequate funds were not appropriated for its administration. Congress at times acts irresponsibly, yielding to pressures and enacting legislation it does not genuinely believe in, and counting on the President to take the odium of vetoing it. The worst situations, of course, develop when the President is of one party and the majority in Congress of another, which has been the case during almost one-fifth of the history of the American presidency. But even when the President's party is in a majority, it often turns out either that the leaders of that majority in Congress are not in sympathy with him or they cannot control their followers.

Significance of Weak Party Discipline

This suggests what has already been asserted about the British system. It is not so much the formal constitutional relationship of the legislature and the executive as the character of the party system that determines the real relationship. As already explained elsewhere, the national political parties in the United States are not disciplined parties with a centralized leadership. The party platform is a collection of vague resolutions which does not lay down a clear-cut party policy. The national central party organization is a temporary committee for fighting elections every four years and not for maintaining disciplined party support of a programme between elections. Unlike the British central party organizations, it cannot veto the nomination of particular persons as party candidates in the constituencies. Attempts by the President, as the leader of his national party, to influence nominations have generally failed. Thus the choice of candidates is dictated by local and sectional considerations which ensure that those elected to Congress will reflect local and sectional interests and will be dependent on these interests for re-election.

To put it concisely, the national parties are loose federations of state parties which lack unity of purpose. They never have clear-cut programmes and, without such a programme and a mandate from the electorate to enforce it, there is no strong urge for rigid party discipline. In times of crisis, a President may come to office, as Franklin Roosevelt did more than once, with a mandate from the nation. His ability to execute it comes more from his appeal to the nation over the heads of Congress than from the disciplined support of his party in Congress. Even if the executive were fused with, and given power to dissolve, the legislature, as in Britain, executive dominance of the legislature would not necessarily result. It would only result if the sectional diversities of the United States were overcome in unified and disciplined national parties.

LEGISLATURE AND EXECUTIVE IN CANADA

The formal relationship of the executive and the legislature in Canada is the same as in Britain. Superficially, the results are the same. The cabinet commands the attention and directs the time and energies of the House of Commons. It prepares the legislative programme and can count with confidence on the support of its majority in the House to carry it through. It has the ultimate threat of dissolution to keep this majority in line. Bitter complaints about cabinet dictatorship and the lack of independence of the private member are commonly heard. Close examination, however, would reveal that party discipline is not so tight as in Britain. Assertions of independence are not as rare because the consequences of revolt are not as disastrous. The member who refuses to obey the party whips may lose the federal patronage and be denied federal funds in the next election but, if he maintains his hold on his constituency, the central organization of his party will think several times before applying insistent pressure to prevent his renomination at the next election. Also, the Canadian cabinet, rather more often than the British, finds it expedient to modify or withdraw particular items of its legislative programme as a result of the pressures that play upon it.

These differences are slight and not of great significance in themselves. If attention is focused solely on events in the House of Commons, party discipline seems to be highly effective. The really important difference is in the content of the programme which party discipline carries faithfully to the statute-book. There is no need to emphasize the generality and imprecision that marks most of the items in the programme of the national parties. In this respect, they resemble the platforms of the national parties in the United States, being framed to appeal to several of the diverse sections and interests of the country. Generally speaking, if we take the peacetime record of the past, the Government of Canada has not been noted for vigorous, far-reaching measures. Even the great depression of the nineteen-thirties did not bring a government or a policy comparable to the Roosevelt Administration and the New Deal in the United States. The executive commands the legislature but only during and since World War II has it forced the legislature to drastic measures or bulky accomplishment in legislation.

Here again the reason lies in the nature of the national political parties. They too are loose federations of provincial parties, and the forcing of a vigorous policy by the executive would threaten the tenuous unity of its majority. The individual member of Parliament, generally resident in the constituency he represents, has a local backing which diminishes his dependence on the national party organization and leadership. His political career is not necessarily ended if he should resist the party line at Ottawa. He may have valuable connections with the autonomous organization of his party in his own province. Since this is generally true of all members of Parliament, the leaders of the national parties are reluctant to try to enforce the comprehensive discipline which grips British parties. Members of Parliament can be held in line in Britain because their personal connection with their constituencies is often slight, and if they are repudiated by the central organization and leadership, their career is likely to be ended, at least in that party.

In fact, the federal cabinet in Canada has less need of a comprehensive discipline, because the positive measures to which the generalities of the party platform commit it are fewer and less drastic than those which British parties undertake. Moreover, the cabinet is not inherently disposed to single-minded aggrandizement of national leadership. As we have seen, the members of the cabinet are ambassadors of provinces and sections as well as national leaders. While they have a large share in framing national policy, they also impose some sectional reservations on it. They get the disciplined support of their party in the House of Commons because they do not ask too much. They get disciplined support because the executive and legislature are fused as in Britain, and they do not ask too much because the federal political parties are loose federations of provincial parties as in the United States.

In concrete terms, the relationship of the executive and the legislature is best illustrated by the case of financial legislation. He who controls the purse occupies a key position in government as in other activities. The control of taxation and public expenditure is of high importance for constitutional government, and on this ground too, financial legislation deserves separate examination. A government required to act in accordance with law must secure specific laws to justify its imposition of taxes and its expenditure of public revenues.

FINANCIAL LEGISLATION IN BRITAIN

A standing order of the British House of Commons provides that all estimates, i.e. proposals for expenditure of public money, must come from the executive and from it alone. The budget is thus necessarily prepared by the executive. In practice, it is prepared by the Treasury, as the department of finance is called. By a process of close consultation between officials of the Treasury and of other departments, a draft of the annual estimates is worked out and submitted to the Treasury several months in advance of the beginning of the next fiscal year.

The Treasury requires every increase in the estimates of a department to be supported by detailed explanation. Since the Chancellor of the Exchequer, the member of the cabinet responsible for finance, must bear the odium of proposing additional taxation, the Treasury is the one department of government unflaggingly devoted to economy. Its attitude toward the estimates submitted by the other departments depends on its forecast of next year's revenues and on the general policy of the government towards increase or decrease of taxation. In any event, the other departments of the government must justify their estimates to a vigilant Treasury, which may veto any item or insist on a general reduction. A department that thinks it has a grievance may appeal to the Prime Minister or to the cabinet as a whole. Generally speaking, however, the Treasury has the last word on the content of the estimates submitted to Parliament.

Role of the House of Commons

Meanwhile, the revenue proposals that are justified or dictated by the estimates are worked out by the Treasury, and after the cabinet has approved them, the Chancellor of the Exchequer presents his budget containing both estimates and revenue proposals to the House. These financial proposals are considered by committee of the whole, known as the Committee of Supply, in such detail as the twenty-six days allotted for such discussion permits. A more thorough screening of a few departmental estimates is undertaken annually by the select committee on estimates. Whether in Committee of Supply or in the estimates committee, the time is taken up in discussing a few groups of expenditures, or "votes," and the others are rushed through with little or no consideration. Millions upon millions of pounds are always voted in haste at the very end. A private member may not move an increase or a shift in the destination of an item in the estimates because that would violate the standing order referred to. He may move that particular items be decreased or entirely disallowed. However, except in very trivial matters, the cabinet regards such a motion as one of want of confidence in the government, and party discipline ensures its defeat. Pressure may persuade the government to modify its financial proposals, but it is now unknown for the House openly to force a revision.

The House of Commons accepts these proposals as reported to it by committee of the whole, and since the House of Lords has no power in money matters, the estimates almost invariably emerge from Parliament in an Appropriation Act, and the revenue proposals in a Finance Act—true copies of the original proposals of the Chancellor of the Exchequer. The most striking indication of the general expectation that the cabinet will carry its financial proposals unchanged is the law enacted in 1913 providing that changes in taxation proposed in the budget speech shall come into effect on the following day.

The system enables the executive, which alone knows in full detail the activities and needs of the various departments of government and the probable yield of the sources of revenue, to draft the financial legislation. It ensures unified responsibility for public expenditure. The appropriations are not arrived at by polling the diverse and unrelated preferences of individual members of Parliament. The executive does not have to countenance raids on the treasury by blocs of members in order to get support for its main proposals. It surveys the entire field of proposed expenditures and enforces a coherent programme. It is unlikely, for example, to appropriate funds for the draining of swamps in aid of agriculture and, at the same time, to authorize expenditures on restoration of swamps for the protection of wildlife. The expeditious enactment of financial legislation is also assured.

It is often said that the Chancellor of the Exchequer is the financial boss in Britain. There is much exaggeration in this view. Despite his strong bias for economy, public expenditures have risen sharply and steadily for the past fifty years. The reasons for this are clear and they operate in the United States and Canada as well. The permanent officials in other departments always see reasons for expanding their activities and extending their establishment. The balance of electoral demand comes down on the side of more government services. The members of Parliament would like to make the best of both worlds and cut taxes while raising expenditures. Since they cannot, they generally acquiesce in or plump for the latter. From their point of view the serious thing about cabinet control of finance is not their inability to reduce estimates but their inability to raise them. The cabinet as a whole responds to these inclinations, and the Chancellor of the Exchequer is always fighting a rearguard action on expenditures.

It is, however, a resolute rearguard action. Incautious department heads who advance inadequately supported or extravagant proposals get badly mauled. In another figure sometimes used to depict the situation, the Treasury is the watchdog of the public purse. Within the lines of policy laid down by Parliament, it enforces strict economy and supervises the household operations of the various departments in aid of efficiency. In this limited sphere, the Chancellor of the Exchequer may be said to be a financial boss. As Parliament does not examine the estimates in full detail, it is necessarily done by an executive agency.

When it comes to the expenditure of the money voted by Parliament, the Treasury, through an accounting officer in each department, sees to it that the money is spent on the purposes for which it was voted. However, Treasury control is not regarded as a sufficient guarantee of probity in such matters. The Comptroller and Auditor-General, appointed by the executive but enjoying the same independence and tenure of office as a judge, audits all the government accounts, reporting irregularities to the Treasury. The most important of his duties is to make an annual report to Parliament. This report is a guide to an active select committee of the House of Commons, the Committee of Public Accounts, which examines and reports to the House on financial irregularities. It is a small committee of fifteen members with a chairman and a majority of its members drawn from the opposition. It probes vigorously in the public accounts, and the government departments take great pains not to incur its censure. Together with the Estimates Committee, it is a very effective instrument for legislative surveillance of the executive.

FINANCIAL LEGISLATION IN CANADA

Subject to minor variations in detail, the legislative-executive relationship in financial matters in the federal government in

Canada follows closely the British pattern. In Canada, the Department of Finance and the Treasury Board carry out most of the functions of the British Treasury. The Treasury Board is a committee of the cabinet composed of the Minister of Finance and five other ministers who have a responsibility corresponding to that of the Chancellor of the Exchequer for settling the financial proposals, subject to the final approval of the cabinet. This responsibility is not concentrated on a single minister nor does the Department of Finance exercise such a searching supervision of the household economy of the spending departments as the Treasury in Britain. Also, the grip of the cabinet on taxation and expenditures is not as strong as in Britain. Logrolling behind the scenes sometimes affects such matters as the revision of the customs tariff and the make-up of appropriations for federal expenditures in the local areas of the country.

One of the most marked differences is in the use made of the public accounts committee. As in Britain, the Auditor-General examines the public accounts and makes an annual report to Parliament. For many years, the public accounts committee of the Canadian House of Commons was moribund. In the ten years preceding the outbreak of World War II, it never met. It was active during the war and was only intermittently active thereafter until revived in 1958. In that year, the long-standing tradition of appointing the chairman from the government supporters was set aside in favour of the British practice of recruiting from the opposition. However, the government failed to follow the British model in all respects, for it still retained a majority of its own supporters on the committee. Moreover, the committee is much larger than its British counterpart, running to fifty members. Limited experiments with an estimates committee, again with British practices in mind, were commenced in 1956, but the Canadian version in operation has not as yet been strikingly successful. Most of these variations from the British budgetary control techniques can be traced to differences in the party systems of the two countries.

The House of Lords in Britain has lost its power over financial legislation. The Canadian Senate has never had its wings clipped, and it claims the power to amend or reject money bills passed by the House of Commons. The rules of the House of Commons declare that its grants of money are not alterable by the Senate.

The only explicit constitutional provisions bearing on the dispute between the two Houses are section 53 of the British North America Act, which provides that money bills shall originate in the House of Commons, and section 54, which, in effect, provides that the cabinet alone can propose appropriations and taxation. It is clear that the Senate cannot amend money bills so as to increase appropriations, but its power to reduce or reject is open to dispute and depends on subtle interpretation of the unwritten portion of the Canadian constitution.

It is not necessary to go into the matter, for two reasons. First, the Senate, as we have already seen, does not venture frequent or prolonged defiance of the House of Commons. It rarely insists nowadays on amending financial legislation. In the railway-building era, the Senate frequently rejected bills providing large appropriations for railways. These bills were one of the Canadian forms of logrolling, and it is doubtful whether the electorate would have supported the House of Commons if the House had tried to make a political issue of the matter. This probably explains why the Senate has often made good its amendments and rejections of money bills in the past. The majority in the House of Commons acquiesced with bad grace in the particular case while denying vigorously the validity of the principle.

Secondly, as the British experience shows, the working of the cabinet system requires that the cabinet should be responsible to the lower House only. To try to make it responsible to two Houses which may be of opposite minds would destroy responsibility. The substance of policy often turns on getting a grant of public money to implement the policy. If the Senate intervened frequently and in detail in finance, it would force a showdown with the popularly elected House in which it would inevitably lose. Its claim to equal powers in finance has merely a nuisance value, which can only be kept on foot if it is not pushed too hard.

FINANCIAL LEGISLATION IN THE UNITED STATES

The worst indictment of the separation of powers in the United States is based on the method of enacting financial legislation. Even those who generally approve the separation of powers are unhappy about its consequences in finance. Revenue bills must originate in the House of Representatives, but aside from this unimportant provision, each House of Congress has a wide initiative in finance. The President makes a budget and proposes it to Congress, but Congress does what it likes with his proposals, when it chooses.

Before 1921, there was not even the semblance of a unified budget. The government departments worked out their own estimates and the Secretary of the Treasury submitted them to the House of Representatives along with an estimate of tax revenues for the coming year. The House at once distributed the estimates to its various committees. In these committees, officials of the departments of government, interest groups, and the different sections and localities of the country all clamoured for appropriations. Each committee responded to these pressures and produced a set of appropriations for the sector of government activity with which it was concerned. The budget, as reported to the House by several committees, consisted of several unrelated proposals tied together in a bundle. A similar process went on in the committees of the Senate after the estimates were passed by the House. No single government department or legislative committee ever looked at the budget as a unified whole. Every department and every committee put in its separate demands without too much concern about what the total was.

In 1921, an advance toward British budgetary practice was made. Legislation in that year provided for the establishment of an executive agency, the Bureau of the Budget, headed by a director appointed by the President and responsible to him alone. His functions resemble those of the Chancellor of the Exchequer, his bias being towards efficiency and economy in the public services. Working with the department officials, the Bureau of the Budget goes carefully into the demands of the departments. The director cuts and trims where he thinks fit and, subject to an appeal by the department to the President, he has the last word. The estimates are the amounts that the President and his advisers, on careful consideration, think necessary for the work of the executive. While the estimates are being prepared, the Bureau makes a forecast of the probable receipts from taxation and decides what modification of the taxation system, if any, should be recommended to Congress. When these estimates and calculations have been completed and drawn together in a budget, the President submits it to both Houses of Congress. The necessity, under present conditions, of executive drafting of financial legislation has been recognized.

The Role of Congressional Committees.

Under the law of 1921, each House had to set up a Committee on Appropriations to which all estimates must go. The estimates for expenditure go first to the appropriations committee of the House of Representatives. They are considered, often in great detail, by the numerous sub-committees of the appropriations committee, which call officials to explain and justify particular proposals for spending, and hear others who wish to support or oppose particular appropriations. The sub-committees often extort undertakings from officials as to how the administrative work to be supported by particular appropriations shall be carried on. In this way, substantial continuous legislative control over administration is secured.

A similar procedure is later followed in the Senate Committee on Appropriations when the appropriations as passed by the House are reported to the Senate. Thus all estimates for expenditure must pass through and be approved by a single committee of each House. This, however, is as far as the copying of the British practice of unified responsibility for appropriations goes.

The appropriations committee of the House reduces some items in the executive proposals and increases others. It may hamstring a particular branch of the administration by cutting its estimates sharply. Through other committees of the House, legislation (inspired by congressional blocs and not by the President) requiring an appropriation of public money for its execution will emerge. In this way, large sums may be added by the appropriations committee to the proposals of the executive. Pork is still distributed from the pork-barrel.

Furthermore, the appropriations committee of the House of Representatives does not draw all the appropriations it recommends into a single appropriation bill. Rather, it sends forward to the House, one after the other, about a dozen bills endorsing appropriations for the various departments and agencies. The House makes minor, but rarely substantial, changes in these bills without ever considering the appropriations as a whole at a given time.

After appropriation bills pass the House, they are sent to the Senate, where further modifications and additions are frequently made by the Senate Committee on Appropriations. Government departments and private interests that were disappointed by the action of the House committee often try their luck again before the Senate committee. Again, when the appropriation bills are reported to the Senate for action, members of the Senate may force significant amendments, usually additions.

After the Senate has added its thoughts to the estimates, the bills go back to the House for its assent to the changes made by the Senate. If, as often happens, the House refuses to accept these as they stand, a conference committee of the two Houses is appointed to find a compromise on which both can agree. When it is found, the bills get their final readings in both Houses and are sent to the President to be signed.

Even in the periods of strong presidential leadership, the action of the legislature may seriously distort the budget as proposed by the President, both by reductions and additions. The appropriations for one of his cherished projects may be cut and his pledges of economy thwarted. He has the power of veto, but Congress rarely gives him a chance to use it. Appropriations known to be obnoxious to him are attached as riders to appropriation bills covering vitally important votes of money. As he cannot veto particular items in a bill but must accept it or reject it as a whole, he has little choice but to accept. The unified responsibility of the British system is still lacking.

The revenue side of the budget is similarly handled by the legislature. The revenue-raising proposals of the Bureau of the Budget go to the Ways and Means Committee of the House and the Finance Committee of the Senate. Although the Constitution provides that revenue bills must originate in the House of Representatives,[1] this does not, in practice, prevent the Senate from introducing new revenue proposals in the guise of amendments to the revenue measure passed by the lower House. Both Houses

[1] The Constitution of the United States, Art. i, sect.7.

alter the revenue proposals of the executive much as they see fit. Officials, representatives of the reluctant taxpayers, and other interests are heard. Logrolling and the push and pull of a great variety of interests are marked features of the framing of tax, as well as appropriation, measures.

Such practices are found on a grand scale, particularly in the revisions of the protective tariff, which has always been a big revenue producer and the scene of unremitting struggle between the various sections and economic interests of the country. The main lines of tariff legislation are fixed by complex bargaining between agriculture, labour, and industry, and the detailed contents of the tariff schedules depend on logrolling between the innumerable industrial and commercial interests, almost all of which want a tariff on some articles and none on others but do not agree at all on what these articles should be. The tariff as made by Congress is not a matter of party policy or executive leadership but of bargaining between a continental array of interests. It should be added, however, that there has been a virtual cessation of tariff-making by Congress in the last twenty-five years. From 1934 until the present, Congress has conferred on the President, usually for successive two- or three-year periods, the power to make reciprocal trade agreements with other countries, and to modify the tariff within certain limits and under certain conditions.

The President cannot depend on getting the kind of taxes he wants. Nor can he depend on getting tax measures that will bring in the revenues he sees to be necessary to meet governmental expenditures. During World War II, for example, Congress more than once cut his tax recommendations very sharply. Congress has always exercised the right to change as it sees fit the appropriations recommended by the President. The executive prepares the budget, but Congress takes it apart and acts on the different parts of it without considering it as a related whole.

The Legislative Reorganization Act

This situation was generally agreed to be so unsatisfactory that in 1946 the Legislative Reorganization Act was passed partly in an attempt to meet the complaints. It provides that, at the beginning of each session, the appropriations committees and the finance committees of both Houses shall meet jointly, and prepare and report to Congress not later than 15 February a proposed "legislative budget" for the coming year. If the estimated expenditures exceed the estimated revenues, the resolution introducing the budget in Congress must contain a clause requiring the public debt to be increased by an amount sufficient to bring the two totals into balance.

It has never been clear how this provision is to be enforced or how the congressional budget it envisages is to be brought into relation with the budget prepared by the President. The original bill out of which the Act developed contained a provision that if Congress should later approve appropriations in excess of the total it had adopted earlier in the financial resolution, the President should be authorized to reduce appropriations by the amount necessary to restore balance. This provision was rejected by Congress, thus limiting the effectiveness that the law is likely to have.

Indeed, other than one attempt to adopt a legislative budget in 1950, most of the provisions of the Legislative Reorganization Act dealing with financial legislation have been ineffective and pork-barrel legislation continues to make a properly planned budget impossible.

The law of 1921 setting up the Bureau of the Budget also provided for the office of Comptroller-General. This official is appointed by the President for a fifteen-year period and cannot be removed except by impeachment and conviction or by a joint resolution of both Houses of Congress. He has two principal functions. First, he makes decisions whether particular expenditures proposed by the executive departments are authorized by the appropriations Congress has made. Second, he investigates and audits all branches of the public accounts to see whether there have been irregularities in the expenditures made, and reports the result of his work to the President and to Congress. Congress, however, has not had active standing committees on the public accounts, and investigations of executive stewardship have been made, if at all, by special congressional committees of investigation appointed from time to time and not solely concerned with financial matters.

It should be recalled here that the Legislative Reorganization Act of 1946 directs the standing committees of both Houses on expenditures (now known as the Committees on Government

Operations), and also the standing committees on particular fields of legislative-executive activity to maintain continuous surveillance over the work of the executive branch of government, checking on both economy and efficiency. The legislation looks to the supersession of special investigating committees and the establishment of more effective checks on all branches of administration.

Weak Control of Public Finance

This account of the enactment of financial legislation points to the greatest weakness of American federal government for present-day purposes. The weakness arises from the impossibility, already noted, of keeping present-day legislation and administration in separate compartments. In an age when governments are expected to enact and administer efficiently a great quantity of complicated and interrelated legislation of the highest importance, it is vital to be able to bring home responsibility for failure. The nation, which elects the President, tends to hold him responsible for failure, but he generally lacks the power to carry his view of what ought to be done. Congress rarely thinks in terms of the whole programme but reacts for and against particular items of it under the stimulus of a great variety of conflicting pressures, intensified by a desire to assert itself against the Administration. Even when it does think in terms of the whole, it lacks the information necessary for fully informed and wise decision and is, in any event, unable to ensure that administration will be carried on in accordance with its view. Moreover, the means through which the electorate could enforce responsibility on Congress are lacking. Party spirit does not dominate Congress; voting commonly does not follow party lines. The parties do not line up for and against an extensive programme in Congress, and nothing therefore would be gained by trying to hold the parties responsible. Where disciplined parties inviting responsibility do not exist, the electorate cannot enforce responsibility. If they did exist, the formal separation of powers probably would not give any great trouble, provided that the President and Congress were of the same party. The majority party would see to it that President and Congress became a harmonious team.

Of course, the present situation is not without advantages.

Any threat of executive dictatorship gets short shrift. Policy is not made in secret party councils but in Congress, where the vital forces of the nation find free expression. Effective integration of policy is difficult, but then it is not as important in Washington or Ottawa as it is at Westminster. In Britain, there is no middle term between the national government and the municipalities. Whatever is demanded of government that cannot be done locally by the municipalities must be done by the national government, which has had to respond to the full impact of the great expansion of government activities.

In the United States and Canada, the states and provinces stand as autonomous governments between the national and municipal governments. Much of what we demand of governments today is carried out by numerous state and provincial governments and, as long as it is done acceptably there, it does not require such close integration and disciplined action at the national level. Because of the federal system, the national government still retains some of the characteristics of an alliance between states for furthering a limited set of common interests. An alliance of states does not need, and no one expects it to have, the close-knit governmental organization necessary for a unitary state.

Much more will be said later about the significance of federalism. For the moment, it is sufficient to realize that federalism is an important factor in the workability of the legislative-executive relationship at Washington and that the future of that relationship is involved in the fate of federalism. If the responsibilities of the national government had not receded substantially from the high point reached in World War II, the states would very likely have been submerged by the enormous power concentrated in the national government. But these responsibilities have receded substantially, although not enough to ensure against a slow erosion of the autonomy of the state governments.

For several years there has been a steady flow of proposals for change, some of which advocate bringing legislative-executive relationships somewhat closer to the British pattern. Such proposals indicate widespread current dissatisfaction with the existing relationships. However, if the state governments, as genuinely independent authorities, can carry a large part of total governmental load, arguments for formal changes designed to secure the efficiency of the British system are not completely convincing.

It is hard to estimate how far formal changes in legislative-executive relations would be effective. The success of the British legislative-executive relationships is due largely to the existence of firmly disciplined political parties. The issue in the United States really is whether the national parties of the United States are capable of comparable discipline. If there are forces at work in the party system and the nation as a whole fostering more effective party unity on more specific and more coherent programmes, formal changes in legislative-executive relationships will aid the development. On the other hand, if the sectional and occupational diversities of the United States continue in strength, preventing any significant growth in the unity of the national parties, keeping them as loose combinations of state parties, such changes are likely to have little effect.

The key to the legislative-executive relationships, indeed the index to the understanding of liberal democratic government, as a whole, is to be found in the state of mind of the electorate, in public opinion. All the analysis of the preceding chapters has been leading to this conclusion. The people may not be able to make the laws, but the state of the public mind, in its divisions, diversities, and confusions as well as in the electoral majorities it produces from time to time, has an influence that is decisive in the long run. Its influence bears powerfully on the way the constitution itself works, as well as on the laws that are made and the manner in which they are administered.

If public opinion is so vitally important, then (it may well be asked) why was it not put in the forefront of the study at the beginning? The answer is that public opinion is the vaguest and most elusive element in government. More can be made of it if the various forms and channels through which it must express itself (the system of representation, the legislature, political parties, and pressure groups) are described first. With these outlined in some detail, attention will now be given to public opinion.

CHAPTER XII

PUBLIC OPINION

DEMOCRATIC government has been defined as government in accordance with the will of the people. The people, in this sense, means the electorate, which, in the countries in question, embraces almost the entire adult population. Taken literally, government in accordance with the will of the electorate would mean that every member of the electorate must be consulted and must agree before a democratic government can embark on a significant line of policy.

It is clear that this is not so. Democratic legislatures often pass, and democratic executives often enforce, legislation that was not in issue at the last election. Nor does the succeeding election always bring a specific verdict of the electorate on such legislation. Even when it does, the enforcement of the legislation in the interim may have had far-reaching consequences which cannot be undone. Also, it has been remarked again and again that the electorate when it is consulted is never unanimous. There is always some dissent in some section of the electorate on whatever proposal is made for government action.

GOVERNMENT BY PUBLIC OPINION

If the familiar definition of democratic government quoted above is to correspond to realities, two qualifications must be introduced. First, government in accordance with the will of the people cannot be taken to mean consultation on every act of government. Rather it must be taken to mean that periodically each member of the electorate is enabled to state his preference between the candidates and the announced policies of two or more political parties. In casting his vote, he may be deciding on the announced policy of parties for the future, on the past record of the parties in and out of power, on the personalities of the candidates, or on some combination of these factors. It would be impossible to discover what factors were decisive for each voter. But this very uncertainty disposes the political parties to take care over their present record, their future programme, and the candidates they sponsor. Where not directly, then indirectly, pronounced attitudes in the electorate have an enormous influence on the behaviour of the political parties, and where a crisis of obviously large significance for the community sharply divides the political parties, rouses prolonged debate, and overshadows other less critical issues, the electorate is certain to get a chance to express itself very directly on the critical question in the next election. If a majority of the electorate is opposed to the policy of the group presently in control of the government, it can change its rulers and bring to power another group of politicians with a policy more to its liking.

This brings us to the second qualification: government in accordance with the will of the people means at most that it is the will of a majority that prevails on controversial questions. The fact that there is a controversy ensures that some portion of the electorate will be dissatisfied with any decision taken. The will of the people is not the will of all. Even then, the majorities are mustered only occasionally and say their say on only a small fraction of the specific decisions that are taken in the name of government.

What has just been said refers only to the influence and control exerted by the electorate through elections. However, in earlier chapters we have seen that the influence of the electorate is not limited to voting in elections every two to four years. Between elections, the political parties are always looking forward to the next election, searching for methods and measures that will be popular and trying to avoid policies that will be unpopular. Party organization, particularly in Britain, and particular politicians everywhere are constantly seeking to plumb opinion in the country. At the same time, they are attempting to influence the development of opinion. Speeches in the legislature are addressed to the country. Political leaders find many other occasions for utterance designed to enlighten, placate, or mould opinion. Elections are intermittent dramatic interventions by the electorate. Between elections, the democratic electorate maintains constant pressure on its rulers through what is generally called public opinion.

Those who are impressed with the effectiveness of this pressure, both in influencing the conduct of government between elections and in shaping the issues and selecting the political leadership for the next election, describe democracy as government by public opinion. The governments of the three countries in question respond to public opinion, but the nature, and particularly the rapidity, of the response differs considerably from one to the other.

BRITISH AND AMERICAN CONTRASTS

In Britain, a relatively high proportion of the electorate gives close attention to government and politics. The political parties have fairly coherent programmes to which they stand committed. The leaders of the political parties who become prime ministers and members of cabinets have generally had long careers in political life, during which the electorate forms an estimate of their characters and acquires an appreciation of their outlook on political issues.

An election in Britain expresses a judgment on party programmes and party personalities, awarding control of the government for the time being to a particular group of persons associated with a particular programme. Public opinion makes a fairly definite choice and then watches attentively for dissension or vacillation within the group, for sharp divergence from or abandonment of the programme. It holds the leaders of the victorious party responsible for coherent direction of the government along certain lines staked out in advance.

The means for enforcing this responsibility are at hand. Steady party discipline and the power of dissolution ensure to the cabinet the power to do the substance of what they have promised. In so far as they fail, the next election can be expected to bring a reckoning. Most important, there is no fixed date for that reckoning, and therefore no assurance of a second chance to redeem any failure to gauge public opinion accurately now. Even though the party majority in Parliament stands firm, any bad misreading of public opinion by the cabinet weakens its moral authority dangerously, and it may be driven to a dissolution and a new election. Hence it is vital to judge public opinion accurately day by day.

Also, any strong evidence that the cabinet is divided within itself on an important question weakens public confidence. In Britain, no one could have been sure that such a disagreement as the one that resulted in the dismissal of Henry Wallace from President Truman's cabinet in 1946 could be patched up without an election. Thus, the persons concerned in the disagreement would have had to pay the closest attention to the state of public opinion across the country at the moment. In any election that did ensue, public opinion would have had its chance to say directly what it thought about the issue of policy out of which the disagreement arose. Elections can always be timed to coincide with issues. Parties therefore attend to both the issues and public opinion with great care.

In the United States, there is less sustained focusing of opinion on national issues. This is due partly to the continental sweep of the country, to the greater social heterogeneity of the electorate, and to the consequent distraction of sectional considerations. It is due partly to other factors. Election dates are fixed. The national parties do not stand for precise programmes. Presidents and cabinets often have not had such long prominent careers in national politics as their counterparts in Britain. In so far as it is not clear what they are pledged to do, it is difficult to hold them strictly and immediately responsible.

Public opinion generally cannot express itself with as sure a knowledge of what is involved in United States elections. Between elections, it has not the means to compel the government to listen. It cannot speak decisively until the fixed date of the next election. So it does not exhibit the habitual alertness of British public opinion. The ultimate response of government to public opinion in the United States may not be less sure than in Britain, but it frequently takes much longer for the response to come.[1]

In Canada, the institution of responsible cabinet government tends to bring a responsiveness to public opinion comparable to that found in Britain. On the other hand, the factors already noted in chapter VIII, which make the Canadian national party system resemble that of the United States, tend to make public opinion

[1]For a contrast of the presidential and parliamentary systems in terms of their responsiveness to public opinion, see Harold D. Lasswell, *Democracy through Public Opinion* (Banta, Menasha, Wis., 1941), pp. 117-22.

elusive and uncertain, and consequently to weaken and delay the response of the government to it.

The frequency with which politicians and others concerned with the actions of government appeal to public opinion for rebuke, support, or justification is a commonplace. They all agree that public opinion must prevail, but there is rarely any large measure of agreement about what the voice of public opinion is uttering on specific questions. Those who see some evidence of popular support for their proposals claim the sanction of public opinion now. Those who cannot deny the popular tide against them at the moment claim the support of enlightened public opinion now, and the support of general public opinion once it has been enlightened. Since, by definition, a controversial issue is one on which substantial bodies of opinion confront each other, both sides generally claim the sanction of public opinion.

WHAT IS PUBLIC OPINION?

Few concepts are as hazy as that of public opinion. Some attempt at definition therefore is necessary. While it may not be possible to find a clear-cut meaning for the phrase, a number of fairly obvious confusions can be cleared out of the way. It will help to consider, first, what is opinion, and second, what makes opinion public.[1]

The word "opinion" is very loosely used in ordinary speech. To many, it includes a belief on any subject under the sun. But the term should be restricted to views entertained on subjects that admit of doubt and are open to controversy. A new and original view on an arithmetic sum is not an opinion but merely an error. Where a proof or demonstration will bring persons of average reasonableness to the same conclusion, the subject does not admit of an opinion. Equally, there cannot be an opinion about a notorious matter of fact, although the questions of fact that fall in this category are fewer than is generally supposed, and much division of opinion arises out of different views as to what the facts

[1]See William Albig, *Modern Public Opinion* (McGraw-Hill, New York, 1956), ch. 1; and Harwood L. Childs, *An Introduction to Public Opinion* (Wiley, New York, 1940), pp. 35–48, for discussion of a variety of suggested definitions and helpful clarification.

relating to a controversial issue really are. Matters that are not debatable are not open to opinion. Nothing that is said about them is likely to modify our ways of living.

Besides the matters that logic or observation have verified, there are many others that cannot be debated in the countries with which we are concerned. These are the generally accepted community views of right and wrong. For example, it is not possible today to debate human slavery, polygamy, or homicide because almost everyone is agreed in condemning them. What we have here is not opinion but consensus. Nothing that is said about them at present is likely to modify social habits or to affect public policy.

Opinion is therefore to be defined as consisting of views on matters that are open to discussion. It must next be asked in what way opinion becomes public opinion. A public opinion is one that determines or influences, or may be expected to influence, what government does. In the first place, its content must have some bearing on the direction public policy is to take. An opinion on the merits of surrealist painting or "rock 'n' roll," even though very widely held, is not public opinion. An opinion on aesthetic values is not likely to affect government directly, although it may be indicative of a public mood that may express itself in political matters. In the second place, an opinion does not become public opinion merely because it expresses a judgment on some aspect of public policy. Isolated opinions held by one or a few persons have little immediate influence. Public opinion is a view relating to government held strongly enough by a considerable number of people to dispose them to push for action.

Public opinion also contains some element of rationality. The views of which it is said at any time to consist are open to discussion, and are shaped by discussion. Almost everyone who talks about public opinion assumes that it can be influenced by the marshalling of facts, and by argument about the significance of the facts. Most of those perhaps who seek to mould public opinion appeal to the emotions as well as to the minds of the public. But the process of persuasion always produces facts, arguments, and discussion on the assumption that further evidence and thought will clarify and modify opinion.

Accordingly public opinion implies something other than mere emotional reactions and prejudices. A wave of indignation over a vicious crime, the general sympathy expressed for the victims of a widely publicized disaster, a host of superficial impressions that are not grounded at all in reflection on the relevant facts, are not public opinion.[1] Public opinion is the product of discussion in which feeling always plays a part but does not entirely determine the result.

This is almost as far as any agreed analysis goes, because cogent objections can be stated against any more precise definition. Many who use the expression assume that public opinion is identical with the opinion of the majority of the electorate, and that on every public question there exists, or can be created fairly quickly by discussion, a clear-cut majority opinion. They personify public opinion, attributing to it a will and an articulate voice which can always be heard if we listen intently.

Public Opinion and the Will of the Majority

The objections to this view have already been pointed out in earlier chapters. On some matters, like the winning of a war once we are involved in it, an overwhelming majority of the electorate is agreed. This is, or approaches, consensus and is scarcely open to debate at all. In genuinely democratic countries at any rate, there are always some fundamental beliefs that almost all approve. At the other extreme, there are a multitude of matters on which majority agreement does not exist at all. Many people have no opinion whatever on deficit financing, and those who have hold a variety of opinions about it. Some are utterly opposed; others approve in certain circumstances and under certain limitations but do not generally agree either on the circumstances or the limitations. Between the two extremes of consensus and utter lack of agreement, there are groups of opinion on many subjects, some of which can muster a clear approving majority in the electorate and others not. If public opinion is by definition confined to specific judgments clearly and unmistakably espoused by a majority

[1] See W. Brooke Graves (ed.), *Readings in Public Opinion*, Introduction by Clyde L. King (Appleton-Century, New York, 1928), pp. xxi-xxiv, where public opinion is distinguished from a number of other popular manifestations.

of the electorate, there is relatively little public opinion to be considered.

In fact, an opinion may be decisive in a given political situation although it is held only by a relatively small minority. Majorities are created by compromise, and one body of opinion may get something it wants in return for helping to create a majority on some unrelated issue. Minorities are sometimes able by vigorous protest to turn aside what seem to be majority demands. The opinions they hold and make effective cannot be denied the character of public opinion.

Furthermore, it is not possible in every circumstance to bring the accepted opinion of a majority of the electorate within the concept of public opinion. Let it be assumed that forty-nine per cent of the electorate in the United States or Britain become avowed Communists, determined to socialize production and distribution and establish the classless society, while fifty-one per cent remain attached to free enterprise. In these circumstances, it might be said that there was a public opinion in favour of free enterprise. Before hastily adopting such a conclusion, let it be assumed further that the Communists liquidate enough of the leaders and lackeys of free enterprise to put the Communists in a slight majority. Is it now to be said that a public opinion in favour of Communism has been created? And if so, would a public opinion in favour of free enterprise be restored if its remaining supporters were to stage a successful counter-revolution restoring their majority by bloodshed?

The illustration is, of course, somewhat fanciful because the political process is not likely to create clear-cut majorities and minorities in this way. It does show, however, that public opinion is not just another name for the opinion of a majority, however created. Moreover, it brings out clearly the fundamental prerequisite for the existence of any public opinion. Public opinion cannot be created by violence. It has to be created by discussion. And there cannot be effective discussion for the purpose between groups that disagree profoundly about the very basis of a just society.[1] They cannot persuade one another on the question what

[1]This point was made clearly many years ago with other illustrations. See Lawrence A. Lowell, *Public Opinion and Popular Government* (Longmans, Green, New York, 1914), rev. ed. pp. 1-7.

government should do next because they do not agree at all on the ends at which government action should be directed. Public opinion cannot exist without some minimum of consensus.

Community Consensus and Public Opinion

In the earlier discussion of political parties, it was argued that the party system will not work except where the people are agreed on some minimum of fundamental matters. Where the parties are sharply divided on the basic principles of a just society, the stage is set for the emergence of a single party which will rule by force and not by discussion and consent. When we say that some minimum of consensus is necessary for the existence and development of public opinion, we are saying the same thing in a different way. To put it more colloquially, there must be common ground on which to meet. We cannot expect to get any measure of agreement on common action unless we are somewhat agreed on the ends to be served by such action. In the broadest sense, the ends to be served are the liberal democratic ideals already discussed.

What has just been said is not intended to show that a peaceful transition to Communism is impossible. It is unlikely but might be possible if it proceeded slowly enough for most of us to slough off our inherited individualistic habits and beliefs and to embrace equally strong convictions of the rightness of collectivism. Over the last fifty years, we have come slowly to what seems to be a consensus on a considerably enlarged sphere of government action that could not have been adopted wholesale in 1900 without revolution. However, it will not be until almost all of us believe in the essential rightness of the Communist ideal that we can hope to reach through peaceful discussion the almost endless decisions about the methods for making the ideal come true. It is no part of the present purpose to discuss this question. The illustration was used to make clear, in terms of current interest, that even the opinion of a majority is not public opinion unless there is an underlying consensus. There must be a public, or a community, to which to appeal, and the public cannot exist where two or more competing all-inclusive ideals are warring within the bosom of a single state.

We have also seen in discussing political parties that there is no agreed analysis of what the fundamental consensus must cover.

Fundamental beliefs are hard to enumerate because we take them for granted and rarely try to analyse them. The deepest of these beliefs are religious in character. If the community has a common religion, we shall find in it, and in the moral code it sanctions, a large element of the consensus. So, for the countries in question here, despite sectarian differences, the Christian view of man's place in the universe, and the moral rules that seem to follow therefrom, are of profound importance. Even those who no longer accept Christian theology give a surprising adherence to Christian morality.

The consensus also finds secular expression. It covers much, although not all, of the criminal law. Some elements of it can only be described generally by such expressions as "a sense of fair play." The beliefs in the worth of individual personality and in individual liberty and equality are the most significant elements. For long, the idea of individual liberty was taken both in practice and belief to include freedom of economic enterprise. While the compelling quality of this particular element of individualistic thought is declining, it probably still has a stronger hold than socialists generally like to believe.

This is not an essay on religion, social morality, and folklore, and it cannot attempt to disentangle and weigh all the varied elements in the consensus. Despite the elusiveness of the subject, which defies summary explanation, it is necessary to emphasize again that there is a body of fundamental ideas to which social and political life is expected to conform. Some of these ideas are held more passionately than others, the relative emphasis given them varies from time to time, and some are always being modified or replaced by others. Nevertheless, these ideas give the nation or community what unity it has. The strength of the consensus largely determines whether the community can hold together under the stress and strain that are inseparable from social life. The consensus helps to hold in check all the divisive tendencies so well exemplified by the activities of pressure groups.

When particular persons or groups flout the fundamental beliefs or fail to conform to them, when events persistently recur that, according to the consensus, ought not to happen, when the aspirations of different groups clash openly and disturb the community's sense of security, there is an agitation to have something done about it. Political action is one of the ways of doing something about it. Generally, there are a number of views on what should or should not be done. Thus discussion is provoked on the nature of the disturbing events, their cause, and the means of their cure. The political process in a democracy consists of a search for solutions to such problems as, for example, what relationships of labour and management will be in harmony with the consensus.

It is not difficult to find supporting evidence for this statement. Minor political issues are sometimes discussed and settled almost entirely on the basis of discovery and analysis of the facts relating to them. But when the claims of strong groups like labour and management clash, the discussion of the facts is supplemented, and often overshadowed, by appeals of both sides to justice and fair play, to individual liberty, to equality, to democracy, and so on. Both sides know they must appeal to the underlying consensus and show that their claims are justified by it, or at least consistent with it. Each side has some confidence that if it can persuade large sections of the more or less neutral onlookers of the identity of its claims with the substance of liberty, equality and democracy it will get something of what it wants.

For instance, in the great steel industry strike in the United States in 1949, the principle of non-contributory pensions for the workers was at issue. In public discussions, the unions maintained that pensions of this kind were necessary for the general welfare of the workers and that the steel companies should provide for the depreciation of their workers through wear and tear just as they set aside sums to cover the depreciation of their equipment (appeals to the belief in the worth of individual personality). They also urged that if the large pensions actually paid to high executives in the industry were justified, then pensions for the workers in the industry were justified too (an appeal to the belief in equality of treatment).

The companies, on the other hand, argued that the workers should be paid for their services in wages, and that if they then wanted a pension scheme they should contribute to it as part of the personal plans made by each of them for taking care of his old age (an appeal to the belief in individual freedom and its corollary, individual responsibility). Each side tried to present its case in ways that would harmonize with the liberal democratic ideals. Public opinion on current issues is formed as discussion gropes for solutions that square with the consensus.

The Elusiveness of Public Opinion

The difficulties of trying to define public opinion may now be restated. It has always been impossible to interest everybody in everything. Some portion of the electorate will take a lively interest in some issues and none at all in others until they reach the level of a national crisis. Thus there is a different public attending to almost every issue. Of the public attending to any one issue, there are some who have a considerable knowledge and a keen interest because the issue affects them directly. There are others— often the majority of the particular public in question—who know little of the facts or of the considerations that bear on any political action that might be taken on the facts. If they are at all open-minded persons, they will tend to become confused and uncertain as they become aware of the welter of facts and argument involved in the issue. At any given moment, many of them are likely to be under the spell of the person who last tried his arts of persuasion on them.

If opinion were polled today, it might show a majority on one side. If it were polled a week later after more fact and argument had been heard, the majority might be on the other side. Then too, the interested public is always changing; some exhaust their interest in the issue while some new development draws others in. As an issue deepens towards crisis, a larger and larger public attends to it, much as the crowd gathers when a street-corner argument develops into a fight. These additions to the public generally have less knowledge of and genuine interest in the issue and are more easily swayed by him who spoke last. On any first-class issue, public opinion is fluid and changing. It may be changing even while it is being polled.

There is, therefore, a different and indeterminate public on almost every issue, and its opinion shifts and fluctuates. Only rarely will the majority of any public also be a majority of the electorate. When we recall that in particular political situations the opinion of small groups is sometimes decisive, and the opinion of larger groups sometimes ineffective, it can be understood why many despair of defining public opinion in terms of specific agreements on particular issues by some specified portion of the electorate. They conclude they cannot identify the authentic voice of public opinion. In short, there is no way of defining public opinion so that you will unfailingly recognize it when you meet it. If this is so, government by public opinion can only be described as the confused process of working out solutions for controversial political issues that the consensus of the community will support, or at least tolerate.[1]

This conclusion is probably too pessimistic. There have always been, among businessmen, newspapermen, and politicians, shrewd estimators of public opinion with an almost uncanny sense of the drift of opinion. They have revealed little of their method, and to outward appearance it seems highly intuitive. But it does indicate possibilities. In recent years, moreover, the public-opinion polls have had enough success to show that there are further possibilities in the measurement of opinion.

MEASURING PUBLIC OPINION

Newspapers revealed an interest in the measurement of opinion over a century ago when they began to conduct "straw votes" as a means of predicting election results. It is a far cry from this casual method of measurement to the refined sampling techniques now being developed and applied by private polling organizations. They divide the population into a number of categories, and select from each category a limited number of persons to be interviewed, on the assumption that the opinions expressed by the sample drawn from each category will be a fairly accurate index to the state of opinion in the category as a whole. Then, if the samples have been selected properly, the views expressed by this public in miniature should come very close to the opinion of the general public.

The margin of error between the opinion of the representative samples and that of the general public can be reduced by increasing the number of persons polled, but the slight increase in accuracy

[1]For a description of public opinion as an organic process rather than an agreement of minds, see Charles Horton Cooley, *Social Process* (Scribner, New York, 1927), ch. xxxi.

has to be balanced against a substantial rise in polling costs. Even for such an important issue as a presidential election in the United States, only between 3,000 and 6,500 voters may be questioned, while a fairly accurate prediction of the results of the Canadian plebiscite on military conscription in 1942 was based on as small a sample as 208 persons in the key provinces of Ontario and Quebec. In making up the representative samples, polling organizations must know the distribution of the population according to region, rural or urban residence, age, sex, occupation, race, and economic status. The samples are checked against official census data, election statistics, and the like to make sure that each category of the public receives its proper weight.

After the samples have been carefully chosen and carefully weighted, it is necessary to guard against possible distortion of the results at various stages in the polling process. The wording of the questions may be ambiguous or may suggest a particular response from the person polled. This difficulty has been overcome, in part, by careful preparation of test questionnaires, which may be revised a dozen times before the final poll is taken. At the interview, the attitude of the questioner or the inflection of his voice may affect the response. Careful selection, and even special training, of interviewers help to guard against error from this source.

With little more than two decades of experience with these refined methods, the public-opinion polls have established a place for themselves, but it is still too early to assess their usefulness accurately. Although the champions of the polls do not suggest that the polls should supplant elections as a means of getting the verdict of public opinion, they do contend that the polls are, in many respects, superior to elections. They make it possible to measure opinion more frequently, and at the moment most appropriate for particular issues. Opinion on particular issues can be polled in isolation, free from the distracting personal factors and the multiplicity of issues that confuse elections. The polls also enable us to inquire whether or not public opinion on an issue like the control of venereal disease, which gets little open public discussion, has crystallized sufficiently to support governmental action.[1]

[1]See George A. Gallup, *A Guide to Public Opinion Polls* (Princeton University Press, 1944), for an explanation of the methods used in polling public opinion, and for support of their accuracy and usefulness.

It has also been argued in the United States that both legislators and administrators can make use of the polls. Members of the legislature might be able to take a firmer stand on public issues if they had a reliable means of testing the claims of the lobbyists to public support. It is sometimes suggested that the standing committees of Congress might use the polls to supplement their public hearings. In the administrative field, the United States Department of Agriculture has made use of polls in the working out of departmental policy. If public opinion polls should come to be widely used by legislators and administrators, they could scarcely be conducted under private auspices. Also, it must be remembered that legislatures claim to be the experts on public opinion, and so are likely to impose sharp limits on the polling of public opinion by government departments.

Accuracy of the Polls

Critics of the polls argue that the basic assumption on which the claim for accuracy in the polls rests is unjustified. They question whether opinion in each of the age, sex, economic, and other categories is homogeneous, whether the opinions expressed by the representative samples can safely be taken to be representative of the opinions held by the public as a whole. They also contend that, as the public concerned varies with each issue, the factors taken into account in making up the sample should vary with each issue.

The polls are also criticized for assuming that every man's opinion is of equal importance. Men have equal voting power, it is true, but unequal influence on the votes of others in an election, and on the opinions of others in open discussion. Therefore, opinion should be assessed qualitatively as well as quantitatively. For example, it is necessary to give additional weight to the opinion of a political leader, although it would be extremely difficult to say how much. Through the use of what are called filter questions, the polling organizations have tried to meet this criticism. These questions explore the information and knowledge on which individual opinions are based. In this way, some approach to qualitative analysis is made possible.

However, in those instances in which the polls are prepared as a commercial product for consumption by the rank and file of newspaper readers, questionnaires normally cover a wide range of topics without going very deeply into the intricacies of any of them. Because of the nature of the market, there is a tendency to select the most recent and lively issues for measurement without sufficient regard for their complexity. If the polls are to measure more than the surface drift of the moment, they must use detailed questionnaires that go more deeply into particular issues, as some polling organizations have done. Only in this way is it possible to estimate the grounds on which an opinion is based, and to judge its intensity and stability.

Critics also urge that, in so far as the questionnaires fail to probe beneath the surface, the polls give a misleading impression of the firmness of opinion on public issues. If a majority appears in the "yes" column, it is popularly taken to be a matured majority opinion. Possibly, however, it may be the result of a considerable number of unreflective, uninformed judgments, judgments that would be quickly modified by open discussion. Also, these opinions are given by people who will never have to assume direct responsibility for them. It is not known how many of them would be prepared to act on the basis of these opinions.

A frequent criticism is that the polls tend to introduce irrational elements into elections. The desire to be on the winning side is sufficiently strong and pervasive to be a factor of some importance in elections. In so far as polls taken in advance of an election suggest a pronounced drift of opinion, the very fact that the drift is indicated is likely to accentuate it. This point has been much discussed in recent years, but without any definite conclusions. It is also urged that the polls tend to undermine the representative system by encouraging the uninformed to make judgments on complex issues, and by suggesting that majorities have made up their minds on such issues. It has already been contended in chapter IX that the electorate is not qualified to rule directly on intricate technical matters. But the majority opinion inferred from the results of a poll does not become law, and as long as many legislators are dubious of the accuracy of the results, the influence of the polls on legislation is not likely to be excessive.

Public confidence in the accuracy of the polls was shaken in 1948 when, against the unanimous prediction of all the reputable polling organizations, Mr. Truman defeated Mr. Dewey in the presidential race. The episode brought about a searching re-examination of polling techniques by the polling organizations themselves and by other interested persons and bodies. No single explanation of the miscalculations was found. Rather, a number of suggested explanations applicable to one or the other of the polling organizations emerged. They were too confident of the accuracy of their methods. They made errors in sampling and in the interpreting of the data secured by sampling. In particular, they guessed wrong on the voting behaviour of the persons who were undecided when they were polled and underestimated the last-minute changes of mind among those who did state a voting preference. Moreover, while eighty-five per cent to ninety per cent of those polled stated a voting preference, only about fifty per cent of the electorate actually voted in the election.[1] The test of these and other explanations will come as the polling organizations refine their techniques in the light of them and try to forecast the next presidential election. While the polls redeemed themselves in 1952 and 1956 by predicting victories for Mr. Eisenhower, there is still reason to believe that they are far from overcoming the difficulties which were so dramatically underlined by the *débâcle* of 1948.

As long as there is any considerable disagreement on the accuracy with which the polls measure opinion, they are not likely to be used widely as part of the governmental machinery for eliciting the will of the people on critical issues. In the meantime, they help to focus the interest of voters on public questions, to make individuals conscious of the opinions that predominate in groups other than their own, and to stimulate the flow of discussion.[2] They enable politicians, officials, and others to get some impression of the nature and intensity of opinion on a variety of questions, and to follow trends of opinion over a period of time. As the techniques are further tested and developed, it may become possible to estimate public opinion on a specific issue at a given moment, not only

[1]For discussions of the polls on the 1948 presidential elections, see Norman C. Meier, and Harold W. Saunders, *The Polls and Public Opinion* (Henry Holt, New York, 1949), and "The Opinion Polls and the 1948 U.S. Presidential Election: A Symposium," *International Journal of Opinion and Attitude Research*, vol. ɪɪ, pp. 309-31, 451-591, vol. ɪɪɪ, pp. 1-46, 157-204.

[2]For discussion pro and con on the polls, see "Public Opinion Polls: Dr. Jekyll or Mr. Hyde?, A Symposium" in *Public Opinion Quarterly*, 4 (1940), pp. 212-84, and Lindsay Rogers, *The Pollsters* (Knopf, New York, 1949).

with accuracy, but in such a way as to create a general conviction of accuracy.

THE LONG-RUN IMPORTANCE OF PUBLIC OPINION

Whether or not the content of public opinion can be usefully tested and measured, there is no doubt about its existence or its massive political influence in the long run. At a given time and place, public opinion seems amorphous and purposeless, "like the windy blisters of a troubled water," as Thomas Hobbes said in another connection. But over a longish period of time and in a deeper perspective set by historical study rather than by contemporary observation, there are surging tides and onrolling waves which at least have direction, if not purpose as well. Some of them beat hard at times on the rugged shores of the community consensus before they recede and change direction. And they do not beat entirely in vain, because the contours of the consensus are gradually changed by their action.

Historians have noted these waves and tides in various countries. In the United States, for example, clearly marked alternating periods of radicalism and conservatism throughout the life of the Republic have been identified. To go no farther back than the beginning of the twentieth century, the Theodore Roosevelt-Woodrow Wilson period was one with unmistakable radical and reforming tendencies, the period from Harding to Hoover marked a sharp swing to conservatism, and the reign of Franklin Roosevelt again brought a pronounced rise of radical temper in the electorate. In the first and last of these periods, a certain type of governmental action was encouraged and readily supported by public opinion; in the intervening period, measures of this same type rarely got effective support from public opinion.

Throughout the nineteenth century, and into the middle of the twentieth, the tides of radical innovation have receded, to be followed by periods of more or less marked movements towards conservatism. Yet the consensus itself has been significantly modified. On the central issue of laissez faire *versus* government intervention in economic and social relationships, of individualism *versus* collectivism, the consensus has come to tolerate, if not actively to support, collectivist measures by government action on a scale that could not have been contemplated a hundred years ago. The reason for the shift is a widespread conviction, rightly or wrongly held, that, in a complex society, a considerable measure of collectivist action is necessary to enable individuals to live fuller lives.

Homage to Public Opinion

Although public opinion is elusive, and even undiscoverable, on particular issues, its receptiveness to suggestion is of immense importance in a democracy. The best proof of this is to be found not in lip-service to the principle that public opinion should rule but in the extraordinary efforts that are made on every hand to estimate and mould public opinion. Along with the expansion of the electorate and the improvement of popular education, and also with the enlarging scope of government activities, have gone continually mounting efforts to gauge and influence opinion. It began with the newspapers, which were unrivaled moulders of opinion in the nineteenth century. In the twentieth century, the falling costs of producing newspapers, books, and pamphlets have added greatly to the bulk, if not to the influence, of the printed word devoted to persuasion. The invention of the radio, television, and the motion picture have provided entirely new possibilities of mass persuasion.

All these instruments of education—or propaganda, as some will have it—are eagerly exploited by a great variety of self-appointed educators of public opinion. As we have already seen, the organized interests have taken up the task. For a considerable time now, they have been spending their millions to educate the public. More recently, most business corporations of any size have found it expedient to maintain departments of public relations, which try to estimate public opinion, to discover how to operate without offending it, and how to move it when collision seems otherwise probable. Public relations counsel hold out the same or more diversified services to those persons and organizations who do not provide them on their own account. What has been referred to as the "engineering of consent" has now brought the techniques of the advertising agency into politics: a candidate is "marketed" as one would market soap or toothpaste! Finally, governments themselves are now establishing public relations services of their own on the ground that the government cannot do what it is expected and required to do unless it too can interpret the detail of its operations to public opinion. Either public opinion is of immense significance, or the leaders of almost every kind of organized activity completely misunderstand their problems.

So much information and argument is now presented to the public on so many issues that any individual who took it all seriously would be utterly bewildered. Most individuals protect their peace of mind by restricting their attention to a relatively narrow range of interests and ignoring all information and counsel that do not bear on it. But this gives no guarantee that the individuals who make up the public will attend to the issues that really do affect them. And the possibilities of persistent misrepresentation and biased argument are now so great that there is much fear of the corruption of public opinion through the instruments of mass persuasion. Some attention—although entirely inadequate—must be given to the potentialities of these instruments and the dangers involved in an irresponsible use of them. First, however, it is necessary to recall certain basic considerations.

FREE DISCUSSION AS THE BASIS OF PUBLIC OPINION

Liberal democratic government is impossible without freedom of thought and speech. Only through free expression is it possible for the people generally to learn what grievances and social maladjustments require governmental action, and to discuss the best means of meeting them. Only through free discussion can the people exercise the influence and control over government that is necessary for effective democracy. This freedom must cover the advancing of opinions that are generally regarded as wrong, because, as has often been remarked, error not infrequently becomes the source of new truth. Even more important, men must be free to argue wrongly as well as rightly, because it is largely through the open exposure of error by discussion—and by sad experience —that we come to understand why we believe what we believe. To see the grounds of error is to see the grounds of truth. To fail to see the grounds of truth is to lack conviction of belief. Liberal democracy requires free competition in ideas. The plethora of ideas which confuse the public is, of course, a consequence of this necessity.

Freedom to think and speak will avail little unless it is supported by the further freedom to assemble peaceably for discussion, in large groups or small, and to associate together for the common purposes discovered by discussion. Not even the all-powerful dictator can enforce directly a ban on thinking. But by rigid control of all the means of communication, and of the right of public meeting and association, he can go far to ensure that the thinker will keep his thoughts to himself. Liberal democracy is dependent also on freedom of peaceable assembly and association.

If the modern democracies were limited in area and population to the size of the ancient city democracies of Greece and Rome, it would be sufficient to ensure each citizen the right to address the assembly of his fellow citizens. The modern democracies, however, comprise tens of millions of people scattered over enormous areas. The fact is too obvious for comment, but its significance is not always fully appreciated. If no one could speak beyond the sound of his voice, the democracies of the United States, Britain and Canada could scarcely have come into existence. Other means of communication which extend the range of effective discussion had first to be invented. Without relatively free access to these other means of communicating opinions, it is unlikely that democracy could have survived, or will survive in the future. Freedom of expression means little if the expression can reach only an infinitesimal fraction of the audience that has to decide.

Historically, the invention of printing, and freedom of the press, preceded the establishment of democracy in Britain and America. Direct government control of the press was abandoned in Britain at the end of the seventeenth century, but a restrictive stamp tax and a rigorous application of the laws against sedition indirectly limited the freedom of the press until the early part of the nineteenth century. In the United States, freedom of the press, as signalized by the First Amendment to the Constitution, was established by the beginning of the nineteenth century.

The printing press, particularly through the newspaper and periodical, was for long the one effective agency for extending communication beyond the natural range of the spoken voice. Most of the great political issues with which the democracies of Britain and America have had to deal have been debated at length in the newspapers before being finally passed on by the legislatures. While legislative action is, of course, formally decisive, the effective determining factor in many issues has been the crystallization of public opinion, in which discussion in the newspapers played a large part. The free press has provided a forum for discussion, and for the clarification of public opinion necessary in a democracy. In recent years, the invention of the motion picture, radio, and television has provided additional means of extended communication. Radio and television particularly supplement the press in the performance of these functions.

The vital service of these means of communication is not limited to the expressing and moulding of opinion. Public opinion on political issues is always concerned with the question whether the government should or should not be required to act in relation to some state of facts, some alleged abuse or maladjustment that puts an unjustifiable burden on some section of the population, or some conflict between two or more groups within the community. Without a considerable knowledge of the facts that constitute the alleged abuse or give rise to the conflict, no useful opinion, either as to the need for governmental action or as to the form it should take, can be matured. The people need accurate information if their intervention in government is not to be entirely irrational.

Faulty Communication of Facts and Opinion

Given the size and population of the modern democracies, the people can have little direct knowledge of the facts of most issues. Their observation is limited to what they see and hear every day in the narrow sphere in which they move. The man who is unemployed for any considerable time has bitter personal knowledge of some of the facts of unemployment. But he does not know, of his own observation, its extent and severity throughout the country. Nor does he know much either of its larger causes or of its broader social effects. If we add to this the fact that normally the bulk of the population has had no serious direct experience with unemployment, it is clear that our own powers of observation with our own senses furnish us with very few of the facts relevant to the question of what to do about unemployment. And if this is true of a phenomenon so widespread at times as unemployment, it is still more true of most of the data with which public opinion is concerned. For example, in any particular labour-management dispute, the immediate facts are directly known to few except the management and a small group of labour leaders.

If the scattered millions composing the electorate are to determine, or even to influence, the solutions to such problems, they need knowledge. The knowledge they need is so varied and extensive that it forbids excessive optimism about democracy. They cannot understand the causes and social effects of unemployment without knowing a good deal about the economy and the complex social structure. This background knowledge could only be imparted to the generality through an organized educational effort obviously beyond the press and other similar channels of communication.

Aside from the background knowledge altogether, the public needs knowledge of the extent and severity of unemployment, the density and degree of destitution arising therefrom, its effects on local and state public finance, and so on. While governments themselves provide statistical compilation and reports on these and similar facts, that does not ensure any wide acquaintance with them. For much of the collecting and reporting of data relevant to the formation of public opinion we have to rely on the newspapers and other newer instruments of communication.

Therefore, in addition to providing forums for discussion, as noted above, a vital service of the press, radio, and television is to provide news, to report the facts that must be acquired and digested before useful public opinion can be formed. Adequate reporting of the facts needed for judgments on the wide range of governmental activities is clearly an enormous job. It is not merely the bulk of the facts that should be reported and the difficulty of discovering them, sifting the significant from the insignificant, and reporting them intelligibly. The communication of facts that one has seen, heard, or otherwise experienced to the people who have not seen, heard, or experienced them, is attended by many hazards. Language, on which the principal reliance must be placed, is far from trustworthy as a means of communication. Television, of course, brings a new visual dimension to language but does not in itself provide any explanation of the situations captured by the camera.

It is first necessary to find words to explain what we have seen. If what we have seen is new or strange to the recipients of our report, it will often be hard to find old familiar words to explain the new experience. Yet we must use the old words, because new words, even if we invented them, would mean nothing to the audience. It would be wrong to say that words failed those who saw and reported the tests of the atomic bomb, but they would probably be the first to admit that they had not been able to convey the full import of what they saw.

There is a further difficulty. Most of the words that must be used for communicating facts, or news, have something more than their bare dictionary meaning for those who hear or read them. For each individual, they are loaded with meanings which vary with the education and experience of the individual. For example, many persons have little or no acquaintance with scientists, but each has a picture in his mind of *the* scientist, some compound of the features of an Einstein, the cartoonist's art, and all he has ever read, heard, and inwardly marked of the activities of scientists. In the same way, highly imaginative pictures are called up in the minds of many people when the words capitalist or communist are used.[1]

Most words thus have for the hearers overtones that are no part of the intention of the honest reporter trying to communicate facts, and that are cunningly exploited by those who want to misrepresent facts. What we believe to be the facts as a result even of what the honest reporter has told us is by no means exactly what he intended to communicate. The overtones block or distort communication to an alarming degree. The blocking and distortion are most marked in relation to issues that arouse deep passions in the electorate.

THE TRANSFORMATION OF THE PRESS

There are serious difficulties in the way of accurate reporting of facts—and also of precise communication of ideas—which have only been hinted at here. The difficulties are so great that fully

---

[1] Walter Lippmann, *Public Opinion* (Macmillan, New York, 1922), ch. vi-x. Under the concept of the "stereotype," Lippmann made clear the serious difficulties in the way of accurate communication. The volume as a whole throws a searching light on the problem of public opinion.

adequate performance of the job by the press would be more surprising than partial failure. There is a widely held conviction today that the press is failing seriously to perform its political functions of reporting news and providing a forum for free discussion. But the reasons given for the failure do not, as a rule, stress the obstacles discussed above. Instead, they emphasize certain technological and economic developments of the last eighty-five years in the newspaper business. Some attention must be given to these developments and their effect on the freedom and effectiveness of the press.

The principal current criticism of the newspapers is that, with the exception of small-town dailies and country weeklies, the publishing of newspapers has become big business, and that the uneasy relations between big business and democracy have manifested themselves in the field of the press in a most serious way. Until well after the middle of the nineteenth century, newspapers were small enterprises with limited circulation serving a relatively small reading public, dominated, if not also owned, by their editors. The strong type of editor was a cross between teacher and preacher, and only incidentally a man of business. In so far as publishing was a business, it was a competitive business which was relatively easy to enter. Every city of any size had several daily papers which competed in the distribution of news and formation of opinion. It was not as easy to go in and out of the newspaper business as of the retail grocery trade, but old papers ceased publication and new ones appeared somewhat after that pattern. Those who thought they had something to say had relatively easy access to this means of communication.

Even as this era of journalism was reaching its peak, the convergence of several lines of social and economic development were preparing a revolution. On the one hand, the increase of population and improvements in popular education were creating a vast body of potential readers of cheap reading matter. On the other hand, a number of technical discoveries and improvements were making mass production of newspapers for mass readers possible. Cheap newsprint from wood pulp, the linotype for typesetting, and startling improvements in the printing press were the main ones.

The Pulitzers and Hearsts, the Northcliffes and Beaverbrooks, and their forerunners, developed the methods for exploiting these possibilities. The circulation of a newspaper could be increased almost indefinitely by lowering its selling price and filling it with features to attract readers who wanted to be amused. As the circulation increased, the new inventions could be progressively applied to multiply output and cheapen the cost per unit. At the same time, the commercial community searching for wider markets for its wares was finding that it paid to advertise, and that a rapidly growing body of potential buyers could be reached through newspapers with a wide circulation. As circulation rose, the revenues of publishers from advertising mounted rapidly too. In this way, the great newspaper fortunes were made, and the papers with a daily circulation in the hundreds of thousands, and even millions, came into existence.

The Tyranny of Circulation

To maintain a newspaper enterprise of anything approaching this magnitude, the publisher has to be a businessman of great capacity. Generally speaking, the publishers who came up or survived in the new era had to have the outlook of businessmen, satisfied that economic considerations should be dominant. The key problem in their business is to maintain, if not to increase, circulation. They cannot recoup themselves for a fall in circulation by any significant increase in the price of the paper, for that would aggravate the decline. Yet, if circulation falls significantly, revenues from advertising fall sharply while the fixed costs represented by their massive plant and equipment continue, and the whole venture is threatened with failure.

The publisher must hold his readers because he is dependent on their patronage. He has to gauge his public and give it what it wants or can be persuaded to want. Since different people want different things of a newspaper, most publishers have sought some guarantee of circulation in sporting news, comic strips, women's fashions and dress patterns, and a host of other features irrelevant to the political functions of a free press. Many have found it expedient to be highly selective in the news they report and to give it the sensational touches that arouse flagging interest. Still others have frankly distorted the news, played upon the passions and prejudices of their readers, debauching rather than clarifying public opinion. These latter explain their success and justify their action by saying that, since the public is vulgar, the press that depends on the public must be vulgar too. They do not profess to mould public opinion but to follow it in its moods and vagaries.[1]

Whether or not the publisher of the great newspaper makes this low estimate of himself, he cannot escape from the calculations of sales, overhead costs, and the prices of the factors of production. Like the other operators of mass-production industries, he is led to seek the advantages of limited competition or monopoly. From this comes the consolidation of newspapers, with the elimination or sharp reduction of competition. It is not clear to what extent this movement has been dictated by sheer economic compulsion, but a monopoly of the advertising and circulation in a large centre of population has a very powerful attraction.

The Decline of Competition

The developments summarized here can be illustrated and, to some extent, measured by approximate figures showing the great rise in circulation and the accompanying decline in the number of daily newspapers in the United States. At the end of 1956, daily circulation in the United States had reached over sixty million, well over twice the number of readers in the first decade of this century; the number of dailies had been cut from the 1910 high of 2,202 to 1,760 in 1956.[2] Furthermore, the decline in competition amongst dailies in metropolitan centres is revealed by the proportion (over eighty per cent) that are now one-paper cities.

In addition, newspaper proprietors have not been content to limit their activities to a single city but have established chains of newspapers absorbing dailies published in a number of cities. Chains developed rapidly up to about 1940 and, although the rate of development has slackened, in 1954 there were ninety-five chains

[1]The transformation of the press in the United States is described in detail in Frank Luther Mott, *American Journalism* (Macmillan, New York, 1941), ch. xxv–xliii. For a short sketch, see William Albig, *Modern Public Opinion*, ch. xvii.
[2]*Editor and Publisher*, April 20, 1957.

controlling over one-quarter of all the dailies in the United States with a circulation close to one-half the total daily circulation.[1] To establish a competitive daily newspaper in a city of any considerable size and finance the venture until the circulation reaches a paying figure is a freedom that only millionaires can exercise.

The huge capital investment involved has helped greatly to bring about a change from individual to corporate ownership of many newspapers. With the adoption of corporate forms has come much of the familiar corporate practice. The great publishing corporations have reached out to control related and associated enterprises as well. For example, they control, or share in the control of the few large news-gathering agencies which now dominate the assembling of the news. Some of them have acquired control of paper mills and pulpwood forests. Big business has not yet swallowed the press but it has bitten deeply into it.

In Britain, the press has undergone a similar transformation, and has been brought even closer to monopoly control. A few huge corporations control almost all the metropolitan newspapers and the bulk of the newspaper circulation in the country. Somewhat similar developments have manifested themselves in Canada, but not on the gigantic scale found in Britain and the United States. There is no need to elaborate these developments because the focus of interest here is not the structure of the press but the significance of the press in the formation of public opinion.

The individuals who control and manage the great and near-great publishing corporations are absorbed in the same or similar problems as are their counterparts in large industrial, commercial, and financial corporations. They talk one another's language and move in the same social circles. The powerful publishers have ceased to resemble, or to associate in any significant way with, teachers, preachers, and the like. They move among bankers, industrialists, and others of the executive class. It would be surprising if their interests and associations did not influence their outlook on many public questions.

One of the critical and continuing issues of public policy, which at times seems to be the issue on which almost all others turn,

[1] Raymond B. Nixon, "Trends in Newspaper Ownership since 1945," *Journalism Quarterly*, 31 (1954), p. 10.

is the appropriate nature and extent of governmental regulation of business and economic life. We have seen that such regulation has made enormous strides in recent years. The business community has resisted this movement consistently, and often bitterly. The press has been far from unanimous in opposition at every stage, but its tone has been predominantly critical. While businessmen as such have the same claim as others to express and support their convictions, concern over the impartiality of the businessman-publisher in reporting and discussing the relations of government, business, and labour is understandable.

The Indictment against the Press

In fact, it is now widely believed that, as a result of the developments sketched above, the greater portion of the press, speaking in terms of circulation rather than of operating units, is no longer an impartial distributor of the news a democracy must have to survive, or an open forum for the airing of all shades of opinion. There are many counts in the indictment against the press, but they fall into two main groups.

First, it is charged that the press has lost interest in its vital political functions of distributing news and providing a forum for discussion. It has become a commercial undertaking, a seller of a commodity or service, and it prepares its wares according to its estimate of the market. In so far as it estimates that the public wants truth to be stranger than fiction, it provides sensation rather than sober accuracy in the news. In so far as it seems that the public wants its prejudices confirmed rather than dispelled, the press will cater to what it thinks are the dominant prejudices among its readers. In so far as it tries to influence market demand, it is guided like any other business by considerations of profit.

Second, it is charged that the press has become the willing tool of the powerful business interests who use it to protect themselves against control and regulation in the public interest. In selecting the events to be reported, in deciding what features of these events are to be emphasized as significant, and deciding the claims to prominence of display in the paper, those who control the press slant the news and distort the understanding of their readers. Even if the particular newspaper is free of outright falsehood, it reports half-truths which conceal important elements of the truth. For example, it has often been charged that the facts of particular labour-management disputes are garbled and misrepresented by the press. Editorial policy, it is claimed, is governed by the business interests and associations of the publishers. They do not generally want to take a line that is critical of businessmen, as such. Even when publishers are disposed to be critical, they are restrained by the advertisers who, it is asserted, will withdraw their advertising from a paper whose editorial and news policy they find objectionable. Moreover, it is charged that the news, and comment on the news, are not strictly separated, and that a good deal of editorial comment masquerades as news in the news columns.

Some critics subscribe to the entire indictment, and others only to parts of it. But, at the extreme, the press is represented as standing astride the channels of communication, determining what we shall learn and understand about what is going on, and deciding what opinions will be expressed or suppressed. It is represented as having a unified outlook on public issues, amounting almost to a conspiracy to distort news and warp opinion. It is represented as being exceedingly powerful, able to determine not only what we shall know but what most of us shall think. Secure in its strategic position, guaranteed against effective competition by the prohibitive cost of launching new organs of news and opinion, it imposes a censorship resembling that maintained by governments before the coming of a free press.

THE DEFENCE OF THE PRESS

The retort on behalf of the press is a qualified admission on the first group of charges, and a denial of the substantial truth of the second group. The newspaper cannot be an organ of news and opinion for the millions composing the electorate unless it maintains circulation. A press that was austere and objective in its marshalling of a vast array of guarded statements of fact would not have a wide reading public. To insist upon such a press would block the communication of facts more seriously than it is blocked at present by writing down to a wide public. The press cannot, it

is asserted, create general prejudices in the public mind. It can
—and sometimes does—exploit those already existing. It cannot
ignore them, because discussion that fails to keep contact with the
prejudices of readers would soon have few readers and almost no
influence. It is impossible to stimulate thought and discussion by
people unless we at least appear to treat their prejudices with respect.
In the broadest sense, it is contended, the public gets the press, as it
gets the government, it deserves. If the mass press is to move on
a different level, the first step is to improve the general education
of the public.

It is also denied that advertisers lay down the law to publishers
or that editorial and news policy has any serious influence on the
placing of advertising. The advertisers' first concern is to reach the
widest possible public. The wider the circulation of a newspaper,
the less open it is to dictation by advertisers. If commercial advertising had not provided rich subsidies to the press, it might have
accepted secret subsidies from other groups whose objectives were
predominantly political rather than economic.

The publisher makes no apology for expressing his own convictions editorially. He also points out that a newspaper of any
considerable size is the work of many journalists, most of whom
are moved by professional pride and convictions of their own.
Their work is subject to supervision but any attempt to dictate to
them continuously in detail would defeat itself. So, their views and
attitudes, as well as those of the publisher, find expression in the
newspaper. The large newspapers contain many features in which
a variety of opinions not in harmony with editorial policy are a
matter of frequent occurrence. The columnists and commentators
have their own public, which the publishers cannot ignore. For
many years, David Low, the consummate British cartoonist, did
much to counteract the editorializing of his then employer, Lord
Beaverbrook. In short, it is argued that the range of fare offered
by the large newspaper is not an inferior substitute for the discussion that used to take place between competitive newspapers.

THE PRESS AS AN ISSUE FOR PUBLIC OPINION

To make a final judgment on the significance of the developments that have transformed the press in the last seventy-five years

would require much more knowledge—and more precise knowledge—than we have at present. One thing, however, is clear. The press, and its freedom or lack of freedom, has become a political issue; itself a subject on which public opinion is to be formed. As such, it affords an excellent illustration of the difficulties that beset the formation of discriminating public opinion. It is easy enough to assemble facts that support the indictment, and just as easy to assemble others for the defence. No doubt, facts enough can be found to convict particular publishers, and also facts enough to ensure honourable acquittal of others. But there are far from enough fully certified facts to decide what, if anything, should be done about the press as a whole. Such facts are extraordinarily hard to discover and formulate as valid general statements. How, for example, is the influence of advertisers on the press as a whole to be discovered and assessed? Some facts bearing on the influence of particular advertisers on particular publishers are known, but even these do not all point one way. There is a considerable diversity of opinion about the influence of advertisers on the press as a whole.

Those who attribute to the press a dominating power over public opinion in Anglo-American countries probably exaggerate its influence. Broadly speaking, the press has been opposed to most items of the rapid expansion of government activities sketched in chapter v. Despite that, the expansion has continued, and even increased its pace. Franklin Roosevelt was elected again and again as President of the United States by large popular majorities, despite opposition by the greater part of the daily press. The decisive victory of the Labour party in the 1945 elections in Britain was won in the face of a predominantly Conservative press. In fact, those who urge the first group of charges against the press are really saying the press has too little influence on public opinion rather than too much.

Nor is the press as close to monopoly control as discussion sometimes seems to suggest. The industry is still competitive, although the competition is, in the terms of the economist, imperfect competition. The competitors are limited in number, protected from the intrusion of outsiders by the large capital requirements for entrance into the industry. But they still struggle—and often struggle fiercely—for their place in the market. They do not engage in price wars, but they do fight for "scoops" in the news. And they must face outside competition from pamphlets, magazines, moving pictures, radio, and television. As long as this continues, there cannot be anything approaching an organized conspiracy to censor the news.

The Press as a Public Utility

Nevertheless, the transformation of the press that has been outlined above gives some ground for thinking that the press has reached, or is rapidly approaching, the status of a public-utility industry, an industry that provides an essential public service under conditions arousing fears of monopoly, or at any rate, under conditions where free competition is no longer an effective regulator in the public interest. In such conditions, unregulated private ownership confers greater power on individuals than the public in the recent past has been prepared to tolerate. The railway, telegraph, telephone, and electric power industries, among others, have reached that stage. Public opinion has sanctioned and maintained governmental regulation, and even government ownership, of these industries.

The real difficulty over the press is that direct government control over the communication of fact and opinion would be a worse evil than the present control of the press, even on the worst interpretation of its effects. If any confirmation were needed, wartime experience has convinced everyone that there is no salvation in a return to censorship. A government edict against the slanting of and suppressing of news would be administratively impossible of enforcement. It would either become a dead letter or it would end in the government's telling the newspapers in detail what to print and what not to print. To give a government agency power to censor fact and opinion would draw all the power-hungry elements in the community into a struggle to get control of the government. |Democracy needs a free press, but it cannot be found through governmental regulation of the press. |

There is thus no reassuring precedent to follow in regulation of this new public utility, and it is highly unlikely that there will be any direct intervention by government in the newspaper industry in the near future. The government-controlled press in the dictatorships, of which something will be said in the last chapter, stands as a warning of what not to do.

Several alternatives have been suggested, but none of them has been elaborated in detail or widely discussed. Two of these may be mentioned. One looks to the restoring of a larger measure of competition in the newspaper industry but has given little hint how this is to be brought about. The other looks toward what is called the constitutionalizing of the press from within, the changing of the publisher from an absolute monarch in his domain to a constitutional one.[1]

The proposal requires that the publisher should recognize his newspaper as a great co-operative undertaking of all those who take part in its publication, and therefore an instrument for expressing their personalities and outlook as well as his own. A profession of journalism still in the making can be expected to turn out journalists loyal to their craft and to the social function it performs. If these can be given a large share in deciding news and editorial policy, limited competition in the newspaper business might become as tolerable as it now is in the professions of law and medicine. There are newspapers in which this constitutional revolution is well under way. A public sufficiently educated to display a strong preference for constitutional over absolute regimes in the newspaper business would greatly accelerate the rate of change.

RECENT INVESTIGATIONS OF THE PRESS

In 1943, a comprehensive private inquiry into the press in the United States was launched by the Commission on the Freedom of the Press, appointed and presided over by Chancellor Hutchins of the University of Chicago. In 1947, the Labour Government in Britain appointed a Royal Commission on the Press to make a similar inquiry. The detailed reports of these commissions were published in 1947 and 1949 respectively. The data and the analysis set forth in these two reports indicate that the problems of the press in both countries are strikingly similar. As a consequence,

[1]See Robert Lasch, "For a Free Press," *Atlantic Monthly*, 174 (1944), pp. 39-44.

both commissions reached a parallel set of recommendations in their reports.

Both commissions rejected government control of the press as being fatal to democracy. Both recommended that existing laws for regulating trusts and monopolies be used to prevent further concentration of the press in still larger units. Both looked to self-regulation of the press as the principal means of checking undesirable tendencies in the press, and of improving performance of its public functions. Both recommended the recognition of journalism as a public profession like law and medicine, and suggested various means of developing professional standards and of increasing the influence of the working journalists on the policies of their newspapers.

To accomplish these objectives, the British Commission recommended the establishment of a General Council of the Press, independent of the government and representatives of proprietors, editors, journalists, and the interested public. This recommendation was adopted, the broad function of the new Council being to "safeguard the freedom of the press and to encourage the sense of public service and public responsibility among all engaged in the profession of journalism." The Council produces an annual report on the state of publishing in Britain and has on the whole lived up to the expectations of its founders.[1] The Hutchins' Commission recommended a council which would be independent of both government and press to make a continuing study of the conduct of the press, to confer with the press itself on ways and means of improvement, and to ensure the widest possible publicity on, and public discussion of, the essential functions of the press in a democracy. No such council has been established but active research centres in the whole field of "communications" now disseminate information upon which a much more mature and effective public opinion might be expected to arise.

BROADCASTING AND PUBLIC OPINION

Radio and television (hereafter described as broadcasting) have become very important instruments of communication. In providing entirely new means of communication, they have helped to maintain a measure of competition in distribution of news and formation of

[1] On the British press generally see Francis Williams, *Dangerous Estate. The Anatomy of Newspapers* (Longmans, Green, London, 1957).

opinion. However, the sharply limited number of wave lengths available made broadcasting semi-monopolistic from the beginning, and posed at once the problem of controlling it in the public interest. Moreover, the need for international agreements to allocate clear channels on an equitable basis has meant that governments have had to retain a much closer contact with broadcasting than with the press. Not only do technical factors limit the number of broadcasting stations, but the amount of material presented over the air is also restricted within the inflexible boundaries of a twenty-four-hour day. Broadcasters, unlike newspaper editors, cannot add a few pages to take care of extra material.

Furthermore, broadcasting is still primarily concerned with its function of entertainment rather than with its function of imparting information or formulating opinion. Even in performing the latter function, broadcasting must depend on the spoken word and the visual image which, while they permit greater dramatization of events, lack the staying qualities of the written word. An appreciation of this limitation probably accounts for the repetitiousness of modern advertising over radio and television. By constricting their reporting of events into brief word-pictures and screen-flashes, both radio and television have helped to increase the interest of the public in the news but, at the same time, they have undoubtedly strengthened the current trend towards the standardizing of ideas for easy assimilation by busy people. The pace of modern civilization gives us less and less time to sift the material from which we are expected to make decisions on increasingly complex issues. Digests, picture magazines, radio, and television best fit this new pattern of existence.

The radio has been widely regarded as a valuable aid to liberal democratic politics. The increase in electoral participation at United States presidential elections, for example, has been attributed to the use of radio in politics. In 1936, when the greater part of the press opposed the re-election of Franklin Roosevelt, extensive use of the radio was said to have counterbalanced the leaning of the press. A substantial portion of the budgets of political parties is now devoted to broadcasting. Some observers have even gone so far as to suggest that radio, and more especially television, have re-established that direct contact between political leaders and followers that characterized Athenian democracy. It is true that leaders can appeal substantially to the whole people as did the leaders in classical times. But broadcasting can only establish a one-way contact: listeners and viewers must remain passive rather than active participants in the discussion of ideas by their leaders. Citizens' forums, Town Halls of the Air, Face the Nation, and the like make possible a limited exchange of ideas on public issues, but this is far from setting up the conditions of Athenian direct democracy. Dictators have taken full advantage of the one-way appeal of broadcasting to indoctrinate masses that are in no position to answer back. Even so, the dictator's appeal is limited because mob hysteria cannot be whipped up easily amongst a scattered radio or television audience. The "fireside chats" of the late President Roosevelt probably exemplify the most effective use of radio as an instrument of democracy and President Eisenhower has similarly revealed the political potential of television.

Broadcasting in the United States

Although there are over 2,000 broadcasting stations in the United States, the whole field has been subject to a concentration of control in the hands of large-scale private enterprise similar to that found in the newspaper world. Four radio and three television networks have about two-thirds of all stations affiliated with them and provide programmes for the major portion of the daily operating period of these stations. Local stations have generally neglected to develop local talent or serve as the mouthpiece for their community. Lucrative "soap operas" fill the daylight hours, and network programmes take up the most popular evening hours under the sponsorship of the few large advertisers who are interested in nation-wide markets. Four advertisers, for example, provide over a quarter of the advertising revenue of one large radio network. The promotion of advertising has also been concentrated in a few companies. "Spot" advertising is reserved for local advertisers who can take advantage of the ready-made audiences built up by the network programmes. While large revenues from advertising permit networks to produce some sustaining programmes of high calibre, the demand of the advertiser for a wide listening audience places the emphasis on programmes with wide popular appeal.

In the United States, use of the air for broadcasting depends on securing a licence from the Federal Communications Commission, an agency of the federal government. In its granting of licences, and its periodic review of licences already granted, the Commission is authorized by Congress to decide whether the "public interest, convenience and necessity" will be served thereby. It is expressly forbidden to interfere with the content of particular programmes. Of course, its power to review licences enables it to pass not only on the adequacy of the technical operation of the station but also on the question whether the programmes offered by the station have served the public interest. However, aside from drawing a line against the obscene, the profane, and the defamatory, the Commission has not tried to work out its own standards for programmes. In 1946, the Commission issued its Blue Book, a set of principles to be observed in programming, but it has only cancelled one or two licences for failure to observe them. A self-administered code of the National Association of Broadcasters to which the bulk of the private stations subscribe, and such voluntary adherence to the Blue Book as is secured, reflect the working compromise that has been established between private ownership and governmental regulation. The compromise seems to suggest that the function of radio is to give the people what they want in the way of entertainment rather than to stimulate the interchange of controversial opinions. This cautiousness prevents radio and television from becoming the political tool of a governing party but it may place undue emphasis on the strictly entertainment function of broadcasting.[1]

Broadcasting in Britain

Since 1927, radio broadcasting in Great Britain has been monopolized by the British Broadcasting Corporation, a semi-autonomous government corporation. In 1954, however, its monopoly of television broadcasting was broken when Parliament created an Independent Television Authority to license and supervise commercially sponsored television. Financed largely by listeners' fees, the Corporation permits no advertising over its stations. Regional organization

[1]See Douglas Waples (ed.), *Print, Radio and Film in a Democracy* (University of Chicago Press, 1942), pp. 66–78, also Charles A. Siepmann, *Radio, Television and Society* (Oxford University Press, New York, 1950).

of programme service gives a limited range of choice for the public. The fact that the Corporation can balance its programmes and direct them to various groups, regardless of their size and purchasing power, enables it to offer a variety of fare. Opinion differs on whether that variety—particularly with the addition of commercial television—is comparable to the range of choice provided by sponsors in the United States. Because the B.B.C. can plan its programmes without thought for advertising revenue it is able to stress the educational value of its offerings, and is, therefore, in a better position than broadcasters in the United States to develop the potential of radio and television as instruments of communication and opinion-formation. However, despite the autonomy of the Corporation, it is frequently charged with favouring the party in power. Such charges are most likely to appear when the B.B.C. is handling controversial or other broadcasts designed to stimulate thought or to make the public familiar with new ideas. Hence, cautiousness in using radio and television as positive instruments of political discussion in Great Britain arises not from the concern for advertising revenues but from a concern for preserving political neutrality. In developing its role as an instrument for the formation of public opinion, the B.B.C. itself tends to become an object of public opinion and criticism.[1]

Broadcasting in Canada

Broadcasting in Canada is carried on under a mixed system of public and private ownership. The Canadian Broadcasting Corporation, a government agency modelled closely on the British pattern, owns and operates some thirty-two radio and television stations. At the same time, there are over two hundred and thirty privately-owned broadcasting stations which, until 1957, operated under licences that could be revoked on recommendation of the Corporation. In 1957, parliament created a new Board of Broadcast Governors which took over the regulatory responsibilities of the Corporation. The C.B.C. was left with its primary function of maintaining national networks—a task which is accomplished in part in conjunction with affiliated private stations. These stations have

[1]R. H. Coase, *British Broadcasting. A Study in Monopoly* (Longmans, Green, London, 1950), also J. C. W. Reith, *Into the Wind* (Hodder and Stoughton, London, 1949).

a restricted range which limits their service to local areas, although most of them are affiliated with the C.B.C. and carry many nation-wide programmes originating both in Canada and in the United States. Though financed in part by parliamentary grants, the C.B.C. —particularly after it came to be faced with the mounting costs of television—has been forced to depend on supplementary revenues from advertising. With these revenues, facilities have been greatly expanded, and sustaining programmes of high quality have been provided alongside the sponsored programmes with their wider audience and more effective salesmanship.

While the C.B.C. is thus placed in a position to purchase the best in the broadcasting entertainment field from the United States and to take advantage of its network monopolies to introduce sustain-ing programmes for special groups of listeners and viewers, the prob-lem of making radio and television positive instruments of democ-racy is just as acute as in the other countries. It is clear that government intervention was necessary to extend broadcasting ser-vices to those sparsely settled areas where private operators, interested in advertising revenues, would not have ventured. It is also apparent, as in the other democracies, that state regulation of broadcasting is required to protect the public interest. But the major problem in Canada, as in Britain, arises from the difficulty of reconciling government operation and regulation with the func-tions of radio and television as means for discussing controversial ideas and exploring critical public issues. During the period when it combined regulatory powers with its operating responsibilities, the C.B.C. was attacked repeatedly for showing bias in handling news reports and controversial broadcasts, and in allocating time to politicial parties. Its successor in the regulatory field, the Board of Broadcast Governors, will undoubtedly face the same complaints.

While some of these charges can be attributed to partisan spleen, they indicate the difficulties that a government-operated broadcasting system encounters if it tries to stress the social or politi-cal functions of radio and television. A government-managed system cannot go beyond a certain point in a positive educative role if it is to be sure of getting general acceptance as a neutral channel of com-munication. The difficulties that arise from charges of political partisanship are not so acute when broadcasting is left in private hands subject to governmental regulation. But then radio comes under the control of a few; it performs such educative functions as advertisers will pay for, and its neutrality comes equally under suspicion.

In the liberal democracies, it is not easy to make broadcasting—whether under private or public auspices—a positive force in enlightening or focusing public opinion. If radio and television are to assert themselves significantly outside the field of entertainment and the news summary, they require much greater encouragement and backing from an enlightened public. Radio and particularly television are still young, and experience with their use and their control is still very limited. But, at the moment, it is plausible to say of broadcasting, as of the press, that we get the kind we deserve.

Pressure groups, public-relations agencies, and propagandists of every kind try to reach the public through all the instruments of mass communications. The breakdown of democracy in continental Europe was accompanied by great blasts of anti-democratic propaganda. As a result, there is considerable demand for the curbing of propaganda. It is by no means clear, however, that the anti-democratic propaganda in Europe would have been at all effective but for the convergence of a number of other favourable conditions. Nor is it at all clear that, given these conditions, any curb on propaganda would have saved the European democracies. Democracy which depends on free discussion cannot afford to limit discussion except on a clear demonstration that it is necessary and will accomplish its purpose and no more. It has rather to trust that one brand of propaganda will be counteracted by another. The trust will be misplaced unless we can assure a fair degree of freedom of access to the instruments of communication. That is why a genuinely free press and an impartially administered broadcasting system are of such critical importance.

GOVERNMENTS COURT PUBLIC OPINION

It has already been stated that, in recent years, democratic governments have begun to pay closer attention to relations between themselves and the public. Departments of government that have complex relationships with a numerous public have set up offices of information and bureaux of public relations to ensure that the government's own version of what it is trying to accomplish is adequately explained. Government publicity has been more widely relied on in the United States than in Britain and Canada. However, its use is on the increase in Britain and Canada. Most of the federal government departments now employ publicity and public relations officers.

Newspapers, magazines, radio, and television are the media of communication most used by governments. A more limited assortment of media provided directly by government itself consists of photographs, exhibits, pamphlets, and moving pictures. Little or no effort is made by government departments to pool these resources or to co-ordinate publicity activities. On the other hand, a central agency for handling all governmental publicity work would be administratively inefficient and politically dangerous. Few publicity offices bother to plan a campaign. Most of them are principally occupied in preparing factual reports of the work and policy of their department. This material is provided partly for the information of those citizens who have a particular interest in the activities of government departments, partly for the edification of the general public and partly to forestall or answer criticisms.

During World War II, the exigencies of war led to the establishment of the Office of War Information in the United States, the Ministry of Information in Britain and the War Information Board in Canada. The functions of these agencies were to interpret their respective countries to other nations abroad, to plan and conduct psychological warfare against the enemy, and to co-ordinate and promote the efforts of these governments to explain the requirements and accomplishments of war organization to their people at home. The result was an immense increase in the efforts put into government publicity. With the close of the war, these establishments were dismantled, or reduced and changed in character. However, the techniques acquired and the experience gained have given an impetus to the extension of governmental information services—notably in the case of the United States Information Agency with its Voice of America and far-flung field offices in many lands.

The reasons for the establishment and likely extension of such services are not hard to find. As government functions increase in number and complexity, the need for sympathetic interpretation of government action becomes more pressing. As we saw in chapters IX and X, government now needs the co-operation of the interests affected to accomplish its purposes, and the general public needs to know what government is trying to do and why. Legislative debate, discussion on the election platform, and other forms of party controversy cannot interpret in adequate detail the specialized effort of many government departments. Government feels the need for special press releases, bulletins, and booklets on a great variety of subjects. It needs to reach the public, and it needs to learn something of the public relations technique of approaching the public.

Here too, the example of the European dictatorships has aroused some concern. When the Nazis captured the government of Germany, they added to the existing departments of government a Ministry of Propaganda and Public Enlightenment, under Dr. Goebbels. The unlimited duplicity of his efforts to explain the German government to the German people is a warning of the lengths to which government-sponsored propaganda can go.

No doubt it would be unduly credulous to believe that democratic governments will always tell the objective truth about themselves. There are plenty of instances where official zeal or partisan spirit, or both, has put a better face on matters than the facts warranted. There is some danger in the strong possibility that, at times, party propaganda will masquerade as government information. But the real menace of government propaganda in the European dictatorships arose rather out of government control of the press and the radio and out of the suppression of all freedom of association and discussion, which silenced all possibility of correction from other sources.

As long as there is a press independent of governmental control and suggestion, government propaganda will be checked by counter-propaganda, and a government that goes too far will defeat its own purposes. In the Anglo-American democracies, there is little evidence at present that the public will give undue credence to statements bearing the stamp of their governments. A healthy suspicion of all pronunciamentos, whether of government or press or broadcaster still remains as one of the principal democratic safeguards. The suspicion may be so robust at times as to defeat legitimate efforts of the government to explain how it is trying to accomplish what the electorate has authorized it to do.

DEMOCRATIC LEADERSHIP AND PUBLIC OPINION

The relation of political leadership to public opinion requires special attention. In chapter x it was concluded that, as a practical matter in a democracy, public policy, the decision what government is to do, always emerges from the competition, clash, and compromise of a great variety of individual and group interests. This might be taken to mean that political leadership is a passive agent which contributes nothing to solutions but waits for the blind jostling of selfish competing interests to reach an equilibrium, out of which the solution emerges automatically. If this were so, we might well despair of political leadership as well as of public opinion. There is, however, an interpretation of democratic politics that assigns important roles to both political leadership and ill-informed, vague, fluctuating public opinion, and rescues them from futility.

The first point to recall is that there is, in a working democracy, a community consensus to which the great bulk of the people subscribe. The consensus does not consist of a set of specific solutions for current problems but rather of a set of beliefs about the ends and purposes that community life should serve. The strongest of these in the democracies in question here is the belief that the community should protect and develop individual personality, and that individual liberty is a highly important means of fostering and expressing personality.

Historically, the general acceptance of the belief in individual liberty was associated with a related belief in the sanctity of private property as a buttress of individual personality. The latter belief is not as unqualifiedly or as widely held as formerly but it is still of great significance, as witness the infrequency of theft and robbery. True, the criminal law forbids theft and robbery, but its edicts could not be enforced effectively if they did not accord with community sentiment, as witness the prohibition law.

There is always much going on in social life that seems to flout or contradict the deeper beliefs, and these beliefs give no obvious directions what to do to bring erring social practice into conformity with them. Massive private property, as represented by present-day capitalist economic organization, seems to limit liberty and dwarf personality for many. How far this is true is not utterly clear, because we do not know what alternative forms of economic organization would do for liberty and personality. Nor is it clear in full detail what restrictions on private property in the form of governmental regulation of economic life will bring a net enlargement of liberty. As chapter v indicates, the electorates have accepted and governments have incorporated into their activities, substantial restrictions on the freedom of businessmen to do what they like with their property. But the debate about what more and what next still goes on. It could scarcely be otherwise in communities that believe both in individual liberty and the sanctity of private property.

It would be easy to laugh at communities that hold doggedly to contradictory beliefs. The beliefs, however, may not be inherently contradictory. What seems to be going on, at any rate, is a tenacious search for a reconciliation between them which can be incorporated in social and economic practice.

This is only one illustration of several that might be given to show that the consensus, of itself alone, rarely makes clear what to do. The consensus does, however, limit what the interests ranged on either side of the dispute can get—and hold—by pressure on the government through political channels. It also limits the choice of solutions for which the politicians can hope to get the support of electoral majorities.

The purpose of discussion is to search for solutions in harmony with the underlying consensus. The function of competing political parties and political leaders is the same. Democratic political leadership calls for two main qualities, which, of course, the actual leaders do not always possess. It calls for ingenuity and imagination in discovering accommodations between conflicting interests which will be at least tolerable to those concerned on both sides. The political leader needs an extensive knowledge and understanding of the conflict for which he proposes a solution. Democratic leadership calls also for men who know by heart the source and course of the deep springs of community belief and feeling, and who therefore see what solutions can be floated and supported on the consensus.

Such leadership is genuinely creative. It creates the necessary equilibrium between group interests. It finds the compromise which public opinion rises surely to support. It redeems the politician from being merely a broker and huckster. It is indispensable in the recurring crises of democratic societies.

The democratic leaders' search is not for the ideal solution. That may be easy to see in a particular crisis, but it is often impracticable of application by a government based on discussion and consent. Lincoln the statesman knew the ideal solution of the slavery question. Lincoln the politician sought long for an accommodation that would limit the evil of slavery without outraging the belief in the sanctity of property and rending the Union, always hoping that, with time and without violence, the ideal solution could be reached. He failed in part, but no political leadership can cope with sectional and group intransigence which disrupts the underlying consensus.

Public Opinion as the Final Judge

On this interpretation, public opinion is not a sovereign legislator framing specific solutions to specific problems. It is rather a judge who hears the political leaders, the advocates of specific competing solutions, and decides between them. More correctly, it is the court of last resort, to which only the more stubbornly contested cases go. The final court of appeal in a judicial system does not render judgment on every dispute. In the same way, the political leaders and permanent officials who make up the government at any given moment make many decisions on which public opinion never renders any perceptible verdict. But just as the lower courts in the judicial system are guided by the precedents and past decisions of the court of last resort, so those who currently control the government are guided by their estimate of what public opinion will stand for or support. Public opinion is always being taken into account, but there is no assurance that the ruling politicians of the moment will not misinterpret it, or even try to circumvent it. Although error may rule perversely in the lower courts for a time, the final tribunal sooner or later brings correction. The democratic hope is that at a certain temperature in public affairs, public opinion will be able to resolve on a judgment that rests squarely and securely on the community consensus.

Although the definition regrettably trails off in vagueness, public opinion is better understood, in the words of Lord Bryce, as something "impalpable as the wind," than as a majority will or general will originating and decreeing solutions to particular political issues. When it is thus understood, some of the obstacles blocking the proper performance by public opinion of its function seem less formidable, although they remain too serious to be ignored.

Public Opinion and Liberal Democracy

The problem of public opinion can now be stated in summary form. It is widely agreed that public opinion must rule in a democracy. But the facts on which the public must form its judgments are almost innumerable, and hard to discover, sift, and interpret correctly. Because of the limitations of language and the emotional overtones of words, communication is often blocked and distorted. The difficulties of communication are intensified because the possibilities of distortion are deliberately exploited in many quarters, because the public is so large and scattered, and because it is hard to persuade large sections of it to attend closely.

The formation of public opinion on the facts, once they are communicated, is a complex process, always influenced by whims and unforeseeable circumstances. The entire public almost never concentrates its thoughts on one specific issue. There is always a movement of individuals in and out of the particular public attending to any one issue. Even among those who give sustained attention over a long period, opinions fluctuate in response to varying moods, the introduction of new facts, and the play of discussion.

Thus it is rarely possible to know whether a majority of the electorate has reached a firm judgment on a question, or what that judgment is. Also, the electorate is unable to formulate satisfactory solutions to many problems in which highly technical considerations have to be taken into account. In such issues, it is generally limited to choosing between alternative solutions proposed to it by political leaders.

If our concepts of democracy and public opinion require that there should be a clear majority decision on every issue, and that the majority should always rule, close study of the actual working of democracy will be disillusioning in the extreme. However, it has been urged here that the substance of democracy as it has been practised in the countries in question here is a flexible system of adjustment between individuals and groups carried on under ultimate popular control rather than the direct enforcement of a popular will. Also, it may be doubted whether many of those who subscribe to the majoritarian view of democracy and public opinion really hold it in any strict literal sense. Associated with the demand that public opinion must always decide and rule is the further insistence that democracy desperately needs leadership if it is to survive. If leadership means anything, it means something more than automatic registration of a majority will. On the interpretation offered here, it consists of ingenuity and imagination in devising, for the adjustment of conflicting interests, compromises that accord with the deeper community beliefs about the fitness of things. Public opinion does not invent these compromises, but it is the final judge of their adequacy.

CHAPTER XIII

THE JUDICIARY AND THE LAW

WE HAVE discussed at some length the organization and functions of legislative and executive powers. We have looked carefully at the influence brought to bear on legislative and executive organs by political parties, pressure groups, and public opinion. Attention must now be turned to the judicial power, the third element in the threefold classification. Here, more similarity and less contrast will be found than was observed in comparisons of legislatures and executives. The United States and Canada have drawn their decisive legal and judicial traditions from Britain. For several reasons, the judiciary is a conservative force in any society and it does not respond to changing fashions and needs as rapidly as other parts of government do. So, in the three countries in question, there is a marked similarity and, in the main, only superficial differences. There is more pointed contrast between the legal and judicial systems of continental Europe, which stem from Roman, or civil, law, and what is often called the Anglo-American system. But even here the differences are often superficial rather than basic, because both common law and civil law systems were moulded by the age-long Western political tradition. The most striking contrast is with the perversions of the civil-law system that the Fascist and Nazi dictators set up in Italy and Germany, and with the Soviet legal and judicial system, all shaped by negations of the Western political tradition. Some of the differences between the civil and common-law systems will be noted.

SELECTION AND TENURE OF JUDGES

The Rule of Law is one of the strongest elements in the liberal democratic creed. It is designed, however, as a means to a further end, the securing of individual freedom under law. The securing of freedom under law has two distinct aspects, or stages. First, the law must mark out, at one and the same time, an area of individual freedom of action and an area of clearly defined prohibitions of individual action, e.g. the criminal law. Further to this, if the law is to provide an equal freedom, it must not deny to some what it concedes to others; it must not establish privilege. Second, the law must prevail; it must be made effective through observance and enforcement. Laws aimed at a good end will come to nothing if they can be disobeyed with impunity. To make the Rule of Law effective, there must be a resolute and impartial judiciary devoted to the impartial administration of justice. Appointment and tenure of judges, and the organization of the courts through which they administer justice, are of the highest importance.

Reference to chapter IV will recall the general rule that British and Canadian judges, and the judges of the federal courts of the United States, are appointed by the executive to hold office during good behaviour, and that they are subject to removal for cause at the instance of the legislature. In Canada, as a modification, the judges of the Supreme Court of Canada and the Exchequer Court of Canada, and of the county and district courts in the provinces, are required to retire at the age of seventy-five. But British judges, judges of the federal courts of the United States, and the judges of the Superior Courts of the provinces of Canada are not subject to compulsory retirement on account of old age. Thus the tenure of these three groups is for life or until voluntary retirement, unless unsatisfactory behaviour gives clear cause for their removal by the legislature. Of course, all the judges referred to above are independent of the executive during their period of tenure. Despite the fact that they often make decisions displeasing to the executive and the legislature, there is almost never any suggestion of removing them in the absence of corruption.

This security of tenure is not so fully enjoyed by the lesser magistrates and justices of the peace. In Britain and Canada, these are appointed by the executive and may be removed by it. In the United States, they are elected for short terms by the electorate. Also, the state judges, as distinct from the federal, in the United States are elected, in most states, by popular ballot for relatively short terms. Being dependent on re-election, they cannot enjoy the same assurance of independence. Election of judges is generally admitted to be an unwise extension of the democratic principle, but there are only a few states in which it has not been made.

Appointment of the judges in Britain and Canada is in the hands of the government of the day, and in the United States the appointment of federal judges is made by the President, with the consent of the Senate. It is thus a form of political patronage. In Britain, this patronage is shared by the Lord Chancellor and the Prime Minister. In Canada, nomination is in the hands of the Prime Minister and the Minister of Justice, but they usually accept the recommendation of the member or members of the cabinet representing the province in which the appointment is to be made. Appointment is still by order-in-council and therefore requires agreement of the cabinet. However, it is substantially correct to say that the particular ministers just mentioned make the appointments. In the United States, the President must get his choice ratified by the Senate, which often insists on a critical investigation of his nominee.

Generally speaking, appointments go to persons who have been active supporters of the party in power. As a rule, the capacity and integrity of prospective appointees are also carefully considered, but in each country there have been instances in which it was difficult to see any merit except services to the party. As there are generally equally capable lawyers in each party, there have been few serious abuses. In fact, there are more complaints today about the general outlook of appointees than over their party affiliations, for reasons yet to be discussed. This is seen most clearly in appointments to the Supreme Court of the United States, where the President, at least, is more genuinely concerned over the broad political philosophy than the party label of his choice.

One limitation on choice must be pointed out. The judges in the Anglo-American system must be chosen from the ranks of the legal profession. No matter how able or learned in the law a man may be, he cannot be a judge in a superior court unless he is a member of the Bar of many years' standing. Almost invariably, lawyers in active private practice are appointed although, in recent years, a number of academic lawyers with distinguished records in teaching and research have been appointed to the Supreme Court and other federal courts of the United States.

This limitation to members of the Bar is not thought to be strange, but natural and inevitable. Yet it is in sharp contrast to the practice of continental Europe,[1] where a lawyer who elects private practice abandons all thought of a judicial career. Continental judges are always trained in law, but are chosen from the civil service and not from the lawyers who appear as advocates in the courts. The young law student who aspires to be a judge goes from his university to the ministry of justice, a department of the central government, as a clerk, and hopes in twenty years to rise by promotion step by step up the rungs of the judicial ladder. When a judge hopes for promotion from a lower to a higher court, he is exposed to the temptation of trying to please his superiors in the ministry of justice, or even the politicians who have influence there. By contrast, in the Anglo-American system filling of the higher judicial posts by promotion has been the exception rather than the rule; but the exceptions are increasing and the judiciary now look hopefully at the next rung on the ladder.

Significance of an Independent Judiciary

Complete independence of the judicial power may seem to sort ill with democracy, which means popular control of governments. In the nineteenth century, this view prevailed in most of the states of the Union, bringing popular election of judges for short terms. Actually, abuses of their security of tenure by appointed judges, have been very rare. The law that the judge gives his oath to uphold is a body of relatively certain rules, and as long as he is true to his oath, there is not much room for popular control of his actions. Also, he is a member of an ancient profession which has, despite apparent exceptions, a great devotion to the ideal of an impartial law. A judge who obviously abandons impartiality or gives an interpretation of the law that lawyers generally think to be obviously wrong, loses caste in the legal

[1]The phrase, "continental Europe," as used in this chapter refers principally to Western Europe and does not include the Soviet Union or those countries of East-Central Europe which now have Communist-dominated governments. They are excluded because their practice in legal matters is quite different in many respects from the long established tradition of Western Europe.

profession. Self-respect and the desire to stand well with their professional brethren are powerful controls on the judiciary. / This is a better safeguard of the impartial administration of justice and the maintenance of freedom under law than putting the judges under direct control of the government.//In the dictatorships, of course, the primary function of the judiciary is not the maintenance of freedom under law, but rather the securing of the overriding interests of society as interpreted by the dictator and the small élite he gathers round him. Accordingly, the judiciary is a tool to be manipulated, not a vital institution to be safeguarded from outside influences.

THE STRUCTURE OF THE COURTS

The judges do not give authoritative interpretations of the law at their own pleasure, or, as a general rule, at the request of the executive or legislature./ They interpret the law while sitting in court to settle disputes between parties appearing before them./ The Anglo-American courts are just as important a part of the judiciary as the judges. A court is not merely a physical location and a collection of equipment like stage properties./It is an institution with a set of officials and records, an atmosphere, and an orderly though complex procedure for hearing and deciding disputes. /

The courts of continental European countries can be described, for the sake of contrast though not with complete accuracy, as branches of a ministry of justice, which is, in turn, an executive department of the central government charged with the administration of justice.[1] The continental judges have security of tenure and independence but they are, nevertheless, in some sense, civil servants. The ministry of justice organizes courts in districts across the country to serve the public somewhat after the fashion of the organization of postal services./Officials of the court are civil servants who keep the records, make and work the rules of procedure in concert with the judges./

The courts in England were always the king's courts with their roots in executive decree of the early Norman kings. But at an

[1]For discussion and contrasts, see R. C. K. Ensor, *Courts and Judges in France, Germany, and England* (Oxford University Press, 1933).

early date in English constitutional history, they became practically autonomous and their development was powerfully influenced by the legal profession. The practicing solicitors are still spoken of as officers of the court. For centuries, the judges and officials were paid, not from the general revenues but, from fees collected from litigants. The judges made—and still make—the rules of court procedure, just as they generated the unique atmosphere of decorum which prevails in a court.

In 1873, the English courts were reorganized on a statutory basis by Parliament, and many of the anomalies and anachronisms of six hundred years of customary accretion were cut away. The salaries of the judges and the sums needed for maintenance of the courts are now permanent charges on the public revenues and do not come up for annual appropriation and debate. The executive does not appoint or exercise control over any significant number of the officials of the courts. Appointment of officials is largely in the hands of the Lord Chief Justice, and they do their work under the direction of the judges. There is no ministry of justice. The Lord Chancellor, a member of the cabinet as well as a judge, has a small administrative department but it exercises very little control. The courts are still largely autonomous and in so far as they need to be ruled, they are ruled by the judges.

In colonial days in America, courts modelled on the English type were created by executive order or act of the legislature. Later, in the United States, the state constitutions prescribed the structure of the state courts in considerable detail and thus limited greatly the power of the state legislatures to modify the judicial system. The national Constitution, by contrast, contains only the briefest of provisions on the federal judicial structure,[1] which has been established almost entirely by Congress.

Once established by whatever means, the courts in the United States and Canada were given much of the autonomy of English courts in the administration of justice. /In Canada, the various court officials are generally appointed by the executive, but the judges make the rules of procedure and direct the work of the officials.| In the United States, some court officials are elected and some appointed. The Supreme Court of the United States makes the rules of procedure for the federal courts. In some states, the

[1]The Constitution of the United States, Art. III and Amendment XI.

state legislatures, and in others the judges, make the rules of procedure, but there is no general executive supervision of the administration of justice. The federal governments of the two countries each have a department of justice with a member of the cabinet at its head, but it is not a ministry of justice in the continental European sense. It is rather the department of the Attorney-General, the legal adviser of the government and its attorney in all legal questions, lawsuits or otherwise, in which the government is interested. The courts and the judges are autonomous in the administration of justice.

The Price of Autonomy

The continental European system has many advantages, particularly in ensuring adequate decentralization of courts for the convenience of local litigants, a simple inexpensive procedure and an expeditious handling of cases. Its weakness and dangers are illustrated by the problem of judicial promotions, already noted. To what extent are impartiality and independence endangered when the executive branch of government participates largely in the administration of justice? The fear of executive interference has always thus far prevented the establishment of ministries of justice of the continental European type in Britain, the United States, and Canada. As a result, there is a confusing multiplicity of courts, each autonomous and separate within the range of matters assigned to it.

In Britain, the judicial system is centralized in London. Apart from the justices of the peace and the county courts, dealing with petty criminal and civil cases respectively, and the assize circuits, there is no adequate decentralization. When large issues are at stake they must go as a general rule to the courts sitting in London, and the litigants must go there too at great expense, a prohibitive burden on the poor. In the United States and Canada, there is satisfactory decentralization for the trial of most matters in the first instance, but appeals must go to the state or provincial capitals or even to the national capital. In continental Europe, on the other hand, the final appeal as well as the original trial is heard in the locality.

In the Anglo-American system, despite many reforms, procedure in the courts is still complicated, adding to cost and often involving delay. It is suited to the convenience and to the sense of professional fitness of the lawyers—every profession tends to develop a distinctive ritual—rather than to the needs of poor litigants. However, it must be said in its defence, that it is admirably suited to protect the rights of those who can afford its expense and delay. The same can be said of the two, or three, or even four successive appeals that may be taken from one court to another, contrasted with the single appeal open to the parties in continental Europe.

The Anglo-American legal profession never forgets the meddling of the Stuarts in the administration of justice, and resists all proposals that a government department should organize and supervise judicial services on a mass-production basis as has been done, for example, in employment office and postal services. It takes justifiable pride and satisfaction in saying that genuinely impartial courts are open to all. Yet, despite substantial steady but slow improvements and a continuing agitation for more, it has no adequate answer to the English judge who retorted, "So is the Ritz Hotel!"

This question cannot be discussed in detail here. It has been sketched for two reasons: to point to the main features of the problem and to bring out the significance of an otherwise dull account of the structure of the courts, which now follows.

THE JUDICIAL HIERARCHY

In each country, the court structure is hierarchical in form with its base on the justices of the peace scattered across the country, and on the magistrates in the urban areas, and its apex in a final central court of appeal. At the lowest level, the justices of the peace are normally laymen without legal training, unpaid or paid only in small fees collected in the course of their work. Their jurisdiction is generally limited to the trial of lesser crimes and misdemeanours but may cover small civil claims as well. In the towns and cities, they are supplemented on the criminal side by police magistrates who are required, in Britain and Canada, to have some legal training.

The next tier of courts in Britain and Canada is county or district courts staffed by judges chosen from the legal profession with permanent tenure whose jurisdiction is limited to civil claims involving relatively small amounts. Generally speaking, no such tier of courts exists in the United States. In some of the larger cities, there are municipal courts of comparable limited civil and criminal jurisdiction. There are, of course, county and district courts in the states of the United States but, as will be seen below, they are courts with general rather than limited jurisdiction. At the next level in all three countries are the courts with general first instance jurisdiction, i.e. courts with authority to try all cases of important civil or criminal consequence. Above this again, there are always courts of appeal to which disappointed litigants have, in most matters, a right of appeal, and there may be, in certain special circumstances, one or even two further appeals to still higher courts. Courts of first instance are generally composed of one judge sitting alone while courts of appeal have a bench of several judges. This pattern may be outlined for each country.

The Courts in Britain

In England and Wales (Scotland and Northern Ireland are both distinct areas for the administration of justice), the county courts are limited in authority to small civil claims. The court with general jurisdiction in the first instance is the High Court of Justice of which there are several divisions all sitting in London. However, judges of this court periodically go on circuit, holding assizes, or sittings, in the "assize towns" across the country. The bulk of the assize work is criminal, but civil disputes may be tried there too. The Court of Criminal Appeals sits in London hearing solely appeals from persons convicted of criminal offences by justices of the peace, stipendiary magistrates, and judges of assize. In civil matters, an appeal lies to the Court of Appeal in London and thence, in some but not in all circumstances, to the House of Lords, which is the highest court of appeal in the realm. The judicial functions of the House of Lords are performed by the Lord Chancellor, nine lords of appeal (eminent lawyers elevated to the House of Lords for this particular purpose), and any peer who has at some time or other held high judicial office.

Only in very special circumstances can an appeal in a criminal case be carried to the House of Lords from the Court of Criminal Appeal. However, the House of Lords has original, or first instance, jurisdiction in a number of matters. Until 1948, peers charged with certain very serious crimes had to be brought to judgment before it. Impeachment proceedings, now obsolete, are also within its jurisdiction.

The Courts in the United States

Each state in the United States has its own judicial hierarchy and there are as many systems as there are states. A common pattern, however, can be discerned. Immediately above the level of justices of the peace, police magistrates, and municipal courts such as juvenile courts, family relations courts, and traffic courts, stand the county or district courts. These courts sitting in the county court houses in the county towns are courts of first instance for almost all civil cases and for criminal cases of a serious nature. They are therefore not at all comparable to the county courts in England. In some states, the county court system still reveals the defects to be expected from a lack of unified responsibility for the whole system. Generally, the judges can sit only in their own court and can only hear cases arising in their own district. So the judge in one county may be idle while the judge in an adjoining county is overwhelmed with work. However, many states have established judicial councils composed of judges, lawyers, state officials, and laymen, which are making progress in meeting this and other defects.

Some states have decentralized district courts of appeal. The presence or absence of intermediate courts of appeal depends largely on the density of population and the volume of litigation in the state. Whether they have such courts or not, every state has, at the apex of the hierarchy, a supreme court, as it is generally called, a final court of appeal sitting at the state capital. In cases that involve an interpretation of the national Constitution and a decision whether or not certain rights can be claimed thereunder, an appeal lies from it to the Supreme Court of the United States in Washington.

Except where some such question arises, the state courts try almost all cases turning on the interpretation of the state constitution and laws. The jurisdiction of the federal courts is set out in section 2 of Article III of the Constitution as restricted by

Amendment xi. It includes a variety of special matters that need not be detailed here. Most of this special jurisdiction of the federal courts turns on the question of the parties to the dispute rather than the subject matter. For example, disputes between two or more states, or between a state and a citizen of another state must be tried in the federal courts regardless of the subject matter of the controversy. Where the dispute is between citizens of different states, it may be tried in the federal courts if the controversy involves $3,000 or more. But the main work of the federal courts is to try cases arising under the laws of the United States, principally laws made by Congress. For example, when the mails are used to commit a fraud, the same act may be at once an offence against the law of a particular state and also an offence against the laws of the United States regulating the use of the post office. For the former offence, the culprit would be tried in a state court, and for the latter, in a federal court.

Thus, there are in the United States two complete and quite separate sets of courts, federal and state, exercising, in each state, jurisdiction over the same people and the same territory. Serious conflicts of jurisdiction are avoided because, generally speaking, the federal courts interpret and apply federal laws, and the state courts interpret and apply the state laws. The jurisdiction of the federal courts is not declared by the Constitution to be an exclusive one. As far as the Constitution goes, cases that the federal courts are competent to try might be tried and decided in the state courts. Congress, however, has provided by statute that in certain types of cases and controversies covered by Article III the federal courts shall have exclusive jurisdiction.

At the lowest level in the federal-court structure stand the district courts in some ninety districts across the United States. At the next level are the circuit courts of appeal, one for each ten federal districts and an additional one for the District of Columbia. These courts were established to take some of the burden of appeals from the district courts off the Supreme Court. So there is now no general right of appeal from the circuit court of appeal to the Supreme Court, except in a very few cases specified by law. Rather, the Supreme Court decides on the circumstances of each application for an appeal whether it will hear it or not. The test applied is whether or not the case raises questions of substantial constitutional or public importance. In addition to hearing appeals, the Supreme Court may act as a court of first instance in a number of matters, particularly disputes in which foreign ambassadors or consuls of foreign powers are involved, and disputes in which a state is a party. The Supreme Court serves as the "living voice" of the Constitution of the United States. Probably in no other democratic country has a court been accorded such powers or acquired such prestige and public respect.

The Courts in Canada

Although Canada is a federal state, its judicial structure shows marked variations from that of the United States. The British North America Act assigns almost the entire administration of justice to the provinces. The establishment and maintenance of the courts, their organization and procedure, with the exception of procedure in criminal matters, are the responsibility of the provincial legislatures and executives. Subject to minor exceptions, all disputes, whatever the persons or subject matter involved and whether or not the decision turns on provincial or federal law, are brought to trial in the provincial courts. For example, the criminal law of Canada is made by the national Parliament, but the prosecution of offenders is invariably in the provincial courts. On the other hand, the judges who dispense justice in these courts are, with minor exceptions, appointed by the federal cabinet because the British North America Act reserves the appointment of superior, county, and district court judges to the central government.

The structure of the courts varies from province to province and a short description of the general pattern will be impressionistic rather than accurate. The first tier above the justices of the peace and the magistrates' courts comprises the county and district courts. Unlike the county courts in England, they generally have both criminal and civil jurisdiction. But they are not, like the county courts in the United States, possessed of general jurisdiction over all criminal and civil matters, however serious and important. The most serious criminal charges and civil claims of large amount or consequence cannot be tried in these courts.

It is the next tier of courts, variously called the High Court of Justice, the Court of Queen's Bench, the Supreme Court, which have general jurisdiction in the first instance. Reasonably adequate decentralization is achieved through sending these judges periodically on circuit throughout the province. At the apex is the Court of Appeals sitting in the provincial capital to which appeals in civil and criminal matters go.

In certain matters, particularly where substantial sums are in question or where an interpretation of the constitution or the validity of federal or provincial legislation is involved, an appeal may be taken from the court of last resort in the province to the Supreme Court of Canada in Ottawa. This is a federal court created by the national Parliament. Its main function, unlike the Supreme Court of the United States, is to hear appeals from the provincial courts. Of rapidly growing importance, however, is the duty imposed on it by an act of the national Parliament to give, at the request of the federal cabinet, advisory opinions on the proper interpretation of the British North America Act and on the constitutional validity of federal or provincial legislation. Much of the judicial interpretation of the legislative powers of the Dominion and the provinces under the British North America Act has been secured in this way in recent years.

There is one other federal court, the Exchequer Court, with a very specialized jurisdiction in the first instance. It hears cases in which the Government of Canada is a party, as when a citizen makes a claim against it or it brings an action to enforce payment of tax or other revenues. It has exclusive jurisdiction to decide disputes arising over copyright, patents, and trade marks. It also has power to decide legal disputes between a province and the Dominion, or between two provinces in so far as particular provinces pass legislation submitting themselves to its decision. There is, therefore, no hierarchy of federal courts in Canada interpreting and applying federal law generally as in the United States.

Until 1949, Canadian litigants could appeal, in certain special circumstances to a still higher court: the Judicial Committee of the Privy Council sitting in London. It is a body specially constituted to hear appeals from the courts of the British Dominions and colonies. Since it must hear appeals from some Dominions and from the colonial Empire, it has to have a wide membership assuring it of experts in the widely differing kinds of laws involved. But for most of its work, the active members of the Judicial

Committee are the Lord Chancellor and the law lords of the House of Lords who are *ex officio* members. It was they who generally gave the final interpretation of the British North America Act.

The main work of the Judicial Committee in relation to Canada was appeals on constitutional questions, which issues were generally carried there as a matter of course from the Supreme Court of Canada or directly from the provincial courts. There was no right of appeal from the Supreme Court of Canada but leave to appeal was granted by the Judicial Committee if the issue at stake was thought to be of first-rate importance. This could almost always be established if a constitutional question was involved, but only rarely where it was not. Yet the fact remains that formerly particular Canadian litigants might have to face as many as four appeals, the latter two at places far distant from their place of residence or business.

The injustice of putting litigants to the expense of carrying an appeal to London and the widespread dissatisfaction in Canada with the Privy Council's interpretation of the British North America Act brought the abolition of all Canadian appeals to that body in 1949. The Supreme Court of Canada is now the final and exclusive court of appeal for Canada.

THE FUNCTIONS OF THE COURTS

It is somewhat misleading to say that the function of the judiciary is to interpret and apply the law. The essential primary function of the judiciary is to hear and decide disputes. Sometimes disputes in the courts are entirely concerned with questions of fact, and judges have only to decide the baffling question which party to believe. Often, however, a dispute involves differing interpretations of the law and, in order to give a decision, the judges may have to determine what is the proper interpretation. But their job is to give a judgment on the dispute, or, at most, a declaratory judgment stating the rights of particular persons arising from a specific set of actual facts, and they generally refuse to give gratuitous opinions on the law that are not necessary for the decision in hand.

The general rule in the Anglo-American system is that the courts cannot be set in motion to grind out interpretations of law in the absence of a dispute between parties with an interest in the result. The courts are always open to hear charges that a particular person has committed a crime or complaints that the civil rights of the complainant have been infringed. The law, however, does not require the courts, or even enable them, to resolve doubtful points that come casually to their attention. Nor does it enable them, except in a few special circumstances, to give advice to perplexed individuals who are in doubt as to what the law requires them to do.

In certain circumstances, through the issue of a writ of mandamus, the courts will order a public official to perform a duty specifically imposed on him by law. In certain other limited circumstances, the courts will issue an injunction restraining particular persons, whether officials or not, from performing acts that, if performed, would be infringements of the rights of other specified persons. Normally, however, it is only when someone comes forward asserting that a wrong has been done, and that he should be compensated or that the culprit should be punished that the courts are set in motion.

Punishment but not Prevention

It follows that in almost all cases the action of the courts is compensatory or punitive and not preventive. As a general rule, individuals cannot be restrained by judicial action merely on the ground of a plausible suspicion that they are about to commit a wrong against the state or another citizen. Thus, in wartime, special legislation has always to be passed by the legislature authorizing the detention of persons who are strongly suspected of seditious aims and traitorous designs not yet put in execution. The abuses to which such powers of detention are always open, and sometimes put, emphasize the wisdom of the rule which restricts very sharply preventive action by the executive or by the courts. Risks of serious wrongdoing are thus incurred. However, freedom to do right involves freedom to do wrong. The law expresses the liberal democratic faith that individual freedom is worth the risk. How is one to be sure that a man is of an irresistibly vicious state of mind? It has been thought better that the risks should be taken and punishment or compensation provided after the event.

The extreme hesitation of the Anglo-American system to embark on preventive action is not just laziness on the part of the judges or untidy administration of justice. It rests squarely on the beliefs in individual freedom and responsibility. If any confirmation of this is needed, it can be found in the practice of the dictatorships. Having no strong faith in the individual and regarding him primarily as a means to more important ends, law in the dictatorships ceases to be primarily concerned with individual rights, and the correlative duties to respect the rights of other individuals. Instead, it puts its main emphasis on the duties of individuals toward the state, and the judges must constantly underline this emphasis in their decisions. If individuals are un-co-operative or grudging in their attitudes, there is every reason to make an example of them. The judiciary is an instrument for safeguarding the regime and promoting the conception of the good life entertained by the rulers.

Accordingly, the courts are not concerned merely with acts done but also with the motives, character, and general attitude of the citizens. In Nazi Germany, for example, the courts often penalized individuals or denied them redress because they had a bad attitude and would no doubt be led into actual transgression if they were not checked beforehand. The Nazi courts had preventive as well as compensatory and punitive functions. Similar instances for Fascist Italy and the Soviet Union could be given.

Executive Consultation of the Judiciary

In this condition of the law in the Anglo-American world it would seem to follow too that neither the executive nor the legislature can require the judges to give authoritative interpretations of the law in the absence of an actual dispute between parties. Broadly speaking, this is true. In the United States, the federal Constitution and the state constitutions prevent it in the absence of constitutional amendment for that purpose. In Britain, the executive is not permitted to consult the judges on the meaning of particular laws or on the legality of particular executive action already taken or proposed to be taken. Of course, the supremacy of Parliament makes it possible for Parliament to enact a law at any time requiring the judges to give such opinions. In Canada, as already noted, the federal Parliament—and most of the provincial legislatures—have enacted legislation requiring the courts to give advisory opinions in constitutional questions, particularly on the meaning of the British North America Act and on the validity of Dominion or provincial statutes. Suggestions for similar legislation have been made in the United States, but thus far only a few states have made the enabling constitutional amendments. Such judicial opinions, when given, are authoritative in the sense that they have the prestige of a considered statement of the court, but ordinarily they are merely advice to the executive and do not form precedents binding the courts in later litigation.

The reason why governments nowadays should want advisory opinions from the judges before disputes arise is very clear, particularly in federal states. Much of to-day's legislation must be actively administered by the executive, and this often requires the setting up of new offices and the employment of hundreds and even thousands of additional civil servants. It often involves also a very drastic readjustment of their practices by numerous individuals and businesses. Unfortunately, however, it is not always easy, in the United States and Canada, to be sure that the legislation is constitutional, and the decision ultimately rests with the courts. Many federal, state, and provincial laws have been held *ultra vires*. For example, in 1937 a Dominion Act to regulate the marketing of agricultural and other natural products was held by the courts to encroach on the exclusive sphere of the provincial legislature, but not before marketing boards under the Act had been put in operation in many parts of the country. Important parts of President Roosevelt's New Deal legislation enacted in 1933 were held unconstitutional by the Supreme Court between 1935 and 1938 after a vast administrative apparatus to enforce it had been set up and put to work. The purpose of advisory opinions by the judges is to get a settlement of the constitutional issue before administrative enforcement of the legislation begins.

In Britain, the judiciary cannot declare legislation unconstitutional, but it must interpret the meaning of legislation when disputes turning on its meaning arise. The judges sometimes give interpretations that surprise and even dismay the executive and upset its programme of enforcement of the law. As a result, there has been some agitation for a law that would enable the executive to get judicial interpretations in advance. Such proposals are resisted on the ground that they would unduly strengthen the hand of the executive and tend to knit the executive and judiciary into one. If the executive can get opinions from the judges beforehand while the individual who resists the intervention of officials in the sphere of his interests cannot, the latter is put at a serious disadvantage.

JUDICIAL CONTROL OF GOVERNMENT OFFICIALS

The force and bearing of this argument cannot be fully appreciated without looking closely at one of the traditional roles of the Anglo-American judiciary. It was pointed out in chapter IV that the judiciary has been relied on to enforce the Rule of Law on citizen and government official alike. If government is to be servant and not master, its actions must be limited by predictable rules which are interpreted and applied by some authority independent of the executive. This has been done in the past mainly by the judges of the same courts that settle disputes between citizen and citizen and, in the absence of a law clearly conferring special powers and privileges on the government official, they have required him to observe the standards applicable to private citizens. In this sense, one law interpreted by one set of judges rules everybody. The Rule of Law, or the supremacy of law as it is generally known in the United States, is a very important principle of Anglo-American constitutions.

/ So the official who is thought to have overzealously exceeded his powers can be brought before an impartial court on the complaint of the aggrieved person. / If the police detain a person on suspicion of crime for any considerable time without bringing him to trial for a specified offence, his jailer can be compelled to appear in the court, and if he cannot show that the detention is lawful, an order for release will be made. Equally, if an official seizes an apparatus which he claims is used for making illicit alcohol in violation of the excise law and which the owner insists is used only for laudable scientific experiment, the owner can have both the fact and the law determined by the judiciary. /

In such disputes, the judges do not lean in favour of the official. If they lean at all, it is the other way. For the Anglo-American legal tradition, of which more will be said later, makes the judiciary a champion of private rights and interests against any suggestion of highhanded action by governments. The independence from the executive which the judge enjoys is not always free from antagonism. So the legal profession and the judges regard any suggestion that the judges should collaborate with the executive as a threat to individual liberty. The judges, it is said, should not be asked to interpret a law giving powers to the executive until they see, in the actual disputes arising, what use the executive is trying to make of the law in question. The dangers involved in such proposals may be exaggerated. Yet the general rule that judges are to decide disputes over the lawfulness of things already done and not to foreclose freedom of action by preventive measures or by interpretations of law in advance of action is an important buttress of constitutionalism.

Today, when great accomplishments are expected of governments, and achievements depend largely on the energy and efficiency of the executive, it is clear why the executive should want to find out from the judges in advance what the judges will uphold. This is particularly true, when the judges are inclined to be unsympathetic to the executive. And it applies with special force because in the Anglo-American system the official is personally liable for damages when he exceeds his powers. The jailer who detains a person unlawfully is liable for heavy damages even though his motives are of the best. Hence when officials are in doubt as to their powers, they are likely to be timid and hesitant in enforcing the law. While this is some protection against executive highhandedness, it also detracts from the vigour of administration. The methods by which constitutionalism has been buttressed are often hindrances to far-reaching governmental action.

European System Contrasted

At this point, it may be useful to introduce a contrast with the European legal and judicial systems that deal with governmental disputes differently from private disputes. In France, for example, the courts that judge between citizen and citizen have no authority to deal with disputes to which the government, or an official of the government as such, is a party. A claim that an official has exceeded his powers in executing his official duties and thus committed a wrong against a private citizen is heard in one of a number of special courts known as administrative courts. These courts are very closely connected with the executive, and the judges who sit in them perform many executive as well as judicial functions. Moreover, the rules of law applied to the settlement of disputes in these courts differ from the rules applied to disputes between citizen and citizen. There is a special body of law called administrative law which governs in the administrative courts.

The only comparably constituted court known to English history is the Court of Star Chamber, which was a branch of the executive and dealt with controversies between the government and the subject. Its memory is infamous because it applied to the officials of the Tudor and Stuart kings a different standard from that applicable to the ordinary citizen and often relied on reasons of state and political expediency to deny redress to citizens in conflict with the Crown. It was abolished three hundred years ago, but even today any suggestion of the creation of administrative courts in the Anglo-American world evokes its image in the minds of the legal profession and others.

It was long thought in these circles that the French administrative courts were similar devices for enabling the executive to escape from the restraints of law. In fact, however, since the beginning of the democratic Third Republic in 1870, whatever may have been true earlier, the administrative courts have been impartial and upright, leaning neither in favour of the official nor the citizen. They give the average citizen better protection against official overzealousness and mistakes than does the Anglo-American system. They are easy of access and have a simple, expeditious procedure. If they find the official at fault, they award compensation to the injured party which is paid not by the official personally but out of the public treasury. In Britain, Canada, and the United States, on the other hand, until a few years ago, the law generally did not impose on the government and the public treasury any responsibility for official wrongdoing. The official himself has always been liable, but a judgment against him is often worthless because he has not the financial resources to meet it.

Despite certain obvious advantages of the continental system, Anglo-American opinion clings to the ideal of a judiciary completely independent of the executive and of one law for citizen and official alike. There is a profound suspicion of any judiciary closely connected with the executive and of any special law for testing the validity of governmental action. To the argument that the French administrative courts were, in fact, impartial it is retorted that what is wanted is not merely justice now, but an assurance of justice in the future.

That assurance is thought to be lacking where the judges are closely linked to the executive, and therefore open to executive pressure. Support for this view is to be found in the experience of Germany and Italy with dictatorship. These two countries had systems of administrative courts on the French model. As soon as the Nazis and Fascists got control of the executive in these two countries, the impartial independence of the administrative courts was overwhelmed, and they became mere tools for consolidating the power of the dictators. So, for that matter, did the French administrative courts under the Vichy regime and German occupation.

However, Britain and the United States have now recognized the obvious justice of the French system in making the public treasury liable for wrongful acts committed by officials in the course of carrying out their duties. In 1946 and 1947, acts were passed by the British Parliament and the United States Congress respectively, giving the right to sue the public treasury in these circumstances. The Canadian Parliament gave its approval to similar legislation in 1953, thereby acknowledging a limited liability of the federal government for damage caused by the negligence or wrongful acts of its servants. In all three countries, however, the official remains personally liable as before, and the injured person may elect to sue him instead of, or along with, the state.

Also, as we shall see in detail later, the legislature in adding continuously to the tasks of the executive often gives special powers and privileges to particular officials and even sets up special administrative tribunals to judge the exercise of these powers.

That is to say, the unsympathetic judiciary finds the legislature cutting down materially its function of judging disputes between officials and citizens. The great enlargement of governmental activities in the last fifty years has affected even the judiciary and has made, despite the protests of the legal profession, substantial breaches in the Rule of Law as it used to be understood.

The upshot of this discussion of the functions of the judiciary is that its primary function is to judge disputes and to interpret the law as far as is necessary for that purpose. Of course, such interpretations are openly made and furnish guides to the meaning of the law for persons who find themselves in circumstances similar to those in which judges have given decisions. The effect of judicial interpretation in a particular case goes far beyond the particular dispute. How far it goes depends on "the law" just as the limits of the judges' power to give interpretations have been said to depend on "the law." In fact, throughout this chapter, a number of conclusions have been ascribed to "the law" and differences between different legal systems have been noted. It is necessary now to inquire what is meant by "the law."

The Origin and Nature of Law

It has been said that the function of the legislature is to make the law. In almost all countries in the world, however, there is a great deal of law in force that has never been made by a legislature. Despite their large annual turnout of legislation, present-day legislatures do no more than add to or make minor alterations in a vast body of law that is derived from other sources. Although it lacks the stamp of a legislature, this body of law regulates far more human relationships and is better observed and enforced than are the laws made by legislatures.

We have here an element of great importance for government and politics which is not generated by the political and governmental mechanisms we have been describing. To explain the origin and growth of law and to define its identifying characteristics would require a large volume. So it must suffice to give summarily some clues to its origin and nature without attempting precise definition. The law, in the sense of a body or system of rules, takes form through the ages just as does a language or a literature, or an art like painting and sculpture. The current generation builds on the past, rejecting parts of it while maintaining or transforming other parts of it. There is always an interaction between the tradition that is handed down and the needs and desires of the present. Just as the Greeks developed certain canons of art and literature that still command respect, and reappear again and again in many different dresses, so the Romans, for example, developed a body of legal rules, principles, and ideas that still retain authority in various guises in modern systems of law.

Every civilization and every society in the course of development secrete, by a process of social chemistry which has never been fully explained, a legal system of more or less distinctiveness. It is closely akin to custom, which is a set of rules and practices with its roots in the past and always being subtly modified and developed in the present. People living together in a society find out almost subconsciously that certain practices and patterns of behaviour are a support, if not a pre-condition, of social life and that other ways of acting are detrimental to or destructive of it. In the most primitive societies, there are always numerous rules to be observed often involving elaborate and intricate ceremonies. At this stage, there may be both law and custom, but it is generally impossible to tell one from the other. Both are enforced by the threat of social ostracism, or worse, and by threats of supernatural punishments.

In these early stages, indeed, it is often impossible to distinguish either law or custom from religion. The priests conduct the ceremonies, interpret the customs, and maintain the authority of the taboos. Sometimes it can be said that the germ of a legal profession is to be found in the priesthood. Legal systems never break entirely free of these early associations. Even today, rules that only recently were no more than custom, now and then become recognized and enforced as rules of law. While no one is now likely to confuse the lawyer and the priest, everyone will have noted how moral and religious feeling help to maintain the authority of the criminal law. Equally, the ideas of justice and fair dealing that find expression in the rules and principles of the law have been impressed on it by moral and religious feeling and by the ethical standards that are honoured in the community.

Law Distinguished from Custom and Religion

It is not easy to say at what point a system of law emerges from custom and religion. Somewhat arbitrarily, we can pick the point at which the priest, who is almost always associated with the interpretation and enforcement of rules of social behaviour in primitive societies, is able to supplement the sanctions of custom and religion by calling on some reservoir of organized physical force to enforce his decrees. When this happens, we can say that the priest has become a judge, and the rules that are enforced in this way are law. Customary rules are obeyed because of habit or fear of censure by one's fellows. The rules of morality are obeyed generally because of a fear of, or a respect and reverence for, divine authority. Most of the law gets support from these sources too. Some even contend that no rule of behaviour can be law unless it accords with the community's sense of what is right and fitting.

In any event, all are agreed that what distinguishes law from custom and morality is the additional sanction of sheriffs, bailiffs, police, jails, and armed forces to be called into operation if needed to coerce the stubborn. So law is defined as the body of rules that is backed by the organized force of the community. The government controls this organized force and thus law has in it a political element lacking in custom and morality. All three are made up of rules for controlling the behaviour of men in society, but law alone conjures up the judge-interpreter, the army, and the policeman.

If this is the nature of law, the judges play a double role. They are agents of the government for determining in what circumstances organized political force is to be turned loose on individuals. They are also agents of the community, as distinct from the government, for seeing to it that disputes are settled according to law, i.e. in ways that do not outrage the community sense of right. In fact, the judges in the Anglo-American world do not think of themselves as agents of the government but as the servants, or the high-priests, of the law.

They have been confirmed in this attitude by the persistence of a belief that was first articulated by the Stoic philosophers before the Christian era. As we saw in chapter II, the Stoics believed in a law of nature, universally binding because it expressed the permanent demands of man's innermost nature. By reflecting on man's essential nature, human reason could unerringly define the right rules for regulating human relationships. Particularly in the United States, lawyers and judges have been deeply influenced by the conception of a law rooted in reason and nature which has a higher validity than the laws made by a legislature. Most of this higher law, they think, is enshrined in the Constitution of the United States, written there by men who had grasped the rational law of nature.

This is the fundamental significance of the substantial independence that Anglo-American judges enjoy. The law they interpret is older than the government and gets much of its support from sources other than the government: custom, morality, reason, and nature. It is on this ground that judges claim to decide whether or not the acts of the government and its officials are according to law. It is partly on this ground that the judges in the United States have made good their power to declare laws made by the legislatures to be void as being contrary to a higher law—the Constitution. It is on this ground that the judges are sometimes, as we shall see, unsympathetic to laws made by the legislature.

Legislation as a Source of Law

However, legislatures do make law, and in ever-growing abundance. In Britain, the law made by the legislature overrides all other law that may be contradictory to it. Everywhere, the law made by the legislature is for the purpose of changing the older law in some respect. Law, like constitutions, must always be capable of change to meet changing conditions and new needs and desires. But deliberate, conscious change by legislatures is largely a modern phenomenon. Never before have legislatures undertaken to change law as radically and as frequently as present-day legislatures do.

Before the Industrial Revolution, law, with its roots in custom, changed slowly as custom always changes. This generally sufficed because the pace of social change that determines the need for change in the law was very slow. By processes that do not concern us here, law was adjusted almost imperceptibly just as social change was imperceptible at any given time. But, as everyone knows, the Industrial Revolution and the continuing technological developments it set going have made more changes in the material conditions of life in two hundred years than had occurred in the previous two thousand. These economic and social transformations have upset the old customary ways of life and have created most of the disorder and maladjustments that legislatures are trying desperately to cure. The law handed down from the past, like the customs by which men lived, fails to maintain order and security in the rapidly changing conditions. Hence the feverish activity of legislatures trying to patch and improvise by deliberate change of and additions to the law. Most of the new governmental functions outlined in chapter v involved substantial changes in the law. Statutes add greatly to the bulk of the law to be interpreted.

A later chapter will explain something of the impact of legislative law making on the inherited legal system and on the work of the judiciary. Here it is important to emphasize that there are inherited legal systems and that, despite their being outmoded in some particulars, they still are of great importance. There are numerous legal systems but only two of them need be commented on; the Roman, or civil-law, system and the English, or common-law, system. Between them, they hold sway over most of the Western world.

Civil Law and Common Law

Roman law had its origin in the custom and religion of the tribes that founded the city of Rome. Over a period of a thousand years, the primitive tribal law of Rome was transformed by the slow piecemeal work of priests, judges, and lawyers into the law of a great empire ruling the then civilized world. It reached its maturity before A.D. 200. When Rome fell, its law fell with it, and the barbarian tribes who overran the Empire brought their own customary law with them, among them the Anglo-Saxons who moved to Britain. By the end of the Middle Ages several systems of law owing little to Roman law had developed in Europe out of the customs of the barbarians, among them the English common law.

The Renaissance, which revived the study of the ancient art and literature, also aroused great enthusiasm for Roman law, a record of which had happily been preserved. The main reason for this enthusiasm is not far to seek. The Renaissance was marked by beliefs in individualism and human rationality. The Roman jurists who were most influential in shaping the Roman law in the stages of its highest development were also Stoic philosophers moved by beliefs in the dignity of the individual, in the brotherhood of man, and in a universal law discoverable by reason. This, by the way, is another instance of the deep roots of the Western political tradition.

Just as the classics became the foundation of the educational system, so the Roman law was adopted in most of continental Europe as the main body of law, superseding, for most purposes, the native law. In the course of time, the countries of Western Europe framed codes of laws suitable to modern conditions but based on Roman law. The modernized Roman system has been adopted in countries as different as Japan and Turkey, and, of course, it was carried to the colonies of the continental European states. Thus Quebec, Louisiana, and South Africa, although now within the orbit of the Anglo-American system, have incorporated in their legal systems varying portions of Roman law.

Scotland went over to the civil law but England did not, retaining her native system of law. This is just another aspect of the remarkable continuity of English political and social development without revolutionary breaks with the past. English law was, by 1500, more fully developed than any of the native systems of continental Europe. It had called into existence a close-knit legal profession maintaining at the Inns of Court in London vigorous law schools where the native tradition was imparted to each succeeding generation of lawyers. These factors aided in resisting the appeal of the classics in the field of jurisprudence. English law made good its claim to survive and become a rival of Roman law in the modern world.

Origin and Development of Common Law

At the time of the Norman Conquest, custom ruled the land and ruled it variously in different parts of England. The administration of justice was entirely in the hands of local assemblies of neighbours who met to deal with deviations from the customary ways of behaviour. The Norman kings pledged themselves to maintain the laws of Edward the Confessor. To help in maintaining order and improving their grip on the kingdom, they gradually took the administration of justice away from the local assemblies and put it into the hands of their own trusted officials.

These officials travelled up and down the country on the king's business, dealing, among other things, with disputes brought to their attention. They were often puzzled over what rules to apply to these controversies. The custom in different areas was often conflicting or divergent and it was difficult to know what the laws of Edward the Confessor were. They did notice, however, that on many matters there was a similarity in custom across the country. They met the difficulty by resolving to apply "the common custom of the realm." In this way they came to talk about the common law—common because it was generally observed throughout the realm.

This is the origin of the name and the system of English law. But it must not be thought that its sole content continued to be common custom. Where customs conflicted or none could be found, the particular officials who gradually came to specialize in judging disputes and relinquished the administrative aspects of the king's business to others, invented new rules, or borrowed from Roman and canon law. To take only one example, the law of property in land came to be perhaps the most distinctive branch of the common law. It was partly based on prevailing custom, but in the main it was developed in great detail by the judges themselves with one dominant purpose in mind: to meet the needs of the feudal system which the Norman kings had brought to England and on which they had to rely for governing the country for three hundred years. The king was the overlord and all England was his estate. Everyone who held land held it of the king, directly or indirectly. The law of property comprised the rules for the orderly administration of this estate. Many other similar, if not striking, illustrations could be given. The law is rooted in custom, but it responds through the creative work of the judiciary to the dominant needs of the time.

This law, which was first shaped for the needs of feudal

England, survived into the modern world and was made over through the centuries into a system of law adequate for a great commercial and industrial civilization and a world empire. Legislation, i.e. law making by a legislature, played no highly significant part in this development until the second quarter of the nineteenth century. It was the work of succeeding generations of judges who never lost touch with the past, but who also responded more or less slowly to changing needs.

The common law was brought to the English colonies on the Atlantic seaboard and there adapted, first to the needs of pioneer America and then later to the needs of industrial America. All British colonies settled by people of British origin took the common law with them and so it spread around the world. It was not, however, generally imposed on conquered colonies settled by non-British European stock. South Africa has its Roman-Dutch law, the version of Roman law adopted in Holland, just as Quebec has a version of the French civil law. However, in the case of Canada, the criminal law is uniform throughout the country and is based on the common law. Also the commercial law of Quebec has been strongly influenced by common law because the commercial class is predominantly of British origin. It is in matters affecting family, property, and personal relations that the civil law rules almost exclusively in Quebec.

The Changing Content of the Common Law

Law must change when new needs can no longer be denied, but its prime function in any given period is to minister to order and stability. For this purpose, the law must have a fair degree of certainty. The sense of security which is the basis of orderly life depends on knowing what others will do or can be held to in the future. Those who plan for the future must be able to find out what the law permits and requires. As a Lord Chancellor of England has said, "Amid the cross-currents and shifting sands of public life, the Law is like a great rock upon which a man may set his feet and be safe."[1] A law that is always changing is uncertain and defeats its own purpose. Moreover, if it is admitted that the judges can change the law, people lose confidence in it and them.

[1]Quoted from Lord Sankey in the *Report of the Committee on Ministers' Powers* (His Majesty's Stationery Office, London, Cmd. 4060, 1932), p. 6.

Accordingly, judges are sworn to apply the law as they find it. For the best of reasons, and with complete honesty and considerable truth, the judge insists that he does not make law but only interprets it.

The explanation of the paradox of certainty and change is that judicial change in the law must be so slow as to be imperceptible, even to judges unless they have a deep knowledge of history. It can be proved that glaciers flow although casual observers will deny it flatly. Similarly, the movement of the law is by a succession of slight shifts in interpretation of some of its rules, the total effect of which will often not be noted in one generation. As long as social and economic change was also slow, this method of adaptation of law might suffice. But by the middle of the nineteenth century, the pace of social change was so rapid, its effects so widespread, and the clamour of new needs so insistent, that leadership in the adaptation of the law was forced on elected legislatures. Conscious and deliberate devising now makes every year a larger supplement to the old, almost unconscious, social process of adaptation.

There is no way of measuring what proportion of the law today is common law and what is statute law made by the legislature. Broadly speaking, the great bulk of private law, the law applicable to relationships between private citizens, is still common law, although modified here and there by statutes. This includes the law of tort (civil wrongs such as trespass, slander, deceit, assault, and so on), the law of personal relations such as those between husband and wife, parent and child, and the law relating to property and contract. In Britain and the United States, it includes the criminal law. In Canada, the bulk of the criminal law has been put in statutory form, the Criminal Code, but this is really little more than a reduction of the common law on the subject to a convenient and authoritative written form.

Most of the recent legislation concerns public law, the law applicable to relationships between government and the individual. Much of the public law is still common law, but statute has added to it in recent years giving new rights and powers to officials and creating new duties and rights for individuals *vis à vis* the government. As we have seen, the great cause of legislation is the extension of government activities. The assumption of these new

functions always requires some adjustment of the relationship
between the government and the individual.

The content of the common law is an arduous study in itself
and little that is useful can be said about it in a short space. But
there are some general characteristics of the system that are
important for a study of present-day government and offer marked
contrasts to the civil law.

Contrasts between Common Law and Civil Law

The common law is unwritten law in the sense that there is
nowhere to be found a compendious set of written rules that
authoritatively state that law. Plenty of books have been written
on all branches of the common law and they are of great assistance
in finding the law. Yet none of them is in any sense binding on the
courts, which must always base their decision on some earlier decision of a court, called a precedent.

For hundreds of years, the cases, or judicial decisions, that
involved a significant interpretation of the law have been collected
together in hundreds of volumes, called the law reports. The report
of a case contains a statement of the facts of the dispute, the judge's
decision, and something of his reason for thinking that the law
justified the decision. That is to say, there is in every case, explicit
or implicit, a statement of the law applicable to the given facts.
To find the law applicable to a dispute arising today, it may be
necessary to consult five precedents, or fifty or more. Anyone who
wishes to master the common law as a whole must master the law
reports, "this codeless myriad of precedent, this wilderness of single
instances."

There was a time when this could be done, but it is past. The
accumulation of precedents is now too great. The principal stock-
in-trade of the lawyer nowadays is a knowledge of how to use the
numerous digests and indices available as guides to the law reports,
and a technique for interpreting what he finds there. He collects
the cases that are similar to the one he has in hand, noting differences and judging of their significance. He then tries to frame a
general rule that will explain these cases. He works inductively
from the particular to the general, and having got it, he applies it
to his own case. The judge does the same, remembering that the
precedents which bind him are decisions in the courts that stand
above his court in the hierarchy. Once the highest court of appeal

has ruled on a particular question, its decision is binding on itself and all lower courts, until the legislature changes the rules.

In contrast, the civil law is written law. It is always to be found in an authoritative code of general rules which the judge is to apply, and he is not permitted to base his decision on precedent to the neglect of the written code. This is a much neater and less cumbersome system and, on the surface, would seem to leave the layman less at the mercy of the lawyer. However, there is a some-what esoteric technique for interpreting the provisions of the code and applying it to facts, which only trained lawyers possess. Also, despite the ban on precedents, the courts do develop settled practices in applying the code, which come to much the same thing. There is a large body of authoritative doctrine over and above the letter of the code.

Both systems have a set of rules for interpreting the meaning of legislation enacted by the legislature. In the civil law, they are few and relatively simple. In the common law, they are much more numerous, having been developed in great detail because every decision of a court interpreting the meaning of some section of a statute is itself a precedent to be followed in later interpretation of the same section. Thus, just as the Supreme Court of the United States has expounded the meaning of the American Con-stitution at great length, so the Anglo-American judiciary amplifies the meaning of all statutes that come into question in cases before it. The Statute of Frauds, for example, enacted by the English Parliament in 1677, contains only a few hundred words. It now takes a substantial book to explain in detail the meaning given it by the courts over the last 300 years. Almost every word in it has been given a special common law meaning which may or may not have been present to the minds of the Parliament that enacted it. The statute has been knit into the fabric of the common law.

This is a necessary process because every piece of legislation, whether socially wise and necessary or not, is upsetting to the legal system, as a system. Like the grain of sand in the oyster, it is an irritant until it is well overlaid with precedent. Great pearls of judicial ingenuity—not to say wisdom—are the result. The inter-pretation of statutes is a creative process adding much to what the legislature has said, and sometimes stultifying, sometimes enlarging, its purpose.

The Individualism of the Common Law

Another important characteristic of the common law is its individualism. We have already noticed the tenderness of judges to individuals and individual rights, and their fairly frequent lack of sympathy with current legislation that restricts in one way or another individual freedom of action. This is partly due to the fact that among the older judges of today, there are still some whose political philosophy was formed before laissez faire was discredited. Many of these are still disposed to think that the government that governs least governs best. This attitude is not nearly as strong in the younger generation of judges who have lived all their lives in an era of extensive governmental activity and whose education has made clear that laissez faire is not a fully adequate politicial philosophy. Laissez faire was abandoned considerably earlier in Britain than in Canada and the United States. So the British judiciary is now almost reconciled to widespread intervention of governments in economic and social life with its aggrandizement of the executive and inevitable inroads on the Rule of Law which were noted in earlier chapters.[1]

In the United States and Canada reconciliation has not proceeded as far as in Britain, but each decade, if not each year, the judiciary in these two countries are showing less hostility and more sympathy to both the objectives and the methods of wide-ranging government activities. The individualism of the Common Law, which has been its most striking feature is steadily being tempered (or eroded as the hostile critics of recent trends would say) by collectivist principles.

Deeply embedded for a long time in the thinking of lawyers trained in the common law has been the principle of no liability without fault. Subject to significant exceptions in special kinds of circumstances, no one should be compelled to pay damages to another unless the injury complained of arose from the neglect or fault of the person to be charged. In many kinds of situations, legislation in recent years requires individuals and corporations to ensure the safety of others, quite irrespective of fault. For example, the workmen's compensation laws require employers to pay into a fund that compensates injured workmen even when the injury was the work-

[1]See pp. 96, 142–5 supra, and also chapter xvi, post, for fuller discussion.

man's own fault. In interpreting legislation of this kind, the judges are slowly acknowledging the merits of the principle which requires those in charge of complex processes, noxious substances, and deceptively innocent-looking machines to ensure the safety of others. They are also coming to recognize that in the common law itself this principle of insurance has a place.

A famous English judge said many years ago that the highest principle of public policy prescribed to judges was that they should not lightly interfere with freedom of contract. The ideal thus expressed was that everyone should be free to make his own bargains and then be required, as a responsible person, to make the best of the bad along with the good. Most of the legislation imposing regulation on business and economic life which was discussed in chapter v restricts freedom of contract in very significant ways. For a long time, the judges did not conceal their dislike of this kind of legislation and narrowed its application wherever they could. Now they are coming to see that the individualistic principle, freedom of contract, is not an absolute principle, and that there are other interests entitled to be shielded by public policy.

The common law has been watchful, since Stuart times, of designs by the government against the property of the subject. Accordingly, legislation imposing taxation has been interpreted strictly. If the intention of the legislature to impose a burden was not expressed in the clearest of language, the courts interpreted it favourably to the taxpayer and against the government. Even here, judicial attitudes are changing and some judges (but not all) are saying that statutes which impose a tax should not be singled out for restrictive interpretation.

The individualistic bias of the judges is moderating in some areas of the law. But it still has great strength. As long as the liberal democratic ideals are adhered to, it will get sustenance from them. For example, in a criminal trial, which is a contest between an individual and the state, the judge acts not as an agent of the government bent on getting a conviction but as an impartial umpire trying to hold the scales of justice evenly. Some of the safeguards available to the accused may be listed:

1. The writ of habeas corpus ensures that he will either be tried within a limited time or released. He cannot be kept in a

dungeon for years while the police torture him into confession or wait for Providence to send further evidence against him.

2. A reasonable time before trial, an indictment, or charge, must be laid against him, setting out a specific offence, alleged to have been committed at a specific date and place.

3. He must have ample time to prepare his defence.

4. He is entitled to the expert assistance of a lawyer before and during the trial.

5. He must be tried in open court where he confronts his judge face to face. The evidence against him must be sworn to by witnesses *viva voce* in the court and there must be full opportunity for cross-examination—a powerful weapon in exposing falsehoods.

6. He cannot be compelled to give evidence that incriminates him. It is his own choice whether he goes into the witness box at all or not.

7. Any reasonable doubt that is unresolved at the conclusion of the case must tell in favour of the accused.

8. He can appeal against a conviction, but the state cannot appeal against an acquittal.[1]

Of course, the habitual criminal thrives on these safeguards. But where they are absent the contest between the individual and the state may be a very unequal one and the government can harry its political enemies through the criminal law. The contest may also be unequal in civil disputes between the government and private persons or interests and there is something to be said for the tendency of the judges to lean in favour of the latter. In Britain, where the matter has been given careful study, it is clear that the government, when it takes action in the courts in civil matters, is a resolute litigant, determined to get its pound of flesh.[2]

The imperatives of public policy are always paramount, and private interests must be subordinated. The unsympathetic attitude of the judiciary to collectivist legislation over a long period, along with other considerations to be explained later, provoked a counterattack by the legislatures in common law countries. In many instances, they have taken away or restricted the power of the judiciary

[1]In Canada, the Crown has a limited right of appeal on a question of law only. A few states in the United States also have exceptions to this rule.
[2]See Carleton Kemp Allen, *Bureaucracy Triumphant* (Oxford University Press, 1931), pp. 68-73 and Appendix II.

to decide disputes that involve the interpretation of such legislation. To give only one example, in Britain and Canada, and in most of the states of the United States, issues in regard to whether a workman is entitled to compensation for industrial accident are no longer decided by the courts but by an executive agency, the Workmen's Compensation Board or the Industrial Accidents Commission. This practice of limiting the power of the judiciary has been extended rapidly in the last thirty years.

Whether the imperatives of public policy require this kind of action or whether less drastic steps would suffice is not yet settled. More will be said about it in discussing the administrative process. It is raised here to show that, as in other fields of government and politics, the growth of governmental functions has had a deeply disturbing effect on the judiciary and the legal system. Long-established techniques for helping to ensure that government shall be servant and not master are being revised.

The characteristics of the Anglo-American judicial system that have been outlined all have an important bearing on government and politics. They make it clear that the independence of the judiciary is not adequately stated by pointing to the fact that the judges cannot be dismissed by the executive. The judges administer justice in courts that are controlled by them and not by civil servants. The greater part of the law they interpret and apply does not depend on the legislature or executive for its authority and vitality. They are the bearers of a legal tradition which dictates impartiality in private disputes, and, in disputes in which the government is concerned, some aloofness from the urgencies finding expression in legislative and executive action. The legal system as a whole has been more concerned with the protection of private rights than with the enforcement of the public interest as conceived by the legislature. Legislatures in haste to bend private rights and interests to meet what they think are the needs of public policy have found these judicial attitudes irksome. However, the judiciary and the common law are gradually adjusting to the conception of what is right and fitting held by legislatures and electorates. The judges are coming to see that the highest principle of public policy is not to maximize individual freedom from restraint but to combine judiciously elements of ordered freedom and enforced equality.

CHAPTER XIV

CIVIL LIBERTIES

IT WILL be recalled from the discussion in chapter II that liberal democratic ideals affirm the essential worth and dignity of every human being. The ultimate aim of democratic politics is to provide the necessary conditions for the fullest and widest realization of human personality. The principal conditions are two. First, there is the indispensable framework of order and general security which government exists to provide. Government provides it by the making and enforcing of laws to which all must equally submit. To be secure in his own person, each must be prepared to help to maintain the same security for others through equal laws equally enforced. The second condition is individual freedom, within the limits imposed by the need for order, to make of ourselves what we can out of our abilities and our own unique experience of life. These two conditions can be summed up together as freedom under law.

When the law marks out a defined area of freedom for individuals and provides a means by which individuals can protect themselves in the exercise of freedom in that area, it can be said to create rights. Each individual then has a right to that area of freedom. However, if the constant aim is to foster and protect human personality, certain kinds of freedom are more important than others, so important in fact that they are basic to the whole enterprise. The principal of these are freedom of religion, freedom of expression, freedom of the person and freedom of public meeting. In the Anglo-American world, a number of these basic freedoms have long been accorded a special emphasis and a special protection which will be discussed in this chapter. They have been variously called fundamental freedoms, civil liberties, or civil rights.

FREEDOM UNDER LAW

Freedom under law is an ideal, a goal to be striven for. To make it effective in our political and social life, both freedom and law have to be defined with some precision and reconciled in the interests of personality. The process of adjustment of the two goes on endlessly, and the precise terms of reconciliation vary from time to time. The changing scope of government activities has required continuous adjustment of the boundary between them in the last fifty years. To define this boundary with precision in the United States, Canada, or Britain, and thus to learn in full detail the scope of individual rights of all kinds, one would have to make an extensive study of the whole legal system.

Liberal democracy approaches the mutual adjustment of freedom and law with a bias towards freedom. As we have already seen, it is broadly correct to say that conduct which is not forbidden by law is permitted. The common law which is still a large part of the law in the three countries has a bias towards individual freedom. But it also circumscribes freedom; witness the criminal law which in Britain and the United States is still largely common law. In Canada, the criminal law has been put in statutory form in the Criminal Code, but the Code is, in the main, an authoritative statement of common law rules. Statute law, made by the legislature, is a rapidly growing part of the law, and it also often puts limits on what individuals are free to do. Between them, common law and statute law define the entire area of individual freedom, largely by the negative process of saying what one may not do.

If individuals break these laws and thereby infringe the rights and freedoms of other individuals, they are exposed to actions in the courts. If X makes a slanderous statement about Y, he infringes Y's right to his good name, and may be sued for damages by way of compensation. If he obstructs a public highway so as to prevent others going about their lawful occasions, he interferes with a lawful freedom of those persons, and the courts will, on a charge being laid, impose a penalty for creating a public nuisance. Where mutual respect and the fear of damages or penalty are not enough to make particular individuals respect the lawful claims of others, the courts are open to give redress. In this way, the law protects individuals against wrongful interference by other individuals.

But individuals need to be protected against the government as well as against their fellows as private persons. A legislature with power to make the laws and an executive with overwhelming force at its command have effective and alarming power to restrict individual freedom. The men who laid the main lines of the modern British constitution at the end of the seventeenth century, and the framers of the United States Constitution, had all had bitter experience with arbitrary governments. One of their most anxious concerns was to limit the power that governments could exercise over individuals.

Accordingly, they selected for special emphasis a number of freedoms thought to be vital to the interests of personality. In Britain, this emphasis led immediately to the Bill of Rights of 1689, a solemn Act of the British Parliament, curbing sharply the powers of the executive branch of government, and to a genuinely independent judiciary free of executive pressure. Also, it led immediately to a strong affirmation of the Rule of Law which subjected public officials of all kinds to the same rules of law and to the same courts as private individuals. Then, over the years, it led to an extraordinarily powerful public opinion in favour of these vital freedoms and opposed to Parliament restricting them by legislation. Canada inherited the Bill of Rights and the Rule of Law as part of her law, established constitutional safeguards of the independence of the judiciary, and also developed a strong public opinion in support of the same vital freedoms. In the United States, the concern for individual freedom led to the Bill of Rights and other clauses in the Constitution, and to the bills of rights in the state constitutions, thus protecting individuals in their exercise of certain rights and freedoms from interference by governments.

The rights and freedoms so protected by constitutional provisions in the United States are generally described as civil rights. Substantially the same rights and freedoms are also protected in Britain and Canada by common law or statute against executive interference, and by a strong public opinion against legislative interference. They are commonly referred to in Britain and Canada as the civil liberties. Civil liberties, or civil rights, are to be distinguished from all the other rights and freedoms that individuals may enjoy under law because they are specially buttressed in one way or another against violation by governments.

The civil rights are to be distinguished from political rights. Political rights are those which give the adult citizen the right to the franchise, qualify him to hold public office and entitle him to direct participation in political life. They are restricted to persons who are citizens, and full recognition of political rights lagged behind the recognition of civil rights, both in Britain and the United States. The civil rights, on the other hand, are rights which protect the individual against political interference in the private sphere of life. Of course, as already noted in chapter xii, political rights cannot be exercised effectively without some at least of the civil rights: freedom of speech, freedom of the press, and freedom of public meeting. But the civil rights were never thought to be dependent on political rights or on political democracy for their validity. They are not restricted to citizens but are conceded, generally speaking, as rights to which a man is entitled because of his human personality. Indeed, for a long time, they were thought to be inherent in man by virtue of his nature (inalienable endowments from his Creator, as Thomas Jefferson said in the American Declaration of Independence) and to rest upon the universal laws of nature as first expounded by the Stoic philosophers.

Civil Liberties: Substantive and Procedural

These fundamental civil rights are all expressly conferred by the Constitution of the United States, and the scope of the limitations they place on government will be discussed later. They are all generally recognized and asserted in Britain and Canada. But solemn declarations and lip-service do not alone guarantee their effectiveness in practice. The Constituent Assembly of the first French republic issued its resounding Declaration of the Rights of Man, but this did not prevent the Reign of Terror three years later, an episode in which the fundamental freedoms were trampled underfoot. Ways and means of assuring their effectiveness are also needed.

The most important of these ways and means is a fair trial without undue delay. Declarations of basic liberties will be of little avail if the government can make arrests on trumped-up charges, and hold its victims without trial or get them convicted in an unfair trial. The first requirement for a fair trial is a judiciary independent of direct control by the government. Others are trial by jury, the right to know the specific charge against one, to confront one's accusers in open court, to have the assistance of a lawyer for one's defence. To prevent undue delay in being brought to trial, there must be a procedure to compel either early trial or speedy release of the accused, such as is provided by habeas corpus. All these procedural rights are conferred in the Constitution of the United States and are equally guaranteed by common law or statute in Britain and Canada.

There are besides a number of weapons that governments bent on persecuting individuals commonly use. They make *ex post facto* laws which turn into crimes acts committed before the law was passed. They make arrests, or search persons and places, on general principles hoping to turn up something, acting on the authority of a general warrant. They require excessive bail from those they have taken into custody. In Britain and Canada, the English Bill of Rights outlaws excessive bail, the common law forbids general warrants, and *ex post facto* criminal legislation would outrage public opinion. The Constitution of the United States outlaws all three abuses. In this way, the protection of individual civil liberties against encroachment by governments is further strengthened.

So there are really two kinds of civil rights. First, there are the essential freedoms that men want for their own sake. These are the substantive civil liberties. Second, there are the means that the Anglo-American genius for practical political devices has established for making them effective. These are the procedural civil rights. Everyone hopes he will never need them. No doubt there is less need for some of them now that political democracy has established a large measure of mutual confidence between government and people. But there is no complete assurance that democratic majorities will always refrain from oppressing minorities, and every criminal trial that arouses public passions reminds us that the struggle for fairness of trial is never over.

For convenience, one term is needed to describe these two kinds of protection for individuals against governments. Both kinds will be called here, civil liberties. This term is perhaps less appropriate than the term, civil rights. But civil rights has acquired a very special meaning in Canada through the use of it to describe a particular area of provincial legislative power in section 92.13 of the British North America Act. As used there, the term, civil rights, is primarily concerned with private law, the legal relationships between person and person in private life. The rights and liberties under discussion here are exclusively in the field of public law, defining relationships between the government and private persons. To avoid confusion, the exclusive term used for the subject now under discussion will be civil liberties.

More will be said later about the scope and significance of some of these civil liberties. Immediately, it is important to see exactly how they are guaranteed to the individual in each country. The method of guarantee is more complex in the United States than in Britain or Canada. We shall look at the simpler British situation first.

Civil Liberties in Britain

It will be recalled that Parliament is supreme in Britain. There is no authority that stands above it and no provision of the constitution it cannot change by majority vote. The only limitation on its power is the customary one of requiring a mandate from the people in an election before carrying through a serious constitutional change. The strongest formal guarantee available for civil liberties is an act of Parliament—which Parliament could change tomorrow. The English Bill of Rights of 1689, from which all American bills of rights borrow, takes the form of an Act of Parliament subject to change or repeal by a majority vote of Parliament. Equally, of course, any rights that depend on the common law can be altered by Parliament. No declaration of rights, however solemn, lies beyond its reach.

Perhaps for this reason, the British people have never made a comprehensive formal statement of their civil liberties. The Bill of Rights itself is mostly concerned with the detail of grievances against the Stuart kings in their high-handed conduct of the executive branch of government, and does not purport to give a general guarantee of the important civil liberties of today. Nothing is said in it in any direct way about freedom of religion, freedom of the press, or freedom of public meeting. It does provide a guarantee of freedom of speech, but only for debates in Parliament. There is no other comparable document in which guarantees of civil liberties in Britain can be found. In the main, they have to be spelled out of the common law, which permits what it does not forbid. In the seventeenth century struggle against the Stuarts, Englishmen appealed to the common law as the basis of their liberties. It still remains the principal source of British civil liberties.

The exact nature of British civil liberties can be made clear by considering more closely the right of freedom of speech. It is nowhere expressly stated as it is in the First Amendment to the Constitution of the United States. It rests rather on the general proposition that what is not forbidden by the common law or by statute is permitted—and protected. To define it, it is necessary to see what kinds of speech or writing entail adverse legal consequences for the speaker or writer.

In the first place, the common law, as modified by statute, sets itself against libel and slander. Any speech or writing which makes false statements injurious to the reputation of any person is a wrong against that person and gives him a right to sue for damages. Libel, i.e. a written slander, is also a criminal offence. Secondly, blasphemy is a criminal offence, and so is the writing and publishing of indecent or obscene literature. The exact definitions of these offences do not matter here. It is enough to note that they place some limits on freedom of expression in the interests of religious sensibilities and sexual morality.

Thirdly, and most important for present purposes, seditious utterances are offences against the criminal law. Seditious libel is broadly defined as "the use of words tending to arouse hatred or contempt for any of the institutions of government, advocating changes in Church or State other than by lawful means, or raising discontent and ill-will among the populace."[1] It would be difficult to carry on vigorous political discussion without committing a technical offence under this law. Not only communists arguing for revolution but democratic socialists persuading the poor that existing society is unfair to them, and members of Her Majesty's Loyal Opposition doing their best to show that the government of the day is stupid and inept could be charged almost daily under this law, and its vague, general terms could be construed as being broad enough to justify conviction. In fact, trials for sedition are extremely

[1]Hiram Stout, *British Government* (Oxford University Press, New York, 1953), p. 40.

rare and occur only when there is incitement to immediate violence and revolt. The reasons why the British government does not even try to use the legal powers it could be construed as having will be considered later.

There are various other limitations on freedom of speech and expression. There are special statutory penalties for trying to arouse disaffection among the police and the armed forces. Dramatic productions, motion pictures, and radio scripts are subject to a relatively mild censorship. This list is not exhaustive but it covers the main restrictions on freedom of expression.

Freedom of speech is what is left after these restrictions and limitations on expression. To be more precise, the individual has a right to say whatever the courts will allow him to say with impunity. For it is only in the courts that action can be taken against him for what he has said. The Rule of Law requires the government to act according to law. Officials cannot detain a person or inflict a penalty on him for what he has said on some vague ground that it is unwise in the public interest or unfair to the government. They can only lay a charge against him in the courts alleging violation of a specific law.

Freedom of the person is secured in the same way. The common law, supplemented by statute, defines the offences for which a man may be convicted and imprisoned. The law also authorizes the detention of the mentally unbalanced in institutions. But the sane man who keeps clear of the criminal law has a right to personal freedom. Anyone, of course, may find himself arrested on suspicion of a crime. But here again the law defines very minutely the lawful power of police or others to arrest, and the right of the suspect to be released on bail pending trial. On very serious charges like that of treason, bail is not allowed. However, if the person arrested is not formally charged and tried speedily for some specific offence he can secure his release on habeas corpus, a proceeding in which the courts will order his gaoler to release him unless the gaoler shows that he is lawfully detained under a specific law. The Rule of Law comes into play here also. Police, gaolers, and other officials who exceed their lawful powers of arrest and detention are personally liable to actions for damages for assault, false arrest, and false imprisonment. Independent courts and procedures ensuring fair trial are also necessary to make personal freedom effective.

Respecting freedom of religion, freedom of the press, and freedom of public meeting, it is enough to say here that freedom of the press has substantially the same protection as freedom of speech and expression, that a wide right of public meeting for all lawful purposes is recognized, and that everyone is free to hold such religious convictions and practice such religious observances as he will. It is true that the Church of England is an established state church but the right of dissent is fully recognized, and there are no longer any civil or political disabilities attached to dissent. The same formula applies to all the basic freedoms. The government cannot penalize anyone for his conduct or hamper him in his actions unless he violates a specific law.

How Civil Liberties are Guaranteed

It must be said again that all these civil liberties are at the mercy of Parliament. Parliament does on occasion limit them. For example, in 1936, Parliament passed the Public Order Act which limited somewhat the right of public procession and meeting. The occasion was the recurring street-fights between Fascists and Communists as they tried to break up one another's meetings thus threatening the most basic of all conditions, that of order and general security. Also, in time of war, Parliament authorizes a degree of censorship of expression, and of detention without trial of persons suspected of enemy association. But in times of peace, the majority in Parliament always shows a tender regard for the basic civil liberties.

Moreover, as we have just seen, the law against sedition is not enforced nearly as drastically as its terms could be construed as justifying. That is to say, the executive, the government of the day, which decides whether or not to launch criminal prosecutions against alleged offenders lets slip almost all its opportunities for pressing charges of sedition. It limits itself almost entirely to prosecuting incitements to immediate violence and attempts to undermine the loyalty of the armed forces and the police.

What is the reason for this forbearance of the executive and of the majority in Parliament? Why has Britain had, without formal constitutional guarantees, the best record in the world for protecting civil liberties? Why is there much more freedom of expressing opinions than a plausible interpretation of the existing law would permit? The answers to all these questions are the same. The British people as a whole have an intense attachment to individual freedom. If the majority party in Parliament were to push through laws sharply restricting civil liberties, it would have to expect defeat at the next election. Equally, if the government undertook widespread prosecutions to enforce the sedition laws to the limit, it would arouse formidable protest. Action of either kind might so undermine confidence in the government of the day as to force an immediate election. Moreover, trials for sedition must take place before a jury. Juries are notoriously more concerned with public opinion than with delicate interpretations of the law, and any attempt by the government to use the sedition laws against its political opponents would likely be frustrated by acquittals.

The British concern for civil liberties expresses itself in the crisis of war as well as in times of peace. When war broke out in 1939, Parliament gave wide emergency powers to the executive. Orders-in-council passed under these powers authorized the detention without trial of persons suspected of enemy or hostile associations. When France fell in 1940 before the Nazi tidal wave, there were in Britain some thousands of German refugees who had fled from Nazi Germany before 1939. There was little doubt that most of these were anti-Nazi and therefore trustworthy, but there was equally no certainty that a considerable number of them were not carefully planted Nazi agents. There was no quick, sure way to tell one from the other. Faced with imminent invasion when treachery from within would likely be fatal, the government detained most of these German refugees. As they were not known to have committed any offence they could not be brought to trial, so they were interned without trial.

Even in this desperate situation when Britain stood alone with the world crumbling about her, British passion for fair play and individual liberty would not be stilled. In Parliament and out, the government was subjected to mounting criticism. The government finally agreed to establish independent advisory committees to screen the persons detained and to advise on their continued detention or release. Over a period of time, these advisory committees investigated the *bona fides* of the German refugees who had been detained and recommended the release of the great majority of them. In most instances, the government followed the advice of the advisory committees. The attachment to civil liberties is both sincere and profound.

The main reason for this unfailing public opinion in support of civil liberties is fairly clear. The British people have lived so long together that they have a deep trust in one another. They feel assured that their fellows will not be roused to precipitate action by the glitter of new ideas. Further, their respect for precedent is enormous. The British are ruled, to an irritating degree, by custom. It has even been suggested that the British are able to enjoy such wide civil liberties because in much of their lives they submit voluntarily to the dictatorship of custom. However that may be, the customs by which they live are permeated with conceptions of fair play and mutual respect.

Notions of fair play and mutual respect rest upon belief in the supreme importance of human personality. So the final sanction for civil liberties in Britain is the liberal democratic ideals. As long as these ideals are widely held and ensure the unity of a people, they afford a better guarantee than the express guarantees of a written constitution. For a written constitution, in the long run, is no stronger than the fundamental beliefs of the people make it.

Civil Liberties in the United States

In the United States, there are two lines of legal defence of civil liberties against governments. The first line of defence is substantially the same as in Britain. What is not forbidden by law is permitted. The main differences are in the details of what is forbidden and in the fact that state as well as federal laws have to be taken into account in discovering what is forbidden. Also, the Rule of Law, or the supremacy of law as it is more often called, is a vital principle in the United States. Except where expressly authorized by law to the contrary, government officials must answer according to the ordinary law in the ordinary courts.

Independent courts are available to test the question whether an official has infringed the rights of individuals as these are defined either by common law or by the statute law of a legislature. This line of defence is a protection of considerable importance.

But there is a second and more formidable line of defence in the federal and state constitutions. As we have already seen, certain specific civil liberties, both substantive and procedural, are written into these constitutions, and thus put beyond the reach of both legislatures and executives. Some of the civil liberties guaranteed in the federal constitution are asserted against the federal government only, some against state governments only, and some against both. But the state constitutions also contain bills of rights which repeat, and often go beyond, the provisions of the federal constitution guaranteeing civil liberties. Except where noted to the contrary, the civil liberties to be discussed here are guaranteed against both state and federal governments.

The principle of limited government in this context means that laws enacted in violation of these guarantees to the prejudice of civil liberties are unconstitutional, and the courts will so declare them. Official action infringing on civil liberties in pursuance of an unconstitutional statute is itself unconstitutional and the courts will so hold. Before valid legislation cutting away these civil liberties could be passed, it would be necessary to amend the constitution, or constitutions as the case may be, so as to take away the protection they afford. Unlike the situation in Britain, a mere legislative majority cannot cut down the guaranteed civil liberties.

The various bills of rights in the American constitutions extend to all persons and not merely to citizens. But they protect civil liberties only against governments and not against private persons or organizations. If hoodlums break up religious services in a church, the remedy is not an appeal to the First Amendment of the United States Constitution but to the ordinary law relating to assault, trespass, and public nuisance.

Many of the civil liberties guaranteed in the federal and state constitutions are stated in general terms without any express qualification. They are not, however, to be taken to be absolute. The substantive freedoms of religion, speech, press, and peaceable assembly set out in the First Amendment, for example, cannot be pressed to the point where they disrupt the indispensable public order and general security that government must provide if it is to be useful at all. It would be almost correct to say that the Supreme Court has inserted the word "reasonable" as a qualification on these freedoms in its interpretation of them. It must be said, however, that in recent years the Supreme Court has put a very high value on the importance of these four freedoms for a liberal democratic society, and will strike down statutes that purport to qualify them unless it is convinced that the qualification is clearly necessary for the preservation of public order.

More will be said on the limits of these rights later. At the moment, the important function of the courts, particularly the Supreme Court of the United States, in defining and safeguarding civil liberties must be stressed. There are limitations, and the Supreme Court has the final word on what they are. Some of them are obvious and occasion no disagreement. As Mr. Justice Holmes once pointed out, no one has the right to shout "Fire" in a crowded theatre. Others are much harder to define, and may even vary from time to time. Much will always depend on the personal outlook of the judges, how strongly they hold the liberal democratic values and how much faith they have in the reasonableness of their fellow-men.

Freedom of Religion

Turning now to the most important of the guarantees, the First Amendment of the Constitution provides that "Congress shall make no law respecting an establishment of religion or prohibiting the free exercise thereof." Judicial interpretation of the clause of the Fourteenth Amendment which forbids the states to deprive any person of "life, liberty or property without due process of law" has held that the "liberty" thus protected against the states includes the four freedoms of the First Amendment. So neither Congress nor state legislatures can set up a state church or interfere with the freedom of the individual to worship God in his own way.

The deepest feelings and the strongest convictions of individuals express themselves in their religion. It sums up their judgment of the inner meaning of their lives, and of their relationship to the cosmic scheme of things. The religious system to which each adheres, even when it takes the form of saying there is no God, is the citadel of his personality.

As long as it was believed that unity of religion was the indispensable foundation of political order, the state prescribed an official religion and required everyone to conform. Dissenters, who always appear when there is any freedom to think at all, were required to assert beliefs they did not hold and persecuted for holding unorthodox beliefs. The final indignity to the individual is to deny him the right to hold and express his innermost convictions. The only escape for the dissenters from this humiliation was to seize the government and turn the tables on their persecutors. So persecution on the one side was matched by seditious conspiracy on the other. In this kind of atmosphere, government by consent and peaceful adjustment of differences is impossible. This is why liberal democracy could not come into existence until religious toleration had been accepted. It was necessary first to see that men have enough in common to support a common system of public order without having to agree on all items of religious faith. This discovery was first made by left-wing Puritans in England and America such as John Locke and Roger Williams. Freedom of religion is a fundamental necessity for liberal democracy.

It should not be thought, however, that it is easy to reconcile the imperative claims of public order and freedom of religion. Deep religious convictions demand more than verbal expression and ceremonial practice; they urge the believer to act on them. A faith that does not inspire action is scarcely a faith at all. Moreover, religious beliefs have a tendency to imperialism; they want truth to prevail. But there is a definite limit to the freedom of individuals that can be allowed in the interests of public order. The defining of what belongs to Caesar and what belongs to God is a difficult and seemingly endless process. It accounts for much of the diversity of opinions and actions in a liberal democracy. More will be said about it later.

To take only a few instances in the United States, religious beliefs have led men to practise polygamy, to refuse the obligations of military service, and to refuse to provide medical services for their children, in defiance of existing law. In these cases the Supreme Court has held that the requirements of public order, national security, and public health justified these laws and that the guarantees of religious freedom do not entitle men to ignore these claims.

In a number of states, the law has required school children to salute the flag and affirm their allegiance to the United States daily. The Jehovah's Witnesses, a zealous religious sect, have regarded this ceremony as idolatrous and have forbidden their children to conform. When the children were expelled from school for refusing to conform, the sect challenged this law as a violation of the guarantee of freedom of religion.

In 1940, a majority of the Supreme Court of the United States upheld the validity of the flag salute law.[1] When the same issue reached the Court again in 1943, it reversed its earlier decision and held the flag salute law invalid on the ground that compelling the salute infringed religious convictions and withholding the salute did not imperil any vital public interest.[2] That is to say individuals are not to be compelled to affirm what they do not believe, but where vital public interests are at stake, they may be required to act in contradiction of their religious beliefs. The doubts and hesitations of the Court on this issue show how difficult it is to divide between God and Caesar.

Freedom of Speech and Press

The First Amendment to the Constitution of the United States forbids Congress to make any law "abridging the freedom of speech or of the press." This guarantee covers both speech and writing in every form and would be more accurately described as freedom of expression. The right it protects is not absolute. Common law and statute impose much the same limitations as in Britain except that a sedition law as widely phrased as the British one would no doubt be unconstitutional. This must not be taken to mean that legislatures in the United States have no power to make laws curbing seditious utterances. Congress in both world wars and various state legislatures, particularly since World War II, have

[1]*Minersville School District* v. *Gobitis,* 310 U.S. 586 (1940).
[2]*West Virginia Board of Education* v. *Barnette,* 319 U.S. 624 (1943).

enacted such laws. The Supreme Court of the United States has not always applied a uniform test in deciding on the validity of such laws. For a long time, the prevailing view of the Court was that utterances which had a "bad tendency" to undermine the belief of Americans in the rightness of their form of government and their established way of life were not entitled to the protection of the First Amendment.[1] In recent years, the Court has tended to lean more heavily in favour of freedom of expression by arguing that the only utterances that can lawfully be curbed are those which threaten paramount public interests "not doubtfully and remotely but by clear and present danger."[2]

What constitutes "a clear and present danger" does not depend primarily on the words used but rather on the circumstances of their use and the conditions of the time. In 1951, for example, when there was still considerable public anxiety about the domestic communist menace in the United States, the Supreme Court upheld the constitutionality of the Smith Act of 1940 and the conviction under the Act of eleven top communist leaders in the United States.[8] The Act makes it an offence to advocate the overthrow of government by force; or to help organize a society that engages in such advocacy; or to become a member of such a society; or to conspire with others to commit any of the first three offences. The majority decision upholding the conviction affirmed the clear and present danger rule. The decisive facts were the conspiring and advocating as part of a tightly organized plan for revolutionary action controlled by the convicted persons themselves and held at the service of the Soviet Union. However, six years later, in a decision which reflected the abatement of public concern over domestic communism, the Supreme Court narrowed the application of the Smith Act in determining that mere advocacy, without incitement to action, was not a crime under the Act.[4]

Other federal statutes directed against communists, notably the Internal Security (McCarran) Act of 1950 and the Communist Control Act of 1954, have also been subjected to careful judicial

[1]*Gitlow* v. *N.Y.*, 268 U.S. 652 (1925).
[2]*Thomas* v. *Collins*, 323 U.S. 516 (1944).
[8]*Dennis* v. *U.S.*, 354 U.S. 298 (1951).
[4]*Yates et al* v. *U.S.*, 354 U.S. 298 (1957).

scrutiny. Although no firm line of court decisions has yet emerged, it is clear that communist groups must register with the government or be prosecuted. Membership in such a registered group is not illegal but the member must contemplate a restriction of his privileges as a citizen and must always face the possibility—under the clear and present danger rule—of prosecution where his teaching or advocacy of violent overthrowal of the government constitutes incitement to action.

Freedom of the Person and of Meeting

In the United States, as in Britain, a person has the right to be free of physical restraint in going about any activity he pleases as long as it is not forbidden by law. In addition, this freedom of the person is further protected by a number of guarantees in federal and state constitutions. To describe the exact scope of them all would require an essay on constitutional law. The most important of them are as follows.

The Thirteenth Amendment of the United States Constitution forbids slavery and involuntary servitude, "except as a punishment for crime whereof the party shall have been duly convicted." It was adopted expressly for the purpose of outlawing negro slavery but it is equally a protection for all. No legislature can enact laws subjecting persons to servitude, and private persons cannot exact forced labour of anyone. The Fifth Amendment forbids Congress, and the Fourteenth Amendment forbids the states, to "deprive any person of life, liberty, or property, without due process of law." The due process clauses, as they are called, are important buttresses of freedom of the person.

The Fourth Amendment, and similar clauses in the state constitutions, affirm "the right of the people to be secure in their persons, houses, papers, and effects against unreasonable searches and seizures. . . ." General warrants are outlawed and, subject to certain exceptions carefully limited by judicial interpretation, no person can be arrested and no person or place searched except upon a warrant sworn out before a judicial officer "describing the place to be searched, and the persons or things to be seized." The main purpose served by "unreasonable searches and seizures" is to compel the person, in effect, to give self-incriminating evidence.

The main purpose of the Amendment then is to prevent self-incrimination before trial.

Anyone who has been arrested must either be charged with a criminal offence and given a fair and speedy trial, or be released. The procedural safeguards of this right contained in common law and statute are much the same in their terms as those found in Britain and have been referred to earlier. The arrested person has also, however, the second line of defence in the Constitution. Among other things, the Constitution of the United States forbids excessive bail, guarantees habeas corpus, public jury trial, the right of the accused to know the charges against him, to confront the witnesses against him in open court, to have counsel, and not to be compelled to be a witness against himself.[1] Broadly speaking, legislatures have no power to take away these procedural civil rights which are designed to ensure that no one will linger in prison without trial and that no one will be convicted without a fair trial.

The First Amendment forbids Congress to abridge "the right of the people peaceably to assemble." This constitutional right is subject to two principal limitations. First, the assembly must be peaceable. Unruly and turbulent meetings that threaten a breach of the peace do not enjoy its protection. Second, those who want to meet must find a lawful place to meet. They cannot assemble on private property without the consent of the owner or tenant, and they have no right to obstruct traffic or passage in public places.

Municipal governments through their ordinances, and local police acting under authority of those ordinances, have considerable, but ill-defined, power to regulate the place and conduct of meetings of any size in the interests of local convenience and order. In actual practice, many such ordinances and much local police action put unconstitutional obstacles in the way of the meetings of unpopular groups. For example, when a privately owned hall is put at the service of an unpopular group, the owner may find his licence cancelled on some subterfuge. To determine how well the right of public meeting is actually protected, it would be necessary to study the conduct of municipal governments across the United States.

[1]See Art. i, sect. 9, and Amendments v to viii inclusive.

Effectiveness of Constitutional Guarantees

There are still other clauses of the United States Constitution affording protection for civil liberties but the principal ones have been discussed sufficiently to show the scope and character of the guarantees of individual freedom against encroachment by the government. How useful these guarantees are to individuals depends, of course, on how well they are observed and enforced. They may be flouted by legislatures and government officials, and if they are, redress can only be had by bringing allegations of in-fringement before the courts, and securing loyal enforcement of them by the courts. Even then, the courts cannot enforce the Constitution in every corner of the United States single-handed. As has been wisely said with particular reference to reliance on the Supreme Court of the United States for the maintenance of free-dom of speech, "Nine men in Washington cannot hold a nation to ideals which it is determined to betray."[1]

Actually, there has been substantial, but by no means wholesale, infringement of the guaranteed civil liberties. Congress and many of the state legislatures have from time to time made, and govern-ments have enforced, laws infringing the constitutional guarantee of freedom of speech. It has often been impossible to secure fair trial for negroes on criminal charges, and it has not always been possible to secure fair trial for widely detested accused persons. Unpopular groups have often found they could not exercise their right of peaceable assembly because local police or mayors put obstacles in their way. Officials charged with enforcing the criminal law have often violated the provisions of the Fourth Amendment outlawing unreasonable searches and seizures. Even when arrests have been lawfully made, the police in many juris-dictions often use "third degree" methods to extract incriminating evidence from the person in custody. Other instances could be given.[2]

Generally speaking, despite constitutional guarantees, civil liberties have not been as well protected in the United States as in

[1] T. R. Powell, quoted in Z. Chafee, *Free Speech in the United States*, revised ed. (Harvard University Press, 1941), at p. x.
[2] For a recent estimate of the effectiveness of the guarantees of civil rights, see Robert E. Cushman, *Civil Liberties in the United States* (Cornell University Press, Ithaca, 1956).

Britain. The fundamental explanation is a simple one. The United States is a young country still creating a national tradition and only slowly absorbing into it an extraordinarily heterogeneous population. There is still much suspicion and hostility between groups of diverse origins and customary ways of life. Much of the worry about disloyalty is due to a feeling of insecurity about persons of foreign origin who may not yet have been wholly won over to the American way of life. To put it in the terms of the earlier discussion about Britain, the American people have not lived long enough together for mutual trust and mutual respect to permeate the entire society. In so far as these are lacking, the difficulty of ensuring respect for the civil liberties of all is correspondingly greater.

This explanation underlines the immense importance of the constitutional guarantees in the United States. Where moral censure of every infringement of civil liberties is not swift and sure, the second line of defence provided by the Constitution is vital. In the first place, persons belonging to hard-pressed minorities can get their civil liberties vindicated and proclaimed if they are able to fight the issue through the courts. Second, the Constitution is a never-ceasing educator in tolerance and fair play. Third, it is a promise and a pledge for the future, counselling patience. As long as the Constitution stands and Americans continue to affirm their loyalty to it, those whose civil liberties are ill protected now still have reason to hope. The limited appeal that communism has had for the negro is probably due in part to a belief that Americans will not always be able to reconcile the generally inferior condition in which the negro still finds himself with loyalty to the constitutional guarantees of civil liberties and to liberal democratic ideals.[1]

In fact, the Constitution is the American conscience. It does not always prevent intolerant and arbitrary action by legislatures and officials. But its promptings never cease, and so far the American people have always repented of unconstitutional excesses, repudiated the leaders associated with these lapses, and repealed

[1]Gunnar Myrdal. *An American Dilemma* (Harper & Bros., New York, 1944), vol. i, ch. 1.

most of the offending legislation. Every generation has produced large numbers of staunch defenders of civil liberties whose devotion renews the pledges of the Constitution. Viewed in this larger perspective and remembering the heterogeneous turmoil of the United States, the achievement has been remarkable, giving still larger promise for the future.

This promise is illustrated by the widespread concern in recent years over ways and means of improving the protection of civil liberties. There are several reasons for this concern. First, the constitutional guarantees discussed above are guarantees against governments only. Lynching is a crime committed by private persons but not a violation of civil liberties by a government. Although lynching is now a rare occurrence, it is still true that intimidation and violence in one form or another by private persons and groups of persons are much greater threats to civil liberties in the United States than actual violations by governments. Second, the question how far there is any legal remedy for infringements by private persons depends on existing federal and state law. It depends on whether the existing laws make it a criminal offence or authorize a civil suit for damages when private persons infringe the civil liberties guaranteed in the Constitution. Where violence or intimidation is used, existing law does provide a remedy, but there are subtler means of violation where no such remedy exists. Third, whether the violation is by a government or a private person, punishment or redress has to be sought in the courts. For this, a person needs financial resources, good legal advice, and the co-operation of the law enforcement officials of the court concerned. Many lack the knowledge or the means to enforce their rights, and co-operation of the law enforcement officials is not always easily secured.

In 1946, President Truman appointed a Committee on Civil Rights to investigate the need for additional legislation and for other more effective procedures for protecting civil liberties. While asserting that civil liberties were being better enforced than ever before, the Committee found an alarming amount of violation in 1947. In its Report, it made many recommendations. The following are particularly pertinent to the present discussion.

The Committee urged legislation by Congress to ensure that every violation of a civil liberty by private persons would be a criminal offence. It asked specially for a federal anti-lynching law. It proposed a joint congressional committee on civil liberties to concern itself with legislative protection, and a permanent Commission on Civil Rights to make a continuous review of the whole question of protection of civil liberties, and report thereon to the President. It recommended that the state governments set up a parallel set of agencies devoted to the same purposes. These recommendations suggest the broad scope of the Committee's proposals. The enforcement of civil liberties was to become a new and vigorous government activity on an extended scale.

Like all proposals for extending government activity, this one had a political background and became focused in a political issue. President Truman committed himself to the implementing of the Report as far as federal action could do so, but only succeeded in rousing the "Dixiecrat" revolt in the Democratic party. Although President Truman made the matter an issue in the 1948 presidential election and won resoundingly, he was subsequently unable to enact civil rights legislation. President Eisenhower's bills also met the same fate until 1957 when Congress finally approved a watered-down compromise civil rights bill which provided for a civil rights commission and strengthened federal enforcement procedures.

The long struggle with Congress over civil rights legislation underlines the basic difficulty. Despite the Constitution, racial and religious prejudices are still important forces in many parts of the United States, and Congress reflects local and sectional feeling. Even if civil liberties were fully "nationalized" and federal laws and federal agencies amply provided for enforcing them, enforcement would run into many of the difficulties experienced in trying to enforce the prohibition laws. For that matter, lynching is now a crime by standard legal definition. The difficulty is to get law enforcement officers to prosecute and juries to convict. State action in a democracy cannot get very far in advance of the sentiments and prejudices of large sections of the people. If it does, it outrages those sections and threatens political unity which is the basis of all hope for the future. For full enforcement of the civil liberties of all, there must be all-embracing mutual trust and mutual respect. Government, of course, can do many things to promote trust and respect, but it cannot be a substitute for the slow, hard process of education.

CIVIL LIBERTIES IN CANADA

Broadly speaking, the fundamental civil liberties with which we are concerned here are substantially the same in Canada as in Britain. What is not forbidden by the law is permitted. The common law, except as amended and supplemented by statute of the appropriate legislature, is the law of Canada and of all provinces except Quebec. Canadian legislatures have not greatly modified the common law rules by which the scope of civil liberties is mainly determined.

In those matters which come within the legislative authority of the provinces, Quebec is ruled by civil law as modified and supplemented by statutes of the Quebec legislature. Therefore, in so far as civil liberties fall within the legislative power of the provinces, the content of these liberties in Quebec depends on civil law rules and on statutes of the Quebec legislature.

However, the resulting differences between Quebec and the rest of the country are not as great as might be expected. First, most of the effective limitations on civil liberties are imposed by the criminal law which is exclusively a matter for the federal Parliament.[1] Second, the Supreme Court of Canada has held specifically that it is beyond the power of provincial legislatures to restrict the freedom of the press and that any such restriction is a matter solely for the Parliament of Canada.[2] Presumably, the reasoning of the Court applies to the other essential civil liberties as well and it is doubtful how far these fall at all within the ambit of provincial authority set out in section 92 of the British North America Act.

As noted earlier, the criminal law in Canada has been codified in the Criminal Code, a statute of the federal Parliament. The

[1]After twenty years on the statute books of Quebec, the Padlock Law was ruled ultra vires by a majority of the Supreme Court partly because it trespassed on the criminal law jurisdiction of the federal government. See *Switzman* v. *Ebling and Attorney-General of Quebec*, 1957, 7 D.L.R. (2nd Series) 337.
[2]Reference re Alberta Press Bill, 1938, S.C.R. 100.

Code is largely a legislative restatement of the common law relating to crimes. For example, it incorporates, by clear implication, the common law definition of sedition. However, the Code adds some illustrative definitions of a qualifying nature on the question of what amounts to a seditious intention. A recent decision of the Supreme Court of Canada suggests that sedition will be more narrowly defined in Canada than it has been under the classical British definitions of the offence.[1] As there is no attempt to enforce the law of sedition to the limit in Britain, it does not necessarily follow that, in actual practice, a wider freedom of expression will be upheld in the Canadian courts than in the British.

Subject to the rather indefinite qualifications noted in the preceding paragraphs, the law relating to civil liberties is essentially the same in both countries. The law in Canada protects freedom of religion, freedom of speech, and freedom of the press from interference by the executive branch of government. It supports freedom of the person from arbitrary arrest and detention without trial, and freedom of public meeting. It provides the safeguards of habeas corpus and fair trial before courts independent of the executive under the protective procedure briefly outlined in chapter XIII.[2]

Unlike the British constitution, the Canadian constitution is partially written in the British North America Act and its several amendments. But the British North America Act does not contain a bill of rights such as is found in the Constitution of the United States. The civil liberties outlined above remain, as in Britain, at the mercy of the appropriate legislature. However, a few matters which have important implications for civil liberties are guaranteed in the Act and put beyond the reach of either federal or provincial legislatures. Section 93 guarantees certain rights of particular religious groups to separate schools. Section 133 guarantees the right to use the English or French language in certain public proceedings. Section 99 ensures security of tenure of office for the judges of the Superior Courts in the provinces.

[1]*Boucher* v. *The King*, (1951), 2 D.L.R. 369. The judgments in this case contain an excellent discussion of the problem of the proper scope for freedom of expression.
[2]See pp. 434-5 *infra*.

These provisions remain amongst the excepted clauses which still can only be altered by an Act of the British Parliament.

While the existing safeguards of civil liberties have been reasonably effective for most persons, there has been a number of disturbing incidents in recent years. In 1937, the Alberta legislature showed itself prepared to restrict freedom of the press. (Actually, the bill in question was held to be *ultra vires* by the Supreme Court of Canada.) In the same year, the Padlock Law was enacted in Quebec. (Subsequently, in 1957, it too was cut down by the Supreme Court.) The Act forbade the printing and distribution of any literature "propagating or tending to propagate communism or bolshevism," and this without any further defining of what communism or bolshevism is or what kind of literature tends to propagate this creed. Also, it authorized the Attorney General, on receipt of proof which satisfied him that a building was being used to propagate communism or bolshevism, to order the closing of such building, thus putting on the owner the burden of trying to get the courts to reverse the order.

Under powers conferred on it by the War Measures Act, the Federal Government passed an order-in-council authorizing the suspension of habeas corpus, an action of which it later took advantage in arresting, detaining, and interrogating at length a number of persons in the espionage investigation of 1946. In 1945, three orders-in-council under the War Measures Act authorized the deportation to Japan of several thousand Canadian citizens of Japanese origin. (In the event, although the privy council upheld their legality, no action was ever taken under these orders.)

Other instances could be given but these are enough to show that Canadian legislatures, and governments acting under authority given them by legislatures, sometimes press upon civil liberties. There is also evidence to show that in some localities, the police ignore the law in attempts to extract incriminating evidence from persons they have arrested, coming close to the "third degree" methods often practised in the United States. Further, it is by no means unknown for municipal authorities to put obstacles in the way of unpopular groups that are trying to distribute literature and/or exercise the freedom of public meeting. The Canadian record on these two points is not as good as that of Britain although markedly better than that of the United States. Finally, in contrast to some parts of the United States where racial feeling often runs strong, a very high standard of fairness of trial of accused persons has been maintained in Canada.

A Bill of Rights for Canada?

In times past, there has been a strong disposition in Canada to be content with the same kind of protection of civil liberties as exists in Britain. After all, it was said, civil liberties are better protected in Britain than in the United States, which shows that the only effective guarantee is a vigilant public opinion. In recent years, there has been a distinct change in attitude. The pressure of the provincial and war time federal legislation noted above on civil liberties has perhaps been the principal cause of the change. It is now being pointed out that even though there may be a national public opinion strongly supporting civil liberties, that has not prevented a provincial public opinion in Quebec in favour of a Padlock Law, and in Alberta in favour of restrictions on freedom of the press. Moreover, it is not at all clear what the distribution of legislative power between the Dominion and the provinces really is respecting civil liberties. The existence of the federal system makes the situation more confused and complex than in Britain.

Further, the Canadian people lack the homogeneity of the British people. Like the United States, Canada is still in the process of absorbing into the national community, large numbers of persons of diverse origins. The process of absorption is slow and the development of mutual respect and mutual confidence between groups of diverse ethnic and cultural origins is still slower. Hence suspicion and latent hostility persist, and may break out from time to time in the form of oppressive legislation directed at the members of minority groups. The obvious parallel with the United States suggests the desirability of a bill of rights in the constitution to prevent legislative encroachment on civil liberties. It is true that civil liberties have been better protected in Britain than in the United States. It is also true that without bills of rights in the federal and state constitutions, civil liberties in the United States would have suffered still greater infringement.

Many of the groups being absorbed into the Canadian community come from countries which have never enjoyed effective civil liberties. One of the vital tasks is to teach them the content and meaning of the Anglo-American constitutional tradition. At present, it is difficult to expound Canadian civil liberties because there is no authoritative statement of them. It would be an immense aid to the education of newcomers and of each generation of young Canadians if they could learn the vital pledges of mutual respect from a bill of rights enshrined in the constitution. What was said earlier about this point for the United States is equally valid for Canada.

Arguments in favour of inserting a bill of rights in the British North America Act received aid and comfort from the Universal Declaration of Human Rights adopted by the General Assembly of the United Nations in 1948. Significantly, the Declaration recites the liberal democratic ideals discussed in chapter II and proclaims as universal human rights the substance of the civil liberties long recognized in the Anglo-American world. Canada voted in favour of the Declaration in the General Assembly, although in the discussions preceding its adoption the Canadian delegates expressed some reservations on points which clearly fell within the powers of provincial legislatures. The Declaration, it was felt, imposed some kind of moral obligation on Canada, as one of the members of the United Nations, to honour its terms. The most effective way to give express recognition of this obligation, many contended, was to incorporate it in the written Constitution.

In response to such considerations, the Saskatchewan Legislature enacted a Bill of Rights in 1947. Among other things, it affirmed the traditional civil liberties in so far as a provincial legislature has power to do so. Of course, the Saskatchewan Legislature can repeal this Act tomorrow, but while it stays on the statute-book it stands as a solemn affirmation of the basic civil liberties.

Moved by similar considerations, the Parliament of Canada set up a joint committee of both houses to explore the matter in 1947 and 1948. Two years later, a Special Senate Committee on Human Rights and Fundamental Freedoms heard much testimony and received strong representations from many quarters urging that a comprehensive bill of rights be inserted in the British North America Act. The Committee approved the idea but noted that some parts of the field of civil liberties were within the jurisdiction of the provincial legislatures. Accordingly, it recommended that any amendment to the Act designed to put civil liberties beyond the control of all legislatures should not proceed without the concurrence of the provinces. It expressed the hope that such concurrence would be reached in time. Meanwhile, as an interim measure, it proposed that the Parliament of Canada should enact a bill of rights covering those aspects of civil liberties which fall within its legislative jurisdiction.

The first step in implementing this recommendation of the Senate Committee was not taken until 1958. In the dying days of the parliamentary session Mr. Diefenbaker, an ardent champion of a bill of rights while in the opposition, introduced a bill "for the recognition and protection of human rights and fundamental freedoms." After a brief discussion, the bill was held over to the 1959 session, re-introduced with government amendments, and approved in 1960. The bill is primarily declaratory only, for it creates no rights that did not exist before and imposes no penalties other than those already provided by common law and other statutes. Whether such legislation, subject as it is to the whims of parliament as long as it is not embodied in the Constitution, will achieve the expectations of its promoters, remains to be seen. In any event, the civil liberties it seeks to protect and identify are essentially negative in character. Constitutional guarantees of them can do no more than require governments to leave individuals alone to exercise the civil liberties as they are able and as they see fit. Actual protection of civil liberties in practice is essentially a judicial function. If a government infringes them, the appropriate and effective remedy is an action in the courts to punish the violation.

Beyond this range of negative rights there is another area of positive rights which in the minds of some should also be incorporated into any bill of rights. The United Nations Declaration on Human Rights, for example, goes much farther than merely proclaiming the fundamental civil liberties that have been discussed so far in this chapter. It goes on to declare that everyone has a right to social security, to education, to just and favourable conditions of work, and to a standard of living adequate for the health and well-being of himself and his family.

The Special Committee of the Senate received representations urging that this enlarged concept of civil rights be incorporated in the proposed bill of rights for Canada. One difficulty with this suggestion is that some of these matters now are, and in the exigencies of the Canadian federal system are likely for a long time to remain, under the jurisdiction of the provincial legislatures. The Committee declined therefore to make recommendations which would have impinged directly on the sphere of the provinces.

However, there is a more fundamental objection to incorporating such rights into a charter of liberty. There will be no dissent from the desirability of affording to every person, in some way or other, the positive benefits of education, security, and an adequate standard of living as outlined in the United Nations Declaration. It does not necessarily follow that they can be effectively guaranteed by provisions in a constitution. Enjoyment of the positive benefits of education and an adequate standard of living cannot be ensured merely by declaring them in a constitution and keeping the courts open to punish violations. If individuals cannot provide these benefits for themselves and their children by their own efforts, then these benefits can only be provided by invoking the whole apparatus of the positive state. There must be a political party which promises these benefits as part of its policy, a firm majority for that party in the legislature, sometimes a vote of public funds to provide the benefits, and always a special administrative arm of the government to supervise and enforce. If public opinion comes out decisively for government action to provide these aids to the good life, they will be provided up to the level that the intelligence, organizing capacity, and resources of the community make possible. Failing this, little or nothing is gained by writing the programme of the positive state into the constitution.

RACIAL AND RELIGIOUS DISCRIMINATION

A matter closely related to the foregoing is the question what, if anything, is to be done by governments about the all too frequent practices of racial and religious discrimination. The most striking illustration of these in North America is the segregation laws of the Southern states of the United States, requiring separate accommodation for negroes and whites in trains, schools, theatres and the like. Aside from these laws, however, there is, in both the United States and Canada, frequent discrimination on racial or religious grounds in employment practices, and in access to housing and places of public accommodation. Most of these practices are not contrary to any existing law, being in the area of economic and other freedom granted to individuals to keep clear of association with persons they do not like.

The Senate Committee heard evidence on racial and religious discrimination in Canada but made no recommendation respecting it. The President's Committee on Civil Rights in the United States recommended legislative and executive action by state and federal governments against many of these discriminatory practices. Ten states have enacted laws, and half-a-dozen major cities have enacted by-laws, directed against discriminatory practices in employment. A number of clauses in the Saskatchewan Bill of Rights Act assert the right of every person to obtain employment, engage in any legal occupation, own or rent property, belong to trade or professional associations, and to enjoy the facilities of places of public accommodation, regardless of his race, creed, or colour. The Ontario Fair Employment Practices Act which came into force in 1951 forbids discrimination in employment on racial or religious grounds.

It would be generally agreed that liberal democratic governments should keep their own skirts clean, avoiding discrimination in all activities over which they have direct and effective control. Aside from setting a good example in this way, there are wide differences of opinion on what can be done by legislation and government action in these fields. Laws against discrimination by private persons obviously create immense problems of enforcement. Governments have found it hard enough to enforce minimum wage and maximum hours laws. To take two examples, how are they to supervise effectively the hiring and firing practices of a multitude of employers and the letting of premises by landlords? Some strong supporters of civil liberties are opposed to such laws on the ground that prejudice and discrimination cannot be prevented by law at all. The whole question of how to deal with racial and religious discrimination is a disputed matter of public policy and no fair statement of the pros and cons can be made in a short space. One important consideration, however, must be pointed out.

Discriminatory practices, particularly in employment and in access to public health services and public education facilities, are a *pro tanto* denial of the liberal democratic ideal of rough equality of opportunity. Despite frequent instances of discrimination, the strength of that ideal is manifest in most of the varied government activities described in chapter v, particularly in the large social security programme designed to promote equality. Indeed the whole development of the positive state is an assertion that the negative approach to civil liberties is not enough. Civil liberties as discussed in this chapter are negative, aimed at securing freedom from outside restraint. But without positive aids and supports, the freedom of the individual in a complex society may be largely illusory. This is commonly expressed by saying what is needed is freedom *for,* and not merely freedom *from,* something. Freedom for the realization of the possibilities of human personality requires health, education, and fair opportunities of employment.

The strength of this conviction in the world today is further illustrated by the United Nations Declaration of Human Rights which states that everyone has a right to social security, to education, to good working conditions, and to an adequate standard of living. These are aspirations easier to phrase than to realize in the life of a society, but they show the strength of the current demands for equality of opportunity. However this is to be accomplished, by positive government action, by changing the hearts of men, or both, pressure for what is called positive freedom seems likely to continue. It is in this context that racial and religious discrimination must be considered.

CIVIL LIBERTIES IN DANGEROUS TIMES

The basis of all civil liberties is a tolerant acceptance of diversity and individual differences. The home of civil liberties is in those countries where liberal democratic ideals have inculcated a deep mutual respect among men, despite their differences. As we saw in chapter II, there is no place for civil liberties in Fascist, Nazi, and Communist regimes. In the Anglo-American countries in the last thirty years, zealous partisans of these regimes have made full use of civil liberties to denounce liberal democratic ideals, and to try to undermine liberal democratic institutions in preparation for dosing us with their own nostrums. Of course, if they were once able to get control of the government, whether through peaceful or violent means, they would immediately destroy all civil liberties. At any rate, these have been their tactics in all countries where they have secured control. The creeds and the practice of modern dictatorships and the threat they make to liberal democratic societies have led to strong demands for reconsidering the whole philosophy of civil liberties.

In considering this question, discussion will be limited to freedom of expression, whether in words or writing. It is the heart of the whole issue. The case for other civil liberties is no stronger than the case for freedom of expression. The analysis that follows deals only with the question what a person should be allowed to say if he can find listeners. It is not concerned with the question what forum, if any, should be made available for opinions we decide to tolerate. It has nothing to do with the question of dismissal of civil servants for radical opinions. These are distinct problems which cannot be discussed here except to say that a government not only is entitled but has a positive duty to its people to be sure of the loyalty of its civil servants. The perplexing point is how to make sure without unfairly prejudicing the position and prospects of the civil servant whose loyalty, while not disproved, is doubtful.

Many who are seriously concerned to defend civil liberties balk at defending them for those who will not admit a reciprocal obligation to defend them for others. Tolerance, they say, must not be extended to the intolerant, freedom must not be allowed to be used to destroy freedom. On what ground can freedom of expression be claimed now by those who will destroy it when they have the power? What principle of fair play is it that requires the acceptance of players who will not play according to the rules?

Further to this issue, it is pointed out that the theory and practice of civil liberties were developed mainly in the Anglo-

American communities. During the latter part of the nineteenth century, these communities established themselves so firmly in the world that the possibility of serious civil disaffection or menacing foreign aggression almost disappeared from the consciousness of their people. They came to regard public order as almost impregnable, something that could be taken for granted. It was easy, and even desirable, in those circumstances to urge civil liberties in almost unqualified terms. It was easy to insist that everyone should be allowed to talk though the heavens fall when nobody believed there was any serious risk that they would fall.

This serene confidence is perhaps best illustrated by Thomas Jefferson in his first inaugural address as President of the United States in 1801 when he said: "If there be any among us who wish to dissolve this union, or change its republican form, let them stand undisturbed as monuments of the safety with which error of opinion may be tolerated where reason is left free to combat it."

Assumptions in the Defence of Free Speech

The most important point about this statement is its assumptions, what it takes for granted. First, it assumes that most men are rational, that they will support what reason shows to be right and true. Second, it assumes the rightness of the union of the American states on a republican basis. It therefore concludes that public order and political unity are impregnable as long as there is freedom of speech. Likewise, John Milton, one of Jefferson's spiritual ancestors in seventeenth century England, urged that truth and falsehood be allowed to grapple, for "who ever knew Truth put to the worse in a free and open encounter?"

Something must be said about these assumptions. It is clear that freedom of expression and discussion will accomplish little unless most of the participants in it are deeply concerned with truth, prepared to follow the argument wherever it goes, and to modify their convictions as the amassing of evidence and the unfolding of logic make their positions untenable. They must be genuine seekers with a sense of curiosity and wonder that is continually refreshed by the flow of discussion. They must be listeners as well as talkers, respectful of what the other side has to say. If, on the other hand, both sides in debate have dogmatic beliefs that will not yield to any demonstration, if they are seeking to convince but unwilling to be convinced, if they are ready to falsify the evidence to gain their point, freedom of speech will drive them further apart instead of bringing them closer together. If the mass of men were as irrational as the Fascists and Nazis said they were, the faith in reason and in freedom of expression would be entirely misplaced. Actually, of course, the experience of the Anglo-American liberal democracies in particular shows that there are conditions in which the faith is justified. The basic problem is to identify these conditions.

Before the members of a society can make fruitful use of freedom of speech, they must be conscious of some underlying unity that transcends difference of opinion. They must believe in one another's reasonableness and have a common loyalty to the pursuit of truth. They must have some measure of agreement on what amounts to proof of the truth of an assertion. If they differ seriously on this point, discussion will not bring them closer together. To be specific, if economic classes can see only their own class interests, there will be one proof which convinces a capitalist and another proof which convinces a proletarian, but no common standard of proof to umpire discussion. A game without generally accepted rules soon ceases to be a game.

If men are as deeply divided in a society made up of economic classes as the prevailing interpretation of Marxist theory says they are, there is no basis for Jefferson's confidence that public order and political unity will stand the shocks that freedom of speech involves. The real basis of Jefferson's confidence as applied to the United States of his day, was the belief that Americans were united in support of the ideals he had stated in the Declaration of Independence, and that they would always uphold a union dedicated to the pursuit of these ideals. Belief in a unity that transcends differences of opinion is the only basis for such confidence today in any of the three countries under discussion. Widespread and firm belief in the liberal democratic ideals is the condition on which freedom of expression is constructive rather than disruptive.

Dangers of Division on Fundamentals

It is possible to see now why some sincere defenders of freedom of speech want to deny it to communists and the holders of other authoritarian creeds like Fascism and Nazism. These creeds deny the liberal democratic ideals, and they reject, either expressly or by implication, the rationality of man. They cannot enter into the fellowship of free men, and they use freedom of speech destructively rather than constructively.

The argument for denial can be made even clearer by looking briefly at John Milton and John Locke, the two great champions of religious toleration in seventeenth century England. Milton, arguing for the right to print and publish without licence from the government, limited his claim for toleration to those of the Protestant faith, to those who accepted the Scriptures as the final standard of proof and of revealed truth. He expressly excluded Roman Catholics because they recognized in the institutionalized authority of their Church another standard of proof and of truth. In its acceptance of the Scriptures, the Protestant group was united on fundamentals and thus able to discuss constructively. John Locke also excluded Roman Catholics because they denied any obligation to keep faith with heretics. That is to say, they were not comprehended within a unity that transcended differences of opinion. He excluded atheists because they cannot be bound by an oath, and hence cannot be contained by any obligation to society. He excluded also those "who give themselves up to the protection and service of another prince," giving as an example, Mohammedans.

Milton and Locke, living in the commotion and strife of seventeenth century England, restricted freedom of expression to those whom they thought could be trusted to use it constructively. Ardent believers in freedom of thought and speech, they did not think public order was sufficiently secure to allow freedom of speech to those who would try to undermine it. When we come to John Stuart Mill who lived in the security and peace of mid-nineteenth century England, we find him arguing for freedom of expression in almost absolute terms. He brushed aside the suggestion that society needs to be protected against subversive and disloyal speech, insisting instead that it is the individual who needs to be protected against society. He did not propose discrimination against Roman Catholics because, in his day, their loyalty to their Church no longer was in active conflict with their loyalty to Britain. The limitations he proposed on freedom of expression would cover libel, slander, and inflammatory incitements to immediate violence, but little else.

Returning now to the present situation, we find the whole world convulsed with the clash of rival systems of ideas which threaten war and imperil the security of the nation states. Within Britain, the United States, and Canada, there are active groups that reject the existing basis of public order and are determined to undermine it, and to overthrow it by force if necessary. In these circumstances, it is not surprising that many find more affinity with Milton and Locke than with Jefferson and Mill. We have lost some of the serene confidence that Jefferson and Mill had in the impregnability of tolerant liberal societies. In Germany and Italy, we have seen freedom of expression destroyed by electorates voting repressive regimes into power. We are alarmed by the danger of a division on fundamentals such as existed between Protestants and Catholics in seventeenth century England. In those communists who take orders from Moscow, we face again the problem of those "who give themselves up to the protection and service of another prince." What is to be said concerning the argument that freedom of expression should be denied to those who cannot be counted on to observe the rules of the game?

The Justification of Freedom of Speech

In the first place, the right to free speech is not absolute. The maintenance of public order and security comes first. That is the justification of laws forbidding inflammatory incitements to violence which endanger public order. In the second place, what constitutes an immediate threat to public order and national security will vary according to circumstances. If the liberal democracies were at open war with the Soviet Union, communist agitation aimed at getting or keeping control of labour unions would fall into that category. If the relationships between the two countries were on a pacific basis, such agitation would not be an immediate threat to public order and national security. But there may be some point in the cold war when it will be. The critical case for discussion is whether to forbid disloyal and subversive talk which aims at present only to undermine belief in the rightness of the liberal democratic order as a preparation for its overthrow by force at some future time.

The test which a liberal democracy should apply to this issue is clear enough. Will the forbidding of such talk further or hamper the realization of liberal democratic ideals? No doubt subversive propaganda wins some converts. Every such convert is a loss. No society can look with complacency on the weakening of belief in its unifying ideals. It is still pertinent, however, to ask why they are converted.

Most of them are converted to a belief in violent solutions because of some rankling sense of injustice, a conviction of the deep inadequacy of existing society. This sense of injustice may be justified or not in particular instances, but it is at least clear that the liberal democratic societies under discussion here are still far from ensuring adequate opportunity for self-realization of all their people. As long as this remains true there will be the discontented, prepared to contemplate rebellion. The only effective way to cope with them is to moderate or remove the discontent by education, remedial laws, or other community action.

It is easy to make laws which impose punishment for subversive propaganda. But in the circumstances just outlined, this will not stop it. It will continue underground. Moreover, repression sharpens the sense of injustice and provides an added argument for desperate measures. There is no doubt at all that the loyalty of the mass of men to liberal democracy has been greatly strengthened by the right to freedom of expression. They have felt that they have a stake in a society that allows them to express the passion they feel about their deepest grievances. Thus repressive laws are likely to fail in their immediate purpose of maintaining loyalty.

The gravest danger in repression is that it excuses the liberal democrat from arguing the case for his ideals and for the highly developed procedures for pursuing them. When he is not openly confronted by the arguments against them, he is not constantly reminding himself and his fellows of the case in favour of them. The surest way to keep beliefs fresh and strong is to exercise them in debate against the strongest criticism of them that can be made. We then know at any moment why we believe what we believe.

Repression would give us, for a time, a false sense of security. We would not be outraged daily by hearing ideas we hate. Because social discontent did not break out in violent expression, we would tell ourselves that there were no serious social maladjustments to be met. We would develop a superficial sense of well-being and fail to brace ourselves, in either knowledge or morale, for the kind of problems we have to meet. This is a sort of aspirin therapy. If we take two or three tablets five or six times a day, we do not know whether we have any aches and pains we should be attending to or not.

Freedom for rebellious and revolutionary utterance is a safety valve which gives warning of the existence of dangerous pressures in society. The only effective way to fight the contagion of disloyalty is to get at its causes. A society that descends to repressive measures is losing faith in its ability to win and keep loyalty. This is bound to be fatal. Authoritarian regimes can continue indefinitely even if they are out of touch with the problems and thoughts of their people. Liberal democracy lives only in the hearts of its citizens. If it cannot be kept alive there by free discussion, it certainly cannot be kept alive by repression.

It would be hard to defend freedom of speech as a sacred personal right of those who will deny it to others if they get a chance. But the merit or lack of merit of the particular claimant is not the issue. The issue is what to do in order to maintain and further the unifying ideals. The answer suggested here is that little or nothing will be accomplished and much will be lost by banning the subversive speech of even confessed revolutionaries.

CHAPTER XV

THE CIVIL SERVICE

THE threefold classification of governmental powers placed the civil service as a minor branch of the executive. This classification was worked out in a period when central governments had very few functions and these were carried out or "executed" by a relatively small number of officials working under close supervision of the Chief of State or his immediate confidants and advisers. Until the end of the laissez faire period, those who expounded the classification were not concerned to improve the efficiency of the central government but rather to devise effective checks on its action. Accordingly, it was rarely thought worth while to treat the civil service as a separate category or to study its distinctive organization.

Yet wherever a central government has established its sway over a wide territory and large population, there has always been a functioning civil service, by whatever derisive term it may have been called. History tells us much about the great ministers of state, the Cecils and the Richelieus, and the magnitude of their accomplishments. It tells us little about the instruments of their will, always a considerable body of officials. As the Norman and Angevin kings strengthened their grip on England, they developed an efficient civil service. Probably the actual order of events was in the reverse: as an effective civil service was developed, the kings improved their hold on the country. Certainly the first step was Domesday Book, a census and a permanent record enabling William I to see the size and character of the kingdom he had won, and to devise instruments of control. The compilation could not have been made without a body of devoted servants who at the time were still a part of the king's household staff. In this body is to be found the germ of the British civil service, and historians are now beginning to trace its development through many vicissitudes, but with unbroken continuity to the present day.

IMPORTANCE OF THE CIVIL SERVICE TODAY

Historians generally concentrate on those aspects of the past that are connected with the urgencies of the age in which they live. Today, the civil service and the tasks of public administration they perform are seen to occupy a position of central importance. We have noted an enormous expansion in the activities of government, and the voluminous detailed work this involves is performed by the civil service. When governments restrict immigration, impose a tariff on imports, or establish a postal service, it is civil servants in the garb of customs and immigration officials and postmen who do the work. When it is decreed that children's allowances or old-age pensions are to be paid by the government, it takes hundreds, if not thousands, of officials to make the investigations, keep the records, pay the claims, and supervise the service. We have already seen something of the range of civil service action that is involved in governmental regulation of various aspects of economic life. At every turn, officials are now expected to do many things which the community wants done quickly and well. The civil service has grown enormously and it spends or distributes a large portion of the national income. Everyone has a vital interest in what it is doing and how it does it.

The decision by the legislature that the government should undertake a particular service is only the first step. The decision to fight a war will come to nothing unless an effective organization for the purpose can be put together. Some of the laws made nowadays are left entirely to the courts to apply, but most of them, on the analogy of war, require positive action by the government. In effect, the legislature declares war on poverty, ill-health, ignorance, and social injustice as internal enemies of the social order and commands mobilization of the civil service to promote health, education, and economic well-being.

Whether the specific measures agreed on are done well or ill, or at all, depends on administration, and administration is, at best, a difficult art. Public administration is greatly complicated in a democracy by the necessary insistence that officials should be kept under control and made responsible to the governed. As we have watched the development of government activities on a large scale, we have come to realize the vital importance of securing efficient organization of and action by the civil service, and at the same time, of ensuring effective control of administration on behalf of the governed. It is not at all clear how these two objectives are to be won. This and the succeeding chapter will attempt an introduction to the problem by discussing the organization of the civil service and the methods currently used for controlling it.

Before going on to these matters, it will be well to get some idea of the magnitudes involved. In 1840, Britain had a population of eighteen millions and the central government employed 17,000 civil servants. In 1957, the population had risen to fifty-two millions but the civil service was close to 650,000 in number. In 1840, the population of the United States was seventeen millions and there were 23,000 civil servants in the employ of the federal government. By 1957, the population had risen to some 165 millions and the federal government employees numbered over two-and-one-half millions. In 1957, the federal civil service in Canada was over 175,000 in number.

The figures for Canada and the United States do not include the very substantial numbers in the state and provincial civil services. For this and several other reasons, the figures for the three countries are not strictly comparable, and they are given here only to show what massive enterprises these governments are. A breakdown of the totals to indicate what these thousands are busied in doing would be significant, but it would introduce complications that would take too much time to explain. As an instance, however, it may be said that in Britain and the United States about a quarter, and in Canada about fifteen per cent, of the total are post-office employees. A relatively few great government services of this kind account for the bulk of the civil servants.

Apart from its sheer size, the present magnitude and importance of the civil service can be measured by the amount of money passing through the hands of government. In 1957, out of a total of nearly £21 billion spent in Britain on all manner of goods and services, government accounted for over £3½ billions, or over seventeen per cent. In the United States, about $86.5 billion, or nearly twenty per cent of total expenditures, was on government account. The amount spent by all levels of government in Canada was much smaller ($5.6 billion) but also accounted for nearly eighteen per cent of all expenditures on goods and services made in the country in 1957.

It should be cautioned that no worthwhile judgment about the wisdom of such expenditures can be made without careful attention to the objects on which the expenditure was made. The public gets a variety of services of great, perhaps inestimable, value in return, and only a small portion of the outlay goes to salaries and wages of civil servants. Also, a large proportion of each total consists of what are called "transfers of income"—sums raised by taxation and distributed to the needy members of the population in the form of social services such as unemployment aid, old-age pensions, and the like. Nevertheless, the civil service has to be relied on largely for seeing to it that government outlay of whatever kind accomplishes the purposes aimed at. There is therefore a vital public interest in its efficiency and the uses to which its energies are put.

For these reasons, it is necessary to discuss the civil service almost as if it were a separate branch of government. To the legislature, judiciary, and executive, we must add the administration, or administrative, as it is often called. It must be remembered however that, unlike the other three, it has no sphere of action in which it can count on going its own way. Formally, as was explained in chapter VI, it is under the direction of the executive, the cabinet or the President, and therefore is a part of the executive. In fact, it is now so vast and its operations so extensive and complex that neither the President nor the cabinet can give close supervision and direction to its activities. Officials take every day a multitude of decisions that are not approved in advance by the responsible executive and often cannot, in practice, be reversed by it. This has led some observers to say that the civil servants are the real governors of the country. This is the substance, such as it is, behind the cries of "bureaucracy," which, of course, means government by officialdom. Some attention will be given to this

matter in the next chapter after the structure and characteristics of
a civil service have been outlined.

HIERARCHICAL ORGANIZATION OF THE CIVIL SERVICE

Subject to minor qualifications, civil service organization is
hierarchical. The old and familiar model to which it can be
compared is military organization. At the base are the great mass
of private soldiers whose duty is to obey, and, at each succeeding
higher level, wider and wider powers of command are lodged until
the commander-in-chief with over-all authority is reached. The
civil service hierarchy can be most easily described by starting at
the top and indicating descending levels of decreasing authority.
At the apex stands the cabinet, or the President, controlling the
civil service, but not a part of it since their tenure is temporary and
political. The service is divided into a number of departments,
each headed by a member of the cabinet who is assisted by a
permanent secretary (to use the British structure as an illustration).
Each department is divided into a number of divisions headed by
an assistant secretary, and each division into a number of sections
headed by a principal. The administrative heads of the sections,
divisions, and departments are assisted in their work of direction
and control by a small number of secretaries and assistants known
as the Cadet Corps of Assistant Principals. In the sections are the
bulk of the civil servants carrying out the work of the government.

Physically, the civil servant may be located in the central
departments in the capital, or in one of the branch offices scattered
through the country, or even in a foreign country. But wherever
he is located, he is firmly fixed somewhere in the hierarchy. If he
has subordinates, they are directly answerable to him, and he in
turn to his immediate superiors. At each level, a great number of
routine operations that can be performed without seeking the
sanction of higher authority are carefully prescribed. Instructions,
requests, or suggestions from the top are sent down the line of
authority step by step, and complaints, information, and requests
for instructions from the lower levels go up in the same way.
One of the great sins against officialdom is to by-pass furtively an

immediate superior in seeking the higher reaches of authority. There are sound reasons for the taboo on such action, but it is clearly one of the reasons for the ponderousness of the government machine when unprecedented situations arise.

It is not quite inevitable that civil service organization should take this hierarchical form, but no other form has yet been discovered that fits the requirements of present-day democratic government. The civil servant exists to serve the community in the way in which the community wants to be served. It has been argued already that the only workable criterion of what the community wants is what the majority party insists on or is prepared to support. The only way of ensuring that the spirit of public policy will be made flesh among us is to have a clear line of authority descending from the political heads of the government to the lowest civil servant. Otherwise, there is no way of galvanizing a civil servant into action at the command of the majority party. Also, it would be impossible for the public to enforce responsibility on the civil service for sins of omission or commission if a search had to be made in every case through the civil service for the particular individuals who acted or failed to act in a given situation. It can be done only if responsibility can invariably be thrown on a few identifiable persons at the top. This necessitates a line of responsibility from the lowest civil servant to the top. Command downward and responsibility upward is the essence of hierarchy.

These considerations do not, of themselves, necessitate the interposition of several levels of authority between the mass of civil servants who do the work and the head of the department at the top. But other factors do make it necessary. Many of the operations of the civil service are performed at great distance from the capital and it is physically impossible to consult the minister on every problem of decision that arises locally. More important, each department of government employs hundreds or even thousands of civil servants, and it is just as impossible for the secretary at the head of the department to supervise personally the activities of each as it is for the general to command each regiment, company, and platoon in detail. There must be several ascending levels of authority at each one of which certain problems of discipline and direction arising from below are drawn off and decided, so as to ensure that only the large and vital questions reach the desks of the busy secretary and his immediate aides. In short, ✳ much of the work of administration has to be decentralized if it is to be done with any efficiency.

The Co-ordination of Specialized Activities

Dividing the civil service into departments is partly for the purpose of delegating the bulk of the decisions that have to be made in running any large organization. It is also for the sake of getting the advantages of specialization which are vital for the success of any large organization. The clerks in a country general store are generally able to serve at any counter. But the great merchandising units of the large cities are department stores with at least a separate sales staff for each department. In the same way, governments find it necessary to set up separate departments to specialize in the regulation of transport, commerce, and labour matters, in supplying services to agriculture and to war veterans, in supervising public health, education, and so on. Yet these departments cannot be water-tight compartments. The department of education is always having to concern itself with questions of the health of children, the regulation of transport is always raising questions that affect labour and agriculture, and the supplying of services to agriculture bristles with problems of education.

No matter how the work is divided, the work of each department impinges on several other departments. The same is true of the division of work within the divisions and sections of each department. So a great part of the work of heads of sections, divisions, and departments is the co-ordination or integration of the several work units under their control. And perhaps the most vital part of the work of the executive, be he President or cabinet, is the co-ordinating of the work of the separate departments of the government. The more the advantages of specialization are sought, the more pressing becomes the task of integration, the settlign of disputes between departments, and ensuring that they do not frustrate one another by working at cross-purposes. The hierarchical organization gives the unity of ultimate command necessary for this purpose.

The same problem exists in corporate private enterprise where frequently the work of tens of thousands of employees has to be organized and directed. Although the problems of large-scale public and private enterprise are by no means identical, students of the vitally important art of management are reaching, in the study of one kind of enterprise, conclusions that can be applied to the other.

Unity of command alone does not ensure co-ordination. There is a strict limit to the number of departments a chief executive can co-ordinate, and the experts would place the number nearer ten than twenty. The reason is that the number of interrelationships increases with the number of departments by geometric progression and soon become too numerous for the mind to grasp. Therefore, the administrative answer to continually increasing activities of government is bigger departments with more levels of decentralization within each of them rather than more departments. Co-ordination can only be maintained by increasing the distance from the apex to the base, thus slowing action and decision still more. This implies that there may be a point at which colossal, highly centralized organization breaks down. Certainly present-day governmental organization makes very heavy demands on administrative skill and ingenuity.

One of the devices for co-ordination is to have one or more departments whose main functions are to control and co-ordinate certain aspects of internal management of all other departments. The commander-in-chief of an army is supported by a staff that is engaged in thinking and planning rather than in active field command. Government also has agencies for this purpose. The most obvious of these is the treasury, or department of finance. We have already seen how this department, through its control over departmental estimates and its power of audit of expenditures, maintains a powerful check on other departments. Sometimes, the treasury, as in Britain, has control over personnel also, thus becoming an efficiency expert for the chief executive and performing for him a great many of the tasks of co-ordination. Other aspects of departmental housekeeping may be similarly centralized.

Such devices make organization still more complex. They are an aid to efficiency and co-ordination only if the administrative skill necessary to operate them is available. For example, a staff agency for planning and co-ordinating the work of the various departments may be attached to the President or cabinet. Rivalry commonly develops between the civil service heads of departments and the staff agency about who is to have the ear of the executive in decisions affecting a particular department, and the department may find a major interest in sabotaging the proposals of the staff agency. Administration may be made worse rather than better by this refinement. There were numerous conflicts of this order between members of President Roosevelt's "brain trust"—and President Eisenhower's "personal staff"—and the administrators in the departments.

THE LINKING OF POLITICS AND ADMINISTRATION

It would merely be confusing to try to describe and contrast in a brief space the administrative structure of the three governments. It is necessary, however, to see at this stage how the political and administrative are linked together. In the course of this exposition, some concrete indications of the structure may be given. In Britain and Canada, the cabinet is the link. It is the agency of final co-ordination, and unity of command is ensured by the conventions of unanimity and collective responsibility. The British administration is divided into about thirty-five departments and the Canadian into more than twenty departments, each headed by a minister. In Britain, some of these ministers are not of cabinet rank. Directly under the minister is a senior civil servant who is the minister's deputy, performing for him most of the work of administering the department. In Britain, he is called the permanent secretary of the department because his post, acquired by promotion within the civil service, gives him security of tenure. In Canada, he is generally known as the deputy minister perhaps because in the colonial period the senior official representing the Whitehall department in Canada was often referred to as the "deputy" of his political chief back in Britain. Whatever the reasons for the difference in title, the much greater complexity of departmental management in recent years has forced a recognition of the need for a permanent officer at the head of each department, and the post has become as secure a job as in Britain even though it is still not always filled by promotion from within the civil service.

Many of the notable accomplishments of British administration are largely due to the teamwork of the amateur minister (who is, after all, a politician and not an administrator) and the permanent civil servant who is expert in the direction of the department. It is through their collaboration that public policy as indicated by elections and party majorities is reconciled with what is administratively possible or inevitable.

The department is divided into divisions, and divisions are subdivided into sections each headed by permanent civil servants—assistant secretaries and principals respectively.[1] These and their secretaries and immediate assistants, and the permanent secretary and his assistants form what is known in Britain as the administrative class of civil servants. They are occupied not in performing the services that their department provides for the public but in administering the departments. They see to it that legislation and other political decisions that come down from above are turned into action. Whether or not the department is an effective working unit depends on the quality of the direction they give. They funnel up to the cabinet all those problems of administration that have political implications, whether they are internal problems of administration or concern the relation of the department to the public. These problems are not sent up in the raw form in which they arise. It is the function of the administrative class to collect all the available data that may bear on the decision and to submit memoranda outlining the alternative courses open and explaining in detail what the consequences of the alternative choices are likely to be.

The minister and the cabinet, who are always having to decide grave questions about people they have never seen and about situations they have never examined at first hand, rely on the administrative class to supply them with every fact and argument that may have a bearing on the decision, except, of course, political expediency in which they themselves are the experts. The circulation up and down through the administrative class sets the tone and temper of the department, determining whether its performance will be mediocre or distinguished. When we come to consider the methods of recruiting civil servants, special attention will have to be given to the selection of the administrative class.

[1] Here again it is British organization that is being used as an illustration.

The President stands at the apex of authority and responsibility in the United States. The members of his cabinet are his subordinates for controlling the departments and keeping him in touch with administration. With the exception of the Postmaster General and the Attorney General, members of the cabinet carry the title of Secretary. Each is the political head of one of the ten executive departments. In addition, there are some sixty-five other executive agencies outside the departments and not under the supervision of any member of the cabinet nor under the direct control of the President. Most of these agencies have developed in the last sixty years as a direct consequence of the rapid growth of the activities of the federal government. For example, depression in the 'thirties and war in the 'forties each brought a great expansion in the activities of the federal government and a new rash of these independent executive agencies. Indeed, at the peak of World War II, they totalled almost a hundred. The dismantling of the war organization and a certain amount of executive reorganization have reduced them to their present number.

The character of these executive agencies, the purposes for which they were created, their rise and fall, and their permutations and combinations are a distinct province of knowledge. The Interstate Commerce Commission and the Federal Trade Commission, briefly noticed in chapter v, now have a long history as agencies for regulating certain aspects of economic life. Others, such as the Securities and Exchange Commission and the National Labour Relations Board, were established for similar purposes in the economic confusion of the 'thirties. Others like the now defunct Reconstruction Finance Corporation and those now drawn together under the Federal Housing and Home Finance Agency were creations of the depression period to provide services for certain groups in the community rather than to apply coercive regulation. Others of earlier creation are the Bureau of the Budget and the Civil Service Commission, set up to assist in the internal housekeeping of the national administration. After World War II, the Atomic Energy Commission and the Economic Co-operation Administration were created to deal with urgent post-war problems affecting the security of the United States. These are merely illustrations to show the range and importance of the independent agencies.

In the next chapter, attention will be drawn to some of the

reasons which were thought to justify giving these agencies independent status outside the regular departments. Meanwhile, it should be noted that in recent years there has been much severe criticism of the wisdom of maintaining this welter of independent executive agencies. Their conduct of administration often has been unsatisfactory. Their conceptions of their particular functions often have been out of harmony with the general policies that the President as the responsible chief executive is trying to enforce. The President has not had the power to direct co-ordinating control of them. The result has been a lack of consistency even to the point of cross-purposes in the administration as a whole. Moreover, even if he had such power as a matter of law, expert judgment is unanimous in saying that the co-ordination of the work of the ten departments and of the scores of executive agencies would be an impossible burden on the President.

Several official investigating bodies, the President's Committee on Administrative Management in 1937 and the two Hoover Commissions on Organization of the Executive Branch of Government 1949–1955, recommended a sharp reduction in the number of independent agencies. In pursuance of these recommendations, several successive Reorganization Acts were passed by Congress between 1939 and 1949, giving the President power to reduce, consolidate, and reorganize the numerous executive agencies. Considerable executive reorganization has been accomplished under these Acts and still further and more drastic reduction of the number of independent agencies are to be looked for as a result of the amendments and extensions made in 1957 to the Reorganization Act of 1949.

To return to the internal structure of the ten regular departments, none of them has an official corresponding to the permanent secretary in Britain. There is not an administrative chief of the department linking it as a whole to the political head. In almost all departments, there is an undersecretary, acting as a deputy for the secretary, and also several assistant secretaries, all political and temporary, likely to go when the secretary goes. Each department is divided and subdivided in a way difficult to describe because there are no standardized terms of description—despite repeated recommendations to that end by the two Hoover Commissions. But each department is divided into bureaux, offices, or services (corresponding to the British division), and each of these is headed by a bureau chief or director under the surveillance of an assistant secretary. As a rule, each assistant secretary gives some over-all supervision to several bureaux or offices within the department.

The bureaux are divided into divisions (corresponding to the British sections) and headed by assistant bureau chiefs. In some departments, these divisions are still further divided into branches, and the branches into sections. Similar division and subdivision is found within the larger of the independent executive agencies. The bureau chiefs, assistant bureau chiefs, and their immediate assistants are the key administrators. With ever lessening exceptions, these are career civil servants who survive changes of government.

This structure as described does not provide adequately for departmental integration and, in recognition of this in recent years, the secretaries of the departments have been surrounding themselves with assistants who help them in planning and co-ordinating the work of the department, and one of whom often acts as a general manager of the department with most of the duties, but not the acknowledged position, of the permanent secretary in British departments. Administrative-political collaboration goes on at the bureau level between the bureau chief and the assistant secretary, and also at the top between the secretary and his acting general manager.

Common Features of Civil Service

With this brief glance at the hierarchical structure and what it involves it should be possible to understand some of the characteristics of a civil service or, to use the terminology of contempt, a bureaucracy. The features to be considered appear in more or less exaggerated form in every large-scale organization where many persons work together to make a common product or to achieve a common result in which the contribution of each is not easily, if at all, distinguishable. They appear in large industrial and commercial corporations, and also in the bureaucracies of the dictatorships. Those selected for discussion are found in more marked degree perhaps in the civil services of democratic states than anywhere else.

That they are so found is mainly due to the fact that the civil service in a democracy works under very peculiar conditions. The control exercised over it from the top is both more lax and more severe than in other bureaucracies. Because of the conflicting and unreconciled interests in the electorate, in the legislature, and in the political parties, direction of the civil service is often vacillating and lacking in vigour. Many groups think it better to let sleeping dogs lie and do not want to rouse the civil service into unwonted activity. There are always influences tending to let the civil service go slack. On the other hand, because the civil service deals so much with the private interests of groups and individuals whose rights must be respected to the letter except in so far as legislation authorizes interference, there is very rigid control of the actions of the service from the top. There is more reliance on the bit and the tight rein than on the spur. The sphere in which the civil service is free to act imaginatively and to explore the way to new pinnacles of achievement is very narrow.

One characteristic has important consequences in all directions. Government usually has an unchallenged monopoly of the activities it carries on. This is obvious in the case of the postal services but no less true in most other things. Government is mainly occupied in doing the things that it has been decided, rightly or wrongly, we will not do, or cannot do effectively, for ourselves, either individually or by voluntary co-operation. This is just as true of the regulation of business as it is of the provision of social security.

The existence of a monopoly means that there is no direct and automatic test of efficiency. Postal rates may be too high, but it cannot be proved by pointing to a competitor who provides the same service at lower rates. Those who are convinced they are being overcharged cannot bring the government to terms by transferring their account to a competitor. Government never has to face the hard choice of increasing the efficiency of its staff or going out of business because more efficient producers are underselling it on the market. As a result, the government is an easygoing employer, satisfied with short hours, a modest pace of work, and easy discipline. Civil servants may be dismissed for political reasons but rarely for slackness or incompetence.

In time of war, the serene calm of the civil service gives way to bustle and feverish activity. Those at the top drive harder because they have a goal that challenges all their powers. Conflicts of interest within the community are set aside while the one supreme aim is being pursued. Also many, if not all, civil servants find an incentive that is often lacking in peace. Where the individual applies himself to a task he has set himself and masters it, there is a savour both to the challenge and the accomplishment. In any large organization, by contrast, it is extremely difficult for any one person in it to grasp the objectives at which the organization is aiming or to see the relation of his duties to that objective. Moreover, we have seen that it is hard to get agreed definitions of the public interest, and civil servants are sometimes lukewarm about the goals at which they are expected to be aiming. Powerful incentives for the rank and file in a large organization are hard to find. Where the public interest can be objectified in the winning of a war, the difficulty is in part overcome. Democracies have not yet found how to give a comparable crystallization of the public interest in time of peace. This helps to explain the frequent criticism that the rank and file of the civil service is stolid, unimaginative, and lackadaisical. They lack a sense of mission.

Consequences of Large Scale Organization

Another feature of large organization is its impersonal character. The owner and operator of the country store comes into direct contact every day with his customers and employees. This is not true either of the manager of the departmental store or of the Postmaster General. When a service is on a mass-production basis, it must be conducted on the assembly-line principle, relying to a great extent on highly standardized and invariable procedures. In addition, central governments are always acting throughout the country at great distances from the centre. Those in control rarely see the persons or situations on which they may have to give final decisions. There are generally several levels of authority between those who make final decisions and those who carry them out.

So the private citizen cannot see those who finally decide unless he can invoke political influence, and the civil servants whom he can see and with whom he has to deal are obliged to treat him distantly and impersonally. They cannot respond to individual cases and appeals as their instinct or reason suggests. They are acting under precise orders or under rules that limit their authority. The relation of the civil servant to his immediate superiors is also impersonal because they too are not free agents but must answer to those above them.

The best index to the impersonal quality of civil service relationships is the pervasiveness of paper work. The standardized procedures by which the departments are run, the rules and regulations which are at once the guide and protection of all subordinates, are only the beginning of the written work. All significant decisions made and actions taken are recorded as permanent evidence of what has been done, and as a guide for the future. Much of the discussion within a department as to what can or ought to be done goes on paper. The complaints, suggestions, and requests for instructions made by subordinates are recorded. If their immediate superior thinks he cannot or should not deal with the issue raised, he records his views and sends the file on. Like a snowball, it picks up comments, suggestions, queries as it moves along.

Busy heads of departments have not time to go through all this information, and they may require an assistant to prepare a *précis* or a memorandum on it. At any stage, the responsible official to whose desk a matter has come may think more information is needed, and someone is detailed to collect it and to comment on what he finds—more material added to a growing file. In the same way, complaints from aggrieved members of the public or questions raised in the legislature set going the procession of files from one desk to another. Most of the administrators deal far more with papers than with persons or concrete situations. There is constant danger that they will identify reality with what they see, that they will regard this paper world as the real world and keeping their desks clean as the acme of accomplishment.

Impersonality and paper work are characteristic of large organization in general. Governments that are strictly responsible to the governed suffer from them in a marked degree. They are expected to act and act vigorously in many matters. It is also insisted that they should do what is right and shun injustice and wrongdoing.

It is not easy to combine these virtues because such governments always act under limited authority. Beyond the margins of that authority they come at once into collision with the vested rights and interests of individuals and groups.

✔ Even where they have clear discretionary power, there is an insistent demand that they act justly. In the public mind, justice means, among other things, equality of treatment. There is no great outcry when a merchant treats one customer differently from another. But if one recipient of unemployment relief or an old-age pension is treated differently from another, the government is likely to be called upon to justify it. A fierce light beats on constitutional governments as well as on thrones. Under the cabinet system, at any rate, political responsibility is concentrated on the political heads of the civil service, and they know that careless action may cost them dearly at the next election.

They therefore tend to limit very narrowly what can be done by their subordinates on their own discretion, and to insist that doubtful matters shall be referred to superiors for decision. They likewise tend to insist that where a discretionary power is to be exercised, the past practice should be consulted to see what has been done in similar cases, and that doubts about whether the past practice covers the present circumstances should also be referred to superiors. The civil servant at the lower levels of authority who deals with living persons and concrete situations is immersed in rules, precedents, and instructions. It requires great circumspection to obey them all, and his caution may make him almost immobile. It is not easy to see how else he can keep out of trouble with his superiors, or the political heads can know what is being done in their names in distant places. The civil servant who will not stay in the rut of routine lives dangerously. In the rut, there is safety and peace.

There is no need to search further for the explanation of red tape. Originally, the term gained currency through the fact that government departments tied up their files with a red binding tape. It is now used as a compendious description of the way these files are built up. To the citizen, red tape means the perverse insistence on the letter of rules and regulations, the completion of inquisitive forms and seemingly irrelevant questionnaires, the noncommittal and evasive letters of civil servants relying on the security of their routine, the passing of the buck to superiors and to other bureaux and other departments. It is infuriating to all who suffer delay or denial in their urgent affairs. In its more extreme forms, it is due to faulty or inefficient organization, or to the stupidity or unnecessary timidity of officials, and therefore can be cured.

But for much of the red tape there is good and sufficient reason not apparent on the surface. It is the necessary concomitant of large organization and constitutional government. Large organization demands departmentalized division of labour, standardized procedures, and routine. Constitutional government demands hierarchical structure with its concentration of authority and responsibility, and extreme caution in exploring the boundary between public duty and private right.

Another common feature of large organization is standardized procedures for dealing with personnel. This is really an aspect of the impersonality already noted, but it deserves separate comment. Effective financial control requires standardization. Financial control has to be worked through a budget of expenditures prepared in advance and adhered to in execution. Budgeting is not possible if each head of a department is free to make what bargains he likes with his subordinates about pay. The only way to prevent this and to stick to a budget is to classify all the positions in the department and assign a fixed rate of pay for each class.

There is another imperative reason for classification. It has already been pointed out that, in a large organization, there is no indisputable criterion of what the services of particular persons are worth. So the employee who works in a niche unseen by the heads of the department has no effective way of bringing his worth forcibly to the attention of his superiors and no assurance that his industry or skill will be noticed or rewarded. Equally, he has no assurance that favouritism among his superiors will not prefer the less deserving in matters of pay and promotion. While he cannot be assured of exact justice, he can be protected against the grosser kinds of injustice, and his morale consequently strengthened, by a classification of the positions in the entire service to the end that there should be no discrimination between employees in the same class—that there should be equal pay for equal work.

There is, of course, plenty of heartache in any classification that seeks to reduce tens of thousands of positions to a relatively small number of categories, because few positions can be exactly equated. Some measure of rough justice can be had by careful allotting of similar jobs to one class, assigning to each class a scale of pay and increases, and fixing the terms of promotion, transfer, vacations, and retirement allowances, if any. Some measure of equity in these matters is a necessity. Most civil servants get little chance for self-expression and little of the satisfaction of personal achievement in their work. The most concrete of the substitutes open to them are pay increases, promotions, and other perquisites. Their concern with equity on such points may become an obsession and have a most serious effect on the *esprit de corps* of the organization.[1] The proof of these assertions is to be found in the importance now attached by large enterprises, whether public or private, to the growing art of personnel management.

CLASSIFICATION AND RECRUITMENT OF THE CIVIL SERVICE

Classification of a civil service is important for still another reason. It is a prerequisite to recruiting the civil service by any other method than political patronage and spoils, a condition of selecting the man for the job instead of the job for the man. If posts are to be filled by merit rather than by political preferment, it is necessary to know what kind of merit is required. Positions must be classified according to the general nature of the work done, and to the qualifications necessary for doing it, so as to arrive at methods of testing the fitness of applicants. This brings up one of the large issues of democratic government, the method of recruiting the civil service. We have seen that large organization, and particularly a civil service, has a number of peculiar characteristics. All these create serious problems of securing and maintaining efficiency. The first step in meeting these problems is to secure a high quality in the personnel. There are also important principles of organization and administration to be observed, but

[1]The above discussion of common features of civil services relies heavily on Herman Finer, *The Theory and Practice of Modern Government* (Holt, New York, 1949), rev. ed. ch. xxvII.

these cannot make the service better than the personnel of which it is composed.

Before turning to methods of recruitment in Britain, the United States and Canada, something should be said generally about classifications. In each country, there are hundreds of classes of positions and the plans on which they are based vary considerably. Yet from the point of view of the kind of work performed rather than of the precise range of duties in each case, a civil service can be divided into five quite distinct grades or classes. It is useful for preliminary appreciation of the make-up of a civil service to set them out:

1. Administrative—the work of general management such as organizing, directing, planning, and co-ordinating.
2. Professional—the class of experts such as doctors, lawyers, economists, entomologists, engineers, and a whole range of scientists concerned with public health, fisheries, forestry, agriculture, and the like.
3. Clerical—all the office workers who, working under supervision, are engaged in the voluminous paper work of the government, including the immediate supervisors concerned with the detail of office management.
4. Skilled industrial workers engaged in maintenance, printing, and government enterprises such as the mint and the arsenals.
5. Unskilled workers employed on various tasks at roughly the level of skill of day labour.

There are a number of civil servants whom it would be difficult to fit into any of these classes, but they are only a small fraction of the total.

In 1850, when laissez faire was at its peak, civil services were the playthings of politics. With the exception of Prussia, which had had for a long time a career service recruited by merit and enjoying security of tenure, those who controlled the governments in most Western countries disposed of civil servants and their posts as they saw fit. Democracy inherited rather than invented political patronage. The favourites of monarchs and ruling cliques were succeeded in government posts by the favourites of politicians. Although the United States and Canada for a time rivalled the excesses of the older regimes, the significant fact is that civil service reform almost everywhere has been carried through under democratic auspices. The zeal of reformers has found enough support in public opinion to make steady advances in the methods of recruiting for the public service.

At the same time, the changing role of government has played an important part. As long as central governments did little but maintain internal order and security from foreign aggression, there was no urgent need for a highly efficient civil service. When governments undertook to regulate many aspects of social and economic life and to provide a wide variety of essential services, the tasks to be performed became too complex and too important to be left in the hands of a civil service haphazardly recruited by patronage. In 1855, when civil service reform began in Britain, it had already been recognized that the central government had to do something about the social confusion caused by the Industrial Revolution. The first steps were taken in the United States in 1883, and extensions of the merit system have on the whole kept pace with the expansion of the activities of the federal government. In Canada, a beginning was made in 1908, but was little effective until 1919. Government's role of regulator and dispenser of services began later and for a considerable time developed more slowly in North America than in Britain. Broadly speaking then, civil service reform in all three countries has followed closely the growing importance of government in the everyday life of the community.

As long as the spoils of office went to the victor in the last election, it was difficult to attract competent persons to temporary insecure service with the government. Even if able men did come to it by chance, a reversal of party fortunes in a few years often put them out just as they were mastering their jobs. *Esprit de corps,* the indispensable condition of efficiency in a large organization, could not be had in these circumstances. Moreover, party politicians had not the necessary techniques, even if they had had the will, to select the many kinds of experts and highly specialized talent that governmental activities now require. Without some recognition of the merit principle, governments could not do the things they do today.

RECRUITMENT IN BRITAIN

The scope and methods of appointment by merit may now be considered. In Britain, the entire civil service has been withdrawn from political patronage. Appointments are under the control of the Civil Service Commission, a board of six members appointed by the executive but enjoying substantial independence from executive pressure. The chief functions of the Commission are to determine qualifications for entrance and to test applicants for the possession of these qualities. Once certified by the Commission, candidates at the top of the list are appointed as positions open up.

Generally speaking, the tests are made by open competitive examination. The largest exceptions to this rule are the skilled and unskilled handworkers, who are recruited through the employment exchanges and certified by interview only. No satisfactory examination has been found for testing a janitor's handiness with a coal scuttle, and even manual skills do not lend themselves easily to testing. Professional and scientific workers are chosen by competitive interview from among those who are already members of the professions or holders of scientific degrees. The clerical group are chosen by open competitive examinations of great variety combined with interviews. The examinations for this group are partly tests of special aptitude and partly tests of general knowledge and intelligence with the emphasis strongly on the latter. The administrative class are chosen by written general examinations of a highly academic type ranging over history, languages, natural science, economics, politics, and philosophy. No attempt is made to test their aptitude for or knowledge about the particular duties to which they will be assigned. It is sought rather to discover those who have the imagination and intellect, the industry and self-discipline necessary to master a number of fields of academic study. These qualities of mind, temperament, and character are further tested by means of interviews. In one optional method of entry used extensively since World War II, the interviews are extended over several days, as groups of candidates are subjected to a careful screening by psychologists and other trained observers.

It must not be thought that all posts are filled by appointment from the outside as they fall vacant. Indeed, almost all the recruiting from the outside in the administrative and clerical classes is from the sixteen to twenty-four age group for posts at the bottom of the particular class for which they are chosen. Almost all the higher posts are filled by promotion. In some instances, promotion is made to depend on the results of a competitive examination among a selected group of candidates. But generally speaking, the Civil Service Commission in Britain is an examining and certifying body only. It has little to do with promotions, which are departmental matters. Nor is it concerned with classifying positions, fixing salary schedules, or with personnel management. These are departmental or Treasury matters.

The wide opportunities for promotion within any one grade or class are closely related to the type of examination. An examination that tests special aptitude for a particular task may give no clue at all to capacity to rise. On the other hand, examinations that test general knowledge and intelligence are likely to discover a civil servant who will quickly learn to master a routine instead of letting the routine master him. He is likely to be able to deal with novel situations and therefore to be worthy of promotion. This kind of ability is of great importance for those in the higher clerical positions, called the executive class in Britain, who have to do with such varied tasks as office management and supervision, compilation of statistics, handling complaints from the public, and so on.

General intelligence and adaptability are most needed, however, in the administrative class. We have already seen that this class, which numbers only about 3,500, occupies the key positions in governmental administration. There is a most intimate relationship between the capacities of this group and the effective execution of laws passed by the legislature. It largely depends on them whether the lessons to be learned in administration of particular laws are brought to the attention of the political heads of the government as material for deciding on changes and amendments. They are concerned with policy as well as administration, and consequently need breadth of mind and interests as well as mastery of routine. These considerations led in Britain to the adoption of the highly academic examination, coupled with the stiff interview procedures, already described. Experience has more than justified the decision. The most serious criticism made of the method of recruiting the administrative class is that for practical purposes the nature of the qualifying examination almost limits membership of the administrative class to graduates of Oxford and Cambridge Universities.

It is not so much that the examinations are difficult as that they are based on the course of studies followed in the ancient universities. So the key group in the civil service is almost exclusively drawn from the upper middle-class, who alone in the past have enjoyed any considerable access to these educational advantages. This situation reflects the traditional class structure and the limited access to higher education in Britain. There is, as a consequence, little disposition to alter the method of choosing the administrative class. Rather, the basis of recruitment can only be broadened as the avenues to university education are opened to able sons of the working class, so that they may thus become eligible candidates for the administrative class.[1]

Recruitment in the United States

The federal Civil Service Commission in the United States is a board of three members appointed by the President, subject to confirmation by the Senate but carrying on its work free of political interference and control. Its main work is to examine and certify candidates for entrance to the federal civil service. It has somewhat wider functions than its British counterpart. It is charged with working out the details of classifications of positions within a general plan adopted by Congress. It participates in the establishing and working of schemes for rating the efficiency of civil servants and it has a power of investigating the fairness of disciplinary measures such as suspension, dismissal, and demotion. It has thus a partial responsibility for personnel management within the service.

On the other hand, the scope of its control of appointments is not as wide as that of the British Commission. It rests with Congress to say what posts shall be filled by competitive tests or other scrutiny of qualifications made by the Commission, and there are still tens of thousands of permanent posts in the service that have not yet been brought under the merit system. Even within the

---

[1]For an intimate account of the administrative class in Britain, see H. E. Dale, *The Higher Civil Service of Great Britain* (Clarendon Press, Oxford, 1941).

classified service, i.e. the classes of positions to be filled by merit, there are numerous exceptions specified by Congress or by presidential orders. The practice of making and continuing temporary appointments, sometimes for years, also makes holes in the merit system even within the classified service. It is to be noted too that none of the higher administrative officials whose appointments must be confirmed by the Senate comes within the jurisdiction of the Commission. These are still a substantial group and include a goodly number of the extremely important bureau chiefs already referred to. Much room for patronage appointments still remains, and these are generally used according to the exigencies of party politics.

Within the classified service, appointments are almost all made on the basis of competitive tests, which may or may not consist of written examinations. Generally speaking, written tests are used to test applicants for the more subordinate positions requiring clerical, manual, or other operative skill to be applied under the close direction of superiors. Applicants for posts requiring professional or scientific knowledge and attainments are usually rated by interview and by evidence of their knowledge and experience derived from sources other than a formal written examination.

The types of examinations given differ markedly from those used in Britain. The civil service examinations in Britain are accommodated to the educational system and try to draw some of the best products of the system into the civil service at an early age with little regard for specialized skills. In the United States, the examinations have always been drafted with an eye to the posts to be filled and are therefore framed to test technical competence. Also, they are open to older age groups than in Britain. There is a much greater variety of examinations, and while they provide a good test of capacity for a particular job they do not test capacity for other work to which the civil servant may be promoted.

Unlike Britain, the United States has not adopted an academic examination on a wide variety of subjects for selecting general administrative capacity, although experiments have been made in that direction since the 1930's. Indeed, the federal Civil Service Commission does not recognize a distinct administrative class. Probably this is in part due to an equalitarian philosophy which dislikes fencing off higher posts as a preserve for those who have enjoyed superior educational advantages. It is partly due to the fact that some of the higher posts are subject to senatorial confirmation and so remain actively political. There is, of necessity, an administrative class, but its ranks are filled either by promotion from other classes in the service or, more rarely, by appointments from outside the service.

The undersecretaries and assistant secretaries are political appointments and change when a new President comes to office, if not before. They, and the bureau chiefs and assistant bureau chiefs are the key administrators. As already noted, a substantial number of the bureau chiefs are still in the unclassified service and open, as far as the law goes, to political pressure and appointment. However, there is a rapidly growing practice to fill these posts by promotion even when they are unclassified and to give the holders of them security of tenure. That is to say, higher administrative work is becoming a career in the United States just as it is in Britain. Nothing more clearly reveals the changing attitudes towards the civil service arising from the necessities of present-day government. The efficient conduct of public administration is now so important to the community and makes such demands on skill and knowledge that it cannot be left to amateur partisans who come and go. It is being recognized that the men who run a department must not only understand it but must feel themselves to be a part of it. It is not easy otherwise to account for the self-restraint of politicians in the face of plums of such size and succulence.

It is believed by many in the United States that this tendency must go further and that all high administrative posts in a department below the rank of assistant secretary must be brought into the career service. Also, it is urged that special attention be paid to the recruiting of an administrative class. It is not enough that posts should be filled by promotion. It is necessary to ensure that there shall be in the service a sufficient number of able men with administrative talent who will look forward to, and deserve, promotion to the highest posts. As matters now stand, most of those who are promoted to be chiefs of bureaux were originally brought into the service as specialists of one kind or another and not as administrators. What is true of them is true also of their immediate assistants and of heads of the divisions into which each bureau is divided. No one would think of recruiting bomber pilots solely by promotion of ground crew who proved themselves handy. In its own way, a government department is just as sensitive an engine with just as close a relation between skilful handling and distinguished performance. On these grounds, it is argued that the British method of recruiting the administrative class should be adopted.

Expert opinion in the United States, however, is not all of one mind on the point. For example, it is pointed out that in Britain there is almost no possibility of promotion from the clerical class into the administrative class, and therefore administrative work has so far been almost exclusively a career for the talents of those lucky enough to be well born and well educated. An unstratified society cannot make such a discrimination but must keep clear the road from the bottom to the top. The office boy who becomes chief of a bureau will bring with him an experience that is a surer guide in departmental matters than the knowledge British administrators get from books and memoranda. Whether or not this contention is sound, it is clear that the contrast between Britain and the United States on this point goes beneath the surface and is founded on marked differences in social outlook and social conditions. These differences have been underlined by the heated controversy aroused by the second Hoover Commission's recommendation in favour of the creation of a Senior Civil Service of non-partisan, experienced officers. In 1958, President Eisenhower issued an order to authorize a "Career Executive Program" along the lines of this recommendation, but the reaction of many officials and students of public administration suggests that the new programme is not wholeheartedly endorsed.

RECRUITMENT IN CANADA

Canadian institutions generally reveal both British and American influences. In the devices for securing the merit system in the civil service, the influences have been predominantly American. The social outlook and conditions in Canada are closer to those of the United States than of Britain, and make the American approach more congenial if not more appropriate. Canada, as well as the United States, had a distressing experience with the spoils system. This experience led reformers to put extraordinary emphasis on combatting patronage in the civil service at the expense of other equally important considerations. The over-emphasis is being corrected rapidly in both countries, but Canadian civil service regulations still express it in striking form. The desire to shield the civil service from the politicians has imposed restrictions that are unworkable and self-defeating.

Since the comprehensive reform of 1918-19, the general rule is that appointments to the federal civil service shall be upon competitive examination with preference to those who head the examination. The examining body is a Civil Service Commission composed of three members appointed by the government of the day and removable during their period of office only by address of both Houses of Parliament. The Commission, however, is much more than an examining body. To prevent political considerations affecting promotions, and transfers from one department to another, the Commission has been put in control of them with power to insist on examinations if it so wishes. Its approval must also be secured for changes in salary scales. The Commission has the immediate responsibility for classifying the positions in the civil service and recommending that existing grades or classes be divided, combined, or abolished. It thus has, subject to interventions of the Treasury Board which will be discussed later, a substantial measure of control over the administrative organization of the departments through its power to make periodic surveys and recommendations. Increases in staff and other significant changes in departmental organization require its approval. Its control over organization, combined with its power to prescribe by regulation the general conditions of work in the service, gives it functions that in Britain are exercised by the Treasury in close conjunction with its financial control.

The statutory powers of the Commission almost entitle it to be called a personnel manager and efficiency expert. The Commission is defective for this purpose because of its independence of the government. Those who are responsible for getting the work of the government done cannot be expected to get the best results when they are subject to external control and delay in personnel matters. Giving such functions to an external agency can only be explained as a heroic attempt to shield the personnel of the service from all the political influences that might be exerted through ministers. In fact, the effort is, in large measure, unnecessary. When politicians cannot get their favourites appointed in the first place, they lose most of their partisan interest in personnel administration.

A plan of classification of positions was adopted in 1919 which follows American rather than British models. It does not recognize a distinct administrative class to which young men are to be directly appointed. It carries further than the United States federal classification an attempt to classify minutely according to the specific duties a post entails. (Under this plan, there are now well over 2,000 classes.) It calls for examinations to test skill and aptitude for specific jobs at the lower levels and aims to preserve the higher posts for persons promoted from the lower ones. For each class, it plots a line of promotion designed to carry the ambitious man to the top.

The examinations called for by the plan are designed to test present knowledge, skill, and aptitude for a particular task rather than general capacity. This method of testing is quite satisfactory for a great number of the positions to be filled. It has not been applied at all to appointments of professional and scientific personnel, which are made on the recommendation of an advisory board that can judge expert qualifications. But its application is still too wide. The use of practical examinations has its worst results in the selection of appointees to clerical posts who are expected to rise by promotion to administrative positions. This method has failed to bring into the lower posts sufficient personnel with capacity to fill the higher posts by promotion.

The lines of promotion are charted, but in most cases they cannot be navigated by those the examination system selects. This is partly due to the refusal of the able and energetic to enter a service where they may have to spend years at stultifying low-paid routine work before a chance of promotion arises. So the higher administrative posts are often filled by bringing in outsiders. As in the United States, urgent need has forced a recognition of the situation. In 1935, an academic examination somewhat resembling the type used in Britain for recruiting administrative talent was introduced for the purpose of attracting and selecting university graduates for administrative posts. The recruits secured under this plan were placed in one of the existing clerical grades and often remained there for a long period engaged in routine operations. In 1946, a further step was taken, and a new class, junior administrative assistant, was set up. Recruits for this class are university graduates chosen by academic examinations for specifically administrative work. The junior administrative assistant is given a period of in-service training designed to fit him for responsible work and promotion in the administrative sphere of the government's operations. We have here the beginnings of a distinct administrative class.

The control of the Civil Service Commission over promotions and transfers is also unsatisfactory. If the administrative head of a department does not control promotions, he is greatly hampered in maintaining a high level of operating efficiency. An external body cannot be fully aware of all the considerations bearing on promotion. In practice, this is largely, though not fully, recognized, and the Commission generally decides on the basis of a rating made by the deputy minister. In the same way, the Commission's supervision over transfers and increases in salary is largely formal. All these matters should be handled by the departments themselves in conjunction with the Department of Finance, and the present arrangement is workable mainly because the Commission withholds its hand.

The situation is unsatisfactory both for the departments and the Commission. The Treasury Board, and ultimately the cabinet, must take the responsibility for the estimates and for all increases in expenditure, whether arising from an upward revision of salaries of civil servants in general or from the promotion of particular civil servants. This fact alone is likely to nullify largely the authority of the Commission over salary schedules and promotions. Also, recommendations of the Civil Service Commission on questions of classification and organization of the civil service must be submitted to the Treasury Board which can then deal with them as it sees fit. The result is a dual control of many important civil service matters. The Treasury Board exercises financial control, as indeed some politically responsible body always must. But it has not the direct responsibility, which should go with its power, for making the civil service efficient and effective.

Such a state of affairs has done nothing to enhance the prestige of the merit system and has given positive aid and comfort to its enemies. A faulty classification, a defective examination system, an impractical promotion scheme, and an unwise division of authority between the departments and the Commission on personnel matters have led to exasperation and antagonism in many quarters and inspired attempts to remove positions from the control of the Commission. The civil service law, which only now after forty years is being thoroughly re-considered with a view to major revision, provides that, subject to certain express exceptions, all appointments shall be upon competitive examination. But numerous exceptions have always been made by various expedients and a high proportion of the positions in the public service have been outside the control of the Commission.[1]

Of course, it is not imperative, or even desirable, that there should be no exceptions to appointment through examinations. Many of these excepted positions have been casual posts of little importance. There is no reason at all for wanting to bring such employment under the control of the Commission. It might also be argued—although not without challenge—that there is no reason why a great number of jobs calling for no special skill should be under the merit system. We have already seen that the party system in North America depends on patronage for getting a good deal of party drudgery done. Keeping a substantial number of minor jobs available for the aspirants to petty office helps to lubricate party mechanisms and will do no serious harm to the public service if it is recognized for what it is, part of the price of party government. The posts that must be protected are the professional and technical and the upper clerical and administrative, because it is on the incumbents of these posts that the success of the complex operations of present-day government largely depends.

In 1946, the Royal Commission on Administrative Classifications in the Public Service criticized severely the dual control of the civil service described here, and recommended that the Treasury Board be given full power over classification and organization, salary scales and general conditions of work, and a large share of responsibility in promotions and transfers. This recommendation of

[1]See the excellent review of the Civil Service Act by the Canadian Civil Service Commission in *Personnel Administration in the Public Service.* December, 1958.

the Commission was not adopted. Whatever the reasons for the reluctance of the government to implement this recommendation, it is true that in the last few years relations between the Civil Service Commission and the Treasury Board have improved. Informal working relationships which define the sphere of action of each body have been established and close co-operation is bringing about improvements in the service. Such informal relationships depend on congeniality of the persons involved, and in the absence of a more formal definition and division of responsibilities, are likely to be unstable.

Administrative Management in the Civil Service

Until the mid 1930's most of the serious study of the civil service was concentrated on problems of recruitment and the merit system. There was a tendency to assume that if good personnel could be attracted to the civil service and the ogre of patronage could be banished, all the important problems would be solved. In recent years, however, the massive and ramified activities of governments have directed attention to questions of efficient organization, and effective control on behalf of the governed. The latter question will be considered in the next chapter. The question how to organize and co-ordinate the work of tens of thousands of civil servants opens a large field, sometimes pretentiously called the science of administration, which cannot be discussed in detail here. It is, however, a matter of immense importance in all countries because of the headlong growth of the welfare state and the serious strains on governmental machinery imposed by a second major war and its aftermath.

The problems of managing a vast civil service have received particularly close and continuous scrutiny over the past two decades in the United States. The division of powers, coupled with the rapid growth in the federal civil service has resulted in the haphazard creation of a great variety of administrative agencies, many of which have managed to live virtually independent lives. This situation was carefully probed in 1936 by the President's Committee on Administrative Management. About ten years later, Congress authorized the appointment of another Committee on Organization of the Executive Branch of Government which became known as the Hoover Commission, after its chairman ex-President Hoover. Its report was published in 1949 and was followed shortly after in 1953 by a Second Hoover Commission which reported in 1955.

It would be impossible to describe in detail the findings and recommendations of these investigative bodies for their results were published in bulky reports and numerous special studies prepared by large staffs of experts. Broadly speaking, the commissions were agreed on their analysis of the defects of existing organization. They found that the President's responsibility as general manager of a vast array of public departments, boards, commissions and agencies was far too great for any one person to shoulder. Not only did the President lack adequate staff assistance to help him keep the complex administrative apparatus under continuous review, he also lacked the means of remodelling and pruning the organization when such measures were obviously necessary. Clearly, the administrative plant can be made to grow more symmetrical and fruitful only as its dead branches and excess foliage are trimmed away.

The central proposal of the first investigating committee was to strengthen greatly the position of the President so as to make him an effective centre of energy, direction, and administrative management. This was accomplished by creating in 1937 a new agency, the Executive Office of the President, consisting of six separate divisions. These divisions have been altered since the original organization was established and it would serve no useful purpose to recount the detailed changes. At present, the Executive Office includes the following divisions: the White House Office, which provides a secretariat for the President; the Bureau of the Budget, designed to follow in its new setting, its earlier functions as the agency for improving general organization and efficiency as well as for financial control; the Council of Economic Advisors, whose function, as already noted in chapter v, is to advise the President on economic matters; the National Security Council, which advises on the co-ordination of foreign policy; the Office of Emergency Management, which is a "stand by" organization that can be brought to life in preparation for war; the Office of Defence Mobilization, which co-ordinates the use of economic resources for war. All these "staff arms" have enabled the President to assume more effectively his constitutional obligation "to take care that the laws be faithfully executed."

Apart from this basic reform, all three investigating bodies agreed that "drastic and sweeping action" was required to reduce the administrative chaos produced by so many independent agencies which (in the words of the President's Committee of 1937) had grown up like the barns, shacks and silos around an old farm. Each committee made many recommendations aimed at the consolidation and reduction of various branches and the re-grouping of administrative functions into a more coherent departmental structure. Over the past fifteen to twenty years, numerous efforts, some more successful than others, have been made to implement these recommendations.

More important than the details of these administrative reforms is the procedure by which the organizational plans have been recommended and implemented. The modern administrative apparatus is too complex and too important to be left solely to the sporadic attentions of committees of inquiry. Congress, too, is obviously incapable of taking the lead in such managerial tasks. As previously noted, the President has gradually acquired the expert staff to assist him in the preliminary tasks of analysing the administrative branch and preparing plans for its reorganization. Therefore, it was a natural step, beginning with the Reorganization Act of 1939, for Congress to confer on the President the power to initiate reorganization plans for its approval. Congress was careful to hedge this grant of power by insisting that it would be subject to periodic renewal— the most recent extension occuring in 1957. In addition to putting a time limit on the President's power to initiate reorganization of the administrative branch, Congress has also retained what amounts to a legislative veto by insisting that either house, within sixty days after submission of the President's plans, can pass a resolution of disapproval.

Despite this rather cumbersome procedure—which in itself is a good example of the tensions created by the separation of powers in the United State—Congress has been remarkably co-operative in accepting the President's lead in the field of administrative management. Only three out of twelve presidential reorganization plans were turned down by Congress between 1939 and 1948. In 1950, when twenty-one such plans were presented, only five were rejected by Congress. It is estimated that seventy per cent of the recommendations made by the First Hoover Commission have now been implemented. Testifying to the widespread interest in and concern for managerial problems in the public service are the "little Hoover Commissions" which have been created by many states and the independent Citizens' Committee on the Hoover Commission which maintained steady pressure on the government to induce it to implement the recommendations of the Commission.

The significance of this whole movement, the criticisms and proposals, has already been pointed out in earlier discussion of the characteristic features and organization of a civil service. Similar criticisms and proposals can be, and have been, made about Canadian and British administration, although in neither is the problem so acute.

In Canada, administrative agencies have been growing rapidly since World War II but the scale is so much smaller than in the United States that there is less chance of the situation getting out of hand merely through defective organization. Nevertheless, there has been much support for a Canadian "Hoover Commission" which would presumably conduct a more thorough investigation of the entire administrative structure than has been possible on the few occasions when royal commissions or special parliamentary committees have been employed. Meanwhile, the Civil Service Commission itself has undertaken a full-scale analysis of the forty-year old Civil Service Act and the regulations made under it. Most of its proposals which were published in December, 1958 are concerned with strengthening the present organization for handling personnel administration, rather than with the problems of departmental reorganization. The latter are the subject of continuous scrutiny by a special branch in the Commission known as the Organization and Methods (O. and M.) Branch. This branch provides expert guidance and, on request of the departments, special studies on ways and means of improving the efficiency of the operating departments. It has no powers of enforcement since each department is able to accept, modify or reject the advice or recommendations of the Commission. Unlike the situation in the

United States, where Congress has insisted on preserving its right to veto executive reorganization plans, the Canadian Parliament has, through the Rearrangement and Transfer of Duties Act, conferred on the cabinet the right to make organizational changes by order-in-council. Of course, for any important change, such as the creation of a new department, parliament's sanction would have to be sought.

It is clear that in the Canadian situation the presence of the cabinet as supreme co-ordinating authority eliminates much of the duality of managerial responsibility that produces confusion in handling the same tasks in the United States. Nevertheless, the cabinet itself needs advice from experts who are in a position to keep a constant watch over the departmental structure. The occasional intervention of outside investigators, such as parliamentary committees or royal commissions and the hiring of experts from private management consultant firms provide a healthy supplement to the work of those in the civil service specifically assigned to such tasks.

In Britain, the size of the civil service and the scope of its operations more nearly approximate the situation in the United States, and the consequent problems of administrative management loom larger than in Canada. Here, too, much reliance has been placed on periodic investigations by royal commissions and such extremely useful parliamentary instruments as the select committee, the Estimates and Public Accounts Committees. The closest equivalent to the Hoover Commission studies has been the classic report from the Haldane Committee on the Machinery of Government— a report which was issued as long ago as 1919. After publication of that report, the Treasury began to build up a small staff of Organization and Methods specialists which was enlarged during World War II and has since become indispensable to the Treasury in undertaking its central responsibilities for supervision and co-ordination of the whole administrative machine.

Clearly, the executive branch in all three countries has now been equipped to handle the difficult and important problems of over-all management. Man has cut an important figure in the world because of his ability to take thought about his actions. The executive branch of government thus equipped, and occupying as it does a strategic position may be expected to strengthen still further its position *vis-à-vis* the legislature and the electorate. All of the investigators mentioned in the previous paragraphs were concerned primarily with the problem of making the administration more efficient for the ever-widening range and complexity of the tasks with which the modern state is confronted. What is of equal concern is the problem of how popular control over this highly intelligent and efficient administration can be achieved. An introduction to this problem will be essayed in the next chapter.

CHAPTER XVI

THE ADMINISTRATIVE PROCESS

THE last chapter dealt mainly with internal aspects of the civil service. Here attention is to be focused on the external relations of the civil service—its connections with and its impact on members of the public. These are of great variety. Almost all the activities of government recounted in chapter v involve action by civil servants affecting some or all members of the public. Sometimes the government provides a service such as the post office or the employment exchange. Sometimes it is mixed service and regulation as in public-health activities. The government maintains diagnostic clinics and laboratories for analysis and also enforces pure-food regulations and a minimum of sanitary measures on municipalities and individuals. Sometimes it is purely regulation, as when employers are required to pay minimum wages and maintain safety devices, and when public utilities are required to provide certain standards of service at fixed rates.

Where a service only is being supplied to the public with or without charge, the public wants little more than efficiency, courtesy, and equality of treatment from the civil servant. If they know their jobs, the public is satisfied with good manners from the post-office clerk and with sympathetic understanding of the plight of the unemployed from the clerks in the employment service. But when civil servants are engaged in regulating our lives, other considerations enter. Here the official has power to require us to do or to refrain from doing something and he is backed by the organized power of the government. He must act firmly and without fear, favour, or discrimination, because he is expected to enforce the public interest even if it is at the expense of private interests. Of course, his firmness will be less galling if it is gloved in courtesy. We do—and should—resent any unnecessary brusqueness by sanitary inspectors, customs officials. and highway police.

Beyond all this, however, is the prime need of good assurance that there will be a limit to the regulating. There must be some

way of ensuring that the sanitary inspector sticks to the sanitary
code, the customs official to the tariff schedule, and the highway
police to the traffic regulations. They cannot be permitted to
follow their intuitions and impose their own personal conceptions
of what we ought to do in the public interest. It is true that their
superiors control them and surround them with instructions that
they must obey. This is small comfort to those whose protests
against official action are met by the answer that orders are orders
and must be carried out. The difficulty is that the officials with
whom the citizen has to deal directly rarely make the decisions
that affect him and he cannot get face to face with those who do.

This fact complicates greatly the problem of controlling the
administrative actions of government. On the one hand, men
will often make decisions they would not make if they had also
the painful duty of imposing those decisions on protesting individuals. On the other hand, men will enforce without question
drastic decisions made by others, decisions they themselves would
shrink from making if they had to explain and justify them to
those affected. So, where regulation enters, the vital question is a
very ancient one, *quis custodiet ipsos custodes*—how to control
the controllers, how to permeate the entire civil service with a
sense of responsibility.

A hundred years ago, the short—and, on the whole, adequate
—answer was that official action was bounded everywhere by the
law and that no one could be required to do, or refrain from
doing, any act except as required by the letter of the law. The
law—either common law or statute law—defined in fairly precise
detail what burdens or restrictions government could impose, and
the courts were available to punish any official who overstepped
or commanded his subordinates to overstep the limits set by law.
Of course, it has never been possible to reduce government to an
automaton carrying out the dictates of clearly defined laws. There
were even then in the hands of the governments in question some
discretionary powers not sharply bounded by law. But such powers
were few, and they did not affect deeply the character of economic
and social life and the terms on which individuals and groups
live together in the community.

This short answer is by no means a complete answer today.
We have noted that the present-day legislature cannot enact all

the laws in all the detail necessary and that it delegates a good deal
of law-making power to the executive. We have also seen that
the power of the courts to sit in judgment on official action has
been progressively limited by legislation in the past fifty years.
There is a widening sphere of action open to the executive which
the courts are not permitted to control. In a broad sense, officials
are still bound by the law; but the difficulty is that, over a substantial part of the field of government, the law gives them a
discretionary power to make rules and regulations, and then to
decide what burdens and restrictions the rules and regulations
justify them in imposing on individuals in concrete situations.

THE DISCRETIONARY POWERS OF THE ADMINISTRATIVE

These discretionary powers are conferred by the legislature on
the executive. The executive in the narrow sense, the President
or cabinet, cannot itself exercise this authority. The decisions to
be taken are so numerous and so often require long study and
expert knowledge that they are of necessity taken by members
of the civil service, or the administration. It is always possible, of
course, but not common for the President or cabinet to intervene.
The manner of exercise of discretionary powers by officials is
often described as the administrative process. Good manners and
courtesy in dealing with the public are, as we have seen, highly
desirable qualities in a civil service, but the success or failure of a
government in its public relations does not necessarily raise constitutional or serious political questions. The rapidly growing
importance of the administrative process does raise important
political and constitutional questions which must be discussed.

In the period between the two World Wars, the controversy
over delegation of legislative and judicial powers to the executive
over-shadowed all other constitutional discussion in Britain,
Canada, and the United States. The debate produced a large,
and sometimes acrimonious, literature. The practice of delegation
was attacked as undermining the very foundations of constitutional
government. According to this view, the legislature, whose
function it is to make whatever laws are needed and to control
the executive, abdicates *pro tanto* when it confers law-making
powers on the executive. The representatives of the people betray
the trust reposed in them when they let an unrepresentative civil

service define what the public interest requires. The Rule of Law, which subjects official action to scrutiny by independent courts, has been a vital safeguard of individual liberty. In so far as the judging of disputes between the government and citizens is taken away from the courts, a most salutary external check on the government is weakened. To allow a government official to judge finally in such disputes is to make the government a judge in its own cause—a violation of the elementary canons of justice. In short, it was argued that the well-tried methods for ensuring that government should be servant and not master are being abandoned.

The practice of delegation was supported on the ground of necessity. Legislatures, it was said, have neither the time nor the technical knowledge to make in full detail all the laws the public now expects them to make. Democratic legislatures would have been completely overwhelmed and discredited long ago if they had not had the wit to limit themselves in many matters to the discussion and settlement of general principles of legislation, leaving the voluminous details to be filled in by the executive with rules and regulations. The common-law courts are quite unsuitable tribunals for deciding the disputes that arise out of much present-day legislation. There are several reasons for their ineptitude. Sometimes it is the sheer number of disputes that the judiciary with its present organization and procedure could not begin to handle expeditiously. Sometimes it is the highly technical issues that arise, calling for expert knowledge which the judges do not possess. Sometimes it is the judges' lack of sympathy with the purposes of the legislation—purposes the public wants carried out whether the judges approve of them or not. In short, according to this contention, the nineteenth-century machinery of government will not meet the twentieth-century needs. Cautious experimenting over the last fifty years has produced the administrative process as a partial answer to the new needs.[1]

[1]Much of the literature on the administrative process is highly technical and not always free from anxiety to prove a case one way or the other. Impartial investigations have been made under public auspices in both Britain and the United States. See *Report of the Committee on Ministers' Powers* Cmd. 4060 (His Majesty's Stationery Office, London, 1932), as well as the more recent *Report from the Select Committee on Delegated Legislation* H.C. 310 (H.M.S.O., London, 1953), and *Final Report of the Attorney General's Committee on Administrative Procedure* (Government Printing Office, Washington, 1941). For a balanced and non-technical account of the administrative process in the United States, see J. Roland Pennock, *Administration and the Rule of Law* (Farrar and Rinehart, New York, 1941).

The outbreak of World War II interrupted the debate, compelling us to concentrate all energies on military objectives. It was resumed on the return of peace with many new arguments made available to both sides by the experience of war organization. In organizing for total war, the democratic governments relied heavily on the administrative process and developed it at a fantastic rate to a point far beyond its peacetime scope. The legislatures, while reserving to themselves the decision on a few great matters of principle, delegated the planning and management of the war to the executive. The laws that assigned to the population their several duties and responsibilities in the common effort were almost entirely made by the executive through rules and regulations and orders-in-council. Very few of the innumerable disputes that arose between the governments and private interests in the war organization ever came before the courts. They were settled either by negotiation or by orders and directives emerging from the executive or from one of the many administrative boards and alphabet agencies that the executive set up to aid in the task of winning the war.

This experience lends support to the view that the administrative process is the inevitable instrument of large-scale governmental operations. At the same time, it is far from refuting the contention that the administrative process has grave dangers for liberal democracy. There were not lacking during the war indications that government by administrative order and decision can easily get out of hand. The debate continues with undiminished vigour.

The place to be accorded to the administrative is one of the big issues facing democratic government. The time has not come to suggest a conclusion. It is much more important at present to try to understand what is involved. Its scope must be fully appreciated. Its character, whether virtuous or vicious, must be estimated and that can only be done by seeing what it does and how it does it. Finally, it cannot be judged at all without some understanding of its causes.

Why Administrative Discretions Are Given

Its causes can be suggested at once, leaving fuller verification to emerge from a discussion of its scope and character. The administrative process is the result of the great expansion in the activities of governments in the last half-century. In chapter v, a distinction was made between the negative state of the nineteenth century and the positive state of the twentieth century, and some of the sweeping social and economic changes contributing to the shift were indicated. In the negative state, laissez faire was the ideal. Within a framework of order provided by government, each person was expected to take care of himself, either by his own efforts or in voluntary co-operation with others. Little was expected of governments. The legislature could itself make whatever small supplementary additions to or modifications of the common law were required. The laws, whether common law or statute, were adequately enforced by the courts' punishing those who broke them and thus deterring the bulk of the population from infringing them. The technique, if not the aim, of government was negative. It contented itself, in the main, with saying, "Thou shalt not."

In the positive state, government ceases to be merely an umpire calling fouls and retiring offending players to the cooler. It becomes a schoolmaster of the old school setting lessons that the citizens positively must learn. The aim of the teaching is to get people to do the things necessary to ensure minimum standards of health, education, safety, and economic well-being for all. The materials set out in chapter v show how numerous are the fields in which government is pushing the realization of one or other of these standards. The attaining of these standards is regarded as so important that, wherever possible, the government defines in great and precise detail the rules of deportment for well-behaved citizens in a complex society. For the same reason, the government takes vigorous steps to enforce observance of the rules and standards. It is not regarded as sufficient in many instances to have the courts punish those who disobey; they must be made to obey. So the government gets into a great deal of inquisitorial and supervisory activity after the fashion of schoolmasters. We are in the era of the positive state because the state is now concerned to get positive results. It says, "thou shalt," and maintains a great inspectorial and enforcement staff to enforce its commands.

The executive is the only branch of government equipped to put energy into getting concrete results. Wars, for example, are directed by the executive and not by legislatures and courts. So the growth of government activities and the shift in the part government is expected to play have aggrandized the executive. The legislature sets the broad objectives of public policy. The executive uses its administrative establishment to expound those objectives in innumerable rules and regulations, and to enforce observance of such rules and regulations. The way in which this enlarges the discretionary power of officials will be made clear by concrete illustration. The illustrations are actual instances of discretionary powers found in one or other of the three countries. Some of the United States and Canadian illustrations are drawn from the state and provincial rather than the federal sphere because government action in the former spheres is often more closely related to common experience and therefore should be easier to understand. The purpose is to indicate the nature of a common development and not to measure its scope in any one of the governments under consideration.

DELEGATION OF LEGISLATIVE POWER TO THE EXECUTIVE

The giving of discretionary power to the executive to make rules of law may be looked at first. In most present-day legislation, the legislature, for whatever reason, does not attempt to make the law in all its concrete detail. It sketches in outline the broad general principles and delegates power to fill in the details. Sometimes in Britain and Canada, the power delegated is very wide. For example, in Canada legislation concerned with the emergency of war authorizes the executive to make such orders and regulations as it "deems necessary for the security, defence, peace, order, and welfare of Canada" as long as the emergency continues. In the United States, certain constitutional restrictions, and the desire of Congress to limit the executive have prevented the grant of such extremely wide legislative powers to the executive.

Usually, the power given is limited to making rules under one particular statute such as the pure-food law or the law regulating the issue and sale of corporate securities. Even here, the power is sometimes stated generally, "to make such rules and regulations as may be necessary for the operation of this Act," and not limited to making rules on certain specified and narrowly limited matters.

Sometimes in Britain and Canada the power is delegated to the cabinet. Such delegations can be readily identified, as they are always exercised by order-in-council. Sometimes it is given to a minister of a particular department, or to a board or commission outside the departmental structure such as the Transport Commission or the Minimum Wage Board. In either case, the rules and regulations so made are generally known as delegated, or subordinate, legislation. In the United States, the rule-making power may be conferred on the President, on one of the secretaries of one of the departments, or on one of the many independent boards and commissions such as the Federal Communications Commission or the Securities and Exchange Commission.

It will be recalled that the separation of powers imposed by the Constitution of the United States reserves the exercise of legislative power to Congress. This might be thought to prevent all delegation to executive agencies of power to make rules and regulations. It does prevent the grant of extremely wide general powers of legislation such as are occasionally given by the legislature to the executive in Britain and Canada. But the Supreme Court has always upheld the validity of the delegation of clearly defined and limited powers to make detailed regulations. In this way, room has been made within the Constitution for extensive subordinate legislation by the executive.

It is impossible to give, in a short space, any accurate impression of the scope and extent of the practice of subordinate legislation. Half the statutes of the British Parliament enacted in the nineteen-twenties gave such power to the executive. Over a hundred statutes, about one half of the acts of the Dominion Parliament in force in 1933, contained provisions authorizing subordinate legislation. Although precise figures are not available for more recent periods, the proportion is now much greater. In sheer bulk, the annual output of subordinate legislation greatly exceeds the annual output of the legislature.

Even in what are called normal times, the number of pages of orders-in-council, rules, and regulations put out by the executive under a statute generally far exceeds the number of pages covered by the statute itself. In periods of emergency, legislative law-making is completely dwarfed by executive rule making. The rules

made in one year under the Agricultural Adjustment Act, one of
the Roosevelt New Deal measures for meeting the great depression
in the United States, covered more pages than all the laws relating
to agriculture passed by Congress since the founding of the
Republic. The rules made under the National Industry Recovery
Act, another of these measures, in the two years of its existence,
filled 10,000 pages.[1] The emergency of war carried this development to hitherto unimagined lengths. In 1946, immediately after
the war, some 1,900 federal statutory provisions in the United
States either authorized or required executive agencies to make
rules and regulations. Many of these were of minor importance,
but the figure gives some idea of the reliance on subordinate
legislation.

Reasons for Subordinate Legislation

Obviously, no legislature could begin to debate and enact a
fraction of the rules that emergencies call for. But even in the
normal activities of present-day governments, the legislature cannot find time for much of the detailed law making. The terms
on which the citizen can use the facilities of the post office, for
example, depend much more on regulations made by the post-
master general than on laws made by the legislature. These
regulations fix the size and weight of packages and determine what
matter shall enjoy mailing privileges at particular rates. They
provide for determining, within the context of the general law
on the subject, what is dangerous, immoral, or fraudulent matter,
and for prohibiting transmission of such matter through the mails.
They also fix, among other things, the conditions of the issue of
money orders and postal notes, of the registration of letters, and
of the insuring of parcels.

The exact scope of the rule-making power relating to the post
office varies from country to country, but in all three, postal regulations cover a very wide field. The legislature could take time to
make these rules, but only at the expense of deliberation on other
matters. The upshot is that in many fields of legislation, the legislature debates and fixes the general policy, and the administration

[1] Ernest S. Griffith, *The Impasse of Democracy* (Harrison-Hilton, New
York, 1939), p. 108.

makes most of the detailed rules thought necessary to carry out ✓ that policy.

Many of the questions to be decided in making post-office regulations require special knowledge. The size and weight of parcels and the scope of insurance and special-delivery facilities, among other things, can only be fixed by those who have had considerable experience in the post-office business and know the general conditions in which it has to be carried on. Whatever regulations are made must be approved and issued by the post-master general, but they are not made by him. They are made by the permanent civil servants who do the work of running the post office.

Often the question what the details of the law should be ✓ depends on expert technical or scientific knowledge. Legislatures are not chosen for their scientific attainments, and experts in the civil service must be relied on. The details of legislation prescribing safety measures in factories and other work places must be adjusted to the conditions of a great variety of industrial establishments. In some instances, it may be enough to require the fencing and covering of exposed machinery. But if protection is to be afforded against physical injury from such risks as explosions and against industrial diseases in the more complicated industrial processes, the measures must be worked out through careful study of the different kinds of risks, and of the kinds of measures that will combat them, in all types of establishments and processes. Expert engineering and other scientific knowledge is vital to success. In one state after another, the fixing of the details of the safety code has been delegated to an administrative agency. Scientific knowledge has been applied, in one way and another, in most spheres of economic and social life, and when government intervenes in these spheres, it must master the elements of science involved as well as take account of economic and political considerations.

Moreover, when government undertakes to regulate economic matters, it must bring a wide knowledge of economic facts to its decisions. A legislature may decide, for example, that employers of labour must pay at least a minimum wage and be content with a maximum number of hours of work per week from each employee. But the minima and maxima must be related to the cost of living and to the state of the labour market. Also, conditions vary so widely in different industries that a single standard of minimum wages and maximum hours often cannot be set for all industries and employments affected by the law. So there is a growing practice in many jurisdictions to leave it to an administrative agency to make orders prescribing, within certain broad limits laid down by the legislature, the exact minima and maxima for different employments. The proportion of apprentices and learners to be allowed in each trade, the minimum scale of payment to them and to handicapped or partially disabled workers are often similarly fixed.

Reliance on copious subordinate lawmaking in this particular field has gone further in Britain and Canada than in the United States, where Supreme Court decisions holding minimum-wage laws to be unconstitutional delayed for a long period extensive experimenting with this kind of legislation. But it does afford a simple illustration of what occurs nowadays in many fields. The complexity of industry and economic life is such that the legislature, after deciding on a broad policy of regulation, has to leave much of the necessary rule making to the administrative.

The intricate regulations that we have seen to be necessary in one sphere of government activity after another can hardly ever be laid down once for all. In some instances, it is by no means clear what should be done, and the regulations must be tentative and experimental. In other instances such as the minimum-wage laws, the interests being regulated discover loopholes in the regulations, and these must be plugged by changes in and additions to the regulations. In any field of regulation, new circumstances and new conditions not contemplated when the law was made emerge from time to time and the rules must be adjusted to them. That is to say, much of present-day legislation is continually in a process of adjustment and change. Adjustment can be made best by a body that can act quickly at any time and that is close to the experience gained in trying to make the law effective. This is another reason for lodging powers of subordinate legislation with the administration.

It is clear that the political executive, the cabinet or President, is no more able to make all these regulations than is the legislature.

Subordinate legislation frequently issues in their name and, because the civil service is under their command, they can modify or veto proposed regulations at any time. If an influential body of opinion is aroused over a piece of subordinate legislation, it will be able to get the political executive to examine carefully the content of the rules and regulations and perhaps to modify it. Short of insistent and convincing external pressure, the political executive accepts without much question what its informed and expert advisers propose on the details of subordinate legislation. Keeping this qualification in mind, it will be convenient henceforth to speak of subordinate legislation being made by the administration, meaning civil servants in government departments or in the independent boards and commissions sometimes set up to assist in the administrative process.

Control of Subordinate Legislation

Because it is often left to civil servants to say how the general principles declared by the legislature shall be applied to concrete situations, they have a substantial discretionary power to determine how the law shall bear on individuals and groups. In fact, it is often impossible to say who will be affected in what ways, and how much, until regulations have been framed and issued. So lobbies and pressure groups are almost as much concerned with the deliberations of the administration in framing regulations as they are with the deliberations of the legislature. With a vital interest in the way civil servants exercise their discretion, the pressure groups likely to be affected are always seeking access to the administration to present their suggestions and protests.

For example, when regulations are to be made under the minimum-wage law, a large number of employers' organizations and several trade unions are likely to ask to be heard. For every exercise of a power of subordinate legislation, there is a cluster of interests with representations to make. They try to persuade the civil servants, or the political executive, or both, how the discretion should be exercised. The legislature, the representatives of the people, has no direct part in the making of these rules. What then ensures that the civil servants will exercise their discretion conformably to the public interest or the will of the legislature?

In the first place, the legislature sets limits to the rule-making power and any rules that go beyond the power granted are invalid. If the minimum-wage board which is authorized to fix minimum wages presumes to fix maximum wages as well, no one need obey the maxima so set. In the Anglo-American system, it is always possible to refuse to obey subordinate legislation on the ground that the legislature never gave the necessary power to make it, and the courts are always open to test such a contention. In this way, subordinate legislation can be kept within the limits laid down by the legislature.

The effectiveness of such a check depends on how clearly the legislature has specified the limits. We have already noticed the power given to the post-office department to make rules on certain specific matters. If the grant of power is limited to particular specified matters, there are reasonably clear limits set to administrative rule-making powers. But often, as in the Post Office Act and many other statutes of the Canadian Parliament, the statute goes on to give the administrative authority in question power to make such rules and regulations as it "deems necessary and expedient for carrying this Act into effect." Where this is done, the courts find it considerably harder to say what the precise limits of the rule-making power are. If the legislature wants to impose sharp control, it should be niggardly in the use of general phrases. But the frequency of such phrases in grants of rule-making power suggests that the legislature is impressed with the need for flexible grants of power.

Secondly, the legislature can require that subordinate legislation shall be laid on the table in the legislature within a stated time after it is made. In this way the legislature knows what regulations have been made and can find opportunities of debating those it does not like. It can, if it so desires, enact a law repealing any or all subordinate legislation. It can go further and repeal the delegation, taking all rule-making power away from a particular administrative agency.

In the United States, Congress has not made any significant use of the device of requiring subordinate legislation to be tabled. In Britain and Canada, Parliament has often but not invariably inserted such a requirement in particular statutes delegating legislative power. However, in practice, little use was made of the opportunity for a long time, and regulations were rarely taken off the table. There are so many of them and their subject matter is so complicated and technical that busy members of the legislature preferred to allot their time to matters that paid larger dividends in public attention. In 1944, however, a select committee of the British House of Commons was established to give sustained scrutiny to the subordinate legislation tabled in the House and to report to the House on particular rules and regulations that seemed to merit special consideration. As a result of the work of this committee, Parliament passed an act in 1946 standardizing some of the procedures for enacting, tabling, and publishing subordinate legislation.

In 1950, the Canadian Parliament passed a somewhat similar act requiring that substantially all subordinate legislation shall be tabled in Parliament and published. Thus far, however, the Canadian House of Commons has not set up a special committee to examine and report to the House on subordinate legislation tabled there. Such a committee is highly desirable but it should not be thought that legislative checks on subordinate legislation are entirely lacking in its absence. If outrageous regulations are made, they will be debated in the House, and someone will have to answer for them. So the administration always keeps the House in mind when framing subordinate legislation.

Thirdly, the political executive that controls the civil service is the instrument of the ruling political party, and the parties are responsive to electoral opinion. Therefore the cabinet or President is concerned with the content of subordinate legislation. Proposed regulations which if enacted might rouse significant sections of opinion are likely to get careful scrutiny by or on behalf of the political executive. Scrutiny is somewhat closer in Britain and Canada than in the United States. As we shall see later, many of the powers of subordinate legislation granted by Congress are placed in the hands of the independent executive agencies of the national government. In their daily work, these agencies are all more or less independent of the President and he generally has not the power to check their rule-making activities.

One of the best indications of what reactions to subordinate legislation can be expected is the attitude of the interest groups concerned. Fourthly, there is therefore, in all three countries, close

I interest group act as a check upon the subordinate legislation

consultation between the executive and interest groups when controversial regulations are being framed or amended, which provides
the most continuous check on subordinate legislation. The nature
of this consultation will be considered more fully at a later point in
this chapter. It should be noted here, however, that the United
States Congress—but not the British and Canadian Parliaments—
often lays down in the statute itself certain requirements as to how
the rule-making authority is to proceed in making rules. In recent
years, there has been a growing tendency for Congress to require
particular administrative authorities to hold a hearing, at which
interested persons and groups are entitled to appear, before regulations are made. In 1946, Congress passed the Administrative
Procedure Act, which requires, as a general rule, that almost all
administrative rule making shall be preceded by a formal hearing.
The procedure to be followed at the hearing is specified in some
detail and resembles that followed in judicial trials.

A fifth kind of check on subordinate legislation exists in the
United States and is of occasional importance. It arises from the
fact that the United States Constitution establishes the separation
of powers and also certain guarantees of private rights which no
governmental agency is entitled to override. If Congress delegates
to the executive, or to an administrative agency, an unfettered
discretion to make rules without imposing, at the same time,
standards or principles to control and limit the exercise of the
discretion, this will be held to be an unconstitutional delegation of
legislative power to the executive. In certain limited kinds of circumstances, the procedure followed by the administrative authority
in fixing its rules and regulations or the content of the rules themselves may be held by the courts to violate due process of law. If
so, the rules in question are invalid. In Britain and Canada, where
such constitutional provisions do not exist, subordinate legislation
is not open to attack on these grounds. The courts can only inquire
whether the legislature has manifestly authorized the rule-making
body to do what it has done.

ADMINISTRATIVE ENFORCEMENT OF THE LAW

When subordinate legislation enacted under the powers given
in a particular statute has defined with some exactness what

individuals are to do or refrain from doing, the executive is ready to enforce the general policy laid down by the statute. As already explained, the requirements of the positive state often cannot be met merely by having the courts impose fines or imprisonment on those who infringe the regulations. The framers of the general policy are not so much concerned to punish offenders as to ensure that the regulations will be obeyed and thus achieve positive results. Accordingly, the legislature often arms the executive with still further powers.

further power given to the executive

In many of the functions of government outlined in chapter v, the administration is authorized to employ inspectors with power to enter premises and conduct investigations to see whether the law is being obeyed. Where particular trades and businesses are being extensively regulated, the legislature often authorizes the administration to require individuals or corporations engaged in one of these businesses to take out a licence or permit. If inspection shows serious infringement of the law, the licence may be cancelled or suspended and the right to engage in that particular business taken away. These are powerful weapons for compelling obedience.

For example, in enforcing certain portions of the pure-food laws, the government does not wait until the poisoned consumer of canned meat starts an action in the courts against the manufacturer. It establishes a permit system, and sends inspectors into the factories to see that the legal conditions on which the permit is issued are being obeyed. If not, it may suspend the permit, or, in some circumstances, refuse to allow the manufacturer to use approved labels, until he takes adequate steps to comply with the law.

This and similar techniques have a very wide application. It is not now regarded as satisfactory that those who carelessly allow disastrous fires to break out should be punished after the event. The victims can sue the culprit for damages, but too often this is just the old precaution of locking the stable after the horse is stolen. The culprit has not the means to make good the damage he has caused. The community is reaching for an enforced standard of safety, and the legislature authorizes the government to employ fire inspectors to enter premises and insist on a minimum of precautions against fire. Minimum standards of sanitation are not sufficiently enforced by keeping the courts open to punish those who ignore the sanitary code. Medical health officers are authorized to inspect premises and to placard those they find are not reasonably fit for human habitation. Similar illustrations could be found in many fields of government activity.

This is what is called administrative, as distinct from judicial, enforcement of the law. In discussing the Anglo-American judicial system we saw that judicial enforcement of the law is, by long tradition, punitive and compensatory rather than preventive. It punishes wrong and does not try directly to compel people to do right. Administrative enforcement does try to prevent wrong-doing. It is no exaggeration to say that this can be a colossal task if it is undertaken in many branches of human affairs. In part, it explains why the negative state could get along numbering its judges in dozens while the positive state must count its civil servants in tens or hundreds of thousands. It also goes far to explain the increasing inroads on the constitutional principle of the Rule of Law, referred to in earlier chapters. This principle was explained as ensuring that government officials could not impose burdens on the citizens by their own decision but could only do so through the decision of a court that the law justified the burden. With few exceptions, this principle ruled in the era of the negative state.

In the last sixty years, the exceptions have eaten deeply into the principle. The owner of premises may find them closed without the courts' having first decided the issue whether they are fit for human habitation or not. The Securities and Exchange Commission in the United States, in its regulation of brokers and stock exchanges, has power in specified circumstances to revoke the licences of brokers and to cancel the registration of securities, thus preventing trading in these securities on a national stock exchange. Commercial disputes over the correct grade of particular lots of grain are settled with virtual finality by officials of the federal Department of Agriculture in the United States, and by officials of the Grain Commission in Canada. Foreigners who enter the United States or Canada may be expelled from either country without ever being able to get the legality or illegality of their entry decided by a court. Here are instances drawn from widely different fields in which the legislature in one or other of the countries under discussion has conferred on administrative authorities the power of deciding issues and/or enforcing the law. The agencies or officials who possess such powers are often called administrative tribunals.

It must not be thought that the courts are excluded from all consideration of the exercise of powers of the kind just described. Sometimes, the statute that grants such powers to administrative agencies expressly provides for a limited appeal from the decision of the agency to the courts. The courts have a varying power to review most kinds of administrative action. The scope of judicial review will be considered later. It is sufficient here to remember that it does exist and that it is considerably broader in the United States than in Britain or Canada.

It may be that some of these instances of administrative power should be approved and others rejected. It is not the present purpose to suggest whether particular inroads on the authority of the courts to settle disputes are justifiable or not. The purpose rather is to examine the nature of the administrative process and see the main reasons for its increasing use. This can only be done by considering still further instances of its use.

ADMINISTRATIVE ADJUDICATION

We have seen that the legislature often cannot make the law in detail for lack of knowledge of all the circumstances to which the law is to be applied. It lays down a general policy in terms of a standard of health or safety that it desires to be achieved. In a significant number of instances, it is recognized that the administration, for the same reasons, cannot make precise rules and regulations, and the legislature makes the best of it by authorizing the administration to apply the standard to particular cases as they arise. For example, it has long been found necessary to have laws regulating railways and other public utilities because of their monopoly position. Such enterprises, if unregulated, always produce a variety of abuses. They charge exorbitant rates, discriminate between those who use the service they provide, and give poor service with a take-it-or-leave-it attitude. It is clear enough, to take the case of railways, that the law should require them to act reasonably. But to define in advance what would be reasonable in all the possible circumstances of railway operation is an impossible task. Thus, on these vital points, the legislature merely says that railways must charge reasonable rates, provide reasonable facilities, avoid unreasonable delay in transporting commodities, and refrain from discrimination against one shipper in favour of another. It then authorizes an administrative agency, the Inter-state Commerce Commission in the United States and the Trans-port Commission in Canada, to apply these standards to particular complaints as they arise, and, in the case of rates, to fix certain standard rates of charges for the future.

Application of Vague Standards

In one sense, the Commission judges disputes between the rail-ways and their customers, interpreting the law as stated in the standard of reasonableness set by the legislature. In another sense, the Commission makes law, not by general rules, but by a special order for each case as it comes up. In fact, the experts on legal theory are not agreed as to whether many of the activities of these Commissions are legislative or judicial. For present purposes, it does not matter which is the correct view. The essential point is that any body authorized to take all the circumstances of a parti-cular case into account has important discretionary power to affect the rights of those who appear before it.

In the United States, for many years attempts were made to regulate railways by minute rules of law interpreted and applied by the judiciary. They were not effective. In Britain, for many years the function of applying to particular cases the vague standards mentioned above was left to the courts. This too was unsatisfactory and was abandoned. The body that is to enforce these standards on railway companies must know the technical ramifications of railway management and engineering as well as the part played by railway transportation in a diversified economy. The courts do not possess this expert knowledge. In the end, in all three countries, the legislature delegated the power of regulating railways to a specialized administrative agency which devotes most, if not all, of its time and energy to railway regulation and which can draw on the expert talent necessary.

There are a great many other instances, always increasing in number, in which the legislature has authorized administrative agencies to apply vague standards to particular cases and thus to modify the rights and liabilities of citizens. Such instances are most commonly found where regulation of some aspect of economic life is being undertaken. The legislature has a view of the desired result, which it embodies in a standard. At the same time, it recognizes the impossibility of foreseeing the almost infinite number of different combinations of circumstances that may arise, and of making precise rules of law to cover them.

In fact, law is not at all a suitable technique for regulating the innermost intricacies of human relationships. Regulation by fixed rules of law is only workable where you can specify particular kinds of conduct as undesirable and forbid them. It is one thing to enact a law making wife-beating a criminal offence. It is an entirely different thing to lay down a complete code of fair and sympathetic treatment of wives by following which a man would fully honour the standard of conduct set by his marriage vows. If comprehensive regulation of marital enterprise ever becomes necessary, it will have to be done by an administrative agency with power to decide according to the particular circumstances of each case.

Law can regulate the margins but not the minutiae of conduct. If the minutiae must be closely regulated, the appropriate technique is military discipline, with every hour and every movement of the soldier subject to command. So where government regulation of a trade or business becomes very extensive, there are at least plausible arguments for government ownership and operation where the necessary discipline can be imposed. Administrative regulation of economic life of the order outlined in chapter v is a halfway house between free private enterprise subject to general rules of law, on the one hand, and state ownership where the government gives all the orders, on the other. It is not yet clear whether the halfway house can be made a permanent stopping place.

Thus there is today a large sphere where the courts no longer judge disputes because there is no law for them to apply. The judgments to be made in many fields of governmental activity involve discretion, and the exercise of discretion requires a judgment on what public policy should be. In a democracy, the legislature and the majority party are the authorities on public policy for the time being. Therefore, discretion in the hands of administrative agencies has to be controlled either by the legislature or by the political executive, which, in turn, is responsible through the legislature and/or the political parties to the electorate. In this way, the discretionary decisions made by administrative agencies can be kept in touch with the policy that the authorities on public policy want to enforce.

Expert and Rapid Decision

Also, the discretion can only be exercised satisfactorily in many instances by those with expert knowledge. An administrative tribunal such as the Interstate Commerce Commission or the Transport Commission generally specializes in one type of problem and can be staffed with experts. The judiciary has to deal with all sorts of disputes and cannot be expected to have a wide range of expertness in railways, sanitary engineering, and so on. Further, as already explained in discussing the judiciary, the courts are sometimes unsympathetic to the aims of present-day legislation. Generally speaking, the judges, until recently, have had little sympathy with governments' efforts to regulate economic life. The case of workmen's compensation legislation, already noticed in chapter v, is a sufficient example. As was noted in chapter xiii, judicial attitudes are slowly changing, but for a long time they provided an additional ground for limiting the jurisdiction of the courts in the kind of matters we are concerned with here.

There is still another class of modern legislation which confers the power of settling disputes on administrative agencies to the exclusion of the courts. This is the legislation making provision for social security. Where it is decided that the government should make certain payments to those persons who suffer from particular types of misfortune, it is necessary, either by statute or by subordinate legislation, to define the conditions for claiming such payments. For example, provincial old-age pensions in Canada are payable only to those who can show that they belong to a certain category of age, residence, need, etc. A claim for a pension, or an application for cancellation of one now being given, raises issues that one might expect to be settled by the judiciary. However, almost invariably, an administrative agency, such as an old-age pensions board is given power to decide whether a pension should be granted or cancelled, reduced or increased in amount.

The reasons for taking claims to social security payments away from the courts are several. Claims for and disputes over pensions, unemployment-insurance benefits, and the like are very numerous. The judicial system with its cumbrous, if not dilatory, procedure could not begin to handle all the claims and disputes that arise, and the delays would amount to denials of justice. Most people who make such claims are needy persons and can afford neither delay nor expense. Accordingly, such cases commonly go to administrative tribunals, which use a summary procedure adapted to the kind of cases arising and which settle all disputes without significant cost to the claimants.

Encroachment of the administrative on the preserves of the judiciary is going on in many fields. It is everywhere related to the assumption of positive tasks by government. It is a response to the demands of the positive state for preventive rather than punitive action, for close collaboration between the making of law and the interpreting and enforcing of law, for expert knowledge, sympathetic interpretation, flexible procedure, and rapid decision in settling claims and disputes. It is impossible to give any meaningful statement of the extent of the encroachment beyond saying that there are scores of administrative agencies with powers of this kind in each of the countries under study here. The significance of the development can be stated most clearly by saying that the more complex the functions assigned to government, the more specialized administrative tribunals must be used to settle the disputes arising.

JUDICIAL REVIEW OF ADMINISTRATIVE ADJUDICATION

The question arises how the administrative can encroach on the sphere of the judiciary in the United States, in view of the prominent place occupied by the separation of powers in the American Constitution. Article III of the Constitution vests the judicial power of the United States in the federal judiciary. Many of the powers to make discretionary decisions that Congress confers on administrative agencies have been held not to involve exercise of the judicial power. Numerous other such powers, however, have undoubted judicial elements. Article III, as interpreted, does not forbid Congress to give the initial exercise of judicial power to an administrative agency, but it does prevent Congress from making such an administrative adjudication final and conclusive. That is to say, where specifically judicial power is so delegated, the decisions made are always open to fairly extensive judicial review by the courts.[1]

The separation of powers thus limits the scope of administrative adjudication in the United States. In Britain and Canada, where the separation of powers is not written into the constitution, Parliament is free to make any administrative adjudication final and conclusive if it wishes.

Apart altogether from the separation of powers, the judiciary in all three countries retains significant power to review administrative decisions that affect the rights of citizens, whether these decisions are specifically judicial or not. This power may arise from the terms of the particular statute conferring administrative powers, or from accepted principles of the common law, supplemented in the United States by the due process clauses of the Constitution. In its broadest outlines, which alone can be discussed in brief space here, this power is much the same in all three countries.

It is for the legislature to say, within the limits, if any, imposed by the constitution, how far administrative adjudication is to go. In many statutes that give the administration power to decide particular issues, provision is made for an appeal to the courts on questions of interpretation of the law. In addition, each such statute always limits the matters that the official is empowered to decide. If the official presumes to decide questions the statute does not authorize him to decide, his decision has no validity, and the courts, on application to them, will so hold. For example, an administrative order may be made under the immigration laws for the deportation of A. B. as an undesirable alien. However, if A. B. claims to be a citizen by birth, he can get the judiciary to decide this question of citizenship. For, while the administra-

[1]*Final report of the Attorney General's Committee on Administrative Procedure*, p. 80.

tion has power to deport aliens, it has no power to deport natural-born citizens. Every power of administrative decision is subject to limits, broad or narrow, and the courts can always be invoked to see that these limits are not transgressed.

there are limits upon administrative decisions.

The courts also retain power to examine the fairness of the procedure of administrative agencies. For example, if the agency fails to give a party notice of proceedings being taken against him or an opportunity to tell his side of the story, the courts will, on request, set aside the decision against him. Also, if the decision is obviously and scandalously wrong, as when there was no substantial evidence to support the finding of fact on which the decision is based, it is possible for the courts to intervene.

Courts have the power to examine the fairness of the administrative agencies.

In Britain and Canada, the power of the courts to review the procedure followed by an administrative agency rests mainly on the common law and so can be modified or removed by an act of the legislature. In the United States, in the absence of a statute imposing more stringent procedural requirements, it rests on the due process clauses of the Constitution and therefore is beyond the power of Congress. Also, the effect of the due process clauses is to extend the scope of judicial review of administrative decisions considerably further in the United States than in Britain or Canada.

The legislature may, if it sees fit, prescribe in detail the procedure that administrative agencies are to follow in making decisions. This is rarely done in Britain or Canada. In recent years, Congress has frequently specified the procedure to be followed by particular agencies. And the Administrative Procedure Act of 1946 already referred to lays down rules of procedure for almost all administrative agencies of the federal government. It also enlarges significantly the possibilities of judicial review of administrative action. It subjects to judicial review a number of agencies hitherto exempt from it and opens to judicial review some kinds of administrative action which, prior to the Act, were not subject to scrutiny by the courts.

> USA

The Administrative Procedure Act is an attempt to recapture for the judiciary much of the ground it has lost through the rise of the administrative process. It is regarded with alarm by some at least of those who hold that flexibility in the administrative process is essential to effective performance of the functions of present-day government.[1] Nevertheless, the American Bar Association which was influential in having the Act passed has not relinquished its determined struggle to arrest these recent developments in administration. The Administrative Procedure Act was its most important counter-offensive, and ten years later, supported by the Second Hoover Commission, it asked Congress to transfer the judicial functions of several commissions to separate courts.

One other important characteristic of judicial review of administrative action should be kept in mind. In the absence of express authorization by the legislature, judicial review does not entitle the courts to try the merits of the case and render a decision settling the issue between the parties. It merely entitles them to quash the administrative decision for some specified defect and, in effect, to require the agency to re-try the case. The reason for this limitation is clear enough. The courts are experts on matters of law and fair play. But the substance of the issue decided by the administrative agency is often a highly technical question as, for example, in railway regulation. The administrative agency rather than the courts is the competent expert on the substance of the matter to be decided by it. Another important limitation arises out of the fact that, in practice, judicial review can only be brought into operation in a fraction of the great numbers of issues dealt with by the administrative agencies.

THE INDEPENDENT REGULATORY BOARDS AND COMMISSIONS

We should now be able to understand the current discussions about the role of boards and commissions in present-day government. The powers of subordinate legislation, administrative adjudication and administrative enforcement of the law discussed in this chapter are conferred on the executive. In Britain, they are, in almost all cases, conferred on one or other of the existing departments of government and the minister at the head of the department is responsible to Parliament for their exercise. But in the United States and Canada, boards or commissions outside the regular departments are often—although not always—set up to

[1]See Frederick F. Blachly and Miriam E. Oatman, "Sabotage of the Administrative Process," *Public Administration Review*, 6 (1946), pp. 213–27.

exercise such powers, particularly when powers to hear and settle claims and disputes are involved. These are known as the independent regulatory commissions.

In setting up independent boards, the legislature takes the view that since the functions to be exercised resemble judicial functions, they should be exercised by bodies with some independence of the government of the day. Accordingly, these agencies are kept outside the departmental structure and they are not directly under the control of the President or the cabinet. In their everyday operations, they are more or less independent both of the executive and the legislature. Important Canadian examples are the Transport Commission, the Grain Commission, and the Unemployment Insurance Commission. Some of the more famous in the United States are the Federal Trade Commission, the Interstate Commerce Commission, the Securities and Exchange Commission, the Federal Communications Commission, and the National Labor Relations Board.

There is widespread, vigorous criticism of the powers and activities of these boards. In part, the criticism is aimed at their independence. They are not judges, members of an ancient profession sworn to uphold the law, yet they have independence of a kind accorded to judges. They are instruments for enforcing the policy of the legislature and the dominant political party, yet they are, to some degree, independent of both legislature and executive. The essence of the criticism, however, is that each of them is a government in miniature violating the doctrine of the separation of powers which large bodies of opinion in Canada think should be respected even though it is not provided for in the constitution. For most, if not all, these boards and commissions also have powers of subordinate legislation. They also have powers of inspection and investigation. They are authorized to launch and carry through prosecutions of offenders against the laws they are administering. In many matters, they are themselves the judges of whether individuals are meeting the requirements of the laws and vague general standards they are administering.

So a board is often, at one and the same time, lawmaker, detective, prosecutor, judge, and jury. Those who make the law also interpret and enforce it. The board is likely to be biased in

favour of the policy it is trying to enforce. Allowing a board or
government department or anyone else to be judge of his own
case leaves something to be desired. It is easy to point to instances
of capricious, if not oppressive, use of this panoply of powers—
abuses that advocates of the separation of powers have always
feared.

On the other hand, it is argued that this combination of legislative, executive, and semi-judicial powers in the hands of a board
or commission is not likely to be seriously abused as long as the
legislature has—as it undoubtedly has—the authority to take back
from these bodies the powers it has given them. Up to a point,
this argument is correct. It is correct only in so far as the legislature has a genuine alternative. If it is necessary that we should
rely ever more heavily on government to perform complex functions, and if these functions can only be performed through the
use of wide administrative discretions, the legislature has not a
genuine alternative. It cannot abolish administrative agencies and
powers; it can merely reshuffle them.

Attacks on the Independence of the Commissions

The independent regulatory boards and commissions of the
federal government in the United States are under heavy fire from
two different directions. On the ground that the President should
be the over-all co-ordinator of administration charged with bringing
all aspects of administrative policy into line with the general policies
of the government, the President's Committee on Administrative
Management recommended in 1937 that almost all the boards
and commissions be brought into one or other of the ten great
departments, where their work would be subject to direction by
the President. Such a step would open the work these commissions
have been performing to direct political influence, but it would
also ensure clear lines of responsibility culminating in the President
who, in turn, is responsible to the electorate for his conduct of
administration.

In the succeeding decade, some limited progress was made in
implementing these recommendations. Then, in 1947, Congress
set up the Hoover Commission to consider in detail the organization of the executive branch of government. This body considered

the position of the independent regulatory commissions with great care. While acknowledging the importance of over-all presidential control of general administrative policy, the Commission thought this could be achieved sufficiently without bringing the independent regulatory commissions inside the government departments, and limited its proposals on this aspect of executive organization to a number of relatively minor recommendations.

The President's Committee on Administrative Management, when recommending the merger of the independent commissions in the departments, did make an express exception for functions of a judicial nature performed by the commissions. It suggested that the officers of the commissions who perform these judicial functions should be made substantially independent of both President and Congress. This accords with another strong body of opinion, particularly in the legal profession, that administrative bodies should not be allowed to perform essentially judicial functions. Following this line of thought, the Administrative Procedure Act of 1946 provided for the withdrawal of the administrative officers who perform functions of this kind from the control of administrative agencies and the conferring on them of an independent status similar to that enjoyed by the judiciary.

There has been no agreement on the wisdom of this step. In 1939, at the instance of the President, the Attorney-General appointed a committee of experts to make a close investigation of administrative procedure in the federal government. A majority of the Attorney-General's Committee on Administrative Procedure, as it was called, refused to recommend such segregation as a general principle, while a minority were strongly in favour of it.[1] There is still the greatest diversity of counsel on what to do about independent boards and commissions, and the administrative process.

The problem of keeping administrative discretion adequately under control remains acute even though the powers are always housed in a government department. Although the device of independent regulatory boards and commissions is little used in Britain, the same arguments are broadly applicable to the British situation. The same combination of discretionary powers is widely

[1] *Final Report of the Attorney General's Committee.* Compare the views of the majority on pp. 43-60 with minority opinions stated on pp. 203-8 and 248-50.

used there. The principal difference is that they are generally given to government departments rather than to independent boards and commissions. This difference has one important consequence. In Britain, anyone who is dissatisfied with the treatment he has received at the hands of the administration can use what influence he has to get redress through political means. He may get members of Parliament to air his grievance in the House of Commons or he can seek direct access to the minister in charge of the department concerned.

This may mean much or little in the cases of particular individuals. It does mean that discretionary administrative powers are always exercised in accordance with the views of the government of the day. Those who can move the ruling political party can influence the use made of the kind of powers we are considering here. But where the powers are in the hands of independent boards, there is no assurance that they will be so immediately responsive to the political pressures that can be exerted on the government through the ruling political party. But it would be wrong to suppose that they are sheltered from all external pressure in the way in which judges are. Whether effective or not, pressure may be applied either through political channels or by representations made directly to the heads of the administrative board.

The Public Corporation in Britain

It should be noted that in one very important field of administration, the operation of the nationalized industries, Britain relies increasingly on agencies outside the government departments and beyond the detailed control of the cabinet. When an industry or business is nationalized, it is not operated under a regular government department but is put in the hands of a public corporation like the British Broadcasting Corporation or the National Coal Board.

These corporations have the same kind of structure as a private corporation except that the shares are publicly owned and the boards of directors are appointed for a fixed term by the government of the day. Once appointed, a board has a wide independence of action in determining policy for the industry and administering its detailed operation. The statutes creating these corporations generally give one or other of the ministers in the cabinet power to give directions to the public corporation on matters of broad general policy but preserve him from any responsibility for short-run policy and day-to-day management.

Control of the public corporation by the public on whose behalf it operates is therefore intermittent and indirect. Only rarely will the statute under which the corporation operates be amended by Parliament. All corporations, however, are required to submit annual reports and financial statements to the minister and to Parliament, and these can be debated. Borrowing for capital purposes requires the consent of the Treasury, and directives on general policy issue from the political executive from time to time.

The public corporation in Britain has an autonomy comparable to that of the regulatory boards and commissions in the United States. It is therefore a very significant exception to the general British insistence that officials who work out and apply public policy must be subject to direct control by a responsible minister. The reason given for the exception is that when the government goes into business, it must apply business methods rather than civil service methods and must be free of the normal political control and meddling imposed through Parliament and the cabinet.

The wide use of the public corporation in Britain today raises sharply a problem noted before: how is a government that does so many things for us to be kept under popular control? British experience with the public corporation over a period of time is likely to throw important light on this question.

INTEREST GROUPS AND ADMINISTRATION

Legislative and judicial control of the administrative process are not of themselves sufficient for keeping the administration from getting out of hand. From the point of view of the interests concerned in any particular aspect of administration, the legislature and courts are too remote and the methods of control too round-about. Thus they always want to have direct access to the administration to press their views and protests on the President or cabinet, or on the officials themselves. We have already seen that there is always a cluster of pressure groups wanting to be heard when subordinate legislation is being framed. Similarly, various interests always want to be heard when the administration has a discretionary power of making decisions in particular cases.

Despite its employment of numerous experts in various subjects, the government is always conscious of inadequate knowledge about the complex matters it is undertaking to regulate. If it is regulating the manufacture and sale of agricultural poisons, it needs to gather information from the manufacturers, distributors, and users of these poisons. The government also knows that it is much easier to enforce its regulations if it can get the co-operation of the interests concerned. But this co-operation is not likely to be had unless the government takes the interests into its confidence, listens to their representations, and makes adjustments here and there in deference to them.

Accordingly, the government generally welcomes the approach of the interests. The administration of many of the more complex activities of government today is carried on by close and continuous collaboration between the political executive, the administrative officials, and the various interests concerned. Generally speaking, there is as much collaboration of this kind where the administration is organized under an independent board as where it is housed in a government department.

It has been said that administration sets the measure of a law. Certainly the decisions taken nowadays by the administration under its discretionary powers are often the vital decisions as far as the individuals and corporations affected are concerned. It follows that in so far as pressure groups find the administration accessible and responsive they are better represented in government than if they had been allowed to elect representatives to the legislature. More than that, the influences that mould administrative action are often decisive in determining the content of a particular government activity. The interests that are well organized and recognized by the government get deference and consideration, while unorganized interests do not. In administration, as in legislation, the importance of group organization emerges clearly. Interests must be effectively organized if they wish to make their weight felt in present-day government.

There is a body of opinion that looks for salvation in a fuller organization of all the significant interests in the community. It doubts whether democratic control of administration can be made effective through the legislature and the judiciary. It wants to develop direct connections between the branches of administration enforcing particular laws and the various sections of the public interested in those laws. In relation to any particular law or government activity some interests will want more vigorous administration and more extended application, while others will want less. Under their pressure and counter-pressure, the administration can shape its action to a form that all the interests will accept and will co-operate in making effective. Democratic government in this way will shed most of its coercive aspects and become a great co-operative enterprise in which all groups share in the administration of those activities which concern them.

This proposal should not be too hastily branded as utopian. Trying to approach the administration *via* the political party, the legislature, and the political executive may involve a long and hazardous detour. There is little doubt that organs of direct consultation will increase in number and importance. Yet two cautions must be put. First, the experience of the United States with this kind of consultation is not wholly reassuring. Because of the number of independent boards and commissions and the inability of the President in recent years to co-ordinate and maintain control of all branches of the administration, administrators in the United States have had in many of their activities more freedom to respond to group pressures and to negotiate with the interests concerned than in Britain and Canada. In too many cases, the result has been that the most powerful interests concerned with a branch of the administration have gained a predominant influence over the administration for a time and diverted it to their purposes.[1]

Secondly, the interests immediately and consciously concerned with a particular field of government action are not the only interests with a stake in the matter. It is often thought that the only interests concerned with the fixing of minimum wages and

[1]See generally, E. Pendleton Herring, *Public Administration and the Public Interest* (McGraw-Hill, New York, 1936).

maximum hours of work are employers and employees. In fact, everyone who is concerned with the level of prices for goods or with health or education has a lively interest in the matter. It is almost impossible to get all the interests with a stake in administrative decisions fairly represented. For this reason, control through the political parties, the legislature, and the political executive, which alone represent the broad general and unorganized interests, is extremely important.

If administrative discretion is to be kept under control, a combination of the older, more indirect, methods of control through the legislature and the political executive, and the newer, more direct, consultation between the administration and the interests affected must be used.[1] The means by which the legislature, and the cabinet or President, control administration have been described in earlier chapters. It remains to indicate briefly how the interested sections of the public make contact with the administration.

In Britain and the United States, when subordinate legislation is to be framed, it is standard practice for the department or administrative agency that has the matter in hand to consult the organized interests. In Canada, the same practice is becoming increasingly common. Copies of the proposed regulations are circulated to the associations and their comments are invited. In the United States, it is common, even where not required by statute, to arrange a conference or public hearing where all sides can make representations. In this way, the administration gets expert knowledge of the complexities it is expected to regulate. It may learn that certain of the proposed regulations are really unworkable, that others rouse violent opposition and attract little support. It hears all the objections before it acts, and decides what concessions or modifications it can afford to make. On the other hand, the fact that the interests are consulted disposes them to co-operate even when the decision goes against them. And after the regulations have been enacted and put into effect, the interests

---

[1]On this question, compare Carl Joachim Friedrich, "Public Policy and the Nature of Administrative Responsibility," *Public Policy: A Yearbook of the Graduate School of Public Administration of Harvard University* (Harvard University Press, Cambridge, 1940), and Herman Finer, "Administrative Responsibility in Democratic Government." *Public Administration Review,* 1 (1940), pp. 335–50.

keep in touch with the administration with complaints and suggestions. When a considerable experience of their operation has accumulated, discussions looking to their revision may be held. There is here a complex interaction between rulers and ruled.

In a less formal way through correspondence and interview with officials, pressure groups make representations about administrative decisions in particular cases. In the United States, officials often attend meetings and conventions of the various associations, addressing them on the policy and work of their department or agency. This is rarely done in Britain and Canada, where officials in government departments are subject to closer check by the political executive and generally refuse to discuss matters of policy in public.

THE USE OF ADVISORY COMMITTEES

Wherever possible, the methods used by pressure groups to influence the legislature are used to urge their views on the administration. These methods are mostly informal and have not yet hardened into a well-established practice. There is, however, one recurring pattern of consultation that is widely used— the advisory committee. This device has been described optimistically as the democratic answer to the challenge of the corporate state. The corporate state meets the problem discussed in this chapter by formally turning over the functions of government to associations or corporations directly representative of interests. In the process, democracy disappears. The advisory committee, it is alleged, meets the need for giving representation to and getting co-operation from the interest groups without destroying democracy. How is this accomplished?

When the government is faced with a complex and arduous task of administration aimed at realizing some objective of the positive state, it can set up a committee representative of the interests affected to advise the administrators. In so far as the interests are organized in active associations, persons who play leading roles in the associations can be put on the committee. Interests that are not organized effectively can also be given representation. A number of persons can be appointed to the committee to speak for consumers or for the general public. Such committees, like the British monarch, have influence but no power to say what the administration shall do. They have the right to advise, to be consulted, and to warn. If they do their job, administration will be carried on under the watchful eye of representatives of those who are directly interested in what is being done.

Through advisory committees, the administration can get quickly and in advance the reactions of various sections of the public on what it proposes to do. It can tap the practical experience and the expert knowledge which are essential to making governmental regulation of complex affairs practicable. By consultation and discussion it can also explain to the representatives of various groups what ends and purposes the government is trying to accomplish. In so far as it succeeds in educating these representatives they, in turn, will carry the explanations to their membership, and the chances of getting co-operation from those who are to be regulated are increased. While the member of the legislature, among other duties, maintains liaison between the government and a territorial constituency, the member of the advisory committee maintains liaison between the government and a functional constituency.

The positive state cannot accomplish what it is trying to do unless it gets widespread co-operation as well as general acquiescence from the public. The advisory committee is calculated to improve the quality of administration, to foster an atmosphere of co-operation, and to make possible continuous scrutiny of the exercise of discretionary administrative powers. It is on these grounds that the advisory committee is sometimes put forward as the democratic answer to the corporate state.

Advisory committees are now widely used as instruments of the administrative process in Britain, Canada, and the United States, and reliance on them is increasing. Generally, they are designed to give representation to interests, organized or unorganized. However, particular persons are often appointed solely because they possess knowledge that the government hopes to be able to use. Advisory committees are useful for the purposes indicated, but they cannot be regarded as an adequate solution for the problems raised in this chapter. In practice, there is continual difficulty in getting able persons to accept membership and take an active interest in the work of the committee. This arises mainly from the fact that the committees are advisory only; they have no power to insist that their recommendations be accepted, and interest therefore tends to flag. It can be maintained, perhaps, if the administration shows itself willing to accept any unanimous recommendation. But any such practice would turn the substance of power over to the advisory committee, and this the administration cannot do. It takes great skill on the part of the administration to get useful results from advisory committees.

The truth is that the organized interests want power and not merely influence in the matters that affect them. If provision is made by the legislature for the government to intervene in the struggle of conflicting group interests, those group interests want to have some share in the control of the administrative agency that tries to regulate the conflict. They have met with some success in this claim. For example, in Canada and the United States, it is not uncommon for administrative agencies that regulate employer-employee relations to be composed of equal numbers of representatives of employers and employees with or without provision for a neutral chairman or other members to represent general public interests. Where the government undertakes to confer benefits on particular organized interests, those interests want a share in administration. So when the legislature provides for compulsory marketing of agricultural produce through a marketing board, the compulsory powers, which only the legislature can confer, are often delegated, in part at least, to boards composed of producers, or of producers, dealers, and processors, of the particular product concerned.[1] The powerful interests want to participate directly in administration and bend the administrative process to their purposes.

THE SIGNIFICANCE OF THE ADMINISTRATIVE PROCESS

This is not necessarily objectionable where the interests that get control are the only interests with a stake in the matter. However,

[1]See Avery Leiserson, *Administrative Regulation* (University of Chicago Press, Chicago, 1942), for a study of the representation of group interests in administration in the United States.

this can only rarely be true. As we have already seen, there are generally wider interests involved. The existence of wider interests which are likely to be prejudiced when administration is diverted to serve narrow and immediate interests is the reason for insisting on the primacy of control through the political parties, the legislature, and the political executive. It is also the reason for the demand, so insistent in the nineteenth century, that civil servants should be neutral tools obeying the hand of the legislature and political executive. The legislature and executive, it was contended, expressed adequately the common good and the national interest, and there was no place for the imaginative civil servant with ideas of his own. Today, by contrast, there is a wide demand that civil servants have a positive constructive attitude toward their work, putting energy and even passion into the accomplishment of great tasks.

This reversal of attitude towards the civil servant is the clearest possible indication of the great change wrought by the rapid growth of governmental functions and the development of the administrative process. Legislatures and executives can no longer express the full content of public policy. The officials are given discretion to expound it in detail. They need, therefore, knowledge, imagination, and a strong will if much is to be accomplished. Yet when civil servants give a marked display of these qualities in their daily work they are accused in many quarters of despotic ambitions. The question remains acute how civil servants can be genuinely creative and still be kept under control. The administrative process as sketched here is the result of tentative groping in the last forty years for an answer to this question.

It must be remembered, of course, that the civil servants who have a substantial discretion to exercise and who are expected to be genuinely creative are very few in number. They are generally senior officials standing close to the top of the hierarchy in each department. The vast majority of civil servants are, as the last chapter indicates, cogs in an impersonal organization, firmly clamped in a restricting routine with little chance to follow their inclinations or sympathies in their work. Indeed, it seems to be a general tendency in large-scale organization to impose a confining discipline on the many and to make overwhelming demands on a few for creative thought and action. The discretionary powers lodged with a few administrators merit the attention given to them here because the decisions they are expected to make are vitally important decisions. More and more the decisions taken in the course of administration affect the character of community life and the basic terms on which economic and social groups in the community live together.

Accordingly, we often hear the charge that the higher officials of the civil service really govern the country. There is no doubt that the political executive relies heavily on these officials for suggestions on policy, on what to do in the public interest. But the final decisions must always rest with the political executive, which is ultimately responsible to the electorate. The political executive must retain the support of a political party and it must take account of the views of organized pressure groups. The civil service is drawing closer to the formulation of policy, but it is still a long way from governing the country. It is, however, undoubtedly true that if government is to be all things to all men, the executive (in the broad sense including President or cabinet, and civil service) must be vigorous, imaginative, and possessed of wide powers. The unsolved problem is how to maintain a powerful executive and at the same time to ensure its continued responsibility to the governed.

All the previous exposition and discussion in this book converge on this point. At the beginning, it was stated that the essence of liberal democracy is a determination that government shall be servant and not master. The constitutions under consideration were framed for that purpose in a day when little was expected of governments. It was explained that the fundamental role of political parties is to enable the governed to change their rulers peacefully, to keep power contingent on their approval, and to construct electoral majorities that will support certain general lines of governmental action.

The great expansion in governmental functions in the last fifty years was sketched and asserted to have imposed great strain on the constitutions in question. In particular, it was seen that the tasks of the legislature and executive have been complicated immensely by the new burdens. A legal and judicial system whose

procedures and traditions were firmly fixed before the great
expansion in governmental functions and designed to support a
negative rather than a positive conception of government was seen
to be unsuited on a number of points for meeting present-day
demands. The rise of pressure groups, some of the divisive tendencies within the political parties, and the widespread dissatisfaction with the present system of representation were traced to the
same source. The principal, although not the sole, effort to adjust
these constitutions to the radically changed conception of the
appropriate functions of government has been the development
of the administrative process.

However, if we are to appreciate the full impact of the growth
of governmental functions on our political systems, the matter
cannot be left at this point. The influences that have expanded
the sphere of governmental action have also had pronounced centralizing tendencies. They have tended to shift to the central
governments functions formerly carried out by municipal governments. In the United States and Canada, they have also tended
to enlarge the functions of the national governments at the expense
of state and provincial governments. Accordingly, it is necessary
to look at the place of federalism and local government in the
liberal democratic constitutions.

CHAPTER XVII

FEDERALISM

THERE are a number of ways in which separate political communities can come together for common purposes. When several
states confer together and agree on a common course of action
in certain specified circumstances such as resistance to a common
enemy, they are bound together by treaty or alliance. When they
go one step further and set up a more or less permanent body of
delegates or ambassadors to make detailed recommendations for
carrying out the treaty or implementing the alliance, their association together is called a confederation. Such was the Congress
finally set up by the American colonies in 1781 under the Articles
of Confederation of 1777 to fight the war against Britain. In a
confederation, the common central body is merely a committee
for deliberating and advising the separate members. It has no
power over the separate states in the association or over the citizens
of these states. A confederation is little more than a "firm league
of friendship," from which the member states have a right to
withdraw.

The next further step is to give irrevocably to the common
central body some portion of the authority hitherto exercised by
each of the member states on its own account. When this is done,
the central body becomes a government with power to act independently of its own volition and not merely a council of
ambassadors. A new state comes into existence to which the
citizens of the member states owe an allegiance and a duty of
obedience. Such are the United States of America brought into
existence by the Constitution of 1789 and the Dominion of
Canada created in 1867. Such unions are federal unions or
federations. The member states or provinces are joined together
not by treaty but by a constitution from which they have no right
to withdraw. It is a marriage and not merely a casual alliance.

Yet, at the beginning at least, a federal union is merely a
marriage of convenience—a practical businesslike arrangement with
no sentimental nonsense. The parties insist on retaining their

distinct identities and personalities; they do not become one flesh. Of course, with the passing of time and the running of a common household, the marriage of convenience may be transformed into the kind of marriage that is made in heaven, where the identities of the several states are merged in an indissolubly united nation.

If and when this happens, the desire for a genuinely independent status in the several participating states will probably disappear. If so, conditions will be ripe for the last step in political unification, the disappearance of autonomous units and the reposing of all final governmental authority in a single central government. This is called the unitary state, of which Great Britain, incorporating the once independent communities of England, Wales, and Scotland, is an example.

Why do separate political communities when uniting together sometimes prefer a federal to a unitary form of government? A federal system is always a compromise between two distinct, and sometimes conflicting, sets of political forces. First, there are the pressing common interests and purposes shared by the several states or provinces. The American colonies on the Atlantic seaboard had just won their independence from Britain and wanted to secure themselves against the assaults of any European imperialism. The British colonies in North America in 1867 feared the aggrandizement of the United States which had emerged from the Civil War as a great military power. Such interests and purposes, among others, can only be protected by presenting a united front. They demand a union.

Secondly, there is the desire of each of the uniting communities to maintain its identity and a large measure of independence. In part, this desire springs from the same mysterious sources as national pride and national exclusiveness. Robert E. Lee, offered the command of the Northern Army at the outbreak of the Civil War, refused it, saying he could not draw sword against his native state, Virginia. His first allegiance was to Virginia and not to the United States. In part, the desire springs from very practical considerations. The conditions of life and the character of the people as moulded by history and the physical environment vary greatly in the states contemplating union. The people of the several states each cherish the unique features of their society and want to maintain them.

No government that fails to take account of these differences will ever be regarded as satisfactory. A government that is locally controlled is far more sensitive to the factors of uniqueness than is a central national government, which is far away and preoccupied with more general issues. The desire to limit the reach of a distant government is the main reason for a federal system. Lacking the urgent common interests, there would, of course, be no union at all. But lacking the insistence on a guaranteed sphere of independence for each of the uniting communities, there would be no reason for a partial union—no case at all for a federal form of government.

Federalism, therefore, is a dual form of government calculated to reconcile unity with diversity. It provides for a common government for common purposes, generally called the federal, or national, government. In the beginning, the common purposes mostly relate to external matters. The aim is to have a common policy *vis-à-vis* the rest of the world. The federal scheme also provides for the continuance of the governments of the several states or provinces in the federation, preserving for them, against the world and against the common government they have set up, control of most matters of internal policy. The most important aspect of a federal system, then, is the distribution of powers and authority between the common government on the one hand, and the state or provincial governments on the other. Hoping to set at rest all later questioning of what this distribution really is, it is written into the Constitution. This distribution of powers firmly established in a written constitution is the distinctive feature of federalism and makes many aspects of politics and government in the United States and Canada markedly different from those of Britain, a unitary state.

The Federal Distribution of Powers

In considering the federal systems of the United States and Canada, the distribution of powers set out in the respective constitutions must be looked at first. It has already been noted in chapter IV that the Constitution of the United States limits the powers of all governments and puts certain matters beyond the reach of either the state or federal government. These matters are said to be reserved to the people. Leaving these aside, some of the more important features of the distribution may be pointed out. Certain specified powers are expressly granted to the national government and it is authorized, in what is known as the elastic clause,[1] to make such laws "as are necessary and proper for carrying into effect," the powers expressly granted. Some powers are expressly forbidden to the national government.[2] While the Constitution expressly prohibits the exercise of certain powers by the states,[3] it nowhere enumerates the powers of the states. As Amendment x makes clear, they hold the residue of powers remaining after the grants to the national government, the express prohibitions to the states, and the reservations to the people are accounted for.

Article i, section 8, enumerates the principal powers granted to the United States.[4] Many of these powers relate, directly or indirectly, to external matters: the raising and supporting of armies and navies, the declaring and prosecuting of wars, the regulation of commerce with foreign nations. In internal matters, the powers of the United States were mostly restricted to the promotion of internal trade and commerce. It was necessary to guard against the states' erecting tariff barriers against one another. Accordingly, in addition to an express prohibition of the levying of duties on imports by the states,[5] the federal government was given power to regulate commerce among the several states. The interstate commerce clause, as it is called, has been the basis of much of the great extension of federal power through judicial interpretation.

Because a common currency and a common standard of weights and measures were needed to promote internal trade and commerce, the federal government was authorized to coin money and to fix its value, and to fix the standards of weights and measures. The powers to establish post offices and post roads, and to grant patents and copyright, were, in part, aimed at the same purpose of facilitating commerce. The only clause that might be thought to have wide general application in internal matters is the one

[1]Art. i, sect. 8, para. 17.
[2]Art. i, sect. 9 and the several Amendments.
[3]These prohibitions are found in Art. i, sect. 10, and in the Amendments xiii, xiv, xv, and xix.
[4]Others of significance vis-à-vis the states are granted in Art. iv, sect. 1, 3, and 4, and in Amendments xiii, xiv, xv, and xix.
[5]See Art. i, sect. 10.

authorizing the federal government "to provide . . . for the general
welfare of the United States," but the context in which it appears
in Article I, section 8, makes it doubtful whether any extensive
power was intended to be granted thereby. It appears not as an
independent grant of power but as one of the purposes for which
the federal government may levy taxes and spend the funds thus
raised.

A few powers are shared by both state and federal governments:
the levying of taxes, the borrowing of money, and the establishment of courts. Because the powers of the states are in the form
of an unspecified residue, no enumeration would be likely to state
them exhaustively. The making and altering of the criminal law
and the laws of marriage and divorce are merely well-known instances of the power of the states to make diverse laws as they see
fit. In fact, as far as the written Constitution goes, the states appear
to be the important authorities on most aspects of property, trade
and commerce, and personal relationships. At least, so one would
infer from a reading of section 8 of Article I and Amendment x.

When the terms of union of the British colonies in North
America were under discussion in the eighteen-sixties, seventy-five
years of experience under the federal Constitution of the United
States were available for guidance. This experience had just culminated in a civil war that threatened to destroy the Union. The
immediate, if not the underlying, cause of the Civil War had been
the claim by the southern states of the right to withdraw from the
Union. Because the powers of the federal government were specific
powers that could be interpreted as having been delegated to it by
the states, the seceding states claimed the right to withdraw the
delegation.

The framers of the Canadian federation wanted to make it
clear from the beginning that such a claim had no semblance of
right in the Canadian federation. Indeed, some of them did not
want a federal system at all but a unitary state with all authority
in one national central government. So the British North America
Act, the statute of the British Parliament that established the
Canadian federal system, tried to limit and qualify the independence of the provinces more sharply than the American Constitution had limited the states. It was provided that the Lieutenant-

Governors, the formal heads of the provincial governments, should be appointed by the federal government and that they should have the power to reserve provincial legislation for the pleasure of the federal cabinet.[1] Also, the federal cabinet was given power to disallow within a limited time any laws enacted by the provincial legislatures.[2] Most important, the opening paragraph of section 91 of the Act, which authorizes the Dominion Parliament "to make laws for the peace, order and good government of Canada" on all matters not exclusively reserved to the provincial legislatures, was intended to make it clear that the residuary powers, the powers not expressly conferred on either Dominion or province, rested with the Dominion, and that the provinces were to have certain specified powers (set out in section 92) and no more. All these provisions were calculated to show that the Dominion did not derive its powers from delegation by the provinces. No room was left for the provinces to argue that their independent status included the right to withdraw from the union.

The powers that the Dominion was to exercise exclusively were set out in section 91. The twenty-nine headings in this section, which purport to be illustrative only and not a definitive statement of the scope of Dominion power, covered a wider range of matters than the corresponding list of federal powers in the Constitution of the United States. They covered such aspects of external relations as a British dependency could expect to control on its own account. They went further than the Constitution of the United States in conferring authority over commercial matters on the federal government. In addition to currency and coinage, they included the power to regulate banking, bills of exchange, interest, and legal tender. Furthermore, in authorizing the Dominion to make laws for "the regulation of trade and commerce," they seemed to confer a wide power of regulating business and commerce. By an exception to section 92.10, the Dominion was given wide control over the transportation and communications industries. By section 121, the provincial legislatures were forbidden to interfere with

[1]British North America Act, sect. 58-60, and sect. 57 as extended by sect. 90.
[2]Ibid. sect. 56 as extended by sect. 90. This power is distinct from, and not to be confused with, the much narrower power of the courts to declare null and void acts of the provincial legislatures that purport to deal with matters reserved to the Dominion Parliament under sect. 91.

freedom of trade between the different provinces. Reflection on these and other powers enumerated in section 91 indicates that the Dominion was intended to have a wider authority in relation to economic life than the federal government in the United States.

Experience in the United States had shown that it was extremely unsatisfactory for the separate states to have exclusive control over the criminal law and over marriage and divorce. Accordingly, these matters, excluding the forms of the marriage ceremony which were left for provincial determination, were put in the sole control of the Dominion. On the other hand, whether for sufficient reasons or not, the framers wished to avoid the duplication of judicial institutions found in the United States, and accordingly the power to constitute courts for the enforcement of both Dominion and provincial law was given to the provinces.[1]

Concurrent, or shared, powers to levy taxes and borrow money were conferred on both the provinces and the Dominion. In addition, concurrent powers over agriculture and immigration were provided for in section 95.

This contrast is by no means an exhaustive discussion of the distribution of powers between the Dominion and the provinces. It is designed mainly to show that the framers intended, in the light of American experience, to strengthen the Dominion *vis-à-vis* the provinces.[2] But, in social and economic matters, what men plan and what ensues are often quite different things. Both these constitutions have been interpreted by the courts on almost innumerable occasions since their adoption and it would be difficult for anyone, looking only at the text of the constitutions, to realize that they mean what the courts have declared them to mean.

JUDICIAL INTERPRETATION OF THE DISTRIBUTION OF POWERS

Except for one significant reversal of the general trend in the years immediately before the Civil War, the Supreme Court of the United States has steadily enlarged the powers of the federal government by interpretations given in disputes coming before it.

[1]*Ibid.* sect. 92.14.
[2]For an extended comparison of the federal aspects of the constitutions of the United States and Canada, see Herbert A. Smith, *Federalism in North America* (Chipman, Boston, 1923), ch. I and III.

By 1959, federal authority had been stretched to the point where it could employ two-and-one-half million civil servants on its legitimate peacetime concerns. The Supreme Court, aided by the arbitrament of arms in the Civil War, has confirmed the indissolubility of the Union and enormously strengthened the position of the federal government *vis-à-vis* the states. Largely, but not entirely, through a liberal interpretation of the federal taxing power, the elastic clause, and the interstate commerce clause, Congress has been given an extremely wide power to regulate trade and commerce and economic life.

Judicial interpretation of the distribution of powers in the Canadian Constitution has gone in the opposite direction. Until 1949, the final authority for judicial interpretation of the Canadian Constitution was the Privy Council in London.[1] The decisions of the Privy Council over a period of fifty years have almost denuded of meaning the general, or residuary, clause contained in the opening paragraph of section 91, except for periods of great national emergency. It is by reliance on this clause in time of war that the federal government substantially supersedes the provincial governments. In times of peace, however, the federal government has been denied any substantial power under it. Thus the peacetime powers of the Canadian Parliament are almost wholly restricted to the matters specifically enumerated in section 91. Even here, the most general clause, "regulation of trade and commerce," has been very narrowly interpreted. Most laws for regulating economic life, such as the manner in which particular trades and industries conduct their business, have been held to be beyond the power of the Dominion and to be solely reserved to the provinces under section 92.13, "property and civil rights in the province." Legislation providing for social services and social insurance has also been held to be a matter for the provinces under property and civil rights.

Indeed, section 92.13 has been so widely interpreted, and the general clause of section 91 so narrowly construed, that it can now be said, without any great exaggeration, that the residuary power rests with the provinces and not with the Dominion. The Privy Council has magnified the provinces, while the Supreme Court of

[1]In 1949, the Supreme Court of Canada in Ottawa became the final court of appeal for constitutional and other cases.

the United States has magnified the federal government. Although the Privy Council has confirmed the provinces in a wide range of powers, it has never said anything to support the right of the provinces to withdraw from Confederation. Nor has any province ever seriously claimed it. The high-water mark of provincialism is the claim frequently made in some quarters that Confederation is a compact between the provinces and cannot be modified without the consent of all the provinces.

It must not be thought, however, that the activities of the federal government today are less numerous and important than they were in, say, 1875. On the contrary, they are vastly greater, having grown steadily since the beginning of the twentieth century. The Dominion did not attempt, in the early years of Confederation, to exercise all the powers that section 91 conferred on it. It was only when it began, from about 1900 on, to expand its activities that it ran into restrictive interpretations by the Privy Council. The decisions of the Privy Council did not prevent the central government from enlarging its activities but they were progressively hampering as the demands for Dominion action grew. The national government could not have carried out during the depression of the nineteen-thirties measures comparable to the New Deal in the United States, because the British North America Act, as interpreted by the Privy Council, reserved most of such measures to the provinces. The activities of the Dominion government have grown but not comparably to those of the federal government in the United States.[1]

FEDERALISM AND THE UNIFIED NATIONAL ECONOMY

The essential feature of a federal system is the co-existence of two governments with authority over the same territory and the same persons. Each of these governments is independent of the other. Each has a sphere in which it alone can rule and cannot be overruled by the other. At the launching of the two federal systems under discussion, it was thought that the sphere of the federal government, on the one hand, and the sphere of the state

[1]See *Report of the Royal Commission on Dominion-Provincial Relations* (King's Printer, Ottawa, 1940), vol. I, pp. 247–59. This volume consists largely of a history of Canadian federalism.

and provincial governments, on the other, could easily be kept separate, that each of the governments would operate in an almost watertight compartment. The matters committed to the federal government were few and appeared not to bear very directly on life in the different states and provinces.[1] The latter would control their own destinies without serious clash with one another or with the federal authority.

This expectation too has been falsified by events. The Civil War in the United States revealed how the states could become dissatisfied with the policies of one another's governments and how one group of states could become so incensed with the policies of the federal government as to secede from the Union. No subsequent issue in either country has threatened civil war, but it has become more difficult, with each succeeding decade, for each government in the federation to carry on in isolation. There are a growing number of interstate and federal-state co-operative arrangements. These arrangements, or the lack of them, are often attended by bickering and quarrelling between the different governments. To overcome the squabbling, the states are counselled either to have more and better co-operation, or to hand over further powers to the federal government so that one government will have control of the whole matter at issue. If present-day federalism is to be understood, it is necessary to see how this has come about.

Revolution in Transport and Communications

The American federation was founded when the Industrial Revolution was just beginning, and the Canadian Dominion was established before the full consequences of the Industrial Revolution had become apparent. To take only one aspect of it, the revolution in transportation and communications was still to come in 1789, and it was still in its early stages in 1867. In these circumstances, the states were of necessity very largely insulated compartments. People lived, not by buying and selling in distant markets beyond the boundaries of their own state, but by producing practically all their needs either on the family farm or in the local community close to home.

Agriculture was still the basic industry and principally con-

[1]Henceforth, in this chapter, the word "state" is to be understood to include "province," unless the context indicates the contrary.

cerned with local markets. The manufacturing industries were still small and mainly occupied in supplying a local demand. Strict accuracy would compel many important qualifications on the description just given. Intercolonial and foreign trade was important on the Atlantic seaboard in 1789 and in the remaining British colonies in North America in 1867, but it had not yet changed the general pattern of economic and social life. Most of the states, at the time the American federations were being launched, were relatively self-contained.

Given security from foreign aggression, events in the sister states and in other parts of the world had but a limited impact on each state. Federal union aimed at providing security from foreign intervention and did so successfully. With the principal conditions of life determined within their own boundaries, the states could have a genuine independence. There followed in each case a golden age of states' rights and provincial autonomy.

All the while, however, the onrushing economic transformation of the modern world was preparing the decline of this golden age. Free trade within the federation, improved transportation facilities, and rapid industrial and commercial expansion led to economic integration within the federation. In the place of the largely self-contained economies of the separate units in the federation, there grew a single unified national economy. Independence gave way to interdependence. Today, if farmers in the agricultural states cannot sell their produce profitably, workmen in the predominantly manufacturing states suffer unemployment, companies fail to pay their expected annual dividends, mortgage payments due to persons in still other states go into arrears. The order of dependence of such events on one another will vary, but it is at least clear that events that take place in one part of the federation have an impact in every other part. In fact, each of the states has become part of a larger whole with no direct power over what happens to the whole.

This momentous development does not of itself alone bring the several governments in the federation into closer contact, co-operation, or conflict. It was not the mere fact of the development of a world economy in the nineteenth century that brought national governments into conflict and war in the twentieth century. It was rather the fact that the people demanded, whether for adequate reasons or not, that their national governments should intervene in economic and social matters that turned economic rivalries into political conflicts.

So, within the federation, if governmental functions had remained limited to those of the mid-nineteenth century, the several governments would not always be coming across one another's paths as they are today. It is the immense increase in governmental activities that produces intergovernmental disputes, demands for better co-operation between them, and arguments for enlarging the powers of the federal government, the government whose arm has the longest reach.

Conflict and Co-operation within the Federal System

Each government working within the sphere assigned to it by the constitution takes action that has repercussions in the spheres of the others. The federal government through its control of tariffs and currency and credit can affect economic conditions in each of the member states. There is scarcely any action it can take on these matters nowadays that does not affect some states favourably and others adversely. This was always true to some extent, but it is more marked now than ever before. On the other hand, the actions taken, or neglected to be taken, by one or all of the states may affect profoundly the matters with which the federal government has to deal.

Equally, action taken by one state government may affect some or all of the sister states. Government regulations covering the grading and marketing of produce in one state almost inevitably affect the trade of other states. Laws passed by one state to relieve debt-ridden farmers in that state affect creditor interests in other states. Moreover, there are many matters on which the government of one state cannot hope to take effective action because some of the factors are beyond its control. If one state makes a levy on the industries within its boundaries for the maintenance of an unemployment insurance fund, it takes the risk that industries will shun it in favour of other states which do not follow suit, and where, therefore, the costs of production are lower. If the federal government is restricting credit, state governments cannot hope to take successful measures for expanding production and employment.

An excellent illustration of the need for interstate and state-federal co-operation is afforded by the predicament in which the oil-producing industry and the oil-producing states of the United

States found themselves in the early nineteen-thirties. The great bulk of the oil production of the country comes from the wells in some half-dozen states, whence most of it flows in interstate commerce to the markets in the other states. Between 1926 and 1931, immensely rich new oil fields were opened and production increased at a fantastic rate. With the onset of the depression at the turn of the decade, the demand for oil failed signally to keep pace with production, and the oil-producing industry suffered a catastrophic decline in prices and consequent cut-throat competition. Each state was faced with the additional problem of conserving an irreplaceable natural resource, which was being wasted by overproduction.

Under the Constitution, production of oil but not its shipment from one state to another is under the control of the state legislatures. A state legislature could pass—and several legislatures in the major oil-producing states had passed prior to 1930—laws limiting and prorating production. But two serious difficulties faced states acting singly and alone. First, oil wells were tapped illegally and the product bootlegged into interstate commerce where control over it could only be exercised by the federal government. Second, it was futile for any one state to impose effective restrictions if the other major oil-producing states failed to act effectively in the same way. The producers in that state would be faced with disastrously low prices in their markets in other states as well as limited in the quantities they could produce and ship.

Complex co-operative arrangements were devised which brought a measure of stability into the oil-producing industry, even if they did not solve the larger problem of wise and effective conservation. Six of the major producing states entered into an interstate compact to restrict the production and marketing of oil. They relied largely on a federal government agency, the Bureau of Mines, to estimate demand and to suggest production quotas for the major oil fields. With these as a basis for discussion, the co-operating states reached agreements on quotas and implemented them by state laws. Congress enacted a federal law forbidding the transportation in interstate commerce of oil produced and shipped in contravention of state laws.[1] The oil-producing industry is, in many respects,

---

[1] Joseph E. Kallenbach, *Federal Cooperation with the States under the Commerce Clause* (University of Michigan Press, 1942), pp. 325-31.

unique, and the severity of the crisis it underwent was due to a fortuitous combination of circumstances. Yet, other illustrations can be given to show that federations are pushed to expedients of this kind under the conditions of a complex interdependent economy.

Another instance of the difficulties that beset the unified national economy in the federation is the rise of trade barriers between the states. These trade barriers are facilitated, although not entirely caused, by the extending regulation of economic life by state governments. They run counter to one of the basic purposes of federal union. As already noted, one of the primary aims of the federal unions of the United States and Canada was to create great free-trade areas, and both constitutions forbid the states to erect barriers against the trade of other states.

In the depression decade between 1930–1939, state governments in both countries resorted to a variety of devices designed to protect home producers against competition from producers in other states. In considerable measure, it was a phenomenon of the depression. To the extent that the national economy failed to work satisfactorily, the states were tempted to try to shelter their own industries from competition from other states so as to provide a secure home market for their own products. The movement assumed much more significant proportions in the United States than in Canada. Much of the Canadian population is found in clusters in relatively small areas, and many of the clusters are separated by great distances and geographical barriers, which limit interprovincial trade. Interprovincial trade in Canada is not nearly as significant as interstate trade in the United States, and there is correspondingly less temptation to seek palliatives for economic distress by interstate trade barriers. Illustration is therefore drawn from the experience of the United States. However, the fact that provincial liquor control boards have been known to favour local breweries against brewers in other provinces shows that the same problem arises in Canada.

The hampering restrictions employed by the states take a multitude of forms. The frank levying of imports or duties on goods coming from other states is forbidden by the Constitution, and therefore barriers to trade have to be masked under the guise of laws that the states have power to enact. One of the most common has been the use of the state taxing power to levy higher rates of taxes on imported products than on native products, or to apply special taxes on non-resident persons or corporations doing business in the state. For example, some states with an important dairy industry have tried in this way to limit the sale of oleo-margarine manufactured in other states. Many states impose a discriminatory tax on imported liquors. Some states impose special taxes on chain stores and higher licence fees on dealers who handle imported products.

All states maintain a variety of laws generally acknowledged to be necessary for the protection of public health and safety. Many states have framed these regulations in such a way, and/or administered them in such a way, as to discriminate against imports from other states. Laws requiring the inspection of milk and dairy herds have been applied so as to exclude milk produced in other states. Laws providing for inspection of, and if necessary, quarantine on plants, fruit, nursery stock, and livestock, to prevent the spread of pests and disease, have been applied at times so as to exclude imports from other states. Economic protection masquerades as biological protection. State laws requiring the grading and labelling of products to protect purchasers against fraud or inferior quality have been framed or applied in such a way as to prejudice imports from other states.

Sometimes the discrimination thought to be involved in the administration of such laws is largely imaginary or unavoidable. In any event, many of the trade barriers erected in many states have originated as retaliatory measures against discriminations, real or imagined. There has been much mutual recrimination between states over laws of this kind, which tends to spread into other aspects of their relationships.

Those discussed above are but a few of the many kinds of trade restrictions that have been employed by some or other of the states. Some of the devices employed are no doubt unconstitutional and can be attacked in the courts. Others could be curbed by Congress acting under the interstate commerce clause of the Constitution. But states acting singly cannot deal with the situation. It was regarded as sufficiently serious to bring representatives of most of the states together in the National Conference on Interstate Trade Barriers in 1939. Following the Conference, the states made a co-operative attack on the abuse and succeeded in halting the movement towards still more irritating trade barriers and in securing the repeal of some of those already existing.[1] The experience with trade barriers provides another illustration of the way in which the states in a federal system fall foul of one another nowadays, and of the need for vigilant co-operative action.

There are many matters in which all governments should act in concert and unison. Failure to do so causes friction and inefficiency. To take a Canadian example, the federal government and its agencies control railway rates and also meet the deficit on the operations of the publicly owned Canadian National Railways. The Canadian National Railways carry about half the total Canadian railway traffic, and in normal times the deficits on its operations are substantial. The provinces build the highways and determine, through motor licences and gasoline tax, the conditions on which motor carriers can use them. For the past three decades or more, the provinces have, in effect, been subsidizing motor carriers by failing to tax them heavily enough to cover their proportionate share of the cost of construction and upkeep of highways. Motor carriers take advantage of the low costs of operation to take business away from the railways and thus to increase the deficits on, and the necessary federal government subsidies to, the Canadian National Railways. Such a situation argues for a single co-ordinated policy of regulating all transportation by rail or road. This can be had only in one of two ways. Either all governments must co-operate closely in the matter or all authority over the regulation of these forms of transport must be transferred to the federal government.

METHODS OF CONSULTATION AND CO-OPERATION

Methods and organs of consultation and co-operation have been developing over a period of years in both the United States and Canada. In Canada, they are still in rudimentary form, going little beyond informal consultation between governments and

[1]On the general subject of trade barriers, see F. Eugene Melder, "Trade Barriers between States," *Annals of the American Academy of Political and Social Science* (1940), 207, pp. 54-61. This volume of the Annals contains a number of articles bearing on the subject matter of the present chapter.

government officials, and occasional Dominion-provincial conferences on critical issues. In the past, these conferences often came
to little because the governments had not taken pains to accumulate
and analyse data in preparation for the work of the conferences.
Delegates who come to conferences inadequately briefed on the
matters to be settled hesitate to agree on anything because they
are not in a position to estimate the consequences of any agreement they might make. However, in recent years, the techniques
of conference have been greatly improved because all governments
are making better preparation for the discussions. While Dominion-
provincial conferences do not always reach agreement, they have
become very effective instruments for patient, detailed exploration and understanding of differences. The United States has
gone further in developing methods and organs of continuous consultation; but even there, there is a crying need for more knowledge
about the facts concerning the number and nature of intergovernmental relationships and the sources and extent of the
frictions that appear.

Interstate Co-operation

One method for co-operation between the states in the United
States is the interstate compact. Article i, section 10, by implication
authorizes the states, with the consent of Congress, to make compacts with one another. The compact has been used with reasonable success in dealing with matters that could be settled once for
all, or for long periods of time, and did not require frequent
re-consideration in the light of changing circumstances. By far
the greater number of interstate compacts have dealt with boundary
disputes, the regulation of boundary waters, interstate rivers,
harbours, and bridges.

In the critical fields of economic life, governmental regulation,
if undertaken, must be revised from time to time as changing circumstances and experience gained in administration require. Also,
economic regulation almost always raises sharp conflicts of interests.
Such conflicts are the stuff of present-day politics, and numerous
state governments are more likely to differ than to agree on the
complex detailed terms of uniform regulations. The oil compact
already referred to is of this character and achieved a measure of

success. On the other hand, the attempt of a number of states to reach a compact on minimum wages and related matters failed in spite of determined efforts.

For a long time, the National Conference of Commissioners on the Uniformity of State Laws in the United States and the Conference of Commissioners on Uniformity of Legislation in Canada have been trying to secure uniform state legislation on particular topics. These conferences are, in a sense, representative of state or provincial governments as the case may be, and they have agreed upon and drafted many uniform laws on various subjects, which they then recommend to state legislatures. Many states have adopted one or more of these laws, but few such laws have been adopted in all states. The greatest success has been achieved with laws that are interpreted and enforced by the judiciary, laws relating to such matters as negotiable instruments, warehouse receipts, sale of goods, and proceedings in the courts. There has been much less success in getting uniformity in laws that require extensive use of the administrative process in their enforcement.

In any event, where use of the administrative process is involved, it is not sufficient to get state legislatures to adopt uniform laws. Where officials have a discretionary power to make rules and decisions and are relied on generally for enforcement, administration sets the measure of the law. Neither uniformity nor effective co-operation can be had without frequent consultation between state executives, or at least between those state officials concerned with particular subjects such as the regulation of insurance companies. Numerous associations of state officials such as the National Association of Supervisors of State Banking, The National Convention of Insurance Commissioners, and The American Association of Motor Vehicle Administrators have been formed to discuss the common or related problems of their members. Comparable bodies in Canada are the Association of Workmen's Compensation Boards of Canada and the Association of Administrators of Labour Legislation. These associations have made some progress in interstate co-operation at the administrative level, subject always to the limits imposed by political considerations.

Because both administrative and political considerations are always involved and must be considered together, the most hopeful development in interstate co-operation is the Council of State

Governments organized in the United States in 1935. A General Assembly of the Council composed of delegates representing both state legislatures and executives meets every second year to discuss both legislative and administrative questions. The Council has established a secretariat which is continuously engaged in research and in the publication of bulletins on the problems of state governments. The Council has also been successful in persuading most of the states to establish permanent commissions on interstate co-operation. From time to time the Council calls conferences on particular problems.

These are some of the methods being used to get uniform or co-operative action by the states.[1] The vigour and success of the work of the Council of State Governments show that there is still a determination to make federalism work and still resourcefulness in finding ways and means. By bringing the states together to find solutions for common problems without abdicating to the federal government, the Council has established a counterpoise to the strong centralizing tendencies of the day. A comparable association of provincial governments in Canada would help to serve the same purpose but one has not yet been established.

Federal-State Co-operation

Illustrations have already been given to show that, in some matters, interstate co-operation is not enough. Federal-state co-operation is also needed. It is often found that power to regulate some particular aspect of economic life is divided by the Constitution between the federal and the state governments. Unless the governments concerned agree on legislation and administration, there is likely to be confusion and conflict in the regulation. To give precise illustrations would require exposition of the complexities of the distribution of powers under the Constitution as interpreted by the courts. It will suffice here to indicate some of the methods of federal-state co-operation in use in the United States and Canada.[2] It must be remembered that in neither

[1]For more extended treatment of interstate co-operation in the United States, see W. Brooke Graves, *American State Government* (Heath, Boston, 1946), 4th ed. ch. xxiv.

[2]For detailed discussion, see Jane Perry Clark, *The Rise of a New Federalism* (Columbia University Press, New York, 1938); J. A. Corry, *Difficulties of Divided Jurisdiction* (King's Printer, Ottawa, 1940) and *The Report of the Commission on Intergovernmental Relations* (U.S. Government Printing Office, 1955).

country has the co-operation achieved been adequate to the growing need.

Federal statutes sometimes adopt the relevant provisions of state law as the federal law to be applied in that state. State laws often adopt the relevant provisions of federal laws or regulations in the same way, as when provincial legislatures and executives in Canada adopt Dominion statutory provisions and administrative regulations relating to the marketing of agricultural products. In the New Deal era, and later in World War II, many state laws were enacted in the United States to aid federal policies on economic recovery and the war effort respectively. Federal and state administrative agencies have co-operated in such fields as railway regulation, road traffic, and enforcement of food and drug legislation. Sometimes attempts are made to fuse the administration of federal and state laws on a particular matter by making state officials federal agents for administering the federal part of the activity, and vice versa. For example, in eight out of ten provinces in Canada, the Royal Canadian Mounted Police are, in effect, provincial officers for provincial law enforcement purposes.

The full range of the devices of interstate and federal-state co-operation, of which examples have been given here, is sometimes described as the new co-operative federalism in contrast to the older federalism, in which state and federal governments went their own separate ways on most matters. The meshing of governmental action so far secured in this way is admitted to be inadequate, but its further development and improvement are put forward as the only alternative to massive centralization under the federal government. There is little doubt that this is true. The great increase in the activities of governments is the main cause of the need for intensive intergovernmental co-operation, and there is no reason to expect in the foreseeable future, any significant decline. Indeed they are more likely to increase. So, if co-operative action does not come to be adequate in particular fields, the alternative is to confer full authority in such fields on the federal government. Because the Canadian provinces could not get together for concerted action in establishing provincial unemployment insurance schemes, they finally accepted an amendment to the British North America Act transferring full constitutional authority over this subject to the Dominion. Some are disposed to think that co-operative federalism is subject to so many frictions and paralysing delays as to put very severe limits on its development.

It is plausible to think that if a single government is put in control of a particular subject, it will be able to work out a unified coherent policy. Reasons will be suggested later for thinking that this is too optimistic a view if wholesale centralization were resorted to, and therefore the utmost effort should be put into making co-operative devices effective. It must be stated, however, that steady co-operation of all or most of the governments in the federation over an extended period is very difficult to maintain. Ultimately, all co-operative enterprises of governments are political matters and cannot be shielded from the impact of politics. Each government, whether state or federal, necessarily responds to the view of the public interest held by the ruling political party or by the combinations of interests that for the time being have the preponderant influence in the councils of governments. Different parties and different combinations of interests may hold power in the different governments at the same time. Diverging conceptions of the public interest are likely to pull some of the meshing gears apart from time to time.

THE TREND TOWARD CENTRALIZATION

Because the fields in which the various governments in the federation come across one another are now so numerous, and because difficulties, delays, and uncertainties always beset co-operative action, some have concluded that federalism is almost obsolete. Because the separate states no longer have an independent economic life of their own, conditions beyond their control may at any time make their independence a sham. When this happens, they become dependent on the federal government. Whether or not this is correct, it is at least clear that the unified national economy in the conditions of widespread governmental activity and regulation strains towards political centralization.

The states acting by themselves could do little to overcome the serious depression of the nineteen-thirties. In the depths of the economic crisis, almost everyone, both in the United States and Canada, looked to the federal governments, echoing Will Rogers' admonition to the President to do *something*—"even if it is only to burn the White House!"[1] The New Deal brought a tremendous upsurge of federal government action in the United States. The federal government undertook large new activities or greatly expanded its former activities in relation to such matters as transport, public utilities, banking and credit, stock and commodity exchanges, labour-capital relations, agricultural production, housing, social security, and conservation. Some of the functions undertaken were later abandoned, but most of them have every appearance of being permanent additions to the work of the federal government.

The persistent centralizing movement could be halted if we could reverse the trend towards ever-greater governmental functions. But the present-day conviction is that business and social life generally must be extensively regulated by governments. When business is organized on a nation-wide scale with many businesses operating in every state, and when labour unions are national, if not international, in scope, the argument for nation-wide regulation of business and labour-capital relations is very strong. Such facts as these reveal the significance of the enlarged interpretation of federal powers by the Supreme Court of the United States. It is a response to a need that is felt. And there has been consternation in many quarters in Canada because the Privy Council denied rather than responded to this need.

Centralizing Tendencies in Public Finance

Another urge to centralization is found in public finance. Here again the reasons are the same, the unification of the economy and the multiplying of governmental functions. In both Canada and the United States, many of the most expensive of the new functions of government are allotted to the states by the distribution of powers in the constitution. For example, highways, education, and many social security measures are primarily their responsibilities. It is thought to be contrary to the interests of the country as a whole that there should be wide disparities in the range and quality of educational and social security services in the several states.

Unfortunately, the capacities of the different states to raise the revenues needed to maintain these services at a uniform level

---

[1]Quoted by Ernest S. Griffith, *The Impasse of Democracy* (Harrison-Hilton, New York, 1939), p. 13.

vary greatly. Some can maintain a high level of services at moderate rates of taxation while others cannot do so even at very high rates of taxation. That is because some states have prospered while others remain chronically poor relations. In most cases, the plight of the latter is largely due to the poverty or lack of variety of their natural resources. Their condition is aggravated, however, by centralizing tendencies in the economic system.

Within the free trade area that the federation maintains, industry and commerce tend to locate in the areas richest in wealth and resources. Manufacturing gravitates to the areas with the best resources of raw materials, industrial skill, and power in form of coal or electricity. Yet the manufacturing industries distribute their products to, and draw their profits from, all parts of the country. The number of products that are nationally advertised is an index of the scope of this business. A similar centralization occurs in the distribution of products. Chain stores and mail-order houses with head offices in a particular state do a nation-wide business, drawing to one point profits that formerly were made and kept by local merchants all over the country. Also, the financial institutions (banks, insurance companies, and trust and loan companies) located in particular areas do business in all areas. These facts explain why, in 1957, twenty-five per cent of the national income of the United States came to be concentrated in the states of New York, New Jersey, Pennsylvania and Delaware.

The net result is the pooling of wealth in the states already blessed by nature with rich resources or strategic position, enabling the governments of these states to tap the pools by corporation tax, income tax on both persons and corporations, and succession duties, while the other state governments are denied comparable access to them. Thus the difficulties of the poorer states in finding tax revenues to support all the activities expected of them are intensified.

There is one government, however, that has ready access by taxation to all pools of wealth in the country, wherever found. That is the federal, or national, government. The poorer states, which find it difficult to finance their activities, and other interests that want a high level of government services, are tempted to argue that income taxes, and succession duties—the taxes that can skim the rich cream pooled by nation-wide business activity—should be

solely in the hands of the national government. Economic centralization gives force to arguments for centralization of the taxation system. When the national government has collected large funds in
this way, it should either make grants to the several states, enabling
each of them to maintain the desired level of government services,
or it should itself take over from the states the more costly functions
of government and administer them.

Federal Grants-in-Aid

Whichever course is adopted, it enhances the importance of the
federal government and diminishes the autonomy and independence
of the state governments. Taking away functions from the state
governments whittles down their status. Giving the federal government a monopoly on income taxes magnifies its power over every
taxpayer and gives it a large fund of revenues to dispose of. Grants
to the state governments out of the fund so collected may be either
conditional or unconditional.

A conditional grant, always called a grant-in-aid, means that the
federal government earmarks grants for particular purposes such
as highway construction, old age pensions, or health insurance and
then requires the state governments to comply with certain specifications as a condition of receiving the grant. On the other hand, if
grants are made unconditionally, no direct control is exercised
over the state governments. But the state governments are each
eager to get as much of this largesse as they can. They constantly
demand larger and larger grants. As the federal government increases the grants in response to pressure, it has to raise its rates of
income tax, thus increasing the general burden of taxation and so
limiting what the states dare to try to raise by levying additional
taxes on their own account. The risk that this process will go on
until the states become largely pensioners of the federal government
prompted one observer to say that a federal state which has a
federal income tax is no longer a federal state.

In the United States and Canada, grants-in-aid have been
in use for many years, aiding various activities carried on by the
state and provincial governments.[1] In 1957, federal grants in the

[1]In Canada, these grants-in-aid are not to be confused with the unconditional Dominion subsidies to the provinces provided for by the British
North America Act, sect. 118.

United States made up about fifteen per cent of the total revenues of the state governments.[1] There were times in Canada in the nineteen-thirties when the federal grants-in-aid made up about a third of the provincial revenues. In some measure then, depending on their amount, these grants require the state governments to dance to the tune of the federal government, which selects the pieces to be played and prescribes the tempo and manner of execution.

This is not a serious interference with state independence as long as the aided activities are only a few of those in which the state governments are engaged. However, grants-in-aid have not thus far been signally successful in reducing the disparities between the financial positions of the various state governments. Generally speaking, the principles on which the amounts of grants allocated to the several states are calculated do not provide sufficiently for discrimination in favour of the poorer states. Common forms are the proportionate grants under which the more a state can afford to spend of its own on the particular service, the more federal assistance it will secure. The poorer states can rarely resist the offer of a proportionate grant and they divert some of their revenues from unaided to aided services in order to earn the federal grant. State budgets thus are often distorted. These undesirable effects are reduced as the proportion contributed by the federal government is raised. For example, the 1956 grants for highway construction provided that the federal government would put up ninety per cent of the cost.

The need for discrimination in favour of the poorer states is clear. The objections to taking account of varying needs are political. If the United States Congress abandons simple rule of thumb in its allocation, it opens up wide possibilities of logrolling. So there is a strong body of opinion which presses for the other alternative of transferring some of the costly functions now performed by state governments to the federal government to be administered as well as financed by it. Such a course eases the financial difficulties of the governments of the poorer states and puts them in a better position to carry the functions that remain to them. In recent years, it has been followed in the allocation

---

[1]*Federal Grants-in-Aid:* Report of the Committee on Federal Grants-in-Aid (Council of State Governments, Chicago, 1949) and *Report of the Commission on Intergovernmental Relations,* op. cit., ch. 5.

of sole responsibility for several of the new social security measures to the federal government. In so far as it is followed, it adds to the power and prestige of the federal government.

The fiscal powers of the federal government are not entirely centralizing in tendency. The difficulties in the way of any one state's undertaking to provide unemployment insurance have already been noted. By the use of a device known as the tax credit,[1] the federal government in the United States was able to remove this difficulty. In the Social Security Act of 1935, Congress levied a tax on the payrolls of all employers in certain specified industries across the country. It also provided that most of this tax would be rebated to employers in those states which established an unemployment insurance scheme complying with certain federal requirements.

In effect, a state that refused to set up such a scheme would be heavily penalized for its refusal, and all states quickly adopted unemployment insurance laws. While this is almost dictation by the federal government to states that did not want to provide unemployment insurance, it is, at the same time, an enabling provision for those that wanted to do so but were restrained by the lack of assurance that other states would do likewise. The capacity of some states to meet what they consider to be serious problems can be enlarged by use of the financial powers of the federal government.

Some of the conditions attached to federal grants-in-aid may have a similar long-run influence. When a federal grant to assist a particular state activity is made on the condition that the state officials who administer the activity have certain qualifications and be appointed by merit, improvements in state administration are likely to result. Federal guidance and leadership such as has developed in the social security programme in the United States may help state governments to help themselves.

Dominion-Provincial Public Finance

Such federal grants-in-aid for stimulating and guiding the development of particular state activities may strengthen rather than weaken state governments. But experience suggests that, in the Canadian environment at least, conditional grants-in-aid are

[1]See Jane Perry Clark, op. cit., ch. x.

not suitable instruments for transferring the large sums needed to enable all the provincial governments to meet the responsibilities put upon them by the electorate and to reduce the wide disparities between them. When large sums are involved, these grants tend to becomes bones of contention between the Dominion and the provinces rather than the basis of close co-operation. At any rate, this was the actual result in the depression period of the nineteen-thirties when the strains on the federal system became so great that a royal commission was appointed to inquire into the desirability of some reallocation of the powers and responsibilities of the provinces and the federal government.

The Sirois Commission, appointed in 1937 to study the problems which had brought several provincial governments to the verge of bankruptcy and had caused unprecedented bickering between the Dominion and the provinces, made an adverse judgment on conditional grants-in-aid and put forward instead a proposal for unconditional grants to be based on the proven fiscal need of each province. Although the Commission made some proposals for increasing the power of the national government to regulate economic life, its main recommendations were primarily financial. These have been the starting-points for most of the later thinking on the subject in Canada and therefore their nature must be briefly indicated.

First, the Commission proposed that certain onerous provincial responsibilities such as relieving unemployment should be placed solely on the Dominion. Second, in return for relief from these burdens, the provinces should surrender entirely to the federal government three vitally important sources of taxation: personal income tax, corporation tax, and succession duties. Third, those provincial governments, which still had a gap between income and outgo after these adjustments should be given by the Dominion an annual unconditional grant large enough to close the gap but subject to certain safeguards designed to prevent abuse.[1] That is to say, each provincial government was to get what it could show to be its fiscal need, and then to be entitled to spend it as it thought best.

These recommendations illustrate the centralizing tendencies referred to earlier. The reception given to the proposals of the

[1]*Report of the Royal Commission on Dominion-Provincial Relations*, vol. II, pp. 75–130.

Commission shows how hard it is to get agreement on a drastic modification of established relationships under a federal constitution. A Dominion-Provincial Conference was called early in 1941 to consider the proposals, but it broke up in disagreement, if not in disorder, before it really got down to serious discussion. Later in 1941, the greater part of the substance of the above proposals was agreed to by the provinces as temporary expedients of wartime finance. In 1945, another Dominion-Provincial Conference was called to plan for post-war reconstruction. The federal government put forward to this Conference a considerably modified form of the proposals made by the Sirois Commission. This Conference also failed to reach an agreement.

The Dominion Government then tried to get each province to agree separately to surrender the three tax sources in question in return for large compensating annual federal grants. By 1947, all provinces except Ontario and Quebec had entered into such agreements for a five year period. On the expiry of these agreements in 1952, they were renewed on terms much more favourable to the provinces and accepted by all provinces except Quebec. When the tax agreements came up again for consideration in 1957, eight provinces once more surrendered these taxes for a five year period. Ontario agreed only in part, and Quebec again refused. The essential point about all this negotiating is that it has ensured the federal government of a near-monopoly of income tax for twenty years (1941 to 1962). There is little prospect of escape from it in the foreseeable future.

In connection with these successive tax agreements, the federal government has made large and increasing grants to the provincial governments. The advice of the Sirois Commission has been heeded, and conditional grants now play only a subordinate part in the structure of Dominion-provincial public finance. The great bulk of the grants are unconditional, allowing each province full freedom in deciding how its grants will be used. These grants have eased greatly the financial strain on the governments of the poorer provinces. Indeed, it is impossible to see how six or seven of the provinces could have carried their responsibilities without them.

Under the arrangements for the years 1957 to 1962, the Dominion makes two kinds of unconditional grants to the provincial governments, regardless of whether they have agreed to surrender their income tax and succession duties or not: (1) equalization grants to minimize the disparities in the capacities of the provinces to raise public revenues and (2) stabilization grants to prevent steep and rapid fluctuations in provincial revenues. The provinces which surrender the aforesaid taxes get additional grants as compensation for so doing. Whatever may be the outcome in the long run, the trend of the last twenty years suggests that Canada will try to meet the central problem of Dominion-provincial public finance mainly by unconditional grants, in contrast to the heavy reliance of the United States on conditional grants-in-aid.

Amendment of the Federal Constitution

The net result of the tendencies in public finance, as in economic and social regulation, is to aggrandize the federal governments at the expense of the states. If these tendencies continue, and if they accelerate as they have in the past forty years, the maintenance of a genuine federal system with its separate and exclusive spheres of governmental power may become impossible. In fact, there are numerous reasons for caution in supporting or acquiescing in these tendencies, which will be considered later. For the moment, it is important to remember that this centralization cannot always take place merely because an electoral majority, and Congress or Parliament, happen to be in favour of it. In many cases, the constitution stands in the way, ensuring to the separate states the sphere of power that they presently possess. Many of the proposals for enlarging the power and responsibilities of the federal government require amendments to the constitution.

Such amendments are not easily carried through. There are always elements in the community that resist, even if they are no more than the state and provincial politicians who do not want to see the range of matters under their direct control narrowed. The richer states in the federation are generally reluctant to see the federal government move into the field of social security because this enables the poorer states to get services at their expense. In Canada, French-speaking Roman Catholic Quebec can be counted on to resist almost every increase of federal power because Quebec distrusts the use to which the federal government will put such power. The English-speaking Protestant majority in Canada as a whole can dominate the federal government, but it cannot control the government of Quebec. The citizens of federal states are increasingly involved in controversies over what amendments should be made to the constitution and in what ways.

The methods prescribed for amending the Constitution of the United States, as described in chapter IV, are not easy but they are quite clear. Moreover, there is not at present any urgent demand for amendments enlarging federal power because the Supreme Court, particularly over the last decade, has been consistently interpreting the Constitution in favour of the federal power. In the critical field of regulation of economic life, the Supreme Court appears to have opened the way for most of the measures Congress is likely to want to adopt. The Supreme Court may change its attitude sometime in the future, but at present it can almost be said that the safeguarding of states' rights depends not on the Supreme Court but on Congress. Since Congress is largely composed of vigorous representatives of local, state, and regional interests, this safeguard is not negligible.

The situation in Canada is quite otherwise. As we have seen, judicial interpretation of the British North America Act has been predominantly in favour of the provinces and against the federal power in the last sixty years. Consequently, the pressure for formal amendment in a centralized direction is very strong. Unfortunately, there is no provision in the British North America Act or elsewhere settling how Canadians are to set about amendments that reduce the powers of the provinces. The Act itself is a statute of the British Parliament, and until 1949, all amendments of the Act of whatever kind had, as a matter of legal formality, to be enacted by the British Parliament. However, in 1949, the British Parliament, at the request of the Canadian Parliament, and without the consent of the provinces, passed an amendment authorizing the Canadian Parliament to amend, by a simple majority of both Houses, the Canadian constitution subject to certain specified exceptions. In the present focus of interest, what this amendment withholds from the Parliament of Canada is much more important than what it puts under its control.

Expressly withheld are the powers of the provincial legislatures (sections 92, 93 and 95), rights of minorities respecting schools (section 93), guarantees respecting the use of the English or French language (section 133), the requirement that there shall be an annual session of Parliament (section 20), and the provision that no House of Commons shall continue for more than five years (section 50). Amendments of the British North America Act respecting these excepted matters must still be made by the British Parliament.

The Search for a Method of Amendment in Canada

Of course, as was pointed out in chapter IV, it has long since been established that the British Parliament will not make amendments except on request from Canada. It is also established by settled practice that these requests are to be made by the Parliament of Canada. Further, it is clear that the Dominion Parliament would not presume to move an amendment which reduced the powers of the provinces or narrowed the express constitutional guarantees afforded by the Act to minorities until the approval of some at least of the provinces had been obtained. It is not clear how many of the provinces must consent to particular amendments or how that consent is to be obtained or how it is to be expressed. So whenever the desirability of any particular amendment is raised, discussion soon goes off on the procedure to be followed in trying to get it. This uncertainty continues with respect to those vitally important sections of the British North America Act, which were expressly excepted from the control of the Parliament of Canada in the 1949 amendment to the Act referred to above.

There have been numerous other earlier amendments to the Act enacted by the British Parliament which need not be discussed here because the methods used in initiating them do not settle the vital issue as to what is to be done when one or more provinces object to a proposed amendment to reduce the powers of the provinces. It is more useful to look at some of the opposing views. Most of those who object, in general, to a reduction of the powers of the provinces tend to uphold a view known as the Compact Theory of Confederation. According to this theory, the constitution adopted in 1867 was a contract or treaty between the separate colonies which became parts of the new Dominion and, therefore, no change in the terms of the contract can be made without the consent of all the parties to it. In this view, the six provinces which later joined the original four are also parties to the contract. It is urged that no amendment reducing the powers of the provinces or affecting the guarantees of minority rights contained in the Act can be made without the consent of all the provinces. Holders of this view would now presumably say the method of amending certain portions of the Act which was adopted in 1949 at the request of the federal Parliament without first securing the consent of the provinces is a violation of the compact.

This is essentially a legal argument but most competent lawyers would deny its validity. It is sufficient to note two, out of the several, points of effective criticism on legal grounds. First, the terms of union which were written into the British North America Act were finally settled by the British government. While they followed, in the main, the Quebec Resolutions, a draft of proposals for union agreed on by the political leaders of the British North American colonies in 1865, they varied from them in important respects, and these variations were never referred back to the colonial legislatures to see whether they agreed with them or not. In other words, there were important terms which were never part of any contract. Secondly, neither the Dominion nor the provinces of Ontario or Quebec could have been parties to any pre-Confederation contract, because they themselves did not exist prior to Confederation but were first brought into existence by it. Furthermore, it is doubtful whether either Nova Scotia or New Brunswick could be said to have been parties to any contract that might have been made because, in neither case, were even the Quebec Resolutions referred to the legislatures of these provinces. The legal argument falls to the ground.

However, if we speak in moral rather than strict legal terms, there is ground for saying that Confederation was a compact, not between the several provinces but between the two races, English and French, which agreed to associate together in the Dominion of Canada on terms of mutual tolerance and respect. The most important reason for a federal union rather than a unitary one was that a unitary state was entirely unacceptable to the French-speaking Canadians. They were willing to come in only on condition that matters affecting language, religion, and basic social relationships were exclusively reserved to the provinces. It might not be a breach of contract but it would be a breach of faith to insist now on withdrawing such matters from the jurisdiction of the provinces without their consent.

Another school of thought holds that there are several different kinds of clauses in the British North America Act, and that a separate method of amendment is appropriate to each. This has been the dominant view at two Dominion-provincial conferences held in 1936 and 1950 on the question of a method of amendment. The 1950 Conference agreed that there were six different types of clauses. Three of these are important for this discussion.

First, certain clauses deal only with the structure and organization of the national government, and should therefore be open to amendment on the motion of the Parliament of Canada without any consent of the provinces being required. Instances might be sections 53–4 prescribing how the Parliament of Canada shall proceed on financial legislation, and section 48 prescribing the quorum for meetings of the House of Commons. Second, there are certain fundamental clauses affecting the rights of race, language, and religion which should not be amended without the consent of all provinces. Instances are section 92.12 (solemnization of marriage), section 93 (guarantee of denominational privileges in education), and section 133 (guarantee of bilingualism in certain aspects of public life).

Third, there is a large number of clauses which concern the Dominion and all the provinces but which are not so fundamental as to require the consent of all provinces for their amendment. Such clauses should be open to amendment "by an Act of the Parliament of Canada and Acts of such majority of the (provincial) legislatures and upon such additional conditions, if any, as may be decided upon." What clauses fall in this third group is, of course, a matter on which there is a considerable division of opinion. Those who want it to be easy to amend the British North America Act tend to enlarge the first and third categories at the expense of the second. Those who want it to be difficult to put through amendments tend to enlarge the second category at the expense of the first and the third. Nor is there any agreement as to what majority of the provincial legislatures, six of the ten, or eight of the ten, should be required for amendment of sections falling in the third category.

There is a pretty general agreement that certain fundamental minority rights guaranteed by the British North America Act should not be modified without the consent of all provinces. Here again the real dispute is over the detailed application of the principle—which clauses protect fundamental rights and which do not. It will not be easy to get general agreement on it. In any direct sense, the transfer of complete authority over social security measures to the Dominion does not abridge any right of race, language, or religion. Indirectly, however, it may, because if people come to look to the federal government as the chief architect of their security against the various mischances of life, relationships within the family and the local community will be affected in numerous ways. In Quebec, in particular, the place of the Church in the social structure would likely be profoundly modified. Thus Quebec is disposed to contend that most of the headings of section 92 are necessary for the protection of minority rights and therefore fall in the second category. There is a wide variety of views as to what are the fundamental clauses of the British North America Act.

There are, of course, still other views as to the appropriate method of amendment.[1] But enough has been said to show that different bodies of opinion come to different conclusions and make any early agreement on a method of amendment improbable. There is no prospect of an early end of the confusion arising in the Canadian federation from this source. The Dominion-Provincial Conference of 1950 on a method of constitutional amendment made a determined effort to reach agreement. In the several sessions of the Conference, agreement was reached on how to amend a large number of sections. However, there were still many sections on which unanimity could not be reached. The Conference narrowed down the differences of view to the essential points but had to conclude its deliberations without composing these differences.

[1]For some of these other views, and for a searching analysis of the whole question of amendment of the British North America Act, see Paul Gérin-Lajoie, *Constitutional Amendment in Canada* (University of Toronto Press, 1951).

Is Federalism Obsolete?

It has been suggested already that, in some quarters, federalism is regarded as obsolete. In many of the problems with which governments are expected to deal, no one government in the federation can act effectively alone. The attempt to act in concert involves so much discussion and delay that many problems are not met at all. What each government does affects the conditions facing the others. They often work at cross-purposes and this adds to the friction. Politicians are not above using the distribution of powers to evade responsibility. To get elected to one of the legislatures in the federation they promise to do things that the constitution reserves to other legislatures, and then try to excuse themselves by blaming the constitution or the other governments in the federation. Therefore, it is urged that no reallocation of powers will sufficiently moderate the friction, the frustration, and evasion of responsibility, and that the states should be abolished.

Associated with this conclusion are others who hold that there is a great deal of overlapping and duplication among the several governments, adding unjustifiably to the ever mounting cost of government. They point to the fact that federal departments of labour, agriculture, health, and so on are duplicated by state and provincial departments of the same name. They say that a country that has to support eleven or fifty-one governments is ridiculously overgoverned and that an immense reduction of government expenditures could be had by abandoning federalism altogether.

Whatever may be the case for abandoning federalism in favour of a unitary state, it cannot be rested on this latter ground. The numerous departments of labour, agriculture, and health are not mainly engaged in duplicating one another's efforts. Some duplication there is, but its cost is negligible relative to the total expenditures of all governments in the federation. At any rate, this was the considered conclusion of the Sirois Commission, which made a careful investigation of the charges of duplication and overlapping in the several governments in Canada.[1] The Commission on Intergovernmental Relations reached a similar conclusion for the United States in 1956.[2]

[1]*Report of the Royal Commission on Dominion-Provincial Relations,* vol. II, p. 183.
[2]*The Report of the Commission on Intergovernmental Relations,* op. cit., Introduction and Part I.

Furthermore, the sums that would be saved by abolishing state and provincial governments are such a tiny fraction of total expenditures of governments in the federation that it would not be worth the upheaval involved. The reason for this is that the cost of upkeep of legislatures, of the internal housekeeping of government departments, and of the salaries of civil servants are but a small part of the current expenditures of governments nowadays. The great outlays of governments are in regulating community life and in providing expensive services for the public. The only really effective way to lower the cost of government is to abolish some of the numerous activities outlined in chapter v. As long as these activities are to be maintained, the abolition of ten or fifty legislatures and governmental establishments would not give any significant relief to the taxpayer.

The question whether the sprawling, poorly co-ordinated federal system is now obsolete, a mastodon blundering about in a streamlined age, is not so easily answered. The first consideration to be kept constantly in mind is that the prime cause of the present confusion in federal systems is the greatly augmented scope of governmental action. If governmental management of the life of the people in peacetime had stayed at the level reached in World War II, there is little doubt that federalism would be obsolete. The federal governments ran the war and decided almost everything connected with it.

The state governments remained in a condition of suspended animation with no substantial sphere of independent initiative. They continued to perform most of the functions they had performed at the outbreak of war and co-operated in the war effort, but decisions at Washington and Ottawa left them little independent choice concerning what they would do. Peacetime governmental operations of wartime magnitude would equally have to be directed by a single central government. State and provincial governments might remain as agents for carrying out the decisions of the federal governments, but they would cease to be principals operating on their own account.

The Continuing Diversity of a Continental Country

However, if governmental activities can be kept substantially below the level they reached in World War II, there is still a great deal to be said for a federal system. The United States and Canada each cover half a continent. Few of the successful unitary states have covered an area greater than that covered by one of the larger states or provinces. It is extremely difficult for a single government to carry on a wide range of activities over so wide an area and carry them on effectively.

The difficulty does not arise merely from the size of the territory; in fact, modern means of transport and communication are overcoming the physical limitations of time and distance. It arises rather out of the diversity of conditions that mark the different parts of a continental country. It was pointed out early in the chapter that the conditions of life and the character of the people vary in the different states at the time of union. These differences are lessened as a common life is shared within the union over a considerable period of time, but they still remain highly significant.

The significant differences have become, in most instances, regional rather than state or provincial in character. It would not be contended that present-day differences between the conditions of life in New Hampshire and Vermont, Georgia and Alabama, New Brunswick and Nova Scotia, Alberta and Saskatchewan are very marked. But there are distinctive differences between the New England region and the deep South, between the maritime region and the prairie region in Canada. Each of the federations in question is made up of a number of distinct regions. The people in each of these regions have common problems and a common outlook on many matters, and their problems and outlook differ markedly from those which form the identifying characteristics of other regions. This is the point made by those who argue in the United States for the amalgamation of groups of states under a smaller number of regional governments. They are not arguing against federalism but for a drastic revision of its territorial pattern.[1]

It may be that some such revision will prove to be necessary if federalism is to be rescued from its present difficulties. However, there is no large support for such a revision at present and no agreement at all on what states, or parts of states, should be combined in the new regions. Only one thing is obvious: provinces

[1]E.g. see William Yandell Elliott, *The Need for Constitutional Reform* (McGraw-Hill, New York, 1935), pp. 191-8.

like Quebec, which, as they stand, are distinct cultural entities, would have to remain as they are. Whatever the outcome of suggestions of this kind, the important point for present purposes is the continuing diversity of conditions in a continental country.

DECENTRALIZATION THROUGH FEDERALISM

If a continental country like the United States or Canada were ruled by a single central government, that government would not be able to adjust all the laws it would have to make and administer to the varying conditions of the different regions. Laws —and even rules and regulations made under them—have to be framed in general terms. In discussing the civil service we saw that, under democratic government at least, there is a general insistence that laws should be administered uniformly with very little discretionary adaptation to special circumstances. We also saw that there are deep underlying reasons for this characteristic of administration.

In fact, uniformity of law and uniform enforcement of it are highly desirable as long as the laws are aimed merely at generally acknowledged anti-social conduct. The definition of murder and its prescribed punishment should be the same everywhere and should be enforced impartially. But when government is regulating everyday life in great detail, diversity of rule and application to meet special circumstances is necessary. This is the reason for the development of the administrative process, which, as we have seen, imposes a considerable strain on the constitutional safeguards of liberal democracy.

The level of minimum wages, the pattern of aid to agriculture and conservation measures, the content of the public-school curriculum should vary according to the cultural and economic conditions of different areas. If general laws on these and a multitude of other matters were enacted and enforced uniformly across the country, there would be deep dissatisfaction over them almost everywhere. Uniformity in these circumstances is sterile, or disrupting, or both.

The reason for adopting federalism in the first place was to arrest the reach of a distant government that is not trusted to take account of unique circumstances in different areas. As long as the

federation with its autonomous states continues to exist, the legislatures of these states adapt the laws, partially at least, to the
special circumstances of particular areas. Consequently there is
less need to rely on the administrative process and less strain on
the constitutional safeguards than there would be if one central
legislature made all the laws for the country. Half a continent cannot
be governed by a highly centralized machine in Ottawa or Washington. It would be necessary to try to decentralize administration by
establishing regional offices under the direction of officials with
discretion to adjust the laws to regional conditions.

If such expedients are desirable in a tight little island like
Britain with a homogeneous population and no great diversity of
conditions, they would be inevitable under the continental conditions of government in North America. If the decentralization
of government which federalism provides were abandoned, it
would become immediately necessary to try to restore it in another
form by setting up regional branches of the national government.

Excessive Rigidity a Weakness of Centralization

The difficulty is, that as long as governments are kept under
control by the governed, there must be fairly narrow limits to
discretionary adaptation of laws to special circumstances. The
regional branches to which the central government would delegate
some discretionary power could not be given enough discretion
to make adequate adjustment. They could not begin to respond
to the unique aspects of life in a particular region as fully as do
the present state governments, each of which must follow the
temper of its own particular electorate and does not need to
concern itself with what is being done in other parts of the
country except in a limited range of matters.

The inability of the regional offices of the national government
to adjust uniform nation-wide laws to varying regional conditions
is not the only difficulty. Many problems with which governments
are expected to deal are peculiar to a particular region and do not
require action on a national scale. The national government would
either deal with these inadequately or ignore them entirely.

There are even now some matters over which federal governments have sole authority but which are of prime importance in

only one or two states. For example, the Dominion Parliament in Canada has exclusive authority over seacoast fisheries. This is necessary because seacoast fisheries involve international negotiation and treaties that the national government alone can undertake. However, the only provinces with a vital interest in seacoast fisheries in the sense that they are the basis of livelihood of a substantial part of the population are Newfoundland, Nova Scotia, and British Columbia. The latter two have complained from time to time that the federal government neglects the fisheries and misunderstands the problems of the industry. Newfoundland, a new Province, has not yet had time to share this grievance.

In the past, at any rate, there has been much substance in the complaint. If one compares the range of services provided for agriculture and the amount of scientific knowledge brought to bear on agricultural problems by the Dominion with what the Dominion has done, until quite recently, to assist the development of the fishing industry, the disparity is so marked as to require explanation. There are a number of explanations, but most of them turn on one central consideration. Agriculture is an important industry in every province and can claim at every stage a livelier interest and a larger sympathy at Ottawa than fisheries. What is a vital concern in all provinces will always have a prior claim to that which is of serious interest to one or two provinces only. Farmers will always have more votes in federal elections than fishermen.

Such a priority is not, in general, a just ground for criticism. But the fact that it exists, and is likely to continue to exist, does suggest that there should be, in a country of great diversities, state—or regional—governments. Wherever possible, these governments should have control over matters of unique concern to that area and they should have a substantial sphere of independent action. Where this is so, the electorates to which the governments are responsible will see to it that vital regional interests are not neglected. Energies will be harnessed to the tasks in hand and not exhausted in futile efforts to get distant governments to do what needs to be done.

So while there are some spheres in which federalism is inefficient, there are more in which decentralized autonomous governments are necessary to efficiency. On these grounds alone it might be concluded that federalism is not obsolete, although particular federal systems may badly need revision. The principal consideration in favour of federalism, however, has not yet been stated.

FEDERALISM AND DEMOCRACY

In Canada and the United States, with their marked sectional differences, it is extremely doubtful whether democratic government could be maintained at all except through the device of federalism. Democracy has been defined as government by consent. It has been urged that the greatest problem in a democracy is to construct electoral majorities that can agree on what the government should do. The problem grows more acute as the number of decisions to be made in the political arenas increases. If all these decisions had to be made in the national arena, so many diverging sectional interests would be brought face to face on so many issues that it would be impossible to get a majority in the electorate or in the legislature that would agree on how all these issues were to be dealt with. Federal, or national, politics in the United States and Canada have been immensely simplified by the fact of a number of lesser political arenas in which a great many issues are settled without ever rising to the level of national politics.

It is not merely, or even mainly, that political squabbles are decentralized in the "insulated chambers" of the states. A lot of little fights may be as serious as one big one. The great triumph of federalism is that many matters that would cause the sharpest conflict if they were thrown into national politics cause little dissension when dealt with separately in each state. Federalism enables many regional interests and idiosyncrasies to have their own way in their own areas without ever facing the necessity of reconciliation with other regional interests. Individuals identify themselves with particular regional interests and find in them a satisfying expression of many facets of their personalities. Federalism is a device for combining unity and diversity in accordance with the requirements of liberal democratic ideals.

Even as things stand at present, the clash of sectional interests in Congress is very marked. It helps greatly to explain why Congress often cannot reach a majority decision on what should be done in the national interest without logrolling. If everything that is done by government in the United States had to be determined by Congress, Congress would exhibit far less unity of purpose than it does now.

In Canada, the federal Parliament and government have been much blamed in the recent past for their failure to deal vigorously with serious matters such as the great depression of the nineteen-thirties. Their vacillation was not due merely to the constitutional limitations on the Dominion. It arose in part from the fact that deep cleavages among the Canadian people prevented them from producing electoral majorities that would support vigorous measures of a specific nature.

The clearest concrete illustration appears in the course of events in Canada in time of war. Twentieth-century wars are national enterprises which require the national government to regulate minutely the most intimate details of life. Under the pressure of war, Canada, for the time being, almost becomes a unitary state. But even the fear of a common enemy is not enough to overcome the basic cultural diversity in the country. Quebec and the rest of the country cannot go along together in prosecuting a total war without disagreements that threaten to create irreconcilable factions. Separatist movements spring from the fact that, in time of war, the common government asks everybody to agree about everything.

Abolition of the federal system would make what has been an expedient of war an everyday necessity. This would be disruptive in the extreme. While the war lasts, a number of divergences of sectional interests are kept in check only by a recognition of the overwhelming necessity of presenting a common front to the enemy. Once the war is over, the check ceases to operate. If it were not for the federal system in Canada, these divergences would clash in the national political arena and convulse the country as does the conscription issue in time of war.

It has already been pointed out that in Canada and the United States the national political parties are federations of provincial and state parties. Each national party appeals to and gets support from persons and groups of diverse interests and attitudes across the country. Each manages to hold its heterogeneous following together because, up until now, national politics have been concerned principally with matters of general interest throughout the country and do not go to the heart of matters on which regional interests and attitudes diverge sharply. These latter matters are mostly within the purview of state and provincial politics. If, however, it were necessary within each national party to come to agreement on these divisive matters, the national parties would scarcely hold together. There is thus some ground for suggesting that the two-party system in national politics in the United States and Canada has been made possible by federalism and that if federalism goes, it will go too. If, as has been contended, democracy and the two-party system are closely related, it would follow that democracy and federalism also have intimate connections in countries of continental extent.

These are some of the reasons for suggesting a close connection between federalism and democracy. They fall short of conclusive proof. In any political situation, the factors involved are so numerous and so hard to estimate that all arguments and conclusions must be taken with a grain of salt. On the other hand, there does not appear to be any adequate ground for thinking that federalism is obsolete. It seems advisable to continue patching up the federal system. Any satisfactory patching, however, is likely to involve an increase in the powers of the federal government. There are a number of pressing problems of nation-wide scope that can only be dealt with adequately by action on a national scale.

Political Unification of Continental Areas

Also, when we say that people have come to think of themselves as Americans or Canadians as well as citizens of particular states or provinces, we mean that they have become conscious of sharing a wider range of common interests with all their fellow citizens throughout the country. It is natural that they should look to the national government to further these interests.

As nationalism grows in strength, the particularism that marks the early stages of a federal system diminishes. In both countries more and more persons come to think in terms of the nation rather than of individual states. Key persons, the leaders in agriculture, business, education and trade unions, attend more and more anxiously to the national governments with decreasing attention to the state governments. Moreover, in an age of conformity, which our times are being called with some justification, individualism declines and so does the particularism of particular regions. Whether desirable or not, conformity is one aspect of a broadening and deepening consensus in both countries. However, the significance of these developments must not be overrated. Increasing conformity is matched by the rebelliousness of "angry young men," and there is no agreement on how far nationalism has overcome particularism in the United States and Canada. In so far as history affords any guide, it suggests that the creation of genuinely united nations out of heterogeneous populations is a long, slow process. Under favourable conditions, the extraordinary means of communication now open to us can speed the process, but they will not accomplish it all at once.

Those who look at the record of the federal systems of the United States and Canada floundering in their difficulties over the past forty years are often impatient with the long, slow process. Whether they are watching the exasperating disagreements of Dominion-provincial conferences in Canada, or the confusion and seeming purposelessness of the United States Congress, they make a comparison with the tidy system of government in Britain. They are inclined to forget that Britain is a small homogeneous country with a national unity matured over many hundreds of years, and therefore not at all comparable with the continental diversity of the United States and Canada. The perspective would be corrected if a contrast were made with the continent of Europe as a whole, which deals with continental political problems by the wasteful and inefficient processes of war.

Laid alongside that contrast, the federations of the United States and Canada seem not only tidy, but also triumphs of civilized efficiency. Such untidiness as they exhibit is due to the fact that each is struggling with the political unification of a continental area. The existence of numerous state and provincial governments in the United States and Canada gives to government, as a whole, a different character from that of Britain, and raises a number of special types of political problems from which British politics is free.

CHAPTER XVIII

LOCAL GOVERNMENT

Up to this point, we have been considering central governments that rule a wide territory operating from a single centre or capital. Even the state and provincial governments in a federal system are central governments in this sense. It will be convenient here to refer to all central governments of whatever kind as senior governments, thus distinguishing them from a very numerous group of subordinate, or junior, governments, each of which has a limited authority in a very narrow locality.

Central governments have never been able to carry on all the activities wanted of government. They have been compelled to rely on a network of local governments which in the aggregate can scarcely be said to be of lesser importance than the senior governments. Municipal government, as it is generally called in North America, touches the lives of more people at more points than do the senior governments. The character of local government and its relation to the senior governments are important factors affecting the working of government as a whole in any country.

Status of Anglo-American Local Government

The place of local government in the constitutional framework must be considered first. Local government is subordinate government. The city or the county, unlike the states or provinces in a federation, has no assured sphere of autonomy that the constitution protects.[1] At any time, a law passed by the appropriate legislature may abolish local government, or modify or take away some of the

---

[1]This statement is subject to some qualification in the United States where about one-third of the states have amended their constitutions to provide a defined sphere of "home rule" for the municipalities in the state. In these states, the state legislature cannot intervene in this sphere at all without first getting the "home rule" amendment of the constitution repealed.

powers exercised by it. The whole structure of local government in Britain and Canada has been created by statute. Local government in the United States is also largely constituted by statute. Many state constitutions, however, contain provisions relating to the structure of local government. Without such statutory and/or constitutional provisions, the government of the city, town, county, or township could not exist legally. It would have no power to require citizens to pay taxes or shovel snow off their sidewalks, and no duty to maintain and repair roads and lighting and sewage systems. These statutes prescribe in abundant detail how local governments are to be set up, how they are to operate, and what powers and duties they are to have.

Thus, as far as the constitution is concerned, the local governments remain subject to the control of the legislature of the appropriate senior government. They have a sphere of operation in which they can do as they like only because a discretion has been conferred on them by statute. The ordinances made by the municipal council are merely another kind of delegated or subordinate legislation and subject to the same controls and limitations as are the rules made by any of the subordinate law-making agencies described in chapter xvi. For example, if the city council makes a by-law requiring the banks to lend money to the needy at three per cent interest, no bank need obey the by-law and the courts would declare it to be invalid. The matters on which the city council has power to make laws are set out in detail in statutes of the legislature, and thus far regulation of banks and rates of interest has never been among them.

In Britain, the local governments derive their authority from, and the limits of their powers are marked out by, Parliament. In the United States and Canada, the constitution assigns local government exclusively to the states and provinces. In the United States, the clauses that assign powers to the federal authority are silent on this subject and therefore the power to create local governments and to exercise control over them is reserved to the states. In Canada, section 92.8 of the British North America Act gives to the provincial legislatures the exclusive power to make laws relating to "municipal institutions in the province." In neither case has the federal government any direct power over the municipalities. They are the creatures of the state or province.[1]

The Tradition of Local Autonomy

The dependent and subordinate position assigned to local government by the constitution tends to obscure one fundamentally important fact. Local government in the Anglo-American world is self-government. There is a long tradition that local governments are not to be district offices of the senior government but institutions through which local affairs are run by local people. For centuries in Britain, local government was run by a self-perpetuating local oligarchy. The country squires as justices of the peace governed the county.

This system was introduced in the American colonies, but it never became rooted there. Local government was rapidly democratized in America; and in the course of the nineteenth century in Britain the justices of the peace were replaced by elected councils chosen by a local electorate and responsible to it. Local democracy is now so firmly established in popular estimation that no legislature would think of using its constitutional powers to abridge it seriously. Local government has a wide sphere of autonomy guaranteed by political considerations and not by the constitution.

So the statutes that prescribe the areas and kinds of local government invariably provide for the election of a local governing body or council by the residents of the area. The statutes also set out in considerable detail the range of matters with which the council has power to deal. The councils are responsible to their electorate and, generally speaking, to no other political authority. Of course, if corruption has been practised in the municipal elections, an action can be brought in the courts to unseat the councillors involved. If the council exceeds its powers or fails to carry out duties imposed on it by law, redress can be sought through judicial proceedings.

It is only in very unusual circumstances, such as a default in payment on municipal bonds, that the senior government can

[1]In this chapter, senior government, in the singular, refers to the state or provincial government in the United States and Canada, or to the central government in Britain.

remove the local council or dictate to it what it shall do. It is true also that there are a number of specific matters to be discussed later in which the senior government has some power of supervision over local governments. Although these powers are steadily increasing, they are still relatively few and, generally speaking, the autonomy of local governments can only be interfered with by the appropriate legislature amending the statutes that define the constitutions of the local governments.

Contrasts between European and Anglo-American Local Government

The practical autonomy of local government within the sphere marked out for it is regarded in Britain and North America as part of the natural order and therefore as scarcely requiring comment. It is by no means inevitable, however, as the very different status of local government in continental Europe shows. Generally speaking—there are significant exceptions—the countries of continental Europe have no tradition of autonomy in local government. The absolute monarchies established strong central authority over local government. In the late nineteenth and early twentieth centuries, there was a trend towards municipal self-government in Europe. The coming of the dictatorships reversed the trend in many countries, and made local government more than ever an instrument of the central authority. The relationship of central and local government in France under the Third Republic affords a fair illustration of the general situation in Europe before the rise of the dictatorships.

A department of the central government, the ministry of the interior, has as its special care the governing of the interior, the local areas of France. In some matters such as education, administration is entirely in the hands of the minister of the interior. The teachers are employees of the central government and the school is as much under its direction as is the local post office. In other matters, such as police, locally elected authorities participate to some extent, but the powers of central direction are so strong as to leave only a shadow of local autonomy. The local police chiefs are appointed by the central government and may receive binding instructions from that source at any time. In still other matters, locally elected authorities have what appears on the surface to be a wide power to govern. Even here, however, the agents of the central government exercise continuous supervision and, on all major questions, bend local government to the desires of the ministry of the interior.

The important units of local government are the department (roughly comparable to the county in Anglo-American countries) and the commune (which may be a rural area or a town or city). In all, there are ninety-seven departments and about 44,000 communes. The legislative authority of the department is a council elected by manhood suffrage. However, the council is far from having unrestricted powers of law making in relation to its locality. As we have seen, the power of the purse is the best test of a legislature's authority. The council must pass the budget of expenditures, but the central government has a wide power to say what it shall and shall not contain.

Nor has the council the pre-eminence over the executive that we might expect a legislature to possess. Under the Third Republic, the chief executive officer who administered the affairs of the department was the prefect, an official of the central government appointed by and solely responsible to the minister of the interior. Under the 1946 Constitution of the Fourth Republic, the president of the department, who is elected by the members of the council from among themselves for a three-year period, has become the chief executive officer. But the prefect continues as the agent of the central government and a sort of resident-supervisor of the administration of the department. However, the effective power of the prefect has not been lessened by this change. If stubborn disputes arise between the prefect and the council of the department, they are resolved by the minister of the interior, who may remove the prefect or even, in certain circumstances, dissolve the council and call a new election.

The laws passed by the French Parliament confine the council of the department to a very narrow sphere, and the prefect is expected to see that it does not act outside this sphere. So when the local aspirations as expressed by the council conflict with the policy of the central government, the prefect has to remember that his masters are in Paris and not in the locality. The department is an administrative area of the central government rather than a unit of effective local self-government.

Within each department, there is a varying number of communes, large and small. Each commune has a locally elected municipal council with power to make laws relating to local matters. The council chooses one of its members as mayor and he is the chief executive of the commune. Once chosen, however, the mayor becomes substantially independent of the council. It cannot dismiss him or directly control him in the work of administration. In an important sense, the mayor too is an agent of the central government. In matters relating to finance, police, and public health, for example, his main function is to enforce decrees of the central government. In many other matters, he is subject to close supervision by the prefect, who can suspend or remove him if he fails to carry out instructions from above.

The council of the commune has a wider sphere of local independence than the council of the department. In the last sixty years, its power to make ordinances, or laws, has been slowly extended. But the range of its independent action is in no way comparable to that enjoyed by municipal councils in Anglo-American countries. In all the genuinely important fields of local government, its decisions are subject to modification by the prefect under certain circumstances. In particular, its freedom in matters of finance is very sharply limited. And recalcitrant councils that resist the tutelage of the prefect can be suspended, and sometimes dissolved, by the higher authorities.

Although the French system of local government provides for the participation of locally elected councils, centralization is its most striking feature. Its character is not seriously misrepresented by charting it in the familiar hierarchical form. At the apex stands the minister of the interior, a member of the cabinet in the national government, from whom orders go to the prefects at the departmental level. The prefect, in turn, passes on edicts and instructions to the mayors who govern the communes at the base of the pyramid.[1] Local government in most European countries

---

[1]There are other intermediate units and officers that need not be considered here. For a sketch of French local government, see Brian Chapman, *Introduction to French Local Government* (Allen and Unwin, London, 1953).

before the era of dictatorships closely resembled the French system.[1] Dictatorship, of course, wherever it has occurred, has enforced still more drastic centralization.

Local government in Britain, Canada, and the United States presents the sharpest contrast to these centralized systems. It is decentralized. Within the wide sphere of operations assigned to them by law, the locally elected councils govern according to their interpretation of the desires of the local electorate. The next election determines whether they have interpreted local opinion correctly or not. Local government in close correspondence to local demands and needs is thus ensured.

Not only do the municipal councils make what laws they think fit; they also appoint and control the officers who enforce these laws and carry on the work of daily administration.[2] While there is a steadily growing number of matters in which the senior government prescribes minimum standards that local governments must observe, the local governments are not obliged to placate officials of the senior government at every turn. It is true, however, that in some states the governor or a state department head has been given power to remove certain kinds of local officials in certain specified circumstances. No matter how dark a view the senior government takes of the behaviour of particular locally elected councils, it cannot suspend or dissolve them. If the council has exceeded its powers or violated the law, the remedy, in almost all cases, is an action in the courts. The only other course generally open to the senior government is to ask the legislature to amend the general law relating to local government. It hesitates to sponsor such a measure because that will bring it into collision with a general public opinion in favour of autonomous local self-government.

AREAS AND AUTHORITIES IN LOCAL GOVERNMENT

Local government requires the division of the country into areas, each with a separate authority or government. The number, type, and extent of these areas vary in each country. What these

[1]Switzerland, where local government has a remarkable degree of autonomy, is one of a few notable exceptions.
[2]Some qualifications of this statement for the United States will be made later.

areas are depends partly on past history and partly on the needs and purposes of the present. The county has been a unit of government in Britain since early times, and it was transplanted to North America in colonial times. The county, or its equivalent, is found everywhere because of the pervasiveness of rural conditions in our past. There may also be smaller urban and rural subdivisions of the county: the town, village, and township in some parts of the United States and in Canada, and the rural district of Britain. Many of these are now too small, either in area or in population, for many purposes, and their importance has declined in favour of the more inclusive county units.

There have always been units of urban government as well. The ancient English boroughs have a long history of local autonomy. The cities and towns of more recent origin in all three countries have been more or less completely separated from the counties or townships in which they lie and have been given charters of self-government. A few great metropolitan centres in each country are special areas with distinctive forms of government. In the United States and Canada, the configuration of the rural units and the names given them vary from state to state and from province to province. Nothing would be gained by attempting detailed description and comparison.

The conditions and needs of rural government differ sharply from those of urban government, and every metropolitan area is in some measure unique. Accordingly, the governmental institutions are more or less adjusted to the differences and there are numerous departures from the common pattern of local government even within a single country. The one great common characteristic has already been discussed. These units are all local democracies practising a wide measure of self-government in a specified list of matters. Also, they are all units of general government and not special areas for special purposes. The city council, for example, has to be a jack-of-all-trades, making decisions in most of the questions of local government that are reserved for local determination.

In Britain, there are very few exceptions to the general authority of the county or city council in local matters. In the United States and Canada, however, there are numerous special areas for special purposes, with separately elected governing bodies. These areas may or may not coincide with the boundaries of the town, city, or county. The most typical example is the school district for the purpose of education, with its board of trustees or board of education. In addition, in the cities and towns in many states and provinces, particular matters are often withdrawn from the jurisdiction of the general council and placed under the authority of special purpose bodies like boards of health, police commissions, and public-utilities commissions.

The questions whether there shall be special authorities for particular purposes and if so, how they shall be chosen, are not left to local choice. They depend on the state or provincial legislation that establishes the structure of local government and defines its functions. Local government, it must be remembered, is subordinate government and cannot frame or alter its own constitution.[1]

Something will be said later about the significance of these special local authorities. At present, it is necessary to look at the characteristics of the general government of local areas. The legislative authority of the city, town, or county is always an elected council chosen by substantially adult suffrage. Although there are some matters in which the local electorate may, or must, participate in the law-making process by referendum, all laws relating to local affairs require an ordinance by the council. The council also has some control over the executive and the administration.

STRUCTURE OF LOCAL GOVERNMENT IN BRITAIN AND CANADA

In Britain and Canada, this control is complete. The council is the executive as well as the legislature, the cabinet as well as the parliament. While the central legislature relies on one small executive committee for all purposes (the cabinet), the local legislatures set up separate executive committees for finance, public works, parks, public welfare, and so on. Each member of the council has a share in the control of one or more branches of administration. Each committee of the council occupies a position

[1]In some states of the United States, the state legislatures authorize alternative forms of structure and organization between which localities are free to choose. A range of choice may exist if the senior legislature permits it. Also, even where state legislation does not offer alternatives, a particular city or county may take the initiative in proposing modifications in its charter for the approval of the state legislature, and of its own citizens in a popular referendum.

comparable to that of the minister in charge of a department of the central government. Indeed, if the chairman of a committee is vigorous and skilful, he may run the committee and thus be himself the equivalent of a minister.

Each committee has a general oversight of administration but does not itself do the work of daily administration. It relies on a civil service, a body of appointed officials and employees, which is very numerous in great cities and almost nonexistent in rural townships. In a large city, the committees of council, like the ministers of large departments of the central government, must rely very heavily on their senior civil servants, restricting themselves to the larger questions of policy. In the smaller units of local governments where the affairs to be managed are few and relatively simple, the committees can—and often do—direct the activity of the civic employees in some detail.

The point to be stressed here is that the municipal civil service, be it large or small, is responsible to a committee of the council, and through it to the council itself. The council not only makes the laws; either directly, or indirectly through senior officials under its control, it determines the effectiveness of law enforcement, hires and fires, purchases supplies, lets contracts, and generally conducts civic housekeeping.

In the senior governments of Britain and Canada, the cabinet co-ordinates the work of the several executive departments, ensuring a degree of harmony in administration as a whole. In the local governments of these countries where each branch of administration is under the supervision of a distinct committee of council, there is need for co-ordination to prevent confusion and working at cross-purposes. The problem is not a serious one until the urban form of government is reached. In the cities, it is met more or less effectively in a number of ways.

The fact of interlocking membership in the various committees helps each committee keep track of what the others are doing. It may be that the finance committee is made up of the chairmen of the other committees; just as in the senior governments administration is integrated through financial control. Also, the mayor of the city is usually a member of all committees of council and of most of the other civic boards and commissions. Furthermore, the committees have no power to make decisions on questions of policy, which must always be settled finally by the council as a whole. That is to say, the council itself performs many of the co-ordinating functions of the cabinet in the senior governments. Finally, in the larger cities, administration is too burdensome and complex for the committees to interfere much in its detail. This is the opportunity of the appointed city officials to exercise a good deal of guidance and authority in administration. In many instances, the city clerk assumes functions approaching those of a general manager.

This description makes no reference to the office of mayor, which is found in all British and Canadian cities. The mayor is the first citizen or chief magistrate of his city, but these are formal titles and do not confer on him any specific governmental functions. Like the King, he has the influence of an exalted position but no significant power. In Britain, he is not popularly elected but is chosen annually by the council, generally from among themselves. Apart from being the chairman of the council, he is largely a figurehead gracing ceremonial occasions. In Canada, following American practice, the mayor is popularly elected, and his standing with the electorate puts him in a stronger position of influence than the British mayor. He is chairman of the council and a member of all committees, but he has no significant powers of his own that are not shared by other members of the council.[1] The real authority both in legislation and administration is the council.

In Britain, the term of office for councillors is three years, with a new mayor or chairman of the council chosen at the beginning of each year. In Canada, the term of office for mayors and members of municipal councils varies. The greater number are still elected annually but two- and three-year terms are becoming increasingly common. One year is too short a period, as it takes a newly elected member of a council a good part of a year to learn how to be useful. The necessity of fighting an election every year discourages many public-spirited but busy men from entering municipal politics. The widespread Canadian practice of a one-year term is borrowed from the United States, where short terms used to be the general rule.

[1]Except in Quebec and British Columbia, where mayors have a qualified power of veto.

Ultra-democratic ideas, which, as we shall see, have had a strong influence on the institutions and practice of local government in the United States, suggested that the more often elected representatives had to go to the people, the closer the control the people would be able to exercise over their government. However, it should be noted that one-year terms are now much less common in the United States than formerly. In most cities, mayors are elected for either two or four years. Some councils are still elected annually, but many of them are chosen for periods running from two to four years.

STRUCTURE OF LOCAL GOVERNMENT IN THE UNITED STATES

In the United States up to the middle of the nineteenth century, the formal organization of municipal government closely resembled the British pattern just described. Legislative and executive authority were concentrated in the council. The mayors of the cities were mostly figureheads, although they were popularly elected and not appointed officers. Two strong sets of influences of the mid-nineteenth century led the state legislatures to introduce the separation of powers into local government and put the executive and legislative powers in different hands.

First, "government of the people, by the people, and for the people" was interpreted as requiring that, wherever possible, those who exercised powers of government should be directly elected. Accordingly, provision was made for direct election of mayors as well as of many of the chief officials of the counties and cities. Clerks, treasurers, auditors, assessors, and others, who in Britain and Canada are appointed by the municipal council, came to be directly elected by the voters in American municipalities. These officers who control a large part of local administration got a direct mandate from the local electorate and became directly responsible to it.

The control of administration was thus largely taken away from the council, and responsibility for administration was diffused among a number of elected officials. The same impulses led to the establishment and direct election of numerous distinct local boards comparable in nature to the school boards already mentioned. Power in local affairs was widely diffused instead of being concentrated in a single elected council. While the trend in this direction has been reversed in the twentieth century, direct election of many administrative officers and boards is still the rule in most counties and in many of the smaller cities in the United States.

The second set of influences was derived from the examples set by the federal and state constitutions. In these constitutions, the separation of powers set the executive apart from the legislature and made it necessary to have the chief executive independently elected. It was plausible to think that a principle that is sound for the nation and the several states must also be valid for the municipality. That is to say, if presidents and governors are directly elected and given wide powers to exercise independently of the legislature, so should mayors. Mayors ceased to be largely figureheads and became elected chief executives with independent powers. They were given a suspensive veto on ordinances passed by the council, the power to hire and fire civic employees, and so on. The extent to which mayors have to get confirmation of their executive decisions by the council varies from state to state. We have already seen how the separation of powers weakens authority and divides responsibility in the federal government of the United States. It has had similar, even more unsatisfactory, results in local government, and a pronounced reaction against it developed about the beginning of the twentieth century.

For a variety of reasons associated with the rapid growth and heterogeneous population of American cities, local government in the second half of the nineteenth century in the United States was marked by many evils and abuses. One contributing factor was the division of legislative and executive authority and the diffusion of responsibility among many elected officials. In the last quarter of the century, there was a rising insistence on drastic reform, and a number of advances towards better local government. Shortly after 1900, the attention of reformers was turned towards the structure of local government itself.

Since then, two principal revisions of the general organization of local government known as the commission plan and the council-manager plan have been adopted by many municipalities. Reorganization of local government in accordance with these plans has made almost no progress in the rural counties or in the larger cities of more than half a million population. A few counties have adopted the manager scheme but still adhere, in the main, to the system of many elected officials and widely diffused authority, and the very large cities are still governed by some variant of the mayor-council plan. At one time, a number of the medium-sized and smaller cities in the United States went over to the commission plan but today they tend to favour the council-manager scheme of local government.

Before speaking more particularly about the commission and council-manager schemes, it should be said the mayor-council form of government is being rapidly transformed in one city after another, largely by strengthening the position of the mayor. This is done by raising the mayor from a figurehead to a chief executive with control over the administrative departments of the city government. The heads of these departments cease to be elected and are appointed and removed by the mayor. They work under his control and supervision. Also, he is often given a predominant influence in finance. It is being widely recognized that efficiency and responsibility in administration cannot be secured adequately under the older practice of diffusion of authority.

The Commission and Council-Manager Plans

Under the commission plan, a small commission, or council, of from three to seven members is elected for a term of two or four years. With the exception of the school board, which is still retained, no other officials or boards are elected by the voters. One of the commissioners is chosen, either by the commissioners themselves or by popular vote, to act as chairman or mayor, but he is rarely given any significant independent powers. The commissioners give full time to the work and are paid substantial salaries. All authority and power, both legislative and executive, is concentrated in the commission.

The separation of powers and the diffusion of authority are eliminated. As a legislative body, the commission enacts by-laws, levies taxes, and appropriates money to the items of expenditure. The day-to-day work of administering the affairs of the city is divided among a number of departments such as finance, works, health, and safety. There are usually an equal number of commissioners and departments so that each commissioner, in addition to being a legislator, is the executive head of a department, directing all its operations.

This structure might be expected to produce the substance of cabinet government: a small executive linking together the legislature and the administration, and concerting among themselves a unified policy both for the legislature and for the separate departments of administration. In practice, however, it has not worked that way. Collective responsibility, which is a vital feature of cabinet government, is lacking.

Each commissioner regards himself as having a distinct mandate from the people for two or four years, and he tends to concentrate his attention on his own department. The commissioners tend to give too much attention to the detail of their departments instead of leaving it to expert permanent officials, and too little attention to co-operative co-ordination of the varied business of the city as a whole. When, as too often happens, each commissioner fights for his own department, the executive does not work as a team, and administrative rivalries weaken the deliberations of the legislature. Lacking a strong, vigilant opposition in the legislature, there is nothing to compel the commissioners to hang together or hang separately.

While commission government is an advance on the forms of organization it superseded, the defects noted, among others, have brought a considerable decline in its popularity in recent years. Some cities that adopted it have abandoned it. Some have gone back to the separation of powers between council and mayor, often giving the mayor a stronger position than before. Others have adopted the council-manager plan, which is the currently favoured plan for reorganizing city government.

The council-manager plan corresponds closely to the commission plan up to the point where responsibility for the day-to-day direction and control of administration is reached. All governing power and responsibility, of a legislative and policy nature, are vested in a small elected council, but the members of the council do not become the active heads of the administrative departments. Instead, the council appoints a city manager who is directly responsible to the council for executing the laws and managing all the affairs of the city. The council also sometimes elects a mayor who is the presiding officer of the council and represents the city on ceremonial occasions. Those who have promoted this arrangement have had the business corporation in mind. The electorate are the shareholders in the city corporation, the council is the elected board of directors and they appoint a general manager who is the operating head of the administration.

Ideally, the line that is drawn is not between legislative and executive but between the making of policy and the carrying out of policy in detail, or administration. The council makes the ordinances, votes the budget, and has general surveillance over administration. The manager puts the council's decisions into effect, advises it on all matters of detail such as drafting a proposed budget, appoints and removes all heads of departments and, subject in most cases to civil service regulations, hires and fires the civic employees. Where the council gets a good manager and can restrain itself from interfering with him in matters of detail, this scheme helps cities to build up a competent expert civil service and to get effective co-ordination of administration. Although these conditions are not always satisfied, the council-manager plan has had a large measure of success.

About two-thirds of the American cities still maintain a more or less marked separation of powers between mayor and council. In these cities, however, the mayor and council are not always the sole authorities in matters of local government. We have noted that the autonomous school district is found in most areas of local government. Schools are controlled by independently elected school boards and not by the council elected for general purposes of local government. Also, in many cities—and in many counties as well—there are other special *ad hoc* authorities, generally elected but sometimes appointed by the governor of the state.

Sometimes the physical boundaries of the authority of these bodies coincide with the boundary of the city or county, and sometimes they combine several areas of local government for a particular purpose. For example, there are often special districts combining two or more municipalities for the purpose of providing roads, parks, health services, fire protection, water supply, and schools. Wherever a special district is created for the exercise of a particular function of local government, an authority independent of mayor or council, or both, is generally created also.

Independent ad hoc Boards

In addition, there are numerous instances where distinct authorities for exercising particular functions within a city or county are set up. The most common are boards of financial control and police commissions. The former usually consist of the mayor and a small board elected by the voters at large. The latter are often appointed by the state government without reference to the wishes of the local council or local electors.

Such *ad hoc* authorities, where they exist, cause still more diffusion of authority and responsibility in local government. Except where their object is to combine two or more counties and/or cities so as to give a larger unit of administration for such services as roads, water supply, or public health, all the criticisms of the separation of powers between the mayor and the council are valid against them also. The adoption of the commission or council-manager plan has frequently involved the abolition of almost all the special authorities and the concentration of the powers of local government in one body.

The most important of the original impulses for establishing *ad hoc* independent boards was disgust with the elected municipal council. In the last half of the nineteenth century, American local government suffered greatly from corruption and boss rule. Political machines often controlled municipal elections and used local government for their own purposes rather than for the good government of the municipality. The establishment of independently elected boards for the exercise of particular functions was intended to take those functions out of politics. We have already seen, however, that there is little hope of curbing machine politics merely by multiplying elections. If the function in question is an important one, the machine politicians will turn their hand to controlling the elections to the board. The *ad hoc* boards have been extremely unsatisfactory, and the present tendency is towards their elimination.

In addition, the withdrawal of important functions from the control of the council lowers the power and prestige of the council.

This, in turn, lowers the calibre of men who seek election to the council, thus providing a fallacious reason for taking still more powers away from the council. Able, public-spirited men are not likely to be willing to give their time and effort to local government unless they see the possibility of solid accomplishment. The surest way to attract them is to concentrate the powers of local government in the general council. This is what has been done in Britain, and British local government is markedly more efficient than American and Canadian local government, where there is more diffusion of authority.

American Influences on Canadian Local Government

Local government in Canada has been greatly influenced by American practice. We have already noted the direct election of mayors and the frequency of short, one-year terms for councils and mayors. The autonomous and independently elected school board is another instance. Canadian cities have never adopted an outright separation of powers between mayor and council with its weakening diffusion of power and responsibility. But there has been a considerable use of independent *ad hoc* authorities for particular purposes, some elected and some appointed.

In the larger urban municipalities in every province, the local police have been "taken out of politics" and placed under a police commission consisting of the mayor, the county judge, and the senior police magistrate (the two latter being appointees of the senior governments). A number of the larger Canadian cities have experimented with boards of financial control.

In some provinces, independently elected public-utilities commissions operate the municipally owned public utilities. In many cities, management of the public library is in the hands of a library board on which the city council has only a minority representation. Other instances in which councils are compelled to share powers of local government with extraneous agencies could be cited. Although the movement has not gone so far as it did in the United States, it has similar unfortunate results in dividing authority and lowering the prestige of the council.

When the commission plan of city government became popular in the United States, it was adopted by a number of Canadian cities, only to be abandoned when its defects became obvious. The council-manager plan has made more progress in Canada and in 1958 had been adopted by over fifty Canadian cities. American influences on Canadian government are more marked in the sphere of local government than anywhere else.[1]

FUNCTIONS OF LOCAL GOVERNMENT

Although the institution of local self-government is common to Britain, the United States, and Canada, it is evident that there are marked differences in structure and organization. Similarly, there is a broad similarity in the kind of functions performed by local government in the three countries and very considerable variations in the detailed scope of the functions undertaken. Even within the same country, state, or province, the scope of the functions of rural and urban government differs greatly. The functions of rural governments are very few while, generally speaking, the larger the city, the more things its government undertakes. It would be burdensome and confusing to list the numerous functions and note the differences. However, if we are to grasp the pressing problems of local government today, it is necessary to see the general character of the functions performed.

The principal purpose of local government is to provide through collective action a number of services that the citizen, standing alone, cannot secure for himself as well or at all. But local governments have never been left free to undertake anything and everything that a majority of the citizens approve. Local governments can only do the things they have been authorized or required to do by the legislature of the appropriate senior government. The statutes enumerate the functions of local government and limit the action of each municipality to its own area.

The functions fall into three broad classes. First, there are the protective services of police, public safety as in fire protection, public health, and sanitation. Secondly, there are certain physical services or facilities, of which roads, streets, and bridges are the best examples. The public utilities such as light, gas, water, power,

[1]William B. Munro, *American Influences on Canadian Government* (Macmillan, Toronto, 1929), ch. III.

and transport, which are increasingly owned and operated by municipalities, fall in the same group. Thirdly, there are what may be broadly described as the welfare services such as education, libraries, parks and other recreation facilities, hospitals, and the care of those for whom some public provision has to be made, because of poverty, advanced age, or other defect.

Just as in the case of the senior governments, functions are always changing in scope and emphasis. In local government too, the trend of activity has been sharply upward, particularly in urban areas. The coming of the automobile compelled much greater outlays on roads, streets, and highways. The demand for better education has imposed steadily rising costs. Greater emphasis on preventive medicine and sanitation measures has raised expenditures on public health. Disturbed economic conditions, with consequent poverty and unemployment combined with an insistence that such distress be relieved at public expense, have multiplied several times the cost of welfare services since the turn of the century. Other expenditures also have tended to rise.

The steady, persistent rise in per capita expenditures of local governments over the last century has created a serious problem in municipal finance. Expenditures are always more easily boosted than revenues. But local governments are in a peculiarly difficult position because much the greater part of the revenues they themselves raise comes from a single source, a tax on real property. Municipalities try to increase their revenues by other kinds of taxes, and by imposing licences and collecting fees of various kinds. In the United States, state governments often share with the local governments the proceeds of such taxes as income tax, gasoline tax, and sales tax. These shared taxes, as they are called, are levied and collected by the state governments, and part of the proceeds is distributed to the local governments, generally without strings attached. While local governments are relying increasingly on these other sources of revenue, their combined yield is almost everywhere considerably less than the proceeds of the tax on land values.

As local expenditures rise, the tax on land values must also rise. This brings an unfortunate tendency into operation. Other factors such as the general level of economic activity remaining constant, sharply rising taxes on real property will depreciate land values, so that local governments are often trying to get more and more revenue from a source that shrinks from and with their every advance.

Furthermore, land values are very sensitive to economic conditions, following the downward swing of depressions and showing the most marked depreciation in the areas hardest hit by economic decline. Unfortunately for local government, the costs of welfare services in particular mount in periods of depression, rising most sharply in the most depressed areas. Thus revenues are hardest to come by when and where they are most needed. Plenty of statistical proof of this predicament could be given, but it is sufficient to recall that many municipalities were bankrupted by the long depression of the nineteen-thirties. And even in the best of times, there is a marked disparity in the financial capacity of different municipalities to maintain a standard level of services.

RELATIONSHIPS BETWEEN LOCAL AND SENIOR GOVERNMENTS

One way of easing the difficulties of the local governments is for the senior governments, which have access to more diversified sources of revenue and whose revenues respond more readily to the buoyancy of the economy, to take over some of the more onerous functions of the local governments. A number of functions have been thus transferred in recent years. In Britain, distress arising from unemployment, poverty, ill-health, and old age is now solely relieved by the central government. In the United States and Canada, a number of welfare problems, which formerly imposed, in one way or another, heavy charges on the funds of local governments, have been taken over by the national, or by state or provincial, governments. Senior governments now provide unemployment insurance and aid to the aged, the blind, needy mothers, and dependent children, thus giving local governments appreciable relief from the burden of welfare services that would otherwise have fallen on them.

Alongside this movement and in some respects antedating it, is another more complex development. The legislatures of senior governments have enacted laws that impose substantial uncontrollable expenditures on local governments, limiting their ability to retrench in the face of declining revenues. Local governments are required to provide certain services and to keep them at a level of quality determined on by the senior government. Elementary education is free to the child but compulsory on the local government. Local governments are required by law to maintain a wide variety of sanitary facilities and public-health precautions. In a host of other matters, some important and some trivial, central governments require local governments to perform specified duties, to employ officials of recognized qualifications, and so on. In Britain, where this development has gone furthest, there are relatively few functions of local government in which the senior government does not impose some minimum standards of obligatory services.

The reasons for the intervention of the central government, whether convincing or not in particular instances, are clear enough. There is thought to be a wider than merely local interest in maintaining a minimum level of such services as education and public health all across the country. Areas of illiteracy and unchecked disease are menaces to the whole society. Yet for various and excellent reasons, these services are not likely to be as well managed and administered by the senior governments as by the local governments. On the other hand, many, if not all, local governments are hard pressed financially to maintain the standards insisted on by the senior government.

Accordingly, the imposition of standards has been accompanied by grants of money from the senior governments to the local authorities. For example, compulsory free education is everywhere assisted by grants, which have risen in amount as the required standards have risen. In Britain, where the senior government imposes many standards, about a third of the annual current expenditures of all local governments were being met by grants from the Treasury at the outbreak of World War II. During World War II, the proportion increased to one-half. Since 1945, the costs of poor relief, maintenance of hospitals, and medical care have been lifted from the local governments, and some new obligations imposed, by Parliament. In 1948 and again in 1958, the whole system of grants-in-aid was revised in an effort to come closer to equalizing the disparate financial resources of different local governments. The proportion now exceeds one-half.

Grants ease the financial position of local governments, but they also limit their independence. The senior government may define in detailed regulations the standard of achievement it expects in particular services, and it employs inspectors to check on performance. Serious failure to comply with the regulations may involve a cut in the grant. The central department of education establishes curricula and tests the product of the schools by periodic examination. Municipalities are frequently required to submit programmes to the senior government for approval before they can qualify for grants.

There is a great deal more to the intervention of the senior government than the drafting of regulations and the prying of inspectors. The departments of the senior government give the local authorities needed encouragement and valuable expert advice. The department of education tries to keep abreast of new movements and new needs in education, and to interpret these to the local school authorities. The senior government provides a number of services for the local authorities that no one of them could provide for itself. Vaccines and serums, diagnostic clinics, and laboratory analysis are provided free of charge. Research in preventive medicine and sanitary engineering is carried on, and the results are available to all local governments. A great work of education in public health is carried on by bulletins, demonstrations, and exhibits. In Britain, this development has gone so far in so many fields that the complex relationships of the central and local governments can best be described as a partnership in the providing and improving of the services supplied by local government.

Nothing comparable to this partnership has yet emerged in the relationships of senior and local governments in the United States and Canada. North America did not have to face the complexities of crowded urban industrial conditions as early as did Britain, and is only now slowly adjusting itself to them. Neither the United States nor Canada has developed the art of local government to the point it has reached in Britain. Municipal civil services, generally speaking, are not nearly as good in quality. Many units of local government are too small, either in area or population, to be effective units of administration for the present-day services required of local government. Little has been accomplished in the way of enlarging these areas. As a consequence of these factors and the financial difficulties of local governments, there has been a tendency in the United States and Canada to take particular services entirely away from local governments and make them solely a responsibility of state or provincial, or national, governments. The tendency has been most marked in public-welfare services and in the construction and maintenance of highways.

Whether this is a desirable tendency or not, it is the existence of federalism with its intermediate level of government that makes it possible. It would be fantastic for the central government in Britain to think of taking over and administering any significant number of the services that local governments supply. It is not so fantastic where the administration of these services can be distributed among fifty or ten governments. Federalism can be employed not only for decentralization but also for a modified centralization.

The Trend towards Centralization

Here we come again upon a persistent trend of present-day politics, the drive towards centralization. In discussing federalism, it was noted that a rising demand for the states and provinces to undertake more expensive functions had created a tendency to centralize more powers in the hands of the federal government. We now see that the pressure for more governmental services at the municipal level has had similar results. The parallel is remarkably close. In each case, general financial weakness of the governments at the lower level and their widely disparate capacity for maintaining the desired services lead to outright centralization of particular services, and to grants-in-aid and extensive control over other services by the government at the higher level.

It is important to note two specific aspects of the centralizing tendency that are not directly connected with what has been said above. First, the senior governments maintain control over borrowing for capital expenditures by the local governments. Generally speaking, local governments are free to fix their tax rates as they like and to spend their revenues as they see fit. Thus they may

undertake at their own discretion any project that they can pay
for out of current income without borrowing. But if they wish to
build a bridge or a town hall or a sewage disposal plant that has
to be financed by borrowing, the consent of the senior government
or one of its administrative agencies must be had before debentures
are issued.

The purpose is to prevent local governments from saddling
the taxpayers of the future with crushing payments of principal
and interest. In over-optimistic mood, many communities will
embark on heavy capital expenditures if not checked. When the
future is to be mortgaged for the sake of the present, the senior
government intervenes to protect the interests of the future.

Formerly, the limitation on borrowing by local governments
was generally fixed by the legislature's setting an upper limit for
each municipality. Today, the legislature states generally the conditions in which borrowing is justified, with or without an upper
debt limit, and requires the local governments to get the consent
of a particular senior government department before raising a
loan. With detailed control over borrowing and increasing collaboration between local and senior governments, the latter are
setting up departments or agencies such as the Bureau of Municipal
Affairs of the Department of Internal Affairs in Pennsylvania, the
Local Government Commission in North Carolina, the Ministry
of Housing and Local Government in Britain, and the Department of Municipal Affairs in Ontario, whose main concern is the
supervision of financial or other aspects of local government.

The second aspect is the contribution of technology and
scientific advance to centralization in government. Many instances
could be offered. For example, before the days of the automobile,
roads and bridges were almost entirely the responsibility of local
governments. The development of motor traffic called for a kind
of road entirely different from that of the horse-and-buggy era.
Most municipalities cannot afford to hire the engineering skill and
knowledge needed to plan and build durable main highways. Most
of them cannot afford to buy the massive machinery necessary for
the maintenance of such roads.

Moreover, if the motorist was to get the most for his money,
it was necessary to plan a network of trunk highways and secondary

feeder roads. Only a senior government with authority over a wide area could plan such a network. These factors go far to explain the lifting of the control of, and the responsibility for, main highways from local governments, and the establishment of central supervision of municipal development and maintenance of secondary roads.

Another instance is peculiarly related to rural local government. A hundred years ago, such control of plant pests and diseases as existed rested largely on municipal regulation. Today it is almost entirely in the hands of senior governments. There are two major causes for this centralization. First, the development of the modern means of transportation has meant that failure of effective control in a few municipalities is a menace to the whole country. Secondly, effective control of plant pests and diseases depends on the skilful use of a vast range of scientific knowledge developed in the past century. Local governments often do not understand, and even where they understand they cannot command, the scientific knowledge and apparatus necessary to combat these enemies effectively.

Consequently, the senior governments now employ a number of scientists who are continually studying plant pests and diseases and devising new means of controlling them. Senior governments have taken power to destroy diseased crops and orchards wherever found and to forbid nurseries from distributing stock without a certificate of health. Almost invariably, advancing science and technology provide impulses to centralization.

It will be noted also that the powers relative to local government that are shifting to the centre are more often exercised by the executive than by the legislature. Local self-government, being subordinate government, has always been subject to ultimate control by the senior government. In the nineteenth century, this control was almost always exercised through rules of law made by the legislature and enforced through actions in the courts. If it was claimed that the local governments had exceeded their powers or failed to perform their mandatory duties, the question had to be determined by the judges. Today the legislature in making laws about local government often legislates in broad general terms and leaves the detailed rules, decisions, and enforcement to a department of the central government. Aggrandizement of the executive and growing reliance on the administrative process are significant features of the changing relationships between local and senior governments.

Decline of Local Autonomy

Through the convergence of a number of different influences, Anglo-American local self-government has substantially less formal autonomy and independence than it had one hundred years ago, or even at the turn of the century. There are some who think that the trend we have been examining threatens to take the "self" out of local self-government. It is difficult to estimate the seriousness of this threat, but no doubt a good deal depends on the vigour and intelligence shown by local democracy. If local governments are determined to understand the complexities of their present-day functions and to improve their civil services sufficiently to meet their problems, central control and supervision and central-local collaboration may help rather than hinder them in surviving. Certainly, local governments need the knowledge, advice, and suggestion which senior governments can supply, and which many local governments cannot easily secure by their unaided efforts.

At any rate, in Britain, where central tutelage has advanced furthest, there has been little evidence that local governments are becoming markedly subservient to the senior government. On the whole, local self-government there has shown remarkable vigour in the last fifty years. Numerous associations of the different kinds of local governments and of local government officers have been formed and they take common counsel on their problems. These local government associations form one of the best-informed and most powerful lobbies the central government has to face, and it is difficult to push through legislation that they resist, and more difficult to administer it effectively. Indeed many seemingly drastic powers of central control over local government are subject to considerable discount, and the central government, to get its way, has had to rely on the arts of persuasion rather than the instruments of coercion.

However, when the Labour Government came to power in 1945, it had a large programme of socialist measures that could only be carried out by government assuming a much larger role in the lives of the British people. The local governments were not suitable agencies for carrying out some parts of the programme. The realization of some of the broad objectives of the Labour Government seemed to require more extensive control and supervision of local governments by the central government. Accordingly, since 1945, there has been a marked increase in the powers of the central government, a corresponding decrease in the powers of the local governments, and a great extension of central control and supervision over the local governments.

The movement has gone so far so quickly that there is now, for almost the first time, widespread and anxious concern about the future of autonomous local self-government in Britain. Of course, it remains to be seen how far the central government can make effective the formal controls it has taken to itself in recent years. If it cannot make them sufficiently effective, the next question is whether there will be a further transfer of powers from the local governments to the central government.

The probable effect of the growing central control of local government is an important question because it seems likely that vigorous local self-government is necessary to the maintenance of democracy in national politics and government. In a general way, the history of democratic experiments in the last hundred years tends to confirm this conjecture. Democracy has had the greatest stability and the highest measure of success in the countries with strong systems of local self-government. On the other hand, in continental Europe, the countries with centralized systems of local government or relatively weaker institutions of local self-government have most easily fallen prey to dictatorships. Of course, these may be accidental coincidences not in any significant way linked as cause and effect. There are, however, some very plausible reasons for thinking there is a great deal more to it than mere coincidence.

LOCAL GOVERNMENT AND DEMOCRACY

In the Anglo-American tradition, local self-government has long been credited with contributing greatly to the working of democracy. Two of the commonest arguments may be looked at first. It is often said that experience on a municipal council is valuable elementary training for budding statesmen and politicians. By being faithful in small things, the municipal councillor learns to handle great affairs when he is called by the electorate to service in national or state politics. Secondly, the mass of citizens get an indispensable political education through discussion of lively local issues and participation in frequent local elections. Such experience helps them to grasp national issues and to exercise their franchise wisely in national politics.

These two contentions are valid as far as they go, but they are far from revealing the essential links between local self-government and democracy. Indeed, they tend to obscure these links because they tacitly assume that it is national, and state or provincial, politics alone which really matter in a democracy, and that local government is merely a training centre and not even a junior league in the game of politics.

We miss the essence of democracy if we think of it mainly as something practised by statesmen in a distant capital and forget that it consists of an attitude of mind towards, and a method of dealing with, all the stresses and strains of living together in a society. If local quarrels were always settled by discussion at the local level and if local communities put their best efforts into making adjustments that are tolerable to all members of the community, there would be less need to tremble at the mention of dictators.

Unfortunately, we have a weakness for big things. The newspapers, which generally give us the kind of news we want, give us exciting front-page accounts of the dramatic events of national and international politics, while the tiresome wrangles of local politicians are decently buried under small headings on an inside page. We do not want to listen to John Smith in a radio discussion on some issue of local government. Rather we want to listen to President Eisenhower, and Prime Ministers Macmillan and Diefenbaker, to hear what the big men are doing about big things. We give too large a share of our attention to these distant exciting events which we cannot adequately understand and on which, therefore, we often cannot make useful judgments. It usually requires a good local scandal to rouse the apathetic local electorate.

The ideal of political democracy demands intelligent, responsible participation by the people in the choice of those who govern and in the approval of the policies by which they are to govern. Intelligent participation requires that the citizen be able to judge the character and qualifications of those who ask for his vote, and to understand the platforms he is asked to support or reject. Responsible participation requires that the citizen, as he votes, should realize that his vote affects the public welfare, that the public welfare will suffer the consequences of his errors in judgment and that he must, therefore, watch his elected representatives and the working out of programmes in practice so as to rectify errors at the earliest possible moment. In the discussion of national government and politics in these pages, numerous reasons have been given for thinking that at present we cannot come at all close to this ideal in the national, state, or provincial political arena. The ideal can, however, be much more closely approached in local government and politics, and that is why democracy, like charity, begins at home.

Some approach to the ideal of intelligent, responsible participation is made in all municipalities where self-government has not degenerated into boss rule. The citizen sees with his own eyes how the men he has elected behave. He can see whether the policies being followed by his local government work well or ill. It is possible for people, even as they go about their own work, to keep track of their local government.

Remoteness of National and Provincial Politics

It is much more difficult to do so in national, or state and provincial, politics. More often than not, voters do not know the candidates between whom they must choose. Moreover, many of the issues in state and national politics are hopelessly abstract to the average citizen; they do not arise out of things that have come concretely to his attention and about which he has knowledge. He does not understand the jugglery by which the budget is balanced, he does not understand the cases for and against the manipulation of currency and credit. Most people are wearied by the parade of statistics marshalled for and against particular governmental

policies, and bewildered by the seemingly convincing, yet inconsistent, arguments put upon particular points by the opposing
candidates and parties.

It must be acknowledged, of course, that the same difficulties
arise in the local politics of large cities. There are numerous
cities in the United States whose affairs equal or surpass in complexity those of the smaller states. But the difficulties are not as
all-pervasive in local as in national or state politics. Even in the
great cities, most of the work and the problems of local government come within the range of the average citizen's knowledge
and understanding. He may not, in fact, attend closely to them.
All that is urged here is that if he did attend closely, he would, on
the whole, be better able to make a useful judgment in local
rather than in state or national politics.

The behaviour of the political parties provides some support
for the general contention made here. In national and state
politics, to a greater extent than in local politics, they try not to
burden the voter too much with reams of facts and statistics.
They try to help him to make up his mind easily by finding simple
issues which will appeal to his feelings and which do not require
sustained attention. Hence, national, and state or provincial,
elections tend, rather more than municipal elections, to emphasize
emotional appeals, and so to fall seriously short of the ideal of
intelligent responsible participation.

It is not suggested that such elections are solely what has been
called registrations of emotions. There are generally some tests of
a rational character, applicable to some, at least, of the claims of
a political party for support, which the voter can apply fairly
easily. Not uncommonly too, some moral issue is at stake, and on
it the average man's judgment is likely to be as good as anyone's.
Yet no one can have failed to note the frequency of cries about
fearsome bogies such as a creeping bureaucracy, the strangling
octopus of socialism, or the insidious infiltration of "reds." And there
can be little doubt that the greater the powers exercised by senior
governments, the more various and complex election issues become,
the less the voter is able to understand and the more he is thrown
back on his emotions.

When a senior government is conducting operations of great magnitude and complexity, how is the voter to know whether it deserves support in the next election—whether it is doing well or ill? For the most part, its record cannot be fairly judged merely by the effects of its policies on the life of any particular voter or his neighbourhood. If a rational judgment is to be made on its record, it must be judged by the way its policies have worked all across the country—statistics again. For these statistics, the voter is at the mercy of the politicians, the writers in the newspapers, the speakers on the radio, about whose integrity and capacity the voter generally knows little or nothing.

This is not a criticism of the average citizen nor is it a criticism of the political parties. Until the electorate is much more highly educated and possessed of a great deal of leisure that they devote to the understanding of political issues, it is hard to see how it could be otherwise. It is a criticism of the assumption that local self-government is just a training ground for democracy that is to be practised elsewhere. It suggests that, for a long time to come, intelligent, responsible citizenship should find its best and most effective expression in local self-government. At the same time, it is not part of the present argument that local governments are always better run and better controlled than are senior governments. Often they are not. All that is said is that the obstacles in the way are less formidable.

The fact that intelligent, responsible citizenship is hard to achieve in national, and state or provincial, politics must not be allowed to obscure its importance or to lessen efforts to achieve it in those fields. There are a great many matters that cannot be dealt with at all by local governments and so must be entrusted to the senior governments. The recent experience with dictatorship in Europe shows clearly that if democracy fails at the national level of government, it automatically disappears at the local level. The conclusion to be drawn from the fact that democracy can be most effectively practised at the local level is that as many matters as possible should be reserved for the decision of local governments. Every increase of centralization, even when it is unavoidable, puts heavier burdens on the citizens' capacity to understand what is going on and to control it.

Decentralization and Political Unity

This brings us to an important reason for linking democracy with local self-government, which has already been discussed in the chapter on federalism. It was urged there that the decentralization afforded by a federal system reduces the number of disputed matters that have to be settled in the national political arena, thus making it much easier to get majorities that can agree on what the national government should be doing.

The same argument applies point for point to the still greater decentralization provided by local self-government, and it need not be restated at length here. It is sufficient to say that the more closely the senior governments can be restricted to the general common interests that unite the citizens, the greater will be national unity and the less will be the danger of the two-party system being splintered into a multiple-party system. One of the best ways of so restricting the senior government is to arrange that local demands and local needs that vary widely will be met by a response to these demands and needs by local governments.

The experience of the French Third Republic with its highly centralized local government tends to support the position just stated. It has already been explained how almost all important decisions in the sphere of local government were decided either by the ministry of the interior in Paris or by one of its agents in the field. When local matters could not be decided at home, the main job of each member of the legislature was to represent his constituency at the point where the decisions were made. Indeed, the French member of the legislature is still preoccupied with lobbying at the ministry of the interior in the interests of his locality.

A frequent combination of professions in French life is that of mayor and member of the Chamber of Deputies. To be a successful mayor, one needs to have close connections with, and some influence over, the ministry of the interior. The most effective connection is membership in the Chamber of Deputies. At each election in the years before the *débâcle* of 1940 at any rate, from fifty to eighty mayors were elected to the Chamber of Deputies, where they formed a powerful mayors' bloc primarily concerned with putting pressure on the department of the interior. Every deputy, whether a mayor or not, has a great many chores to do at the ministry of the interior. According to the constitutional forms, the central government controls and directs local affairs. In actual practice, local affairs and interests invade the central government, hoping to control its decisions.

French localities must think of their own interests, and they must send to the legislature men who will be determined champions of local needs and interests. If the local water supply is not adequate and more up-to-date facilities cannot be purchased without the consent of the department of the interior, it is inevitable that a high proportion of parish pump politicians will go to the legislature. A Chamber of Deputies with its gaze thus introverted has not enough interest in, time for, or understanding of, broad questions of the national interest. Politicians biased towards local interests find it extremely difficult to find common ground on which to base national political parties united in a common view of the national interest. This, it may be suggested, is one of the roots of the multiple-party system in France, although by no means the only one. Localism has always played too important a part in French national politics. Countries with a vigorous system of local self-government are freed of such distractions.

Centralization and the Coup d'Etat

One other and rather different aspect of the significance of local self-government may be selected for attention. In most countries of continental Europe, a central department of the interior has had a large measure of control over local government. Usually this includes pretty complete control of the local police forces. Unlike the local police in the Anglo-American system, the *gendarmerie* are virtually agents of the central government in the localities, taking orders from the centre. Thus control of the department of the interior was one of the great prizes for which Nazi and Fascist parties contended when they were fighting their way to power.

For example, the first government in which Hitler participated in Germany was a coalition with the Nationalist party, each party getting half the posts in the cabinet. But in that cabinet, Hitler's lieutenants, Goering and Frick, got control of both the Prussian and Reich ministries of the interior. That gave them leverage on the local governments and control of the police across the country. They were thus enabled to fasten their grip on the country in an incredibly short time. This helps somewhat to explain how the Nazis, who never got forty per cent of the total vote in a free election, were able to carry through a revolution without firing a shot—except, of course, the shots of the local police acting under their orders.

A highly centralized system of local government eases the task of a would-be dictator, while local self-government helps to assure its people against the sudden *coup d'état*. Even where there is no immediate need to guard against such eventualities, an effective system of local self-government acts as a counterpoise to the senior government or governments. All forms of human organization tend to expand and aggrandize themselves unless and until checked by stronger forces. It is therefore extremely important, at a time when the powers of central governments are expanding very rapidly, to have active, energetic local centres of political life that are determined to retain a sphere of independence for themselves.

On occasion, indeed, they may resist the central government too strongly, clinging doggedly to powers they can no longer exercise effectively. But we must reckon with the bad which the good often carries with it. The point to be remembered is that the senior governments which are in ultimate control of the weapons of coercion in the society are checked not only by legislatures, electorates, and courts but also by independent local governments in which many men of modest ambition find an outlet for their energies and their desire to render public service. These men can be counted on to resist centralizing pretensions and to compel those who urge more centralization to prove its necessity to the hilt.[1]

These are some of the reasons for thinking there is a close connection between local self-government and liberal democratic senior governments. Still others could be given. The fact that dictators always destroy the autonomy of local government also suggests a connection. It does not follow, however, that local

[1]For this and other considerations in favour of local self-government, see Herman Finer, "The Case for Local Self-Government," *Public Administration Review*, 3 (1943), pp. 51-8.

self-government will continue to bolster liberal democracy in the twentieth century unless it is substantially modified and improved.

Financial weakness and the necessity for governments to possess technical scientific knowledge are not the only factors in the movement to shift the responsibility for certain services from the local to the senior governments. Many units of local government, particularly rural ones, are too small to carry some of the newer functions of government. The civil services of most American and Canadian municipalities are not of a sufficiently high quality to perform many municipal functions efficiently. As the things that local governments are expected to do become more numerous and complex, a considerable overhauling of municipal organization is imperative.

CHAPTER XIX

DEMOCRACY AND DICTATORSHIP

THE preceding chapters have outlined and compared in a general way the main features of the structure and working of government in the United States, Britain, and Canada. The description given falls far short of what would be necessary to explain the complex operations of these three governments as going concerns. No one will know them well unless he observes them at work and reads widely in books that give detailed exposition. The caution given at the beginning may be repeated; the working of any system of government is the study of a lifetime.

No system of government can be understood even in an elementary way without some reference to the ends it is designed to serve. For this reason, the discussion began with a consideration of ideals of government. The basic structure and much of the actual working of government in the United States, Britain, and Canada is a response to liberal democratic ideals. Similarly, the practical implications of the Communist ideals explain the essential character of government in the Soviet Union. The practice of the Nazi and Fascist dictatorships becomes more intelligible when related to their rejection of democratic ideals. While the hostility and bitterness between the Western democracies, on the one hand, and the Soviet Union, on the other, are to be explained partly on the ground of a clash of material interests, they also spring from sharply different conceptions of social, economic, and political organizations.

The clash between the Soviet Union and the genuinely liberal democratic societies is the central political fact in the world today. In all three countries under discussion here, there are still small minorities crusading for Communist ideals. They insist that liberal democratic ideals are shams and that liberal democratic government is merely a cloak for exploitation of the masses. Democracy is subject to challenge from within. It is also subject to challenge

631

from without. It is impossible to say at what moment citizens of the liberal democratic states may be required to risk their lives in what is essentially a struggle over social and political ideals.

In still larger perspective, there are the confusions and doubts within the ranks of the liberal democrats themselves. While holding firmly to the value of individual personality as the ultimate ideal, they are much more perplexed than they were fifty years ago on the appropriate means of serving that ideal. Specifically, as we saw in discussing the differences of opinion between individualists and democratic socialists in chapter v, there is disagreement on how far we can permit the government to go in organizing our lives without making it our master. The collapse of democracy under internal strains in many countries in Europe in the last generation shows that democratic government is not impregnable, that there are conditions in which it will not work. There is no generally accepted explanation of why it has failed in these instances. This adds to the perplexity. So at every point, we are compelled to go beyond an examination of the structure and working of particular governments and ask what purposes they are designed to serve and how their structure and operation are related to those purposes. It is important to grasp the essential features of democratic beliefs and to see their implications for government and politics. When this has been done, one is better able to estimate the significance of changing trends in democratic government.

For these reasons, description has been limited to the main outlines of the governments of Britain, the United States, and Canada, thus reserving a good deal of space for elementary analysis of the significance of what has been described. It was pointed out at the beginning that liberal democratic government is expected to serve two principal related ends or purposes. First, democracy, defined as government by the people, for the people, seeks to ensure a close correspondence between what the people want and what the government does. For government is an instrument for the purposes of the men associated together in the state. Secondly, a democracy that is liberal seeks adequate guarantees of a large sphere of freedom of thought and action for individuals as the indispensable means of serving the claims of individual personality.

The manner and degree in which the main institutions of government in the three countries contribute to these ends have been discussed. An attempt has been made to explain the essential functions that the different organs of government are expected to perform and the nature of the difficulties in the way of a satisfactory performance. There is immensely more to be said on all these matters and many students of the subject would question some of the explanations suggested here. Yet there is no doubt that these are the matters of vital import, and there is little use in the study of government and politics unless it contributes to an understanding of them.

Summary of Trends in Democratic Government

We have seen that the main institutions of government do not remain unchanged from one generation to another. They have been considerably modified in the last half-century in all three countries. The modification has come about in response to the rapidly expanding activities of government. The new activities have not only added greatly to the total of government business but have also made the conduct of that business much more complicated and difficult. It is no longer possible to make a clear-cut classification of the powers of government into legislative, executive, and judicial. It was shown that in many fields nowadays the law is being made in the course of its administration, or execution, and that it is being administered while it is being made. Not only is it clear that the judges sometimes make law while they are interpreting it and applying it to particular cases but also that the administration often exercises judicial functions when it rules on claims and disputes in the course of administration.

The fact is that the administration has become in some measure a government within a government. It makes a great deal of law by rules and regulations and orders-in-council, it executes and enforces the law generally, and it exercises substantial powers of a judicial nature. Some students of the subject urge that if analysis is to be realistic we must add a fourth power, the administrative, to the classification. It is at least clear that the older classification does not sufficiently explain the facts.

If the tripartite classification of the powers of government is now inadequate, the doctrine of the separation of powers which rests on this classification is also defective.[1] Whether or not the separation of powers is necessary to protect the liberties of the citizen against the government—a point on which liberal democrats are in disagreement among themselves—there is no doubt that governments cannot perform efficiently their present-day tasks if they are bound by rigid separation of powers. This is conceded even in the United States, where the separation of powers is written into the Constitution, and much thought is being given to ways and means of greater legislative-executive collaboration. In all three countries, it is still generally and strongly believed that the judiciary should be independent of both legislature and executive. Judicial independence has been maintained, but at the cost of taking the power to adjudicate on numerous matters away from the judiciary and reposing it with the administrative. Indeed, the clear proof that strict adherence to the separation of powers interferes with the performance of the present-day tasks of government is the rise of the administrative in which are frequently joined powers of legislating, of executing, and of judging.

It does not necessarily follow, of course, that the administrative will swallow the other powers. The legislature still fixes the broad objectives and methods of administrative action and the judiciary still applies certain canons of legality to administrative discretion. It may be possible to limit the mingling of legislative, executive, and judicial powers to certain areas of governmental activity. New and better devices of control may be devised. Much depends on whether the functions of government continue for an indefinite period to grow more numerous and complex.

Frequent reference has been made to the aggrandizement of the executive. The rise of the administrative is the most striking aspect of that aggrandizement, for the administrative is always under the control and direction of the executive. The administrative is a part of the executive, and they have been treated separately here only for purposes of exposition. Another important factor in

[1]For a view that classification of governmental action in terms of powers is outmoded, and an attempt to classify in terms of dynamic processes, see Ernest S. Griffith, *The Modern Government in Action* (Columbia University Press, New York, 1942).

the strengthening of the executive is its indispensability in law making. The legislature cannot make effective laws on most subjects without constant reliance on the data and experience gathered by the executive in the course of administration. In Britain and Canada, the executive has gained an almost unchallenged initiative in legislation, and even in the United States the trend is clearly in that direction.

The members of the legislature, coming from all walks of life and having a short tenure of office, which frequently is not renewed by the electorate, are the amateurs in government. They have an advantage in being closer to the currents of public opinion than the civil service, but even the most intelligent of them are at a decided disadvantage in technical matters when ranged against expert civil servants with permanence of tenure. The legislatures have not taken adequate steps to adjust their procedure to the increased tempo and growing complexity of government. So, while they still make the big decisions on policy, they are becoming much more dependent on the executive to invent policies for them to approve. Moreover, governmental administration has so wide a range and so many ramifications which can only be understood after long, patient, and skilled investigation that legislatures are steadily becoming less effective critics of administration. They criticize, but they often do not know what to criticize or what to regard as a satisfactory answer to their criticisms. Perhaps the most serious aspect of the aggrandizement of the executive is that the intricacies of the administrative machine and of the operations it is performing leave the legislature in a state of bewilderment.

The legislature makes the important decisions on policy, fixing the general line that government is to take. But the legislature does what the ruling political party wants it to do. Although the authority of the majority party is not so extensive in the United States Congress, it controls the legislature in Britain and Canada. If the legislature is weak, it is partly because the political parties have been slow to establish secretariats to help them to formulate policy, to explore ways of putting their policies into practice, and to study administration in detail to see how the policies of the opposing party work out in practice. In fact, the parties have brought vote-gathering to a fine art, but they have only recently begun to take comparable pains to study public policy and its administration. The parties have only just begun to adapt themselves to the great expansion of governmental functions.

Whatever the weakness of a two-party system, it is an improvement on the shifting coalitions of a multiple-party system. Government is expected to do every day so many things of vital importance that it must act vigorously and consistently if the tasks are to be accomplished. These requirements are not likely to be met unless one party has a clear majority in the legislature. However, the great range of governmental action and the consequent rise of numerous pressure groups which seek to influence or control governmental action are constant threats to a vigorous two-party system. One of the most significant features of American politics is the internal weakness of the national parties. Blocs in Congress often act like splinter parties. As already noted, part of the alarm over the activities of pressure groups in Washington is justified bcause of the weakness of the discipline maintained by the majority party in Congress. Britain has the best disciplined party system, even though political life was confused during the inter-war years by the existence of three parties. The two-party system seems now to have reasserted itself after a period of coalition government from 1931 to 1945. In Canada, the slow swing of the political pendulum has tended towards a one-party-dominant situation with a confusion of smaller opposition parties which the overwhelming victory of the Progressive Conservatives in 1958 may help to clarify. Firmness, vigour, and coherence in public policy are needed as never before, and these can only be secured by well-disciplined majorities which can offset the divisive forces in contemporary democratic societies.

The courts have maintained their independence, but the scope of their authority is being narrowed and the discretionary powers of government officials correspondingly increased. How greatly the rule of law is threatened by this development depends on how far it goes. An essential safeguard of liberal democracy would be lost if a numerous officialdom with wide powers were completely free from control by the judiciary. On the other hand, the judges cannot—and never could—supervise all governmental action. Today, they are not entirely satisfactory interpreters of much of the legislation under which officials hold their powers. The truth is that the judges are best fitted, by tradition and training, to interpret and apply the common law. The common law with its roots in custom has been largely made up of general rules of conduct applicable to all, rules that are observed in most instances because they accord with the community sense of right. In those relatively few instances in which common law rules were not obeyed voluntarily, the loose organization and the dilatory procedure of the Anglo-American judicial system sufficed for a long time to enforce obedience.

The rapid economic and social changes of the last hundred years have upset habitual and customary ways of life, causing much insecurity. The common law has not yet been able to adapt itself adequately to these changes. Attempts are therefore made to adapt the law by legislation. But, as we have seen, much of the legislation now being passed does not make law in the sense of establishing general rules of conduct for all. Rather it authorizes administrators to make different orders for different situations, and to enforce them. In many human relationships, law is being superseded by discretionary administration. The scope of the judicial power narrows, because judges are not administrators but interpreters of law.

The great growth in the functions of government has not merely modified the relationship of the legislative, executive, and judicial powers; it has also altered the relationship between the different levels of government. When government is required to do many things and when everything it does has numerous effects on other aspects of life which in turn may have to be regulated, the advantage goes to the government with the longest reach, because it can control more of the factors involved. Thus local government loses authority to the senior government and comes under its direct and detailed supervision. In a federal system, the state governments lose powers to the national government. They become less able to fend for themselves, and their autonomy within the federal system is restricted, if not threatened with extinction. The trend towards centralization has been a marked feature of the last half-century.

In summary form, these are the trends which can be observed in liberal democratic government. They do not, of themselves, prove that democracy faces a grave crisis. On three points, however, they are indicative of crisis. First, the party system on which democracy must rely to direct the government and to ensure that it obeys the will of the people is subjected to very sharp strain by the diverse demands of pressure groups of various kinds. Secondly, judicial scrutiny of executive action, which has played a very important part in ensuring that government shall be servant and not master, is being steadily relaxed. Thirdly, centralization of authority with the senior governments, and aggrandizement of the executive within the senior governments, are creating heavy concentrations of power which, if not closely controlled, will get out of hand. There could be crisis in this combination of trends.

Those who talk about a crisis of democracy do not all agree about its nature. To some, the crisis is spiritual. That is to say, the people of the democracies have not been able to grasp and keep hold of an adequate conception of the good life and of a just society. The crisis arises because they do not know what they want or ought to want. Others regard the crisis as primarily institutional, or governmental. The democracies, they say, have failed to adapt their constitutions and machinery of government to the enormous demands made upon governments for services and regulations of various kinds. Still others insist that the crisis arises from the inherent impossibility of reconciling democracy and a large sphere of individual liberty with massive governmental operations which affect almost every aspect of life.

It is possible that each of the three is partially valid but it would take us too far afield to go into the matter here. There can be no useful exploration of the crisis of democracy until the nature of democratic government and its main institutions are understood. It may aid understanding if we take up briefly again the comparisons between dictatorship and democracy which were suggested at the outset. The governmental institutions of the dictatorships are in marked contrast to those we have been examining. Yet some of them look like projections of recent trends in liberal democratic government.

STRUCTURE OF GOVERNMENT IN THE DICTATORSHIPS

The Nazi and Fascist regimes in Germany and Italy have been destroyed, and the Soviet dictatorship, we are told, is really a new kind of democracy.[1] There are great differences in the ideals and the social results of these three systems of government. Each is, or was, a distinct system differing very markedly from the others in the details of organization. Despite these differences, there is a striking similarity in the general pattern of the structure of the three governments.

The dictatorships recognize the distinction between legislative, executive, and judicial power and maintain, as a matter of form, distinct organs for the exercise of each kind of power. But the principle of the separation of powers is not recognized and therefore exercises no restricting influence on governmental organization. In fact, there is a concentration of power in the executive which was most clearly marked in Nazi Germany and is less openly avowed in the Soviet Union where many democratic forms were copied in the last revision of the constitution in 1936. To put it more accurately, all power is concentrated in the leadership of the one political party which either constitutes or controls the executive.

The most significant similarity between dictatorial regimes is the supremacy of the one party. All other political parties are proscribed. The opposition to the government cannot combine in an opposing political party and compete for the favour of the electorate. In each case, the party controls election of members to the legislature. In Russia, only one candidate is nominated for each seat in the legislature. Almost all the voters go to the polls and they vote almost unanimously for the "official" candidates. The same was true in Nazi Germany. In Fascist Italy, popular elections as a means of electing the legislature came to an end in 1939 when the legislature became largely composed of representatives of occupational groups. However, the Fascist party controlled the choice of representatives by these groups. Under these circumstances, legislatures are always composed of those who will follow the orders of the party. They cease to be freely representative of the various interests and impulses in the community.

In fact, the legislature ceases to be a significant organ of government. The German Reichstag under Hitler enacted only seven statutes in seven years. The Italian Chamber of Deputies

[1]For the purpose of grammatical ease in this comparison, it will often be convenient to refer to the Fascist and Nazi systems in the present tense as if they still existed.

had no power to consider or enact any measures which had not been approved by Mussolini. The Supreme Council of the U.S.S.R. is bicameral, with some 1,300 members divided about evenly between the two chambers. These are too large for effective deliberation, and, in any event, they meet for only two or three weeks during the year to hear addresses from party leaders and to ratify actions taken by the government. Almost all legislative functions are performed by a small executive committee, or Presidium, of the Supreme Council consisting of thirty-odd members. This committee together with the Council of Ministers (or cabinet) might be said to form the executive. But the final authority in all important decisions, whether legislative or executive in nature, is a still smaller and unofficial body, the Presidium or executive committee of the Communist party. It is the board of high strategy for the party and for the government, composed of a variable number—usually about 15—of the leading members of the party.

In Nazi Germany and Fascist Italy, the executive consisted of those whom the party leader chose to assist him in determining policy and in administering the various departments of government. For all practical purposes, the party leadership and the executive were identical. In the Soviet Union, the Supreme Council chooses both the executive committee of the Supreme Council and the Council of Ministers but the Communist party has a decisive influence in the choice. The laws, in each case, are made by executive decree and generally confer wide discretionary power which is unchecked by judicial supervision. Legislative and executive power is concentrated in the leader and in those who share his confidence or power.

The judiciary under the dictatorships remains an important institution for settling disputes between private citizens and interpreting the law applicable to such disputes. New judicial functions arise from the revision of the criminal law to include a number of political offences against the regime. Generally, special tribunals for defence of the state against its internal enemies are established, but sometimes persons accused of political offences are tried in the ordinary courts. Great care is therefore taken to ensure that the judges shall have the appropriate attitude towards cases coming before them. The Nazis and Fascists, in Germany and Italy, purged the courts of all judges who were unsympathetic to the new dispensation. In the Soviet Union, the Communist party has exercised effective control over the appointment or election of judges and usually adds lay "assessors" capable of exercising a strong influence on the decisions of the courts.

The ordinary courts have no authority to deal with disputes between citizens and the government or government officials. In Germany and Italy before the rise of the dictatorships, there were special administrative courts for this purpose similar to the French administrative courts briefly described in chapter XIII. Under the dictatorships, as we have already noted, these courts lost their independence completely and became mere tools of the administration. Even then, many matters were withdrawn from their jurisdiction. A government with unlimited decree power does not need judges to interpret the law. If the law does not accomplish the purpose for which it was enacted, it can be interpreted or modified without delay by another decree.

Moreover, under these dictatorships, the nature of law and the functions of the judiciary differ sharply from the prevailing Anglo-American ideas. The common law in Britain and America puts its main emphasis on the rights of individuals against other individuals and against the government. The function of the judiciary is to declare and enforce these rights when particular disputes arise. In the dictatorships, on the other hand, where the government regulates all aspects of life without exception, the emphasis of the law is on the duties of the individual to obey the government, and the judiciary in its decisions must constantly underline this emphasis. The judiciary is an instrument for safeguarding the regime and promoting its conception of the good life.

Accordingly, the courts are not concerned merely with acts done but also with the motives, character, and general attitude of those who come before them. Under the Nazi rule in Germany, as was explained in chapter XIII, the courts often took action against individuals not because of their deeds but because they were unsatisfactory persons and would no doubt betray the regime if they had a chance. In other words, the primary purpose of the Nazi courts was not to protect individuals but to protect the Nazi regime.

The clearest description of the functions of the judiciary in a dictatorship is given in a Soviet law of 1938 relating to the judiciary. It is there declared that the general purpose of the courts is "to educate the citizens of the U.S.S.R. in a spirit of devotion to the fatherland and to the cause of socialism, in the spirit of an exact and unfaltering performance of Soviet laws, careful attitude towards socialist property, labour discipline, honest fulfilment of State and public duties, respect towards the rules of the Socialist Commonwealth."[1] The entire emphasis is on the duties of the citizen and the first imperative for the courts is to educate the citizen in the socialist way of life. Soviet jurists have often retorted that the Anglo-American judiciary has also been primarily concerned with protecting a way of life, with enforcing the rule of bourgeois capitalism. There is a substantial element of truth in the retort. It would be reasonably accurate if it went further and asserted that the Anglo-American judiciary has striven, consciously or unconsciously, to maintain the liberal democratic way of life including the capitalist economic system.

A wide sphere of individual liberty involves constant striving and competing which would be destructive of liberty if there were not clear definitions of what the individual is entitled to do, and what he must refrain from doing so as to preserve the rights of others. Accordingly, the judiciary in a liberal democratic system must put a heavy emphasis on individual rights. In a society where other values are supreme, the judiciary must defend those values. The only point being made here is that the courts in the dictatorships, whether Fascist or Communist, are defending different ways of life.

Another striking feature common to the three dictatorships in question is the destruction of the independent organization of group interests. Pressure groups, as such, are abolished. With the elimination of capitalism in the Soviet Union, most of the diverse economic interests associated with it also disappeared. (According to socialist theory, the abolition of profit and private property automatically dissolves the diversity of economic interests and replaces it with one common interest, the maximum productivity

[1]Quoted in James T. Shotwell (ed.), *Governments of Continental Europe* (Macmillan, New York, 1940), p. 852.

of the economy as a whole.) Such group interests as remained ultimately lost their freedom to agitate and to press their point of view on the government. For example, the trade union organization has come under the control of the Communist party and the principal function of the trade unions is not to protect the interests of the workers but to ensure labour discipline and efficiency in pursuit of the objectives of the government.

In Germany and Italy, the dictators did not tear down the existing social and economic structure with its wide diversity of organized group interests. Rather they reconstructed the jumble of divergent group interests by sternly co-ordinating each of them with the aims of the party and the government. By pressure and compulsion, associations representing group interests were persuaded to elect as their officers party members or party sympathizers. The associations ceased to be independent organizations lobbying the government and became instruments by which the government enforced its drastic policies on the groups of which the nation was composed. Under party leadership and control, many groups of the type discussed in chapter x became more highly organized than ever before and the government delegated to them wide powers of self-government. However, it was not genuine self-government. The associations lost their autonomy and vitality and became merely administrative departments of the government for executing the government's policy under rigorous party discipline.

The modern totalitarian dictatorships cannot tolerate independent group life. It has already been pointed out that the political parties in the democracies are, in large measure, combinations of group interests. If the dictators allowed groups their independence, many of them would combine to oppose the government. That is to say, opposing political parties would, in fact, be formed despite the ban on them. Therefore, the organized groups had either to be liquidated, or co-ordinated and knit into the governmental structure.

When Hitler came to power, Germany was a federal state. One of his first acts was to destroy the autonomy of the separate states or provinces. Autonomous states were just as intolerable to the Nazi party as were autonomous associations of group interests. All possible centres of resistance to the programme of the party had to be destroyed. The separate states remained only as administrative divisions of the country ruled by a governor, or party boss, responsible only to the Fuehrer.

The Union of Soviet Socialist Republics, on the other hand, is organized as a federation of fifteen socialist soviet republics, i.e., states or provinces. In the Soviet constitution, much is made of the autonomy of the several republics even to the point of conferring on them a formal right of secession. Within firmly fixed limits the Soviet regime has given substantial cultural autonomy to the constituent republics, particularly in matters of race and language. But aside from this, the autonomy of the several states is largely illusory and Soviet federalism has little resemblance to the federalism of the United States and Canada.

In the first place, the powers of the national central government are very wide and extremely vague, thus affording possibilities of expansion by interpretation. In particular, its powers include the final determination of the economic plan and the supervision of its execution. Since the economic plan may involve regulation and adjustment of almost every aspect of life, there is little dependable substance left to the autonomy of the republic. Secondly, the Communist party dominates the governments of the constituent republics and ensures co-ordination of those governments within the system. Thirdly, separatist agitation within the constituent republics has been interpreted by the Soviet courts as a vicious form of counter-revolutionary activity, i.e., treason. Soviet federalism is not, in any significant sense, a mitigation of the overwhelming concentration of governmental power.

Substantially the same can be said of local government in the Soviet Union. There are numerous units of local government in each of which the people elect a governing council which has authority over a considerable range of local affairs. However, the Communist party is active in guiding the elections, and the requirements of the economic plan which are fixed by the national government limit narrowly the alternative courses of action open to the locally elected council in many matters. In Germany and Italy, the dictatorships co-ordinated local government as they co-ordinated everything else. Popular election of local councils was abolished and local government committed to a party boss who was responsible to the central government and not to the people of the local community. As in France, local government in Germany and Italy had always been subject to a large degree of direction and supervision by the central government. Under the dictators, local government was completely subjected to the central department of the interior which might intervene at any time in any way it thought fit.

In an earlier chapter, it was pointed out that, as the functions of government have expanded in scope and complexity, democratic governments have had to court public opinion more assiduously. They need the co-operation and not merely the acquiescence of the citizens, and government departments seek to influence public opinion through publicity consciously directed at that purpose. While there is danger that government publicity may be diverted into subtle propaganda for the party in power, the danger is limited by the fact that private enterprise and competition in the spread of information and ideas is carried on ceaselessly through many channels of communication largely or entirely free of government control.

In the dictatorships, on the other hand, open competition in the spread of information and ideas is as intolerable to the leaders as are competing political parties. The one political party settles authoritatively what is to be done in the public interest and it does not allow its decisions to be shaken by open discussion. Government in the dictatorships has an extremely wide range of functions. Dictators also need co-operation from their citizens, and they spare no effort to mould opinion. Furthermore, since the public interest is paramount, and the actions to be taken in the public interest have been authoritatively settled, it follows that everyone should support these actions. Thus the dictators want unity, and even unanimity, of opinion, and they use every device known to propagandists to secure it or, at any rate, to create the impression that it has been secured. Government in the dictatorships controls and directs all the media of communication.

Only a few illustrations of the methods used can be given here. Government publicity is no longer left to the unco-ordinated efforts of several government departments but is centralized under a single agency. The Ministry of Propaganda and Public Enlightenment under the guiding genius of Dr. Goebbels in Germany is the best example of this centralized control of government propaganda on all fronts. The press comes completely under government control. In the picturesque but accurate description of Walther Funk, the Nazi Minister of Economics, it is "no longer a barrel organ out of which everybody is permitted to squeeze whatever melody he likes, but a highly sensitive and far-sounding instrument or orchestra on which and with which only those shall play who know how, and in whose hands the Fuehrer himself has placed the conductor's baton."[1]

The measures by which the press was controlled in Italy are typical. Newspapers had to secure a license from the government. Journalists were enrolled (mainly through party organizations) in a professional register. A government Press Bureau issued minute instructions on what news was fit to print, and all newspapers had to file copies with the government so that their loyalty could be checked. Much of the news came from inspired party or government sources. As a result, the newspapers in the dictatorships came to have a dull-gray uniformity.

Radio has been similarly controlled. In the Soviet Union, the government operates the radio through a public corporation. The same device was used in Germany. Working through a system of government-subsidized receiving sets with limited range, and through mass listening groups, Dr. Goebbels made radio his most effective instrument of propaganda. In Italy, radio was in the hands of a private monopoly rigorously regulated by a commission in the Ministry of Propaganda.

Other media of communication have been controlled and used in the same thorough fashion as the press and the radio. The Soviet Union, with a large population just emerging from illiteracy, has relied heavily on public posters and moving pictures for the moulding of opinion. Literature, art, and the sciences are all under government censorship or control. Education, which has been notably advanced by the Communist dictatorship, has also been drawn into the service of party dogma. The rulers see to it that education is not confined to the schools but is carried on in the professional, recreational, cultural, and occupational associations. In Germany

---

[1]Quoted in William Albig, *Public Opinion* (McGraw-Hill, New York, 1939), p. 251.

and Italy also, the dictators carried party education into the schools, the party youth organizations, and all the various associations that, as we have already seen, were largely agencies of the government.

In this way, the dictator eliminates all widespread public discussion of ideas and information that challenges or throws doubts upon the policy of the government. To fill the void thus created, all the channels of communication are used to bring to the people the "facts" they should know and the ideas they must accept. The highly centralized governmental organization binds the citizen's body and efforts to the tasks set him by the leaders. The highly centralized propaganda machine tries to shackle his mind as well.

Completely lacking in respect for the values of individual personality, the modern dictatorships see no point in maintaining guarantees of individual liberty. Indeed, these regimes were established on the assumption that the interests of all individuals are identical with the interests of society and of the state. Consequently, no one can be allowed to assert his individuality when that assertion clashes with government policy as defined by the leaders.

Immediately on coming to power in Germany, the Nazis abolished freedom of the person, of speech, of the press, and of public meeting. They set up a rigid censorship, a secret police system, and the infamous concentration camps. Although they had made the courts subservient to them, they rarely troubled to use the judicial process on those who were thought to be politically dangerous. Thousands of Germans were bundled off to concentration camps to be tortured, killed, or to languish indefinitely, without having had a trial at all. No one had any rights he could hope to maintain against the government.

A comparable, although not quite so thoroughgoing, destruction of civil liberties took place in Fascist Italy through the instrumentality of censorship, control of all meetings and associations, secret police and bogus trials of persons charged with political crimes. By these methods, an apparatus of terror was established in both countries which ensured the docility of the great bulk of the population. The few who had the courage to think of resisting the government could not agitate openly. They were compelled to go into underground subversive movements. Civil liberties were entirely destroyed.

The Soviet Union, as we have seen, pays lip service to the basic values of the Western tradition. Thus the Soviet constitution contains a bill of rights expressly guaranteeing most of the civil liberties upheld in the Anglo-American world. But, as we have also noted, constitutional provisions alone do not guarantee civil liberties. Assurance of fair trial by an independent judiciary with power to enforce the constitution is also necessary.

In practice in the Soviet Union, the civil liberties are systematically denied and overridden. First, the judiciary, like all other institutions of Soviet government, is dominated by the Communist party. Second, persons charged with "political crime," a nebulous category which covers almost any action thought by the Communist party to be contrary to the public interest, can be arrested and banished to the forced labour camps without having had a trial at all. Third, the secret police, aided by informers, are empowered to arrest and sentence persons unfortunate enough to incur the enmity of the Communist party. The guarantees of civil liberties in the Soviet constitution are little more than a scrap of paper because the essential procedures, a clearly defined and precisely limited criminal law, confinement of official action by the Rule of the Law, habeas corpus, impartial courts, and assurance of fair trial, are lacking.

Conclusions

It can be seen, therefore, that while liberal democratic government is marked by a division of power, both functionally and geographically, among a number of authorities which operate as checks on one another, the one-party dictatorship is marked by an utter concentration of power. The power so concentrated in the hands of a small clique of party leaders is not checked in any way by judicial institutions and it is no longer contingent on the party winning the next election. For the one party takes no chances on losing the next election. The only way to break its rule is by revolution. And revolution is almost impossible because all unofficial organizations which might become centres of opposition are stamped out. The secret police are everywhere, and every meeting which lacks official blessing meets under the shadow of the forced labour camp.

There are many who say that the democracies are travelling the totalitarian road. They support their view with a variety of arguments. As far as governmental structure is concerned, they point to the trends in democratic government which have been discussed here and insist that the general pattern of government in the dictatorship is, in the main, a projection of these trends. This view is not entirely groundless. It is clear enough that liberal democracy cannot survive where power is concentrated as it is in the dictatorships. Yet the democracies are still a long way from such a concentration of power and it is open to them to halt these trends before they reach the monolithic state. There is now much more concentration of power in the democratic governmental structure than there was in 1900 and this is not without its alarming aspects. But it is not necessarily beyond human ingenuity to find improved methods of control as counterpoises to the aggrandizement of the executive and the growing predominance of national over local, and state or provincial, governments.

This is the crux of the matter. If the government is going to perform many positive services for the community, there must be greater concentration and less dispersion of power than that which marked the age of laissez faire. But wherever power is lodged, devices are needed to ensure that it can be called to account. The more power is concentrated, the more nicely calculated the means of controlling it must be. The elaboration of new and more effective controls has not kept pace with the growing concentration of power. More thought must be given to such controls in the immediate future. And it is not going too far to say that some caution will have to be exercised in adding still further to the positive functions of government. However, if the democratic ideal of the supreme importance of individual personality is clearly understood and firmly held by the bulk of the people and if enough persons with an informed intelligence participate actively in democratic politics, the needed controls can probably be devised and the required caution is likely to be exercised.

SELECTED REFERENCES

Chapter I: The Study of Government

Alfred DeGrazia: *The Elements of Political Science*, ch. I and II. Alfred
    A. Knopf, New York, 1952.
David Easton: *The Political System*. Alfred A. Knopf, New York,
    1953.
Raymond Gettell: *Political Science*, 2nd. ed., ch. I-III. Ginn & Co.,
    New York, 1949.
A. D. Lindsay: *The Modern Democratic State*. Oxford University
    Press, London, 1943.
Leslie Lipson: *The Great Issues of Politics*, ch. I-IV. Prentice-Hall,
    New York, 1954.
R. M. MacIver: *The Modern State*, pp. 1-22. Clarendon Press,
    Oxford, 1926.
————*The Web of Government*, ch. I. Macmillan, New York, 1947.
Charles E. Merriam: *Systematic Politics*, ch. I and II. University of
    Chicago Press, 1945.
Joseph S. Roucek, et al: *Introduction to Political Science*, ch. I-III.
    Thomas Y. Crowell, New York, 1950.
Richard Carlton Snyder and H. Hubert Wilson: *Roots of Political
    Behavior*, ch. I-II. American Book Co., New York, 1949.

Chapter II: Ideals of Government

Hillman M. Bishop and Samuel Hendel: *Basic Issues of American
    Democracy*, 3rd. ed., sections I-II. Appleton-Century-Crofts, New
    York, 1956.
John Bowle: *Western Political Thought*. Oxford University Press,
    New York, 1948.
William Ebenstein: *Today's Isms*, 2nd. ed. Prentice-Hall, New York,
    1958.
Irwin Edman: *Fountainheads of Freedom*. Reynal and Hitchcock,
    New York, 1941.
William Y. Elliott and Neil A. McDonald: *Western Political Heritage*.
    Prentice-Hall, 1949.
Arthur Koestler: *Darkness at Noon*. Jonathan Cape, London, 1940.
Laurence Stapleton: *The Design of Democracy*, ch. I-IV. Oxford Uni-
    versity Press, New York, 1949.
Richard Carlton Snyder and H. Hubert Wilson: *Roots of Political
    Behavior*, ch. X-XII. American Book Co., New York, 1949.
T. E. Utley and J. Stuart Maclure: *Documents of Modern Political
    Thought*. Cambridge University Press, 1957.
Frederick Watkins: *The Political Tradition of the West*. Harvard
    University Press, Cambridge, 1948.

CHAPTER III: FORMS OF GOVERNMENT

Aristotle: *Politics,* Bk. v and vi.

Carl Becker: *Modern Democracy,* ch. i and ii. Yale University Press, New Haven, 1941.

Herman Finer: *The Theory and Practice of Modern Government,* rev. ed., ch. v. Henry Holt and Co., New York, 1949.

Carl J. Friedrich: *Constitutional Government and Democracy,* rev. ed., ch. i. Ginn & Co., Boston, 1950.

Raymond Gettell: *Political Science,* 2nd. ed., ch. xii. Ginn & Co., New York, 1949.

R. Kranenburg: *Political Theory,* ch. iv. Oxford University Press, London, 1939.

R. M. MacIver: *The Web of Government,* ch. vii-ix. Macmillan, New York, 1947.

Nathaniel Micklem: *The Idea of Liberal Democracy.* Christopher Johnson, London, 1957.

The Republic of Plato, tr. by Francis Macdonald Cornford, ch. xxxi and xxxii. Oxford University Press, New York, 1945.

Joseph S. Roucek, et al: *Introduction to Political Science,* ch. viii-ix. Thomas Y. Crowell, New York, 1950.

CHAPTER IV: CONSTITUTIONS AND THE SEPARATION OF POWERS

Walter Bagehot: *The English Constitution,* World's Classics ed.

R. K. Carr, Marver H. Bernstein, D. H. Morrison, *The National Government: American Democracy in Theory and Practice,* 3rd. ed., ch. iii-v. Rinehart and Co., New York, 1959.

Gwendolen M. Carter, John H. Hertz and John C. Ranney: *Major Foreign Powers,* 3rd. ed., part i, ch. ii. Harcourt, Brace, New York, 1957.

H. McD. Clokie: *Canadian Government and Politics,* new rev. ed., ch. iii. Longmans, Green, Toronto, 1951.

Edward S. Corwin: *The Constitution and What It Means Today.* 11th ed. Princeton University Press, 1954.

Robert MacGregor Dawson: *The Government of Canada,* 3rd. ed., rev., ch. i, ii, and iv. University of Toronto Press, 1957.

Sir W. Ivor Jennings: *The Law and the Constitution,* 3rd. ed., ch. i-iv. University of London Press, 1943.

W. P. M. Kennedy: *The Constitution of Canada,* 2nd. ed., ch. xxii. Oxford University Press, London, 1937.

C. B. Swisher: *American Constitutional Development,* rev. ed. Houghton, Mifflin, New York, 1956.

K. C. Wheare: *Modern Constitutions.* Oxford University Press, London, 1951.

CHAPTER V: THE EXPANSION OF GOVERNMENT ACTIVITIES

Henry J. Abraham: *Government as Entrepreneur and Social Servant.* Public Affairs Press, Washington, D.C., 1956.

M. Anshen and F. D. Wormuth: *Private Enterprise and Public Policy.* Macmillan, New York, 1954.

Carl Becker: *Modern Democracy,* ch. III. Yale University Press. New Haven, 1941.

J. A. Corry: *Growth of Government Activities since Confederation* (mimeo.). King's Printer, Ottawa, 1940.

D. N. Chester and F. M. G. Willson: *The Organization of British Central Government.* Allen and Unwin, London, 1957.

Marshall Edward Dimock: *Business and Government.* Henry Holt, New York, 1953.

Herman Finer: *The Theory and Practice of Modern Government,* rev. ed., ch. II-IV. Henry Holt, New York, 1949.

W. Brooke Graves: *American State Government,* 4th. ed., ch. XX and XXI. Heath, Boston, 1953.

Hiram Miller Stout: *British Government,* ch. XVIII-XX. Oxford University Press, New York, 1953.

CHAPTER VI: THE EXECUTIVE—THE MAINSPRING OF GOVERNMENT

Sir Gilbert Campion, et al: *British Government since 1918,* ch. II. Allen and Unwin, London, 1950.

B. E. Carter: *The Office of Prime Minister.* Princeton University Press, 1956.

Gwendolen M. Carter, John H. Hertz and John C. Ranney: *Major Foreign Powers,* 3rd. ed., part I, ch. V. Harcourt, Brace, New York, 1957.

H. McD. Clokie: *Canadian Government and Politics,* new rev. ed., ch. VI. Longmans, Green, Toronto, 1951.

Robert MacGregor Dawson: *The Government of Canada,* 3rd. ed. rev., ch. VIII-XI. University of Toronto Press, 1957.

Herman Finer: *The Theory and Practice of Modern Government,* rev. ed., ch. XXIII and XXVI. Henry Holt, New York, 1949.

William E. D. Halliday: "The Privy Council Office and Cabinet Secretariat in Relation to the Development of Cabinet Government," *Canada Year Book, 1956.*

Sir W. Ivor Jennings: *Cabinet Government,* 2nd. ed., ch. I-III, IX, XI, and XIII, Cambridge University Press, 1951.

Harold J. Laski: *Parliamentary Government in England,* ch. II and VIII. Allen and Unwin, London, 1938.

—— *The American Presidency.* Allen and Unwin, London, 1940.

Clinton Rossiter: *The American Presidency.* Harcourt, Brace, New York, 1956.

CHAPTER VII: THE LEGISLATURE: ITS FUNCTIONS AND PROCEDURE

T. K. Bailey and H. D. Samuel: *Congress at Work.* Henry Holt, New York, 1952.

James M. Burns: *Congress on Trial: The Politics of Modern Law-Making.* Harper & Bros., New York, 1949.

Gwendolen M. Carter, John H. Hertz and John C. Ranney: *Major Foreign Powers*, 3rd. ed., part I, ch. IV. Harcourt, Brace, New York, 1957.

H. McD. Clokie: *Canadian Government and Politics*, new rev. ed., ch. V. Longmans, Green, Toronto, 1951.

Robert MacGregor Dawson: *The Government of Canada*, 3rd. ed., rev., ch. XV-XIX. University of Toronto Press, 1957.

Alfred DeGrazia: *The American Way of Government*, ch. XXIII-XXVI. John Wiley and Sons, New York, 1957.

Herman Finer: *The Theory and Practice of Modern Government*, rev. ed., ch. XVII-XX. Henry Holt, New York, 1949.

Sir W. Ivor Jennings: *Parliament*, 2nd. ed., ch. IV-VI, VIII, XI, and XII. Cambridge University Press, 1957.

Harold J. Laski: *Parliamentary Government in England*, ch. III and IV. Allen and Unwin, London, 1938.

K. MacKenzie: *The English Parliament. A Study of its Nature and Historic Development*. Penguin Books, Harmondsworth, Middlesex, 1950.

Eric Taylor: *The House of Commons at Work*. Penguin Books, Harmondsworth, Middlesex, 1951.

Norman Ward: *The Canadian House of Commons: Representation*. University of Toronto Press, 1950.

CHAPTER VIII: POLITICAL PARTIES

Hugh A. Bone: *American Politics and the Party System*, 2nd. ed., ch. XI-XXVI. McGraw-Hill, New York, 1955.

Gwendolen M. Carter, John H. Hertz and John C. Ranney: *Major Foreign Powers*, 3rd. ed., part I, ch.III. Harcourt, Brace, New York, 1957.

H. McD. Clokie: *Canadian Government and Politics*, new rev. ed., ch. IV. Longmans, Green, Toronto, 1951.

Robert MacGregor Dawson: *The Government of Canada*, 3rd. ed., rev., ch. XXI-XXIII. University of Toronto Press, 1957.

Herman Finer: *The Theory and Practice of Modern Government*, rev. ed., ch. XII-XVI. Henry Holt, New York, 1949.

Pendleton Herring: *The Politics of Democracy*. W. W. Norton, New York, 1940.

Ivan Hinderaker: *Party Politics*. Henry Holt, New York, 1956.

V. O. Key: *Politics, Parties and Pressure Groups*, 3rd. ed., ch. VII-XIII, and XXIV. Thomas Y. Crowell, New York, 1953.

Harold J. Laski: *Parliamentary Government in England*, ch. II. Allen and Unwin, London, 1938.

Robert T. McKenzie: *British Political Parties*. St. Martin's Press, London, 1955.

Samuel Lubell: *The Future of American Politics*, 2nd. ed., rev., Anchor Books, New York, 1956.

E. E. Schattschneider: *Party Government*. Rinehart and Co., New York, 1942.

John R. Williams: *The Conservative Party of Canada: 1920-1949.* Duke University Press, Durham, North Carolina, 1956.

CHAPTER IX: REPRESENTATION

Walter Bagehot: *The English Constitution,* World's Classics ed., ch. v.

David E. Butler: *The Electoral System in Britain, 1918-1951.* Clarendon Press, Oxford, 1953.

Alfred DeGrazia: *Public and Republic: Political Representation in America.* Alfred A. Knopf, New York, 1951.

Herman Finer: *The Theory and Practice of Modern Government,* rev. ed., ch. xxii. Henry Holt, New York, 1949.

Carl J. Friedrich: *Constitutional Government and Democracy,* rev. ed., ch. xiv-xvi and xxii. Ginn and Co., Boston, 1950.

F. A. Hermens: *The Representative Republic.* University of Notre Dame Press, 1958.

J. Hogan: *Election and Representation.* Blackwell, Oxford, 1945.

Sir W. Ivor Jennings: *The British Constitution,* 3rd. ed., ch. i. Cambridge University Press, 1950.

Enid Lakeman and James D. Lambert: *Voting in Democracies.* Faber and Faber, 1955.

Harold J. Laski: *The Dangers of Obedience,* ch. iii. Harper & Bros., New York, 1930.

John Stuart Mill: *Representative Government,* ch. vii.

CHAPTER X: PRESSURE GROUPS

Hugh A. Bone: *American Politics and the Party System,* 2nd. ed., ch. v-x. McGraw-Hill, New York, 1955.

Stuart Chase: *Democracy under Pressure.* Twentieth Century Fund, New York, 1945.

Henry W. Ehremann, ed.: *Interest Groups on Four Continents.* University of Pittsburgh Press, 1958.

The Federalist, no. X.

Sir W. Ivor Jennings: *Parliament,* 2nd. ed., ch. vii. Cambridge University Press, 1957.

V. O. Key: *Politics, Parties and Pressure Groups,* 3rd. ed., ch. ii-vi. Thomas Y. Crowell, New York, 1953.

Dayton D. McKean: *Party and Pressure Politics,* ch. xviii-xxix. Houghton Mifflin, Boston, 1949.

Henry M. Magid: "Freedom and Political Unity," *Journal of Ethics,* 51 (1941), pp. 144-57.

K. Schriftgiesser: *The Lobbyists.* Little, Brown, Boston, 1951.

Richard Carlton Snyder and H. Hubert Wilson: *Roots of Political Behavior,* ch. v. American Book Co., New York, 1949.

J. D. Stewart: *British Pressure Groups: Their Role in Relation to the House of Commons.* Oxford University Press, London, 1957.

David B. Truman: *The Governmental Process.* Alfred A. Knopf, New York, 1951.

Chapter XI: The Relationship between the Executive and the Legislature

S. H. Beer: *Treasury Control: The Coordination of Financial and Economic Policy in Great Britain.* Oxford University Press, London, 1956.

W. E. Binkley: *President and Congress.* Alfred A. Knopf, New York, 1947.

A. E. Buck: *Financing Canadian Government,* ch. ii-vi. Public Administration Service, Chicago, 1949.

James M. Burns: *Congress on Trial: The Politics of Modern Law-Making.* Harper & Bros., New York, 1949.

Robert MacGregor Dawson: *The Government of Canada,* 3rd. ed., rev., ch. xix. University of Toronto Press, 1957.

Herman Finer: *The Theory and Practice of Modern Government,* rev. ed., ch. xxi. Henry Holt and Co., 1949.

Pendleton Herring: *Presidential Leadership.* Farrar & Rinehart, New York, 1940.

Sir W. Ivor Jennings: *Parliament,* 2nd. ed., ch. ix and xv. Cambridge University Press, 1957.

Harold J. Laski: "The Parliamentary and Presidential Systems," *Public Administration Review,* 4 (1944), pp. 347-59.

Herbert S. Morrison: *Government and Parliament: A Survey from the Inside.* Oxford University Press, London, 1954.

Don K. Price: "The Parliamentary and Presidential Systems," *Public Administration Review,* 3 (1943), pp. 317-34.

Roland Young: *This Is Congress,* ch. viii. Alfred A. Knopf, New York, 1943.

Chapter XII: Public Opinion

William Albig: *Modern Public Opinion.* McGraw-Hill, New York, 1956.

Hugh A. Bone: *American Politics and the Party System,* 2nd. ed., ch. i-iv. McGraw-Hill, New York, 1955.

Hadley Cantril: *Gauging Public Opinion.* Princeton University Press, 1944.

Zechariah Chafee, Jr.: *Government and Mass Communication.* University of Chicago Press, 1947.

R. H. Coase: *British Broadcasting.* Longmans, Green, London, 1949.

Wilfred Eggleston: "The Press of Canada," in *Royal* (Massey) *Commission Studies.* King's Printer, Ottawa, 1951.

The Commission on Freedom of the Press: *A Free and Responsible Press.* University of Chicago Press, 1947.

Carl J. Friedrich: *Constitutional Government and Democracy,* rev. ed., ch. xxiv. Ginn & Co., Boston, 1950.

George Gallup: *A Guide to Public Opinion Polls,* 2nd ed. Princeton University Press, 1948.

William Ernest Hocking: *Freedom of the Press: A Framework of Principle.* University of Chicago, 1947.

Walter Lippman: *Public Opinion*. Macmillan, New York, 1922.

A. Lawrence Lowell: *Public Opinion and Popular Government*, rev. ed., ch. i-iv. Longmans, Green, New York, 1914.

J. L. McCamy: *Government Publicity*. University of Chicago Press, 1939.

Carlton McNaught: *Canada Gets the News*. Ryerson Press, Toronto, 1940.

Norman C. Meier and Harold W. Saunders (eds.): *The Polls and Public Opinion*. Henry Holt and Co., New York, 1949.

Frank Luther Mott: *American Journalism*, ch. xxv-xliii. Macmillan, New York, 1941.

N. J. Powell: *Anatomy of Public Opinion*. Prentice-Hall, New York, 1951.

Report of the Committee on the Analysis of Pre-election Polls and Forecasts of the Social Science Research Council, *Public Opinion Quarterly*, 12 (1948-49), p. 599.

Report of the Royal (Fowler) *Commission on Broadcasting*. Queen's Printer, Ottawa, 1957.

Report of the Royal Commission on the Press, 1947-1949, Cmd. 7700. H.M. Stationery Office, London, 1949.

Lindsay Rogers: *The Pollsters*. Alfred A. Knopf, New York, 1949.

Charles A. Siepmann: *Radio, Television, and Society*. Oxford University Press, New York, 1950.

Chapter XIII: The Judiciary and the Law

Henry J. Abraham: *Courts and Judges: An Introduction to the Judicial Process*. Oxford University Press, New York, 1959.

Thurman W. Arnold: *The Symbols of Government*, ch. vii. Yale University Press, 1935.

Peter Archer: *The Queen's Courts*. Penguin Books, Harmondsworth, Middlesex, 1956.

Edgar Bodenheimer: *Jurisprudence*, ch. ii-v. McGraw-Hill, New York, 1940.

Benjamin N. Cardozo: *The Nature of the Judicial Process*. Yale University Press, 1921.

Gwendolen M. Carter, John H. Hertz and John C. Ranney: *Major Foreign Powers*, 3rd. ed., part i, ch. vii. Harcourt, Brace, New York, 1957.

Robert MacGregor Dawson: *The Government of Canada*, 3rd. ed., rev., ch. xx. University of Toronto Press, 1957.

Alfred DeGrazia: *The American Way of Government*, part vii. John Wiley, New York, 1957.

R. C. K. Ensor: *Courts and Judges*. Oxford University Press, London, 1933.

W. Brooke Graves: *American State Government*, 4th. ed. ch. xvi-xviii. Heath, Boston, 1953.

John Chipman Gray: *Nature and Sources of Law*, 2nd ed. Macmillan. New York, 1927.

R. H. Jackson: *The Supreme Court in the American System of Government*. Harvard University Press, 1955.

R. M. Jackson: *The Machinery of Justice in England*, 2nd. ed. Cambridge University Press, 1953.

Sir W. Ivor Jennings: *The Law and the Constitution*, 3rd. ed., appendices II and III. University of London Press, 1943.

R. M. MacIver: *The Modern State*, ch. VIII. Clarendon Press, Oxford, 1926.

Roscoe Pound: *The Spirit of the Common Law*. Marshall Jones, Boston, 1921.

Munroe Smith: "The Elements of Law," in *Studying Law*, edited by A. T. Vanderbilt, pp. 171-376. Washington Square Publishing Corporation, New York, 1945.

CHAPTER XIV: CIVIL LIBERTIES

H. S. Ashmore: *An Epitaph for Dixie*. McGraw-Hill, New York, 1958.

Hillman M. Bishop and Samuel Hendel: *Basic Issues in American Democracy*, 3rd. ed., section III. Appleton-Century-Crofts, New York, 1956.

Robert K. Carr: *Federal Protection of Civil Rights*. Cornell University Press, Ithaca, 1947.

Zechariah Chafee, Jr.: *The Blessings of Liberty*. Lippincott, New York, 1956.

Sir Alfred Denning: *Freedom under the Law*. Stevens, London, 1949.

A. V. Dicey: *The Law of the Constitution*, 9th. ed., ch. I, IV, and VIII. Macmillan, London, 1939.

Walter Gellhorn: *Individual Freedom and Governmental Restraint*. Louisiana State University Press, 1956.

Ivan Hinderaker, ed.: *American Government Annual 1958-59*, ch. I and II. Henry Holt, New York, 1958.

Sir W. Ivor Jennings: *The Law and the Constitution*, 3rd. ed., ch. VIII. University of London Press, 1943.

Law and Order in Canadian Democracy: A Series of Lectures prepared by the Royal Canadian Mounted Police. King's Printer, Ottawa, 1950.

John Locke: *A Letter Concerning Toleration* in *Of Civil Government and Toleration*. Cassell & Co., London, 1905.

Adolf Löwe: *The Price of Liberty*. Hogarth Press, London, 1937.

Alexander Meiklejohn: *Free Speech*. Harper & Bros., New York, 1948.

John Stuart Mill: *On Liberty*. Oxford University Press, London, 1933.

John Milton: *Areopagitica*, in *Complete Poetry and Selected Prose of John Milton*. The Modern Library, New York, 1931.

Proceedings of the Special Committee on Human Rights and Fundamental Freedoms. King's Printer, Ottawa, 1950.

Arthur M. Schlesinger, Jr: *The Vital Center*, ch. IX. Houghton Mifflin, Boston, 1949.

To Secure These Rights: The Report of the President's Committee on Civil Rights. Simon and Schuster, New York, 1947.

CHAPTER XV: THE CIVIL SERVICE

Paul H. Appleby: *Big Democracy.* Alfred A. Knopf, New York, 1945.

G. A. Campbell: *The Civil Service in Britain.* Penguin Books, Harmondsworth, Middlesex, 1955.

Sir Gilbert Campion, et al: *British Government since 1918,* ch. III. Allen and Unwin, London, 1950.

Taylor Cole: *The Canadian Bureaucracy,* ch. I-IV. Duke University Press, 1949.

H. E. Dale: *The Higher Civil Service of Great Britain.* Clarendon Press, Oxford, 1941.

Robert MacGregor Dawson: *The Government of Canada,* 3rd. ed., rev., ch. XII and XIII. University of Toronto Press, 1957.

Alfred DeGrazia: *The American Way of Government,* part VIII. John Wiley, New York, 1957.

Frank Dunhill: *The Civil Service: Some Human Aspects.* Allen and Unwin, London, 1956.

Samuel Edward Finer: *A Primer of Public Administration.* Muller, London, 1950.

Herman Finer: *The Theory and Practice of Modern Government,* rev. ed., ch. XXVII, XXX, and XXXIII. Henry Holt and Co., New York, 1949.

Carl J. Friedrich: *Constitutional Government and Democracy,* rev. ed., ch. II. Ginn and Co., Boston, 1950.

Arthur W. Macmahon and John D. Millett: *Federal Administrators,* ch. I-V and XVII-XXIV. Columbia University Press, 1939.

W. J. M. Mackenzie and J. W. Grove: *Central Administration in Britain.* Longmans, Green, London, 1957.

Fritz Morstein Marx: *The Administrative State.* University of Chicago Press, 1958.

Personnel Administration in the Public Service. Report of the Civil Service Commission of Canada, Ottawa, December, 1958.

Report of the President's Committee on Administrative Management, *Administrative Management in the Government of the United States.* United States Government Printing Office, Washington, 1937.

Reports of the Two (Hoover) Commissions on the Organization of the Executive Branch of the Government, *Task Force Reports on Personnel and Civil Service.* U.S. Government Printing Office, Washington, 1949 and 1955.

Report of the Royal Commission on Administrative Classifications in the Public Service. King's Printer, Ottawa, 1946.

O. G. Stahl: *Public Personnel Administration,* 4th. ed. Harper & Bros., New York, 1956.

Leonard D. White: *Introduction to the Study of Public Administration,* 4th. ed. Macmillan, New York, 1955.

CHAPTER XVI: THE ADMINISTRATIVE PROCESS

Carleton K. Allen: *Bureaucracy Triumphant.* Oxford University Press, London, 1931.

Sir Gilbert Campion, et al: *British Government since 1918,* ch. IV and V. Allen and Unwin, London, 1950.

Cecil T. Carr: *Concerning English Administrative Law.* Columbia University Press, New York, 1941.

Robert MacGregor Dawson: *The Government of Canada,* 3rd. ed., rev., ch. XIV. University of Toronto Press, 1957.

John Dickinson: *Administrative Justice and the Supremacy of Law,* ch. I-V. Harvard University Press, Cambridge, 1927.

Final Report of the Attorney General's Committee on Administrative Procedure, United States Government Printing Office, Washington, 1941.

Herman Finer: "Administrative Responsibility in Democratic Government," *Public Administration Review,* 1 (1940), pp. 335-50.

Carl L. Friedrich: "Public Policy and the Nature of Administrative Responsibility," *Public Policy: A Year Book of the Graduate School of Public Administration of Harvard University.* Harvard University Press, Cambridge, 1940.

E. Pendleton Herring: *Public Administration and the Public Interest.* McGraw-Hill, New York, 1936.

Rt. Hon. Lord Hewart: *The New Despotism.* Benn, London, 1929.

C. S. Hyneman: *Bureaucracy in a Democracy.* Harper & Bros., New York, 1950.

Sir W. Ivor Jennings: *The Law and the Constitution,* 3rd. ed., ch. VI and appendix I. University of London Press, 1943.

J. Roland Pennock: *Administration and the Rule of Law.* Farrar & Rinehart, New York, 1941.

Report of the Committee on Ministers' Powers, Cmd. 4060. H.M. Stationery Office, London, 1932.

Report of the Committee on Administrative Tribunals and Enquiries, Cmd. 218. H.M. Stationery Office, London, 1957.

Bernard Schwartz: *Law and the Executive in Britain.* New York University Press, New York, 1949.

John Willis (ed.): *Canadian Boards at Work.* Macmillan, Toronto, 1941.

CHAPTER XVII: FEDERALISM

A. Anderson: *The Nation and the States, Rivals or Partners?* University of Minnesota, 1955.

Hillman M. Bishop and Samuel Hendel: *Basic Issues in American Democracy,* 3rd. ed., sections IV and V. Appleton-Century-Crofts, New York, 1956.

A. E. Buck: *Financing Canadian Government,* ch. X, XIII. Public Administration Service, Chicago, 1949.

George C. S. Benson: *The New Centralization.* Farrar & Rinehart, New York, 1941.

Jane Perry Clark: *The Rise of a New Federalism*. Columbia University Press, New York, 1938.

H. McD. Clokie: *Canadian Government and Politics*, new rev. ed., ch. vii. Longmans, Green, Toronto, 1951.

Commission on Intergovernmental Relations: A Report to the President for Transmittal to the Congress. U.S. Government Printing Office, Washington, 1955.

J. A. Corry: *Difficulties of Divided Jurisdiction*. King's Printer, Ottawa, 1940.

Donald Davidson: *The Attack on Leviathan*. University of North Carolina Press, Chapel Hill, 1938.

Robert MacGregor Dawson: *The Government of Canada*, 3rd. ed., rev., ch. ii and iv-vii. University of Toronto Press, Toronto, 1957.

The Forty-Eight States. The American Assembly, New York, 1955.

J. W. Fesler: *Area and Administration*. University of Alabama Press, 1949.

A. R. M. Lower, F. R. Scott, et al.: *Evolving Canadian Federalism*. Duke University Press, Durham, N.C., 1958.

Paul Gérin-Lajoie: *Constitutional Amendment in Canada*. University of Toronto Press, 1950.

W. Brooke Graves: *American State Government*, 4th. ed., ch. xxiv and xxvi. Heath, Boston, 1953.

A. W. Macmahon: *Federalism: Mature and Emergent*. Doubleday, New York, 1955.

A. M. Moore and J. H. Perry: *Financing Canadian Federation*. Canadian Tax Foundation, Toronto, 1953.

Report of the Royal Commission on Dominion-Provincial Relations, bk. i. King's Printer, Ottawa, 1940.

Richard Carlton Snyder and H. Hubert Wilson: *Roots of Political Behavior*, ch. ix. American Book Co., New York, 1949.

K. C. Wheare: *Federal Government*, 3rd. ed. Oxford University Press, New York, 1953.

CHAPTER XVIII: LOCAL GOVERNMENT

C. R. Adrian: *Governing Urban America*. McGraw-Hill, New York, 1955.

William Anderson (ed.): *Local Government in Europe*. Appleton-Century, New York, 1937.

George C. S. Benson: *The New Centralization*, ch. ii, iii, vii, and ix. Farrar & Rinehart, New York, 1941.

A. E. Buck: *Financing Canadian Government*, ch. xii. Public Administration Service, Chicago, 1949.

Gwendolen M. Carter, John H. Hertz and John C. Ranney: *Major Foreign Powers*, 3rd. ed., part i, ch. vi, part ii, ch. v. Harcourt, Brace, New York, 1957.

Sir Gilbert Campion, et al.: *British Government since 1918*, ch. vi. Allen and Unwin, London, 1950.

K. G. Crawford: *Canadian Municipal Government*. University of Toronto Press, 1954.

Alfred DeGrazia: *The American Way of Government*, parts xv and xvi. John Wiley, New York, 1957.

Herman Finer: *English Local Government*, 4th. rev. ed. Methuen, London, 1950.

—— "The Case for Local Self-Government," *Public Administration Review*, 3 (1943), pp. 51-8.

W. Brooke Graves: *American State Government*, 4th. ed., ch. xx-xxiii. *Heath*, Boston, 1953.

Ernest S. Griffiths: *The Impasse of Democracy*, ch. xvii. Harrison-Hilton, New York, 1939.

W. Eric Jackson: *Local Government in England and Wales*. Penguin Books, Harmondsworth, Middlesex, 1945.

Sir John Maud and S. E. Finer: *Local Government in England and Wales*. Home University Library. Oxford University Press, London, 1953.

William Bennett Munro: *American Influences on Canadian Government*, ch. iii. Macmillan, Toronto, 1929.

Thomas J. Plunkett: *Municipal Organization in Canada*. The Canadian Federation of Mayors and Municipalities, Montreal, 1955.

CHAPTER XIX: DEMOCRACY AND DICTATORSHIP

D. W. Brogan: *The Free State*. Hamish Hamilton, London, 1945.

Gwendolen M. Carter, John H. Hertz and John C. Ranney: *Major Foreign Powers*, 3rd. ed., part v. Harcourt, Brace, New York, 1957.

Herman Finer: *Road to Reaction*. Little, Brown, Boston, 1945.

Ernest S. Griffith: *The Impasse of Democracy*. Harrison-Hilton, New York, 1939.

—— *The Modern Government in Action*. Columbia University Press, 1942.

Friedrich Hayek: *The Road to Serfdom*. University of Chicago Press, 1944.

Hans Kohn: *The Twentieth Century*. Macmillan, New York, 1949.

R. M. MacIver: *The Web of Government*, ch. viii and ix. Macmillan, New York, 1947.

—— *The Ramparts We Guard*. Macmillan, New York, 1950.

Robert G. Neumann: *European and Comparative Government*, part v. McGraw-Hill, New York, 1955.

J. Roland Pennock: *Liberal Democracy: Its Merits and Prospects*. Rinehart & Co., New York, 1950.

Arthur M. Schlesinger, Jr.: *The Vital Center*. Houghton Mifflin, New York, 1949.

Julian Towster: *Political Power in the U.S.S.R., 1917-1949*. Oxford University Press, New York, 1948.

Rebecca West: *The Meaning of Treason*. Viking Press, New York, 1947.

INDEX

Nazis: low respect of, for human personality, 46-7; deny rationality, 47; exalt the nation and the state, 48-9, 51; deny freedom and equality, 50-1; never got a majority in a free election, 628; and control of ministry of interior, 628

New Brunswick, 174, 182, 582, 587

New Deal: and growth of civil service in United States, 144; framed by President and his advisors, 162; an example of presidential leadership, 335; important parts of, held unconstitutional, 417; and expansion of government activities, 572

Newfoundland, 182, 590

Nova Scotia, 174, 182, 582, 567, 590

Occupational representation. See Functional representation

Office of Defence Mobilization, 163, 507

Office of Emergency Management, 163, 507

Officials: control of, by judiciary, 418-22; personality liable for wrongdoing, 419, 421; position of, in continental Europe, 419-20; relations of, with interest groups, 541-7. See also Civil service and Civil servants

Oligarchy: tendencies towards, in political parties, 228, 230, 240; in the British party system, 240-1, 332; in the United States party system, 244. See also Parties, political

One-party system: necessity of purges in, 232-3; a feature of modern dictatorships, 639, 643, 645. See also Dictatorship

Ontario, 89, 174, 182, 578-9, 582

Ontario Hydro Electric Power Commission, 106

Opposition, the: functions of, 197; influence of, 339

Opposition, His Majesty's Loyal, 154

Orders-in-Council: use of, by Canadian Cabinet, 176, 177; use of, in wartime, 516; signify formal decision by cabinet, 519. See also Administrative process and Legislation, subordinate

Ordinances, power of President to make, 161

Organization, large-scale: and monopoly, 117-18; and oligarchy, 230, 332; civil service, an instance of, 480-3; features of civil service due to, 487-93; impersonal character of, 489-90; red tape, a concomitant of, 492; personnel matters in, 492-3; disturbing tendency in, 548-9. See also Civil service

Organization and Methods, 509-10

Organizations, reform, as pressure groups, 315

Organizations, women's, as pressure groups, 310

Overlapping and duplication, in federal governments, 585

Ownership, government: examples of, 124-5; extension of, in Britain, 131-2; views of socialists on, 133-4, 136-7; views of individualists on, 138; conditions urging, 531

Padlock Law, 105-6, 459n., 461-2

Paper work, in civil service, 490-1

Parliament (Britain): origin of, 92; place of, in British constitution, 93-6; supremacy of, 93-6, 416-17; delegates powers to executive, 94; takes powers from the judiciary, 94; formal role of, in amendment of British North America Act, 108, 580; can amend British constitution, 107, 111; dissolution of, 152-3, 167, 329; has no power over British Dominions, 154; composed of two chambers, 164, 180; effects control of administration through cabinet, 168; not the active centre of decision, 193, 196; has inadequate knowledge of administration, 214; fixes powers of local governments, 596. See also House of Commons and House of Lords

Parliament (Canada): powers of, under British North America Act, 104-5, 555-7; and amendment of constitution, 108, 580-4; and civil liberties, 460-1. See also House of Commons and Senate

Parliament Act (1911), 186, 331

Parliamentary secretary, functions of, in Britain, 169; in Canada, 176-7

Parties, political: extra-constitutional growth by custom, 111-12; and appointments to upper chambers in